- **1,063 respondents:** Instructors enlightened us on course dynamics in a nation-wide Introductory Spanish Course Survey.

- **83 symposium attendees:** Some of the brightest minds in the discipline created solutions to address core course needs.

- **57 student focus group attendees:** Students at seven different schools gave us a window into their study habits and biggest course challenges.

- **144 editorial reviewers:** Introductory Spanish instructors directly informed the development of *Experience Spanish* content.

- **140 webinar attendees:** Instructors reviewed samples of Connect Spanish online and provided feedback in real time.

- **479 survey respondents:** Instructors and students weighed in on content, functionality, and design questions throughout the process.

- **24 Editorial and Cultural Advisory Board members:** These boards provided expert feedback to the editorial and digital teams.

- **11 Digital Advisory Board members:** This board reviewed digital content and functionality, contributing invaluable user input.

- **11 Cultural and Curricul...** ...ted cultural content and created lesson plans for Connect Spanish.

- **23 Beta Test Schools:** At each beta test school, instructors swapped out a unit to pilot *Experience Spanish* and completed a review on the results.

- **968 Beta Test Student Participants:** We also captured substantial student feedback on the beta test, which helped us refine the final product.

# NTRODUCTORY SPANISH, AND IT'S IN YOUR HANDS!

## **Experience** a program that helps *you* administer *your* course more **efficiently** and **effectively**...

It lessens the burden of the instructor to "guess" about how to organize her time in presenting concepts (less time on easier ones, more on the difficult ones).

Lisa Nalbone, *University of Central Florida*

It helps guide students to proficiency at their own speed, reduces the teachers' workload, and appeals to students who live their lives immersed in digital settings.

Deanna Mihaly, *Eastern Michigan University*

## **Experience** a program that helps *you* achieve **consistent learning outcomes** across diverse instructional settings...

*Experience Spanish* includes an innovative online tool that will allow students to reach higher levels of proficiency by guiding them through a series of task-based activities that not only incorporate structure and vocabulary but also a cultural component.

Neysa L. Figueroa, *Kennesaw State University*

I like that the technology component is fully integrated and not added on as an afterthought.

Gillian Lord, *University of Florida*

# XPERIENCE SPANISH AND EXPERIENCE THE WORLD!

# Blackboard

# Do More

**McGraw-Hill Higher Education and Blackboard have teamed up.
What does this mean for you?**

**1. Your life, simplified.** Now your students and you can access all McGraw-Hill Connect™ and Create™ content (i.e., text, learning aids, teaching tools, homework, and so on) directly from within your Blackboard course. Say goodbye to the days of logging in to multiple applications, and say hello to true single sign-on.

**2. Deep integration of content and tools.** Not only do you get single sign-on with Connect™ and Create™, you also get deep integration of McGraw-Hill content and content engines right in Blackboard. Whether you're choosing a book for your course or building Connect™ assignments, all the tools you need are right where you want them—inside of Blackboard.

**3. Seamless gradebooks.** Are you tired of keeping multiple gradebooks and manually synchronizing grades into Blackboard? We thought so. When a student completes an integrated Connect™ assignment, the grade for that assignment automatically (and instantly) feeds into your Blackboard grade center.

**4. A solution for everyone.** Whether your institution is already using Blackboard or you just want to try Blackboard on your own, we have a solution for you. McGraw-Hill and Blackboard can now offer you easy access to industry leading technology and content, whether your campus hosts it or we do. Be sure to ask your local McGraw-Hill representative for details.

# EXPERIENCE
# SPANISH

## Un mundo sin límites

María J. Amores
*West Virginia University*

José Luis Suárez García
*Colorado State University, Fort Collins*

Michael Morris
*Northern Illinois University*

The McGraw·Hill Companies

Connect
Learn
Succeed™

Published by McGraw-Hill Higher Education, an imprint of The McGraw-Hill Companies, Inc., 1221 Avenue of the Americas, New York, NY 10020. Copyright © 2012 by the McGraw-Hill Companies, Inc. All rights reserved. No part of this publication may be reproduced or distributed in any form or by any means, or stored in a database or retrieval system, without the prior written consent of The McGraw-Hill Companies, Inc., including, but not limited to, in any network or other electronic storage or transmission, or broadcast for distance learning.

✪ This book is printed on recycled, acid-free paper containing a minimum of 50% total recycled fiber with 10% postconsumer de-inked fiber.

3 4 5 6 7 8 9 DOW/DOW 0 9 8 7 6 5 4 3 2

ISBN: 978-0-07-353439-8 (Student Edition)
MHID: 0-07-353439-0

ISBN: 978-0-07-328010-3 (Instructor's Edition, **not for resale**)
MHID: 0-07-328010-0

Vice President and Editor-in-Chief: *Michael Ryan*
Editorial Director: *William R. Glass*
Publisher: *Katie Stevens*
Senior Sponsoring Editor: *Katherine K. Crouch*
Director of Development: *Scott Tinetti*
Senior Development Editor: *Allen J. Bernier*
Editorial Coordinators: *Margaret Young, Erin Blaze, Laura Chiriboga*
Executive Marketing Manager: *Hector Alvero*
Faculty Development Manager: *Jorge Arbujas*
Media Project Manager: *Thomas Brierly*
Senior Production Editor: *Mel Valentín*

Design Manager: *Andrei Pasternak*
Cover Designer: *Irene Morris/Andrei Pasternak*
Art Editor: *Robin Mouat*
Interior Designer: *Maureen McCutcheon*
Illustrator: *Harry Briggs*
Visual (Photo) Coordinator: *Sonia Brown*
Photo Researcher: *Sonia Brown*
Buyer II: *Tandra P. Jorgensen*
Permissions Coordinator: *Veronica Oliva*
Composition: *Aptara®, Inc.*
Printing: *RR Donnelly & Sons*

Cover Image: Charles Krebs/Stone/Getty Images

Credits: The credits section of this book begins on page C-1 and is considered an extension of the copyright page.

**Library of Congress Cataloging-in-Publication Data**

Amores, María.
  Experience Spanish / María J. Amores, José Luis Suárez García, Michael Morris.—1st ed.
     p. cm.
  Includes bibliographical references and index.
  ISBN-13: 978-0-07-353439-8 (alk. paper)
  ISBN-10: 0-07-353439-0 (alk. paper)
  1. Spanish language—Textbooks for foreign speakers—English. 2. Spanish language—Grammar. 3. Spanish language—Spoken Spanish. I. Suárez García, José Luis. II. Morris, Michael. III. Title.
  PC4129.E5A534 2011
  468.2'421—dc22
                                                                    2010041624

The Internet addresses listed in the text were accurate at the time of publication. The inclusion of a website does not indicate an endorsement by the authors or McGraw-Hill, and McGraw-Hill does not guarantee the accuracy of the information presented on those sites.

www.mhhe.com

# Experience Spanish Preface

*Experience Spanish* was built from the ground up by thousands of instructors and students of introductory Spanish who participated in our extensive research.

Our objective was to better understand how the changing nature of second language courses is affecting the experience of students and instructors.

## WHAT DID WE LEARN FROM THE RESEARCH?

Introductory Spanish instructors want to motivate learners to develop confidence and ownership of their communication skills.

- **40%** of faculty said they are dissatisfied with their students' ability to communicate in Spanish when they complete the introductory course and would like a tool that helps their students gain the confidence they need to successfully communicate in Spanish beyond the classroom.

Instructors who have students coming in with varying levels of language proficiency would like to get everyone on the same page.

- **50%** of faculty said they spend more time than they would like dealing with variation in student preparedness and would like a tool that helps them level the playing field.

Instructors also strive for consistent learning outcomes across diverse instructional settings, whether their courses are face-to-face, hybrid, or fully online.

- **60%** of faculty said they find it difficult to achieve consistent course outcomes across different course formats and would like a tool that helps them deliver a seamless learning experience regardless of how their students choose to experience their course.

Many instructors would like to more efficiently handle issues of course administration.

- **43%** of faculty said they are spending more time than they would like on administrative tasks related to delivering their courses and would like a tool that helps them to better manage their workload.

# THE RESULT?

We listened. We know that your students are changing. Technology is changing. The idea of the "classroom" is changing. Now, the way your students experience Spanish can change as well!

*Experience Spanish* is a first. Its groundbreaking adaptive diagnostic and synchronous and asynchronous conversation tools create a 24/7 learning environment never before possible. With *Experience Spanish*, instructors can tailor the environment while students tailor the experience, allowing everyone to take ownership of learning.

# Experience a Program That Motivates **Students** to Develop Their **Communication Skills**

In a recent survey, nearly one-thousand faculty told us about their experiences teaching introductory Spanish. Seventy-nine percent indicated that the development of cultural competence was either "very important" or "extremely important" as a course outcome. This research, in addition to anecdotes from the classroom, reveals that students with a positive attitude toward the target culture are more motivated to participate in class, continue their language study beyond the required sequence, and retain their language skills after finishing their language study.

"These readings will captivate their interest and aid their learning. I also think it will motivate them to practice and learn more beyond the classroom."

Ana E. Almonte,
*Hudson Valley Community College*

With these findings in mind, the cultural features of *Experience Spanish*, including the **Entrada cultural** and **Expresiones artísticas** pages and the **Nota cultural** boxes in each chapter, as well as the unique **Conexiones culturales** spreads, were designed to give students important glimpses into the Hispanic world and promote cross-cultural comparisons and connections.

On the digital side of *Experience Spanish*, students are transported into an immersive world called **Mundo interactivo** where they experience the thrill of mastering relevant, task-based communication scenarios in real-world contexts. With synchronous and asynchronous voice chat functionality, students can easily engage in communication practice online. This experience helps students gain the confidence to use their Spanish skills in the classroom and in their communities. Professors have access to a suite of media-rich content and tools to tailor their students' experience and provide targeted feedback at just the right moments to maximize learning.

"What I love about this is that you are covering multiple modalities—listening comprehension; speaking and writing—in a contextualized thread. It's a logical use of the basic language skills that builds up to the ultimate goal of speaking."

Todd Hughes, *Vanderbilt University*

*Experience Spanish* also offers instructors the necessary tools to help their students develop communicative proficiency in all four skill areas: listening and reading comprehension and written and oral production. Activities in *Experience Spanish* focus on the exchange of information about students' experiences and also on the Hispanic world they explore throughout the materials. In each chapter, select activities and the **Lectura cultural** sections expose students to aural and written language, drawing attention to listening and reading skills. **Palabra escrita**, included in every main chapter, focuses on the development of extended writing.

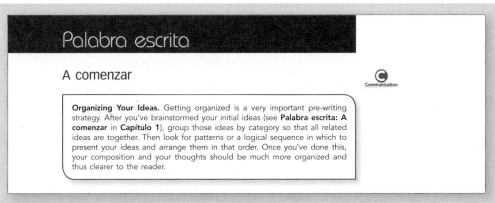

When learners have the opportunity to use Spanish to communicate their own ideas, they are more motivated to excel.

"The writing guide is wonderful."

Bethany J. Sanio,
*University of Nebraska—Lincoln*

At its core, *Experience Spanish* puts beginning learners on the path to communicative and cultural competency.

# Experience a Program That Addresses *Students'* Varying Levels of **Language Proficiency**

Introductory Spanish classrooms typically contain a mix of true beginners, false beginners, and even heritage speakers in the same classroom. Based on our research, we learned that the varying levels of language proficiency among students represent one of the greatest course challenges for the majority of introductory Spanish instructors.

"The adaptive diagnostic tool is very promising. It provides the individualized feedback students need to take responsibility for their own learning and it stresses mastery."

**Sandra L. Watts,** *University of North Carolina at Charlotte*

*Experience Spanish* offers a powerful adaptive diagnostic tool that allows students to identify those grammatical structures they haven't yet mastered and receive an individualized study program for mastering them. Thanks to input from students and instructors around the country, we identified the top grammar points that are most challenging in for Spanish learners. These points are presented as modules within this diagnostic tool that helps students concentrate their study time around the areas where they need the most practice. You can simply say, "Go work on preterite vs. imperfect"—and off they go!

In addition to addressing the variety of student levels in your classes, the *Experience Spanish* program also appeals to students with diverse study habits. According to ethnographic research conducted by McGraw-Hill, four student types have emerged across disciplines.

### Forward Learners

### Interrupted Learners

### Short-Term Learners

### Delayed Learners

We took into consideration the diversity of student populations across the country and even within a single classroom when we designed the interactive content of *Experience Spanish*. For example, for the Forward Learners, we provide a wealth of practice activities online and guide their workflow with options for additional practice. For the Interrupted Learners, we offer content downloadable to a laptop or iPad, giving them the ability to study anywhere, anytime. The Short-Term Learners can use the diagnostic tool to hone in on their weak areas so that they can use their study time more efficiently. And when the Delayed Learner is cramming at the last minute, he or she will find all the study tools they need in one convenient location.

*Experience Spanish* appeals to the individual needs of a wide variety of students by presenting interactive content and diagnostic tools that bring everyone to the same level of mastery.

# Experience a Program That Helps *You* Administer *Your* Course More **Efficiently** and **Effectively**

Syllabus creation. Communicating with students outside of class. Assigning and grading homework. These are just a few of the administrative tasks that occupy instructors' time and thus rob them of valuable opportunities to enrich the teaching and learning experiences. Imagine a resource that efficiently handles these tasks and does so in a way that also allows you to easily tailor your course to your goals and needs. Nearly half of the instructors surveyed told us that course administration issues are a huge obstacle to effective teaching.

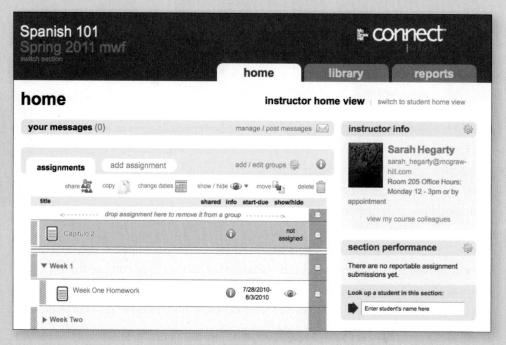

*Experience Spanish* provides the online tools to reduce the amount of time and energy that instructors have to invest in administering their course. For example, when creating assignments, instructors can easily sort according to a variety of parameters that are important to their course in particular. You can sort and assign based on language acquisition skill, grammar structure, vocabulary theme, the amount of time the activity takes, or the activity type (multiple-choice, fill-in-the-blank, and so on).

*Experience Spanish* also allows instructors to easily monitor students' progress thanks to a user-friendly and highly intuitive online gradebook that gives instructors the opportunity to provide individualized feedback and guidance based on performance. The gradebook also allows instructors to upload and assign their own materials as well as easily select and organize activities, while knowing exactly how they map back to course goals and objectives.

Since high-quality customer support is so critical when working with digital tools, the dedicated *Experience Spanish* support team stands at the ready to answer student and instructor questions whenever they arise.

We listened. The *Experience Spanish* program provides the tools you need to administer your course effectively so that you can focus on what is most important: your students' progress.

# Experience a Program That Helps *You* Achieve **Consistent Learning Outcomes** Across Diverse Instructional Settings

The context for teaching and learning can take many forms in today's world, including traditional face-to-face courses, fully online courses, and hybrid offerings. Nearly one-third of the programs across the country are now offering hybrid or online sections. Given these trends, *Experience Spanish* is uniquely designed to provide consistent outcomes no matter which of these formats is used.

The content of *Experience Spanish* is comprised of an array of integrated print and digital offerings, giving you the maximum flexibility to choose the most appropriate format for your courses. At the same time, you can be assured that regardless of the format, all content is directly tied to course learning objectives that are consistent across all components of the program.

Can students in an online course attain the same level of oral communicative language proficiency as those in a traditional classroom setting? With *Experience Spanish*, the answer is yes! For example, in-class communicative activities are replicated in the online environment, allowing students to pair up with virtual partners for communication practice.

The video program is another example of flexibility; whether you have your students view the video online or you prefer to show the video in class, you can incorporate it into your face-to-face or online sections, depending on what works best for you. Related activities can be done in class or online, so students receive the same amount of exposure and practice no matter what the class format.

And you won't want your students to miss out on the video! Shot exclusively for *Experience Spanish* in Argentina, Costa Rica, the Dominican Republic, Los Angeles, Mexico, Peru, and Spain, the *Experience Spanish* video program consists of two components:

**Concurso de videoblogs** is based on a videoblogging contest in the aforementioned countries. Competing to win the contest, the bloggers take a documentary approach that allows learners to view life and culture in those regions and to hear different Spanish dialects.

"Congratulations to whoever designed a video that includes culture and normal conversation as well as imitates authentic speech."

Bethany J. Sanio, *University of Nebraska—Lincoln*

"The topic is interesting and relevant. Students will be motivated to learn more."

Michael Vrooman, *Grand Valley State University*

The **Conexiones culturales en vivo** video segments correspond to the **Conexiones culturales** section at the end of **Capítulos 3, 5, 7, 9, 11,** and **13** and give students an opportunity to compare topics and themes of importance across different Spanish-speaking countries.

Just like the video, each component of the *Experience Spanish* program ensures a seamless transition from the face-to-face classroom to the virtual classroom and everything in between.

# About the Authors

**María J. Amores** received her Licenciatura en Filología Hispánica from the Universidad de Sevilla and her Ph.D. in Spanish Applied Linguistics with a concentration in Second Language Acquisition from Pennsylvania State University. She is currently an Associate Professor of Spanish at West Virginia University, Morgantown, where she coordinates and supervises the Basic Spanish Program and teaches undergraduate and graduate courses in language, culture, methodology, and linguistics. Her research is oriented toward pedagogical issues related to the teaching of writing and to the professional development of graduate teaching assistants. Professor Amores has published various articles on these topics in *Dimension, The Northeast Conference on the Teaching of Foreign Languages Review,* and *Foreign Language Annals.* She has also conducted several in-service workshops at national institutions for language instructors at the public school (K-12) levels, and at international institutions for teachers of Spanish as a second language.

**José Luis Suárez García** received his Ph.D. from the University of Illinois at Urbana-Champaign in 1991. He is currently a Professor of Spanish and Graduate Coordinator at the Department of Foreign Languages and Literatures at Colorado State University in Fort Collins. He regularly teaches Spanish Golden Age and other courses on Peninsular Literature and Culture and has taught Spanish language at all levels. Professor Suárez has published several reviews, articles, and books on Spanish Golden Age literature and culture, medieval bibliography, poetic and dramatic theory, and contemporary theater. He has been a guest speaker at the prestigious Jornadas de Teatro Clásico in Almagro, the Jornadas de Teatro de Almería, and has been a Panelist for the Post-Performance Roundtable Discussions at the XX Festival del Siglo de Oro in El Paso, Texas. Some of his publications have appeared in *Criticón, Journal of Spanish Studies, La Corónica, Journal of Hispanic Philology, Anales de Literatura Española,* Editorial Castalia, Universidad de la Rioja, and Editorial Universidad de Granada.

**Michael Morris** received his Ph.D. in Foreign Language Education from the University of Iowa in 1997. He is currently an Associate Professor of Spanish and Foreign Language Education at Northern Illinois University, where he teaches courses in Spanish language and linguistics as well as language teaching methodologies. He also coordinates the first- and second-year Spanish program and oversees the foreign language teacher certification program. His research focuses on the analysis of foreign language teachers' beliefs regarding instruction and the relationship of these beliefs to their classroom practices, as well as foreign language classroom assessment. He has given many in-service presentations to elementary, secondary, and college level teachers at the local, state, and national levels as well as abroad. His work has appeared in *Foreign Language Annals, Hispania, The Modern Language Journal, The Journal of Graduate Teaching Assistant Development,* and the annual volume of the American Association of University Supervisors and Coordinators.

# Acknowledgments

We would like to thank the overwhelming number of friends and colleagues who served on boards of advisors or as consultants, completed reviews or surveys, and attended symposia or focus groups. Their feedback was indispensible in creating the *Experience Spanish / Connect Spanish* program. The appearance of their names in the following lists does not necessarily constitute their endorsement of the program or its methodology.

## Digital Board of Advisors

Miriam Barbaria
*Sacramento City College*

María Bolívar
*San Diego Mesa College*

José Cruz
*Fayetteville Technical Community College*

Anne Hlas
*University of Wisconsin—Eau Claire*

Todd Hughes
*Vanderbilt University*

Gillian Lord
*University of Florida*

Elizabeth Mares
*College of DuPage*

Ana Menéndez-Collera
*Suffolk County Community College*

Juan Manuel Soto Arriví
*Indiana University—Bloomington*

María (Mónica) Montalvo
*University of Central Florida*

Yolanda González
*Valencia Community College*

## Editorial Board of Advisors

Lina Cofresi
*North Carolina Central University*

Annette Dunzo
*Howard University*

Ronna Feit
*Nassau Community College*

Leah Fonder-Solano
*University of Southern Mississippi*

Próspero García
*University of Massachusetts—Amherst*

Anne Prucha
*University of Central Florida*

Michelle Ramos-Pellicia
*George Mason University*

Maritza Salgueiro-Carlisle
*Bakersfield College*

Horacio Xaubet
*North Carolina Central University*

## Cultural Board of Advisors

Ana E. Almonte
*Hudson Valley Community College*

Ana Dávila-Howard
*Ferris State University*

José Escorcia
*University of Missouri—Columbia*

Martina Fehr-Canela
*Santa Rosa Junior College*

Jane Gibson
*Central Texas College*

Gema Hernández
*Florida State College at Jacksonville*

Yolanda Hernández
*College of Southern Nevada— Las Vegas*

Nuria Ibáñez-Quintana
*University of North Florida*

Alejandro Mandel
*Xavier University*

Purificación Martínez
*East Carolina University*

Eugenia Múñoz
*Virginia Commonwealth University*

Elizabeth Olvera
*University of Texas at San Antonio*

Kay Raymond
*Sam Houston State University*

Eva Solano
*University of North Florida*

Norma Urrutia
*Xavier University*

## Cultural and Curricular Consultants

Nelly Cañas
*Greenville Technical College*

Susann Davis
*Western Kentucky University*

María Fidalgo-Eick
*Grand Valley State University*

Alfonso García-Osuna
*Kingsborough Community College*

Todd Hernández
*Marquette University*

Talía Loaiza
*Austin Community College*

Andrea Lucas
*Sacramento City College*

Bernard Manker
*Grand Rapids Community College*

Jan Underwood
*Portland Community College*

Andrés Villagrá
*Pace University*

Michael Woods
*Oregon State University*

# Reviews

Susana Ackerman
*Santa Rosa Junior College*

Silvia P. Albanese
*Nassau Community College*

Frances Alpren
*Vanderbilt University*

Ana E. Almonte
*Hudson Valley Community College*

Tyler Anderson
*Mesa State College*

Janet Banhidi
*Marquette University*

Lisa A. Barboun
*Coastal Carolina University*

Andrew Bennett
*University of Missouri—St. Louis*

Sarah Bentley-Quintero
*Portland Community College*

Leela Bingham
*San Diego Mesa College*

Ryan N. Boylan
*Gainesville State College*

Kristy Britt
*University of South Alabama*

Elaine S. Brooks
*University of New Orleans*

Nancy Broughton
*Wright State University*

Lillie Rose Busby
*Sam Houston State University*

Julia Emilia Bussade
*The University of Mississippi*

Martha Caeiro
*University of Missouri—St. Louis*

Lilian Lizeth Cano
*University of Texas at San Antonio*

Beth Cardon
*Georgia Perimeter College*

María Carmen García
*Texas Southern University*

Oriol Casañas
*University of Denver*

Ronald C. Cere
*Eastern Michigan University*

Margaret Chaves-Smith
*Vance-Granville Community College*

An Chung Cheng
*University of Toledo*

José Juan Colín
*University of Oklahoma*

Marcos Contreras
*Modesto Junior College*

José Cruz
*Fayetteville Technical
Community College*

Ana Dávila-Howard
*Ferris State University*

Elfe Dona
*Wright State University*

Deborah M. Edson
*Tidewater Community College,
Virginia Beach Campus*

Anne M. Edstrom
*Montclair State University*

Denise Egidio
*Guilford Technical Community College*

Vickie R. Ellison
*Kent State University*

Eddy Enríquez Arana
*Pennsylvania State University*

Luz Marina Escobar
*Tarrant County College*

Fabio Espitia
*Grand Valley State University*

Dina Fabery
*University of Central Florida*

Ronna S. Feit
*Nassau Community College*

Carlo Ferguson-McIntyre
*Truckee Meadows Community College*

María Fidalgo-Eick
*Grand Valley State University*

Neysa L. Figueroa
*Kennesaw State University*

Joan Fox
*University of Washington*

María Fussell
*University of Nevada, Las Vegas*

Khedija Gadhoum
*Clayton State University*

Muriel Gallego
*Ohio University*

Marlon Garren
*Asheville Buncombe Technical
Community College*

Judith Garson
*Santa Rosa Junior College*

Amy George-Hirons
*Tulane University*

Jane Gibson
*Central Texas College*

Arcides González
*Florida State College at Jacksonville*

Yolanda González
*Valencia Community College*

Andrew Gordon
*Mesa State College*

Sergio Guzmán
*College of Southern Nevada*

Marilyn A. Harper
*Pellissippi State Community College*

Patricia Harrigan
*Community College of
Baltimore County*

Alan Gerard Hartman
*Mercy College*

Richard A. Heath
*Kirkwood Community College*

Karla Hernández
*San Diego Mesa College*

Yolanda Hernández
*College of Southern Nevada*

Anne Hlas
*University of Wisconsin—Eau Claire*

Mary Ann Horley
*University of North
Carolina at Greensboro*

Carmen Jany
*California State University—
San Bernadino*

Caridad Jiménez
*Pensacola Junior College*

Qiu Y. Jiménez
*Bakersfield College*

Dallas Jurasevic
*Metropolitan Community College*

Adam Karp
*American River College*

Marianna Kunow
*Southeastern Louisiana University*

Joseph La Valle
*Gainesville State College*

Andrew Lawton
*Florida State College at Jacksonville*

David Leavell
*College of Southern Nevada*

Kathleen Leonard
*University of Nevada, Reno*

John Llorens
*American River College*

Talía Loaiza
*Austin Community College*

Leticia P. López
*San Diego Mesa College*

Nuria R. López-Ortega
*University of Cincinnati*

Augusto Lorenzino
*Temple University*

Alejandro Mandel
*Xavier University*

Laura Manzo
*Modesto Junior College*

Dawn M. Meissner
*Anne Arundel Community College*

Sergio Martínez
*San Antonio College*

James A. McAllister
*University of New Orleans*

Dave McAlpine
*University of Arkansas at
Little Rock*

ACKNOWLEDGMENTS

Peggy McNeil
*Louisiana State University*

Nelly McRae
*Hampton University*

Mercedes Meier
*Coastal Carolina Community College*

Wendy Méndez-Hasselman
*Palm Beach State College*

Deanna Mihaly
*Eastern Michigan University*

Dennis Miller, Jr.
*Clayton State University*

Ljiljana Milojevic
*Ocean County College*

Theresa Minick
*Kent State University*

María (Mónica) Montalvo
*University of Central Florida*

María Eugenia Moratto
*University of North
Carolina at Greensboro*

Norma Mouton
*Sam Houston State University*

Carrie Mulvihill
*Des Moines Area Community
College—Urban Campus*

Lisa Nalbone
*University of Central Florida*

Ruth F. Navarro
*Grossmont College*

Dana Nichols
*Gainesville State College*

Cynthia Nicholson
*Asheville-Buncombe Technical
Community College*

Elizabeth Olvera
*University of Texas at San Antonio*

Ann M. Ortiz
*Campbell University*

Lucía Osa-Melero
*University of Texas at Austin*

Mirta Pagnucci
*Northern Illinois University*

Marilyn Palatinus
*Pellissippi State Community College*

Tammy Pérez
*San Antonio College*

Derek A. Petrey
*Sinclair Community College*

Inmaculada Pertusa
*Western Kentucky University*

Erica Piedra
*Sacramento City College*

Anne Prucha
*University of Central Florida*

Marian Quintana
*George Mason University*

David Quintero
*Seattle Central Community College*

Bill B. Raines
*Guilford Technical
Community College*

María T. Redmon
*University of Central Florida*

Claire Reetz
*Florida State College at Jacksonville*

Anna Regalado
*Rio Hondo College*

John Riley
*Greenville Technical College*

Angelo J. Rodríguez
*Kutztown University of
Pennsylvania*

Cristina Ofelia Rodríguez Cabral
*North Carolina Central University*

R. Joseph Rodríguez
*University of Houston*

Marcela Ruiz-Funes
*East Carolina University*

Laura Ruiz-Scott
*Scottsdale Community College*

Victoria Russell
*Valdosta State University*

Christine Sabin
*Sierra College*

Celia Samaniego
*Cosumnes River College*

Bethany J. Sanio
*University of Nebraska—Lincoln*

Mark Schaaf
*Indiana University—Purdue
University Indianapolis*

Louis Silvers
*Monroe Community College*

Victor Slesinger
*Palm Beach State College*

Juan Manuel Soto Arriví
*Indiana University, Bloomington*

Cristina Szterensus
*Rock Valley College*

Gilberta H. Turner
*University of Texas at San Antonio*

Jan Underwood
*Portland Community College*

Norma Urrutia
*Xavier University*

Iris Yolanda Van Derdys-Ortiz
*Springfield College*

Natalia Verjat
*Tarrant County College*

Andrés Villagrá
*Pace University*

Paul Vincent
*Grossmont College*

Hilde Votaw
*University of Oklahoma*

Michael Vrooman
*Grand Valley State University*

Melanie J. Waters
*University of Illinois at Urbana-
Champaign*

Sandra L. Watts
*University of North Carolina at
Charlotte*

Mary West
*Des Moines Area Community College*

Justin White
*Florida Atlantic University*

Helga Winkler
*Moorpark College*

Susanna Williams
*Macomb Community College*

Marjorie J. Zambrano-Paff
*Indiana University of Pennsylvania*

## Symposia

María Nieves Alonso Almagro
*Suffolk County Community College*

Pilar Alcalde
*University of Memphis*

Debra Andrist
*Sam Houston State University*

Maxi Armas
*Triton College*

Miriam Barbaria
*Sacramento City College*

Lisa Barboun
*Coastal Carolina University*

Aymara Boggiano
*University of Houston—Houston*

Emma Brombin
*Daytona Beach College*

Beth Cardon
*Georgia Perimeter College*

Margaret Chaves-Smith
*Vance-Granville
Community College*

Alicia Cipria
*University of Alabama*

José Cruz
*Fayetteville Technical
Community College*

Octavio de la Suaree
*William Paterson University*

Marisol del-Teso-Craviotto
*Miami University*

Rosa Dávila
*Austin Community College*

Christopher DiCapua
*Community College of Philadelphia*

Carolyn Dunlap
*Southwestern University*

Deborah Edson
*Tidewater Community
College—Virginia Beach*

Héctor M. Enríquez
*University of Texas at El Paso*

José Escorcia
*University of Missouri—Columbia*

Donna Factor
*El Camino College*

Janan Fallon
*Georgia Perimeter College*

Neysa L. Figueroa
*Kennesaw State University*

Leah Fonder-Solano
*University of Southern Mississippi*

Inés García
*American River College*

Próspero García
*University of Massachussetts—Amherst*

Mariche García-Bayonas
*University of North Carolina
at Greensboro*

Alfonso García-Osuna
*Kingsborough Community College*

Blanca Gill
*Consumnes River College*

Amy Ginck
*Messiah College*

Yolanda González
*Valencia Community College*

Marilyn Harper
*Pellissippi State Technical
Community College*

Eda Henao
*Borough of Manhattan
Community College*

Luisa Howell
*Mount San Antonio College*

Nuria Ibáñez-Quintana
*University of North Florida*

Magalí Jerez
*Bergen Community College*

Valerie Job
*South Plains College*

Linda J. Keown
*University of Missouri*

Alejandro Latínez
*Sam Houston State University*

David Leavell
*College of Southern Nevada*

Jeff Longwell
*New Mexico State University*

Ceydy Ludovina
*American River College*

Bernard Manker
*Grand Rapids Community College*

Elizabeth Mares
*College of DuPage*

Rob Martinsen
*Brigham Young University*

Mary McKinney
*Texas Christian University*

Nelly McRae
*Hampton University*

Ana Menéndez-Collera
*Suffolk County
Community College*

Linda Miller Jensen
*Tidewater Community College*

Ljiljana Milojevic
*Ocean County College*

Nancy T. Mínguez
*Old Dominion University*

Teresa Minick
*Kent State University*

Deborah Mistron
*Tennessee State University*

María (Mónica) Montalvo
*University of Central Florida*

Oscar Moreno
*Georgia State University*

Javier Morin
*Del Mar College*

Carlos Pedroza
*Palomar College*

Tammy Pérez
*San Antonio College*

Teresa Pérez-Gamboa
*University of Georgia*

Maribel Pinyas
*Portland Community College*

Kristina Primorac
*University of Michigan*

Marian Quintana
*George Mason University*

David Quintero
*Seattle Central Community College*

Sheila Rivera
*University of Central Florida*

Susana Rivera-Mills
*Oregon State University*

Laura Ruiz-Scott
*Scottsdale Community College*

Kimberley Sallee
*University of Missouri—St. Louis*

Oneida Sánchez
*Borough of Manhattan
Community College*

Bethany J. Sanio
*University of Nebraska—Lincoln*

Patricia Scarfone
*Orange Coast College*

Daniela Schuvaks Katz
*Indiana University—Purdue
University Indianapolis*

March Jean Sustarsic
*Pikes Peak Community College*

Daniel Thornhill
*Florida Atlantic University*

Jan Underwood
*Portland Community College*

Adriana Vega Hidalgo
*University of North
Carolina at Charlotte*

Andrés Villagrá
*Pace University*

Hilde M. Votaw
*University of Oklahoma*

Michael Vrooman
*Grand Valley State University*

Melanie J. Waters
*University of Illinois at
Urbana-Champaign*

Sarah Williams
*University of Pittsburgh*

Susanna Williams
*Macomb Community College*

Justin White
*Florida Atlantic University*

Olivia Yáñez
*College of Lake County*

# Focus Groups

## ACTFL 2009 Digital Focus Group

Mark Darhower
*North Carolina State University*

Eddy Enríquez Arana
*Pennsylvania State University*

Yolanda González
*Valencia Community College*

Elena Grajeda
*Pima Community College*

María (Mónica) Montalvo
*University of Central Florida*

Kimberley Sallee
*University of Missouri—St. Louis*

Lester Sandres Rapalo
*Valencia Community College*

Mary West
*Des Moines Area Community College*

Helga Winkler
*Moorpark College*

## NECTFL 2010 Digital Focus Group

Silvia P. Albanese
*Nassau Community College*

Ronna Feit
*Nassau Community College*

Karen Martin
*Texas Christian University*

Mary McKinney
*Texas Christian University*

Ana Menéndez-Collera
*Suffolk County Community College*

María Nieves Alonso Almagro
*Suffolk County Community College*

## Atlanta Focus Group

Andrew Bennett
*University of Missouri—St. Louis*

Wendy Bennett-Turner
*Pellissippi State Community College*

Ryan N. Boylan
*Gainesville State College*

Sara Burns
*Gainesville State College*

Beth Cardon
*Georgia Perimeter College*

Rosa Chávez-Otero
*University of Georgia*

Andrea DiBenardo
*Georgia Perimeter College*

Fabio Espitia
*Grand Valley State University*

Janan Fallon
*Georgia Perimeter College*

Marilyn Harper
*Pellissippi State Community College*

María Mumford
*North Carolina Central University*

Dana Nichols
*Gainesville State College*

Teresa Pérez-Gamboa
*University of Georgia*

John Riley
*Greenville Technical College*

Dora Schoenbrun-Fernández
*San Diego Mesa College*

Veronica Tempone
*Indian River State College*

## Student Focus Groups

We would also like to thank the following students for their time and important perspective during the development of this program.

*From American River College*

Tracy Baltierra
Daniel Day
Erika Fuentez
Ben Haueter
Olivia Joiner
Sean McDade
Katie Newton
Veronica Pardo
Alyona Pivnitskaya
Kishonn Prince
Kayla Robinson
Kristin Valentine
William C. Webb, II.

*From Hunter College*

Lola Abudu
Carissa Boncardo
Kendra Clarke
Nina González
Vevica Gooden
Lynuda L. La Rocque
Kisha McMeo
Aurerose Piana
Esra Samrioglu

*From Pace University*

Francesca Carter
Nikkita Dadlani
Casi DeSarro
Alexis Gruttadauria
Adam Maltese
Alexandra Newton
Jasmine Parker
Angela Plura
Candace Pond
Xenia Torres

*From Suffolk Community College*

Ben Javidfar

*From the University of Missouri—Columbia*

James Beverley
Jordan Fowler
Samantha Greenfield
Stephanie Johnson
Kristen Kuehn
Wren Tolan

*From the University of Missouri—St. Louis*

Matthew B. Beesley
Courtney Harmon
Stephanie Johnson
Zach King
Jennifer White

*From the University of Oklahoma—Norman*

Stephanie Anderson
Chris Applegate
Sarah Bloss
Chinh Doan
Nicole Egli
María Hernández
Alyssa Loveless
Daniel Page

*From the University of Wisconsin—Madison*

Felicia Barrios
Jenna Erickson
Courtney Kuehn
Luke Nevermann
Spencer Schubert

The authors wish to thank the following friends and professional colleagues. Their feedback, support, and contributions are greatly appreciated.

▶ Jonathan Carlyon, Francisco Leal, (Chile), María del Pilar Isabel Máynez Vidal (Universidad Autónoma de México), Nereida Perdigón (Venezuela), Ángel Tuninetti (West Virginia University), Lillian von der Walde Moheno (Universidad Autónoma de México) for their insights into Latin American cultures

▶ The graduate teaching assistants at West Virginia University, especially: Susana Mazuelas, Elena Gandolla, and Manuel Villaescusa for contributing to some of the cultural features

▶ International Studies Abroad (ISA) for their invaluable assistance with the DVD Program, especially the following people. They made it possible for us to film in so many locations from around the Spanish-speaking world.

- Gustavo Artaza, *President/CEO*
- Dr. Rafael Hoyle, Ph.D., *Executive Vice President of Academic Affairs*
- Arturo Artaza, *Executive Vice President University Relations and Marketing in Austin*
- Dominick Luciano, *Senior Director of University Relations and Marketing Manager*
- Christian Vargas, *ISA San José, Costa Rica Resident Director*
- Michelle McRaney DeWinder, *ISA Lima, Peru Resident Director*
- Guillermo Cáceres, *ISA Buenos Aires, Argentina Resident Director*
- Alma Montes, *ISA Guanajuato, Mexico Resident Director*
- Jonathan Lapiax, *ISA Santiago, Dominican Republic Assistant Resident Director*
- Laura Reyes Ruiz, *ISA Granada, Assistant Director of European Operations*
- Eugenio Aguilar, *ISA Granada*
- Lorena Herrera, *ISA Granada*
- Marisa Revelles, *ISA Granada, Resident Director*
- Liliana Valenti (Coquí), *ISA Buenos Aires*
- María Sol Alonso, *ISA Buenos Aires*
- María Elena Arroyo, *ISA Lima*

▶ The staff of the Museo de Arte de Lima for their hospitality and for allowing us to film inside the museum

▶ Mona Miller, *Director of EuroLearn*, for her support of the video project in the initial stages

▶ The bloggers and other people who participated in the **Concurso de videoblogs** segments

- Héctor Iván Bernal (Los Angeles)
- Miguel Anguiano, Elena, Alejandra, and Chucho (Mexico)
- Ana Gallego Coin, Carlos and Julia, Eugenio and Lorena, as well as Miguel González Dengra, Concha García, and their children Carlos and Julia (Spain)
- Juan Carlos, Pedro, Catalina and her mother Leticia, and our special thanks to Don Carlos, «el pintor de carretas» in Sarchí (Costa Rica)
- Merfry Rijo de Contreras (Dominican Republic)
- María Elena Arroyo and Graciela (Peru)
- Federico Villar and Sol (Argentina)

▶ The various film crews in Argentina, Costa Rica, Dominican Republic, Los Angeles, Mexico, Peru, and Spain, especially

- Jennifer Rodes (Klic Video Productions, Los Angeles)
- Xavier Roy (Froggie Productions)
- Manuel Vílchez (Spain)

▶ Christa Neumann, who first proposed the project and provided initial guidance

- Allen J. Bernier, for his tireless editorial assistance and help as the book took shape. His role went beyond the call of duty, and we are especially appreciative.

- My husband, Jim Rentch, who kept "the home fires burning" for several years. My deepest thanks for his help and support. —*María J. Amores*

- Courtenay Suárez, for her help with many ideas and suggestions on language and culture, and for always taking care of our family. I would not have made it without her support! —*José Luis Suárez García*

- The rest of our friends and family members for their support, love, and understanding throughout this process. We love you all very much, and we couldn't have done it without you. ¡Mil millones de gracias!

## Contributing Writers

Rodney Bransdorfer, Susanna Coll-Ramírez, Juan Carlos de los Santos, Frank Freeman, Mercedes Freeman, Mary Goodrich, Mar Freire Hermida, Carla Iglesias-Garrido, Misha Maclaird, Pennie Nichols, Andrew Noverr, Kimberley Sallee, Bethany J. Sanio, Julie Sellers, Scott Tinetti

## Product Team

**Editorial:** Allen J. Bernier, Susan Blatty, Erin Blaze, Meghan Campbell, Laura Chastain, Laura Chiriboga, Laura Ciporen, Katherine K. Crouch, William R. Glass, Jennifer Kirk, Lynne Lemley, Beth Mejia, Christa Neumann, Pennie Nichols, Michael Ryan, Kimberley Sallee, Katie Stevens, Scott Tinetti, Margaret Young

**Digital:** Victoria Anderson, Nathan Benjamin, Maria Betancourt, Sunil Bheda, Cherie Black, Gennady Borukhovich, Jay Chakrapani, Jeff Collins, Kyle Constance, Xavier de Cardenas, Aoife Dempsey, Sarah Hegarty, Stephanie Hom, Neil Kahn, Roja Mirzadeh, Dennis Plucinik, Sanjay Shinde, Catherine Vanderhoof, Jenny Woo

**Art, Design, and Production:** Harry Briggs, Thomas Brierly, Sonia Brown, Christina Gimlin, Sarah Hill, Patti Isaacs, Tandra Jorgensen, Glenda King, Robin Mouat, Andrei Pasternak, Brian Pecko, Natalia Peschiera, Terri Schiesl, David Staloch, Mel Valentín

**Marketing and Sales:** Hector Alvero, Jorge Arbujas, Julie Bickar, Audra Bussey, Deo Díaz, Mackenzie Dunn, Carolyn Ghazi-Tehrani, Craig Gill, Meredith Grant, Helen Greenlea, Suzanne Guinn, James Headley, Rolando Hernández, James Koch, Greg Moore, Bruce Moser, Kim Nentwig, Alexa Recio, Ricardo Reilova, Katie Reynolds, Dan Ryan, Maureen Spada, Dawn Stumpf, Janet Taborn

- Extra special thanks go out to Helen Greenlea, Maureen Spada, and Suzanne Guinn for their direction and leadership for all of us in the market development activities of this project. They did an incredible job and without a doubt took the concept of Market Development to a whole new level.

**Media Partners:** Aptara, BBC Motion Gallery, Dartmouth Publishing Inc., Eastern Sky Studios, Klic Video Productions, Laserwords, LearningMate Solutions, Tricon Infotech, UVCMS

# Contents

**Conexiones culturales** Los pasatiempos y los deportes: El fútbol

*El fútbol: Deporte internacional*
*La historia del fútbol y la FIFA*
*La Copa Mundial*

*Las selecciones nacionales*
*Las ligas femeninas*
*Lionel Messi*

| Grammar | Writing & Video | Reading & Culture |
|---|---|---|

**Conexiones culturales** La naturaleza: Los parques nacionales

*El Yunque (Puerto Rico)*
*El Parque Nacional Tortuguero (Costa Rica)*
*Las Torres del Paine (Chile)*

*La Sierra Nevada (España)*
*Las Islas Galápagos (Ecuador)*

**Conexiones culturales** La música y la danza: La guitarra

*El flamenco (España)*
*Los mariachis (México)*
*La guitarra clásica: Andrés Segovia (España)*

*Carlos Santana (los Estados Unidos)*
*El Buena Vista Social Club: Compay*
*Segundo (Cuba)*

| Grammar | Writing & Video | Reading & Culture |
|---|---|---|

**Conexiones culturales** La vida moderna: Los medios de comunicación
*El Internet*
*Los teléfonos celulares*
*Los medios sociales*
*La televisión en español*
*La prensa*

En el **National Puerto Rican Day Parade,** *Manhattan*

# Entrada cultural

## Hispanics in the United States

Cultures

En El Paso, Texas

En la Calle Ocho, Miami

*Shakira*

The United States has a varied and fascinating blend of ethnic cultures, of which Hispanic culture is one of the richest and most important. Several factors interact to create this cultural wealth: the differing origins of Hispanics (Mexico, Central America, the Caribbean, South America, and Spain), the historical tendency of different groups to reside in different areas (Cubans in Florida, Puerto Ricans in New York, and Mexicans in states that border Mexico), and the sheer numbers of Hispanics who now live throughout this country. They live in large cities, small towns, and rural areas. They work as doctors, judges, teachers, shopkeepers, factory workers, and on farms. They represent an integral part of the United States.

In the United States, as of 2007, Hispanics represented more than 15 percent of the total population, or more than 45 million people. They comprise the most numerous minority group in the country, and projections indicate that by 2050 Hispanics will constitute 25 percent of the estimated 400 million people who will live in the United States at that time.

Examples of the contributions of Hispanics to American contemporary culture are found everywhere: in architecture, in painting, and in depictions that combine traditional forms with modern influences. We hear them every day in the Latin music created in the United States, as well as in the works of popular singers from Hispanic countries. Television broadcasts dozens of programs in Spanish, Hispanic actors star in U.S. movies, and Americans read the works of Hispanic authors. We hear the influence of Spanish in spoken American English, and we see it in the written language as well. American cuisine also contains many foods of Hispanic origin. Did you know that the turkey eaten on Thanksgiving is of Central American origin? And did you know that potatoes originated in the Andean region where Peru and Bolivia are now located? Imagine a summer picnic without potato salad! Certainly there are few people in the United States in the 21st century who are unfamiliar with tortillas and the foods we make with them, which originated in Mexico and Central America. Look at the photos on this page. Can you think of other examples of Hispanic culture that we see on a daily basis?

| ¿Cómo te llamas? ¿Cuál es tu nombre? | What's your (*fam.*) name? |
| ¿Cómo se llama usted? ¿Cuál es su nombre? | What's your (*form.*) name? |
| Me llamo... Mi nombre es... | My name is . . . |
| Soy... | I'm . . . |
| Mucho gusto. Encantado/a.* | It's a pleasure (to meet you). |
| Igualmente. | Likewise. |
| ¿De dónde eres? | Where are you (*fam.*) from? |
| ¿De dónde es usted? | Where are you (*form.*) from? |
| Soy de... | I'm from . . . |

▶ To say good-bye to someone, you can use:

| Adiós. | Good-bye. |
| Hasta luego. | See you later. |
| Hasta mañana. | See you tomorrow. |
| Hasta pronto. | See you soon. |
| Nos vemos. | See you later. (*lit.* We'll see each other.) |

▶ Here are a few polite expressions that you should know.

| Gracias. | Thank you. |
| De nada. | You're welcome. |
| No hay de qué. | Don't mention it. |

### ACTIVIDADES

**A. Saludos y despedidas.** Finish the dialogues by matching the responses in column B with the blanks in column A.

| A | B |
|---|---|
| 1. —Buenos días, señor Osorio. | a. —Bien. Hasta luego. |
| —_____ | b. —Buenos días, señora Martínez. ¿Cómo está usted? |
| —Bien, gracias. ¿Y usted? | |
| —_____ | c. —Nos vemos. |
| —Adiós. | d. —Hola, Miguel. ¿Qué tal? |
| 2. —_____ | e. —Muy bien, gracias. |
| —Bien, gracias. ¿Y tú? | |
| —_____ | |
| —Hasta mañana. | |
| —_____ | |

*Use **encantado** if you're male, **encantada** if you're female.

---

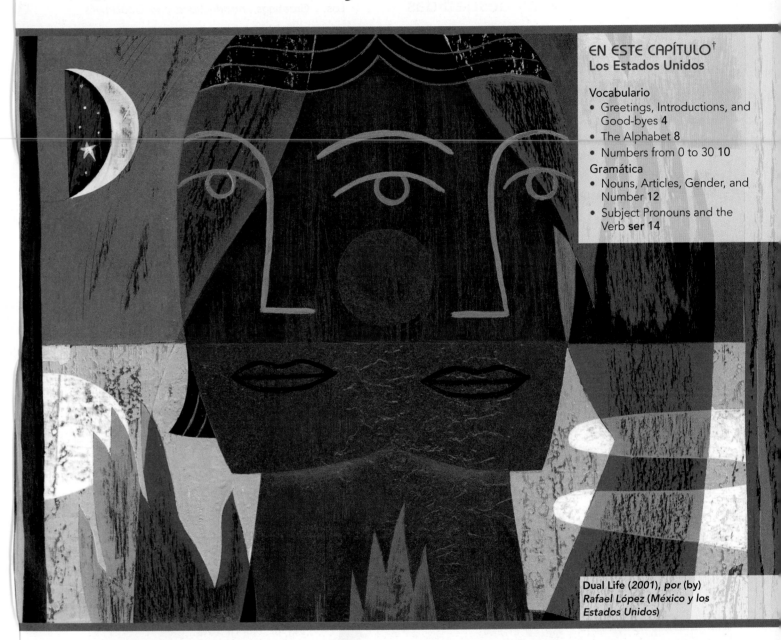

Dual Life (2001), por (by) *Rafael López (México y los Estados Unidos)*

**EN ESTE CAPÍTULO†**
**Los Estados Unidos**

Vocabulario
• Greetings, Introductions, and Good-byes 4
• The Alphabet 8
• Numbers from 0 to 30 10

Gramática
• Nouns, Articles, Gender, and Number 12
• Subject Pronouns and the Verb **ser** 14

1. How would you define the term *culture*?
2. What are some similarities and differences between your culture and another culture that you're familiar with?
3. In your opinion, what do you think the painting *Dual Life* represents?

 connect™
|SPANISH

www.connectspanish.com

*¿Somos... *Are We Similar?*
†En... *In This Chapter*

# Vocabulario del tema*

## Los saludos, las presentaciones y las despedidas°

Los... *Greetings, Introductions, and Good-byes*

**1.**

—Hola, Paula. ¿Cómo estás?
—Bien, gracias. ¿Y tú?
—Muy bien, gracias.

**2.**

—Buenos días, profesora Peña. ¿Cómo está usted?
—Bien, profesor Galeano. ¿Y usted?
—Muy bien, gracias.
—De nada.

**3.**

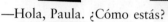

—Hasta luego, Jorge.
—Adiós, Luis.

**4.**

—Hola. ¿Cómo te llamas?
—Me llamo Jaime García.
—Mucho gusto.
—Igualmente.

**5.**

—Hola. Soy Guillermo. ¿Cuál es tu nombre?
—Mi nombre es Rosa María.
—Mucho gusto, Rosa María.
—Encantada, Guillermo. ¿De dónde eres?
—Soy de San José. ¿Y tú?
—Soy de Nueva York.

**Observe (Note)**

Throughout *Experience Spanish*, you'll find translations for vocabulary and grammar presentations at the bottom of the page.

*del... thematic
**1.** Hi, Paula. How are you? / Fine, thanks. And you? / Very well, thanks. **2.** Good morning, Professor Peña. How are you? / Fine, Professor Galeano. And you? / Very well, thank you. / You're welcome.
**3.** See you later, Jorge. / Good-bye, Luis. **4.** Hello. What's your name? / My name is Jaime García. / Nice to meet you. / Likewise. **5.** Hi, I'm Guillermo. What's your name? / My name is Rosa María. / Nice to meet you, Rosa María. / It's a pleasure, Guillermo. Where are you from? / I'm from San José. And you? / I'm from New York.

## Nota cultural

### ADDRESSING PEOPLE IN FORMAL AND FAMILIAR SITUATIONS

*Como usted mande, mi amor.*

Spanish has two ways of directly addressing a single person as *you*. **Usted** is used in formal situations, such as with a professor or in a business context. **Tú** is used in familiar situations, such as with family and friends. However, in some Hispanic cultures, it's common for relatives to use **usted** with each other as a sign of respect.

Sometimes native speakers will knowingly go against the rules of appropriateness to establish distance from someone on purpose, or even to express humor. Let's say a husband and wife are in the habit of addressing each other with **tú**. Then one day, one of them starts giving the other a list of things to get done around the house. The spouse receiving the list of chores might respond with the phrase, "**Como usted mande, mi amor.**[a]" Had the speaker instead used **tú**, the phrase could have been viewed as funny; however by switching to **usted**, the speaker adds a level of sarcasm that makes the response even funnier.

If you're ever unsure whether to use **tú** or **usted**, remember the following simple rule: use **usted** until you're told it's OK to use **tú**. It's better to be inappropriately formal than insultingly familiar.

[a]*Como... As you command, my love.*

**SITUACIONES** Indicate whether you should use **tú** or **usted** forms to address people in the following situations.

| | TÚ | USTED |
|---|---|---|
| 1. You bump into your Spanish professor at the library. | ☐ | ☐ |
| 2. You greet a classmate in the hallway. | ☐ | ☐ |

▶ To greet someone, you can use one of these expressions.

| | |
|---|---|
| **Hola.** | Hello. |
| **Buenos días.** | Good morning (*until midday meal*). |
| **Buenas tardes.** | Good afternoon (*until evening meal*). |
| **Buenas noches.*** | Good evening (*after evening meal*). |

▶ Here are some expressions you can use to talk about yourself and find out more about someone else.

| | |
|---|---|
| **¿Cómo estás?** | How are you (*familiar*)? |
| **¿Cómo está usted?** | How are you (*formal*)? |
| **¿Qué tal?** | How's it going? |
| **Muy bien.** | Very well. |
| **Bien.** | Fine. |
| **Regular.** | So-so. |
| **No muy bien.** | Not very well. |
| **¿Y tú?** | And you (*fam.*)? |
| **¿Y usted?** | And you (*form.*)? |

*****Buenas noches** can also be translated as *Good night* and thus used as a way of saying good-bye to someone, as in **Buenas noches, hasta mañana.** (*Good night, see you tomorrow.*)

**B.** Respuestas (*Answers*) lógicas. Listen to the expressions and select the appropriate answer.

1. **a.** Encantado.  **b.** Me llamo Andrea.  **c.** ¿Cuál es tu nombre?
2. **a.** Mi nombre es Rose.  **b.** Mucho gusto.  **c.** Soy Rose.
3. **a.** Lisa.  **b.** Hola. Encantada.  **c.** ¿Cómo te llamas?
4. **a.** Me llamo Ana.  **b.** Soy de Pennsylvania.  **c.** Muy bien, gracias.
5. **a.** Encantada.  **b.** Hasta luego.  **c.** Buenos días.
6. **a.** Buenas tardes.  **b.** No muy bien.  **c.** De nada.

**C.** A conocerlo/la (*Getting to know you*). Answer the questions about yourself, using a complete sentence whenever possible.

1. ¿Cómo se llama usted?
2. ¿Cómo está usted?
3. ¿De dónde es usted?

**D.** Entrevista (*Interview*). Find a classmate that you haven't met yet and have a short conversation with him/her in Spanish. Be sure to do the following:

Communication

1. Greet him/her and introduce yourself.
2. Ask what his/her name is.
3. Ask how he/she is or how it's going.
4. Ask where he/she is from.
5. Say good-bye to him/her.

---

## Nota cultural

Cultures

### LOS SALUDOS

¡Hola! ¿Qué tal?

It is very common for people from Hispanic cultures to shake hands, hug each other, and even kiss each other on the cheek when greeting or saying good-bye to someone. Typically, women kiss each other on the cheek whether they are already acquainted or meeting for the first time. The same is true when a man and a woman meet. It is more common for two men to shake hands, although they may hug each other if they are close friends.

Recently, there has been a greater tendency among young men in Spain who are long-time friends to kiss each other on both cheeks when greeting and saying good-bye, just as women do.

PREGUNTAS Answer the questions.

1. What do you think about the Hispanic way of greeting people?
2. How does the Hispanic way of greeting people compare to how people greet each other in non-Hispanic cultures?

# El abecedario°

El... *The Alphabet*

The Spanish alphabet (**el abecedario** or **el alfabeto**) consists of 29 letters. The letter **ñ** follows **n** in alphabetized lists, and the letters **k** and **w** only appear in words borrowed from another language, for example: **kilo, whisky.**

| \multicolumn{4}{c}{THE SPANISH ALPHABET} | | | |
|---|---|---|---|
| LETTER | NAME(S) OF LETTER | \multicolumn{2}{c}{EXAMPLES} | |
| a | a | Argentina | Adiós. |
| b | be, be grande, be larga, or be de burro | Bolivia | Buenos días. |
| c | ce | Colombia | ¿Cómo estás? |
| ch | che | Machu Picchu | Mucho gusto. |
| d | de | República Dominicana | despedida |
| e | e | España | Encantado. |
| f | efe | Francia | frase |
| g | ge | Guinea Ecuatorial | Gracias. |
| h | hache | Honduras | Hasta luego. |
| i | i | Islas Galápagos | Igualmente. |
| j | jota | San José | jueves |
| k | ka | Kenya | kilo |
| l | ele | Lima | libro |
| ll | elle *or* doble ele | Barranquilla | Me llamo... |
| m | eme | Maracaibo | Muy bien. |
| n | ene | Nicaragua | nacionalidad |
| ñ | eñe | Cataluña | mañana |
| o | o | Oviedo | otro |
| p | pe | Panamá | palabra |
| q | cu | Quito | ¿Qué tal? |
| r | ere | Rosario | Regular. |

## THE SPANISH ALPHABET

| LETTER | NAME(S) OF LETTER | EXAMPLES | |
|---|---|---|---|
| s | ese | Sucre | saludo |
| t | te | Tierra del Fuego | Buenas tardes. |
| u | u | Uruguay | uno |
| v | ve, uve, ve chica, ve corta, *or* ve de vaca | Venezuela | Nos vemos. |
| w | doble ve *or* ve doble | Winnipeg | página Web |
| x | equis | México | extranjero |
| y | i griega | Guayaquil | ya |
| z | ceta *or* zeta | Zaragoza | zanahoria |

## ACTIVIDADES

**A. Buscando en el mapa** (*Searching on the map*). Review the sample words and phrases in the third column of the preceding chart. Did you notice that they're all place-names? See how many of these place-names you can find on the three regional maps inside the back cover of *Experience Spanish*. ¡OJO! (*Careful!*) All but two of these place-names can be found on the maps.

Cultures

**B. Buscando en el diccionario**

**PASO 1.** Review the sample words and phrases in the fourth column of the preceding chart and jot down any whose meaning you don't know.

**PASO 2.** Now, using the Spanish-English Vocabulary near the back of *Experience Spanish* or a Spanish-English dictionary, look up the meanings for at least ten of the words that you jotted down in **Paso 1.**

**C. ¡A deletrear!** (*Let's do some spelling!*)

**PASO 1.** Jot down this information.

1. your full name
2. your best friend's full name
3. the name of the first street on which you remember living
4. the name of the city where you were born
5. the name of a place in the Spanish-speaking world that you would like to visit

**PASO 2.** Now, working with a partner, spell aloud each answer that you jotted down in **Paso 1.** Your partner should jot down each letter as you say it with the goal of guessing what you're trying to spell. Did you successfully spell each item, and did your partner understand? If not, try again. Then switch roles.

Communication

Uno, dos, tres, cuatro, cinco.

# Los números de 0 a 30°

*Los... Numbers from 0 to 30*

| | | | |
|---|---|---|---|
| 0 cero | 8 ocho | 16 dieciséis | 24 veinticuatro |
| 1 uno | 9 nueve | 17 diecisiete | 25 veinticinco |
| 2 dos | 10 diez | 18 dieciocho | 26 veintiséis |
| 3 tres | 11 once | 19 diecinueve | 27 veintisiete |
| 4 cuatro | 12 doce | 20 veinte | 28 veintiocho |
| 5 cinco | 13 trece | 21 veintiuno | 29 veintinueve |
| 6 seis | 14 catorce | 22 veintidós | 30 treinta |
| 7 siete | 15 quince | 23 veintitrés | |

◐ Note the accents on **dieciséis, veintidós, veintitrés,** and **veintiséis.**

◐ When used as an adjective, **uno** changes to **un** for masculine and **una** for feminine.

Hay sólo* **un** hombre aquí.     *There's only one man here.*
Tengo sólo **una** tía.     *I have only one aunt.*

◐ **Veintiuno** changes to **veintiún** or **veintiuna** when used as an adjective.

Tengo **veintiún** dólares.     *I have $21.*
Hay **veintiuna** rosas aquí.     *There are twenty-one roses here.*

◐ You may see the numbers 16–19 and 21–29 written out in a longer but less common form.

| | | | |
|---|---|---|---|
| **diez y seis** | **diez y siete** | **diez y ocho** | **diez y nueve** |
| **veinte y uno** | **veinte y dos** | **veinte y tres** | **veinte y cuatro...** |

---

## Nota comunicativa

Communication

### Hay AND ¿cuántos/as?

The verb form **hay** is used in Spanish to mean *there is* or *there are*. Can you guess what **no hay** means? (If you said *there isn't* or *there aren't*, you're right.)

**Hay** doce libros en el escritorio.     *There are twelve books on the desk.*

**¿Cuántos/as?** is used before plural nouns to ask *how many?* **¿Cuántos?** is used before masculine plural nouns and **¿cuántas?** before feminine ones. You'll learn more about gender agreement (masculine vs. feminine) later in this chapter and in **Capítulo 1.**

—¿**Cuántos estudiantes** hay en esta clase?     *How many students are there in this class?*
—Hay veinticinco.     *There are twenty-five.*
—¿**Cuántas personas** hay en esta foto?     *How many people are there in this photo?*
—Hay siete personas.     *There are seven people.*

---

*According to the Real Academia Española (*Royal Spanish Academy*), which is the official governing body of the Spanish language, the adverb **sólo** (*only*) does not require an accent, except in cases of possible confusion with the adjective **solo/a** (*alone*). However, throughout the *Experience Spanish* program, the adverb **sólo** will always appear with an accent as a matter of style. You should check with your instructor to find out if he or she will require the accent on this adverb for grading purposes.

## ACTIVIDADES

**A. Los números.** Write out the numbers.

MODELO 4 → cuatro

1. 10
2. 14
3. 7
4. 21
5. 6
6. 12
7. 28
8. 5
9. 15
10. 16
11. 8
12. 1

**B. ¿Cuántos dijo?** (*How many did he/she say?*) Listen to some short phrases, each containing a number. Jot down the number you hear, as in the model.

| Vocabulario práctico | | | |
|---|---|---|---|
| **hombres** | men | **libros** | books |
| **mi** | my | **escritorio** | desk |
| **familia** | family | **teléfonos celulares** | cell phones |
| **clase** | class | **computadoras** | computers |
| **hoy** | today | **laboratorio** | laboratory |
| **mujeres** | women | | |

MODELO (*you hear*)  Hay siete hombres en mi familia. →
(*you write*)  siete

**C. Matemáticas.** With a partner, take turns reciting the mathematical expressions aloud as in the model. ¡OJO!  + (**más**), − (**menos**), = (**son**).

Communication

MODELO 2 + 2 = 4 →
Dos más dos son cuatro.

1. 2 + 3 = 5
2. 3 + 4 = 7
3. 10 − 4 = 6
4. 1 + 8 = 9
5. 20 − 9 = 11
6. 23 − 8 = 15
7. 14 + 12 = 26
8. 2 + 27 = 29
9. 30 − 17 = 13
10. 16 + 12 = 28
11. 24 − 22 = 2
12. 21 − 14 = 7

**D. ¿Cuántos hay?** Answer the questions with complete sentences, as in the model.

MODELOS ¿Cuántos profesores hay en la clase? →
Hay un profesor en la clase.
Hay una profesora.

1. ¿Cuántas horas (*hours*) hay en un día?
2. ¿Cuántos días hay en una semana (*week*)?
3. ¿Cuántas semanas hay en el mes (*month*) de febrero, normalmente (*usually*)?
4. ¿Cuántos días hay en el mes de septiembre?
5. ¿Cuántos hombres hay en la clase hoy?
6. ¿Y cuántas mujeres hay?

# Gramática

## P.1 Nouns, Articles, Gender, and Number

**GRAMÁTICA EN CONTEXTO**

### Un viaje al suroeste de los Estados Unidos

- **el carro**
- **la Ruta** 66
- **los amigos**
- **las vistas**

- **un museo** en el Gran Cañón
- **una iglesia** en San Antonio
- **unos recuerdos**
- **unas montañas** en Colorado

*El Valle (Valley) de los Monumentos, Utah*

### COMPRENSIÓN

**PASO 1.** Give the correct plural form of each article.

**MODELO** un museo → unos museos

1. la ruta → _____ rutas
2. el carro → _____ carros
3. una iglesia → _____ iglesias

**PASO 2.** Give the correct singular form of each article.

**MODELO** los amigos → el amigo

1. unas montañas → _____ montaña
2. unos recuerdos → _____ recuerdo
3. las vistas → _____ vista

---

In Spanish, nouns identify people, places, things, and ideas, and they are either masculine or feminine in gender. Definite articles (**el/la/los/las** = *the*) and indefinite articles (**un/una/unos/unas** = *a, an; some*) must agree in gender and number with the noun they accompany, as shown in the following charts.

### DEFINITE ARTICLES (*the*)

|  | MASCULINE |  | FEMININE |  |
|---|---|---|---|---|
| SINGULAR | el **libro** | the book | la **plum**a | the pen |
| PLURAL | los **cuadern**os | the notebooks | las **ventan**as | the windows |

### INDEFINITE ARTICLES (*a, an; some*)

|  | MASCULINE |  | FEMININE |  |
|---|---|---|---|---|
| SINGULAR | un **libro** | a book | una **plum**a | a pen |
| PLURAL | unos **cuadern**os | some notebooks | unas **ventan**as | some windows |

---

GRAMÁTICA EN CONTEXTO *A Trip to the Southwestern United States* / • *the car* • *(the) Route 66* • *the friends* • *the views/sites* • *a museum in the Grand Canyon* • *a church in San Antonio* • *some souvenirs* • *some mountains in Colorado*

## GENDER

**A.** Most nouns ending in **-o** or nouns that refer to male beings are masculine.

**el cuaderno** (*notebook*)                **un hombre** (*man*)

**B.** Most nouns ending in **-a** or those denoting female beings are feminine.

**la mesa** (*table*)                **una mujer** (*woman*)

**C.** Most nouns that refer to people have corresponding masculine and feminine forms. Here are some simple rules to remember.

1. Masculine nouns ending in **-o** have a corresponding feminine form ending in **-a.**

   **el compañero de clase** (*male classmate*)        **un amigo** (*male friend*)
   **la compañera de clase** (*female classmate*)      **una amiga** (*female friend*)

2. Generally, masculine nouns that end in a consonant form their feminine counterparts by adding an **-a** to the consonant.

   **el profesor / la profesora**        **un alemán** (*German [man]*) **/ una alemana**

3. Nouns ending in **-ante** and **-ista** use the same form for both masculine and feminine. The article or the surrounding context will determine the gender.

   **el estudiante / la estudiante**        **un dentista / una dentista**

**D.** Nouns that refer to places, things, or ideas (i.e., not people) still must be either masculine or feminine; however, there's often no apparent logic for which gender such nouns carry. Here are some general rules to remember.

1. Most nouns ending in **-ión** and **-d** are feminine.

   **la acción** (*action*)        **una universidad** (*university*)

2. Most nouns ending in **-l, -n, -r,** and **-s** are masculine.

   **el fin** (*end*)              **el amor** (*love*)
   **un papel** (*paper*)          **un mes** (*month*)

3. Many nouns ending in **-ma, -pa,** or **-ta** are masculine even though they end in **-a.**

   **el problema**        **un mapa**        **el atleta** (*athlete*)

4. Nouns ending in **-e** don't follow any rule and their gender needs to be memorized.

   **el café** (*café; coffee*)        **una clase**

5. Some common nouns are irregular and don't follow the rules. The gender of these nouns needs to be memorized.

   **el día**        **una mano** (*hand*)

## NUMBER

**A.** Nouns that end in a vowel form the plural by adding **-s.**

**cuaderno → cuadernos**

**B.** Nouns that end in any consonant except **-z** add **-es** to form the plural.

**mujer → mujeres**

**C.** To form the plural of nouns ending in **-z,** change the **-z** to **-c** and add **-es.**

**lápiz** (*pencil*) **→ lápices**

## ACTIVIDADES

**A. Los artículos definidos.** Give the definite article (**el/la/los/las**) of each noun. **¡OJO!** Some nouns can be either masculine or feminine.

1. _____ actor
2. _____ sistema
3. _____ amigos
4. _____ tendencias
5. _____ cantante (*singer*)
6. _____ televisión
7. _____ artista
8. _____ libertad (*freedom*)

**B. Los artículos indefinidos.** Give the indefinite article (**un/una/unos/unas**) of each noun.

1. _____ comunidad
2. _____ elección
3. _____ tema ,
4. _____ deporte
5. _____ novelas
6. _____ influencias
7. _____ escritor
8. _____ día

**C. ¿Singular o plural?** With a partner, change the phrases from singular to plural, or vice versa.

MODELOS   un saludo → unos saludos
las despedidas → la despedida

1. la universidad
2. los profesores
3. un optimista
4. los días
5. una flor (*flower*)
6. la clase
7. un escritorio
8. unas estudiantes

## P.2 Subject Pronouns and the Verb **ser**

Expressing *to be*

### GRAMÁTICA EN CONTEXTO

### Una página de *Facebook*

Hola. **Yo** me llamo Antonio.

- **Soy** inteligente, flexible y liberal.
- No **soy** pesimista.
- **Soy de** Guadalajara, México.

Mi amiga se llama Ana.

- **Es** independiente y responsable.
- No **es** inflexible para nada.
- **Es de** La Paz, Bolivia.

**¿Y usted?** Complete the statements using the cues.

1. Yo soy _____, _____ y _____. No soy _____.
   ☐ conservador(a)    ☐ inteligente       ☐ optimista
   ☐ independiente     ☐ (im)paciente      ☐ pesimista
   ☐ (in)flexible      ☐ liberal           ☐ (ir)responsable
2. Soy de _____ [*place-name*].

GRAMÁTICA EN CONTEXTO **A Facebook Page** / Hello. My name is Antonio. • I'm intelligent, flexible, and liberal. • I'm not a pessimist. • I'm from Guadalajara, Mexico. / My friend's name is Ana. • She's independent and responsible. • She's not at all inflexible. • She's from La Paz, Bolivia.

Like English, Spanish uses pronouns to refer to the subject of a verb. Review the chart.

| SUBJECT PRONOUNS AND THE VERB **ser** (*to be*) | | | |
| --- | --- | --- | --- |
| SINGULAR | | PLURAL | |
| **yo** soy | I am | **nosotros** somos<br>**nosotras** somos | we are |
| **tú** eres | you are (*fam.*) | **vosotros** sois<br>**vosotras** sois | you are (*fam. Spain*) |
| **usted (Ud.\*)** es | you are (*form.*) | **ustedes (Uds.\*)** son | you are (*form. Spain; fam., form. elsewhere*) |
| **él** es<br>**ella** es | he is<br>she is | **ellos** son<br>**ellas** son | they are |

**A.** The masculine plural subject pronouns **nosotros, vosotros,** and **ellos** have corresponding feminine forms. The feminine forms can only be used if a group consists of *all* women. The masculine forms are *always* used for groups of all men as well as when referring to mixed groups.

**Nosotras** somos de Miami.  *We're from Miami* (all women).
**Ellos** son inteligentes.  *They're intelligent* (all men or a mixed group).

**B.** In many parts of Spain, **vosotros/as** forms are used in familiar situations and **Uds.** forms in formal ones. Elsewhere, **Uds.** forms are used in both formal and familiar situations.

¿Cómo sois vosotros?  *What are you* (fam. Sp.) *like?* (*How would you describe yourselves?*)

¿Cómo son Uds.?  *What are you* (*form. Sp.; fam., form. elsewhere*) *like?* (*How would you describe yourselves?*)

**C.** Subject pronouns in Spanish are optional in most cases. They're typically only used to avoid confusion, to add emphasis, or to stress an opposition, as in the following example.

Yo soy de Phoenix. ¿De dónde eres tú?  ***I'm** from Phoenix. Where are **you** from?*

**D.** Ser is used with adjectives to describe people and things.

El profesor **es** inteligente y muy paciente.  *The professor is smart and very patient.*

**E.** Ser is used with **de** to express origin.

—¿De dónde **son** Uds.?  *Where are you from?*
—**Somos** de Nueva York.  *We're from New York.*

**F.** When **de** is followed by the definite article **el,** the two words are combined to form the contraction **del** (**de** + **el** = **del**).

Fernando es **del** estado de Texas.  *Fernando is from the state of Texas.*

---

\*The subject pronouns **usted** and **ustedes** are usually abbreviated **Ud.** and **Uds.,** respectively. *Experience Spanish* will use **Ud.** and **Uds.** from now on.

## Nota comunicativa

### BASIC NEGATION

Insert the word **no** before a verb to make it negative.

| | |
|---|---|
| **No soy** de los Estados Unidos. | *I'm not from the United States.* |
| **No somos** de aquí. | *We're not from here.* |

---

### ACTIVIDADES

**A. ¿Cómo soy yo?** Indicate whether or not these adjectives correctly describe you.

¿Es Ud... ?

| | SÍ | NO | | | SÍ | NO |
|---|---|---|---|---|---|---|
| 1. altruista | ☐ | ☐ | | 6. independiente | ☐ | ☐ |
| 2. idealista | ☐ | ☐ | | 7. inocente | ☐ | ☐ |
| 3. realista | ☐ | ☐ | | 8. paciente | ☐ | ☐ |
| 4. materialista | ☐ | ☐ | | 9. responsable | ☐ | ☐ |
| 5. optimista | ☐ | ☐ | | 10. flexible | ☐ | ☐ |

> **Observe**
>
> The adjectives in activity A are cognates (**cognados**). Cognates are words that are similar or identical in form and meaning in two or more different languages.

> **Observe**
>
> If you use an adjective to describe more than one person, place, thing, or idea, the adjective must be in the plural.
>
> Julia y David son **inteligentes.**
>
> Use the same rules to make adjectives plural that you learned earlier in this chapter for making nouns plural: Add **-s** to words ending in a vowel; add **-es** to words ending in a consonant.

**B. No soy así** (*I'm not like that*). Say whether or not these adjectives correctly describe you. If they don't, then say who (either a real person or a character from a book, movie, or TV show) that adjective correctly describes, as in the model.

| Vocabulario práctico | | | |
|---|---|---|---|
| **sí** | yes, indeed | **a veces** | sometimes |
| **pero** | but | **un poco** | a little |

MODELOS   cruel →

   No, yo no soy cruel, pero Hannibal Lecter sí es cruel.
   No, yo no soy cruel, pero Hannibal Lecter y Jason de *Friday the 13th* sí son crueles.
   Sí, soy un poco cruel a veces.

| | | |
|---|---|---|
| 1. impaciente | 5. superficial | 9. extravagante |
| 2. rebelde | 6. inflexible | 10. liberal |
| 3. arrogante | 7. irresponsable | 11. sentimental |
| 4. pesimista | 8. elegante | 12. inteligente |

**C.** Y tú, ¿cómo eres? Describe yourself to a partner using the adjectives that you learned in activities A and B.

Communication

MODELO  ESTUDIANTE 1: ¿Cómo eres, Amy?

ESTUDIANTE 2: Soy optimista, idealista, independiente y rebelde. Y tú, ¿cómo eres?

ESTUDIANTE 1: Yo soy idealista, independiente y optimista, pero no soy rebelde. Soy flexible.

**D.** ¿Y cómo son estas (*these*) personas?

PASO 1.  Read the selections about some people from the Hispanic world who have become famous in this country.

**SALMA HAYEK,** having already gained popularity as an actress in Mexico, left for Los Angeles with the dream of becoming an equally successful actress in the United States. She soon realized that there would be more challenges than she had anticipated. One such challenge was her very thick accent in English, which closed many opportunities for her. She worked very hard, took English lessons, studied acting, and eventually overcame all of the challenges to become one of Hollywood's leading actresses.

**JAVIER BARDEM** was famous in his native Spain before he became popular in this country. In 2000, he was the first Spanish actor to be nominated for an Oscar for his portrayal of Reinaldo Arenas, a gay Cuban writer, in *Before Night Falls*. The excitement after his nomination was such that fans mobbed him on the streets of Madrid and paparazzi waited at his doorstep. King Juan Carlos even invited him to dinner! In 2008, Bardem finally became the first Spanish actor to win an Oscar, for his role in *No Country for Old Men*.

PASO 2.  With a partner, answer the questions about the people described in **Paso 1.** ¡OJO! For item 3, mention what characteristics both actors have in common. Use adjectives that you learned in activities A and B and elsewhere.

Communication

1. ¿Cómo es Salma Hayek?
2. ¿Cómo es Javier Bardem?
3. ¿Cómo son los dos (*both of them*)?

**Observe**

You already know that adjectives must agree in number with the nouns they modify. They must also agree in gender with those nouns.

Alejandra es de Colombia. Es **colombiana.**

# Nota interdisciplinaria

## GEOGRAFÍA: LOS PAÍSES Y LAS NACIONALIDADES

Spanish is the official language of more than twenty countries. Review the list of country (**país**) names and nationalities (**nacionalidades**) and locate each country on the map.

| PAÍS | NACIONALIDAD | PAÍS | NACIONALIDAD |
|---|---|---|---|
| Argentina | argentino/a | Honduras | hondureño/a |
| Bolivia | boliviano/a | México | mexicano/a |
| Chile | chileno/a | Nicaragua | nicaragüense |
| Colombia | colombiano/a | Panamá | panameño/a |
| Costa Rica | costarricense | Paraguay | paraguayo/a |
| Cuba | cubano/a | Perú | peruano/a |
| Ecuador | ecuatoriano/a | Puerto Rico | puertorriqueño/a |
| El Salvador | salvadoreño/a | República Dominicana | dominicano/a |
| España | español(a) | Uruguay | uruguayo/a |
| Guatemala | guatemalteco/a | Venezuela | venezolano/a |
| Guinea Ecuatorial | ecuatoguineano/a | Estados Unidos | estadounidense |

# Lectura cultural

As you study Spanish, you will undoubtedly encounter words that you've never seen or heard. However, there are several strategies you can use to help you understand the overall message of a text. For example, read the title and any subheadings to anticipate the main topic and subtopics. Look at photos and photo captions. Review any charts or bulleted lists that may give you more clues about the specific points a text is trying to convey. And finally, look for cognates, words that are spelled almost the same and that have the same meaning in both English and Spanish.

As you read the following text for the first time, see how many cognates you can find. Then read the text again to see how well you can understand the overall message, without using a dictionary. We understand there are a lot of words in this selection that you won't know. However, try not to be bothered by this fact, and instead focus on the cognates to see how much you can guess. You may be surprised at how much you can understand.

## Biografía: Cristina García

Cristina García, una autora famosa, nació[a] en La Habana, Cuba, en 1958, pero se mudó a[b] los Estados Unidos con su familia en 1961. Sus padres le contaban[c] muchas historias de Cuba y de las costumbres[d] cubanas.

En su primera novela, *Dreaming in Cuban* (en español, *Soñar en cubano*), García describe las experiencias de Pilar, una cubana que se mudó a los Estados Unidos de joven.[e]

*Cristina García*

Muchos años después,[f] Pilar vuelve a[g] Cuba para conectarse con su familia y con su identidad cultural.

[a]*was born*   [b]*se... she moved to*   [c]*Sus... Her parents used to tell her*   [d]*customs*   [e]*de... as a young girl*
[f]*Muchos... Many years later*   [g]*vuelve... she returns to*

**PASO 1.** Make a list of all the cognates that you found in the reading.

**PASO 2.** Based on your list from **Paso 1** and your understanding of the overall message, indicate which of the statements you believe best summarizes the reading.

1. ☐ Cristina García has worked for several newspapers and continues to enjoy her life as a reporter.
2. ☐ Cristina García has been very active in the anti-Castro movement in the Cuban community in Miami.
3. ☐ Cristina García is a Cuban-American novelist who has written about searching for one's cultural identity.

# Vocabulario

## Los saludos, las presentaciones y las despedidas / Greetings, Introductions, and Good-byes

| | |
|---|---|
| Hola. | Hello. |
| Buenos días. | Good morning (*until midday meal*). |
| Buenas tardes. | Good afternoon (*until evening meal*). |
| Buenas noches. | Good evening (*after evening meal*). |
| ¿Cómo estás? | How are you (*fam.*)? |
| ¿Cómo está usted (Ud.)? | How are you (*form.*)? |
| ¿Qué tal? | How's it going? |
| Muy bien. | Very well. |
| Bien. | Fine. |
| Regular. | So-so. |
| No muy bien. | Not very well. |
| ¿Y tú? | And you (*fam.*)? |
| ¿Y usted? | And you (*form.*)? |
| ¿Cómo te llamas? ¿Cuál es tu nombre? | What's your (*fam.*) name? |
| ¿Cómo se llama usted (Ud.)? ¿Cuál es su nombre? | What's your (*form.*) name? |
| Me llamo... Mi nombre es... | My name is . . . |
| Soy... | I'm . . . |
| Mucho gusto. Encantado/a. | It's a pleasure (to meet you). |
| Igualmente. | Likewise. |
| ¿De dónde eres? | Where are you (*fam.*) from? |
| ¿De dónde es usted (Ud.)? | Where are you (*form.*) from? |
| Soy de... | I'm from . . . |
| Adiós. | Good-bye. |
| Hasta luego. | See you later. |
| Hasta mañana. | See you tomorrow. |
| Hasta pronto. | See you soon. |
| Nos vemos. | See you later. (*lit.* We'll see each other.) |

## Los números de 0 a 30 / Numbers from 0 to 30

cero, uno, dos, tres, cuatro, cinco, seis, siete, ocho, nueve, diez, once, doce, trece, catorce, quince, dieciséis, diecisiete, dieciocho, diecinueve, veinte, veintiuno, veintidós, veintitrés, veinticuatro, veinticinco, veintiséis, veintisiete, veintiocho, veintinueve, treinta

## Los pronombres personales / Personal Pronouns

| | |
|---|---|
| yo | I |
| tú | you (*sing. fam.*) |
| usted (Ud.) | you (*sing. form.*) |
| él | he |
| ella | she |
| nosotros/as | we |
| vosotros/as | you (*pl. fam. Sp.*) |
| ustedes (Uds.) | you (*pl. form. Sp.; pl. fam., form. elsewhere*) |
| ellos/as | they |

## Las descripciones / Descriptions

| | |
|---|---|
| ¿Cómo eres? | What are you (*fam.*) like? |
| ¿Cómo es usted (Ud.)? | What are you (*form.*) like? |

## Las nacionalidades / Nationalities

argentino/a, boliviano/a, chileno/a, colombiano/a, costarricense, cubano/a, dominicano/a, ecuatoguineano/a, español(a), guatemalteco/a, hondureño/a, mexicano/a, nicaragüense, panameño/a, paraguayo/a, peruano/a, puertorriqueño/a, salvadoreño/a, uruguayo/a, venezolano/a

## Los verbos / Verbs

| | |
|---|---|
| ser (*irreg.*) | to be |
| soy | I am |
| eres | you (*sing. fam.*) are |
| es | he/she is, you (*sing. form.*) are |
| somos | we are |
| sois | you (*pl. fam. Sp.*) are |
| son | they are, you (*pl. form. Sp.; pl. fam., form. elsewhere*) are |

## Otras palabras y expresiones / Other Words and Expressions

| | |
|---|---|
| a veces | sometimes |
| el abecedario | alphabet |
| ¿cuántos/as? | how many? |
| de | from |
| del | from the |
| De nada. | You're welcome. |
| el / la / los / las | the |
| Gracias. | Thank you. |
| hay | there is/are |
| no | no; not |
| No hay de qué. | Don't mention it. |
| el país | country |
| pero | but |
| sí | yes |
| sólo | only |
| un poco | a little |
| un(a) | a |
| unos/as | some |
| y | and |

# ¿Qué estudia Ud.?*

*Unos estudiantes en el campus universitario*

1. Why did you decide to take Spanish in college?
2. Are there Hispanic students at your institution? Is the Hispanic population large there? Do you know where the majority comes from?
3. Do Hispanic students have an association? Do you participate in some of the activities they may organize? Which ones?

www.connectspanish.com

*¿Qué... What Do You Study?

21

## Vocabulario del tema

### En el salón de clase°

En... *In the Classroom*

la pizarra – the board

el pizarrón (blanco)

el reloj

la profesora

la pared

la puerta

la ventana

el marcador

el borrador

la mesa

la computadora portátil

el cuaderno

el diccionario

el libro de texto

el estudiante

la estudiante

el papel

el lápiz

el celular

el escritorio

la silla

la mochila

el bolígrafo

| la computadora | computer |
| la goma | eraser (*for pencil*) |
| la tarea | homework |

## Las personas

| el/la bibliotecario/a | librarian |
| el/la compañero/a de clase | classmate |
| el/la compañero/a de cuarto | roommate |
| el hombre | man |
| la mujer | woman |
| el/la profesor(a) | professor; teacher |

## Los edificios y los lugares°          Los... *Buildings and Places*

| la biblioteca | library |
| el centro estudiantil | student union |
| el despacho | (individual) office |
| el estadio | stadium |
| la Facultad de... | School of . . . |
|   Bellas Artes |   Fine Arts |
|   Ciencias |   Science |
|   Educación |   Education |
|   Letras |   Humanities |
|   Leyes |   Law |
|   Medicina |   Medicine |
| la librería | bookstore |
| la oficina | (main) office |
| la residencia (estudiantil) | (student) dorm |
| el salón de clase | classroom |
| el teatro | theater |

Cognados: la cafetería, el campus, la clínica, el gimnasio, el hospital, el laboratorio
(de computadoras), la universidad

## Las materias y las carreras°          Las... *Classes and Majors*

| la administración empresarial | business administration |
| las ciencias políticas | political science |
| la contabilidad | accounting |
| el derecho | law |
| la economía | economics |
| la estadística | statistics |
| la física | physics |
| la informática | computer science |
| la ingeniería | engineering |
| las lenguas (extranjeras) | (foreign) languages |
|   el alemán |   German |
|   el árabe |   Arabic |
|   el chino |   Chinese |
|   el español |   Spanish |
|   el francés |   French |
|   el inglés |   English |
|   el italiano |   Italian |
|   el japonés |   Japanese |
| las matemáticas | math |

| el periodismo | journalism |
| la química | chemistry |
| la sicología | psychology |

**Cognados:** la anatomía, la arquitectura, el arte, la astronomía, la biología, la filosofía, la geografía, la historia, la literatura, la medicina, la música, la sociología

### ACTIVIDADES

**A. Asociaciones.** Match the classes with their corresponding majors.

**MATERIAS**

1. la física, las matemáticas, la ingeniería ____
2. las ciencias políticas, las leyes __d__
3. el arte, la música __a__
4. la contabilidad, la estadística, la economía ____
5. la anatomía, la genética, la biología ____

**CARRERAS**

a. Bellas Artes
b. Administración Empresarial
c. Medicina
d. Derecho
e. Arquitectura

---

## Nota cultural

### MARIO MOLINA

El doctor Mario Molina es de Veracruz, México, y actualmente[a] es profesor en el Departamento de Química y Bioquímica de la Universidad de California, San Diego. Es famoso porque ganó[b] el Premio Nóbel de Química en 1995[c] por sus estudios sobre[d] la descomposición de la capa[e] de ozono.

[a]*currently*  [b]porque... *because he won*  [c]mil novecientos noventa y cinco
[d]por... *for his studies about*  [e]*layer*

---

**B. Más asociaciones.** Match the majors with their corresponding person, thing, or concept.

1. Física: ____   a. la literatura   b. la cafetería   **c.** Albert Einstein
2. Filosofía: ____   **a.** Platón (*Plato*)   b. Mona Lisa   c. la novela
3. Informática: ____   **a.** una computadora   b. Sigmund Freud   c. un estadio
4. Historia: ____   **a.** Cristóbal Colón (*Christopher Columbus*)   b. un despacho   c. la sicología
5. Química: ____   a. el centro estudiantil   **b.** Mario Molina   c. el japonés

**C. Los edificios.** Fill in the blanks with the correct building or place.

1. María toma (*takes*) clases de biología y química en _____.
2. Irene levanta pesas (*lifts weights*) en _____.
3. Álvaro toma música y arte en _____.
4. Miguel come (*eats*) en _____.
5. José compra (*buys*) los libros en _____.
6. Isabel toma clases de francés y japonés en _____.
7. Carolina y Juan estudian (*study*) en _____.
8. Alejandra toma apuntes (*notes*) en _____.

<table>
<tr>
<td>

**Observe**

</td>
<td>

Remember to use the definite article (**el/la/los/las**) with titles when referring to someone in the third person.

Mi profesora de inglés es **la profesora Wilson.**
(referred to in third person, use article)

*My English professor is professor Wilson.*

*but*

Buenos días, **señor Martínez.**
¿Cómo está Ud.?
(addressed directly, no article)

*Good morning, Mr. Martínez.*
*How are you?*

</td>
</tr>
</table>

**D.** ¿Qué (*What*) hay en tu (*your*) mochila? With a partner, finish the statements using the vocabulary you've learned so far in this chapter and in the **Capítulo preliminar.** Then switch roles.

Communication

1. En mi (*my*) mochila hay…
2. En mi despacho/cuarto hay…
3. En el salón de clase veo (*I see*)…
4. Este (*This*) semestre/trimestre tomo (*I'm taking*)… [número] materias:… [lista de materias]
5. Estudio (*I study*) en… [lugar]
6. Mi materia favorita es…
7. Mi profesor favorito / profesora favorita es… [nombre]

## Nota interdisciplinaria

Connections

### MÚSICA: HISPANIC INFLUENCE ON MUSIC IN THE U.S.

*Los Tigres del Norte*

From its beginnings in the jazz clubs of the 1930s, to the *salsa* explosion and regional movements like *Tejano* and *Chicano rock*, to its eventual cross-over into pop music, it can't be denied that Latin music is on the rise in this country. After the early influence of Puerto Ricans and Cubans in New York, the focus shifted to Miami as the Mecca for Latin singers who stormed the music charts, propelled by producers such as Emilio and Gloria Estefan. By the 1980s, *rumba* and *mambo* sounds were replaced by *conga* style and more recently, by Latin pop and Latin rock. On the border with Mexico, *Los Tigres del Norte* are, without a doubt, the best known example of *Norteño* music, updating traditional-style border ballads with contemporary themes.

The Miami sound went international thanks to Ricky Martin and after him, Enrique Iglesias, Jon Secada, and many others. Shrugging off the blandness of some Latin pop, a street music emerged called *reggaeton*, which is now popular in many parts of the country. You don't need to travel to the Caribbean or Miami to enjoy Latin music. It's everywhere!

**PREGUNTAS** With a partner, answer the questions. Then share your ideas with the class.

1. Are you familiar with any other Latin musicians, singers, or genres of music other than those mentioned in the text? Who? Do you remember any song in particular?
2. Have you ever been to a Latin music concert? When? Where? What band or musician?

# Gramática

## 1.1 Descriptive Adjectives

**GRAMÁTICA EN CONTEXTO**

### El nuevo semestre

ROSA MARÍA: ¿Cómo son tus clases este semestre?

JAVIER: Todas mis clases son **interesantes.**

ROSA MARÍA: ¡Qué padre! Tengo tres clases **aburridas** este semestre y solamente una clase **interesante.**

JAVIER: ¿Y cómo son tus profesores?

ROSA MARÍA: Mi profesora de historia es muy **inteligente** y **simpática,** pero los otros profesores no son tan **buenos.**

### ¿CIERTO O FALSO? (*True or False?*)

|  | CIERTO | FALSO |
|---|---|---|
| 1. Rosa María toma tres clases interesantes. | ☐ | ☒ |
| 2. La profesora de historia de Rosa María es simpática. | ☒ | ☐ |
| 3. Todas las clases de Javier son aburridas. | ☐ | ☒ |

*(handwritten note in margin: Qué padre – that's great!)*

### FORMATION

**A.** Descriptive adjectives must agree in gender and number with the person, place, or thing that they modify.

Carmen es muy **simpática.**
Fernando y Josefina son **puertorriqueños.**

*Carmen is very nice.*
*Fernando and Josefina are Puerto Rican.*

| DESCRIPTIVE ADJECTIVES | | |
|---|---|---|
| Gender / Number Agreement | | |
|  | MASCULINE | FEMININE |
| SINGULAR | un amigo alto | una amiga alta |
| PLURAL | unos amigos altos | unas amigas altas |

**B.** Masculine adjectives that end in any vowel other than **-o** or in most consonants are the same in the feminine singular, and simply add **-s** or **-es** to form the plural.

---

GRAMÁTICA EN CONTEXTO *The New Semester / **ROSA MARÍA:** What are your classes like this semester? **JAVIER:** All of my classes are interesting. **ROSA MARÍA:** How cool! I have three boring classes this semester and only one interesting class. **JAVIER:** And what are your professors like? **ROSA MARÍA:** My history professor is very intelligent and nice, but my other professors aren't as good.*

|  | MASCULINE | FEMININE |
|---|---|---|
| SINGULAR | elegante<br>pesimista<br>fiel | elegante<br>pesimista<br>fiel |
| PLURAL | elegantes<br>pesimistas<br>fieles | elegantes<br>pesimistas<br>fieles |

**C.** Adjectives that end in **-dor** and most masculine adjectives of nationality add **-a** to form the feminine singular, **-es** to form the masculine plural, and **-as** for the feminine plural.

|  | MASCULINE | FEMININE |
|---|---|---|
| SINGULAR | trabajador<br>español | trabajadora<br>española |
| PLURAL | trabajadores<br>españoles | trabajadoras<br>españolas |

## POSITION

**A.** Adjectives usually follow the nouns they modify.

Es una clase **interesante**.      *It's an interesting class.*
Son **estudiantes inteligentes**.      *They are smart students.*

**B.** The adjectives **bueno/a** and **malo/a** may precede or follow the nouns they describe. However, when they precede a noun, the **-o** is dropped in the masculine singular form.

*es un libro bueno*

Es un **buen libro**.      *It's a good book.*
Es una **película mala**.      *It's a bad movie.*

**C.** The adjective **grande** can also precede or follow a noun, but when preceding a noun it's shortened to **gran** and means *great* or *impressive.*

Quebec es una **gran ciudad**.      *Quebec is a great city.*
Los Ángeles es una **ciudad grande**.      *Los Angeles is a large city.*

## SOME COMMON ADJECTIVES

Here are some common adjectives that you have already seen or that you will need to know as you continue your Spanish studies.

*atrevida – daring*
*mentiroso – liar*

| | | | |
|---|---|---|---|
| **alto/a** | tall | **fácil** | easy |
| **bajo/a** | short | **difícil** | difficult |
| **bonito/a** | pretty | **rubio/a** | blond(e) |
| **guapo/a** | handsome; pretty | **moreno/a** | dark-haired; dark-skinned |
| **feo/a** | ugly | **pelirrojo/a** | redheaded |
| **trabajador(a)** | hardworking | **simpático/a** | nice |
| **perezoso/a** | lazy | **antipático/a** | mean |
| **interesante** | interesting | **grande** | large |
| **divertido/a** | fun | **pequeño/a** | small |
| **aburrido/a** | boring | | |

## ACTIVIDADES

**A.** ¿Cómo es Ud.? Describe yourself using these adjectives or others you have learned.

Soy..., pero no soy...

| | | | |
|---|---|---|---|
| alto/a | feo/a | pelirrojo/a | simpático/a |
| antipático/a | guapo/a | perezoso/a | trabajador(a) |
| bajo/a | moreno/a | rubio/a | ¿ ? |
| bonito/a | | | |

**B.** Explorando (*Exploring*) la cultura hispana. Match the phrases in column A with those in column B to form sentences about Hispanic culture.

Hombre, *por Fernando Botero, pintor y escultor colombiano* (1932– )

Don Quijote, *por Pablo Picasso, pintor español* (1881–1973)

| A | B |
|---|---|
| **1.** Las pinturas (*paintings*) de Picasso y Dalí son ___. | **a.** una novela española universal |
| **2.** Botero es ___. | **b.** muy atractivos |
| **3.** *Don Quijote* es ___. | **c.** famosas en el mundo (*world*) |
| **4.** Enrique Iglesias es ___. | **d.** un pintor y escultor colombiano |
| **5.** Javier Bardem y Penélope Cruz son ___. | **e.** divertida y alegre (*upbeat*) |
| **6.** La salsa es ___. | **f.** un cantante hispano famoso |

## Nota comunicativa

**Communication**

### UNSTRESSED POSSESSIVE ADJECTIVES

Unstressed possessive adjectives show ownership of something or someone, agree in gender and number with the person or thing being possessed, and always precede the noun they modify.

**Mi libro** de filosofía es interesante.  *My philosophy book is interesting.*
**Vuestra mamá** es muy inteligente.  *Your mother is very smart.*
**Sus apuntes** de clase son claros.  *His class notes are clear.*

| UNSTRESSED POSSESSIVE ADJECTIVES | | | |
|---|---|---|---|
| **mi(s)** | my | **nuestro**/a/os/as | our |
| **tu(s)** | your (*fam.*) | **vuestro**/a/os/as | your (*fam. Sp.*) |
| **su(s)** | your (*form.*) | **su(s)** | your (*form. Sp.; fam., form. elsewhere*) |
| **su(s)** | his/her | **su(s)** | their |

Because **su(s)** has so many interpretations, you can instead use a phrase with the preposition **de** in the following formula to avoid confusion:

**el/la/los/las** + *person/thing being possessed* + **de** + *owner*

| POTENTIALLY UNCLEAR | CLARIFIED WITH **de** PHRASE |
|---|---|
| **Su clase** es interesante. (*Whose class? His, hers, yours, theirs?*) | **La clase de Esteban** es interesante. *Esteban's class is interesting.* |
| **Su libro** es viejo. (*Whose book?*) | **El libro del profesor** es viejo. *The professor's book is old.* |

*[handwritten: use context clues, or de]*

**C. Mis experiencias.** Write sentences based on the cues, according to your own experience or background.

**MODELO** deporte favorito →
        Mi deporte favorito es el béisbol.

1. universidad favorita
2. profesor favorito
3. clase más (*most*) fácil
4. novela favorita
5. clase más difícil
6. clase favorita

**Communication**

**D. Entrevista**

**PASO 1.** Interview a classmate using these questions, and then switch roles. Provide as many details as you can.

1. ¿Cuál (*What/Which*) es tu ciudad de origen?
2. ¿Cuál es tu carrera?
3. ¿Cuál es tu clase más difícil?
4. ¿Cuál es tu clase más fácil?
5. ¿Cuáles son tus clases favoritas?

**PASO 2.** Report to the class what your classmate and you have and do not have in common.

**MODELO** La ciudad de origen de Amy es San Antonio, Texas. Mi ciudad de origen es Los Ángeles, California. Nuestra clase más difícil es química.

**Observe**

*[handwritten: which is your career]*

The interrogative **¿cuál?** has a plural form: **¿cuáles?**

  **¿Cuál es** tu carrera?

  **¿Cuáles son** tus libros?

# 1.2 Introduction to the Verb **gustar**

## Las cosas que me gustan

Hola, me llamo Paco, soy estudiante universitario y **me gustan** muchas cosas de mi universidad. Primero, **me gusta** mi residencia, porque mi compañero de cuarto, José, es muy buena onda. **A él le gusta** mucho el fútbol americano y **nos gusta** ir a los partidos de nuestro equipo los sábados. Segundo, **me gustan** mis clases por lo general. **Me gustan** mucho mis clases de química, informática y matemáticas. **Me gusta** un poco mi clase de literatura porque es interesante, pero es difícil. Y **no me gusta** mi clase de filosofía, porque es muy aburrida. Finalmente, **me gusta** mucho la vida nocturna cerca de mi universidad. ¿Y a ti? ¿Qué **te gusta** más de tu universidad?

### ¿CIERTO O FALSO?

|  |  | CIERTO | FALSO |
|---|---|:---:|:---:|
| 1. | A Paco le gusta su universidad. | ☒ | ☐ |
| 2. | No le gusta su residencia. | ☐ | ☒ |
| 3. | Le gusta mucho su clase de literatura. | ☒ | ☐ |
| 4. | Le gustan las matemáticas, pero no le gusta la filosofía. | ☒ | ☐ |
| 5. | No le gusta la vida nocturna. | ☒ | ☐ |

Spanish uses a special construction with the verb **gustar** (*to be pleasing*) to express likes and dislikes.

| | |
|---|---|
| **Me gusta** la clase de química. | *I like Chemistry class.* (lit. *Chemistry class is pleasing to me.*) |
| —¿**Les gustan** las lenguas extranjeras? | *Do you like foreign languages?* (lit. *Are foreign languages pleasing to you* [pl.]?) |
| —Sí, **nos gustan** mucho. | *Yes, we like them a lot.* (lit. *They are very pleasing to us.*) |

You'll learn more about the grammar of this construction in later chapters. However, for now, you only need to know the following details.

| gustar (to like [to be pleasing]) | | | |
|---|---|---|---|
| me **gusta(n)**... | I like . . . | nos **gusta(n)** | we like . . . |
| te **gusta(n)**... | you (*sing. fam.*) like . . . | os **gusta(n)** | you (*pl. fam. Sp.*) like |
| le **gusta(n)**... | you (*sing. form.*) like . . . | les **gusta(n)** | you (*pl. form. Sp.; pl. fam., form. elsewhere*) like . . . |
| le **gusta(n)**... | he/she likes . . . | les **gusta(n)** | they like . . . |

GRAMÁTICA EN CONTEXTO *The Things I Like /* Hello, my name is Paco, I'm a college student, and I like a lot of things about my university. First, I like my dorm, because my roommate, José, is really cool. He likes football a lot, and we like to go to our team's games on Saturdays. Second, I like my classes, generally speaking. I like my chemistry, computer science, and math classes a lot. I like my literature class a little because it's interesting, but it's hard. And I don't like my philosophy class, because it's really boring. Finally, I really like the nightlife near my university. And you? What do you like most about your university?

**A.** Use **gusta** when the thing being liked is singular.

**Me gusta** la clase de español.     *I like Spanish class.*
¿**Le gusta** nuestro campus?     *Do you like our campus?*

**B.** If the thing being liked is plural, use **gustan**.

—¿**Te gustan** los deportes?     *Do you like sports?*
—Sí, **me gustan**.     *Yes, I like them.*

**C.** Notice how **me, te, le, nos, os,** and **les** change to indicate who likes the thing mentioned (*to whom it is pleasing*).

—¿Qué clases **os gustan** más?     *What classes do you like most?*
—Nos **gustan** más el periodismo     *We like journalism and French the*
y el francés.     *most.*

**D.** To express dislike for something, insert **no** before the **me, te, le, nos, os,** or **les.**

**No me gusta** la estadística.     *I don't like statistics.*
**Me gustan** las ciencias políticas, pero     *I like political science, but*
**no me gustan** los políticos.     *I don't like politicians.*

**E.** To clarify who **le** or **les** is referring to, insert **A** (or **a**) + [*person's name or pronoun*] at the beginning of the phrase.

**A Yanina le gusta** mucho la     *Yanina likes computer science a lot.*
informática.
**A Ana y a María no les gusta** la     *Ana and María don't like*
economía.     *economics.*
**A él no le gustan** las matemáticas.     *He doesn't like math.*

## ACTIVIDADES

**A. Me gusta la clase de...** Finish the sentences to form truthful sentences for you.

1. Me gusta mucho mi clase de...
2. Me gusta un poco mi clase de...
3. No me gusta mi clase de...
4. Me gustan mis clases de...
5. No me gustan mis clases de...
6. Me gusta(n)... porque es / son...

**B. Otros gustos**

**PASO 1.** Jot down at least five things that you like and five that you don't, as in the models. **¡OJO!** You can use the cues in the **Vocabulario práctico** box. Remember to use the definite article (**el/la/los/las**) before a noun.

> **Vocabulario práctico**
>
> **el español, la química, la historia, la literatura,...**
> **el/la cantante** (*singer*) _____
> **la película** (*movie*) _____
> **el béisbol, el fútbol americano, el fútbol** (*soccer*)**, el basquetbol, el vólibol**
> **la música rock, la música hip hop, la música rap, la música country, la música clásica, la música latina, el reggaetón, el jazz**
> **la comida** (*food*) **mexicana, la comida italiana, la comida china, la pizza, los mariscos** (*shellfish*)**, la comida rápida** (*fast food*)**, la comida del centro estudiantil, la comida de la cafetería**

**MODELOS** Me gusta el español.
No me gusta la música clásica.
Me gustan las cantantes Shakira y Christina Aguilera, pero no me gusta
Luis Miguel.

Communication

**PASO 2.** Now share your answers with a classmate and ask him/her what he/she likes and dislikes.

**MODELOS** E1: ¿Te gusta el español?
E2: Sí, me gusta (el español).
E1: ¿Te gusta la comida china?
E2: No, no me gusta.
E1: ¿Te gustan las películas de Harry Potter?
E2: Sí, me gustan mucho.

---

## Nota comunicativa

Communication

### QUESTION WORDS

You've already learned a few question words in *Experience Spanish,* for example:

| | | |
|---|---|---|
| **¿Cómo** te llamas? | **¿De dónde** eres? | **¿Cuántos** libros hay en tu mochila? |
| **¿Cómo** eres? | **¿Cuál** es tu nombre? | **¿Cuántas** personas hay en la clase? |

Some other common question words that you should know include: **¿qué?, ¿cuándo?, ¿quién(es)?,** and **¿cuánto?**

| | |
|---|---|
| **¿Qué** clase te gusta más? | **What** class do you like most? |
| **¿Cuándo** es el examen? | **When** is the exam? |
| **¿Quién** es tu compañera de cuarto? | **Who** is your roommate? |
| **¿Quiénes** son tus profesores? | **Who** are your professors? |
| **¿Cuánto** cuesta este bolígrafo? | **How much** does this pen cost? |

---

Communication

**C.** ¿Qué te gusta hacer (*to do*)? With a partner, ask and say what you both like to do.

**MODELO** E1: ¿Qué te gusta beber (*to drink*)?
E2: Me gusta beber café.
E1: ¿Qué no te gusta beber?
E2: No me gusta beber Coca-Cola.

1. **beber**      café, chocolate, Coca-Cola, té, limonada, agua (*water*)
2. **comer** (*to eat*)      tacos, enchiladas, hamburguesas, pizza, pasta
3. **estudiar** (*to study*)      historia, español, informática, matemáticas,...
4. **hablar** (*to speak*)      español, con (*with*) mis amigos, por teléfono (*on the phone*)
5. **escuchar** (*to listen to*)      la música rock, la música country, el jazz,...
6. **tocar** (*to play*)      el piano, la guitarra, el violín, la batería (*drum set*)
7. **jugar** (*to play*)      al béisbol, al basquetbol, al vólibol, al fútbol (americano)
8. **vivir** (*to live*)      en la residencia, en la casa de mis padres, en mi casa, en un apartamento, solo/a (*alone*), con un compañero / una compañera de cuarto

### Observe

When you use an infinitive verb form (e.g., **estudiar**) after **gustar, gustar** should *always* be singular. This is true even if a plural noun follows the infinitive or if you use a series of infinitives.

Me **gusta beber** té.

Nos **gusta comer** enchiladas.

Le **gusta estudiar, hablar** y **jugar.**

# Palabra escrita*

## A comenzar

Communication

> **Generating Your Ideas / Brainstorming.** This pre-writing strategy consists of writing down all the ideas that come to mind about the subject of your composition. Jot down more ideas that you could possibly use, even those that seem irrelevant to you at this point. They may be very useful later on in the writing process! Brainstorming ideas may take the form of short sentences or simple words, and the information can be visually arranged on the page in different ways. Brainstorming, specifically, takes a listing form and is called, **"lluvia de ideas** (*rain [shower] of ideas*)" in Spanish.

You are going to start the process of writing a brief composition that you will finalize in the **Palabra escrita: A finalizar** section of your *Manual de actividades.* The topic of this composition is **Mi universidad.** The purpose of your composition will be to tell the reader about your university.

**A.** Lluvia de ideas. With a partner, jot down as many ideas about your university as you can for these categories.

1. number and origin of students
2. number of professors
3. academic programs: quantity and popularity
4. cultural and social events that your institution offers for students

**B.** A verificar (*Let's verify*). Check your university's website to make sure that the information is accurate. You may want to add more details. Share your information with the class and jot down any additional ideas that you gain from that experience.

**C.** A escribir (*Let's write*). Now write a first draft of your composition with the ideas and information that you jotted down in activities A and B. ¡OJO! Keep your work in a safe place. You'll need it again when you do the **Palabra escrita: A finalizar** section in your workbook.

---

*written

## Carlos Callejo

*Our History, 1995, El Paso County Courthouse*

Carlos Callejo, muralist and painter, was born in El Paso, Texas. Eventually he moved to Los Angeles, where he lived and studied art at California State University, Los Angeles, and at the Otis Art Institute. After thirty years, he returned to his native El Paso to paint several murals for that city, most notably at the El Paso County Courthouse. His work displays influences from Mexican muralists and themes that focus on the Chicano community, its history, and its values.

   Callejo's mural, *Our History,* fills several walls of the third-floor atrium at the El Paso County Courthouse. It depicts the history of El Paso, its sister city to the south, Ciudad Juárez, and the surrounding region, while communicating themes of justice, equality, ethnic diversity, and hope for the future.

# Vocabulario del tema

## Actividades típicas en la universidad

1. caminar y charlar con una amiga
2. estudiar y escuchar música
3. comprar los libros
4. mirar la televisión
5. jugar al fútbol
6. tocar el piano

| andar en bicicleta | to ride a bicycle |
|---|---|
| bailar | to dance |
| buscar (algo) | to look for (something) |
| charlar | to chat |
| hablar (por teléfono) | to speak (on the phone) |
| jugar (a) | to play (*a game, sport*) |
| al* béisbol | baseball |
| al fútbol americano | football |
| al basquetbol | basquetball |
| al vólibol | volleyball |
| lavar la ropa | to wash clothes |
| navegar en Internet | to surf the Internet |
| tocar | to play (*a musical instrument*) |
| tomar | to take; to drink |
| tomar apuntes | to take notes |
| tomar una clase | to take a class |
| trabajar | to work |

### ACTIVIDAD

Clasificaciones.

**PASO 1.** Indicate whether you're more likely to do these activities during the week (**entre semana**), on the weekend (**fin de semana**), on any day of the week (**cualquier día de la semana**), or never (**nunca**).

| | ENTRE SEMANA | FIN DE SEMANA | CUALQUIER DÍA DE LA SEMANA | NUNCA |
|---|---|---|---|---|
| 1. bailar en un club | ☐ | ☐ | ☐ | ☐ |
| 2. trabajar | ☐ | ☐ | ☐ | ☐ |
| 3. andar en bicicleta | ☐ | ☐ | ☐ | ☐ |
| 4. mirar la televisión | ☐ | ☐ | ☐ | ☐ |
| 5. estudiar en la biblioteca | ☐ | ☐ | ☐ | ☐ |
| 6. tocar un instrumento musical | ☐ | ☐ | ☐ | ☐ |
| 7. charlar con un amigo / una amiga | ☐ | ☐ | ☐ | ☐ |
| 8. buscar algo en el Internet | ☐ | ☐ | ☐ | ☐ |
| 9. jugar al béisbol | ☐ | ☐ | ☐ | ☐ |
| 10. tomar apuntes | ☐ | ☐ | ☐ | ☐ |

**PASO 2.** Now interview classmates to find out if and when they do the activities listed in **Paso 1**. Do you have any shared interests?

MODELO E1: ¿Miras la televisión?
E2: Sí.
E1: ¿Cuándo?
E2: Entre semana.

---

*When the preposition **a** is followed by **el,** they contract to form **al.**

# Los días de la semana°

| | | | noviembre | | | |
|------|--------|----------|--------|---------|--------|---------|
| lunes | martes | miércoles | jueves | viernes | sábado | domingo |
| 1 | 2 | 3 | 4 | 5 | 6 | 7 |
| 8 | 9 | 10 | 11 | 12 | 13 | 14 |
| 15 | 16 | 17 | 18 | 19 | 20 | 21 |
| 22 | 23 | 24 | 25 | 26 | 27 | 28 |
| 29 | 30 | | | | | |

| | |
|---|---|
| el día | day |
| los días entre semana | weekdays |
|   lunes |   Monday |
|   martes |   Tuesday |
|   miércoles |   Wednesday |
|   jueves |   Thursday |
|   viernes |   Friday |
| el fin de semana | weekend |
|   sábado |   Saturday |
|   domingo |   Sunday |
| la semana | week |

## ¿Cuándo?  When?

| | |
|---|---|
| esta mañana | this morning |
| esta tarde | this afternoon |
| esta noche | tonight |
| hoy | today |
| mañana | tomorrow |
| pasado mañana | the day after tomorrow |
| el lunes (martes, miércoles,... ) | on Monday (Tuesday, Wednesday, . . . ) |
| los lunes (martes, miércoles,... ) | on Mondays (Tuesdays, Wednesdays, . . . ) |
| el lunes (martes, miércoles,... ) que viene | next Monday (Tuesday, Wednesday, . . . ) |
| la semana que viene | next week |
| todos los días | every day |
| entre semana | during the week |
| por la mañana | in the morning |

| | |
|---|---|
| por la tarde | in the afternoon |
| por la noche | in the evening, at night |
| antes (de) | before |
| después (de) | after |

## ¿Con quién(es)?  |  ## With Whom?

| | |
|---|---|
| el/la amigo/a | friend |
| el/la esposo/a | husband/wife |
| la mamá | mom |
| el/la mejor amigo/a | best friend |
| el/la novio/a | boyfriend/girlfriend |
| el papá | dad |

● Days of the week are not capitalized in Spanish, unless there's some special reason to do so.

● To indicate what day it is, use the day of the week without the definite article **el.**

| | |
|---|---|
| Hoy es lunes. | *Today is Monday.* |
| Mañana es martes. | *Tomorrow is Tuesday.* |

● To express *on* + [*day of the week*], use the day of the week with the definite article **el.**

| | |
|---|---|
| El examen es el **viernes.** | *The exam is on Friday.* |

● To indicate that something happens on the same day every week, use the day of the week as a plural noun with the definite article **los.**

| | |
|---|---|
| Me gusta estudiar en casa los **sábados.** | *I like to study at home on Saturdays.* |

### ACTIVIDADES

**A.** ¿Qué día es? Referring to the calendar on page 37, listen to your professor and indicate whether the statements he/she makes are true or false.

MODELO  (*you hear*) El día 4 es jueves. →
        (*you indicate*) Cierto.

| CIERTO | FALSO | | CIERTO | FALSO |
|---|---|---|---|---|
| **1.** ☐ | ☐ | **4.** | ☐ | ☐ |
| **2.** ☐ | ☐ | **5.** | ☐ | ☐ |
| **3.** ☐ | ☐ | **6.** | ☐ | ☐ |

**B.** Si (*If*) hoy es... Again, referring to the calendar on page 37, match the answers in column B with the statements in column A.

| A | B |
|---|---|
| 1. Si hoy es miércoles, mañana es ____. | a. domingo |
| 2. Si hoy es viernes, pasado mañana es ____. | b. el jueves que viene |
| 3. Si hoy es lunes, pasado mañana es ____. | c. jueves |
| 4. Si mañana es martes, hoy es ____. | d. lunes |
| 5. Si pasado mañana es lunes, hoy es ____. | e. miércoles |
| 6. Si hoy es el día 11, el día 18 es ____. | f. sábado |

**C.** ¿Cuándo te gusta… ? Using the chart as a reference, complete the sentences to make true statements about when you like to do certain things.

|  | LUNES | MARTES | MIÉRCOLES | JUEVES | VIERNES | SÁBADO | DOMINGO |
|---|---|---|---|---|---|---|---|
| **por la mañana** |  |  |  |  |  |  |  |
| **por la tarde** |  |  |  |  |  |  |  |
| **por la noche** |  |  |  |  |  |  |  |

MODELOS  Me gusta estudiar los sábados por la mañana.

*or*

Los sábados por la mañana me gusta estudiar.

1. Me gusta estudiar _____.
2. _____ me gusta lavar la ropa.
3. Me gusta mirar la televisión _____.
4. _____ me gusta bailar con mis amigos.
5. Me gusta hablar por teléfono con mi mamá (papá, mejor amigo/a) _____.
6. _____ me gusta jugar al béisbol (fútbol, basquetbol,… ).
7. Me gusta navegar en Internet _____.
8. _____ me gusta andar en bicicleta.

# ¿Qué hora es?°

¿Qué… *What Time Is It?*

1. **Es la una.**

2. **Son las siete.**

3. **Son las diez y cuarto. (Son las diez y quince.)**

4. **Son las ocho y media. (Son las ocho y treinta.)**

5. **Son las cuatro y diez.**

6. **Es la una y veinte.**

7. **Son las nueve menos cuarto/quince.**

8. **Es la una menos veinte.**

## Otras palabras y expresiones

| | |
|---|---|
| ¿A qué hora... ? | At what time . . . ? |
| a la(s) + *time* | at + *time* |
| de la mañana | in the morning |
| de la tarde | in the afternoon |
| de la noche | in the evening, at night |
| en punto* | sharp, exactly |
| mediodía | noon |
| medianoche | midnight |

**Repaso: el reloj**

▶ Use es la **una...** for times between 1:00 and 1:59 but **son las...** for all other times.

▶ Use y **cuarto** to indicate *quarter past* and y **media** to indicate *half past*.

▶ To add minutes to a time, use y and the number.

▶ To indicate time that is approaching the hour, use **menos** and the number.

▶ To find out what time something happens, use **¿A qué hora... ?** To answer, use **A la(s)** + *time*.

| | |
|---|---|
| —¿A qué hora es la clase de español? | *What time is Spanish class?* |
| —A las doce y media. | *At 12:30.* |

▶ To indicate A.M. or P.M., use **de la mañana** (tarde, noche).

| | |
|---|---|
| Son las siete y quince **de la mañana**. | *It's 7:15 in the morning.* *(It's 7:15 A.M.)* |
| Es la una **de la tarde**. | *It's 1:00 o'clock in the afternoon.* *(It's 1:00 P.M.)* |
| Son las once **de la noche**. | *It's 11:00 o'clock at night.* *(It's 11:00 P.M.)* |

▶ To emphasize an exact time of day, use **en punto**.

| | |
|---|---|
| Son las tres en punto. | *It's exactly 3:00 o'clock.* |
| —¿A qué hora es el partido? | *What time is the game?* |
| —A la una en punto. | *At 1:00 sharp.* |

▶ To express *midnight* or *noon*, use **medianoche** or **mediodía**, respectively.

| | |
|---|---|
| Es medianoche. | *It's midnight.* |
| —¿Cuándo es la fiesta? | *When is the party?* |
| —Mañana a mediodía. | *Tomorrow at noon.* |

---

*The phrase **en punto** is typically only used at the top of the hour. **Son las nueve** en punto.

CAPÍTULO 1 ¿Qué estudia Ud.?

**A.** ¿Qué hora es? Taking turns with a partner, say what time is shown on the following clocks.

Communication

MODELO (*you see*)    A.M.

(*you say*)   Son las ocho y dieciséis de la mañana.

| | | | |
|---|---|---|---|
| A.M. | P.M. | A.M. | P.M. |
| 1. | 2. | 3. | 4. |
| P.M. | A.M. | P.M. | A.M. |
| 5. | 6. | 7. | 8. |
| A.M. | P.M. | P.M. | A.M. |
| 9. | 10. | 11. | 12. |

**Observe**

Note that **de** is used in the expressions **de la mañana (tarde, noche)** when referring to a specific time, but **por** is used when no specific time is stated.

   —¿Cuándo es tu clase de historia?

   —A las 9:00 **de la mañana.** (*specific time*)

*but*

   —**Por la mañana.** (*general, no specific time stated*)

**B.** ¿Cómo es tu horario (*schedule*)?

**PASO 1.** On a separate sheet of paper, create an empty chart similar to the one in activity C on page 39.

**PASO 2.** Now ask a partner these questions and fill out your chart from **Paso 1,** based on his/her responses. **¡OJO!** Don't let your partner see your chart. Both you and your partner should answer in complete sentences.

**MODELO** E1: ¿Cuándo te gusta estudiar?
E2: Me gusta estudiar los lunes por la mañana.

1. **a.** ¿Qué clases tomas (*are you taking*)? [*Jot down his/her responses.*]
1. **b.** ¿A qué hora es tu clase de _____? [*Finish your question based on your partner's response to question 1a. You should repeat this question for each class your partner is taking.*]
2. ¿Cuándo te gusta lavar la ropa?
3. ¿Qué día o qué días de la semana te gusta mirar la televisión?
4. ¿Cuándo te gusta hablar por teléfono con tu mamá (papá)? ¿Qué día(s)? ¿A qué hora?
5. ¿Cuándo te gusta charlar con tu novio/a, esposo/a, mejor amigo/a?

**PASO 3.** Check with your partner to see if you filled out the chart correctly.

**PASO 4.** Now share the information you learned about your partner in **Pasos 2** and **3** with another student.

**MODELOS** A [*name of your partner*] le gusta estudiar los lunes por la mañana.
Su clase de _____ es los lunes, miércoles y viernes por la tarde.
Todos los días le gusta charlar con su novio.

---

## Nota cultural

Cultures

### EL RELOJ DE 24 HORAS

| AEROPUERTO - CUERNAVACA | | CUERNAVACA - AEROPUERTO | |
|---|---|---|---|
| 6:30 | 15:45 | 4:00 | 12:00 |
| 7:30 | 16:30 | 4:30 | 12:40 |
| 8:15 | 17:15 | 5:00 | 13:20 |
| 9:15 | 18:00 | 5:30 | 14:15 |
| 10:30 | 18:45 | 6:00 | 15:00 |
| 11:15 | 19:30 | 7:00 | 16:00 |
| 12:00 | 20:15 | 8:00 | 16:40 |
| 12:45 | 21:00 | 9:00 | 17:15 |
| 13:30 | 22:00 | 10:00 | 18:15 |
| 14:15 | 23:00 | 10:40 | 19:30 |
| 15:00 | | 11:20 | |

MEXICO D.F. **55-49-35-05 AL 08**
CUERNAVACA **(73) 18-46-38 Ó 18-91-87**
TIEMPO APROX. DE RECORRIDO: **1 HR. 40 min.**

It is a common practice in the Hispanic world to use the 24-hour clock in schedules for television programs, buses, trains, movies, and the like. In North America, this is often known as *military time.* To convert the P.M. hours of military time to the 12-hour clock that you're probably more accustomed to, simply subtract twelve from the hours. Thus, 14:00 would become 2:00 P.M., and 19:00 would be 7:00 P.M.

Spanish speakers rarely use the 24-hour clock in conversation. When asked for the time, they will normally respond using the 12-hour system, for example, **"Son las dos de la tarde"** to mean *It's 2:00 P.M.*

**ACTIVIDAD** Convert the following times to military time.

1. 9:00 A.M.
2. 4:30 P.M.
3. 8:15 P.M.
4. 10:46 P.M.
5. 12:00 A.M.

# Gramática

## 1.3 Present Tense of Regular -ar Verbs

### GRAMÁTICA EN CONTEXTO

**Un día típico de Raúl**

[*Raúl le **manda** un e-mail a su amigo Alberto sobre sus clases este semestre.*]

Hola, Alberto:

¿Qué tal? Aquí todo bien. **Tomo** cuatro clases este semestre, y mi clase favorita es francés a las diez de la mañana. ¡La profesora sólo **habla** en francés! Es un poco difícil, pero me gusta mucho. Después, **trabajo** en la cafetería hasta las dos, y luego **estudio** en la biblioteca por la tarde. Por la noche, **paso** tiempo con mi novia: **miramos** la televisión, **cenamos** en algún restaurante o simplemente **descansamos** y **pasamos** un rato juntos. Si mi novia **necesita** estudiar, **hablo** por teléfono con mis padres o leo mi e-mail.

¿Y tú, Alberto? ¿Cuántas clases **tomas**? ¿**Hablas** francés? ¿Cuándo y dónde **estudias**? ¿**Trabajas** este semestre?

Hasta pronto,
Raúl

### ¿CIERTO O FALSO?

Raúl...

|  | CIERTO | FALSO |
|---|---|---|
| 1. toma cuatro clases este semestre. | ☐ | ☐ |
| 2. trabaja en la biblioteca. | ☐ | ☐ |
| 3. estudia por la tarde. | ☐ | ☐ |
| 4. no mira la televisión con su novia. | ☐ | ☐ |
| 5. habla por teléfono con sus padres a veces (*at times*). | ☐ | ☐ |

**A.** The base of the Spanish verb system is the infinitive. Infinitives are not conjugated, which means that they have no subject associated with them.

| **estudiar** | *to study (infinitive; no subject; not conjugated)* |
|---|---|
| yo **estudio**, tú **estudias**, él **estudia** | *I study, you study, he studies (conjugated verbs)* |

Spanish has three types of infinitives: those that end in **-ar, -er,** or **-ir,** which are commonly referred to as **-ar, -er,** and **-ir** verbs, respectively. For now, we'll focus on just the **-ar** verbs. (You'll learn about **-er** and **-ir** verbs in **Gramática 1.4.**)

---

GRAMÁTICA EN CONTEXTO *A **Typical Day for Raúl** / Raúl is sending an e-mail to his friend Alberto about his classes this semester. Hi, Alberto: / How's it going? Everything's fine here. I'm taking four classes this semester, and my favorite class is French at 10:00 A.M. The professor only speaks French! It's a little difficult, but I like it a lot. Afterward, I work in the cafeteria until 2:00, and then I study in the library in the afternoon. At night, I spend time with my girlfriend: We watch television, eat out at some restaurant, or simply rest and spend some time together. If my girlfriend needs to study, I talk on the phone with my parents, or I read my e-mail. / And you, Alberto? How many classes are you taking? Do you speak French? When and where do you study? Are you working this semester? / Later, Raúl.*

**B.** To conjugate an -ar verb in the *present tense*, remove the -ar from the infinitive (**habl-**) and add the present tense endings **-o, -as, -a, -amos, -áis,** and **-an.**

| PRESENT TENSE OF **-ar** VERBS | | | |
|---|---|---|---|
| **habl**ar (*to speak*) | | | |
| **(yo) habl**o | I speak | **(nosotros/as) habl**amos | we speak |
| **(tú) habl**as | you speak | **(vosotros/as) habl**áis | you speak |
| **(Ud.) habl**a | you speak | **(Uds.) habl**an | you speak |
| **(él/ella) habl**a | he/she speaks | **(ellos/as) habl**an | they speak |

**C.** Note in the preceding chart that the subject pronouns (**yo, tú, Ud.,** . . . ) are in parentheses. This is because they are usually considered optional in Spanish. That is, the conjugated verb forms already include the subject (**hablo** = *I speak*). The subject pronouns are used only to add emphasis or to clarify and avoid confusion.

Yo **hablo** inglés y español.　　　　　*I speak English and Spanish. What*
　¿Qué **hablas tú**?　　　　　　　　　　*do you speak?*

Accordingly, you will often see no subject stated in a sentence. This means that you will have to learn to look and/or listen for the verb endings in order to know who or what the subject of a sentence is.

**D.** The preceding chart shows only one simple translation of the Spanish present tense. However, present tense verbs have other meanings, depending on the context.

**Bailo** cada fin de semana.　　　　　*I dance every weekend.*
¿**Caminas** a la universidad?　　　　　*Do you walk to the university?*
—Juan, ¿qué haces?　　　　　　　　　*Juan, what are you doing?*
—**Hablo** por teléfono.　　　　　　　　*I am speaking on the phone.*
Mañana **trabajo** todo el día.　　　　　*Tomorrow I will work all day.*

**E.** You learned a few -ar verbs in the **Vocabulario del tema** section of this **Tema** (p. 35). Here are some more **-ar** verbs and expressions that you should know.

| COMMON -ar VERBS | | | |
|---|---|---|---|
| **cenar** | to eat dinner | **pasar tiempo** | to spend time |
| **contestar** | to answer | **pasar un rato** | to spend some time |
| **desayunar** | to eat breakfast | **practicar** | to practice |
| **descansar (un rato)** | to rest (a bit) | **practicar un deporte** | to participate in a sport |
| **escuchar** | to listen to | **regresar (a)** | to return, go back (*to a place*) |
| **llamar (por teléfono)** | to call (on the phone) | **sacar buenas/malas notas** | to get good/bad grades |
| **llegar** | to arrive | **sacar un DVD** | to check out a DVD |
| **llevar** | to carry | **terminar** | to finish |
| **navegar en Internet** | to surf the Internet | **tomar** | to drink |
| **pagar (por)** | to pay (for) | | |

**F.** Some verbs are commonly followed by the infinitive of another verb. When this happens, only the first verb is conjugated, just as in English.

**desear** + *inf.* to desire/want to (*do something*)

> Deseo **regresar** a casa ahora, por favor.
>
> *I want to go back home now, please.*

**necesitar** + *inf.* to need to (*do something*)

> Necesitamos **estudiar** para el examen.
>
> *We need to study for the exam.*

## ACTIVIDADES

**A.** ¿Qué hacen estas personas (*do these people do*)? Match the conjugated verb forms in column B with the phrases in column A to form logical sentences.

|  | A |  | B |
|---|---|---|---|
| 1. | Juana ____ con sus amigas todos los días. | a. | Miramos |
| 2. | Valentín __g__ música mientras (*while*) estudia. | b. | tocas |
| 3. | Estela y Yolanda siempre (*always*) ____ buenos apuntes. | c. | toco |
| 4. | Los viernes (yo) ____ un DVD y __k__ la ropa. | d. | toman |
| 5. | —¿Estudia y ____ Ud.? | e. | trabaja |
|  | —Sí, ____, pero no trabajo. | f. | charla |
| 6. | —Maricela, ¿tocas algún (*any*) instrumento musical? | g. | escucha |
|  | —Sí, __c__ el piano. ¿Y qué __b__ tú? | h. | estudio |
| 7. | —¿Qué programas de televisión __i__ Uds.? | i. | miran |
|  | —____ NCIS, *Criminal Minds* y *Sobreviviente* (*Survivor*). | j. | saco |
|  |  | k. | lavo |

**B.** Otras actividades diarias (*daily*). Fill in the blanks with the correct form of the verbs from the list. **¡OJO!** You'll need to use some verbs more than once.

| descansar | llamar | llevar | pasar |
|---|---|---|---|
| escuchar | llegar | navegar | tomar |

1. Rosalinda _____ a sus clientes por teléfono.
2. Keesha _____ en Internet antes de (*before*) sus clases.
3. Tomás y su novia, Elena, _____ un rato juntos (*together*).
4. ¡Huy (*Gosh*), Ana! _____ muchas cosas en tu mochila. Pesa (*It weighs*) mucho, ¿no?
5. —David, ¿A qué hora _____ tú a la universidad entre semana?
   —Bueno (*Well*), _____ a las nueve en punto. Luego (*Then*), _____ un café y _____ un rato.
6. —¿Qué tipos de música _____ Uds.?
   —Normalmente _____ música rock, pero a veces nos gusta _____ música latina.

**C.** ¿Qué haces tú (*do you do*)? Answer the questions with complete sentences as in the model. **¡OJO!** The **Vocabulario práctico** might help you answer item 7.

MODELO   ¿A qué hora cena Ud. normalmente (*usually*)? →
         Normalmente ceno a las cinco.

| **Vocabulario práctico** | | |
|---|---|---|
| la música country | la música latina | la música rock |
| la música hip hop | la música rap | |

(Continúa.)

1. ¿Baila Ud. bien o mal?
2. ¿A qué hora desayuna normalmente?
3. ¿Saca buenas o malas notas normalmente?
4. ¿Qué lleva en su mochila en este momento (*at this moment*)?
5. ¿Trabaja? ¿Dónde trabaja? ¿Cuántas horas (*hours*) trabaja a la (*per*) semana?
6. ¿Quién en la clase de español probablemente (*probably*) toca un instrumento musical? (Adivine si no sabe. [*Guess if you don't know.*])
7. ¿Qué tipo(s) de música escuchan Ud. y sus amigos?

Expressing Actions in the Present (Part 2)

# 1.4 Present Tense of Regular -er and -ir Verbs

## GRAMÁTICA EN CONTEXTO

### Un nuevo amigo porteño

[*Augusto y Natalia toman una clase de biología juntos. Augusto saluda a Natalia después del primer día de clase.*]

AUGUSTO: Buenos días. Tú hablas español, ¿no?

NATALIA: Hola. Sí, hablo español. Mi familia es cubana. Me llamo Natalia. ¿Cómo te llamas?

AUGUSTO: Me llamo Augusto. Soy porteño, es decir, soy de Buenos Aires, Argentina.

NATALIA: ¡Argentina! Mucho gusto, Augusto. ¿Te gusta la Universidad de Miami?

AUGUSTO: Pues, claro. Hay muchos estudiantes internacionales y clases muy interesantes.

NATALIA: ¿Y **comprendes** bien el inglés?

AUGUSTO: Sí, claro, *I speak English.* En mi familia, todos **aprendemos** inglés desde pequeños. **Leo** y **escribo** muy bien en inglés.

NATALIA: ¿**Vives** aquí en el campus?

AUGUSTO: Sí, **vivo** en Eaton, en una de las residencias.

NATALIA: Mi amigo Sam **vive** en Eaton también. No hay una cafetería en Eaton, ¿verdad?

AUGUSTO: No, **comemos** en otras cafeterías. Yo **como** en la cafetería Hecht/Stanford. Pero muchos residentes de Eaton **comen** en Mahoney/Pearson también.

NATALIA: Bueno, **asisto** a otra clase en diez minutos. Nos vemos en clase en dos días.

AUGUSTO: Sí, Natalia. Hasta luego.

---

GRAMÁTICA EN CONTEXTO *A New Friend from Buenos Aires* / Augusto and Natalia take a biology class together. Augusto greets Natalia after the first day of class. / **AUGUSTO:** Good morning. You speak Spanish, don't you? / **NATALIA:** Hi. Yes, I speak Spanish. My family is Cuban. My name is Natalia. What's your name? **AUGUSTO:** I'm Augusto. I'm porteño, that is, I'm from Buenos Aires, Argentina. / **NATALIA:** Argentina! It's a pleasure, Augusto. Do you like the University of Miami? / **AUGUSTO:** Well, of course. There are a lot of international students and interesting classes. / **NATALIA:** And you understand English well? **AUGUSTO:** Yes, of course, I speak English. In my family, we all learn English from a very young age. I read and write very well in English. / **NATALIA:** Do you live here on campus? / **AUGUSTO:** Yes, I live in Eaton, in one of the dorms. / **NATALIA:** My friend Sam lives in Eaton too. There isn't a cafeteria in Eaton, right? / **AUGUSTO:** No, we eat in other cafeterias. I eat in the Hecht/Stanford cafeteria. But many students eat in Mahoney/Pearson too. / **NATALIA:** Well, I attend another class in ten minutes. We'll see each other in class in two days. / **AUGUSTO:** Yes, Natalia. See you later.

¿Y UD.?

1. ¿Comprende Ud. bien el español? (Comprendo... )
2. ¿Vive Ud. en el campus? (Vivo... )
3. ¿Come Ud. en la cafetería? (Como... )
4. ¿Asiste a otras clases hoy? (Asisto... )

**A.** To form the present tense of **-er** and **-ir** verbs, remove the **-er/-ir** from the infinitive (**com-/viv-**) and add the present tense endings, as shown in the following chart. Note that the endings are the same for both **-er** and **-ir** verbs except in the **nosotros/as** and **vosotros/as** forms.

| PRESENT TENSE OF **-er** AND **-ir** VERBS | | | |
|---|---|---|---|
| **comer** (to eat) | | **vivir** (to live) | |
| como | comemos | vivo | vivimos |
| comes | coméis | vives | vivís |
| come | comen | vive | viven |

**B.** Here are some common **-er** and **-ir** verbs you should know.

| COMMON **-er** AND **-ir** VERBS | | | |
|---|---|---|---|
| **-er** VERBS | | **-ir** VERBS | |
| aprender | to learn | abrir | to open |
| aprender a + *inf.* | to learn to (do something) | asistir (a) | to attend, go to (a class, event) |
| beber | to drink | escribir | to write |
| comer | to eat | describir | to describe |
| comprender | to understand | recibir | to receive |
| correr | to run; to jog | vivir | to live |
| leer | to read | | |
| vender | to sell | | |

### ACTIVIDADES

**A.** ¿Qué hacen? (*What are they doing?*)

PASO 1. Indicate the correct verb to complete each sentence.

1. Tú no ____ esta lección.
2. Uds. ____ a clase de lunes a viernes.
3. Mis amigos y yo ____ café por la mañana.
4. El profesor ____ en la cafetería con sus estudiantes.
5. Este semestre ____ a hablar español y alemán.
6. Olga y Paloma ____ sus libros al final (*at the end*) del semestre.
7. Por la mañana, ____ por el parque con mi amiga Inés.
8. La profesora de historia ____ el período colonial.

a. corro
b. venden
c. comprendes
d. bebemos
e. aprendo
f. asisten
g. come
h. describe

**PASO 2.** Restate each sentence from **Paso 1** to describe you and/or your friends. Change information in the sentence as necessary.

MODELO   No comprendo la Lección 3.
         Nosotros no comprendemos las matemáticas.

**B.** En la universidad

**PASO 1.** Study the image, then indicate which sentence describes a scene in this image. Correct the incorrect sentences.

1. ☐ Antonio bebe café y lee su e-mail.
2. ☐ Penélope, Úrsula y Héctor escriben su tarea.
3. ☐ Los profesores asisten a clase.

**PASO 2.** With a partner, come up with four more sentences that describe the image from **Paso 1.** Use the sentences in **Paso 1** as models.

Communication

**C.** Entrevista. Interview a partner using these questions. Then switch roles.

1. ¿Qué bebes por la mañana?
2. ¿Cuántos libros llevas en tu mochila normalmente?
3. ¿Dónde vives?
4. ¿A cuántas clases asistes los lunes?
5. ¿Dónde comes entre semana?

# Lectura cultural

## ANTES DE LEER

You are going to read a text about associations for Latin American students at some institutions in the United States and Canada. Which of the following types of information would you expect to find in the reading?

☐ objetivos de las asociaciones
☐ programas de actividades de recreación
☐ servicios sociales para los estudiantes y la comunidad
☐ carreras de los estudiantes latinoamericanos
☐ programas de actividades culturales

## Asociaciones de estudiantes latinoamericanos

*En Stanford University*

En muchas universidades estadounidenses, y en algunas[a] canadienses, hay organizaciones o asociaciones de estudiantes latinoamericanos. El objetivo de estas organizaciones es promover[b] la lengua y la cultura latinoamericanas en el campus y en la comunidad. Los socios[c] son estudiantes de diferentes países de habla hispana[d] y, con frecuencia, de Brasil. Sin embargo,[e] las asociaciones invitan a participar en sus actividades a todas las personas de la comunidad.

Las actividades son numerosas y muy diversas. La mayoría[f] de las asociaciones organizan torneos[g] de fútbol, *picnics* en donde sirven comida hispana,[h] fiestas tradicionales o conciertos de música latina. Algunas organizaciones realizan también[i] servicios sociales en la comunidad. Por ejemplo, ofrecen[j] clases de español gratis, organizan intercambios entre[k] estudiantes de universidades hispanas y su universidad en Norteamérica, o ayudan económicamente a[l] estudiantes de Latinoamérica. Algunas asociaciones organizan actividades culturales como festivales de cine, exposiciones[m] de arte o foros en línea[n] para hablar de temas de la actualidad[ñ] en Latinoamérica.

[a]*some* [b]*promote* [c]*members* [d]*de... Spanish-speaking* [e]*Sin... However* [f]*majority* [g]*tournaments* [h]*sirven... they serve Hispanic food* [i]*realizan... also provide* [j]*they offer* [k]*intercambios... exchanges between* [l]*ayudan... they help financially* [m]*exhibitions* [n]*foros... online forums* [ñ]*de... current*

Los programas de las organizaciones tienen[o] muchos objetivos y todos contribuyen a la diversidad de la universidad y la comunidad. Además,[p] estas asociaciones ofrecen a los estudiantes latinoamericanos una oportunidad de mantener[q] su lengua, su cultura y su identidad.

[o]*have* [p]*In addition* [q]*maintain*

## DESPUÉS DE LEER

**A.** Comprensión. Provide the following information, based on the reading.

1. nacionalidad de los socios de las asociaciones
2. objetivo de las asociaciones
3. actividades de recreación
4. actividades culturales
5. servicios a la comunidad y a los estudiantes
6. beneficios para los socios

Communication

**B.** Temas de discusión. With a partner, answer the questions. Then share your ideas with the class.

1. ¿Hay una asociación de estudiantes latinoamericanos en su universidad? ¿De qué países son los estudiantes de la asociación?
2. ¿Cuántas asociaciones de estudiantes hay en su universidad? ¿Qué tipos de actividades organizan para los estudiantes y la comunidad?

## Los Ángeles: Héctor

Presentación del concurso

Héctor es de Texas y toda[a] su famila habla español en casa. Pero ahora[b] Héctor vive y estudia en Los Ángeles. En el vídeo, Héctor habla de la influencia hispana en Los Ángeles y presenta su idea para un concurso de videoblogs en el mundo hispano.

[a]*all of*   [b]*now*

### ANTES DE VER°

Antes... *Before watching*

Answer the questions, based on your own experiences in your area.

1. What types of Hispanic influence are apparent in your community?
2. What kind of Hispanic food is available? Do you like it? Why or why not?
3. What do you think of the blogging culture in the world today? Do you like to blog? Why or why not?

| Vocabulario práctico | |
|---|---|
| **Un agua horchata,[†] por favor.** | An horchata, please. |
| **pupusas** | *Salvadoran dish similar to an empanada* |
| **empanadas** | *thick, stuffed pastry* |
| **¿Con leche o sin leche?** | With milk or without milk? |
| **Uds. van a aprender** | You're going to learn |
| **Estamos en Granada** | We're in Granada |
| **les va a gustar** | you're going to like it |
| **porteño** | from Buenos Aires |
| **¿Recuerdan el tango?** | Do you remember that tango? |
| **querido** | dear, beloved |

### DESPUÉS DE VER

**A. Comprensión.**   Answer the questions, based on Héctor's video.

1. What features or aspects of Los Angeles does Héctor present in his video?
2. What suggestions does Héctor offer for practicing your Spanish in Los Angeles?
3. What is Héctor's plan for the blogging competition? Who are the bloggers? Where are they from?

**B. Temas de discusión.**   With a partner, answer the questions.

1. What images or topics from the video segment were most interesting to you and why?
2. Do you think Héctor's blogging competition will be interesting? Why or why not?

---

*\*Competition*
*†***Agua horchata** or just **horchata** is a cold drink made of water, rice, almonds, cinnamon, vanilla, and sugar.

51

## En el salón de clase — In the Classroom

| | |
|---|---|
| el bolígrafo | pen |
| el borrador | eraser (*for whiteboard*) |
| la computadora portátil | laptop |
| el cuaderno | notebook |
| el escritorio | desk |
| la goma | eraser (*for pencil*) |
| el lápiz | pencil |
| el libro de texto | textbook |
| el marcador | marker |
| la mesa | table |
| la mochila | backpack |
| el papel | paper |
| la pared | wall |
| el pizarrón (blanco) | whiteboard |
| la puerta | door |
| el reloj | clock; watch |
| la silla | chair |
| la tarea | homework |
| el (teléfono) celular | cell (phone) |
| la ventana | window |

Cognados: la clase, la computadora, el diccionario, el teléfono

## Las personas

| | |
|---|---|
| el/la bibliotecario/a | librarian |
| el/la compañero/a de clase | classmate |
| el/la compañero/a de cuarto | roommate |
| el/la estudiante | student |
| el hombre | man |
| la mujer | woman |
| el/la profesor(a) | professor; teacher |

## Los edificios y los lugares — Buildings and Places

| | |
|---|---|
| la biblioteca | library |
| el centro estudiantil | student union |
| el despacho | (individual) office |
| el estadio | stadium |
| la Facultad de… | School of . . . |
| Bellas Artes | Fine Arts |
| Ciencias | Sciences |
| Educación | Education |
| Letras | Humanities |
| Leyes | Law |
| Medicina | Medicine |
| la librería | bookstore |
| la oficina | (main) office |
| la residencia (estudiantil) | (student) dorm |
| el salón de clase | classroom |
| el teatro | theater |
| el trabajo | work (*general*) |

Cognados: la cafetería, el campus, la clínica, el gimnasio, el hospital, el laboratorio (de computadoras), la universidad

## Las materias y las carreras — Classes and Majors

| | |
|---|---|
| la administración empresarial | business administration |
| la contabilidad | accounting |
| el derecho | law |
| la economía | economics |
| la estadística | statistics |
| la física | physics |
| la informática | computer science |
| la ingeniería | engineering |
| las lenguas (extranjeras) | (foreign) languages |
| el alemán | German |
| el español | Spanish |
| las matemáticas | math |
| el periodismo | journalism |
| la química | chemistry |
| la sicología | psychology |

Cognados: la anatomía, el árabe, la arquitectura, el arte, la astronomía, la biología, el chino, las ciencias políticas, la filosofía, el francés, la geografía, la historia, el inglés, el italiano, el japonés, la literatura, la medicina, la música, la sociología

## Los adjetivos — Adjectives

| | |
|---|---|
| aburrido/a | boring |
| alto/a | tall |
| antipático/a | mean |
| bajo/a | short |
| bonito/a | pretty |
| buen, bueno/a | good |
| difícil | difficult |
| divertido/a | fun |
| fácil | easy |
| feo/a | ugly |
| gran, grande | large |
| guapo/a | handsome; pretty |
| interesante | interesting |
| mal, malo/a | bad |
| moreno/a | dark-haired; dark-skinned |
| pelirrojo/a | redheaded |
| pequeño/a | small |
| perezoso/a | lazy |
| rubio/a | blond(e) |
| simpático/a | nice |
| trabajador(a) | hardworking |

## Los adjetivos posesivos — (Unstressed) Possessive Adjectives

| | |
|---|---|
| mi(s) | my |
| tu(s) | your (*sing. fam.*) |
| su(s) | your (*sing. form.*); his; her |
| nuestro/a/os/as | our |
| vuestro/a/os/as | your (*pl. fam. Sp.*) |
| su(s) | your (*pl. form. Sp.; pl. fam., form. elsewhere*); their |

## Las palabras interrogativas — Question Words

| | |
|---|---|
| ¿cómo? | how? |
| ¿cuál(es)? | what?, which? |
| ¿cuándo? | when? |
| ¿cuánto? | how much? |
| ¿dónde? | where? |
| ¿quién(es)? | who? |
| ¿qué? | what? |

| Actividades típicas en la universidad | Typical Activities at the University |
|---|---|
| andar en bicicleta | to ride a bicycle |
| bailar | to dance |
| buscar (algo) | to look for (something) |
| caminar | to walk |
| cenar | to eat dinner |
| charlar | to chat |
| comprar | to buy |
| contestar | to answer |
| desayunar | to eat breakfast |
| descansar (un rato) | to rest (a bit) |
| escuchar (música) | to listen to (music) |
| estudiar | to study |
| hablar (por teléfono) | to speak (on the phone) |
| jugar (a) | to play (a game, sport) |
| al basquetbol | basquetball |
| al béisbol | baseball |
| al fútbol americano | football |
| al fútbol | soccer |
| al vólibol | volleyball |
| lavar la ropa | to wash clothes |
| llamar (por teléfono) | to call (on the phone) |
| leer el e-mail | to read/check one's e-mail |
| llegar | to arrive |
| llevar | to carry |
| mirar la televisión | to watch TV |
| navegar en Internet | to surf the Internet |
| pagar (por) | to pay (for) |
| pasar tiempo | to spend time |
| pasar un rato | to spend some time |
| practicar | to practice |
| practicar un deporte | to participate in a sport |
| regresar (a) | to return, go back (to a place) |
| sacar buenas/malas notas | to get good/bad grades |
| sacar un DVD | to check out a DVD |
| terminar | to finish |
| tocar | to play (a musical instrument) |
| tomar | to take; to drink |
| tomar apuntes | to take notes |
| tomar una clase | to take a class |
| trabajar | to work |

| Otros verbos | |
|---|---|
| abrir | to open |
| aprender | to learn |
| aprender a + inf. | to learn to (do something) |
| asistir (a) | to attend, go to (a class, event) |
| beber | to drink |
| comer | to eat |
| comprender | to understand |
| correr | to run; to jog |
| describir | to describe |
| desear + inf. | to desire/want to (do something) |
| escribir | to write |
| gustar | to like (lit. to be pleasing) |
| leer | to read |
| necesitar + inf. | to need to (do something) |
| recibir | to receive |
| vender | to sell |
| vivir | to live |

| Los días de la semana | Days of the Week |
|---|---|
| el día | day |
| los días de entre semana | weekdays |
| lunes, martes, miércoles, jueves, viernes | |
| el fin de semana | weekend |
| sábado, domingo | |
| la semana | week |

| ¿Cuándo? | When? |
|---|---|
| antes (de) | before |
| después (de) | after |
| entre semana | during the week |
| esta mañana | this morning |
| esta tarde | this afternoon |
| esta noche | tonight |
| hoy | today |
| mañana | tomorrow |
| pasado mañana | the day after tomorrow |
| el lunes (martes, miércoles,... ) | on Monday (Tuesday, Wednesday, . . . ) |
| los lunes (martes, miércoles,... ) | on Mondays (Tuesdays, Wednesdays, . . . ) |
| el lunes (martes, miércoles,... ) que viene | next Monday (Tuesday, Wednesday, . . . ) |
| la semana que viene | next week |
| todos los días | every day |
| por la mañana | in the morning |
| por la tarde | in the afternoon |
| por la noche | in the evening, at night |

| ¿Con quién(es)? | With Whom? |
|---|---|
| el/la amigo/a | friend |
| el/la esposo/a | husband/wife |
| la mamá | mom |
| el/la mejor amigo/a | best friend |
| el/la novio/a | boyfriend/girlfriend |
| el papá | dad |

| ¿Qué hora es? | What Time Is It? |
|---|---|
| a la(s) + time | at + time |
| ¿A qué hora? | At what time? |
| de la mañana | in the morning |
| de la noche | in the evening, at night |
| de la tarde | in the afternoon |
| en punto | sharp, exactly |
| Es la una. | It's one o'clock. |
| medianoche | midnight |
| mediodía | noon |
| menos cuarto/quince | quarter to |
| Son las dos (tres, cuatro,... ). | It's two (three, four, . . . ) o'clock. |
| y cuarto/quince | quarter past |
| y media/treinta | half past |

| Otras palabras | |
|---|---|
| sí | yes |
| también | also, too |

# Entrada cultural

## México

Cultures

*Offshore oil platform in the Gulf of Mexico*

*Social and ethnic diversity in Mexico City*

In the pre-Columbian region of what is Mexico today, a number of indigenous peoples, including the Mayans and the Aztecs, lived and created highly developed civilizations that flourished for 4,000 years before the Spanish arrived in 1519. Advancements in mathematics, astronomy, art, medicine, and architecture such as pyramids and temples are only part of these civilizations' legacy. During the conquest by Spain and the following colonial period, the pre-Hispanic cultures blended with Spanish social and religious traditions, and interracial mixing among indigenous people and Spanish colonizers created new ethnic groups. This ethnic blend, known in Spanish as **mestizaje,** has been and still is present in Mexican society and is the foundation of Mexican cultural identity. As such, today Mexico is a multicultural and multiethnic country, where Spanish coexists officially with numerous indigenous languages, and where its people show their deep-rooted traditions and beliefs.

The convergence of cultures can be observed in the various forms of Mexican lifestyle. While Mexican villagers generally follow the ancient way of life, urban people from large cities follow models similar to those in Europe and of its northern neighbor, the United States. The mixture of cultures is shown in Mexican folk art traditions such as colorful textiles and pottery, originated from indigenous and Spanish crafts. It is represented in its architecture in the fact that indigenous archeological ruins exist side-by-side with magnificent colonial buildings, such as churches or haciendas, and with modern skyscrapers or office buildings. The influence of different cultures, mostly indigenous and European, is also reflected in Mexican music. Traditional sounds include the well-known mariachi, rancheras, and corridos. However, contemporary music like pop, hip hop, rap, and rock, both in English and in Spanish, are popular among Mexicans, and ancient sounds are still played in certain contexts.

Mexico's richness is also present in its unique diversity of flora and fauna and in its abundance of natural resources, such as petroleum, natural gas, various metals and minerals, oceans that yield copious quantities of seafood, and fertile land for agriculture. Certainly, the inequality of income distribution still exists. However, Mexico is working to establish more democratic institutions to eradicate poverty among rural populations.

Due to its diversity, it is difficult to generalize about Mexico. While Mexicans may differ in many ways, they have in common a capacity for warmth and kindness toward people who show an interest in their culture and way of life.

*Woman with typical embroidered blouse and black clay pottery from Oaxaca, Mexico*

# ¿Qué hace Ud. en su tiempo libre?*

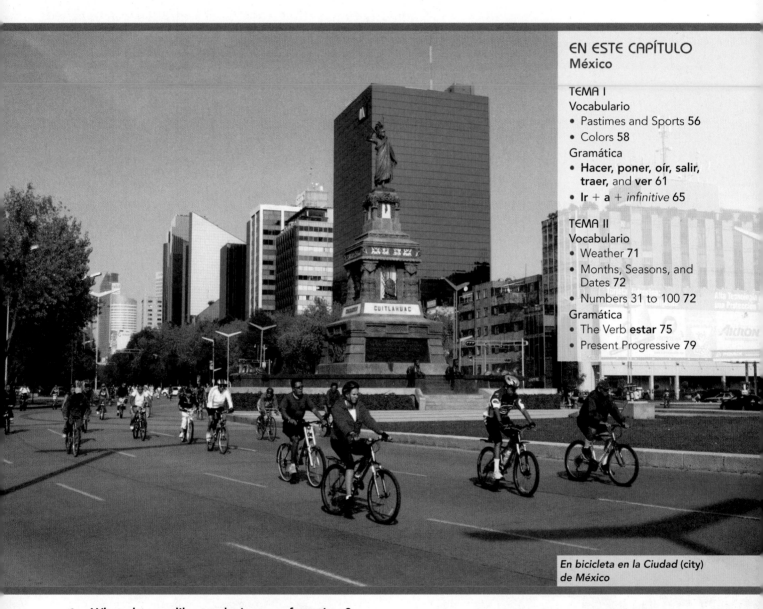

**EN ESTE CAPÍTULO**
**México**

**TEMA I**
**Vocabulario**
- Pastimes and Sports 56
- Colors 58

**Gramática**
- **Hacer, poner, oír, salir, traer,** and **ver** 61
- **Ir + a +** *infinitive* 65

**TEMA II**
**Vocabulario**
- Weather 71
- Months, Seasons, and Dates 72
- Numbers 31 to 100 72

**Gramática**
- The Verb **estar** 75
- Present Progressive 79

*En bicicleta en la Ciudad (city) de México*

1. **What do you like to do in your free time?**
2. **Do you enjoy going to musical or other cultural events? What kind?**
3. **Do you participate in any sports? In organized leagues or just among friends?**

**McGraw Hill** **connect**™
**|SPANISH**
www.connectspanish.com

---

*¿Qué... What Do You Do in Your Free Time?*

## Vocabulario del tema

### Los pasatiempos° y los deportes

Los… *Pastimes*

| la calle | street | el pasatiempo | pastime |
| la fiesta | party | los ratos libres | free time |
| la natación | swimming | el tiempo libre | free time |
| el partido | game (*single occurrence*) | | |

Cognados: el golf, el tenis

Repaso: andar en bicicleta, bailar, caminar, cantar, descansar (un rato), escuchar (música), leer, mirar la televisión, navegar en Internet, practicar un deporte, sacar un DVD, tocar un instrumento musical; el/la amigo/a, el basquetbol, el béisbol, el fin de semana, el fútbol americano, el vólibol

**Observe**

The verb **jugar** has some irregularities in the present tense.

| | |
|---|---|
| **jue**go | **jug**amos |
| **jue**gas | **jug**áis |
| **jue**ga | **jue**gan |

**Juego** al fútbol todos los sábados.     *I play soccer every Saturday.*

You'll learn more about similar irregular verbs in **Capítulo 3**. For now, you'll just need to recognize these forms of **jugar** when you see them.

## ACTIVIDADES

**A.** Los pasatiempos y los deportes

**PASO 1.**   Jot down as many related words as possible from the **Vocabulario del tema** presentation for each drawing.

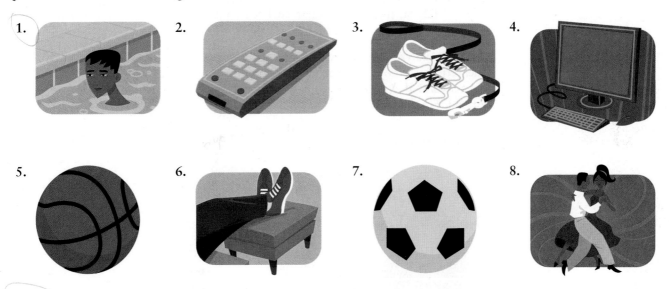

1.

2.

3.

4.

5.

6.

7.

8.

**PASO 2.**   Now organize the words you jotted down in **Paso 1** into the categories of **Pasatiempos** and **Deportes.** Which ones are **pasatiempos**? Which are **deportes**?

**B. Asociaciones.** Match the activities in column B with the people or things in column A.

| | A | | B |
|---|---|---|---|
| 1. | ____ Michael Phelps | **a.** | sacar |
| 2. | ____ en Internet | **b.** | jugar al fútbol |
| 3. | ____ la televisión | **c.** | caminar |
| 4. | ____ la fiesta | **d.** | practicar la natación |
| 5. | ____ Manu Ginóbili | **e.** | bailar |
| 6. | ____ el parque | **f.** | jugar al basquetbol |
| 7. | ____ Lionel Messi | **g.** | navegar |
| 8. | ____ el DVD | **h.** | mirar |

**C. Mis ratos libres**

**PASO 1.** Indicate the things you like to do in your free time.

Me gusta...

1. ☐ practicar deportes
2. ☐ nadar en la piscina
3. ☐ bailar
4. ☐ andar en bicicleta
5. ☐ caminar por el parque

6. ☐ escuchar música
7. ☐ mirar la televisión
8. ☐ descansar
9. ☐ leer novelas
10. ☐ escribir poemas

Communication

**PASO 2.** With a partner, use the phrases in **Paso 1** to ask each other what you like to do in your free time. Follow the model. Feel free to include other activities in your questions.

**MODELO** E1: ¿Te gusta patinar en línea en tus ratos libres?
E2: Sí, me gusta patinar en línea en mis ratos libres. / No, no me gusta practicar deportes en mis ratos libres.

**PASO 3.** Analyze your answers in **Paso 1** to answer the question: **¿Eres activo/a o sedentario/a?** If most of the answers you indicated are for items 1–5, you can respond **Soy activo/a.** If you indicated more answers for items 6–10, you should probably respond: **Soy sedentario/a.**

## Los colores

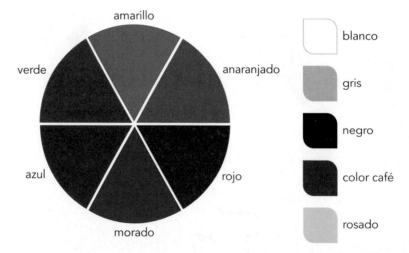

- When used as adjectives, colors must agree in gender and number with the nouns they modify: **el edificio blanco, la bicicleta roja.**
- Note that some colors have only one form for masculine and feminine: **el edificio gris, la bicicleta gris.**

◉ And **color café** requires the use of **de** before it.

**Es de color café.**     *It's brown.*

**D.** Las habitaciones (*bedrooms*) de Laura y Gustavo

**PASO 1.**   List the things in color that you see in the two bedrooms. Follow the model.
**¡OJO!** You can use the **Vocabulario práctico** in the margin, next to the drawings.

**MODELO**  En la habitación de Laura hay una bicicleta rosada,…

La habitación de Laura

| Vocabulario práctico | |
|---|---|
| **el bate de béisbol** | baseball bat |
| **la gorra** | baseball cap |
| **la pelota** | ball |
| **la raqueta de tenis** | tennis racquet |
| **los zapatos de tenis** | tennis shoes |

La habitación de Gustavo

Communication

**PASO 2.** With a partner, compare what Laura and Gustavo do in their spare time. Follow the model.

**MODELO** Laura juega al tenis y al fútbol, camina y...

## Nota cultural

Cultures

### LOS CUATES

A well-known Mexican Spanish word is **cuate/a.** If a Spanish speaker introduces his or her friend as a **cuate/a,** you know for sure that he or she is a Mexican. A **cuate/a** is a close friend, someone you may have known for years. **Cuates** are the friends you play soccer with every day after school or those who invite you to their birthday parties. Generally, **cuates** are friends who live in your neighborhood with whom you grew up and that you see all the time. As you grow up, your circle of **cuates** can increase, decrease, or you can completely change one group for another. As a young adult, **cuates** are now the people you go out with on a Saturday night or with whom you meet in a sports bar to watch your favorite team.

PREGUNTA With a partner, answer the questions. Then share your ideas with the class.

1. How would you translate the term **cuate/a** into English?
2. Do you have some friends that you consider closer than others? What do your friends mean to you? What activities do you do together?

CAPÍTULO 2   ¿Qué hace Ud. en su tiempo libre?

# Gramática

## 2.1 Hacer, poner, oír, salir, traer, and ver

### GRAMÁTICA EN CONTEXTO

### Los fines de semana

[*Dos amigos charlan enfrente de la biblioteca.*]

JULIO: Oye, Rodrigo, ¿qué **haces** los fines de semana?

RODRIGO: Bueno, depende. Los sábados son para descansar, pero siempre **hago** ejercicio o juego al tenis por la mañana. Después, regreso a casa, **pongo** la televisión y **veo** un partido de fútbol o béisbol, o **hago** otra cosa para descansar. Pero en la noche, siempre **salgo** con mis cuates.

JULIO: ¿Y los domingos?

RODRIGO: Ja, ja… los domingos, **hago** todo lo que debo hacer. Es decir, **traigo** mis libros a la biblioteca y **hago** la tarea aquí, porque hay mucho ruido en la residencia. Necesito silencio, pero en la residencia siempre **oigo** música, una televisión o algo…

JULIO: Mmm… Comprendo. Bueno, ¡nos vemos!

¿Y Ud.? Indicate which of these things you usually do on the weekends. ¡OJO! For item 6, mention something else that you do on weekends.

|  | SÍ | NO |
|---|---|---|
| 1. Hago la tarea. | ☐ | ☐ |
| 2. Pongo la radio o la televisión. | ☐ | ☐ |
| 3. Veo películas (*movies*). | ☐ | ☐ |
| 4. Salgo con mis cuates. | ☐ | ☐ |
| 5. Estudio en un lugar donde no oigo nada (*anything*). | ☐ | ☐ |
| 6. ¿ ? | | |

**A.** The verbs **hacer, poner, salir, traer,** and **ver** have some irregular conjugations.

| hacer (*to do; to make*) | | poner (*to put, place*) | |
|---|---|---|---|
| hago | hacemos | pongo | ponemos |
| haces | hacéis | pones | ponéis |
| hace | hacen | pone | ponen |

GRAMÁTICA EN CONTEXTO *Weekends* / [*Two friends chat in front of the library.*] / *JULIO:* Hey, Rodrigo, what do you do on the weekends? *RODRIGO:* Well, that depends. Saturdays are for resting, but I always exercise or play tennis in the morning. Then, I go back home, turn on the television, and watch a soccer or baseball game, or I do something else to relax. But at night, I always go out with my buds. *JULIO:* And on Sundays? *RODRIGO:* Ha, ha . . . on Sundays, I do everything that I should do. That is, I bring my books to the library and I do my homework here, because there is a lot of noise in the dorm. I need silence, but in the dorm I always hear music, a television, or something . . . *JULIO:* Hmm . . . I understand. Well, see ya!

| salir (to leave, to go out) | | traer (to bring) | |
| --- | --- | --- | --- |
| salgo | salimos | traigo | traemos |
| sales | salís | traes | traéis |
| sale | salen | trae | traen |

| oír (to hear) | | ver (to see; to watch) | |
| --- | --- | --- | --- |
| oigo | oímos | veo | vemos |
| oyes | oís | ves | veis |
| oye | oyen | ve | ven |

**B.** The verbs **hacer, poner,** and **salir** are often used in a variety of expressions, sometimes with alternate meanings. Here are a few common expressions.

| | |
| --- | --- |
| **hacer una fiesta** | to throw a party |
| Penélope **hace una fiesta** cada viernes. | *Penélope throws a party every Friday.* |
| **hacer ejercicio** | to exercise |
| Alberto y Jaime **hacen ejercicio** todos los fines de semana. | *Alberto and Jaime exercise every weekend.* |
| **poner** | to turn on (*an electrical appliance*) |
| Por la mañana, **pongo** la radio. | *In the morning, I turn on the radio.* |
| **salir (con)** | to go out (*with*) |
| ¿Sabes que Gloria **sale** con Roberto? | *Do you know that Gloria is going out with Roberto?* |
| **salir de** | to leave from (*a place*) |
| **Salgo** de la casa a las 8:00. | *I leave the house at 8:00.* |
| **salir para** | to leave for (*a place*) |
| Mañana **salimos para** Chicago. | *Tomorrow we leave for Chicago.* |

**C.** For most Spanish speakers, the verbs **mirar** and **ver** can be used interchangeably when referring to watching something like television or a movie. Note, however, that only **ver** can be used to mean *to see.*

| | |
| --- | --- |
| Los lunes Eugenio **mira/ve** su programa favorito en la televisión. | *On Mondays Eugenio watches his favorite program on television.* |
| ¿**Ves** al hombre alto? Es mi papá. | *Do you see the tall man? He's my dad.* |

### ACTIVIDADES

**A.** ¿Cuántas veces a (*times per*) la semana? Indicate which activities you do. Then, tell how many times per week you do the activities that you checked. **¡OJO!** For item 9, mention some other activity that you do and how many times per week you do it.

1. ☐ Salgo con mis amigos a andar en bicicleta _____ veces a la semana.
2. ☐ Pongo la televisión y veo telenovelas (*soap operas*) _____ veces a la semana.
3. ☐ Pongo la radio y hago la tarea (*homework*) _____ veces a la semana.
4. ☐ Traigo mi perro (*dog*) al parque a jugar _____ veces a la semana.

5. ☐ Hago ejercicio en el gimnasio _____ veces a la semana.
6. ☐ Salgo de casa antes de las 8:00 de la mañana _____ veces a la semana.
7. ☐ Traigo mis libros de texto a clase _____ veces a la semana.
8. ☐ Veo las noticias (*news*) en la televisión _____ veces a la semana.
9. ☐ ¿ ? _____ veces a la semana.

**B. Mis viajes (*trips*) a México.** Complete the sentences with the correct form of **hacer, poner, oír, salir, traer,** or **ver.**

1. Cada año (*Each year*), nosotros _____ un viaje (*trip*) a México. ¡Me gusta México!
2. Cuando estoy de vacaciones (*on vacation*) en México, yo nunca (*never*) _____ la televisión. Prefiero (*I prefer*) salir a escuchar música y comer.
3. Rosa, ¿_____ (tú) esa música? Son mariachis. Es típico ver a mariachis en México, D.F.* ¿Te gusta?
4. Cuando estoy en Guadalajara, siempre (*always*) _____ a pasear por el centro histórico.
5. Cuando vamos a las playas (*beaches*), mis hermanos _____ sus juguetes (*toys*) para jugar en la arena (*sand*).
6. Mi padre visita todos los museos y _____ muchas exposiciones de arte.
7. Mi madre y mi hermana visitan los mercados donde _____ mucha cerámica (*pottery*) y tejidos (*woven goods*).
8. Lo mejor de viajar (*The best thing about traveling*) en México es hablar español. ¡Nosotros _____ y practicamos español todo el día (*all day long*)!

**C. ¿Qué haces los fines de semana?**

**PASO 1.** Form sentences that are true for you using the phrases from each column.

**MODELO** hacer la tarea → Hago la tarea los domingos por la noche.

| | | |
|---|---|---|
| hacer la tarea<br>ver deportes en la televisión<br>salir con mis amigos<br>poner la radio y escuchar música<br>practicar deportes<br>hacer ejercicio<br>poner la computadora y leer mi e-mail<br>salir a bailar<br>ver películas | **+** los viernes<br>los sábados<br>los domingos<br>los fines de semana **+** | por la mañana<br>por la tarde<br>por la noche |

**PASO 2.** With a partner, ask questions about what you do on the weekends, based on **Paso 1.** Each of you should make up at least one additional question.

Communication

**MODELO** hacer la tarea → ¿Cuándo haces la tarea?

**D. Los deportes en México**

**PASO 1.** Complete the reading about sports in Mexico. Choose the correct word in parentheses when there are choices. For all other items, use the correct form of **hacer, oír, poner, salir, traer,** or **ver.**

Cultures   Recycle

(*Continúa.*)

---

*México, D.F. (sometimes shortened to simply **el D.F.** [el de-efe]) is Mexico City. **D.F.** stands for **Distrito Federal.**

*Un aro (ring) en una cancha de pelota de Chichén Itzá*

Los deportes en México tienen[a] una larga[b] historia. (**El/La**[1]) juego de pelota[c] data desde[d] la época precolombina.[e] En las versiones más recientes, el jugador[f] ____[2] una pelota por (**un/una**[3]) aro de piedra.[g]

El deporte más popular en México hoy en día (**es/son**[4]) el fútbol. La Primera División de México, fundada[h] en 1943, incluye[i] dieciocho clubes, los mejores equipos[j] de México. México también tiene un equipo nacional muy (**bueno/buena**[5]). Cuando los aficionados[k] ____[6] para ver el equipo nacional, ____[7] los partidos[l] en el estadio más grande de México, el Estadio Azteca, en México, D.F.

Aunque el fútbol es el deporte más popular, el béisbol también (**es/eres**[8]) muy popular. La Liga Mexicana de Béisbol se fundó[m] en 1925 con seis equipos. Hoy en día (**es/hay**[9]) dieciséis equipos en esta[n] liga nacional. ¡Y algunos mexicanos juegan en las Grandes Ligas[ñ]! Cuando Ud. ____[10] (**su/sus**[11]) televisión y ____[12] partidos de béisbol en este[o] país, ____[13] a los reporteros hablar de beisbolistas[p] mexicanos, ¿no?

---

[a]*have* [b]*long* [c]*juego... ball game* [d]*data... dates from* [e]*época... pre-Columbian period* [f]*player* [g]*aro... stone ring* [h]*founded* [i]*includes* [j]*mejores... best teams* [k]*fans* [l]*games* [m]*se... was founded* [n]*this* [ñ]*Grandes... Major Leagues* [o]*this* [p]*baseball players*

**PASO 2.** Complete these items based on what you learned in **Paso 1.**
**¡OJO!** Some items may have more than one answer.

1. Empareje (*Match*) el deporte con la descripción.
   ____ el fútbol
   __c__ el béisbol
   ____ el juego de pelota
   **a.** un deporte precolombino
   **b.** la Primera División de México
   **c.** la Liga Mexicana
2. Hay ____ equipos de béisbol en la Liga Mexicana.
   **a.** seis          **b.** dieciséis          **c.** dieciocho
3. Los mexicanos van al Estadio Azteca para ver los partidos del equipo nacional de ____.
   **a.** pelota          **b.** béisbol          **c.** fútbol
4. Muchos atletas mexicanos juegan ____ en las Grandes Ligas.
   **a.** a la pelota          **b.** al béisbol          **c.** al fútbol
5. El juego de pelota data desde ____.
   **a.** 1925          **b.** 1943          **c.** antes de 1492
6. Hay aros de piedra en ____.
   **a.** Chichén Itzá          **b.** el Estadio Azteca          **c.** las Grandes Ligas

**PASO 3.** With a partner, talk about traditional and popular sports in your area. Use the questions to get started.

1. ¿Cuáles son algunos de los deportes tradicionales en este país? ¿Cuáles son populares en su región?
2. ¿Qué deportes ven Uds. en la televisión?
3. ¿Qué deportes practican Uds.? ¿En qué ligas o equipos juegan? (Juego... / Jugamos... )

**PASO 4.** Search the Internet for information about one of these topics. Share your results with the class.

1. la historia del juego de pelota en Mesoamérica
2. la Primera División de México (fútbol)
3. los beisbolistas mexicanos en las Grandes Ligas

CAPÍTULO 2 ¿Qué hace Ud. en su tiempo libre?

## 2.2 Ir + a + infinitive

**GRAMÁTICA EN CONTEXTO**

### Una fiesta

[*Elisa habla de sus planes y de los planes de su hermano.*]

Este sábado mis compañeras de cuarto y yo **vamos a hacer** una fiesta. Yo **voy a invitar** a nuestros amigos, y Elena **va a comprar** la comida. Mariana y Lucía **van a decorar** el apartamento. La noche de la fiesta, **vamos a poner** música y todos **van a bailar**. ¡**Va a ser** una fiesta divertida!

Al contrario, mi hermano Claudio **va a estudiar** todo el fin de semana con sus compañeros de clase. **Van a pasar** horas en la biblioteca y no **van a venir** a la fiesta. Claudio no **va a pasar** un fin de semana divertido.

**Comprensión.** With whom do you associate these descriptions, with Elisa (**E**) or with her brother Claudio (**C**)?

|  | E | C |
|---|---|---|
| 1. Va a estudiar. | ☐ | ☐ |
| 2. Va a hacer una fiesta. | ☐ | ☐ |
| 3. Sus compañeros van a pasar horas en la biblioteca. | ☐ | ☐ |
| 4. No va a pasar un fin de semana divertido. | ☐ | ☐ |
| 5. Va a bailar. | ☐ | ☐ |

**A.** One way to express your future plans is to use the verb **ir** (*to go*), followed by the preposition **a** and an infinitive: **Ir + a +** *infinitive*. Here are the present tense forms of **ir**.

| ir *(to go)* | |
|---|---|
| voy | vamos |
| vas | vais |
| va | van |

—¿Qué vas **a hacer** el sábado?  *What are you going to do this Saturday?*

—Voy **a nadar** en la piscina con mis amigos.  *I'm going to swim in the pool with my friends.*

**B.** **Ir** + **a** can also be used with nouns to express destination. Note that the question word **¿adónde?** is often used with **ir.**

**Vamos al** partido de béisbol
el viernes.

*We're going to the baseball game on
Friday.*

—¿**Adónde** vas después del partido?

*Where are you going after the game?*

—Voy **a** la fiesta de Jaime.

*I'm going to Jaime's party.*

### ACTIVIDADES

**A.** ¿Qué van a hacer el fin de semana que viene? Match each drawing with the most logical sentence.

a.

b.

c.

d.

e.

f.

g.

h.

1. ____ Mis padres van a bailar el sábado por la noche.
2. ____ Mis amigos y yo vamos a jugar al fútbol el domingo por la tarde.
3. ____ Ernesto y Antonio van a ver la televisión el sábado.
4. ____ Vas a escuchar música todo el fin de semana.
5. ____ Uds. van a patinar en línea en el parque el sábado por la mañana.
6. ____ Tú y tus amigos van a nadar el domingo.
7. ____ Voy a andar en bicicleta el viernes por la tarde.
8. ____ Elena va a sacar un DVD el viernes por la noche.

**B.** ¿Adónde van? Tell where each person is going based on what he/she needs. **¡OJO!** There can be more than one answer for some items.

MODELOS   Lucía necesita el libro de texto para la clase de biología. →
                  (Ella) Va a la librería.
                  Necesito un sándwich. → Voy a la cafetería.

1. Nora necesita nadar.
2. Necesito hacer ejercicio.
3. Uds. necesitan andar en bicicleta.
4. Necesitas comer.
5. Uds. necesitan hacer la tarea.
6. Mi compañero de clase y yo necesitamos buscar unos libros para la clase de literatura.
7. Ud. necesita comprar más cuadernos.

**C.** Una encuesta (*survey*): ¿Qué van a hacer este semestre/trimestre?

**PASO 1.** Survey your classmates to find out who will do the following things this semester/trimester. For items 6 and 7, make up two questions of your own. Then ask each person at least two questions from your list. Write the names of people next to the things they will do.

**MODELO** E1: ¿Vas a comprar cinco libros de texto este semestre?
E2: No, no voy a comprar cinco libros de texto; voy a comprar tres.
E1: ¿Vas a tomar seis exámenes finales?
E2: Sí, voy a tomar seis exámenes finales este semestre.

1. escribir cuatro informes (*reports*)
2. pasar por lo menos (*at least*) cinco horas por semana en la biblioteca
3. leer tres novelas
4. hacer ejercicio todos los días
5. correr dos millas (*miles*) por semana
6. ¿ ?
7. ¿ ?

**PASO 2.** Now report to the class who will do what this semester.

**MODELO** Elena y Tom van a comprar cinco libros de texto. Jesse va a tomar seis exámenes finales.

**D.** ¿Qué vamos a hacer esta tarde?

Cultures

Recycle

**PASO 1.** Complete the narration about pastimes in Mexico. Use the present tense of the verbs in parentheses. Indicate the correct word when two appear in parentheses.

*Unos mariachis en el zócalo* (central plaza)

(Continúa.)

México es un país grande, con diversas ciudades y pueblos.[a] Las actividades y los pasatiempos de los residentes varían[b] según el clima, (el/la[1]) geografía y la situación económica. Pero no importa[c] si Ud. (ir[2]) a una ciudad grande o a una aldea,[d] siempre (*Ud.:* ir[3]) a encontrar[e] un zócalo. Como en otros países hispanohablantes, la plaza (ser[4]) el corazón del pueblo.[f]

Aunque[g] (*nosotros:* ver[5]) a gente[h] en el zócalo durante el día, las actividades se aceleran por (el/la[6]) tarde y la noche. Todo el mundo[i] (salir[7]) al zócalo: los viejos, los jóvenes… todos[j] (ir[8]) allí. Algunos[k] (pasear[9]) por el zócalo y (hablar[10]) con amigos y vecinos.[l] (Los/Las[11]) fines de semana, especialmente los sábados, los mariachis (tocar[12]) música. Muchos (bailar[13]) o (mirar[14]) bailar a las personas. Los niños (ir[15]) con sus padres a jugar. Los jóvenes (buscar[16]) a sus amigos y novios o novias. A veces, los adultos (hacer[17]) negocios[m] en el zócalo. Indudablemente,[n] el zócalo es un centro de mucha actividad y vida.[o]

---

[a]ciudades… *cities and towns*  [b]*vary*  [c]*no… it doesn't matter*  [d]*village*  [e]*find*  [f]corazón… *heart of the town*
[g]*Although*  [h]*people*  [i]Todo… *Everyone*  [j]viejos… *old, young… everyone*  [k]*Some (people)*  [l]*neighbors*
[m]*business*  [n]*Without a doubt*  [o]*life*

**PASO 2.** Indicate the zócalo activities mentioned in **Paso 1. ¡OJO!** For item 8, give another activity based on the reading.

1. ☐ leer
2. ☐ jugar
3. ☐ hacer ejercicio

4. ☐ tocar música
5. ☐ limpiar
6. ☐ pasear

7. ☐ buscar a…
8. ☐ ¿ ?

Communication

**PASO 3.** With a partner, imagine that you're in Mexico and about to go to a zócalo. Take turns saying what you're going to do there. **¡OJO!** You can use activities from **Paso 2,** but you should come up with at least two additional activities based on **Paso 1.**

MODELOS  Vamos a jugar.
Vamos a escuchar música.

# Palabra escrita

## A comenzar

Communication

> **Organizing Your Ideas.** Getting organized is a very important pre-writing strategy. After you've brainstormed your initial ideas (see **Palabra escrita: A comenzar** in **Capítulo 1**), group those ideas by category so that all related ideas are together. Then look for patterns or a logical sequence in which to present your ideas and arrange them in that order. Once you've done this, your composition and your thoughts should be much more organized and thus clearer to the reader.

You are going to start the process of writing a brief composition that you will finalize in the **Palabra escrita: A finalizar** section of your *Manual de actividades*. The topic of this composition will be **La pasión por los deportes**. The purpose of your composition will be to tell the reader about what sports are popular in your area.

**A. Lluvia de ideas.** With a partner, answer these questions, based on what you've learned in **Tema I.**

1. ¿Cuáles son los deportes más populares en este país? ¿Y en su estado o provincia?
2. ¿Qué deportes practica Ud.?
3. ¿Qué deportes le gusta mirar en la televisión?
4. ¿Qué otras actividades deportivas (*sports*) hace Ud.?
5. ¿Qué actividad deportiva va a hacer Ud. el fin de semana que viene?

**B. A organizar** (*Let's organize*) **sus ideas.** Review your ideas and organize them into categories and in a logical order, as suggested in the strategy box. Look for additional details on the Internet. Share your information with the class and jot down any additional ideas that you gain from that experience.

**C. A escribir.** Now write a first draft of your composition with the information that you provided in activities A and B. **¡OJO!** Keep your work in a safe place. You'll need it again when you do the **Palabra escrita: A finalizar** section in your *Manual de actividades*.

## Diego Rivera

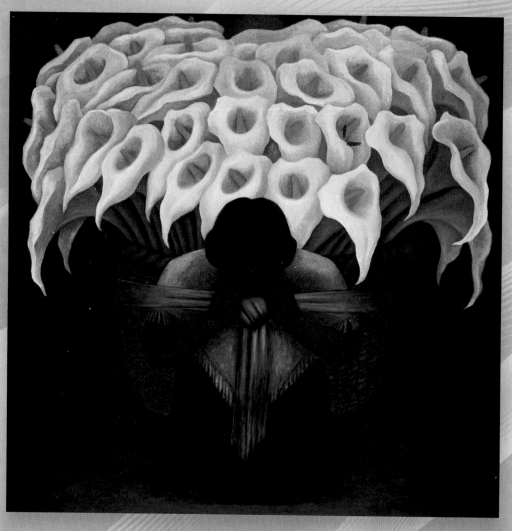

El vendedor de alcatraces, *1942*

Diego Rivera (1886–1957) is one of the most important Mexican painters of the 20th century. He studied in Europe, where he was influenced by such famous painters as Picasso, Renoir, and Cézanne. When he returned to Mexico, he became famous for his mural paintings, which frequently depict social and class themes in Mexico. His murals adorn numerous buildings in Mexico, as well as in other countries. His historical murals in the Presidential Palace, located in the Zócalo of Mexico City, are among his more famous and popular works. In 1929, he married Frida Kahlo (1907–1954), who became a famous and iconic modern artist in her own right.

In *El vendedor de alcatraces* Rivera portrays the theme of working-class men and women. The woman in this painting, looking at the ground while carrying a large bundle of lilies on her back, thus represents and personifies the burdens of the working class.

## Vocabulario del tema

### ¿Qué tiempo hace?°

¿Qué... *What's the weather like?*

**Hace (mucho) frío.**

**Está\* nevando. / Nieva.**

**Está\* lloviendo. / Llueve.**

**Hace (mucho) viento.**

**Está (muy) nublado.\***
**Hay (muchas) nubes.**

**Hace fresco.**

**Hace (mucho) calor.**

**Hace (mucho) sol.**

**Hace (muy) buen/mal tiempo.**     It's (very) good/bad out.

▶ The verb **hacer** (*to do; to make*) is used to describe many weather conditions. For example, the phrase that expresses *It's cold* (**Hace frío**) literally means, *It makes cold*. With these expressions, use **mucho**, not **muy**, to express *very*.

—¿Qué tiempo hace?          *What's the weather like?*
—Hace mucho calor hoy.      *It's very hot today.*

---

\*The verb **estar** can be used for some weather expressions. You'll learn more about **estar** later in this chapter and in future chapters.

# Los meses, las estaciones y las fechas°

Los... *Months, Seasons, and Dates*

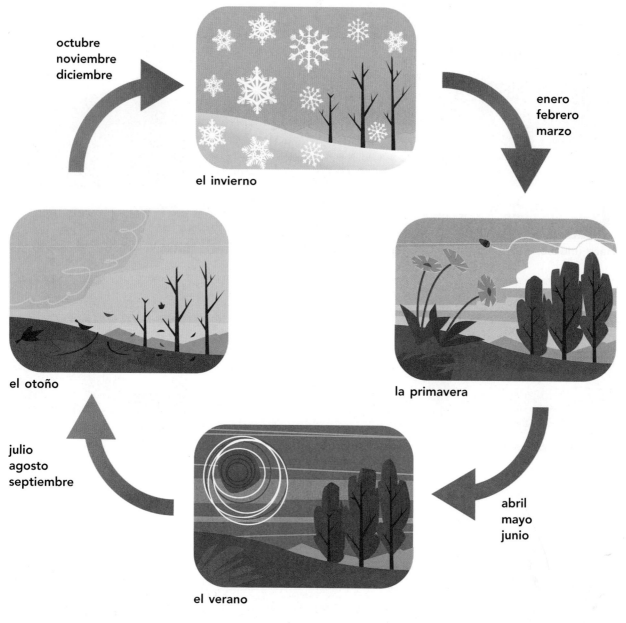

octubre
noviembre
diciembre

el invierno

enero
febrero
marzo

el otoño

la primavera

julio
agosto
septiembre

abril
mayo
junio

el verano

Cognado: el calendario

el almenati (the almanac)

## Los números de 31 a 100

In **Capítulo preliminar** you learned numbers 0 through 30. Here you'll learn more numbers to be able to talk about temperature.

| | | | |
|---|---|---|---|
| 31 treinta y uno | 35 treinta y cinco | 39 treinta y nueve | 70 setenta |
| 32 treinta y dos | 36 treinta y seis | 40 cuarenta | 80 ochenta |
| 33 treinta y tres | 37 treinta y siete | 50 cincuenta | 90 noventa |
| 34 treinta y cuatro | 38 treinta y ocho | 60 sesenta | 100 cien |

◗ Note the pattern for the 30s. 40 through 99 use the same pattern.

| | | |
|---|---|---|
| **41 cuarenta y uno** | **63 sesenta y tres** | **85 ochenta y cinco** |
| **52 cincuenta y dos** | **74 setenta y cuatro** | **96 noventa y seis** |

◗ Months, like days of the week, in Spanish are usually in lowercase letters.
◗ To express dates, use the formula: **el** + *day* + **de** + *month*. ⁺del + year

Hoy es el 3 de mayo.            *Today is May 3ʳᵈ.*
Nuestro aniversario es          *Our anniversary is (on) June 26ᵗʰ.*
el 26 de junio.

## ACTIVIDADES

**A. ¿Qué tiempo hace?** Match each drawing with the corresponding sentence. **¡OJO!** There may be more than one correct answer for some items.

1. _____

2. _____

3. _____

4. _____

5. _____

6. _____

7. _____

| | | |
|---|---|---|
| **a.** Hace calor. | **e.** Hace viento. | **i.** Hace fresco. |
| **b.** Nieva. | **f.** Está lloviendo. | **j.** Está nublado. |
| **c.** Hace mucho frío. | **g.** Hace buen tiempo. | **k.** Hace muy mal tiempo. |
| **d.** Está nevando. | **h.** Llueve. | **l.** Hace sol. |

**B. El pronóstico del tiempo** (*weather forecast*). With a partner, give a logical weather description for the following places and times. **¡OJO!** Remember that the seasons in the southern hemisphere are "opposite" of those in the northern hemisphere.

Ⓒ Communication

1. el mes de junio en Miami, Florida
2. el mes de noviembre en Quebec
3. el mes de octubre en Dallas
4. el mes de enero en Aspen
5. el mes de febrero en Buenos Aires
6. el mes de agosto en Sydney, Australia

## Nota interdisciplinaria

**MATEMÁTICAS: Más, menos, por, entre, son**

In Spanish, the plus sign (+) is pronounced **más.** Review the following pronunciations of other mathematical symbols.

$+ \rightarrow$ **más**        $\times \rightarrow$ **por**        $= \rightarrow$ **son**

$- \rightarrow$ **menos**        $:^* \rightarrow$ **entre / dividido entre**

Tres **más** ocho **son** once.            *Three plus eight equals eleven.*
Siete **por** nueve **son** sesenta y tres.   *Seven times nine equals sixty-three.*
Veinticuatro **entre** seis **son** cuatro.    *Twenty-four divided by six equals four.*

ACTIVIDAD Say the following math problems aloud, including the correct answer.

**1.** $32 + 19 =$ ____    **2.** $94 : 2 =$ ____    **3.** $74 - 8 =$ ____    **4.** $10 \times 10 =$ ____

**C. Un poco de matemáticas.** Say and complete each formula aloud in Spanish.

**MODELO**  (*you see*) $4 + 8 =$ ___ →
(*you say*) Cuatro más ocho son doce.

**1.** $90 : 3 =$ ___        **3.** $54 + 14 =$ ___        **5.** $12 \times 5 =$ ___        **7.** $21 \times 4 =$ ___
**2.** $13 + 7 =$ ___        **4.** $66 : 11 =$ ___        **6.** $89 - 15 =$ ___        **8.** $100 - 65 =$ ___

Communication

**D. Fechas.** With a partner, give important dates in your life, in the school year, or in the calendar year.

**MODELO**  Mi cumpleaños (*birthday*) es el catorce de mayo.

**1.** mi cumpleaños / el cumpleaños de ____
**2.** el día de la independencia de este país
**3.** los exámenes parciales (*midterm*) y finales
**4.** la Navidad (*Christmas*)
**5.** el Día de Acción de Gracias (*Thanksgiving*)
**6.** el primer día de las vacaciones de primavera (*spring break*)
**7.** el primer día de primavera (verano, otoño, invierno)
**8.** ¿ ?

---

*Traditionally the : symbol is used in Spanish to denote division. However, thanks to the proliferation of modern electronics produced outside of the Spanish-speaking world, most Spanish speakers today use the symbol that appears on those electronic devices: ÷.

# Gramática

## 2.3 The Verb estar

**GRAMÁTICA EN CONTEXTO**

### Una conversación telefónica

[*A continuación está parte de una conversación telefónica entre dos amigas, Andrea y Carmen.*]

ANDREA:  Aló [...ᵃ] ¿Cómo **estás**, Carmen? [...ᵇ] Muy bien, gracias. ¿Dónde **estás**? [...ᶜ] Pues, yo **estoy** en un café. Ven, te invito. [ ...ᵈ] **Está** en la Avenida Juárez, cerca del zócalo. [...ᵉ] ¡Excelente! Hasta pronto.

Comprensión. Here are Carmen's answers, but they're not in chronological order. Put them in order by matching them with the gaps in what Andrea said above. ¡OJO! The first one has been done for you.

1. _____ ¡Perfecto! Nos vemos dentro de poco (*in a little while*).
2. _____ **Estoy** en casa. ¿Por qué?
3. _____ ¡Gracias! ¿Dónde **está** el café?
4. _a_ Hola.
5. _____ **Estoy** bien, gracias, Andrea. ¿Y tú?

You have already learned many of the uses of the verb **ser,** which is one verb in Spanish that means *to be*. In this section you will learn some of the uses of the verb **estar,** another Spanish verb that is equivalent to the English verb *to be*. Keep in mind that **ser** and **estar** are never interchangeable, and that each verb is used in specific contexts.

Here are the present tense forms of **estar.**

| estar (*to be*) | |
|---|---|
| estoy | estamos |
| estás | estáis |
| está | están |

**A.** One main use of **estar** is to tell where something or someone is located.

El parque Chapultepec **está** en la Ciudad de México.

*Chapultepec Park is in Mexico City.*

Mis padres **están** en casa hoy.

*My parents are at home today.*

---

GRAMÁTICA EN CONTEXTO **A Telephone Conversation** / [*Below is part of a telephone conversation between two friends, Andrea and Carmen.*] **ANDREA:** *Hello.* [...ᵃ] *How are you, Carmen?* [...ᵇ] *Fine, thank you. Where are you?* [...ᶜ] *Well, I'm in a café. Come on over, I'm buying.* [...ᵈ] *It's on Juárez Avenue, near the zócalo.* [...ᵉ] *Excellent! See you soon.*

In addition to the preposition **en**, there are several other prepositions of location that are used with **estar**. Here are some of the most common prepositions of location.

| | | | |
|---|---|---|---|
| cerca (de) | close (to) | enfrente de | in front of |
| lejos (de) | far (from) | detrás de | behind |
| encima de | on top of | a la derecha (de) | to the right (of) |
| debajo de | under | a la izquierda (de) | to the left (of) |

Estamos cerca de la Biblioteca Nacional.

*We are close to the National Library.*

adentro (de)    inside (of)

El Museo de Antropología está a la derecha.

*The Museum of Anthropology is to the right.*

El Estadio Olímpico no está lejos de aquí.

*The Olympic Stadium isn't far from here.*

---

## Nota comunicativa

Communication

### THE VERB quedar TO DESCRIBE LOCATION

The verb **quedar** (*to be situated*) can be used interchangeably with **estar** to describe the location of buildings or some other relatively permanent structure.

—¿Dónde **están (quedan)** las canchas de tenis?

*Where are the tennis courts?*

—**Quedan (Están)** detrás del edificio de educación física.

*They are behind the physical education building.*

---

**B.** **Estar** is also used to describe people's emotions and the current conditions of people and things. Here are some common adjectives used with **estar.**

| | | | |
|---|---|---|---|
| aburrido/a | bored | limpio/a | clean |
| alegre | happy | loco/a | crazy |
| asustado/a | scared | nervioso/a | nervous |
| cansado/a | tired | ocupado/a | busy |
| contento/a | content, happy | preocupado/a | worried |
| emocionado/a | excited | regular | so-so |
| enfermo/a | sick | sorprendido/a | surprised |
| enojado/a | angry | sucio/a | dirty |
| furioso/a | furious | triste | sad |
| irritado/a | irritated | | |

Todos **están contentos** porque hace muy buen tiempo.

*Everyone is happy because it's nice out.*

**C.** Here are two common adverbs used with **estar.**

| | |
|---|---|
| bien | fine, well |
| mal | bad, not well; sick |

—¿Cómo estás?

*How are you?*

—Estoy bien, gracias.

*I'm fine, thanks.*

**A. ¿Dónde están?** Tell where everyone is this summer, based on the map.

MODELO  el profesor (Cabo San Lucas) → El profesor está en Cabo San Lucas.

1. Uds. (México, D. F.)
2. Mary (Tijuana)
3. yo (Guadalajara)
4. Horacio y Mark (Acapulco)
5. tú (Cancún)
6. Josi y yo (Oaxaca)

**B. ¿Cómo están?** Finish the descriptions of the summer trips of the people from activity A using the verbs **estar** and **quedar.**

MODELO  Cabo San Lucas queda en Baja California. El profesor está muy bien porque descansa en la playa (*beach*) todos los días.

1. México, D. F. _____ en el valle (*valley*) de México. Uds. _____ muy ocupados en la capital.
2. Tijuana _____ en la frontera (*border*) con California. Mary _____ mal porque hace mucho calor y hay mucha contaminación (*pollution*).
3. Guadalajara _____ en el estado de Jalisco. Yo _____ un poco triste porque llueve mucho aquí en el verano.
4. Acapulco _____ en la costa (*coast*) del Pacífico, en el estado de Guerrero. Horacio y Mark _____ muy cansados todas las tardes porque practican muchos deportes acuáticos como el *windsurf* y el buceo (*scuba diving*).
5. Cancún _____ en la Península de Yucatán. (Tú) _____ muy contento porque hace muy buen tiempo.
6. Oaxaca _____ en las montañas (*mountains*). Josi y yo _____ alegres porque hace muy buen tiempo y hacemos excursiones todos los días.

**C. Cuando...** With a partner, describe how you feel and what you usually do in these circumstances.

**MODELO** Cuando tomo un examen muy difícil... → estoy muy nervioso/a.

1. Cuando llueve todo el día...
2. Cuando hace mucho calor...
3. Cuando está nevando...
4. Cuando mis amigos están ocupados y estoy solo/a (*alone*)...
5. Cuando paso mucho tiempo en la biblioteca...
6. Cuando salgo a bailar...
7. Cuando veo mucho la televisión...

Cultures   Recycle

**D.** Los problemas climáticos y ambientales (*environmental*)

**PASO 1.** Complete the reading about a few of the weather-related environmental issues in Mexico.

*Algunas dunas en Baja California*

Muchas personas creen que en todo México hace calor todo el año. Pero no es así.[a] México (**ser**[1]) un país muy grande con diferentes regiones climáticas. (**Los/Las**[2]) problemas más grandes son los desastres naturales en la costa, la desertificación en el norte,[b] la deforestación en el sur[c] y la contaminación[d] en (**los/las**[3]) ciudades grandes.

Los desastres naturales más comunes (**ser**[4]) los huracanes en la costa. En las costas del Pacífico y del Caribe, típicamente (**hacer**[5]) calor todo el año, y (**los/las**[6]) estaciones (**estar**[7]) marcadas[e] por la lluvia y las tormentas.[f] Entre junio y noviembre, llueve mucho y (**ser**[8]) frecuentes los huracanes y tormentas tropicales.

El altiplano[g] (**estar**[9]) en el interior de México entre dos cordilleras.[h] En el norte del altiplano, cerca de los Estados Unidos, el clima (**ser**[10]) árido y la desertificación

---

[a]*like that*  [b]*north*  [c]*south*  [d]*pollution*  [e]*marked*  [f]*lluvia... rain and storms*  [g]*highlands*  [h]*mountain ranges*

es un (**gran/grande**[11]) problema. La industria de la ganadería[i] acelera el problema y el gobierno (**buscar**[12]) medidas para combatirlo.[j]

Al otro extremo del país, en los bosques tropicales que (**estar**[13]) en el sur, el problema es la deforestación. ¿Qué medidas (*nosotros:* **necesitar**[14]) tomar para combatir este problema mundial[k]?

Otro problema mundial es la contaminación. México, D.F. (**ser**[15]) una ciudad de más de 20 millones de residentes, con unos 8 millones de coches.[l] La contaminación de los coches (**quedar**[16]) atrapada[m] entre las tres montañas que (**estar**[17]) alrededor de[n] la capital. El Plan Verde (**ser**[18]) un esfuerzo[ñ] monumental del gobierno para combatir la contaminación a todos los niveles.[o] Para reducir el *smog*, el plan es construir[p] techos[q] verdes, es decir,[r] plantar jardines, árboles[s] y otras plantas (**debajo/encima**[19]) de los edificios de la ciudad.

---

[i]*cattle*  [j]*medidas… measures to combat it*  [k]*worldwide*  [l]*cars*  [m]*trapped*  [n]*alrededor… surrounding*  [ñ]*effort*  [o]*levels*  [p]*to build*  [q]*roofs*  [r]*es… that is*  [s]*trees*

**PASO 2.**  With a partner, talk about each of these issues. What is it? **¿Es un problema o una de las causas del problema? ¿O es una solución o un recurso** (*resource*)**?** Where does it occur? Discuss possible actions.

Communication

**MODELO**  la desertificación → La desertificación es un problema. El problema de la desertificación está en el norte de México / en el altiplano.

1. la deforestación
2. el clima árido
3. los huracanes
4. la industria de la ganadería
5. los 8 millones de coches
6. los bosques tropicales
7. los techos verdes
8. el *smog*

**PASO 3.**  With a partner, research **El Plan Verde.** What does the plan encompass? What other cities are taking similar measures? Choose one aspect of the project to explore and present your findings to the class.

Communities

## 2.4 The Present Progressive

Expressing Actions in Progress

**GRAMÁTICA EN CONTEXTO**

### El fin de semana

Es el fin de semana, pero Mariana no **está trabajando. Está estudiando.** También **está bebiendo** un refresco, **comiendo** una hamburguesa y **leyendo** su e-mail.

¿Y Ud.? Tell who is doing these activities in the classroom. **¡OJO! nadie** = *nobody.*

1. ¿Quién está leyendo el periódico?
2. ¿Quién está mirando el reloj?
3. ¿Quién está mandando (*sending*) un mensaje de texto?
4. ¿Quién está contestando una pregunta?
5. ¿Quién está hablando con el profesor / la profesora?

---

**GRAMÁTICA EN CONTEXTO** *The Weekend / It's the weekend, but Mariana isn't working. She's studying. She's also drinking a soda, eating a hamburger, and reading her e-mail.*

In Spanish, the present progressive is formed by using the present tense of the verb **estar** with a verb form called the *present participle* or *gerund*. This structure is equivalent to the English structure *to be* + ____ *-ing*, and like its English counterpart, refers to actions that are in progress at the moment.

—¿Qué estás haciendo?        *What **are you doing** (right now)?*
—Estoy mirando la televisión.        *I'm **watching** television.*

**A.** The gerund is formed by dropping the **-ar**, **-er**, or **-ir** ending from the infinitive and adding **-ando** for **-ar** verbs or **-iendo** for **-er** and **-ir** verbs.

### THE PRESENT PROGRESSIVE: Estar + -ando/-iendo

| | INFINITIVE | PRESENT PARTICIPLE (GERUND) | TRANSLATION |
|---|---|---|---|
| **-ar** VERBS | **jugar** | **jugando** | playing |
| **-er** VERBS | **hacer** | **haciendo** | doing; making |
| **-ir** VERBS | **salir** | **saliendo** | going out; leaving |

**B.** A spelling change of **-i-** to **-y-** in the **-iendo** ending is required to form the gerund of **-er** or **-ir** verbs whose stem ends in a vowel.

### THE PRESENT PARTICIPLE: -yendo

| INFINITIVE | FORMATION | PRESENT PARTICIPLE (GERUND) | TRANSLATION |
|---|---|---|---|
| **creer** | **cre + iendo** | **creyendo** | believing |
| **leer** | **le + iendo** | **leyendo** | reading |
| **oír** | **o + iendo** | **oyendo** | hearing |

**C.** Spanish uses the present progressive less frequently than English. Thus, you should get in the habit of using the simple present tense or **ir** + **a** + *inf.* in Spanish when you would typically use *to be* + *-ing* in English, and only use the present progressive in Spanish when you want to emphasize the fact that something is happening *right now, at this very moment.*

—¿Qué haces hoy?        *What are you doing today?*
—Voy a estudiar con Pablo.        *I'm studying (going to study) with Pablo.*

—¿Qué estás haciendo?        *What are you doing (right now)?*
—Estoy leyendo el periódico, pero después voy al cine.        *I'm reading the newspaper (right now), but later I'm going to the movies.*

**A. ¿Qué están haciendo?** Match the sentences in column A with those in column B to describe what people are doing at this moment.

| A | B |
|---|---|
| 1. ____ Los niños están en el parque. | **a.** Está llamando a su mejor amiga. |
| 2. ____ Hace mucho frío afuera y no deseo salir. | **b.** Estamos estudiando en la biblioteca. |
| 3. ____ Hace fresco. Hace muy buen tiempo. | **c.** Estoy tomando mucha agua. |
|  | **d.** Están practicando fútbol. |
| 4. ____ Mañana tenemos un examen difícil. | **e.** Estamos paseando por la calle. |
| 5. ____ Paloma está triste. | **f.** Están hablando con la profesora en su oficina. |
| 6. ____ Uds. tienen problemas en la clase de sicología. | **g.** Estoy leyendo una novela en casa. |
| 7. ____ Tengo mucho calor. |  |

**B. Ya (*Already*) estamos haciendo eso (*that*).** Leonora is saying what everyone needs to do. Explain that everyone is already doing everything already.

**MODELO** Necesitas leer la lección. → Ya estoy leyendo la lección.
Teresa necesita buscar el libro. → Ya está buscando el libro.

1. Uds. necesitan hacer la tarea.
2. Pedro necesita poner la radio.
3. Tus amigos necesitan traer el videojuego (*videogame*).
4. El profesor necesita preparar su clase.
5. Yo necesito limpiar la casa.
6. Nosotros necesitamos sacar unas fotos.
7. Ud. necesita hacer ejercicio.

**C. ¿Dónde están y qué hacen?** With a partner, talk about where these people are and what they are doing right now. If you're not sure, invent logical sentences. **¡OJO!** Come up with another person for items 5 and 6.

Communication

**MODELO** nuestro/a profesor(a) → Nuestro profesor está en clase. Está explicando la lección.

1. tu compañero/a de cuarto
2. tu mejor amigo/a
3. tu mamá/papá
4. nosotros/as
5. ¿ ?
6. ¿ ?

**D. ¡Están patinando en el hielo (*ice skating*)!**

Cultures

Recycle

**PASO 1.** Complete Estela's explanation of the ice rink in Mexico City's Zócalo. Give the correct form of the verbs in parentheses. When the cue *PP* appears, use the present progressive of the verb. When there are two words, choose the correct word.

(Continúa.)

*La pista de hielo (ice rink) en el Zócalo de México, D.F.*

¡Qué onda! Me llamo Estela y soy del D.F. Esta tarde, mis amigos y yo estamos en el Zócalo. ¡(*Nosotros, PP:* Esperar[1]) nuestro turno para patinar en el hielo! Todos los años en el invierno, (*ellos:* poner[2]) una pista de hielo aquí en el Zócalo. La pista es de tres mil metros cuadrados[a] y acomoda a mil doscientas[b] personas a la vez.[c] ¡Es enorme! ¡Y es gratis[d]! Este año los patines[e] también (ser[3]) gratis.

La cola[f] que (*nosotros, PP:* hacer[4]) para entrar en la pista de hielo es muy larga. Siempre (*nosotros:* llegar[5]) muy temprano, a (los/las[6]) 8:00 de la mañana. Pero aún así,[g] (esperar[7]) unas cinco o seis horas. Y después de esperar tantas horas, el tiempo en la pista (estar[8]) limitado a setenta y cinco minutos.

La larga espera[h] no es el único[i] problema con la pista. Como en el D.F. no (hacer[9]) mucho frío en (el/la[10]) invierno, por la tarde cuando hace (mucho/mucha[11]) sol, a veces el hielo se derrite.[j] También (*yo:* necesitar[12]) confesar que nosotros los capitalinos[k] no (patinar[13]) muy bien. Por eso,[l] son frecuentes los pequeños accidentes.

Con todos los inconvenientes,[m] ¡es muy divertido y una experiencia única[n] en la capital! Aunque todos (*PP:* esperar[14]) muchas horas, (*ellos:* pasar[15]) el tiempo hablando de las maravillas[ñ] que (ir[16]) a hacer en el hielo.

---

[a]*tres... three thousand square meters*   [b]*mil... one thousand two hundred*   [c]*a... at the same time*   [d]*free (of charge)*   [e]*skates*   [f]*line*   [g]*aún... even so*   [h]*wait*   [i]*only*   [j]*se... melts*   [k]personas de México, D.F.   [l]*Por... That's why*   [m]*nuisances*   [n]*unique*   [ñ]*wonders*

**PASO 2.**   Indicate whether the sentences are true (**C**) or false (**F**), based on Estela's description.

|  | C | F |
|---|---|---|
| **1.** Es posible patinar en el hielo todo el año en el Zócalo. | ☐ | ☐ |
| **2.** No hace mucho frío en la capital en el invierno. | ☐ | ☐ |
| **3.** La entrada (*entrance fee*) a la pista es muy cara (*expensive*). | ☐ | ☐ |

4. Ud. no necesita traer patines a la pista.
5. La pista no es muy grande.
6. Es necesario esperar muchas horas para entrar en la pista.
7. Muchas personas patinan de seis a ocho horas.
8. Los residentes de México, D.F. son expertos en patinar.

**PASO 3.** With a partner, invent two venues for entertaining a community. You can use established places or invent places. You will give clues about what people are doing there and the class will try to guess what the venue is. Use the **Vocabulario práctico** for ideas and look up words you might need.

Communication

| Vocabulario práctico | |
| --- | --- |
| el campo de fútbol (americano) | soccer (football) field |
| la cancha de tenis/basquetbol | tennis/basketball court |
| el gimnasio, el parque, la piscina, la pista de hielo | |

**MODELO** Muchas personas están patinando en el hielo. → Es una pista de hielo.

# Lectura cultural

**ANTES DE LEER**

Cultures

You are going to read an article about pastimes in Mexico City. Before you read the passage, answer these questions. Then share your ideas with the class.

1. ¿Qué le gusta hacer a Ud. en su tiempo libre?
2. En su opinión, ¿cuáles son los pasatiempos más comunes entre los estudiantes de su universidad?

## La Ciudad de México

*El Zócalo de la Ciudad de México*

La Ciudad de México es una gran metrópolis en donde hay entretenimiento[a] para gente de diversos gustos y aficiones. Las personas interesadas en la historia pueden[b] visitar los innumerables museos y sitios de interés que hay en la ciudad. El Zócalo, por ejemplo, cuenta con[c] preciosos edificios del gobierno,[d] como el Palacio Nacional, en donde se exhiben famosos murales del artista Diego Rivera. Cerca del Zócalo está el Templo Mayor, un sitio arqueológico de ruinas aztecas donde se puede[e] apreciar la historia del Imperio azteca. También es interesante pasear por las calles de la ciudad y observar la magnífica arquitectura colonial de ciertos distritos. La zona de Coyoacán, con sus casas pintadas de colores vivos —sobre todo, morados, rojos y verdes— es especialmente atractiva. En este lugar hay muchos cafés literarios en donde se puede escuchar música y disfrutar de un ambiente bohemio y estimulante.

La Ciudad de México también ofrece la oportunidad de hacer actividades al aire libre.[f] Hay parques naturales ideales para correr, caminar o andar en bicicleta. Además,[g] para los aficionados al golf, la Ciudad de México cuenta con espléndidos campos[h] de fama nacional e internacional.

Finalmente, para los amantes[i] de la noche, la ciudad ofrece muchas opciones: restaurantes de exquisitos menús internacionales y locales, cafés, cantinas, bares, discotecas, teatros y conciertos. Un lugar de diversión es La Plaza Garibaldi, un lugar donde se congregan los populares mariachis para entretener[j] con sus canciones tradicionales a la multitud de asistentes.[k]

---

[a]*entertainment*  [b]*can*  [c]*cuenta... has*  [d]*government*  [e]*se... one can*  [f]*al... outdoors*  [g]*Besides*  [h]*courses*  [i]*lovers*  [j]*entertain*  [k]*attendees*

## DESPUÉS DE LEER

**A.** ¿Cierto o falso? Skim the article and indicate if the statements are true (**C**) or false (**F**).

|   | C | F |
|---|---|---|
| 1. En la Ciudad de México hay pasatiempos para personas de gustos diferentes. | ☐ | ☐ |
| 2. La Ciudad de México ofrece la oportunidad de hacer actividades culturales. | ☐ | ☐ |
| 3. Por las noches, la Ciudad de México no es muy animada. | ☐ | ☐ |
| 4. No hay lugares para hacer ejercicio o practicar deportes. | ☐ | ☐ |

**B.** Comprensión. Read the article again and list the activities that people can do at these places and times.

1. en el Zócalo
2. en el Palacio Nacional
3. en la Plaza Garibaldi
4. en el Templo Mayor
5. en el parque cerca de la ciudad
6. por la noche
7. en Coyoacán

Communication

**C.** Lugares interesantes. With a partner, and using the text as a model, make a list in Spanish of interesting places where you live and some activities that people can do there. Then share the information with the rest of the class.

## México: Miguel

El fútbol en México

Cultures

Miguel es de México y vive en Guanajuato. En su blog habla del fútbol, el deporte nacional de México. También nos lleva por (*he takes us around*) la bella (*beautiful*) ciudad de Guanajuato.

### ANTES DE VER

Los deportes. Answer the questions.

1. Do you consider yourself a diehard or fair-weather fan when it comes to supporting your favorite sports teams? Explain.
2. What do you like to do before and after watching a sporting event?
3. Where is a good place to enjoy a sporting event in your area?

### Vocabulario práctico

| | | | |
|---|---|---|---|
| **desde muy chicos** | from a young age | **regresamos** | we return |
| **¡Por supuesto!** | Of course! | **desafortunadamente** | unfortunately |
| **¡Ni modo!** | No way! | **no tenemos** | we don't have |
| **¡Claro!** | Of course! | **tú sabes** | you know |
| **jugo de naranja** | orange juice | **quiero ver** | I want to watch |

### DESPUÉS DE VER

**A.** ¿Cierto o falso? Indicate whether the statements are true (**C**) or false (**F**), according to Miguel's blog. Correct the statements that are false.

|  | C | F |
|---|---|---|
| 1. Both friends are fans of the same team. | ☐ | ☐ |
| 2. There is no famous soccer team in Guanajuato. | ☐ | ☐ |
| 3. At the restaurant, Miguel orders **limonada** and **enchiladas**. | ☐ | ☐ |
| 4. The game starts at 3:00 P.M. | ☐ | ☐ |
| 5. Chucho is very sad because his team is losing. | ☐ | ☐ |

**B.** Temas de discusión. With a partner, answer the questions. Then share your thoughts with the class.

Communication

1. How do sports affect young people? What are the mental, physical, and psychological advantages and disadvantages of one sport over another?
2. What are some of the most dangerous sports? Which ones are the least dangerous or not dangerous at all? Why?

# Vocabulario

| Los pasatiempos y los deportes | Pastimes and Sports |
|---|---|
| jugar (ue) al dominó | to play dominos |
| nadar (en la piscina) | to swim (in the swimming pool) |
| pasar tiempo con el/la novio/a | to spend time with one's boyfriend/girlfriend |
| pasear (con el perro) | to take a walk, stroll (with the dog) |
| patinar (en línea) | to (inline) skate |
| sacar fotos | to take photos |
| tomar el sol | to sunbathe |
| la calle | street |
| la fiesta | party |
| la natación | swimming |
| el partido | game (*single occurrence*) |
| el pasatiempo | pastime |
| los ratos libres | free time |
| el tiempo libre | free time |

**Cognados: el golf, el tenis**

## Los colores

amarillo, anaranjado, azul, blanco, color café, gris, morado, negro, rojo, rosado, verde

| Algunos verbos irregulares | Some Irregular Verbs |
|---|---|
| estar (*irreg.*) | to be |
| estar + gerund | to be (*doing something*) |
| hacer (*irreg.*) | to do; to make |
| ir (*irreg.*) | to go |
| ir + a + *inf.* | to be going to (*do something*) |
| poner (*irreg.*) | to put, place; to turn on (*lights; an electrical appliance*) |
| oír (*irreg.*) | to hear |
| salir (*irreg.*) | to go out; to leave |
| traer (*irreg.*) | to bring |
| ver (*irreg.*) | to see; to watch |

| ¿Qué tiempo hace? | What's the Weather Like? |
|---|---|
| Está lloviendo. / Llueve. | It's raining. |
| Está nevando. / Nieva. | It's snowing. |
| Está (muy) nublado. / Hay (muchas) nubes. | It's (very) cloudy. |
| Hace (muy) buen/mal tiempo. | It's (very) nice/bad out. |
| Hace (mucho) calor. | It's (very) hot. |
| Hace fresco. | It's cool. |
| Hace (mucho) frío. | It's (very) cold. |
| Hace (mucho) sol. | It's (very) sunny. |
| Hace (mucho) viento. | It's (very) windy. |

## Los números de 31 a 100

treinta y uno, treinta y dos, treinta y tres, treinta y cuatro, treinta y cinco, treinta y seis, treinta y siete, treinta y ocho, treinta y nueve, cuarenta, cincuenta, sesenta, setenta, ochenta, noventa, cien

| Los meses | Months |
|---|---|
| enero, febrero, marzo, abril, mayo, junio, julio, agosto, septiembre, octubre, noviembre, diciembre | |

**Cognado: el calendario**

| Las estaciones | Seasons |
|---|---|
| el invierno, la primavera, el verano, el otoño | |

| Las preposiciones de lugar | Prepositions of Location |
|---|---|
| a la derecha (de) | to the right (of) |
| a la izquierda (de) | to the left (of) |
| cerca (de) | close (to) |
| debajo de | under |
| detrás de | behind |
| encima de | on top of |
| enfrente de | in front of |
| lejos (de) | far (from) |

| Los estados físicos y emocionales | Physical and Emotional States |
|---|---|
| aburrido/a | bored |
| alegre | happy |
| asustado/a | scared |
| cansado/a | tired |
| contento/a | content, happy |
| emocionado/a | excited |
| enfermo/a | sick |
| enojado/a | angry |
| furioso/a | furious |
| irritado/a | irritated |
| limpio/a | clean |
| loco/a | crazy |
| nervioso/a | nervous |
| ocupado/a | busy |
| preocupado/a | worried |
| regular | so-so |
| sorprendido/a | surprised |
| sucio/a | dirty |
| triste | sad |
| bien *adv.* | fine, well |
| mal *adv.* | bad, not well; sick |

| Otras palabras | |
|---|---|
| creer | to believe |
| quedar | to be located (*buildings*) |
| el/la joven | young person |
| ¿adónde? | (to) where? |
| conmigo | with me |
| contigo | with you (*sing. fam.*) |
| cuando | when |
| para | for |
| por | for; by |

# La vida diaria*

Trabajando en la cocina

1. What domestic chores do you typically do in your daily life?
2. What activites do you enjoy doing? Which ones do you like the least?
3. What do you do for fun? What do you do to relax?

*La... Daily Life

**SPANISH**

www.connectspanish.com

# TEMA I: Las obligaciones y los quehaceres

## Vocabulario del tema

### Los quehaceres domésticos

① hacer (*irreg.*) la cama

sacudir los muebles

② pasar la aspiradora

barrer el piso

③ doblar la ropa

planchar la ropa

④ cocinar

lavar los platos

sacar la basura

## Otros quehaceres

arreglar el cuarto
cortar el césped
lavar
  los platos
  la ropa
limpiar (la casa)
poner (*irreg.*) la mesa
quitar la mesa
secar (la ropa)
trabajar en el jardín
trapear (el piso)

## Other Chores

to tidy/clean up the room
to mow the lawn (cut the grass)
to wash
  the dishes
  clothes
to clean (the house)
to set the table
to clear the table
to dry (clothes)
to work in the garden/yard
to mop (the floor)

## Los aparatos domésticos

la aspiradora
la estufa
el horno
el (horno de) microondas
la lavadora
el lavaplatos
la licuadora
la secadora

## Appliances

vacuum cleaner
stove
oven
microwave (oven)
washer, washing machine
dishwasher
blender
dryer

## ¿Con qué frecuencia?

una vez a la semana
una vez al mes

## How often?

once a week
once a month

Repaso: **diario/a, todos los días**

### ACTIVIDADES

**A.** El horario de quehaceres

PASO 1.   Indicate which chores you do or you think should be done daily (**todos los días: D**), weekly (**una vez a la semana: S**), or monthly (**una vez al mes: M**). Add one daily, one weekly, and one monthly chore to the list.

| | D | S | M | | | D | S | M |
|---|---|---|---|---|---|---|---|---|
| **1.** arreglar el cuarto | ☐ | ☐ | ☐ | | **7.** sacudir los muebles | ☐ | ☐ | ☐ |
| **2.** lavar la ropa | ☐ | ☐ | ☐ | | **8.** trapear el piso | ☐ | ☐ | ☐ |
| **3.** hacer la cama | ☐ | ☐ | ☐ | | **9.** lavar los platos | ☐ | ☐ | ☐ |
| **4.** sacar la basura | ☐ | ☐ | ☐ | | **10.** ¿ ? | ☑ | ☐ | ☐ |
| **5.** cortar el césped | ☐ | ☐ | ☐ | | **11.** ¿ ? | ☐ | ☑ | ☐ |
| **6.** barrer el piso | ☐ | ☐ | ☐ | | **12.** ¿ ? | ☐ | ☐ | ☑ |

PASO 2.   With a partner, talk about how often you do specific chores: **todos los días, una vez a la semana, una vez al mes.**

Communication

MODELO   E1: Hago la cama todos los días. ¿Y tú?

        E2: No, sólo hago la cama una vez a la semana. Pero barro el piso todos los días.

**B.** Los aparatos domésticos. Complete each sentence with a logical word from the **Vocabulario del tema.**

1. Preparo el desayuno (*breakfast*) en la _____ pero hago pasteles (*cakes*) en el _____.
2. Siempre lavo los platos a mano (*by hand*) porque no tengo _____.
3. Uso la _____ y la _____ para lavar y secar la ropa.
4. _____ y _____ el piso de la cocina (*kitchen*) una vez a la semana. Para limpiar las alfombras (*rugs*), paso la _____.
5. No me gusta planchar _____, pero a veces es necesario.

**C.** ¿Lógico o ilógico? Indicate if the following sentences are logical (**lógico: L**) or not (**ilógico: I**). If a sentence isn't logical, change it so that it is.

|  | L | I |
|---|---|---|
| 1. Uso la secadora después de sacar la ropa de la lavadora. | ☐ | ☐ |
| 2. No tengo lavaplatos, por eso uso la aspiradora. | ☐ | ☐ |
| 3. El piso está sucio (*dirty*), por eso sacudo los muebles. | ☐ | ☐ |
| 4. Hago la cama por la noche, después de estudiar. | ☐ | ☐ |
| 5. Primero voy a lavar la ropa, luego voy a secar la ropa, después, voy a doblar la ropa. | ☐ | ☐ |
| 6. Antes de poner la mesa, quitamos la mesa. | ☐ | ☐ |
| 7. Alberto va a tender (*hang out*) su ropa porque no tiene secadora. | ☐ | ☐ |
| 8. Cuando llueve, me gusta trabajar en el jardín. | ☐ | ☐ |

**D.** ¡Vamos a limpiar!

**PASO 1.** List five chores from the **Vocabulario del tema** that need to be done in your room or at your house right now.

**PASO 2.** Share your list with a partner. For each item, complete one of the sentences to explain why it needs to be done and when you're going to do it.

No me gusta ____, pero voy a ____.
No tengo tiempo para ____, pero voy a ____.

**MODELOS** E1: No me gusta trapear el piso, pero voy a trapear el fin de semana que viene.
E2: No tengo tiempo para lavar los platos, pero voy a lavar los platos esta noche.

**E.** Compañeros de casa

**PASO 1.** Imagine that you and a partner are housemates and that you're going to divide up the chores around the house. Make a list of daily, weekly, and monthly chores, and assign each chore to one person or the other. **¡OJO!** You can use your answers from activity A, **Paso 1** earlier in this section to get started. Include as many chores as you can think of.

**PASO 2.** Now share your results of **Paso 1** with the class.

**MODELO** Sue va a sacar la basura todos los días. Las dos (*both of us*) vamos a cocinar todos los días. Yo voy a cortar el césped una vez a la semana.

# Nota interdisciplinaria

Connections

## SOCIOLOGÍA: CHANGING GENDER ROLES IN MEXICO

Traditionally, Mexican women were responsible for chores such as caring for children, cooking, and cleaning. However, it is becoming more common for Mexican men to help with such tasks. There are several reasons for this change. Mexican women generally have more formal education now than at any time in the past, and they have a greater sense of their potential to shape new societal expectations for males and females. However, more conventional attitudes toward what constitutes "women's work" still exist in some more traditional parts of the country, depending on women's social status, where they live, their family income, and whether they are single, married, or divorced.

In rural areas where access to education for women is often limited, men generally work outside their home to provide for their families, while women devote themselves to housekeeping. This situation is also true for women from working-class families in urban areas. In the case of unmarried or divorced women and widows, they may work one or even two jobs to support the family, but they also retain responsibility for domestic tasks.

In contrast, families of greater economic means often employ young women to help with running their households. These young women frequently come from poorer families in rural areas where jobs are scarce, and they may send some of their wages back to their families to provide economic support for them. While in some upper-class families these young women may be regarded as servants, in others they are treated almost as members of the family by their employers.

**PREGUNTAS** With a partner, answer the following questions. Then share your ideas with the class.

1. What social forces are driving changes in the traditional status of women in Mexico? Are they the same forces that, in your opinion, may exist in every country?
2. What are the roles of women in your community? Are these roles changing? How do they compare to what you have just learned about Mexican society?

# Gramática

## 3.1 Deber/Necesitar + *infinitive*

### GRAMÁTICA EN CONTEXTO

### Una semana ocupada

Esta semana mis compañeros de cuarto y yo **debemos limpiar** nuestro apartamento. Manuel **necesita pasar** la aspiradora, y yo **debo lavar** los platos. Mis compañeros de cuarto **necesitan trabajar** todas las noches, y yo **debo estudiar**. ¡Y alguien **debe ir** de compras!

¿Y Ud.? Indique cuáles de las siguientes actividades Ud. debe hacer o necesita hacer el fin de semana que viene.

1. ☐ Debo estudiar.
2. ☐ Debo ir de compras.
3. ☐ Necesito lavar los platos.
4. ☐ Necesito limpiar mi cuarto.
5. ☐ Necesito salir.
6. ☐ Debo sacar la basura.
7. ☐ Necesito trabajar.
8. ☐ ¿ ?

The verb **deber** + *inf.* is used to express that someone must or should do something. **Necesitar** + *inf.* expresses that someone needs to do something. Generally speaking, **necesitar** expresses a slightly stronger sense of obligation than **deber**. Both verbs have regular conjugations.

| deber (*should, must*) | |
|---|---|
| debo | debemos |
| debes | debéis |
| debe | deben |

| necesitar (*to need*) | |
|---|---|
| necesito | necesitamos |
| necesitas | necesitáis |
| necesita | necesitan |

| | |
|---|---|
| Esta tarde debo limpiar mi alcoba. | *This afternoon I should clean my room.* |
| Los niños nunca deben jugar en la calle. | *Children should never play in the street.* |
| Muchos padres necesitan trabajar horas extras. | *Many parents need to work extra hours.* |
| No necesitas poner la mesa hasta las siete. | *You don't need to set the table until 7:00.* |

### ACTIVIDADES

**A.** ¿Qué debe hacer Ud. esta semana?

**PASO 1.** Indicate which of these activities you need to do or should do this week.

---

GRAMÁTICA EN CONTEXTO **A Busy Week** / This week my roommates and I should clean our apartment. Manuel needs to vacuum, and I should wash the dishes. My roommates need to work every night, and I should study. And someone should go shopping!

|     | SÍ | NO |
| --- | --- | --- |
| 1. Debo planchar la ropa. | ☐ | ☐ |
| 2. Necesito arreglar el cuarto. | ☐ | ☐ |
| 3. Necesito sacudir los muebles. | ☐ | ☐ |
| 4. Debo hacer la cama. | ☐ | ☐ |
| 5. Debo lavar los platos. | ☐ | ☐ |
| 6. Necesito trapear. | ☐ | ☐ |
| 7. Debo lavar la ropa. | ☐ | ☐ |
| 8. Necesito cortar el césped. | ☐ | ☐ |

**PASO 2.** Share your answers from **Paso 1** with a partner. Do you need to do the same things this weekend? Be ready to share your responses with the class like in the model.

**MODELO** Yo necesito arreglar mi cuarto. Julia debe arreglar su cuarto también.

**B. Los quehaceres.** Complete the sentences with the correct form of **necesitar** in the first blank and the correct form of **deber** in the second.

1. Mis compañeros de cuarto y yo _____ lavar la ropa. También _____ doblar la ropa.
2. Yo _____ cortar el césped y tú _____ trabajar en el jardín.
3. Julio _____ pasar la aspiradora y Camilo _____ barrer el piso.
4. Manuel, tú _____ poner la mesa, y después de comer (*after eating*), _____ quitar la mesa.
5. Gabriel y León, Uds. _____ barrer el piso. También _____ trapear.
6. Finalmente, nosotros _____ arreglar el cuarto y _____ hacer la cama.

**C. ¿Qué debes hacer?**

**PASO 1.** Ask a partner what he/she should or needs to do at specific or general times. **¡OJO!** Your partner can use the following cues in his/her answers.

| arreglar mi cuarto | lavar los platos | sacudir los muebles |
| --- | --- | --- |
| cocinar | planchar la ropa | trapear |
| cortar el césped | sacar la basura | ¿ ? |

**MODELOS** esta noche →
　　　　E1: ¿Qué debes hacer esta noche?
　　　　E2: Debo sacar la basura.

　　　　*or*

　　　　E1: ¿Qué necesitas hacer esta noche?
　　　　E2: Necesito hacer la tarea y ver mi programa favorito en la televisión.

1. a las 4:30 de la tarde hoy
2. mañana por la mañana
3. el lunes que viene
4. mañana a las 7:00 de la noche
5. el fin de semana que viene
6. pasado mañana
7. esta noche
8. el mes que viene

**PASO 2.** Now share your results from **Paso 1** with the class.

**D. La familia García necesita limpiar su nueva casa**

**PASO 1.** Complete the situation between la señora García and her family with the correct form of the verb in parentheses.

[*Señora García wants to gather her family (her children, María Elena and Betito, and her husband, Esteban) and have them help her with the household chores.*]

(Continúa.)

—*Gracias por ayudarme (helping me) con los platos, mamá.*
—*Por nada, mi vida.*

SRA. GARCÍA: ¡Chicos!ᵃ ¡María Elena! ¡Betito! ¡Bajen,ᵇ por favor! (*Yo:* **Necesitar**¹) limpiar la casa pero Uds. (**deber**²) ayudar.ᶜ

[*María Elena and Betito arrive.*]

MARÍA ELENA: Sí, mamá. ¿Qué onda?ᵈ

SRA. GARCÍA: (*Nosotros:* **Necesitar**³) limpiar la casa hoyᵉ y todos (**deber**⁴) ayudar. María Elena, (*tú:* **deber**⁵) lavar los platos y poner la mesa.

MARÍA ELENA: Sí, mamá.

SRA. GARCÍA: Betito, (*tú:* **deber**⁶) barrer el piso y sacar la basura.

BETITO: Sí, mamá.

SRA. GARCÍA: Después, los dosᶠ (**necesitar**⁷) arreglar su cuarto porque es un desastre... ¡Dios mío!ᵍ

[*Sra. García puts her hand on Esteban's shoulder.*]

Y tú, mi amor... (**deber**⁸) cortar el césped, porque yo no puedo.ʰ

ESTEBAN: Claro que sí, mi vida.ⁱ ¿Y qué vas a hacer tú?

SRA. GARCÍA: ¿¡Yo!? Pues, todo lo demás.ʲ (*Yo:* **Necesitar**⁹) sacudir los muebles, pasar la aspiradora y después trabajar en el jardín.

ESTEBAN: Entendido.ᵏ Bueno,ˡ chicos... ¡A trabajar!

---

ᵃ*Kids!* ᵇ*Come downstairs* ᶜ*help* ᵈ*¿Qué... What's up?* ᵉ*today* ᶠ*los... the two of you* ᵍ*¡Dios... My God!* ʰ*I can't* ⁱ*mi... my dear (lit. my life)* ʲ*lo... the rest* ᵏ*understood* ˡ*Well*

---

## Nota cultural

Cultures

### ¿QUÉ ONDA?

*¿Qué onda?*

The phrase **¿qué onda?** is a popular Mexican expression meaning *what's up?* Other expressions using the word **onda** include **buena onda** and **mala onda.** Both can be used to refer to people or situations. Compare the following statements.

| | |
|---|---|
| **Juan es buena onda.** | *Juan is a good/cool guy.* |
| **Paco es mala onda.** | *Paco is a jerk.* |
| **¡Qué buena onda!** | *Sweet! How cool!* |
| **¡Qué mala onda!** | *What a bummer!* |

---

**PASO 2.** Describe what these people end up doing in the situation from **Paso 1.**

MODELO Esteban →
Esteban corta el césped.

1. María Elena...
2. Betito...
3. La señora García...

**PASO 3.** En parejas (*pairs*), contesten (*answer*) las preguntas.

1. ¿Qué quehaceres necesitan hacer Uds. este fin de semana?
2. ¿Qué quehaceres domésticos les gustan menos?
3. ¿Qué deben hacer en casa esta semana?
4. ¿Para qué clases necesitan estudiar esta semana?
5. ¿Qué tarea deben hacer esta noche para la clase de español?

## 3.2 Tener, venir, preferir, and querer

**GRAMÁTICA EN CONTEXTO**

### La familia mexicana

México **tiene** una larga historia de la familia tradicional y extendida, en la que la esposa o la madre mantiene el hogar, y el esposo o el padre **tiene** trabajo fuera de la casa. Pero en estos días, en algunas familias mexicanas, ambos padres trabajan, y en muchos casos sólo la familia nuclear vive en la casa. Con estas situaciones **vienen** otros cambios. Por ejemplo, la madre ya no **tiene** la ayuda de su madre o su suegra en casa, y no **tiene** tiempo para hacer todos los quehaceres. A veces, las familias emplean a una muchacha para limpiar y cocinar, pero en otros casos si **quieren** ahorrar dinero, **prefieren** compartir los quehaceres.

**Comprensión.** Match the phrases in each column to form sentences based on the reading.

1. En muchas familias mexicanas, la madre y el padre ___
2. Hoy, muchas madres mexicanas ___
3. Históricamente, en la casa mexicana, la madre ___
4. Muchas parejas (*couples*) mexicanas ___

a. tiene todas las responsabilidades domésticas.
b. no tienen la ayuda de su madre o suegra.
c. prefieren hacer los quehaceres juntos (*together*).
d. tienen un trabajo fuera de la casa.

---

The **yo** forms of **tener** and **venir** have the irregular ending **-go.** With the exception of the **nosotros** and **vosotros** forms, all other forms of **tener, venir, preferir,** and **querer** change the -e- of the verb stem to -ie-. These are called stem changing verbs and they are more fully presented in **Gramática 3.3.**

| tener (*to have*) | |
|---|---|
| tengo | tenemos |
| tienes | tenéis |
| tiene | tienen |

| venir (*to come*) | |
|---|---|
| vengo | venimos |
| vienes | venís |
| viene | vienen |

| preferir (*to prefer*) | |
|---|---|
| prefiero | preferimos |
| prefieres | preferís |
| prefiere | prefieren |

| querer (*to want*) | |
|---|---|
| quiero | queremos |
| quieres | queréis |
| quiere | quieren |

**A.** The verb **tener** is used in many common expressions that are expressed with *to be* in English. You have already seen that **tener calor** and **tener frío** are used to express *to be hot* and *to be cold*, respectively. Here are a few other **tener** expressions that you will need to know.

---

GRAMÁTICA EN CONTEXTO **The Mexican Family** / *Mexico has a long history of the traditional and extended family, in which the wife or mother maintains the home and the husband or father has a job outside the house. But these days, in some Mexican families, both parents work, and in many cases, only the nuclear family lives in the house. With these situations come other changes. For example, the mother no longer has the help of her mother or mother-in-law at home, and she doesn't have time to do all of the chores. Sometimes, families employ a young woman to clean and cook, but if they want to save money, they prefer to share the chores.*

| | |
|---|---|
| tener... años | to be . . . years old |
| tener (mucho) calor | to be (very) hot |
| tener cuidado | to be careful |
| tener éxito | to be successful |
| tener frío | to be cold |
| tener ganas de + *inf.* | to feel like (*doing something*) |
| tener miedo (de) | to be afraid (of) |
| tener prisa | to be in a hurry |
| tener razón | to be right |
| no tener razón | to be wrong |
| tener (mucha) sed | to be (very) thirsty |
| tener sueño | to be sleepy |
| tener (mucha) suerte | to be (very) lucky |

**B.** The verbs **preferir** and **querer** express preference and desire for things when followed by nouns, but they are also often used to express preference and desire for actions when followed by a verb in the infinitive.

| | |
|---|---|
| Yo **prefiero** vivir en un barrio del centro, pero mi esposo **quiere** vivir en el campo. | *I prefer to live in a downtown neighborhood, but my husband wants to live in the country.* |

### Nota comunicativa

Communication

**Tener que** + *inf.*

Earlier in this chapter you saw two ways to express obligation, with the verbs **deber** and **necesitar**. Another way of expressing obligation in Spanish is with the expression **tener que** + *inf.*, which means to have to (*do something*).

| | |
|---|---|
| Hoy **tenemos que lavar** la ropa. | *Today we have to do laundry.* |
| ¿A qué hora **tienes que estar** en casa? | *What time do you have to be home?* |

### ACTIVIDADES

**A. Un mensaje telefónico.** Listen as your instructor recites a telephone message that Susana left for her friend, María, and indicate whether the statements are true (**C**) or false (**F**).

| Vocabulario práctico | | | | | |
|---|---|---|---|---|---|
| **llámame** | call me | **abrazo** | hug | **chau** | good-bye |

|  | C | F |
|---|---|---|
| 1. Susana no tiene que trabajar esta tarde. | ☐ | ☐ |
| 2. Susana prefiere mirar la televisión. | ☐ | ☐ |
| 3. Susana no quiere tomar café. | ☐ | ☐ |
| 4. Anita también quiere salir con Susana y María. | ☐ | ☐ |
| 5. Anita prefiere salir a las cinco. | ☐ | ☐ |
| 6. Anita quiere ir al cine. | ☐ | ☐ |

**B. Nuestras actividades.** Complete the sentences with the correct form of **tener, venir, preferir,** or **querer.**

1. Todos los fines de semana, mis amigos _____ a mi casa.
2. No me gusta hacer ejercicio en mis ratos libres. Yo _____ tomar una siesta.
3. El fin de semana que _____, mis amigos y yo _____ levantar pesas.

4. ¿Cuándo _____ (tú) que trabajar?
5. Elisa no _____ estudiar el fin de semana que _____.
6. ¿(Tú) _____ jugar a las cartas o jugar al billar (*pool*)?
7. Después de clase, mis compañeros de cuarto y yo _____ a casa.
8. Voy a tomar una siesta porque _____ sueño.

**C. Mis actividades.** En parejas, contesten las preguntas.

Communication

1. ¿Qué cosas prefieren Uds. hacer durante el verano como pasatiempos? ¿Y durante el invierno?
2. ¿Qué días tienen que asistir a clase?
3. ¿Qué quieren hacer después de clase hoy?
4. ¿Qué tienen que hacer este fin de semana?
5. ¿Qué quieren hacer este fin de semana?
6. ¿Qué deben hacer este fin de semana?

**D.** Los balnearios (*Spas; Water parks*) de Morelos, México

Cultures   Recycle

**PASO 1.** Complete la lectura con la forma correcta de los verbos entre paréntesis.

Si Ud. (**querer**[1]) relajarse,[a] (*Ud.:* **tener**[2]) que ir a uno de los balnearios de Morelos con sus aguas termales.[b] Hay actividades para todos. A los niños les gustan las piscinas. ¡Muchos niños no (**querer**[3]) salir de la piscina ni[c] para comer! Para las personas que (**tener**[4]) ganas de disfrutar de la naturaleza,[d] hay jardines bonitos. Si un huésped[e] (**preferir**[5]) hacer ejercicio, también hay gimnasios.

Muchas personas van al balneario de Oaxtepec para descansar. A veces no (*ellos:* **querer**[6]) hacer ejercicio; (*ellos:* **preferir**[7]) tomar un baño termal. Otras personas (**querer**[8]) tener un tratamiento de barro[f] natural.

*Las Estacas, un balneario y campamento (campsite) de Morelos*

Celia Bermúdez, de la Ciudad de México, dice: «Nosotros (**tener**[9]) suerte porque vivimos cerca de muchos balnearios lindos.[g] Mi familia y yo (**venir**[10]) aquí para las vacaciones porque está a solamente cien kilómetros de[h] la capital. A mis hijos les gusta nadar, y mi esposo siempre (**querer**[11]) jugar al dominó con los otros hombres. Pero yo (**preferir**[12]) pedir un tratamiento facial y un masaje. Hay de todo».[i]

Celia (**tener**[13]) razón: hay de todo. ¡Ud. (**tener**[14]) que visitar un balneario para experimentarlo[j]!

---

[a]*relax*  [b]*thermal*  [c]*not even*  [d]*disfrutar... enjoy nature*  [e]*guest*  [f]*mud*  [g]*beautiful*  [h]*está... it's only 100 kilometers from*  [i]*Hay... There's a little of everything.*  [j]*para... to experience it*

**PASO 2.** Indicate whether the statements are true (**C**) or false (**F**), based on the reading in **Paso 1.** Change the false statements so that they are true.

|  | C | F |
|---|---|---|
| 1. No hay muchas actividades diferentes en los balnearios. | ☐ | ☐ |
| 2. Los balnearios están cerca de México, D.F. | ☐ | ☐ |
| 3. Las personas que van a un balneario pueden tomar un baño termal. | ☐ | ☐ |
| 4. En los balnearios no hay gimnasios. | ☐ | ☐ |

**PASO 3.** With a partner, answer the questions.

Communication

1. ¿Qué actividades y servicios ofrecen (*offer*) los balnearios en su región? ¿Son semejantes a las actividades mencionadas en el **Paso 1** o diferentes? Expliquen.
2. ¿Cuáles son algunos lugares populares para los turistas en su región? ¿Visitan Uds. esos (*those*) lugares? ¿Qué hacen las personas allí?
3. Imagínense (*Imagine*) que Uds. están en un balneario. ¿Qué actividades prefieren hacer?

Communities

**PASO 4.** Search for **balnearios** on the Internet and compare the activities offered at water parks in Spanish-speaking countries with those offered at water parks in this country. Share your results with the class.

## Nota cultural

Cultures

### FOOD AND SOCIAL NORMS

*En el Café de Tacuba, en México, D.F.*

Eating out and dining etiquette, as with all aspects of culture, may differ from country to country, depending on people's beliefs and values. In Mexico, if you invite someone to eat in a restaurant, it is expected that you will pay the bill. Requesting separate checks is considered socially unacceptable by most Mexicans. The dress code at a restaurant is quite strictly observed. In formal restaurants, it is expected that men will dress in suit and tie and women will wear formal dresses. In less formal locations, business casual attire is appropriate, but wearing very casual clothing is regarded as impolite, especially for dinner. While eating, it is customary to keep both hands above the table, to use knife and fork—except for food like tacos or tostadas—and to engage in good conversation.

With the exception of large cities such as Mexico City and Monterrey, Mexico's rhythm of life is calm and laid back. This relaxed attitude is reflected in all aspects of daily life, including eating practices. As such, social breakfasts, lunches, and dinners, whether at a restaurant or at a person's home, are generally lengthy. People may spend two or more hours enjoying their meal and chatting with each other. Leaving immediately after eating is regarded as rude and insulting.

**PREGUNTAS** In small groups, answer the questions. Then share your ideas with the rest of the class.

1. Inviting someone to a restaurant may have different connotations in different cultures. What does it mean to you? And to people in your community?
2. Compare Mexican dining etiquette—dress code, time spent during meals, manners at the table—to that in your community. Is it similar or different? How?

# Palabra escrita

## A comenzar

Communication

> **Developing Your Ideas: Collecting Information (Part 1).** Another way to generate ideas is by collecting information about the topic of your composition. This strategy is necessary when the subject of your composition goes beyond your personal experience and knowledge. The resources you use to collect information are varied, ranging from searching Internet sources, to administering questionnaires to people, to simply interviewing your classmates. It all depends on the topic of your composition. For the purpose of this composition, you will interview your classmates.

You are going to start the process of writing a brief composition that you will finalize in the **Palabra escrita: A finalizar** section of your *Manual de actividades*. The topic of this composition is **Las obligaciones y los quehaceres.** The purpose of your composition will be to tell the reader about the things that your classmates and you have to do or should do in a typical week.

**A.** Lluvia de ideas. Brainstorm a list of things that correspond to each category.

1. los quehaceres que no me gustan
2. los quehaceres que prefiero hacer
3. las cosas que tengo que hacer en una semana típica
4. las cosas que debo hacer en una semana típica

**B.** Entrevistas

**PASO 1.** First formulate the questions that you will need to ask your classmates to find out what chores they don't like, which ones they prefer, and what they have to do or should do in a typical week.

**PASO 2.** Now interview *at least* three classmates (in Spanish), using the questions you formulated in **Paso 1.** As you interview each classmate, jot down their responses.

**C.** A organizar sus ideas. Review the information you've collected to see if you notice any patterns. Are there preferences or obligations that all of you have in common? Are there things that only one or two of you do? If you don't see any patterns, you probably need to collect some more information. Interview a few more classmates like you did in activity B and repeat this activity C.

**D.** A escribir. Now write a first draft of your composition with the ideas and information that you collected in activities A, B, and C. **¡OJO!** Keep your work in a safe place. You'll need it again when you do the **Palabra escrita: A finalizar** section in your *Manual de actividades.*

## La Catedral Metropolitana

Cultures

*La Catedral Metropolitana, en el Zócalo de la Ciudad de México*

Mexico City's Metropolitan Cathedral is the largest church in Latin America and the heart of the world's largest Roman Catholic diocese. It is located on the north side of the Zócalo, which is known officially as the Plaza de la Constitución. Built over a number of years (1525–1813), many architectural and decorative styles were integrated into the structure, including classical, baroque, and neoclassical styles. Inside the cathedral, the sacristy, the choir, and the Altar de los Reyes—with sculptures of kings and queens who have been canonized—are masterpieces of these different artistic styles. The facade is divided into three sections, which are flanked by the two monumental bell towers that rise 67m[a] above the Zócalo.

[a]*220 feet*

## Vocabulario del tema

### Las distracciones y otros pasatiempos

jugar (ue) al billar

jugar (ue) a las cartas

tomar una copa

levantar pesas

tomar una sauna

hacer (irreg.) yoga

asistir a la iglesia

| | |
|---|---|
| escuchar música | to listen to music |
| hacer (*irreg.*) ejercicio | to exercise |
| ir (*irreg.*) | to go |
| al cine | to the movies |
| a la mezquita | to the mosque |
| a la sinagoga | to the synagogue |
| jugar (ue) a los videojuegos | to play videogames |
| pasarlo bien/mal | to have good/bad time |
| tomar un café | to have coffee |
| tomar una siesta | to take a nap |
| ver un DVD / una película | to watch a DVD/movie |

Cognados: el jacuzzi, el masaje, la meditación, la sauna

Repaso: caminar, correr, jugar (ue) al dominó, mirar la televisión; la piscina, el yoga

## ACTIVIDADES

**A. Después de un día difícil**

PASO 1.   Indicate the activities you prefer to do after a hard day. ¡OJO! You can include other activities that you learned in **Capítulo 2.**

1. ☐ escuchar música
2. ☐ hacer ejercicio
3. ☐ hacer yoga
4. ☐ ir a la iglesia (mezquita/sinagoga)
5. ☐ ir al cine
6. ☐ jugar a las cartas
7. ☐ jugar a los videojuegos
8. ☐ jugar al billar

9. ☐ jugar al dominó
10. ☐ levantar pesas
11. ☐ tomar un café
12. ☐ tomar una copa
13. ☐ tomar una sauna
14. ☐ tomar una siesta
15. ☐ ¿ ?
16. ☐ ¿ ?

PASO 2.   Tell where you might go to do each of the activities in **Paso 1.** ¡OJO! You can use words from the **Vocabulario práctico** or names of specific places in your area.

**Vocabulario práctico**

| | |
|---|---|
| el bar | el gimnasio |
| el café | la mezquita |
| la casa | la sinagoga |
| el club | el templo |
| la discoteca | la universidad |

MODELOS   Voy al gimnasio a levantar pesas.
Me gusta ir a la sinagoga Beth Shalom los sábados.

**B. Asociaciones.** Match the sentences in column A with those in column B to form logical continuous thoughts.

**A**

1. Jorge necesita estudiar más esta noche. ___
2. Nora va a una fiesta con su amiga. ___
3. A Íñigo le gusta hacer ejercicio. ___
4. La familia Gómez es muy religiosa. ___
5. Horacio pasa mucho tiempo en el bar. ___
6. Nancy desea ver la nueva película de Guillermo del Toro. ___
7. Pablo está muy cansado. ___

**B**

a. Va a tomar una copa y bailar.
b. Necesita tomar una siesta.
c. Levanta pesas todos los días.
d. Debe tomar café.
e. Va al cine esta noche.
f. Va a la iglesia todos los domingos.
g. Le gusta jugar al billar.

**C.** Consejos. With a partner, offer at least two suggestions for the person(s) in these situations. ¡OJO! Use **deber, necesitar,** or **tener que** in your answers. Follow the model.  Communication

MODELO Esteban tiene mucho trabajo y está muy estresado. →
Esteban debe hacer yoga o quizás (*maybe*) levantar pesas.

1. Marina necesita perder peso (*lose weight*).
2. A Angélica le gustan mucho las películas, pero no tiene televisión.
3. Alberto está cansado, pero tiene que trabajar por la noche.
4. Marcos está en casa. Hace mal tiempo, y Marcos está muy aburrido.
5. Amalia y Carmen están muy nerviosas. Mañana tienen un examen.
6. Son las 8:00 de la mañana. Daniel tiene que asistir a sus clases, pero no tiene energía.

**D.** Las obligaciones y las diversiones

PASO 1.   Create logical sentences using phrases from each column, adding words as necessary.

MODELO  Antes de un examen, me gusta hacer yoga.

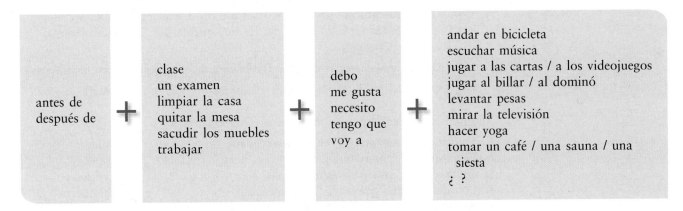

| antes de<br>después de | + | clase<br>un examen<br>limpiar la casa<br>quitar la mesa<br>sacudir los muebles<br>trabajar | + | debo<br>me gusta<br>necesito<br>tengo que<br>voy a | + | andar en bicicleta<br>escuchar música<br>jugar a las cartas / a los videojuegos<br>jugar al billar / al dominó<br>levantar pesas<br>mirar la televisión<br>hacer yoga<br>tomar un café / una sauna / una<br>   siesta<br>¿ ? |

PASO 2.   With a partner, ask and answer questions based on your sentences from **Paso 1.** Your partner should guess if your sentences are true or false for you.  Communication

MODELO  E1: ¿Qué te gusta hacer antes de un examen?
E2: Me gusta hacer yoga (antes de un examen).
E1: No, no es cierto.
E2: Sí, es cierto. Asisto a las clases de yoga en el centro estudiantil.

**E.** Mi profesor(a)

PASO 1.   Write three sentences telling what you think your instructor likes to do to relax, is going to do to relax today, and doesn't have time to do.

1. A mi profesor(a) le gusta…
2. Esta tarde mi profesor(a) va a…
3. Mi profesor(a) no tiene tiempo para…

PASO 2.   As a class, take turns asking your instructor questions, and try to ask follow-up questions, as in the model.  Communication

MODELO  ESTUDIANTE:   ¿A Ud. le gusta jugar a los videojuegos?
PROFESOR(A): Sí, me gusta jugar a los videojuegos.
ESTUDIANTE:   ¿Y cuál es su videojuego favorito?
PROFESOR(A): Bueno (*Well*), mi videojuego favorito es… Me gusta mucho.

# Gramática

## 3.3 More Stem Changing Verbs

### GRAMÁTICA EN CONTEXTO

#### ¿Qué podemos hacer después de clase?

Un túnel en la Gran Pirámide de Cholula

[*Ignacio y Lourdes, estudiantes de la Universidad de las Américas, piensan pasar tiempo con su nuevo amigo, Andrew. Andrew es un estudiante extranjero de Toronto.*]

IGNACIO: ¿Qué prefieren hacer primero?

LOURDES: Quiero comer algo, pero no en la universidad porque **almuerzo** aquí casi todos los días. Vamos al Mercado de Cholula donde **sirven** unas quesadillas deliciosas.

ANDREW: Después, ¿**podemos** ir a la pirámide?

LOURDES: Claro. ¡Tienes que visitar nuestra pirámide!

IGNACIO: ¿A qué hora **piensan** volver? Tengo otro examen mañana.

LOURDES: No estoy segura. ¿A qué hora **cierran** el parque y el museo?

IGNACIO: **Podemos** preguntar en el mercado. De todos modos, Andrew, no **puedes** ver todo en un día. Es muy grande, con la iglesia, el museo, los túneles…

ANDREW: ¿Túneles arqueológicos? ¿**Pierden** a muchas personas en los túneles?

IGNACIO: ¡No, hombre! Hay mapas y si **pides** un guía, no pasa nada.

Comprensión. Complete cada oración con el verbo correcto.

1. Lourdes casi siempre ___ en la universidad.
2. El parque ___ por la tarde.
3. Ignacio ___ a casa para estudiar más.
4. Lourdes ___ una quesadilla en el mercado.
5. Andrew no ___ ver todo el parque en un día.

a. pide
b. puede
c. vuelve
d. almuerza
e. cierra

You have already seen in **Gramática 3.2** how verbs like **querer** and **preferir** have a change to their stem vowel. Many other common verbs in Spanish have spelling changes in their stems when conjugated in the present tense. These changes affect all forms except **nosotros** and **vosotros**. The patterns can be seen in the following verb charts. There are three types of stem change in the present tense: e → ie, o → ue, and e → i. Note that the shape of the outline around the verb forms with the stem changes resembles a shoe or boot, and that is why these verbs are sometimes referred to as "shoe" verbs.

GRAMÁTICA EN CONTEXTO *What Can We Do After Class?* / Ignacio and Lourdes, students at the University of the Americas, plan to spend time with their new friend, Andrew. Andrew is a foreign student from Toronto. / **IGNACIO:** What do you prefer to do first? / **LOURDES:** I want to eat something, but not at the university because I have lunch here almost every day. Let's go to the Cholula Market where they serve some delicious quesadillas. / **ANDREW:** Afterwards, can we go to the pyramid? / **LOURDES:** Of course. You have to visit our pyramid! / **IGNACIO:** What time do you plan to return? I have another exam tomorrow. / **LOURDES:** I'm not sure. What time do they close the park and museum? / **IGNACIO:** We can ask at the market. At any rate, Andrew, you can't see everything in one day. It's very big, with the church, the museum, the tunnels . . . / **ANDREW:** Archeological tunnels? Do they lose many people in the tunnels? / **IGNACIO:** No, man! There are maps and if you ask for a guide, nothing will happen.

## STEM CHANGE e → ie

| pensar (to think) | | perder (to lose) | |
|---|---|---|---|
| pienso | pensamos | pierdo | perdemos |
| piensas | pensáis | pierdes | perdéis |
| piensa | piensan | pierde | pierden |

Other common verbs with an e → ie stem change:

| cerrar | to close |
|---|---|
| empezar | to begin |
| entender | to understand |
| tender (la ropa) | to hang clothes |

## STEM CHANGE o → ue

| almorzar (to have lunch) | | volver (to return) | |
|---|---|---|---|
| almuerzo | almorzamos | vuelvo | volvemos |
| almuerzas | almorzáis | vuelves | volvéis |
| almuerza | almuerzan | vuelve | vuelven |

Other common verbs with an o → ue stem change:

| dormir | to sleep | mostrar | to show |
|---|---|---|---|
| encontrar | to find | poder | to be able |
| jugar* | to play | | |

## STEM CHANGE e → i

| pedir (to ask for; to order) | | servir (to serve) | |
|---|---|---|---|
| pido | pedimos | sirvo | servimos |
| pides | pedís | sirves | servís |
| pide | piden | sirve | sirven |

Other common verbs with an e → i stem change:

| conseguir† | to get, obtain |
|---|---|
| seguir† | to continue; to follow |

---

*jugar is the only u → ue stem changing verb in Spanish. As you saw in **Capítulo 2**, jugar is generally followed by **a** when speaking about playing a game or sport; for example, **jugar al tenis**.

†(con)seguir → (con)sigo, (con)sigues, (con)sigue,...

**A.** Several stem changing verbs can be followed by an infinitive. Note that the expression **pensar** + *inf.* translates as *to plan to.*

Mucha gente **prefiere** tomar vacaciones en agosto.
*Many people prefer to take vacations in August.*

Los jóvenes **quieren** hacer muchas actividades al aire libre.
*Young people want to do a lot of outdoor activities.*

Pablo no **puede** salir con nosotros.
*Pablo can't go out with us.*

Nosotros **pensamos** viajar a la costa este fin de semana.
*We are planning to travel to the coast this weekend.*

**B.** Some stem changing verbs form common expressions with the addition of a preposition.

1. **empezar** + **a** + *inf.* = *to begin to (do something)*
   Ahora muchas personas empiezan a investigar las posibilidades del ecoturismo.
   *Now many people are beginning to investigate the possibilites of ecotourism.*

2. **pensar** + **en** + *noun* = *to think about (something)*
   Todos debemos pensar en el medio ambiente.
   *We should all think about the environment.*

3. **volver** + **a** + *inf.* = *to (do something) again*
   ¿Vuelves a visitar tu pueblo pronto?
   *Are you going to visit your town again soon?*

**C.** The verb **soler** is always followed by an infinitive.

**soler (ue)** + *inf.* = *to usually (do something)*
Suelo levantar pesas todos los días.
*I usually lift weights every day.*

**D.** The formula **seguir** + *gerund* is used to express a continuing action or situation. Note that the translation of **seguir** varies depending on the context.

¿Sigues trabajando en la agencia de viajes?
*Are you still working at the travel agency?*

Seguimos buscando los vuelos más económicos.
*We keep looking for the least expensive flights.*

**E.** Stem changing **-ir** verbs have a stem change in their gerund form as well.

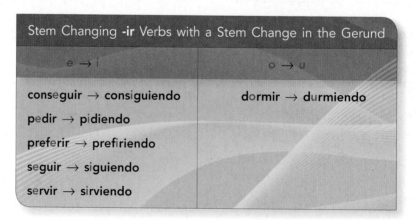

| Stem Changing **-ir** Verbs with a Stem Change in the Gerund ||
| :--- | :--- |
| *e → i* | *o → u* |
| conseguir → consiguiendo | dormir → durmiendo |
| pedir → pidiendo | |
| preferir → prefiriendo | |
| seguir → siguiendo | |
| servir → sirviendo | |

## ACTIVIDADES

**A. Asociaciones.** Give at least one infinitive whose meaning you associate with each of these words.

1. la siesta
2. una pizza
3. la lección
4. las cartas

5. la ropa
6. a casa
7. la puerta
8. las llaves (*keys*)

**B. Un día típico.** Llene (*Fill in*) los espacios en blanco con la forma correcta de los verbos entre paréntesis.

1. Yo _____ (**empezar**) a estudiar la lección.
2. Mis amigos _____ (**jugar**) al billar.
3. Tú _____ (**pedir**) una hamburguesa.
4. La profesora _____ (**pensar**) tomar café.
5. Los estudiantes _____ (**almorzar**) en la cafetería.
6. Tú _____ (**poder**) levantar pesas después de clase.
7. Nosotros _____ (**entender**) la lección y no necesitamos estudiar más.

**C. Descripciones.** With a partner, describe what these people do, want, think, and so on, by combining one element from each column to form complete sentences.

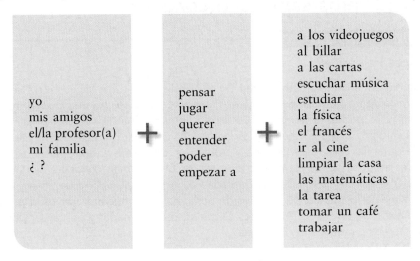

yo
mis amigos
el/la profesor(a)
mi familia
¿ ?

+

pensar
jugar
querer
entender
poder
empezar a

+

a los videojuegos
al billar
a las cartas
escuchar música
estudiar
la física
el francés
ir al cine
limpiar la casa
las matemáticas
la tarea
tomar un café
trabajar

**D. En Cuernavaca**

 Cultures     Recycle

**PASO 1.** Complete la conversación entre Jennifer y la señora Reyes con la forma correcta de los verbos entre paréntesis, según (*according to*) el contexto.

SRA. REYES: ¿Qué (*tú:* **pensar**[1]) hacer esta tarde, Jennifer?

JENNIFER: No sé. Mis amigas y yo (**querer**[2]) salir juntas.[a]

SRA. REYES: ¿Cuándo (*Uds.:* **pensar**[3]) salir?

JENNIFER: A las seis. Ellas (**almorzar**[4]) a las dos. Luego (*ellas:* **dormir**[5]) la siesta.

SRA. REYES: Bueno, Cuernavaca es la Ciudad de la Eterna Primavera[b] así que (*Uds.:* **poder**[6]) hacer muchas actividades afuera,[c] como pasear por el zócalo o visitar el Jardín Borda. ¿(*Uds.:* **Jugar**[7]) a las cartas? Es una opción si no quieren estar afuera. También hay un cine cerca de la casa.

JENNIFER: El cine es una buena idea. Hay una película que yo (**querer**[8]) ver. Necesito saber a qué hora (*la película:* **empezar**[9]). Y ¿a qué hora (**cerrar**[10]) el café de la esquina?[d]

SRA. REYES: A las once. ¿Por qué?[e]

---

[a]*together*  [b]*la... The City of Eternal Spring*  [c]*outside*  [d]*de... on the corner*  [e]*¿Por... Why?*

(Continúa.)

JENNIFER: Porque^f después, (*nosotras:* **poder**^11) tomar un café y charlar.

SRA. REYES: Es una buena idea. (*Ellos:* **Servir**^12) pasteles^g deliciosos en ese^h café.

JENNIFER: Gracias por la idea, señora. ¡A mis amigas y a mí nos gusta mucho Cuernavaca!

^f*Because* ^g*pastries* ^h*that*

**PASO 2.** Answer the questions, based on **Paso 1.**

1. ¿Qué piensa hacer Jennifer esta tarde?
2. ¿A qué hora quieren salir Jennifer y sus amigas? ¿Por qué?
3. Según la señora Reyes, ¿qué pueden hacer Jennifer y sus amigas?
4. ¿A qué hora cierra el café? ¿Qué sirven allí (*there*)?

Communication

**PASO 3.** With a partner, answer the questions.

1. ¿Qué actividades piensan Uds. hacer después de clase? ¿Y el fin de semana que viene?
2. Cuando quieren pasarlo bien con sus amigos, ¿adónde prefieren ir? ¿Qué prefieren hacer?
3. ¿Qué actividades pueden hacer los estudiantes extranjeros en su ciudad? Expliquen.

---

Expressing *to know* and *to be familiar with*

# 3.4 The Verbs **saber** and **conocer**

**GRAMÁTICA EN CONTEXTO**

### ¿Conoces Palenque?

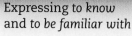

*Las Cascadas de Agua Azul en Chiapas, México*

Luis estudia en la Universidad Iberoamericana en la Ciudad de México. Esta semana está muy contento porque va a **conocer** Palenque, las ruinas de una ciudad maya. Va con Sofía y sus padres y hermanos. **Conoce** a Sofía de una de sus clases, y ahora son buenos amigos. El viaje a Palenque es largo, y es una ruta montañosa y difícil, pero el padre de Sofía, Julio, **sabe** llegar sin problemas. **Conoce** bien todo el sur de México porque es arqueólogo y viaja mucho por esa región. También **conoce** un lugar ideal para pasar el día con la familia: las Cascadas de Agua Azul. **Sabe** que Sofía y Luis, y especialmente los hermanos menores de Sofía, no van a querer pasar toda la semana sacando fotos de las ruinas. Allí en las cascadas, pueden nadar y descansar después de explorar las pirámides de Palenque.

Comprensión. Indique quién probablemente dice estas cosas (*says these things*): Luis (**L**), Julio (**J**) o los dos (**LD**).

| | L | J | LD |
|---|---|---|---|
| 1. No sé llegar a Palenque. | ☐ | ☐ | ☐ |
| 2. Conozco a Sofía. | ☐ | ☐ | ☐ |
| 3. Conozco bien las ruinas mexicanas. | ☐ | ☐ | ☐ |
| 4. Sé que Palenque es una ciudad maya. | ☐ | ☐ | ☐ |
| 5. Conozco bien a mis hijos. | ☐ | ☐ | ☐ |
| 6. Sé nadar. | ☐ | ☐ | ☐ |

---

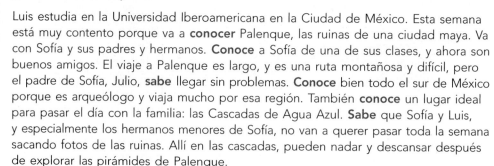

GRAMÁTICA EN CONTEXTO / *Are You Familiar with Palenque? / Luis studies at the Ibero-American University in Mexico City. This week he is very happy because he is going to get to know Palenque, the ruins of a Mayan city. He's going with Sofía and her parents and brothers. He knows Sofía from one of his classes, and now they're good friends. The trip to Palenque is long, and it's a mountainous and difficult route, but Sofía's father, Julio, knows how to get there without any problem. He's well acquainted with all of southern Mexico, because he's an archeologist and he travels a lot through that region. He also knows an ideal place to spend the day with his family: Blue Water Waterfalls. He knows that Sofía and Luis, and especially Sofía's younger siblings aren't going to want to spend the whole week taking pictures of ruins. There at the falls, they can swim and relax after exploring the pyramids of Palenque.*

In Spanish, both **saber** and **conocer** express *to know*. The present tense forms of these verbs are shown below. Note the irregular **yo** forms: **sé** and **conozco**.

| saber (*to know*) | | conocer (*to know, be acquainted with*) | |
|---|---|---|---|
| sé | sabemos | conozco | conocemos |
| sabes | sabéis | conoces | conocéis |
| sabe | saben | conoce | conocen |

Both of these verbs express *to know*, but they are not interchangeable.

**A.** **Saber** means to know in the sense of knowing facts or specific bits of information. When followed by an infinitive, it expresses to know how (*to do something*).

—¿Sabes el teléfono de Carlos?

*Do you know Carlos's telephone number?*

—No, pero sé el teléfono de su hermana.

*No, but I know his sister's number.*

David no sabe descansar. Debe pasar un día en el balneario.

*David doesn't know how to relax. He should spend a day at the spa.*

**B.** **Conocer** expresses familiarity or acquaintance with people, places, and things. When used with people, it can also mean to meet (for the first time), depending on the context.

—¿Conocen Uds. al nuevo pastor de la iglesia?

*Do you all know the new pastor at the church?*

—Sí, conocemos al pastor y a su mujer también.

*Yes, we know the pastor and his wife, too.*

## Nota comunicativa

### THE PERSONAL a

Did you notice the **a** following the verb **conocer** in the previous examples? This use is called the personal **a**, and there is no English equivalent. It is used to indicate when a person is a direct object of a verb. You will learn more about this use of the personal **a** and about direct objects in **Gramática 5.1.**

### ACTIVIDADES

**A. ¿Saber o conocer?** Indicate whether you associate **saber** or **conocer** with each concept.

|  | SABER | CONOCER |
|---|---|---|
| **1.** el número de teléfono de su profesor(a) de español | ☐ | ☐ |
| **2.** la dirección (*address*) del rector / de la rectora (presidente/a) de la universidad | ☐ | ☐ |
| **3.** a los padres de su mejor amigo/a | ☐ | ☐ |
| **4.** México, D.F. | ☐ | ☐ |
| **5.** hablar español | ☐ | ☐ |
| **6.** jugar al billar | ☐ | ☐ |
| **7.** a todos sus compañeros de clase | ☐ | ☐ |
| **8.** dónde está la biblioteca | ☐ | ☐ |

**B. El sabelotodo** (*know-it-all*). Javier is trying to impress Marta. Complete their conversation with the correct form of **saber** or **conocer,** as appropriate.

JAVIER: Yo _____¹ a muchas personas famosas.

MARTA: ¿Sí? ¿_____² (Tú) a Daddy Yankee?

JAVIER: Sí, y también _____³ (yo) dónde vive. Tengo su número de teléfono.

MARTA: ¿Sí? ¿Y él también _____⁴ tu número de teléfono?

JAVIER: Por supuesto.ᵃ Y mi familia y yo también _____⁵ a muchos atletas famosos. Por ejemplo, mis hermanos _____⁶ a todos los jugadores de la Liga Mexicana y _____⁷ sus direcciones.

MARTA: ¿De verasᵇ? ¡Obviamenteᶜ no _____⁸ (tú) impresionar a las mujeres!

---

ᵃPor... *Of course*  ᵇDe... *Really?*  ᶜ*Obviously*

**C. Entrevista**

**PASO 1.** Interview a classmate using these questions. Then switch roles. Provide as many details as you can.

1. ¿Qué ciudades de este país conoces?
2. ¿Qué ciudades de otros países conoces?
3. ¿Qué restaurantes de aquí conoces?
4. ¿Qué actividades sabes hacer?
5. ¿Cuántos números de teléfono sabes de memoria? ¿Por qué son importantes?
6. ¿Conoces bien a todos tus profesores? Explica.

**PASO 2.** Now share your results of **Paso 1** with the class.

**D. ¡Bienvenidos (*Welcome*) a México, D.F.!**

**PASO 1.** Complete la situación con la forma correcta del verbo entre paréntesis. **¡OJO!** Cuando hay dos verbos, escoja (*choose*) primero el verbo correcto.

*El Palacio Nacional en el D.F.*

GUÍA: ¡Bienvenidos a México, D.F.!

SR. GÓMEZ: Gracias. Nosotros (**necesitar**¹) información.

GUÍA: Por supuesto. ¿Qué (*Uds.:* **querer**²) hacer? ¿(*Uds:* **Conocer/Saber**³) la ciudad?

SR. GÓMEZ: No, pero nuestros amigos viven cerca. Ellos (**venir**⁴) aquí para el fin de semana.

GUÍA: En ese casoᵃ su familia (**deber**⁵) tomar un *tour* por la Plaza de la Constitución. Van a ver el Zócalo, el Palacio Nacionalᵇ y la Catedral Metropolitana.

SRA. GÓMEZ: ¿A qué hora (**empezar**⁶) el *tour*?

GUÍA: En dos horas.

SR. GÓMEZ: Muy bien. (*Nosotros:* **Almorzar**⁷) y después (**volver**⁸) para el *tour*. ¿Qué más nos recomienda?ᶜ (*Nosotros:* **Preferir**⁹) hacer diferentes actividades.

GUÍA: ¿Les gusta la historia?

JUANITO: ¡Sí! Yo (**conocer/saber**¹⁰) mucho de la historia mexicana. La estudiamosᵈ en clase.

GUÍA: Muy bien. Entonces tú (**tener**¹¹) que visitar el Museo Nacional de Antropología. (*Yo:* **Pensar**¹²) que Uds. también (**deber**¹³) ir a Xochimilco.ᵉ A todos los turistas les gustan mucho las trajinerasᶠ de Xochimilco.

---

ᵃEn... *In that case*  ᵇel... *City Hall* (lit. *National Palace*)  ᶜ¿Qué... *What else do you recommend to us?*
ᵈLa... *We study it*  ᵉ*city of floating gardens and canals near Mexico City*  ᶠ*flat-bottom boats*

SRA. GÓMEZ: ¡Qué buena idea! (*Nosotros: Poder*[14]) invitar a nuestros amigos. Mi amor, ¿(*tú: conocer/saber*[15]) su número de teléfono?

SR. GÓMEZ: Sí. Los llamo en seguida.[g] Señor guía, gracias por su ayuda.

[g]Los... *I'll call them right away.*

**PASO 2.** Conteste las preguntas, según el **Paso 1.**

1. ¿Qué prefieren hacer los Gómez?
2. Según el guía, ¿qué actividades deben hacer los Gómez?
3. ¿Quién sabe mucho de la historia de México?
4. ¿Qué van a hacer los Gómez esta tarde?

**PASO 3.** En parejas, contesten las preguntas.

Communication

1. ¿Qué pueden hacer los turistas en la ciudad donde Uds. viven? ¿En su región? ¿En su estado/provincia?
2. Cuando Uds. viajan, ¿qué actividades prefieren hacer? ¿Visitar museos? ¿Conocer lugares históricos? ¿ ? Expliquen.

**PASO 4.** Search the Internet for one or more of the places mentioned in **Paso 1** (el Zócalo de México, D.F., el Palacio Nacional, el Museo Nacional de Antropología, Xochimilco) or others in or near Mexico City. Compare the activities available to tourists there with those available in your city or region. Share your results with the class.

Comparisons

Communities

## Nota cultural

Cultures

### LA VIRGEN DE GUADALUPE

*La imagen original de la Virgen de Guadalupe*

The Virgin of Guadalupe is Mexico's most popular revered religious image and the focal point of many pilgrimages. On December 12, *the Virgin's* official feast day, thousands of Mexican Catholics visit the Basilica of Guadalupe in Mexico City to venerate her and to bring her offerings in petition or thanks for good providence. The history that led up to this occasion goes back to the 16th century.

According to traditional stories, the Virgin of Guadalupe appeared to an indigenous man, Juan Diego, at the top of Tepeyac Hill, on December 12, 1531, and asked for a chapel to be built at that site in her honor. When Juan Diego told his story to the bishop, the bishop told Juan Diego to return and ask the Virgin for a miracle to prove her request. The Virgin granted his wishes and the bishop ordered a chapel to be built on the hill, near the same location where the current Basilica stands in Mexico City today.

The Virgin of Guadalupe was officially recognized by the Roman Catholic Church in 1737 and eventually named Patroness of Mexico and the Americas. The Virgin of Guadalupe is not only a religious icon, but a symbol of today's Mexican culture as well. Images of her are seen everywhere: in churches, homes, stores, taxis, buses, offices, and even in tattoos.

**PREGUNTAS** En parejas, contesten las preguntas.

1. Do you think that praying to religious icons like the **Virgen de Guadalupe** is valuable? Why or why not? If not, then why do you suppose that so many people in Mexico hold her in such high regard?
2. Do you know of other cultures that have significant cultural icons? Which ones? How do people relate to those icons in their daily lives?
3. Had you ever heard about the **Virgen de Guadalupe** before reading this **Nota cultural?** If so, what have you heard? Search the Internet for some information and share your findings with the class.

mil
novicientos
noventa y
cinco

# Lectura cultural

Cultures

You are going to read an account of a young Mexican lady named Leticia Guerrero. Leticia, or Leti, as her family and friends call her, is a college student in Cuernavaca, Mexico. In addition to her studies, she has a job and helps with the chores around the house, but she still finds time to go out with friends. Before attempting the **Antes de leer** activity, review the following **Nota comunicativa** to learn how to ask and explain why people do certain things.

---

## ▌ Nota comunicativa

Communication

### ¿Por qué? AND porque

In Spanish, like in English, when someone is asked *why* (**por qué**) he/she does or did something, the response almost always includes the word *because . . .* (**porque...** ).

—¿**Por qué** te gusta ir al cine
los viernes?

—(Me gusta ir al cine los viernes)
**Porque** es cuando salen las
películas nuevas.

*Why do you like to go to the
movies on Fridays?*

*(I like to go the movies on Fridays)
Because it's when the new
movies come out.*

---

## ▌ ANTES DE LEER

Mi vida diaria

**PASO 1.** Conteste las preguntas.

1. ¿Cómo es su vida diaria? ¿Tiene Ud. mucho trabajo entre semana? ¿Por qué?
2. ¿Qué le gusta hacer para descansar? ¿Por qué?
3. ¿Cuáles son sus pasatiempos preferidos para los fines de semana? ¿Por qué?

Communication

**PASO 2.** Change the questions in **Paso 1** to questions using **tú** forms so that you can use them to interview a classmate. Then interview a classmate, switch roles, and provide as many details as you can.

**PASO 3.** Now share the results of your interview in **Paso 2** with the class.

**MODELO** La vida diaria de David es muy tranquila (*calm*), porque sólo tiene tres clases por semana y no tiene que trabajar.

---

## Los fines de semana de Leticia

Hola. ¿Qué tal? Me llamo Leticia, pero mi familia y mis amigos me llaman Leti. Estoy estudiando una maestría[a] en Educación y Tecnología Educativa en la Universidad Internacional de Cuernavaca. El programa es muy difícil y tengo que estudiar mucho. Además de estudiar,[b] trabajo por la tarde. Me gusta mi trabajo, pero toma mucho tiempo. Entre semana, apenas tengo[c] tiempo para estudiar, porque siempre llego tarde[d] a casa. En la noche miro la televisión o juego a las cartas con mis papás para descansar un poco antes de ir a dormir. Una gran ventaja[e] de mi universidad es que sólo hay clases de lunes a jueves. Así que[f] tengo un largo fin de semana libre para estudiar y descansar.

---

[a]*master's*  [b]*Además... Besides studying*  [c]*apenas... I hardly have*  [d]*late*  [e]*advantage*  [f]*Así... So*

¿Y qué hago los fines de semana? Bueno, lo primordial[g] para mí es estudiar y hacer toda la tarea que no pude[h] hacer durante la semana anterior. Así que suelo hacer la tarea los viernes antes y después del trabajo. Después, en la noche, prefiero ir a un café al aire libre,[i] como Los Arcos cerca del zócalo, o tal vez[j] a la Ex Hacienda de Cortés, a tomar una copa con unos amigos. O sea,[k] los viernes prefiero hacer algo tranquilo después de una larga semana, pero a otros amigos no. A ellos les gusta salir a bailar en las discotecas hasta la madrugada[l] y volver a hacer lo mismo al día siguiente.[m] Eso no lo aguanto yo.[n]

Los sábados por la mañana, ayudo a[ñ] mi mamá con los quehaceres, por ejemplo, barrer y trapear el piso, sacudir los muebles, limpiar los baños y arreglar mi cuarto. Por la tarde, me gusta cocinar y darle a[o] mi mamá la oportunidad de no tener que

La Catedral de Cuernavaca

cocinar un día de la semana. De esa manera,[p] ella puede descansar en el patio, leer o escuchar música, ir de compras o hacer lo que le dé la gana.[q]

Luego en la noche es cuando lo paso bien con mis amigos. Una cosa que me gusta mucho es bailar. Y por «bailar» quiero decir:[r] bailar salsa, cumbia, merengue y cualquier otro tipo de música latina. Por eso, mis amigos y yo vamos a Zúmbale, el mejor club de música latina en vivo de Cuernavaca. Los sábados es difícil entrar a Zúmbale porque siempre hay una larga cola.[s] Pero tengo enchufe[t]. Es que mi primo Manolo trabaja en la puerta y siempre nos deja[u] pasar sin esperar y sin pagar el cóver. Qué buena onda, ¿no? Allí, pasamos la mayor parte de la noche bailando, tomando unas copas y bailando más.

Los domingos, duermo hasta tarde por la bailada[v] de la noche anterior y después voy a misa[w] con mis padres a la Catedral de Cuernavaca. La Catedral es grande, y es casi imposible entender lo que dicen por los altavoces,[x] gracias al eco. Pero a mi mamá le gusta porque después puede ver y charlar con sus amigas.

En la tarde, el domingo es para la familia, y a mi papá le gusta llevarnos a un lugar fuera de Cuernavaca. A veces vamos a Tepoztlán o a lugares como Taxco, Xochicalco, Las Estacas, las Lagunas[y] de Zempoala, las Grutas[z] de Cacahuamilpa y otros. Pero, desafortunadamente no tengo tiempo para hablar de esos lugares, porque tengo que ir al trabajo. Nos vemos, ¿eh? ¡Hasta luego!

---

[g]lo... *the essential thing*  [h]*no... I couldn't*  [i]*al... open air*  [j]*tal... maybe*  [k]*O... In other words*  [l]*early morning (before sunrise)*  [m]*lo... the same thing the following day*  [n]*Eso... Me, I can't handle that.*  [ñ]*ayudo... I help*  [o]*darle... give*  [p]*De... That way*  [q]*lo... whatever she feels like*  [r]*quiero... I mean*  [s]*line*  [t]*a connection*  [u]*nos... he allows us*  [v]*long dancing session*  [w]*mass (Catholic church service)*  [x]*lo... what they say throught the loudspeakers*  [y]*ponds*  [z]*Grottos (Caves)*

**A.** ¿Qué hace Leti?

**PASO 1.**   Conteste las preguntas.

1. ¿Qué hace Leti entre semana?
2. ¿Cuántos días tiene el fin de semana de Leti? ¿Cuáles son? ¿Por qué?
3. ¿Qué hace Leti los viernes?
4. ¿Qué hace la mamá de Leti los sábados? ¿Por qué?
5. ¿Qué hace Leti los sábados por la mañana? ¿Y por la tarde?
6. ¿Qué hace Leti los sábados por la noche? ¿Por qué?
7. ¿Qué hacen Leti y su familia los domingos por la mañana? ¿Y por la tarde?

**PASO 2.**   Ahora comparta sus respuestas del **Paso 1** con un compañero / una compañera de clase.

Communication

**B.** ¿Qué hay que hacer en Cuernavaca?
Leti mentions a few things she likes to do and places she likes to go in Cuernavaca. Search the Internet to find out more about the places she mentions or to find out what else there is to do in Cuernavaca that interests you. Share your findings with the class.

Communication

**C.** ¡Vamos en camino! (*Let's hit the road!*)
At the end of the reading, Leti mentions some places outside of Cuernavaca, Mexico. Choose one of the places, search the Internet to find out more about it, answer the following questions, and share your results with the class.

1. ¿Cómo se llama el lugar?
2. ¿En qué estado de la República Mexicana está?
3. ¿Qué puede hacer allí?
4. ¿Sabe Ud. si hay algún lugar similar en este país? ¿Cómo se llama? ¿Conoce ese lugar? ¿Qué puede hacer una persona que va allí?

Comparisons

**D.** Comparaciones.
Write a brief paragraph in which you compare your weekend activities from **Antes de leer** with Leti's weekend activities.

## México: Miguel

**Cultures**

Guanajuato

### ANTES DE VER

Answer the questions.

1. After completing the **Concurso de videoblogs** section of **Capítulo 2,** what did you think the city of Guanajuato was like?

2. Do you think that Guanajuato would be a good place to do the following activities? (Select as many as you think would apply.)
   a. ☐ descansar
   b. ☐ andar en motocicleta
   c. ☐ salir a comer
   d. ☐ visitar museos
   e. ☐ ir de compras
   f. ☐ ¿ ?

3. Do you think Guanajuato may be a good place to visit? Why? What caught your eye in Miguel's blog from **Capítulo 2?**

### Vocabulario práctico

| | | | |
|---|---|---|---|
| **por todas partes** | everywhere | **piña** | pineapple |
| **tortas** | sandwiches | **se conservan bien** | are well-preserved |
| **licuadas** | shakes | **callejones estrechos** | narrow alleyways |
| **aguas frescas** | fruit drinks | **beso** | kiss |
| **sandía** | watermelon | **demasiado moderna** | too modern |

### DESPUÉS DE VER

**A.** ¿Cierto o falso? Indicate whether the statements are true (**C**) or false (**F**), according to Miguel's blog. Correct the statements that are false.

|  | C | F |
|---|---|---|
| 1. Elena and Alejandra are Miguel's sisters. | ☐ | ☐ |
| 2. Guanajuato is a large city with a lot of downtown traffic. | ☐ | ☐ |
| 3. At Mercado Hidalgo, you can find almost anything. | ☐ | ☐ |
| 4. The Plaza de la Paz is a modern plaza with many private buildings. | ☐ | ☐ |

**B.** Temas de discusión. With a partner, complete the tasks. Then share your results with the class.

**Communication**

1. Summarize some unique elements of Guanajuato.
2. Of the small alleyways in Guanajuato, the one known as **el Callejón del Beso** is the most famous. Write a few sentences to describe it.

# Vocabulario

## Los quehaceres domésticos — Domestic Chores

| | |
|---|---|
| arreglar el cuarto | to tidy/clean up the room |
| barrer (el piso) | to sweep (the floor) |
| cocinar | to cook |
| cortar el césped | to mow the lawn (cut the grass) |
| doblar la ropa | to fold clothes |
| hacer (*irreg.*) la cama | to make the bed |
| lavar | to wash |
|   los platos |   the dishes |
|   la ropa |   clothes |
| limpiar (la casa) | to clean (the house) |
| pasar la aspiradora | to vacuum |
| planchar (la ropa) | to iron (clothes) |
| poner (*irreg.*) la mesa | to set the table |
| quitar la mesa | to clear the table |
| sacar (la basura) | to take out (the trash/garbage) |
| sacudir (los muebles) | to dust (the furniture) |
| secar (la ropa) | to dry (clothes) |
| tender (ie) (la ropa) | to hang (clothes) |
| trabajar en el jardín | to work in the garden/yard |
| trapear (el piso) | to mop (the floor) |

## Los aparatos domésticos — Appliances

| | |
|---|---|
| la aspiradora | vacuum cleaner |
| la estufa | stove |
| el horno | oven |
|   el (horno de) microondas |   microwave (oven) |
| la lavadora | washer, washing machine |
| el lavaplatos | dishwasher |
| la licuadora | blender |
| la secadora | dryer |

## ¿Cón qué frecuencia? — How Often?

| | |
|---|---|
| una vez a la semana / al mes | once a week/month |

Repaso: diario/a, todos los días

## Expresiones con el verbo *tener*

| | |
|---|---|
| tener... años | to be . . . years old |
| tener (mucho) calor | to be (very) hot |
| tener cuidado | to be careful |
| tener éxito | to be successful |
| tener frío | to be cold |
| tener ganas de + *inf.* | to feel like (*doing something*) |
| tener miedo (de) | to be afraid (of) |
| tener prisa | to be in a hurry |
| tener que + *inf.* | to have to (*do something*) |
| tener razón | to be right |
|   no tener razón |   to be wrong |
| tener (mucha) sed | to be (very) thirsty |
| tener sueño | to be sleepy |
| tener (mucha) suerte | to be (very) lucky |

## Las distracciones — Entertainment/Hobbies

| | |
|---|---|
| hacer (*irreg.*) ejercicio | to exercise |
| hacer (*irreg.*) yoga | to do yoga |
| ir (*irreg.*) | to go |
|   al cine |   to the movies |
|   a la iglesia |   to church |
|   a la mezquita |   to the mosque |
|   a la sinagoga |   to the synagogue |
| jugar (ue) | to play |
|   al billar |   pool |
|   a las cartas |   cards |
|   a los videojuegos |   videogames |
| levantar pesas | to lift weights |
| pasarlo bien/mal | to have a good/bad time |
| tomar | to have |
|   un café |   a cup of coffee |
|   una copa |   a drink (*alcoholic*) |
| tomar una siesta | to take a nap |
| tomar una sauna | to spend time in a sauna |
| ver (*irreg.*) | to watch |
|   un DVD |   a DVD |
|   una película |   a movie |

Cognados: el jacuzzi, el masaje, la meditación, la sauna
Repaso: caminar, correr, escuchar música, jugar (ue) al dominó, mirar la televisión, nadar en la piscina

## Otros verbos

| | |
|---|---|
| almorzar (ue) | to eat lunch |
| cerrar (ie) | to close |
| conocer (zc) | to know, be acquainted with |
| conseguir (*like* seguir) | to get, obtain |
| deber + *inf.* | to should, ought to (*do something*) |
| dormir (ue) | to sleep |
| empezar (ie) | to begin |
|   empezar a + *inf.* |   to begin to (*do something*) |
| encontrar (ue) | to find |
| entender (ie) | to understand |
| mostrar (ue) | to show |
| necesitar + *inf.* | to need to (*do something*) |
| pedir (i) | to ask for; to order |
| pensar (ie) (en) | to think (about) |
|   pensar + *inf.* |   to plan to (*do something*) |
| perder (ie) | to lose |
| poder (ue) | to be able |
| preferir (ie) | to prefer |
| querer (ie) | to want |
| saber (*irreg.*) | to know |
| seguir (i) | to continue; to follow |
|   seguir + *gerund* |   to keep / still be (*doing something*) |
| servir (i) | to serve |
| soler (ue) + *inf.* | to usually (*do something*) |
| tener (*irreg.*) | to have |
| venir (*irreg.*) | to come |
| volver (ue) | to return (*to a place*) |
|   volver a + *inf.* |   to (*do something*) again |

Repaso: descansar, estudiar, hacer (*irreg.*), necesitar, trabajar

## Otras palabras y expresiones

| | |
|---|---|
| la cosa | thing |
| el lugar | place |
| entre | between |
| ¿por qué? | why? |
| porque | because |
| según | according to |

# Los pasatiempos y los deportes

Connections

## ANTES DE VER

¿Cuánto sabe Ud. de los pasatiempos y los deportes en el mundo hispano? Indique si las oraciones son ciertas (C) o falsas (F).

| | C | F |
|---|---|---|
| 1. El fútbol es un deporte de gran importancia en los países hispanos. | ☐ | ☐ |
| 2. El fútbol no es un deporte popular entre (*among*) los niños (*children*) mexicanos. | ☐ | ☐ |
| 3. Costa Rica tiene fama por la variedad de actividades que se puede hacer al aire libre (*outdoors*). | ☐ | ☐ |
| 4. En la República Dominicana, los jóvenes juegan sólo al fútbol. | ☐ | ☐ |
| 5. Los beisbolistas dominicanos no son conocidos (*well-known*) en este país. | ☐ | ☐ |

### Vocabulario práctico

| | | | |
|---|---|---|---|
| **la porra** | group of fans (*Mex.*) | **sueñan con ser** | (they) dream of being |
| **apoya** | supports | | |
| **el senderismo** | hiking | **en cualquier lugar** | anywhere |
| **montar a caballo** | horseback riding | | |
| **disfrutar de** | to enjoy | **han ganado** | they have won |
| **emocionante** | thrilling | **los centros de entrenamiento** | training centers |
| **la tirolina** | ziplining | | |

## DESPUÉS DE VER

Complete las oraciones con información verdadera (*true*), según el vídeo. Use palabras de la lista. ¡OJO! Algunas palabras no se usan.

| | | | |
|---|---|---|---|
| bate | ecoturismo | fútbol | porras |
| béisbol | equipo | insectos | senderismo |

1. El _____ es muy popular en la vida (*life*) hispana.
2. Las _____ mexicanas son muy dedicadas a su equipo favorito.
3. Costa Rica ofrece (*offers*) actividades relacionadas con el _____.
4. La biodiversidad de la naturaleza (*nature*) costarricense consiste en muchas variedades de plantas, animales e _____.
5. El _____ es el deporte más popular en la República Dominicana.
6. Para jugar al béisbol, sólo se necesitan (*are needed*) un _____, una pelota, unos guantes (*gloves*) y unos amigos.

## LA HISTORIA DEL FÚTBOL Y LA FIFA

Aunque el fútbol moderno data del siglo XIX,[a] había antecedentes del[b] fútbol en China hacia el año 200 a.C.[c] La FIFA (Fédération Internationale de Football Association, en francés) es la institución que hoy en día[d] controla las reglas del fútbol.

[a]data... *dates back to the 19th Century*   [b]había... *there were precursors to*
[c]hacia... *from around the year 200 B.C.* [a.C. = antes de Cristo]   [d]hoy... *nowadays*

## LA COPA MUNDIAL

La FIFA también organiza la Copa Mundial de fútbol, un torneo[a] que se juega cada cuatro años. El lema[b] de la FIFA hace conexiones entre el deporte y el mundo: «Por[c] el juego. Por el mundo». Aquí se ve la selección nacional española tras[d] su victoria en la Copa Mundial de 2010.

[a]*tournament*   [b]*slogan*   [c]*For*   [d]*after*

## ACTIVIDADES

**A.** Comprensión. Indique si las oraciones son ciertas (**C**) o falsas (**F**).

|  | C | F |
|---|---|---|
| 1. La Copa Mundial se juega cada cuatro años. | ☐ | ☐ |
| 2. La FIFA organiza la Copa Mundial. | ☐ | ☐ |
| 3. Laura del Río juega para un equipo profesional en España. | ☐ | ☐ |
| 4. Lionel Messi es un famoso beisbolista dominicano. | ☐ | ☐ |
| 5. El fútbol se originó (*originated*) en Francia en el siglo XIX. | ☐ | ☐ |

**B.** Conexiones. En parejas, contesten las preguntas.

1. ¿Se juega el fútbol en la región donde Uds. viven? Expliquen.
2. ¿Cuáles son los deportes más populares en la región donde viven?
3. ¿Cuáles son sus deportes favoritos y por qué?

**C** Connections

**C.** A investigar más. Busque información en el Internet y en su libro de texto para hacer una investigación sobre algún pasatiempo o deporte que le interesa a Ud. (*that interests you*). En su informe (*report*), debe:

1. presentar una descripción breve de la actividad.
2. explicar en qué estación/estaciones del año se practica más.
3. explicar quién(es) hace(n) esta actividad.

**D.** Temas de discusión. En grupos pequeños, comenten *uno* de estos (*these*) temas y escriban algunas conclusiones breves en español. Luego, compartan sus conclusiones con la clase.

**C** Communication

1. los deportes en la vida diaria
2. la importancia de los pasatiempos en la vida estudiantil

## LAS LIGAS FEMENINAS

¡El fútbol es popular entre las mujeres también! Se practica mucho en las escuelas y universidades y hay ligas y equipos femeninos profesionales. La liga profesional femenina de los Estados Unidos también goza de[a] futbolistas internacionales, como Mónica Ocampo, de México, y Laura del Río (foto), de España.

[a]goza... *has*

## LIONEL MESSI

Lionel Messi es un futbolista argentino de fama internacional. Messi juega en el F.C.[a] Barcelona como delantero.[b] Es popular por la calidad[c] de su fútbol, sus goles y sus premios.[d]

[a]Fútbol Club  [b]*forward*  [c]*quality*  [d]*awards*

## ASÍ SE DICE: EL LENGUAJE DEPORTIVO

el basquetbol = el baloncesto (*Sp.*)

correr = hacer (*irreg.*) jogging

el fútbol = el balompié

la pelota = el balón, la bola, el esférico

surfear = correr las olas, hacer (*irreg.*) surfing

goalie = el arquero, el golero, el guardameta, el portero

indoor soccer = **el futbito** (*Sp.*), **el fútbol sala, el futsal**

innings (**béisbol**) = **las entradas, los innings**

to snowboard = **hacer** (*irreg.*) **snowboard**

to waterski = **esquiar** (**esquío**) **sobre el agua**

Girasoles en Andalucía

# Entrada cultural

## España

Cultures

Flamenco en Sevilla

Inmigrantes en las Islas Canarias

El Alcázar de Segovia

España forma, con Portugal y Gibraltar, la Península Ibérica. La posición geográfica de la península ha facilitado[a] durante su historia el asentamiento[b] de numerosos pueblos como los fenicios, romanos, visigodos, árabes y judíos.[c] Los romanos introducen el latín, base del español de hoy, en la península. Después llegan los visigodos y establecen el cristianismo. Más tarde, los árabes dominan la península durante ocho siglos y dejan su influencia en la arquitectura, en la cocina y en la lengua. Durante ese tiempo un gran número de judíos coexiste con árabes y cristianos y colaboran en proyectos artísticos y científicos. Estos pueblos, con tradiciones culturales muy diversas, determinan la riqueza[d] cultural de la España de hoy.

Esta riqueza está presente en las costumbres y tradiciones de los españoles, en el arte y en la magnífica arquitectura. Un gran número de monumentos son Patrimonio de la Humanidad.[e] Está presente también en la diversidad lingüística. El español, o castellano, es la lengua oficial del país, pero hay otras lenguas que son oficiales, cada una en su región: el catalán en Cataluña, el gallego[f] en Galicia y el vascuence en el País Vasco. La música española presenta estilos muy variados también. La música folclórica más popular incluye el flamenco, típico del sur del país, y la jota, baile característico de varias regiones del norte de la península. En la actualidad, ritmos occidentales como el pop, el rock, el rap y el hip hop son influyentes y coexisten con la música tradicional.

El efecto de otras culturas continúa en la sociedad española contemporánea. En la década de los 90, España empieza a recibir una gran cantidad de inmigrantes de países latinoamericanos como Ecuador, Colombia, Argentina, Bolivia, Perú y la República Dominicana, y de diferentes zonas de África, Asia y Europa. Esta intensa inmigración está creando una diversidad racial, cultural, lingüística y religiosa con implicaciones significativas en la cultura y el futuro de España.

---

[a]*ha... has made easy*  [b]*settlement*  [c]*Jewish people*  [d]*richness*  [e]*Patrimonio... UNESCO World Heritage Sites*
[f]*Galician*

118

# El fútbol

## EL FÚTBOL: DEPORTE INTERNACIONAL

El fútbol es el deporte más popular y con más aficionados del mundo. Se practica con dos equipos de once personas y una pelota. En los Estados Unidos se llama *soccer*, pero en Inglaterra[a] se llama *football*.

[a]*England*

## LAS SELECCIONES NACIONALES

Cada país hispano tiene una selección nacional de fútbol. Sus partidos son un gran evento social e histórico. Algunos partidos, como Argentina contra[a] Brasil, atraen[b] la expectación[c] mundial por el prestigio de los dos equipos. En los Estados Unidos el fútbol es popular también y su equipo sigue creciendo[d] en el *ranking* mundial. Aquí se ve la selección argentina de 2010.

[a]*against*  [b]*attract*  [c]*excitement*  [d]*sigue... continues to grow*

# ¿Cómo es su familia?

*Una familia española*

1. ¿Tiene Ud. una familia grande o pequeña? ¿Cuántas personas hay en su familia?

2. ¿Viven todos los miembros de su familia en la misma región o viven por todas partes de este país? ¿Vive algún pariente en otro país actualmente (*currently*)? ¿dónde?

3. Cuando Ud. piensa en el concepto de «la familia», ¿a quiénes incluye? ¿sólo a los padres y hermanos o a todos los miembros y todas las generaciones de la familia? ¿y a los parientes políticos (*in-laws*)? ¿y a las mascotas (*pets*)?

SPANISH

www.connectspanish.com

## Vocabulario del tema

### Las relaciones familiares°

Las... *Family Relationships*

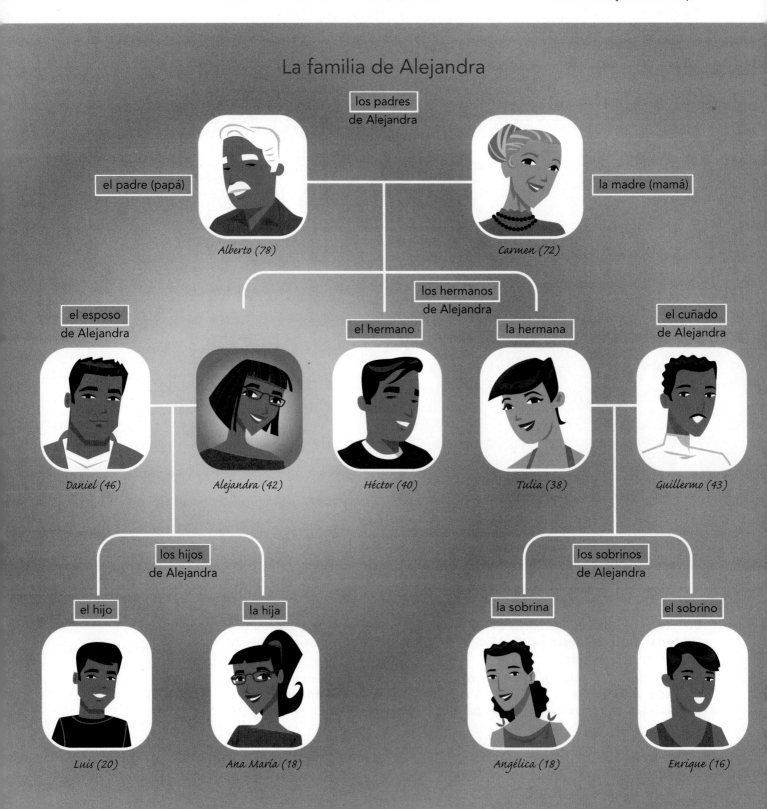

La familia de Alejandra

los padres de Alejandra

el padre (papá) — Alberto (78)

la madre (mamá) — Carmen (72)

los hermanos de Alejandra

el esposo de Alejandra — Daniel (46)

Alejandra (42)

el hermano — Héctor (40)

la hermana — Tulia (38)

el cuñado de Alejandra — Guillermo (43)

los hijos de Alejandra

el hijo — Luis (20)

la hija — Ana María (18)

los sobrinos de Alejandra

la sobrina — Angélica (18)

el sobrino — Enrique (16)

| | |
|---|---|
| los abuelos | grandparents |
|   el/la abuelo/a |   grandfather/grandmother |
| los nietos | grandchildren |
|   el/la nieto/a |   grandson/granddaughter |
| los parientes | relatives |
| los primos | cousins |
|   el/la primo/a |   (male/female) cousin |
| los tíos | aunts and uncles |
|   el/la tío/a |   uncle/aunt |

## La familia política     In-Laws

| | |
|---|---|
| el/la cuñado/a | brother-in-law / sister-in-law |
| la nuera | daughter-in-law |
| el/la suegro/a | father-in-law / mother-in-law |
| el yerno | son-in-law |

## Las mascotas

| | |
|---|---|
| el gato | cat |

Repaso: el perro

### ACTIVIDADES

**A.** ¿Cierto o falso? Indique si las oraciones son ciertas (**C**) o falsas (**F**), según el árbol genealógico (*family tree*) de la página 120. Corrija (*Correct*) las oraciones falsas.

|  | C | F |
|---|---|---|
| 1. Alejandra es la nieta de Alberto. | ☐ | ☐ |
| 2. Alberto y Carmen tienen cuatro nietos. | ☐ | ☐ |
| 3. Tulia y Guillermo tienen cuatro hijos. | ☐ | ☐ |
| 4. Héctor y Tulia son primos. | ☐ | ☐ |
| 5. Daniel y Alejandra son los abuelos de Enrique. | ☐ | ☐ |
| 6. Tulia tiene dos sobrinos. | ☐ | ☐ |
| 7. Ana María tiene dos tíos. | ☐ | ☐ |
| 8. Daniel es el cuñado de Tulia. | ☐ | ☐ |

**B.** ¿Quién es?

**PASO 1.** Identifique a cada persona, según el árbol genealógico de la página 120.

1. Es la hermana de la madre de Angélica.
2. Son hermanas y tienen un hermano.
3. Es la abuela de Enrique.
4. Tiene cuatro sobrinos.
5. Son los nietos de Carmen.
6. Es el cuñado de Tulia.
7. Son los tíos de Luis.
8. Es el esposo de Tulia.

**PASO 2.** Write four sentences like those in **Paso 1**, without revealing the name of the person you describe. Then read your sentences to a partner while he/she guesses the names of the people described. Then switch roles.

MODELO E1: Es la hermana de Enrique. ¿Cómo se llama?
         E2: Se llama Angélica.

## Nota cultural

Cultures

### LOS APELLIDOS[a]

En la mayoría de los países de habla española las personas tienen dos apellidos: el primer[b] apellido del padre y el primer apellido de la madre. Tradicionalmente, el apellido del padre es el primero y el apellido de la madre es el segundo.[c] Mire este nombre: Marina Guzmán Núñez. De acuerdo al método tradicional de nombrar a un hijo, *Guzmán* sería[d] el apellido del padre de Marina, y Núñez sería el apellido de su madre.

Sin embargo, las convenciones han cambiado.[e] En España, desde 1999, cuando van a ponerles nombre a sus hijos, los padres pueden colocar[f] el apellido de la madre primero y después el apellido del padre. Incluso los hijos, cuando son mayores de edad (en España, 18 años), pueden escoger el nombre que quieren primero. Así, Marina, a los 18 años, puede ser Marina Guzmán Núñez (a la manera tradicional), o Marina Núñez Guzmán (la nueva posibilidad).

---

[a]*surnames* [b]*first* [c]*second* [d]*would be* [e]*han... have changed* [f]*place*

**PREGUNTAS** En parejas, contesten las preguntas y después compartan sus respuestas con la clase.

1. ¿Cuántos apellidos tienen los españoles? ¿Es una costumbre en España solamente o en otros países hispanos?

2. En general, ¿qué apellido llevan las personas de su país? ¿Es posible escoger el apellido de la madre?

## Los números a partir de° 100

a... *Beyond*

| | | |
|---|---|---|
| 100 cien | 500 quinientos/as | 1.000 mil |
| 101 ciento uno | 600 seiscientos/as | 2.000 dos mil |
| 200 doscientos/as | 700 setecientos/as | 1.000.000 un millón (de) |
| 300 trescientos/as | 800 ochocientos/as | 2.000.000 dos millones (de) |
| 400 cuatrocientos/as | 900 novecientos/as | |

▶ For numbers between 100 and 200, use **ciento.**

**Ciento uno, ciento dos, ciento tres... ciento noventa y nueve**

▶ The hundreds from 200 to 900 will show gender agreement.

**Doscientos** uno, **doscientos** dos... **doscientos** noventa y nueve hombres

**Trescientas** tres... **cuatrocientas** siete... **novecientas** cinco mujeres

▶ The indefinite article is not used before one thousand.

**Mil dólares**                    **Cinco mil dólares**

▶ To express years in Spanish, the numbers are said using **mil.**

1492   **mil** cuatrocientos noventa y dos

1959   **mil** novecientos cincuenta y nueve

1776   **mil** setecientos setenta y seis

2001   **dos mil** uno

CAPÍTULO 4   ¿Cómo es su familia?

▶ To express dates that include years, use the formula: **el** + *day* + **de** + *month* + **de** *year*.

Hoy es **el** 30 **de abril de** 2012.      *Today is April 30, 2012.*

▶ Use the indefinite article for one million. The preposition **de** is required before a noun.

**un** millón **de** personas      *a million people*
**tres** millones **de** personas      *three million people*

---

## Nota comunicativa

Communication

### ASKING SOMEONE'S AGE WITH tener

You have already learned several expressions with **tener,** including **tener... años,** to express age. To ask how old someone is, use the question **¿Cuántos años tienes?** for someone you would refer to as **tú** or **¿Cuántos años tiene Ud.?** for someone you would refer to as **Ud.**

| | |
|---|---|
| —¿Cuántos años tienes? | *How old are you (sing. fam.)?* |
| —Tengo veintidós años. | *I'm twenty-two (years old).* |
| | |
| —¿Cuántos años tiene Ud.? | *How old are you (sing. form.)?* |
| —Tengo cuarenta y tres años. | *I'm forty-three (years old).* |

---

**C.** **¿En qué año nació** (*was he/she born*)? Look at the ages listed in parentheses below the names of people in the family tree on page 120. Imagine that the current year is 2012 and, based on their ages, say in what year these people were born. ¡OJO! Say the years in Spanish.

**MODELO** Alejandra → Nació en mil novecientos setenta (1970).

1. Alberto     3. Daniel     5. Guillermo     7. Enrique
2. Carmen     4. Tulia     6. Luis     8. Angélica

**D.** El divorcio en España

Cultures

**PASO 1.** Read the summary of a report about divorce rates in Spain. Don't worry if you don't understand all of the words. Try to get the gist of the summary.

---

### EL EFECTO DEL «DIVORCIO EXPRÉS» EN ESPAÑA

En 2005, el gobierno de España introdujo[a] un proyecto de ley[b] para el «divorcio exprés», que permite el divorcio sin la separación física. En 2006, se registraron[c] 126.952* divorcios en España, un aumento[d] de 74,3* por ciento en comparación con 2005. El aumento más grande fue[e] entre los recién casados:[f] 945 parejas se divorciaron[g] en el primer año de matrimonio, un aumento de 330,6 por ciento.

---

[a]*introduced*   [b]*proyecto... bill*   [c]*se... were registered*   [d]*increase*   [e]*was*   [f]*recién... newlyweds*   [g]*se... divorced*

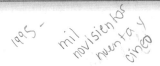

---

*Note that in Spanish, the decimal point we use in English becomes a comma and the comma a period. If you need to read the punctuation of a number, the words are **punto** (period) and **coma** (*comma*). Generally you will only read punctuation for numbers with decimals, so, for example, 65,2 would be **sesenta y cinco coma dos.**

**PASO 2.** Conteste las preguntas con los números y años correctos. ¡OJO! Diga (*Say*) sus respuestas en voz alta (*aloud*).

1. ¿En qué año aprobaron (*did they approve*) la ley para el «divorcio exprés» en España?
2. ¿Cuántos divorcios se registraron en 2006?
3. ¿En qué porcentaje (*percentage*) aumentaron (*increased*) los divorcios en 2006?
4. ¿Cuántas parejas recién casadas se divorciaron en 2006?

## Para describir a la gente°

*People*

| | |
|---|---|
| cariñoso/a | affectionate |
| delgado/a | thin |
| gordo/a | fat |
| hermoso/a | pretty |
| jubilado/a | retired |
| listo/a | smart |
| orgulloso/a | proud |
| torpe | clumsy |
| tranquilo/a | calm |
| travieso/a | mischievous |
| unido/a | close (*relationship*) |
| viejo/a | old |

**Cognados:** extrovertido/a, obediente, responsable
**Repaso:** alto/a, bajo/a, bonito/a, bueno/a, feo/a, guapo/a, joven (jóvenes), moreno/a, nervioso/a, pelirrojo/a, perezoso/a, rubio/a, trabajador(a)

**E. ¿Cómo son?** Complete las descripciones de la familia de Marisol con palabras de la lista.

| | | | |
|---|---|---|---|
| cariñoso/a | guapo/a | listo/a | travieso/a |
| extrovertido/a | jubilado/a | pelirrojo/a | unido/a |

1. En mi familia, todos somos morenos. No tengo parientes _____.
2. Mi abuelo ya no trabaja. Está _____.
3. Mi hermana trabaja mucho en la escuela y es buena estudiante. Es muy _____.
4. Mi prima Agustina es preciosa, pero no es muy obediente. Es _____.
5. En mi familia hacemos muchas cosas juntos. Somos una familia muy _____.
6. Mi primo Sebastián es muy popular en la escuela porque es muy _____. Pero no tiene novia porque también es muy tímido.
7. Mi tía Victoria hace muchas cosas para nosotros. Me gusta ir a su casa porque es muy _____ y paciente.
8. Mi tía Beatriz es simpática y _____. Tiene muchos amigos muy interesantes.

Communication

**F. ¿De quién hablo?** With a partner, take turns describing people in the drawing on page 120, without giving their names so that the other can guess. Invent some details about their personalities. Follow the model.

**MODELO** E1: Es travieso y joven. Le gusta seguir a su primo Luis por todas partes.
E2: Es Enrique.

**G. Entrevista.** Entreviste a un compañero / una compañera de clase con las preguntas. Luego, cambien de papel (*switch roles*).

1. ¿Cómo se llaman tus padres?
2. ¿Cuántos hermanos tienes? ¿Cómo se llaman y cuántos años tienen?
3. ¿Qué mascota o mascotas tienes? ¿Cómo es/son? (Describan la personalidad de sus mascotas.)
4. ¿Cuántos abuelos vivos (*living*) tienes? ¿Dónde viven? ¿Cuándo visitas / ves a tus abuelos?
5. ¿Cómo eres tú? ¿Eres muy extrovertido/a? ¿Eres travieso/a?
6. ¿Quién es tu pariente favorito? ¿Cómo se llama? ¿Cuántos años tiene? ¿Por qué es tu pariente favorito?

# Gramática

## 4.1 Por and para

*Expressing by, for, through, . . .*

**GRAMÁTICA EN CONTEXTO**

El Parque Casilda Iturriza en Bilbao

### La comida de los domingos

[*Ryan va a estudiar en la Universidad de Deusto de Bilbao por un año y vivir con una familia vasca en el barrio Indautxu. Es su primera semana con la familia y su nuevo «hermano» español, Quique, explica la rutina de los domingos.*]

QUIQUE: Los domingos, toda la familia come en casa de mis abuelos. Mi mamá y mis tías ayudan a mi abuela **por** la mañana porque preparan mucha comida **para** la familia. Nosotros debemos llegar a la casa de mis abuelos **para** la 1:30. La comida siempre es a las 2:00.

RYAN: ¿Dónde viven tus abuelos?

QUIQUE: Viven en la Calle Cosme Echevarrieta. Podemos caminar **por** el Parque Casilda Iturriza **para** llegar más rápido.

RYAN: ¿No vamos **por** autobús?

QUIQUE: No, sólo tenemos que caminar **por** seis o siete manzanas. Está cerca. No debes hacer otros planes **por** la tarde. ¡Comemos mucho! Y luego hablamos **por** una o dos horas después de la comida. ¡Es muy bueno **para** aprender sobre los deportes y la política del País Vasco, y **para** practicar el español!

**GRAMÁTICA EN CONTEXTO** *Sunday Meals / Ryan is going to study at Deusto University in Bilbao for a year and live with a Basque family in the Indautxu neighborhood. This is his first week with the family and his new Spanish "brother," Quique, explains the Sunday routine. /* **QUIQUE:** *On Sundays, all of the family eats at my grandparents' house. My mom and my aunts help my grandmother in the morning because they prepare a lot of food for the family. We should arrive at my grandparents' house by 1:30. Lunch is always at 2:00. /* **RYAN:** *Where do your grandparents live? /* **QUIQUE:** *They live on Cosme Echevarrieta Street. We can walk through the Casilda Iturriza Park to get there faster. /* **RYAN:** *We're not going by bus? /* **QUIQUE:** *No, we only have to walk for six or seven blocks. It's close. You shouldn't make other plans for the afternoon. We eat a lot! And later we talk for one or two hours after lunch. It's very good for learning about sports and politics in the Basque Country and to practice Spanish!*

**Comprensión.** Empareje (*Match*) las frases de las dos columnas para formar oraciones lógicas según la conversación entre Ryan y Quique.

1. Ryan y Quique salen para ____.
2. Los parientes de Quique se sientan a la mesa por ____.
3. La abuela, la madre y las tías de Quique preparan comida para ____.
4. Quique y Ryan van a caminar por ____.
5. Empiezan a preparar la comida por ____.

a. toda la familia los domingos
b. la casa de los abuelos antes de la 1:30
c. la mañana
d. el parque
e. más de dos horas los domingos

---

You have probably noticed the many occurrences of the prepositions **por** and **para** in Spanish. You may already know that they both can mean *for*. However, they are not interchangeable, and they each have several English equivalents in addition to *for*. Some of the most common and most important uses of each are presented here.

### Uses of **por**

**A.** **Por** is used to express *in* when referring to the periods of the day. Remember that **de** is used when giving the exact time of day: **Son las 8:00 de la mañana.**

| | |
|---|---|
| **por** la mañana | in the morning |
| **por** la tarde | in the afternoon |
| **por** la noche | in the evening/at night |
| Mi padre tiene que trabajar **por** la noche, pero mi madre trabaja **por** la mañana. | *My father has to work at night, but my mother works in the morning.* |

**B.** **Por** means *by* or *by means of* when used with modes of transportation or communication.

| | |
|---|---|
| Mis abuelos no viajan **por avión** porque tienen miedo de volar. | *My grandparents don't travel by air because they are afraid of flying.* |
| Mis hermanos y yo nos hablamos frecuentemente **por teléfono.** | *My siblings and I talk to each other frequently by telephone.* |

**C.** **Por** expresses movement *through* or *along*.

| | |
|---|---|
| El perro sale **por la puerta**, pero el gato sale **por la ventana.** | *The dog leaves through the door, but the cat leaves through the window.* |

**D.** **Por** is used in many fixed expressions. Here are a few of the most common.

| | | | |
|---|---|---|---|
| **por ejemplo** | for example | **por fin** | finally |
| **por eso** | that's why | **por lo general** | in general |
| **por favor** | please | **por lo menos** | at least |

### Uses of **para**

**A.** **Para** + *inf.* means *in order to* (*do something*). Note that in English we often mean *in order to* but only say *to*.

| | |
|---|---|
| Debemos llegar a las 6:00 **para tener** suficiente tiempo. | *We should arrive at 6:00 (in order) to have enough time.* |

**B.** **Para** indicates *who* or *what* something is destined for or to be given to.

| | |
|---|---|
| El vídeo es **para mi sobrina** y el juguete es **para mi sobrino.** | *The video is for my niece and the toy is for my nephew.* |

**C.** **Para** is used to express *toward* or *in the direction of.*

Mañana mis tíos salen **para Málaga.**    *Tomorrow my aunt and uncle leave for Málaga.*

**D.** **Para** is used to express deadlines.

El informe es **para el jueves.**    *The report is for Thursday.*

**A.** Asociaciones. Indique quiénes dirían (*would say*) las oraciones: los padres (**P**) o los hijos (**H**)?

|   | P | H |
|---|---|---|
| 1. ¡Debes salir para clase en dos minutos! | ☐ | ☐ |
| 2. Tengo que terminar la composición para el miércoles. | ☐ | ☐ |
| 3. No me gusta estudiar por la tarde. | ☐ | ☐ |
| 4. Voy a comprar una bicicleta para Antonio. | ☐ | ☐ |
| 5. Necesito un cuaderno para la clase de biología. | ☐ | ☐ |
| 6. No debes hablar por teléfono después de las 10:00 de la noche. | ☐ | ☐ |
| 7. Necesito usar la computadora para escribir la tarea. | ☐ | ☐ |
| 8. No deben pasar por esa (*that*) calle por la noche. | ☐ | ☐ |

**B.** Una mañana típica. Complete la descripción de una mañana típica de Sofía con **por** y **para.**

_____¹ la mañana, mi padre prepara el café _____² mamá mientras ella nos despierta[a] _____³ la escuela. Mis hermanos tienen que salir a las siete y media _____⁴ tomar el autobús. Yo también voy a la escuela en autobús, pero mi autobús pasa _____⁵ nuestra casa a las ocho. No puedo ver la televisión _____⁶ la mañana, _____⁷ eso escucho mi *iPod* o leo mientras espero el autobús.

A veces el autobús llega un poco tarde,[b] y como mis padres salen _____⁸ el trabajo a las ocho en punto, espero sola por unos minutos. Tengo que estar en mi clase a las ocho y veinte en punto, y cuando el autobús llega tarde, tengo que correr _____⁹ llegar a tiempo.

_____
[a]nos... *wakes us up*   [b]*late*

**C.** Mascotas para la familia

**PASO 1.** En parejas, contesten las preguntas sobre el anuncio.

1. ¿Cómo pueden ser buenas las mascotas para los niños?
2. ¿Cómo pueden ayudar las mascotas a las personas mayores?

**PASO 2.** Ahora contesten estas preguntas personales.

1. ¿Qué mascotas tienen Uds.? ¿Por qué prefieren ese tipo de animal? Expliquen.
2. ¿Cómo se llaman sus mascotas?
3. ¿Qué hacen para pasar tiempo con sus mascotas?
4. ¿ ?

# Mascotas para toda la familia

¿Qué espera Ud.?

- para enseñar la responsabilidad
- para aliviar el estrés y la depresión
- para pasar momentos divertidos
- por el cariño que la mascota les trae a todos

*¡Las mascotas son buenas para todos!*

**D.** Mi nombre, mi santo y mi cumpleaños (*birthday*)

**PASO 1.**   Complete la descripción con la forma correcta de las palabras entre paréntesis. Si hay dos palabras, escoja (*choose*) la palabra correcta.

*¡Feliz cumpleaños!*

En los países hispanos, especialmente en España, muchos
padres nombran[a] a sus hijos por un santo. Aunque[b] España
es hoy un país moderno y liberal, (**mucho**[1]) españoles,
influidos[c] por su largo pasado[d] católico, todavía[e] conservan
esta tradición religiosa.

(**Por/Para**[2]) los niños, es divertido tener el nombre de
un santo, porque pueden celebrar dos fiestas: su cumpleaños
y el día de (**su/sus**[3]) santo. (**Por/Para**[4]) ejemplo, si el cumpleaños de Pedro es (**el/la**[5]) 22 de febrero, (*él:* **ir**[6]) a hacer
una fiesta el 22 de febrero (**por/para**[7]) celebrar su cumpleaños.
(**Por/Para**[8]) el 29 de junio, va a celebrar el día de su santo, San Pedro. También hay
santas. Ana, (**por/para**[9]) ejemplo, nació el 12 de junio y (*ella:* **celebrar**[10]) su cumpleaños
ese[f] día. Pero su familia también (**hacer**[11]) otra fiesta el 26 de julio en honor de su
santa, Santa Ana.

No (**todo**[12]) las familias hacen fiestas (**por/para**[13]) celebrar el día del santo, pero
sí hacen fiestas de cumpleaños. Y la fiesta (**ser**[14]) una celebración familiar. En este[g]
país, las fiestas de cumpleaños son (**por/para**[15]) los niños y (**su**[16]) amigos, pero en
España y otros países hispanohablantes, aunque los amigos (**asistir**[17]) a las fiestas,
por lo general, los padres, los hermanos, los abuelos, los primos, los tíos y los sobrinos
son los invitados[h] principales.

---

[a]*name*  [b]*Although*  [c]*influenced*  [d]*past*  [e]*still*  [f]*that*  [g]*this*  [h]*guests*

**PASO 2.**   Empareje las frases para formar oraciones lógicas según el **Paso 1.**

1. El día del santo refleja (*reflects*) ____
2. En las fiestas de cumpleaños en España,
   los parientes son, por lo general, ____
3. Algunos españoles hacen una fiesta ____
4. Típicamente en este país, las fiestas
   de cumpleaños son para los niños ____
5. El 26 de julio es ____

a. el día de Santa Ana.
b. y sus amigos.
c. para celebrar el día del santo.
d. la tradición católica de España.
e. los invitados más importantes.

**PASO 3.** Entreviste a un compañero / una compañera con las preguntas. Luego, cambien de papel.

1. ¿Qué significado (*meaning*) tiene tu nombre? ¿Es el nombre de un santo? ¿de un pariente? ¿de una persona famosa?
2. ¿Cuándo hace fiestas tu familia?
3. ¿Cómo celebras tu cumpleaños? ¿Haces una fiesta con tu familia? ¿con tus amigos? ¿Dónde haces la fiesta?

## 4.2 Demonstrative Adjectives and Pronouns

*Expressing this, that, these, and those*

**GRAMÁTICA EN CONTEXTO**

### Esta es mi ciudad.

*La Coruña*

[*Terry visita a la familia de su amiga Sabela en La Coruña, Galicia. Esta tarde, Sabela y Terry pasean por el Paseo Marítimo y hablan de la familia y la ciudad de Sabela.*]

SABELA: Casi toda mi familia es del pueblo de Beo, pero ahora todos vivimos en **esta** ciudad. En **aquel** pueblo… bueno, en casi todos los pueblos de **esta** provincia, no hay muchas oportunidades para trabajar.

TERRY: Pero **esta** ciudad es maravillosa, ¿no? **Este** paseo es estupendo. Bordea toda la ciudad y las playas. ¿Cómo se llama **esa** playa en el centro que acabamos de pasar?

SABELA: **Esa** es la playa Orzán, la otra es Riazor.

TERRY: Y la torre…

SABELA: Sí, **aquella** torre es el símbolo de **esta** ciudad. Se llama la Torre de Hércules y es de los tiempos romanos. Tienes razón. **Esta** es una ciudad maravillosa. Y **este** verano, ¡tienes que volver para celebrar las Hogueras de San Juan! ¡**Ese** es el festival favorito de mi familia!

Comprensión. Empareje los lugares con las descripciones más lógicas.

1. ____ la Torre de Hércules
2. ____ la ciudad de La Coruña
3. ____ el festival de San Juan
4. ____ el Paseo Marítimo
5. ____ el pueblo de Beo
6. ____ las playas de Orzán y Riazor

a. Aquel es el más largo de Europa.
b. Ese es el favorito del verano.
c. Esta tiene más de 2.000 años.
d. Esas están en el centro.
e. Esta tiene muchas atracciones.
f. Aquel no tiene muchas oportunidades.

---

**GRAMÁTICA EN CONTEXTO** / ***This is My City.*** / *Terry visits the family of her friend Sabela in Galicia. This afternoon, Sabela and Terry stroll along the* Paseo Marítimo *and they're talking about Sabela's family and city. /* **SABELA:** *Almost all my family is from the town of Beo, but now we all live in this city. In that town . . . well, in almost all of the towns of this province, there are not many opportunities to work. /* **TERRY:** *But this city is marvelous, isn't it? This promenade is great. It skirts the whole city and the beaches. What is the name of that beach downtown that we just passed?* **SABELA:** *That is Orzán beach, and the other one is Riazor. /* **TERRY:** *And the tower . . . /* **SABELA:** *Yes, that tower over there is the symbol of this city. It's called the Tower of Hercules and it's from Roman times. You're right. This is a marvelous city. And this summer, you have to come back to celebrate the San Juan Bonfires! That is my family's favorite festival!*

**A.** Demonstrative adjectives express *this*, *that*, *these*, and *those*. In English, *this* and *these* refer to things that are close to the speaker, while *that* and *those* indicate things that are farther from the speaker. However, a further distinction is made in Spanish between things that are relatively far and those that are even farther away from the speaker. Like typical adjectives in Spanish, these adjectives also must agree in number and gender with the item that they describe. The following chart shows the forms of the demonstrative adjectives in Spanish. Note that the masculine singular forms do not end in **-o** like most other adjectives.

| DEMONSTRATIVE ADJECTIVES (*this, that, these,* and *those*) | | | | | |
|---|---|---|---|---|---|
| | SINGULAR | PLURAL | SINGULAR | PLURAL | SINGULAR | PLURAL |
| MASCULINE | **este** (*this*) | **estos** (*these*) | **ese** (*that*) | **esos** (*those*) | **aquel** (*that [way over there]*) | **aquellos** (*those [way over there]*) |
| FEMININE | **esta** (*this*) | **estas** (*these*) | **esa** (*that*) | **esas** (*those*) | **aquella** (*that [way over there]*) | **aquellas** (*those [way over there]*) |

—Isabel, **este** joven es mi primo Jorge.      *Isabel, this young man is my cousin Jorge.*

—**Esa** mujer alta es mi tía Pati.      *That tall woman is my aunt Pati.*

—¿Y quién es **aquel** hombre guapo?      *And who is that handsome man over there?*

**B.** Demonstratives can also be used as pronouns. The English equivalents are generally expressed with *one*, as in *this one* or *that one*. The forms of the pronouns are identical to the adjectives shown in the preceding chart and examples.

—Y tu hermano, ¿es **ese** hombre o **aquel**?      *And your brother. Is he that man or the one over there?*

—Es **ese. Aquel** es un amigo de la familia.      *He's that one. The one over there is a friend of the family.*

**C.** When *this* and *that* are referring to unknown objects or to an entire situation, the neuter pronouns **esto, eso,** and **aquello** are used.

¿Qué es **esto**?      *What is this?*

¡**Eso** es horrible!      *That's horrible!*

¿Qué es **aquello** que se ve allí?      *What is that over there?*

**A.** Estas familias. Indique qué familia describe cada oración.

1. _____ La hija de aquellos padres no tiene hermanos.
2. _____ Esa familia es grande.
3. _____ Este abuelo ayuda con sus nietos.
4. _____ Esos muchachos son gemelos.

5. _____ Estos padres necesitan ayuda porque trabajan.
6. _____ Aquella muchacha (*girl*) es hija única (*an only child*).

**B.** En una fiesta familiar. Complete los diálogos con los demostrativos correctos.

1. —Quiero hablar con tu primo, pero no sé quién es.
   —(*That*)[1] muchacho en el sofá es mi primo David. (*That* [*over there*])[2] muchacho cerca de la ventana es mi primo Esteban. ¿A cuál quieres conocer?

2. —(*This*)[3] fiesta es muy divertida. Gracias por invitarme.[a]
   —No hay de qué. (*This*)[4] noche, después de la fiesta, mis hermanos y yo vamos a salir a bailar. ¿Quieres ir con nosotros?
   —¡Claro! ¿Van a (*that* [*over there*])[5] discoteca nueva en el centro[b]?
   —Sí. La música que tocan allí es muy buena.

3. —¿Quiénes son (*those*)[6] hombres?
   —Son mis tíos, los hermanos de mi madre. No son de aquí.

4. —¡(*This*)[7] casa es muy grande y bonita! Es la casa de tus abuelos, ¿verdad?
   —Sí.
   —¿Y dónde están tus abuelos?
   —(*Those* [*over there*])[8] dos personas que están en la cocina son mis abuelos.

[a]*inviting me*  [b]*downtown*

Cultures  Recycle

**C.** La unidad (*unity*) de la familia vasca

**PASO 1.** Complete la lectura sobre las familias vascas con la forma correcta de las palabras entre paréntesis. Cuando *PP* aparece con un verbo, use el presente progresivo (**estar** + **-ando/-iendo**).

*Una pareja (couple) vasca vota con la ayuda (help) de sus hijos en unas elecciones regionales en Bilbao.*

Los vascos son un grupo étnico en España y Francia que viven en una región de Europa llamada el País Vasco. El País Vasco tradicionalmente comprende[a] siete provincias: cuatro en el norte[b] de España y tres en el sur[c] de Francia. La mayoría de los vascos vive en España. Por eso, (**mucho**[1]) personas asocian el vasco con España.

El origen de (**este**[2]) pueblo[d] y su idioma es un misterio. Sin embargo, los vascos comparten (**mucho**[3]) características culturales con las demás regiones españolas. Como el resto de los españoles, los vascos (**ser**[4]) muy unidos y (**ese**[5]) unidad se refleja en las familias, sobre todo, en prácticas sociales como las comidas.

Tradicionalmente, en España, la comida principal (**ser**[6]) entre las 2:00 y las 4:00 de (**el/la**[7]) tarde. Los hijos y el padre (**regresar**[8]) a casa, donde la madre, la sirvienta, o (**mucho**[9]) veces la abuela, tiene la comida preparada. Comen juntos y pasan (**ese**[10]) momentos conversando. (**Este**[11]) tradición (*PP:* **cambiar**[12]) poco a poco en las zonas urbanas, donde algunas compañías internacionales imponen[e] un horario[f] estadounidense. Sin embargo, las escuelas, los lugares de trabajo y muchos padres (**seguir**[13]) el horario tradicional y casi siempre la familia (**comer**[14]) y pasa tiempo junta.

Una diferencia entre el País Vasco y el resto de las regiones españolas respecto a la familia es que la tasa de natalidad[g] en el País Vasco (**ser**[15]) inferior a la media[h] española incluso a la media europea. (**Este**[16]) fenómeno se debe[i] en parte al desarrollo industrial de la sociedad vasca, muy superior al de otras regiones españolas. La industrialización ofrece más puestos[j] de trabajo para todos y la mujer vasca tiene más oportunidades en (**este**[17]) mercado laboral. Como consecuencia, las mujeres vascas tienden a[k] casarse cuando son mayores y, (**por/para**[18]) eso, tienen pocos hijos.

---

[a]incluye  [b]*north*  [c]*south*  [d]*people*  [e]*impose*  [f]*schedule*  [g]tasa... *birthrate*  [h]*mean*  [i]se... *is due*  [j]*positions*
[k]tienden... *tend*

**PASO 2.**  En parejas, contesten las preguntas.

1. ¿Qué importancia tienen las comidas en este país? ¿Son importantes para la unidad familiar?
2. En este país, ¿cuáles son algunas de las dificultades de las madres que quieren trabajar?

Communication

# Palabra escrita

## A comenzar

Communication

> **Selecting a Topic.** When selecting a topic to write about, keep in mind the following recommendations. First, choose a topic that interests you. Writing about a topic that interests students has proven to result in better writing samples. Second, write from your own personal experience whenever possible. This will reduce the amount of outside research you have to do. Third, choose a topic that's within the scope of your purpose. In other words, select a focused topic that doesn't force you to write a lot more than what is expected of you. If your topic is too broad, your composition could either be too long, or too confusing (lacking focus), or both. Remember: you don't want to lose your audience.

You are going to start the process of writing a brief composition that you will finalize in the **Palabra escrita: A finalizar** section of your *Manual de actividades*. The general topic of this composition is **La familia,** but you will choose the specific subtopic you want to write about. You can write a description of your family, a statement about what "family" means or what is important about family, an anecdote or description of a favorite relative, and so on. The purpose of your composition will be to tell the reader about the family-related topic you choose.

**A.** Lluvia de ideas. En parejas, hagan una lluvia de ideas sobre estos temas y otros que se les ocurran (*that come to mind*).

1. temas posibles sobre la familia
2. palabras o frases que describen a su familia
3. palabras o frases que describen a la familia ideal
4. palabras o frases que describen a su pariente favorito
5. la importancia de la familia
6. una definición de «la familia»
7. ¿ ?

**B.** A organizar sus ideas. Repase sus ideas e indique las que más le interesen a Ud. (*the ones that interest you most*). Luego, escoja un tema. Haga una lluvia de ideas sobre otros detalles que Ud. puede incluir. Organice sus ideas, compártalas (*share them*) con la clase y apunte otras ideas que se le ocurran durante el proceso.

**C.** A escribir. Ahora, haga el borrador de su composición con las ideas y la información que recopiló (*collected*) en las actividades A y B. **¡OJO!** Guarde bien su trabajo. Va a necesitarlo (*need it*) otra vez para la sección de **Palabra escrita: A finalizar** en el *Manual de actividades*.

# Diego Velázquez

Las meninas, *1656*

Diego Rodríguez de Silva y Velázquez (1599–1660) fue[a] el pintor principal en la corte del rey[b] Felipe IV. Es uno de los pintores más importantes del siglo XVII español.

    *Las meninas* es una obra representativa del Barroco español, un estilo conocido por los detalles y ornamentación. En el centro de este cuadro, se representa a la Infanta Margarita con dos meninas o damas de honor.[c] También vemos al pintor autorretratado[d] y a los reyes — Felipe IV y doña Mariana — reflejados en el espejo al fondo.[e]

---

[a]*was*  [b]*king*  [c]*damas… ladies-in-waiting*  [d]*in a self-portrait*  [e]*espejo… mirror in the background*

## Vocabulario del tema

### Otras relaciones familiares

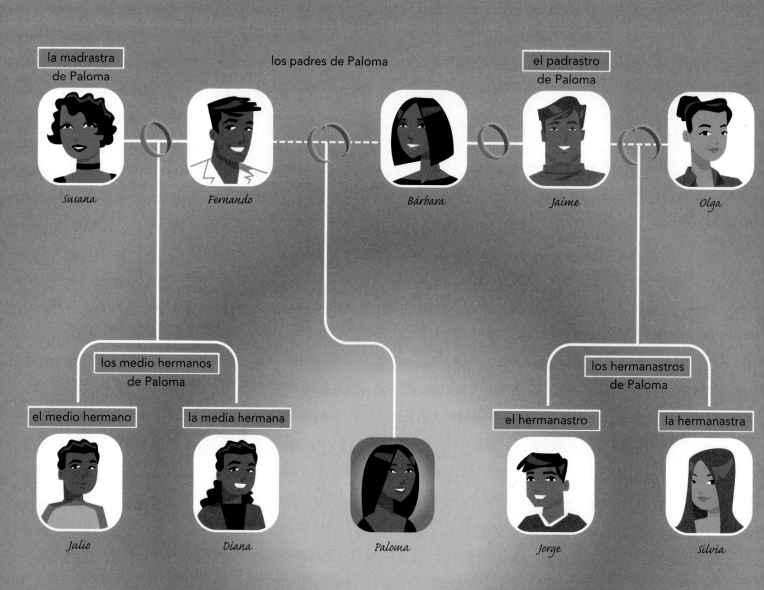

La familia de Paloma

la madrastra de Paloma

los padres de Paloma

el padrastro de Paloma

Susana

Fernando

Bárbara

Jaime

Olga

los medio hermanos de Paloma

los hermanastros de Paloma

el medio hermano

la media hermana

el hermanastro

la hermanastra

Julio

Diana

Paloma

Jorge

Silvia

Paloma es la hijastra de Susana y Jaime. Es la media hermana de Julio y Diana y la hermanastra de Jorge y Silvia.

| | |
|---|---|
| **el/la ahijado/a** | godson/goddaughter |
| **los /las gemelos/as** | twins |
| **el/la hijastra/o** | stepson/stepdaughter |
| **el/la hijo/a adoptivo/a** | adopted son/daughter |
| **el/la hijo/a único/a** | only child |
| **la madrina** | godmother |
| **el padrino** | godfather |
| **el/la primo/a segundo/a** | second cousin |

**Observe**

Some Spanish-speakers do not distinguish between **medio hermanos** (*half siblings*) and **hermanastros** (*stepsiblings*). They use **hermanastros** for both.

## Los eventos familiares

| | |
|---|---|
| **el bautizo** | baptism |
| **la boda** | wedding |
| **el cumpleaños** | birthday |
| **el divorcio** | divorce |
| **el matrimonio** | marriage; married couple |

**Cognado: la ceremonia civil**

## El estado civil°

°El... *Marital Status*

| | |
|---|---|
| **casado/a** | married |
| **divorciado/a** | divorced |
| **separado/a** | separated |
| **soltero/a** | single |
| **viudo/a** | widowed |

## ACTIVIDADES

**A.** Correcciones. Corrija las oraciones, según el dibujo (*drawing*) de la página 136.

1. Olga es la madrastra de Silvia.
2. Paloma tiene tres hermanastros.
3. Silvia es la hijastra de Susana.
4. Paloma y Jorge son medio hermanos.
5. Susana y Fernando están divorciados.

**B.** Definiciones

**PASO 1.** Empareje cada oración con la palabra o expresión definida.

1. ____ No tiene hermanos.
2. ____ Tiene ex esposo.
3. ____ Es una mujer con ahijado.
4. ____ Son hermanos que nacieron (*were born*) el mismo día.
5. ____ Su esposo ya murió (*has already died*).
6. ____ Tienen la misma madre pero sus padres son diferentes.
7. ____ No está casada y no tiene ex esposo.
8. ____ Vive con padres no biológicos.

a. divorciada
b. los gemelos
c. los medio hermanos
d. la hija adoptiva
e. el hijo único
f. la madrina
g. soltera
h. la viuda

**PASO 2.** Escoja cuatro palabras del **Vocabulario del tema** de los **Temas I** y **II** de este capítulo y escriba una definición en español para cada palabra. Puede usar las oraciones del **Paso 1** como modelo.

**PASO 3.** En parejas, túrnense (*take turns*) para leer las definiciones del **Paso 2** y adivinar qué palabras definen.

### C. Mis compadres

**PASO 1.** Lea la selección sobre los padrinos (*godparents*).

El compadrazgo[a] es una tradición en muchas familias hispanas. La costumbre de designar un padrino tiene orígenes cristianos y judíos. El padrino y la madrina participan en sacramentos religiosos, como el bautismo en la tradición cristiana y la circuncisión en la tradición judía, como también confirmaciones y bodas. Pero también participan en fiestas y otras celebraciones familiares. Son parte de la familia y los padres y padrinos tienen una relación especial: son compadres.

La idea es que los padres y los padrinos comparten la crianza[b] de un hijo. Los padrinos pueden ser parientes (tíos del ahijado, por ejemplo), pero en muchos casos, son buenos amigos de los padres. Un hijo o hija típicamente tiene dos padrinos: una madrina y un padrino. Pero pueden tener más.

---

[a]*co-parenthood*  [b]*upbringing*

**PASO 2.** ¿Cierto o falso? Corrija las oraciones falsas.

|  | C | F |
|---|---|---|
| 1. El compadrazgo es la tradición de adoptar hijos. | ☐ | ☐ |
| 2. La tradición del padrino no es exclusiva de los cristianos. | ☐ | ☐ |
| 3. El papel de los padrinos es estrictamente secular. | ☐ | ☐ |
| 4. A veces un ahijado o una ahijada tiene más de dos padrinos. | ☐ | ☐ |
| 5. Mi padrino es el compadre de mis padres. | ☐ | ☐ |

### D. Mi familia

**PASO 1.** Dibuje el árbol genealógico de su propia familia o de una familia imaginaria. Ponga espacios en blanco (*blank*) en vez de (*instead of*) los nombres de todos sus parientes. Ponga su propio nombre en el lugar correcto.

**PASO 2.** En parejas, intercambien los árboles genealógicos y túrnense para describir y nombrar los miembros de su familia. Cada persona debe tratar de llenar todos los espacios en blanco del árbol de la otra persona, según las descripciones que recibe.

**MODELO**  E1: Mi padre se llama Tom. Tiene cuarenta y cinco años.
E2: [*writes "Tom (45)" on the blank for E1's father*]
E1: Mis padres están divorciados y tengo una madrastra que se llama Lily. Lily tiene 53 años.
E2: [*writes the name "Lily (53)" on the blank for E1's stepmother*]

# Nota interdisciplinaria

Connections

## SOCIOLOGÍA: LA NUEVA FAMILIA ESPAÑOLA

*Una familia española*

La familia tradicional, formada por un hombre y una mujer casados y sus hijos, es el modelo más común en España, pero no es el único. Desde finales del siglo XX, nuevos tipos de familia conviven[a] con la familia clásica y gozan de[b] plena[c] aceptación social. Madres solteras, segundas o terceras parejas,[d] hijos adoptados de otros países del mundo, madres o padres separados con sus hijos, personas que viven solas o matrimonios mestizos entre españoles e inmigrantes han transformado[e] mucho la estructura familiar en España.

*Una madre soltera con su hija*

[a]*coexist*  [b]*enjoy*  [c]*total*  [d]segundas... *second or third spouses*  [e]han... *have transformed*

**PREGUNTAS** En parejas, contesten las preguntas. Después, compartan sus respuestas con la clase.

**1.** Según el texto, ¿cómo es la estructura de la familia tradicional española?

**2.** ¿Cuáles son algunos de los ejemplos de los nuevos modelos de familia en España?

## 4.3 Más/Menos... que...

**GRAMÁTICA EN CONTEXTO**

### Las familias de mis hijos

La Plaza de San Antonio, Cádiz

[*Trey, un estudiante estadounidense, vive con Eduardo y Flor y sus cuatro hijos en Cádiz, España. Esta tarde pasea por la Plaza de San Antonio con la abuela. La abuela habla de las familias de su hija Flor y de su hijo Vicente.*]

| | |
|---|---|
| ABUELA: | Vicente y su familia viven en Córdoba. Vicente es **mayor que** su hermana Flor. Tiene 45 años. Flor sólo tiene 39. Pero Vicente y su esposa Eva tienen **menos** hijos **que** Flor y Eduardo. Vicente sólo tiene dos hijos: una hija de 15 años y un hijo de 9 años. |
| TREY: | Interesante, porque Daniel, el hijo mayor de Flor, ya tiene 19 años. |
| ABUELA: | Vicente y Eva se casaron **más** tarde **que** Flor y Eduardo. Y a Flor le gusta tener una familia grande. Eva es **menos** hogareña **que** Flor. No quiere **más** de dos hijos. |
| TREY: | Pues, yo soy hijo único, así que las familias de sus hijos son **más** grandes **que** mi familia. |

### ¿CIERTO, FALSO O NO SE DICE (NSD)?

| | C | F | NSD |
|---|---|---|---|
| 1. La abuela tiene más hijos que su hijo Vicente. | ☐ | ☐ | ☐ |
| 2. El hijo de Vicente es mayor que el hijo mayor de Flor. | ☐ | ☐ | ☐ |
| 3. Flor es menor que Vicente. | ☐ | ☐ | ☐ |
| 4. Eva y Vicente tienen más años de casados que Flor y Eduardo. | ☐ | ☐ | ☐ |
| 5. Daniel es menor que Trey. | ☐ | ☐ | ☐ |

Speakers use comparisons to communicate that two (or more) persons or things have the same characteristic and they want to indicate which person or thing has more or less of the characteristic, or if they possess it equally. In Spanish, it is possible to compare adjectives, adverbs, nouns, and verbs.

**A.** When speakers want to say that a person or thing has more or less of a characteristic than another person or thing, they use the formula **más/menos** + *adj./adv.* + **que**.

Generalmente, la sociedad mexicana es más conservadora que la sociedad española.

*Generally, Mexican society is more conservative than Spanish society.*

En España probablemente la gente vive menos religiosamente que en Latinoamérica.

*In Spain, people probably live less religiously than in Latin America.*

---

**GRAMÁTICA EN CONTEXTO** *My Children's Families* / Trey, an American student, lives with Eduardo and Flor and their four children in Cádiz, Spain. This afternoon, he's strolling through the San Antonio Plaza with the grandmother. The grandmother talks about the families of her daughter Flor and her son Vicente. / **ABUELA:** Vicente and his family live in Córdoba. Vicente is older than his sister Flor. He's 45. Flor is only 39. But Vicente and his wife Eva have fewer children than Flor and Eduardo. Vicente only has two children: a 15-year-old daughter and a 9-year-old son. / **TREY:** Interesting, because Daniel, Flores's older son, is already 19. / **ABUELA:** Vicente and Eva married later than Flor and Eduardo. And Flor likes having a large family. Eva is less domestic than Flor. She doesn't want more than two children. / **TREY:** Well, I'm an only child, so your children's two families are bigger than my family.

**B.** When speakers want to say that two or more nouns are not equal, they use the formula **más/menos** + *noun* + **que.**

En España **más** adultos viven con sus padres **que** en este país.

*In Spain, more adults live with their parents than in this country.*

**Observe**

Use **más/menos de** when making a comparison that includes a quantity or numeric amount.

Hay **más de cien** personas aquí, y **menos de la mitad** sabe de qué hablamos.

*There are more than a hundred people here, and less than half (of them) know what we're talking about.*

**C.** When speakers want to say that two actions are unequal in some way, they use the formula *verb* + **más/menos** + **que.**

Hoy en España las mujeres se dedican **menos** al hogar **que** en el pasado.

*Today in Spain women dedicate themselves to the home less than in the past.*

**D.** Some comparative forms of inequality do not follow the **más/menos** + *adj./adv.* + **que** pattern. There are two special comparative forms for age: **mayor que** (*older*) and **menor que** (*younger*). Also, *better than* and *worse than* are expressed with the words **mejor que** and **peor que.**

Mi abuelo paterno es **mayor** que mi abuelo materno.

*My paternal grandfather is older than my maternal grandfather.*

Nuestra tía Rosa es **menor que** nuestra tía Berta.

*Our aunt Rosa is younger than our aunt Berta.*

Nuestra nueva casa es **mejor que** la antigua.

*Our new house is better than the old one.*

El barrio de ellos está **peor que** antes.

*Their neighborhood is worse than (it was) before.*

## ACTIVIDADES

**A. ¡Más que tú!** Indicate the correct word to complete the sentence for you. The answers you choose should be logical for the sentence and true for you. The words may be used more than once.

1. Este semestre paso ___ tiempo con mis amigos que el semestre pasado (*last*).
2. Mi mejor amigo es ___ que yo.
3. Mi madre es ___ paciente que mi padre.
4. Los gatos son ___ cariñosos que los perros.
5. Estoy ___ cansado/a en la noche que en la mañana.
6. Mis notas (*grades*) son ___ este semestre que el semestre pasado.
7. Mi abuelo es ___ que mi abuela.
8. Tengo ___ libros que el profesor / la profesora.
9. Trabajo ___ que mis padres.
10. Soy ___ responsable este año que el año pasado.

a. más
b. menos
c. mejor
d. mejores
e. peor
f. peores
g. mayor
h. mayores
i. menor
j. menores

Communication

**B.** Encuesta

**PASO 1.** Circulate and ask your classmates these questions. Ask at least three different students each question.

1. ¿Cuántos hermanos tienes?
2. ¿Cuántas mascotas tienes?
3. ¿Cuántas horas estudias los fines de semana?
4. ¿Cuántas clases tomas este semestre?
5. ¿Cuántas horas trabajas por semana?
6. ¿Cuántos años tienes?

**PASO 2.** Comparta sus resultados del **Paso 1** con la clase como en el modelo.

**MODELO** Angie es mayor que Ryan.

**C.** ¡¿Vives con tus padres?!

Cultures

Recycle

**PASO 1.** Complete the conversation between Jesús and Wendy with the correct form of the words in parentheses. When cues for comparatives are given, use the corresponding comparative forms. ¡**OJO!** You may need to use the irregular forms **mejor, peor, mayor,** and **menor** for some items. A "+" sign means "*more than;*" a "−" sign means "*less/fewer than.*"

*En la Universidad de Sevilla*

WENDY: Jesús, ¿quieres tomar un café?

JESÚS: Claro. ¡Te invito!

WENDY: Ah, es decir[a] que tú vas a pagar por el café, ¿verdad? ¡Ahora, después de cuatro semanas aquí, (*yo:* **entender**[1]) esa expresión!

JESÚS: Es verdad. Hablas español mucho (+ **bueno**[2]) que el mes pasado.

WENDY: Pues,[b] ¡gracias! Y acepto el café. ¿Qué (*tú:* **hacer**[3]) esta tarde?

JESÚS: (*Yo:* **Tener**[4]) que pasar por mi casa y luego (*yo:* **ir**[5]) a la biblioteca para buscar unos libros. Mis clases son (+ **difícil**[6]) que nunca[c] este año.

WENDY: ¿Tu apartamento (**quedar**[7]) cerca de aquí?

---

[a]es... *that is to say*   [b]*Well*   [c]*ever*

JESÚS: Bueno, vivo con (**mi**[8]) padres. Tienen un piso[d] cerca del centro.

WENDY: ¿(*Tú:* **Vivir**[9]) con tus padres?

JESÚS: Pues, claro.

WENDY: Pero tú eres (+ *edad*[10]) que yo. Tienes 24 años, ¿no?

JESÚS: Sí, pero aquí en España es normal vivir con los padres a mi edad cuando estudias o trabajas en la misma ciudad. Mi hermana (**tener**[11]) 30 años y (**vivir**[12]) con mis padres también.

WENDY: ¡Guau! ¡Los padres españoles deben ser (+ **paciente**[13]) que los padres en mi país!

JESÚS: No es cuestión[e] de paciencia. Para nosotros, es (− **práctico**[14]) vivir en un apartamento durante los estudios universitarios.

WENDY: Yo sé que en mi país la economía está (+ **mal**[15]) que antes y son más los estudiantes que viven con sus padres, pero todavía es (+ **común**[16]) vivir en una residencia o en un apartamento. En mi país, somos (+ **independiente**[17]) que los estudiantes españoles.

JESÚS: Pues, no estoy de acuerdo con eso. No somos (− **independiente**[18]) que vosotros por vivir con nuestros padres. Y (**vuestro**[19]) familias no son (− **unido**[20]) que las nuestras por salir de casa a los 18 años. Tenemos costumbres diferentes. Es todo.

_____
[d]*flat* [e]*matter*

**PASO 2.** Indique si las oraciones son ciertas (**C**) o falsas (**F**), según el **Paso 1.** Corrija las oraciones falsas.

|  | C | F |
|---|---|---|
| **1.** Wendy habla español mejor que Jesús. | ☐ | ☐ |
| **2.** Las clases de Jesús este semestre son menos fáciles que el semestre pasado. | ☐ | ☐ |
| **3.** Wendy es menor que Jesús. | ☐ | ☐ |
| **4.** Según Jesús, las familias españolas son más grandes que las familias de este país. | ☐ | ☐ |
| **5.** Los estudiantes de este país son menos dependientes que los estudiantes de España. | ☐ | ☐ |
| **6.** En este país, la economía está mejor que antes. | ☐ | ☐ |

**PASO 3.** En parejas, contesten las preguntas.

1. ¿Dónde viven Uds.? ¿Viven con sus padres, en un apartamento o en una residencia? Expliquen por qué.

2. ¿Qué piensan de la siguiente idea?: Los estudiantes que viven en un apartamento con amigos son más independientes que los estudiantes que viven con sus padres. ¿Están de acuerdo? Expliquen sus respuestas.

3. ¿Cuántos adultos que viven con sus padres conocen Uds.? ¿Por qué viven con ellos?

Communication

# Nota cultural

## DON QUIJOTE DE LA MANCHA

*Don Quijote y Sancho Panza*

*Don Quijote de la Mancha* (1605), del escritor español Miguel de Cervantes (1547–1616), narra la historia de Don Quijote, un hidalgo enloquecido[a] por la lectura de libros de caballería.[b] Se cree un caballero andante[c] y decide salir de su pueblo con su vecino[d] Sancho Panza para luchar contra[e] las injusticias. Don Quijote idealiza la realidad a la manera de los libros de caballería y en sus viajes le ocurren muchas aventuras cómicas, como la famosa lucha contra los gigantes[f] que, en realidad, son molinos de viento.[g] Sus aventuras siempre terminan en humillación para Don Quijote. La novela es una parodia divertida de la literatura caballeresca,[h] pero el personaje de Don Quijote simboliza también el idealismo y la lucha contra la realidad hostil.

La novela es considerada una obra maestra de la literatura española y universal y ha tenido[i] una enorme influencia en el mundo del arte y la cultura de todo el mundo. Vemos la presencia de Don Quijote en la literatura, en el cine, en obras musicales, en la pintura y en la escultura. Además, la palabra **quijote** es hoy parte de la lengua española y es sinónimo de **idealista** o **poco práctico**. Don Quijote trasciende la ficción y para muchos españoles, es un personaje real que continúa vivo.

---

[a]hidalgo... *crazed country gentleman* [b]*chivalry* [c]caballero... *knight-errant* [d]*neighbor* [e]luchar... *to fight against* [f]*giants* [g]molinos... *windmills* [h]literatura... *chivalresque literature* [i]ha... *has had*

**PREGUNTAS** En parejas, contesten las preguntas. Después, compartan sus ideas con la clase.

1. ¿Por qué está loco Don Quijote?
2. ¿Qué detalle del texto indica que Don Quijote es idealista?
3. ¿Conocen Uds. héroes de ficción que luchan por causas nobles? ¿Cuál(es)?

## 4.4 Tan, tanto/a/os/as... como...

Making Comparisons of Equality

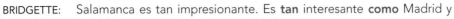

### Salamanca

*[Joe y Bridgette estudian un año en la Universidad de Salamanca. Hablan con su amigo español, Miguel.]*

**La Plaza Mayor de Salamanca**

| | |
|---|---|
| BRIDGETTE: | Salamanca es tan impresionante. Es **tan** interesante **como** Madrid y Barcelona. |
| MIGUEL: | ¡Más! Yo creo que es más interesante. |
| JOE: | Y tiene **tanta** importancia histórica **como** las ciudades mayores de España. La Plaza Mayor de Salamanca es **tan** importante **como** las plazas de Madrid. |
| MIGUEL: | Es verdad. No tenemos **tantas** plazas **como** Madrid, pero la Plaza de España y la Plaza Mayor de Madrid no son **tan** bonitas **como** nuestra Plaza Mayor. |
| BRIDGETTE: | Y las otras universidades de España no tienen **tanta** fama **como** vuestra universidad. |
| JOE: | Pero, ¡las clases son exigentes! En la Universidad de Toronto, nunca estudio **tanto como** tengo que estudiar aquí. |
| BRIDGETTE: | ¡No es verdad! Yo trabajo **tanto como** antes. Pero en Canadá, no tenemos **tantas** distracciones **como** aquí. Siempre estamos de excursión porque hay tantas atracciones interesantes. |

Comprensión. Empareje las frases de las dos columnas para formar oraciones lógicas.

1. La Plaza Mayor de Salamanca es ____ la Plaza de España.
2. Las clases de la Universidad de Salamanca son ____ las de Toronto.
3. Salamanca no tiene ____ Madrid.
4. La historia de Salamanca es ____ la de Barcelona.
5. Joe no estudia ____ Bridgette.

   **a.** tan bonita como
   **b.** tantos habitantes (*inhabitants*) como
   **c.** tanto como
   **d.** tan larga como
   **e.** tan difíciles como

---

**A.** When speakers want to say that a person or thing has as much of a characteristic as another person or thing, they use the formula **tan** + *adj./adv.* + **como.**

| | |
|---|---|
| Creo que los museos de arte son **tan** interesantes **como** los museos de historia. Visito los museos de historia **tan** frecuentemente **como** los de arte. | *I think art museums are as interesting as history museums. I visit history museums as frequently as art museums.* |

---

GRAMÁTICA EN CONTEXTO **Salamanca** / Joe and Bridgette are studying for a year at the University of Salamanca. They are talking to their Spanish friend, Miguel. / **BRIDGETTE:** Salamanca is so impressive. It's as interesting as Madrid and Barcelona. / **MIGUEL:** More! I think it's more interesting. / **JOE:** And it has as much historical importance as the larger cities of Spain. The Plaza Mayor of Salamanca is as important as the plazas in Madrid. / **MIGUEL:** It's true. We don't have as many plazas as Madrid, but the Plaza de España and the Plaza Mayor in Madrid are not as pretty as our Plaza Mayor. / **BRIDGETTE:** And the other universities in Spain aren't as famous as your university. / **JOE:** But the classes are demanding! At the University of Toronto, I never study as much as I have to study here. / **BRIDGETTE:** That's not true! I work as much as before. But in Canada, we don't have as many distractions as here. We're always on an outing because there are so many interesting attractions.

**B.** When speakers want to say that two or more nouns are equal in quantity, they use the formula **tanto/tanta/tantos/tantas** + *noun* + **como.** Note that **tanto,** as an adjective, must agree in number and gender with the noun that is being compared.

En España existen **tantas** estructuras familiares alternativas **como** en este país.

*In Spain, as many alternative family structures exist as in this country.*

**C.** When speakers want to say that two actions are equal in some way, they use the phrase **tanto como.**

Mis hermanos estudian **tanto como** yo.
A los jóvenes españoles les gusta salir con sus amigos **tanto como** a los jóvenes de este país.

*My siblings study as much as I do.*
*Spanish young people like to go out with their friends as much as youth in this country.*

---

## Nota comunicativa

Communication

### SUPERLATIVES

When we refer to something in English as the biggest, fastest, smallest, best, worst, and so on, we are expressing superlatives. In Spanish, superlatives are very similar in structure to comparisons. The only differences are the inclusion of a definite article (**el, la, los, las**) and an optional expression with **de** that expresses the group to which the subject is being compared. Compare the following sentences. The first is a typical comparison and the second a typical superlative.

Mi tío Arnoldo es **más alto que** mi tío Federico.

*My uncle Arnoldo is taller than my uncle Federico.*

Mi tío Arnoldo es **la persona más alta de** la familia.

*My uncle Arnoldo is the tallest person in the family.*

Often, the expression with **de** is not included if the context is already clear.

El fútbol es el **deporte más popular** (del mundo).

*Soccer is the most popular sport (in the world).*

Rusia es **el país más grande** (del mundo).

*Russia is the largest country (in the world).*

---

CAPÍTULO 4 ¿Cómo es su familia?

## Nota comunicativa

**Communication**

### -ísimo/a

One way of expressing extremes in Spanish is with the word **muy** (*very*).

Su primo Rogelio es **muy** inteligente.     *Her cousin Rogelio is very inteligent.*

To emphasize even more, you may string together multiple uses of **muy** or, for variety, you may use the suffix **-ísimo/a** attached to an adjective or adverb.

Mi abuela es muy, muy vieja. = Mi abuela es **viejísima.**
*My grandmother is very, very old.*

El pastel de cumpleaños es muy, muy delicioso. = El pastel de cumpleaños
  es **deliciosísimo.**
*The birthday cake is very, very delicious.*

As always with adjectives in Spanish, the ending **-ísimo/a** must agree in number and gender with the noun it modifies. Also, the formation of these words depends on the ending of the original adjective.

If the adjective ends in a consonant, the **-ísimo/a** ending is directly attached:
  **difícil → dificilísimo/a.**

If the adjective ends in a vowel, the vowel is dropped before adding the ending: **inteligente → inteligentísimo/a.**

If the final consonant of an adjective root is **c, g,** or **z,** spelling changes must be made to maintain the original sound: **rico → riquísimo; largo → larguísimo; feliz → felicísimo.**

---

### ACTIVIDADES

**A. Mi familia.** Indique qué oraciones describen su familia.

1. ☐ Mi padre trabaja tantas horas como mi madre.
2. ☐ Comemos juntos tanto como solos (*alone*).
3. ☐ Paso tanto tiempo con mi familia como con mis amigos.
4. ☐ Hablo con mi hija tanto como con mi hijo.
5. ☐ Mis amigos son tan importantes como mi familia.
6. ☐ Mis hermanos me ayudan (*help me*) tanto como mis tíos.
7. ☐ Tengo tantos tíos como abuelos.
8. ☐ Mi abuelo paterno es tan viejo como mi abuela materna.

**B. Unos chicos españoles.** Haga comparaciones de igualdad usando **tan, tanto/a/os/ as... como,** según la información en la tabla.

**MODELOS**  Isabel habla tantos idiomas como Teresa.
        Isabel no recibe tantos e-mails como Lucía.

|  | ISABEL | TERESA | LUCÍA | MANOLO |
|---|---|---|---|---|
| **1.** idiomas que habla | 1 | 1 | 2 | 2 |
| **2.** e-mails que recibe cada día | 5 | 13 | 15 | 13 |
| **3.** hermanas que tiene | 3 | 1 | 2 | 2 |
| **4.** películas que ve cada año | 5 | 20 | 20 | 50 |
| **5.** edad (años) | 20 | 20 | 25 | 28 |

**C. Entrevista.** En parejas, entrevístense sobre sus familias. Usen las oraciones y preguntas para empezar.

1. Yo tengo ___ hermanos. ¿Tienes tantos hermanos como yo? ¿Cuántos hermanos y cuántas hermanas tienes? ¿Cómo se llaman? ¿Son mayores o menores que tú?

2. Yo tengo ___ mascotas. ¿Tienes tantas mascotas como yo? ¿Qué tipo de mascotas tienes? ¿Cuántos años tiene(n)? Mi perro/gato es ___ que tu ___.

3. Yo sólo tengo ___ abuelo(s) vivo(s) y tiene(n) ___ años. ¿Tienes tantos abuelos como yo? ¿Son tan viejos como mis abuelos? ¿Dónde viven?

**D.** Las tradiciones de mi familia

**PASO 1.** Complete the conversation in which Wendy and Jesús continue to talk about families with the correct form of the words in parentheses. For verbs with the cue *PP*, give the present progressive form (**-ando/-iendo**). When cues for comparatives are given, use the corresponding comparative forms. **¡OJO!** You may need to use the irregular forms **mejor, peor, mayor,** and **menor** for some items.

*Una niña baila flamenco después de su primera comunión.*

WENDY: Tienes razón. Tenemos que tener en cuenta[a] que, aunque tenemos costumbres diferentes, las costumbres de un país son (= **válido**[1]) (**como/que**[2]) las costumbres de otro.

JESÚS: Así es. En nuestro país, algunas tradiciones familiares están (*PP:* **cambiar**[3]) porque ya no[b] es (= **fácil**[4]) encontrar trabajo en la ciudad de uno como en el pasado.

WENDY: Pero creo que son más las familias (**español**[5]) que siguen (*PP:* **ser**[6]) unidas.

JESÚS: Bueno, sí. Las familias extendidas en tu país no se reúnen[c] tanto (**como/que**[7]) las familias de España. Y creo que la familia nuclear también (**hacer**[8]) más cosas juntas aquí. Como (*tú:* **saber**[9]), la familia española come junta (**por/para**[10]) lo menos una vez casi todos los días y los parientes (**asistir**[11]) a casi todas las celebraciones, cumpleaños, aniversarios, días festivos... todo. Para las vacaciones, muchos hijos adultos (**ir**[12]) con (**su**[13]) padres, incluyendo a veces a los abuelos también, a pasar tres o cuatro semanas en la playa[d] o en las montañas.[e]

WENDY: ¡Qué divertido! En mi familia no pasamos (= **tiempo**[14]) juntos. Mi hermano (+ *edad*[15]) nunca[f] pasa las vacaciones con nosotros, ni[g] viene a nuestras fiestas. No vive muy lejos, pero ahora pasa (+ **tiempo**[16]) con su novia y con sus amigos (**como/que**[17]) con nosotros. Pero en mi familia sí comemos y hacemos algunas actividades juntos. Pero yo probablemente no paso con mi familia (= **tanto**[18]) tiempo (**como/que**[19]) tú.

JESÚS: Es una costumbre diferente, y aunque yo prefiero nuestra costumbre de pasar tiempo con mis padres y mis hermanos, las dos costumbres (**tener**[20]) igual valor.[h]

[a]tener... *keep in mind*  [b]ya... *no longer*  [c]se... *get together*  [d]*beach*  [e]*mountains*  [f]*never*  [g]*nor*  [h]*value*

**PASO 2.** Indique las palabras correctas para completar las oraciones, según el **Paso 1.**

1. Las costumbres de mi país son ___ válidas ___ las costumbres de tu país.
   **a.** tanta / como   **b.** más / que   **c.** menos / que   **d.** tan / como

2. En España, es ___ difícil ___ antes encontrar trabajo en la ciudad de uno.
   **a.** tan / como   **b.** más / que   **c.** menos / que   **d.** tanta / como

3. Las familias nucleares en España típicamente hacen ___ cosas juntas ___ en este país.
   **a.** tantas / como   **b.** más / que   **c.** menos / que   **d.** tanto / como

4. Wendy pasa ___ tiempo con su familia ___ Jesús.
   a. tanta / como    b. más / que    c. menos / que    d. tanto / como
5. Jesús cree que las costumbres de este país tienen ___ valor ___ las de su país.
   a. tanto / como    b. más / que    c. menos / que    d. tantas / como

PASO 3. En parejas, contesten las preguntas.

Communication

1. ¿Qué actividades hacen Uds. con su familia?
2. ¿Cuántas veces por año pasan tiempo con su familia extendida? ¿Qué hacen juntos?
3. Para Uds., ¿por qué es importante pasar tiempo con su familia? Si no es importante para Uds., ¿con quién es importante pasar tiempo?

# Lectura cultural

Ud. va a leer un artículo publicado en la sección **Mi mundo** de la revista *Siempre mujer*. El artículo informa sobre una encuesta realizada por la revista *Time*. Habla de los cambios recientes en los roles familiares del hombre y de la mujer, como consecuencia de la incorporación de la mujer al mundo del trabajo.

Cultures

### ANTES DE LEER

En parejas, contesten las preguntas. Después compartan sus ideas con la clase.

1. Piensen en sus familias y en la familia típica de su comunidad. ¿Quién tiene mayor responsabilidad de cuidar de la casa y de los hijos?
2. ¿Qué miembros de su familia trabajan fuera de la casa? ¿Tienen un trabajo a tiempo completo (*full time*) o a tiempo parcial? ¿Y cuál es la situación en otras familias que Uds. conocen bien?
3. En general en su comunidad, ¿quién cuida de la casa y de los hijos si la mamá y el papá tienen un trabajo a tiempo completo fuera de la casa?

## Los nuevos roles familiares

¿La mujer trabaja y el hombre cuida los niños? Claro que sí.[a] Hoy en día, las relaciones de pareja son una constante negociación.

No es una sorpresa que cada vez sean[b] más las mujeres que trabajan, sobre todo en estos tiempos de crisis económica, cuando cualquier aporte salarial[c] es bien recibido.

Según un estudio realizado por la revista *Time:*

- En 1970 la mayoría de los niños creció[d] bajo el cuidado de sus madres, quienes eran[e] amas de casa. Hoy en día, sólo el 30 por ciento puede decir lo mismo.

[a]Claro... *Of course*  [b]*there are*  [c]cualquier... *any financial contributions*  [d]*grew up*  [e]*were*

- Sin embargo, ante la sociedad, la mujer sigue siendo la responsable de la crianza[f] de los chicos.

- El 44 por ciento de las mujeres encuestadas no estuvo de acuerdo con que fuera[g] el hombre quien trabajara fuera de la casa y la mujer quien se encargara[h] de los hijos, mientras que el 57 por ciento de los hombres estuvo de acuerdo.[i]

- En cuanto a las prioridades en la vida femenina, la mayoría de las mujeres dijo[j] que estar saludables,[k] ser autosuficientes, tener solvencia económica y un trabajo a tiempo completo era lo más importante para ellas.

- Para los hombres, la salud, el trabajo, la casa y el dinero son igualmente importantes, pero en menor escala. Esto indica que ahora los roles familiares son compartidos.

- Además, el 85 por ciento de las mujeres dijo sentirse cómodas[l] de trabajar fuera de la casa, y el 79 por ciento de los hombres dijo que ahora está mucho mejor visto y más aceptado que ellos se encarguen del hogar, mientras que[m] ellas trabajan.

*__Fuente:__*[n] *Estudio* What Women Want Now, *publicado en la revista* Time.

---

[f]*raising*   [g]*no estuvo... did not agree that it was*   [h]*se... was in charge*   [i]*estuvo... agreed*   [j]*said*   [k]*healthy*
[l]*dijo... said they felt comfortable*   [m]*mientras... while*   [n]*Source*

## DESPUÉS DE LEER

**A.** ¿Cierto o falso? Indique si las oraciones son ciertas (**C**) o falsas (**F**). Corrija las oraciones falsas con información específica del artículo.

|  | C | F |
|---|---|---|
| 1. Hasta los años 70 la mayoría de las mujeres era (*were*) ama de casa. | ☐ | ☐ |
| 2. En estos tiempos, sólo un 30 por ciento de las mujeres cuida del hogar y de los niños. | ☐ | ☐ |
| 3. Hoy día, los hombres y las mujeres tienen prioridades diferentes en la vida. | ☐ | ☐ |
| 4. A las mujeres de hoy no les gusta trabajar fuera de casa, pero necesitan el dinero. | ☐ | ☐ |
| 5. El hombre de hoy día acepta más cuidar del hogar que en el pasado. | ☐ | ☐ |

**B.** Temas de discusión. En grupos pequeños, contesten las preguntas. Después, compartan sus respuestas con la clase.

1. ¿Qué prioridades tienen los hombres y las mujeres de hoy, según el artículo?
2. El texto sugiere (*suggests*) que la mujer trabaja fuera de casa y es la responsable del hogar y la familia. Según sus propias experiencias, ¿ocurre lo mismo en su comunidad? Expliquen.
3. ¿Piensan Uds. que hoy día los hombres se encargan del hogar y de los hijos más que en el pasado?
4. En su opinión, ¿qué piensa la sociedad, en general, de un hombre que cuida del hogar mientras su esposa trabaja fuera de la casa?
5. Imagínense (*Imagine*) su futuro. ¿Les gustaría (*Would you like*) cuidar de su casa y de sus hijos y no tener profesión? ¿Son similares las respuestas de los hombres de la clase a las de las mujeres?

# España: Ana

## La vida familiar en Granada

Cultures

Ana Gallego es de Granada, España, y trabaja en teatro y televisión. En su blog conocemos su preciosa ciudad y aprendemos sobre la familia española.

### ANTES DE VER

Conteste las preguntas.

1. Según lo que Ud. ya sabe, ¿cómo es la familia típica española de hoy?
2. ¿Cómo se compara la familia española con su propia familia?

### Vocabulario práctico

**Parque García Lorca**

| | | | |
|---|---|---|---|
| **mostraros** | show you | **¡pues anda que tú!** | look who's talking! |
| **homenaje** | honor | **basta ya** | stop, that's enough |
| **bienvenidos** | welcome | **tener la fiesta en paz** | live in peace |

### DESPUÉS DE VER

**A.** Comprensión. Indique si las oraciones son ciertas (**C**) o falsas (**F**), según el blog de Ana. Corrija las oraciones falsas.

|  | C | F |
|---|---|---|
| 1. El segmento comienza en un parque famoso de Granada. | ☐ | ☐ |
| 2. Ana habla de la vida rural y la vida urbana. | ☐ | ☐ |
| 3. En el parque hay una gran variedad de flores y árboles. | ☐ | ☐ |
| 4. García Lorca es un director de cine español. | ☐ | ☐ |
| 5. Concha y Miguel son profesores de matemáticas. | ☐ | ☐ |
| 6. Concha habla de sus hijos y sus padres. | ☐ | ☐ |
| 7. Ana no conoce a Carlos ni a Julia. | ☐ | ☐ |

**B.** Temas de discusión. En parejas, contesten las preguntas. Después, compartan sus ideas con la clase.

Communication

1. ¿Creen Uds. que la familia de Concha y Miguel es una familia típica en España? Expliquen.
2. ¿Cómo es la relación entre los miembros de la familia que visita Ana?
3. Contesten la pregunta que Ana hace al final de su *blog*: ¿Es parecida la familia de Concha y Miguel a su propia familia? Mencionen algunas semejanzas y diferencias.

# Vocabulario

## Las relaciones familiares — Family Relationships

| | |
|---|---|
| el/la abuelo/a | grandfather/grandmother |
| los abuelos | grandparents |
| el/la ahijado/a | godson/goddaughter |
| el/la esposo/a | husband/wife |
| el/la gemelo/a | twin |
| el/la hermanastro/a | stepbrother/stepsister |
| el/la hermano/a | brother/sister |
| los hermanos | siblings |
| el/la hijastro/a | stepson/stepdaughter |
| el/la hijo/a | son/daughter |
| el/la hijo/a adoptivo/a | adopted son/daughter |
| el/la hijo/a único/a | only child |
| los hijos | children |
| la madrastra | stepmother |
| la madre | mother |
| la madrina | godmother |
| el/la medio/a hermano/a | half brother/sister |
| el/la nieto/a | grandson/granddaughter |
| los nietos | grandchildren |
| el padrastro | stepfather |
| el padre | father |
| los padres | parents |
| el padrino | godfather |
| los padrinos | godparents |
| el pariente | relative |
| el/la primo/a | cousin |
| el/la primo/a segundo/a | second cousin |
| el/la sobrino/a | nephew/niece |
| los sobrinos | nephews and nieces |
| el/la tío/a | uncle/aunt |
| los tíos | aunts and uncles |

## La familia política — In-Laws

| | |
|---|---|
| el/la cuñado/a | brother-in-law/sister-in-law |
| la nuera | daughter-in-law |
| el/la suegro/a | father-in-law/mother-in-law |
| el yerno | son-in-law |

## Las mascotas — Pets

| | |
|---|---|
| el gato | cat |

Repaso: el perro

## Los números a partir de 100

cien, ciento uno, ciento dos, ciento tres,... ciento noventa y nueve
doscientos/as, trescientos/as, cuatrocientos/as, quinientos/as, seiscientos/as, setecientos/as, ochocientos/as, novecientos/as
mil, dos mil,...
un millón (de), dos millones (de),...

## Para describir a la gente

| | |
|---|---|
| cariñoso/a | affectionate |
| delgado/a | thin |
| gordo/a | fat |
| hermoso/a | pretty |
| jubilado/a | retired |
| listo/a | smart |
| orgulloso/a | proud |
| torpe | clumsy |
| tranquilo/a | calm |
| travieso/a | mischievous |
| unido/a | close (relationship) |
| viejo/a | old |

Cognados: extrovertido/a, obediente, responsable
Repaso: alto/a, bajo/a, bonito/a, bueno/a, feo/a, guapo/a, joven (jóvenes), moreno/a, nervioso/a, pelirrojo/a, perezoso/a, rubio/a, trabajador(a)

## Los eventos familiares

| | |
|---|---|
| el bautizo | baptism |
| la boda | wedding |
| el cumpleaños | birthday |
| el divorcio | divorce |
| el matrimonio | marriage; married couple |

Cognado: la ceremonia civil

## El estado civil — Marital Status

| | |
|---|---|
| casado/a | married |
| divorciado/a | divorced |
| separado/a | separated |
| soltero/a | single |
| viudo/a | widowed |

## Otras palabras y expresiones

| | |
|---|---|
| para | for; toward |
| para + inf. | in order to (do something) |
| por | in; by; by means of; through; along |
| por ejemplo | for example |
| por eso | that's why |
| por favor | please |
| por fin | finally |
| por lo general | generally |
| por lo menos | at least |

## Los demostrativos — Demonstratives

| | |
|---|---|
| este/a | this (one) |
| estos/as | these (one) |
| ese/a | that (ones) |
| esos/as | those (ones) |
| aquel, aquella | that (one) over there |
| aquellos/as | those (ones) over there |
| esto | this (concept, unknown thing) |
| eso, aquello | that (concept, unknown thing) |

## Las comparaciones — Comparisons

| | |
|---|---|
| más/menos... que | more/less . . . than |
| mayor/menor que | older/younger than |
| tan, tanto/as/os/as... como | as . . . as |
| el/la/los/las más/menos... de | the most/least . . . of/in |

# ¡Hogar, dulce hogar!*

*Una calle de Frigiliana, uno de los Pueblos Blancos de Andalucía*

1. ¿Cómo son las viviendas (*dwellings*) en la región donde Ud. vive?
2. ¿Dónde vive durante el año académico, en una casa, en una residencia estudiantil, en un edificio de apartamentos? ¿en otro lugar?
3. ¿Qué parte de su casa o apartamento le gusta más? ¿por qué?

www.connectspanish.com

*Hogar… *Home, Sweet Home!*

153

# TEMA I: ¿Hay una vivienda típica?

## Vocabulario del tema

### Las viviendas

① el barrio / el vecindario

la calle

la casa

el jardín

② la casa adosada

la cochera

el coche

③ el estudio

el edificio de apartamentos

el piso / el apartamento

④ el noveno piso

el bloque de pisos

el balcón

el segundo piso

el primer piso

la planta baja

**154** ciento cincuenta y cuatro

CAPÍTULO 5 ¡Hogar, dulce hogar!

| | |
|---|---|
| las afueras | outskirts; suburbs |
| el ascensor | elevator |
| la avenida | avenue |
| el bulevar | boulevard |
| el campo | country(side) |
| la casa adosada | townhouse |
| el centro | downtown |
| el/la vecino/a | neighbor |
| | |
| amueblado/a | furnished |
| céntrico/a | central, centrally located |
| lleno/a de luz | bright; well-lit |
| oscuro/a | dark; dim |
| de al lado | next-door |
| sin amueblar | unfurnished |

**Cognados:** el chalet, el patio
**Repaso:** el césped, la ventana; tranquilo/a

---

## Nota comunicativa

Communication

### ORDINAL NUMBERS

Here are some of the more common ordinal numbers in Spanish.

| | | | |
|---|---|---|---|
| **primer, primero/a** | first | **sexto/a** | sixth |
| **segundo/a** | second | **séptimo/a** | seventh |
| **tercer, tercero/a** | third | **octavo/a** | eighth |
| **cuarto/a** | fourth | **noveno/a** | nineth |
| **quinto/a** | fifth | **décimo/a** | tenth |

Ordinal numbers can be used as adjectives or pronouns, and they agree in number and gender with nouns they modify or replace.

| | |
|---|---|
| Vivimos en la **segunda casa** a la derecha. | *We live in the second house on the right.* |
| Mi casa es la **quinta** desde la esquina. | *My house is the fifth from the corner.* |

The adjective forms **primer** and **tercer** are used to refer to masculine singular nouns. When used as masculine singular pronouns, they end in an **-o.**

—¿Es este el **primer piso**? (*adjective*)
—No, es el **tercero.** (*pronoun*)

---

**A. Opción múltiple.** Su profesor(a) va a leer algunas descripciones. Indique la opción correcta para cada descripción.

1. a. el piso
   b. la casa
   c. la casa adosada

2. a. el estudio
   b. el bulevar
   c. el vecino

3. a. las afueras
   b. céntrico
   c. la avenida

4. a. el bloque de pisos
   b. el estudio
   c. la planta baja

5. a. el jardín
   b. el patio
   c. el balcón

6. a. el centro
   b. la cochera
   c. el vecindario

7. a. las calles
   b. el bloque de pisos
   c. el campo

8. a. la avenida
   b. el barrio
   c. el noveno piso

## Nota cultural

Cultures

### LAS CORRALAS

*Una corrala*

Las corralas son un tipo de vivienda característica del Madrid tradicional. Estos modelos se originan en el siglo XVI por la necesidad de acomodar a muchos emigrantes de ciudades españolas a la capital. Pero su gran expansión ocurre en el siglo XIX, convirtiéndose en el alma[a] de Madrid. Las corralas son escenarios de famosas obras de teatro, de musicales y de películas, y sus habitantes inspiraron[b] grandes obras literarias.

La corrala generalmente tiene cuatro plantas[c] y en cada planta se distribuyen las viviendas, todas asomadas a[d] un patio central o corredor. Estas pequeñas viviendas, de menos de 30 metros cuadrados, tienen dos dormitorios, una cocina y un comedor, y en la mayoría de las corralas sus vecinos todavía comparten baños comunitarios. Los apartamentos no tienen ventanas al exterior y es en el patio donde transcurre la vida social de la comunidad.

[a]*soul* [b]*inspired* [c]*stories* [d]asomadas... *opening on to*

**PREGUNTAS** En parejas, contesten las preguntas. Después, compartan sus ideas con la clase.

1. ¿Por qué se originan las corralas en Madrid? ¿Cuándo aparece este tipo de arquitectura?
2. ¿Por qué creen Uds. que los habitantes de las corralas pasan la mayor parte del día en el patio?

**B.** La palabra intrusa (*that doesn't belong*). Indique la palabra que no corresponde a la serie y explique por qué.

MODELO **a.** el barrio     **b.** el vecindario     ⓒ céntrico     **d.** el vecino

         **Céntrico** no es parte de la zona donde una persona vive.

1. **a.** el centro     **b.** el bulevar     **c.** amueblado     **d.** la avenida
2. **a.** el estudio     **b.** el ascensor     **c.** el piso     **d.** la casa
3. **a.** la ventana     **b.** el balcón     **c.** la cochera     **d.** el campo
4. **a.** la planta baja     **b.** sin amueblar     **c.** el primer piso     **d.** el segundo piso
5. **a.** oscuro     **b.** tranquilo     **c.** lleno de luz     **d.** el vecino

**C.** Tipos de viviendas en España

PASO 1. Lea la información sobre las viviendas en España.

La mayoría de los españoles vive en pisos o en casas adosadas porque no se dispone de[a] mucho espacio. En las ciudades grandes predominan los pisos, pero en los pueblos pequeños es más típico que la gente viva en casas adosadas. Algunas personas viven en chalets en las afueras de las ciudades y de los pueblos. Otras personas tienen un chalet como segunda vivienda lejos de su ciudad de origen para pasar las vacaciones. En los estudios y apartamentos viven generalmente las personas solteras. Finalmente, hay en España pueblos muy pequeños en zonas rurales donde la gente que trabaja en el campo vive en casas similares a los «farmhouses» de este país.

[a]no... *is not available*

**PASO 2.** En parejas, hagan una lista de los tipos de viviendas que se mencionan en el **Paso 1.** Después indiquen una característica de cada una de ellas.

MODELO   Tipo de vivienda: casas adosadas
         Característica:    La mayoría de los españoles vive en casas adosadas, especialmente en los pueblos.

**PASO 3.** En grupos, y siguiendo el modelo del **Paso 2,** hagan una descripción de los tipos de viviendas de la región geográfica donde Uds. viven. ¿Son esos tipos de viviendas semejantes o diferentes a los tipos de viviendas en España? Compartan sus ideas con la clase.

**D.** Entrevista

**PASO 1.** Entreviste a un compañero / una compañera con las preguntas. Luego, cambien de papel.

1. ¿Vives solo/a, con compañeros de cuarto o con tu familia?
2. ¿Qué tipo de vivienda tienes aquí? ¿En qué parte del pueblo / la ciudad está ubicada?
3. ¿Qué tipo de vivienda tiene tu familia? Descríbela.
4. ¿Vive tu familia en una ciudad pequeña o en una ciudad grande? ¿En qué parte de la ciudad vive?
5. ¿Cómo es el vecindario? ¿Te gusta tu vecindario? ¿por qué?
6. ¿Cómo es la relación con tus vecinos? ¿Son Uds. amigos? ¿Hacen actividades sociales juntos?

**PASO 2.** Ahora compartan los resultados del **Paso 1** con la clase.

---

## Nota interdisciplinaria

### ARQUITECTURA: LOS PARADORES ESPAÑOLES

*El Parador Nacional de Ronda*

Los paradores españoles son hoteles dentro de edificios históricos, como antiguos palacios, castillos[a] o monasterios. La arquitectura de los edificios varía según el año de su construcción original. Por ejemplo, hay paradores de estilo románico,[b] gótico, renacentista, barroco, etcétera. Hay aproximadamente noventa paradores por toda España. Muchos paradores están en el centro histórico de las ciudades. Otros están en sitios naturales. Sin embargo, todos comparten espléndidas vistas del lugar donde se encuentran.[c]

El interior de estos monumentos —claustros,[d] salones, etcétera— está restaurado, pero mantienen el estilo y el ambiente original. Algunos paradores incluso tienen piscinas, saunas y gimnasios. Las habitaciones tienen todas las comodidades[e] modernas, como aire acondicionado, minibar y baños completos. Sin embargo, muchos mantienen el espíritu del pasado, pues están amuebladas con piezas[f] de la época original.

[a]*castles*   [b]*romanesque*   [c]*se... they're found*   [d]*cloisters*   [e]*comforts*   [f]*pieces*

PREGUNTAS En parejas, contesten las preguntas. Después compartan sus respuestas con la clase.

1. ¿En qué tipos de edificios están situados los paradores españoles? ¿En qué lugares de España hay paradores?
2. ¿Cómo es la arquitectura de los paradores? ¿Cómo es el interior de los edificios?
3. ¿Cómo son las habitaciones?

## 5.1 Direct Object Pronouns

**GRAMÁTICA EN CONTEXTO**

### La nueva casa

*[Una familia pone los muebles en su nueva casa. Hablan
los padres mientras que los niños los ayudan.]*

PAPÁ: Aquí está la nueva mesa. ¿Quién tiene las
sillas?

MAMÁ: Yo **las** tengo, amor.

PAPÁ: ¿Y el sofá?

MAMÁ: **Lo** tienen Federico y Bárbara, pero es muy pesado para ellos.

PAPÁ: **Los** ayudo.

MAMÁ: Oye, ¿dónde está Liliana? No **la** veo.

PAPÁ: Está en el salón.

MAMÁ: Necesitamos **cuidarla** porque es muy joven. ¡Liliana!

PAPÁ: Llama a Federico y Bárbara también. Todos vamos a descansar un
rato. **Los** invito a tomar un helado.

MAMÁ: Ay, gracias, amor. ¡Federico, Bárbara, Liliana,… !

Comprensión. Complete los diálogos con las palabras de la lista.

| la | las | los | te |
|---|---|---|---|

1. —¿Quién tiene la mesa?
   —Yo _____ tengo.
2. —No veo a los niños. ¿Dónde están?
   —Yo _____ veo. Están en la cocina.
3. —Necesitamos las cortinas. ¿Dónde están?
   —No sé. No _____ tengo.
4. —¿Me ayudas con la cómoda (*chest of drawers, dresser*)?
   —Sí, _____ ayudo.

---

A direct object receives the action of the verb in a sentence and generally answers
the question *what?* or *who?*

¿Miran Uds. la televisión en el salón?    *Do you all watch television in the
living room?*

Here, the subject **Uds.** is performing the action in the sentence, while the direct object
**la televisión** receives the action of the verb **miran**. Again, the direct object answers
the question *What (do you watch)?*

---

GRAMÁTICA EN CONTEXTO **The New House** / *A family is putting furniture in their new house. The
parents talk while the children help (them). /* **PAPÁ:** *Here is the new table. Who has the chairs? /* **MAMÁ:**
*I have them, darling. /* **PAPÁ:** *And the couch? /* **MAMÁ:** *Federico and Barbara have it, but it's very heavy
for them! /* **PAPÁ:** *I'll help them. /* **MAMÁ:** *Hey, where's Liliana? I don't see her. /* **PAPÁ:** *She's in the living
room. /* **MAMÁ:** *We need to take care of her because she's very young. Liliana! /* **PAPÁ:** *Call Federico
and Barbara too. We're all going to take a break. I'm treating you all to some ice cream. /* **MAMÁ:** *Oh,
thank you, darling. Federico, Bárbara, Liliana, . . . !*

| DIRECT OBJECT PRONOUNS | | |
|---|---|---|
| | SINGULAR | PLURAL |
| FIRST PERSON | me | nos |
| SECOND PERSON | te | os |
| THIRD PERSON | lo/la | los/las |

**A.** Direct object pronouns are used to avoid having to repeat the direct object over and over in a conversation or in writing. Each third person form must agree in number and gender with the noun that it replaces, and all direct object pronouns precede the conjugated verb.

—¿Usa Miguel Ángel **el ordenador** en casa?  
*Does Miguel Ángel use the computer at home?*

—Sí, **lo** usa en casa.  
*Yes, he uses it at home.*

—¿Tiene el dormitorio una mesita y una lámpara?  
*Does the room have a night table and a lamp?*

—Sí, **las** tiene.  
*Yes, it has them.*

—¿**Te** saludan Teresa y Susana cuando **te** ven?  
*Do Teresa and Susana greet you when they see you?*

—Sí, **me** saludan cuando **me** ven en la calle.  
*Yes, they greet me when they see me on the street.*

**B.** In a negative sentence, the word *no* is placed just before the direct object pronoun.

—¿Tienen piscina las casas en España?  
*Do the houses in Spain have pools?*

—No, generalmente **no las** tienen.  
*No, generally they don't have them.*

**C.** In the case of a conjugated verb followed by an infinitive, the direct object pronoun may be placed just before the conjugated verb or attached to the infinitive.

—¿Puedes llamar**me** más tarde en casa?  
*Can you call me later at home?*

—Sí, **te puedo** llamar.  
—Sí, **puedo llamarte.**  
*Yes, I can call you.*

**D.** If the verb is in the present progressive form, the pronoun may be placed immediately before the conjugated form of **estar,** or attached to the end of the gerund. When pronouns are attached to a gerund, a written accent marks the original stressed syllable.

—¿Estás limpiando la cocina?  
*Are you cleaning the kitchen?*

—Sí, **la estoy** limpiando.  
—Sí, estoy **limpiándola.**  
*Yes, I'm cleaning it.*

**E.** Remember to use the personal **a** before a direct object noun if it refers to a person or personified entity, such as the family pet. (Note: **Duque** is a common name for a dog.)

—¿Vas a llamar **a Elena** esta tarde?  
—*Are you going to call Elena this afternoon?*

—Sí, **la** voy a llamar (esta tarde).  
—*Yes, I'm going to call her (this afternoon).*

—¿Ves **a Duque?**  
—*Do you see Duque?*

—No, no **lo** veo.  
—*No, I don't (see him).*

TEMA I   ¿Hay una vivienda típica?       ciento cincuenta y nueve   |159

**A.** El apartamento de Laura. Su profesor(a) va a leer una descripción del nuevo apartamento de Laura. Conteste las preguntas.

| Vocabulario práctico | | | |
| --- | --- | --- | --- |
| **usar** | to use | **amable** | friendly |
| **sentarse** | to sit | **casi** | almost |

1. El apartamento de Laura tiene muchas ventanas.
   a. Las abre todas las mañanas.
   b. No las abre todas las mañanas.
2. El apartamento también tiene balcón.
   a. Laura lo usa mucho.
   b. Laura no lo usa mucho.
3. Laura toma café en el balcón.
   a. Lo toma por las mañanas
   b. Lo toma por las tardes.
4. El edificio tiene un jardín.
   a. Laura lo ve desde su apartamento.
   b. Laura no lo ve desde su apartamento.
5. Laura tiene vecinos.
   a. Los llama todos los días.
   b. Los ve casi todos los días.
6. El edificio tiene ascensor.
   a. Laura lo usa.
   b. Laura no lo usa.

**B.** En casa. Complete las oraciones con el pronombre de objeto directo correcto, según el contexto.

1. Tu ropa está sucia. ¿Por qué no _____ lavas?
2. Ellos tienen muchos libros. _____ tienen en su mochila.
3. La casa de mi mamá tiene muchas ventanas, pero no _____ abre todos los días.
4. Profesora, Ud. debe usar la cochera. ¿(*Ud.*) _____ ve allí?
5. ¿Tú quieres ir al cine con nosotros? _____ llamamos antes de salir.
6. Nosotros estamos muy contentos porque tú vas a dar una fiesta. ¿_____ vas a invitar?
7. Tengo que cortar el césped. _____ corto todos los fines de semana.
8. Yo no conozco a Federico. No sé por qué él dice que _____ conoce.

Communication

**C.** Entrevista. Entreviste a un compañero / una compañera de clase con las preguntas. Luego, cambien de papel. ¡**OJO**! Cambien los sustantivos de objeto directo por (*into*) pronombres.

MODELO ¿Vas a cortar el césped hoy? →
　　　　Sí, lo voy a cortar / Sí, voy a cortarlo.
　　　　No, no lo voy a cortar. / No, no voy a cortarlo.

1. ¿Vas a usar la computadora hoy?
2. ¿Conoces a tus profesores?
3. ¿Debes lavar las ventanas de tu casa?
4. ¿Vas a llamar a tus amigos hoy?
5. ¿Traes todos tus libros a clase?
6. Cuando hay ascensor en un edificio, ¿lo usas Ud.?
7. ¿Ves a tus vecinos con frecuencia?

**D. Los patios andaluces**

**PASO 1.** Llene los espacios en blanco con el pronombre de objeto directo correcto, según el contexto.

Los patios andaluces son una joya[a] de esta región del sur de España, y Ud. puede conocer \_\_\_\_\_[1] en nuestro *tour* especial por los patios de Córdoba.

Estos patios son interiores —es decir, la gente no \_\_\_\_\_[2] ve desde la calle. Son una parte central de la casa y muy íntima. La familia también \_\_\_\_\_[3] considera una parte central de la vida familiar.

Los patios andaluces reflejan[b] la influencia árabe. Los visitantes \_\_\_\_\_[4] ven inmediatamente en su forma geométrica y ordenada. Las flores[c] y las plantas son una parte importante de esta forma. Los jardineros[d] \_\_\_\_\_[5] ponen en lugares cuidadosamente escogidos para hacer resaltar[e] sus colores. Las paredes también son comunes en los patios, y la gente \_\_\_\_\_[6] construye para definir el espacio. De manera semejante, los patios incluyen los arbustos, los árboles y los senderos[f] y la gente \_\_\_\_\_[7] incorpora en forma geométrica.

*Un patio en Córdoba*

¿Quiere Ud. tener una experiencia inolvidable[g]? \_\_\_\_\_[8] invitamos a venir a Córdoba.

[a]*gem*  [b]*reflect*  [c]*flowers*  [d]*gardeners*  [e]*hacer… to make stand out*  [f]*los arbustos… bushes, trees, and paths*
[g]*unforgettable*

**PASO 2.** Conteste las preguntas, según el **Paso 1.**

1. ¿A qué ciudad va el *tour*?
2. ¿Cómo son los patios andaluces? Descríbalos.
3. ¿Cómo ponen los jardineros las plantas y las flores en los jardines?
4. ¿Cómo se usan (*are used*) los arbustos, los árboles y los senderos?
5. ¿Qué incluye el *tour*?

**PASO 3.** En parejas, contesten las preguntas.

Communication

1. ¿Qué jardines públicos o parques hay en su región? ¿Los visitan Uds.? Expliquen.
2. ¿Es importante el jardín o el patio para la familia en su región? Expliquen.
3. ¿En qué actividades participan las familias en los jardines y parques públicos de su región? ¿En cuáles participan Uds.?

**PASO 4.** Busque más información en el Internet sobre los patios andaluces. Compárelos con los jardines y parques en su región. Después, comparta sus resultados con la clase.

Comparisons  Communities

# 5.2 **Ser** and **estar** Compared

## Los últimos chismes

[*Nidia llama a Paula para contarle los últimos chismes. Primero, lea lo que dice Nidia.*]

Aló… ¿Paula? **Soy** yo, Nidia. ¿Cómo **estás**? […ª] ¿Dónde **estás**? […ᵇ] ¿Qué **estás** haciendo? […ᶜ] ¿**Estás** ocupada, o puedes hablar un momento? […ᵈ] Bueno, te tengo unas noticias. **Son** muy interesantes. Federica va a casarse con su nuevo novio mañana. […ᵉ] Su novio se llama Franco Ibarra. […ᶠ] **Es** de España. […ᵍ] ¡Ay, chica! **Es** alto, moreno, guapo y rico. […ʰ] La boda **es** en la Iglesia del Rosario. Y no lo vas a creer: van a vivir en una casa enorme en la playa. […ⁱ] **Es** de los padres de Franco… Pero mira, ¿qué hora **es**? […ʲ] ¿Tan tarde? Lo siento, pero me tengo que ir. […ᵏ] Adiós.

**Comprensión.** A continuación aparece la otra parte de la conversación: las respuestas de Paula. Pero no están en el orden correcto. Léalas y luego emparéjelas con los comentarios y preguntas de Nidia.

1. _____ ¿De quién es la casa?
2. _____ ¡De veras! ¿Quién es su novio?
3. _____ ¿De dónde es?
4. _____ Estoy en la biblioteca.
5. _____ ¿Dónde es la boda?
6. _____ Estoy bien.
7. _____ Son las 3:20.
8. _____ Hasta luego.
9. _____ No, no estoy ocupada.
10. _____ ¿Cómo es?
11. _____ Estoy estudiando.

**A.** You have already worked with many of the uses of the verbs **ser** and **estar**, both of which translate as *to be* in English. This side-by-side comparison should help clarify those uses.

----

GRAMÁTICA EN CONTEXTO **The Latest Gossip** / Nidia calls Paula to tell her the latest gossip. First, read what Nidia says. / Hello. Paula? This is Nidia. How are you? […ª] Where are you? […ᵇ] What are you doing? […ᶜ] Are you busy, or can you talk for a minute? […ᵈ] Well, I have some news for you. It's very interesting. Federica is going to marry her new boyfriend tomorrow. […ᵉ] Her boyfriend's name is Franco Ibarra. […ᶠ] He's from Spain. […ᵍ] Oh girl! He's tall, dark, handsome, and rich. […ʰ] The wedding is in the Church of the Rosary. And you'll never believe it: they're going to live in an enormous house on the beach. […ⁱ] It's Franco's parents' . . . But look, what time is it? […ʲ] That late? I'm sorry, but I have to go. […ᵏ] Good-bye.

| USES OF THE VERB **ser** | USES OF THE VERB **estar** |
|---|---|
| **1. Ser** is used to give the time of day or year, the month, the date, and the day:<br><br>Hoy **es** el 15 de mayo. El año **es** 2011. **Es** martes. **Es** primavera.<br>*Today is the 15th of May. The year is 2011. It is Tuesday. It is spring.* | **1. Estar** is used to tell where someone or something is located at a given moment.<br><br>Mi familia **está** en la playa.<br>*My family is at the beach.* |
| **2. Ser** indicates possession.<br><br>¿La computadora **es de** Manuel? No, **es de** Ana María.<br>*Is the computer Manuel's? No, it's Ana María's.* | **2. Estar** is used to talk about the feelings or appearance of a person or thing at a specific point in time. Often, speakers do this to emphasize a change from the person or thing's usual qualities.<br><br>Los niños **están** muy cansados hoy. No tienen la energía de siempre.<br>*The children are very tired today. They don't have their usual energy.*<br><br>No puedes usar el coche porque **está** descompuesto/roto.<br>*You can't use the car because it's broken down.* |
| **3. Ser** indicates origin and nationality.<br><br>¿**Es** Marisol de España? Sí, **es** española.<br>*Is Marisol from Spain? Yes, she's Spanish.* | **3. Estar** is used to form the present progressive tense, which is used to state that an action is in progress at this moment.<br><br>En este momento **estoy** leyendo el periódico en línea.<br>*At the moment I'm reading the newspaper on line.* |
| **4. Ser** describes the inherent qualities of a person or thing. These qualities may be physical or related to a person's personality.<br><br>El piso **es** precioso, lleno de luz y tranquilo.<br>*The apartment is cute, well-lit, and quiet.*<br><br>Vosotros **sois** muy amables.<br>*You (all) are very kind.* | |
| **5. Ser** gives a definition, or it identifies someone or something.<br><br>El comedor **es** mi parte favorita de la casa.<br>*The dining room is my favorite part of the house.* | |

**B.** In some cases, the meaning of an adjective changes depending on whether **ser** or **estar** is used. Remember that **ser** refers to inherent qualities, while **estar** refers to current conditions or to indicate a change from the norm.

| | |
|---|---|
| **Verónica es aburrida.** | *Verónica is boring.* |
| **Verónica está aburrida.** | *Verónica is bored.* |
| **Rodrigo es muy listo.** | *Rodrigo is very clever.* |
| **Rodrigo está listo.** | *Rodrigo is ready.* |
| **Marcos es rico.** | *Marcos is rich.* |
| **La comida está rica.** | *The food tastes delicious.* |

## ACTIVIDADES

**A. Buscando una nueva casa.** Lea las descripciones de una casa que Rogelio y Margarita piensan comprar. Indique si las características de la casa le parecen (*seem to you*) atractivas o no.

|  | SÍ | NO |
|---|---|---|
| **1.** La casa es muy pequeña. | ☐ | ☐ |
| **2.** Las ventanas están limpias. | ☐ | ☐ |
| **3.** La casa es de ladrillo (*brick*.) | ☐ | ☐ |
| **4.** Las flores del jardín están muertas (*dead*). | ☐ | ☐ |
| **5.** Los vecinos son amables (*friendly*). | ☐ | ☐ |
| **6.** La puerta está rota (*broken*). | ☐ | ☐ |
| **7.** El refrigerador es de los años 70. | ☐ | ☐ |
| **8.** El barrio es tranquilo. | ☐ | ☐ |

**B. El álbum de fotos.** Llene los espacios en blanco con la forma correcta de **ser** o **estar,** según el contexto.

*Emilia está hablando con Alberto, su amigo.*

Mira[a] mis fotos, Alberto. En esta, ves a mi amiga Adriana. Ella _____[1] de Toledo… Mis amigos y yo _____[2] en la playa de Málaga en esta foto… Y aquí ves a mi tía Magdalena. Ella _____[3] muy inteligente. _____[4] arquitecta. En esta foto, mi cuarto _____[5] sucio, y mis papás _____[6] enojados… Esta _____[7] la foto de la casa de mi hermana. (La casa) _____[8] en Madrid. Mira, aquí _____[9] (tú) en mi casa para mi cumpleaños… Sí, son mis tíos. (Ellos) _____[10] de Granada… ¿Qué _____[11] haciendo yo en esta foto? Este…[b] Ay, _____[12] las tres menos cuarto. ¡Tengo que irme![c]

———————
[a]*Look at*  [b]*Um…*  [c]*leave*

**C. Dos estudiantes.** Revise los dibujos de dos estudiantes universitarios. Luego, conteste las preguntas. **¡OJO!** Puede inventar otros detalles si es necesario.

A            B

1. ¿Dónde están David y Felipe en este momento?
2. ¿De quién es el cuarto A? ¿y el cuarto B?
3. ¿De dónde son David y Felipe?
4. ¿Cómo está el cuarto de David? ¿y el de Felipe?
5. ¿Dónde está la ropa de David?
6. ¿De quién es el cartel del club de fútbol de Barcelona?
7. ¿Quién está contento?

**D.** La leyenda (*legend*) del acueducto de Segovia

Cultures   Recycle

**PASO 1.** Complete la lectura con la forma correcta del verbo entre paréntesis. **¡OJO!** Cuando hay dos verbos entre paréntesis, escoja primero el verbo correcto.

*El acueducto de Segovia, España*

Uno de los sitios más impresionantes que Ud. (poder[1]) ver en España es el acueducto de Segovia. (Estar/Ser[2]) muy grande y muy interesante. (Tener[3]) una longitud de aproximadamente 2.400 pies[a] y 88 arcos elegantes. El acueducto data del siglo I[b] y (estar/ser[4]) una construcción romana. No obstante,[c] hay una leyenda que ofrece[d] una versión diferente de su historia.

Según la leyenda, una mujer (trabajar[5]) en una casa en Segovia. Ella (traer[6]) agua desde el Río Frío todas las mañanas. El trabajo (estar/ser[7]) muy duro[e] y las otras empleadas de la casa no (querer[8]) ayudarla.

Un día, la mujer (volver[9]) a casa con un gran jarro[f] de agua. (Estar/Ser[10]) las seis de la mañana, y ella (estar/ser[11]) muy cansada. «¿Por qué (*yo:* tener[12]) que trabajar tan duro?» (pensar[13]) ella. «(*Yo:* Necesitar[14]) una solución».

---

[a]*feet*   [b]*data... dates from the 1st century*   [c]*No... Nevertheless*   [d]*offers*   [e]*hard*   [f]*jug*

De repente, ella (ver[15]) a un ser muy extraño.[g]

—Quién (estar/ser[16]) tú?

—¿No me (*tú:* conocer/saber[17])? Soy el diablo.[h] (*Yo:* Querer[18]) ayudarte.

—¿Cómo?

—Tú y yo (ir[19]) a hacer un pacto. Yo te (hacer[20]) un acueducto.

—¿Y qué me (*tú:* pedir[21]) a cambio[i]?

—Tu alma.[j]

—No (*yo:* conocer/saber[22])...

—Tú (estar/ser[23]) trabajando mucho. (*Tú:* Necesitar[24]) mi ayuda.

—Está bien. Pero con una condición: El gallo[k] (cantar[25]) a las 5:00 de la mañana. Si tú no terminas[l] el acueducto para las 5:00 de la mañana, yo no te doy[m] mi alma.

—Trato hecho.[n]

Esa noche, la mujer no (dormir[26]) bien. (*Ella:* Pensar[27]) solamente en su pacto con el diablo y (tener[28]) miedo. (Hacer[29]) muy mal tiempo y llueve mucho. Pero la mujer (conocer/saber[30]) que no es una tormenta[ñ] común: El diablo está trabajando.

Finalmente, (estar/ser[31]) las 5:00 de la mañana. Cuando la mujer y las otras empleadas (salir[32]) de la casa, (ver[33]) un gran acueducto. Pero, afortunadamente para la mujer, al acueducto le falta la última piedra.[o] El diablo (estar/ser[34]) furioso, pero la mujer (estar/ser[35]) muy contenta y aliviada porque el diablo no va a tener su alma. Y ahora, Segovia (tener[36]) un acueducto elegante y útil.

---

[g]un... *a very strange being*  [h]*devil*  [i]*a... in exchange*  [j]*soul*  [k]*rooster*  [l]*finish*  [m]no... *I won't give you*  [n]Trato... *Deal*  [ñ]*storm*  [o]le... *is missing the last stone*

**PASO 2.** Conteste las preguntas, según el **Paso 1.**

1. ¿Dónde está el acueducto? ¿Cómo es?
2. ¿Dónde trabaja la mujer de la leyenda? ¿Qué hace ella en su trabajo?
3. ¿Cómo está la mujer cuando conoce al diablo?
4. ¿Qué quiere el diablo? ¿Cómo piensa ayudar a la mujer?
5. ¿Cuál es el trato entre el diablo y la mujer? ¿Cuál es la condición de la mujer?
6. Al final, ¿qué pasa? ¿Cómo está la mujer? ¿Y el diablo?

# Palabra escrita

## A comenzar

Communication

> **Developing Your Ideas Through Description.** The purpose of a descriptive piece of writing is to provide the reader with sensory information about the subject being presented, for example, how it sounds, smells, or looks. In other words, the writer wants to help the reader to see or feel the topic the way he/she does. To achieve this, adjectives and other linguistic conventions need to be chosen carefully. A useful pre-writing activity is to write sentences or brief paragraphs about how a person, place, thing, or event makes you feel and why.

You are going to start the process of writing a brief composition that you will finalize in the **Palabra escrita: A finalizar** section of your *Manual de actividades*. The topic of this composition is **Un lugar especial en el hogar.** The purpose of your composition will be to describe a certain area or room in your home (or a favorite relative's home that you're familiar with) and to explain to the reader why it is special to you.

**A.** Lluvia de ideas. En parejas, hagan una lluvia de ideas sobre estas preguntas.

1. ¿Cual es el lugar especial para Uds. en el hogar? ¿Dónde está?
2. ¿Cómo es?
3. ¿Qué hacen allí?
4. ¿Cómo se sienten Uds. (*do you feel*) cuando están allí?
5. ¿Por qué es un lugar especial para Uds.?

**B.** A organizar sus ideas. Repase sus ideas y asegúrese de (*make sure*) que describen bien el lugar y que comunican las emociones que Ud. siente (*feel*) cuando está en ese lugar. Organice sus ideas, compártalas (*share them*) con la clase y apunte otras ideas que se le ocurran durante el proceso.

**C.** A escribir. Ahora, haga el borrador de su composición con las ideas y la información que recopiló (*collected*) en las actividades A y B. ¡OJO! Guarde bien su trabajo. Va a necesitarlo otra vez para la sección de **Palabra escrita: A finalizar** en el *Manual de actividades*.

# Antoni Gaudí

El arquitecto catalán Antoni Gaudí (1852–1926) fue[a] el máximo representante del Modernismo y un pionero en las vanguardias artísticas del siglo XX. Mientras vivía, muchos críticos y artistas no entendían ni apreciaban[b] el arte de Gaudí, pero actualmente,[c] su obra es emblemática de la modernidad de Barcelona.

La Sagrada Familia, su obra maestra, es una catedral neogótica de grandes dimensiones. Sus capiteles miden[d] más de 100 metros cada uno y dominan toda Barcelona. Este proyecto fue para Gaudí una obsesión personal, pero en 1926 —después de trabajar en la catedral unos treinta y cinco años, y antes de completarla— Gaudí murió[e] en un accidente. La catedral permaneció inacabada[f] durante años, pero en 1979 se reiniciaron[g] las obras, siguiendo la idea original de Gaudí.

[a]*was* [b]*no… didn't understand or appreciate* [c]*today* [d]*measure* [e]*died* [f]*permaneció… remained unfinished* [g]*se… resumed*

La Catedral de la Sagrada Familia, Barcelona

## Vocabulario del tema

### Los cuartos y los muebles de la casa

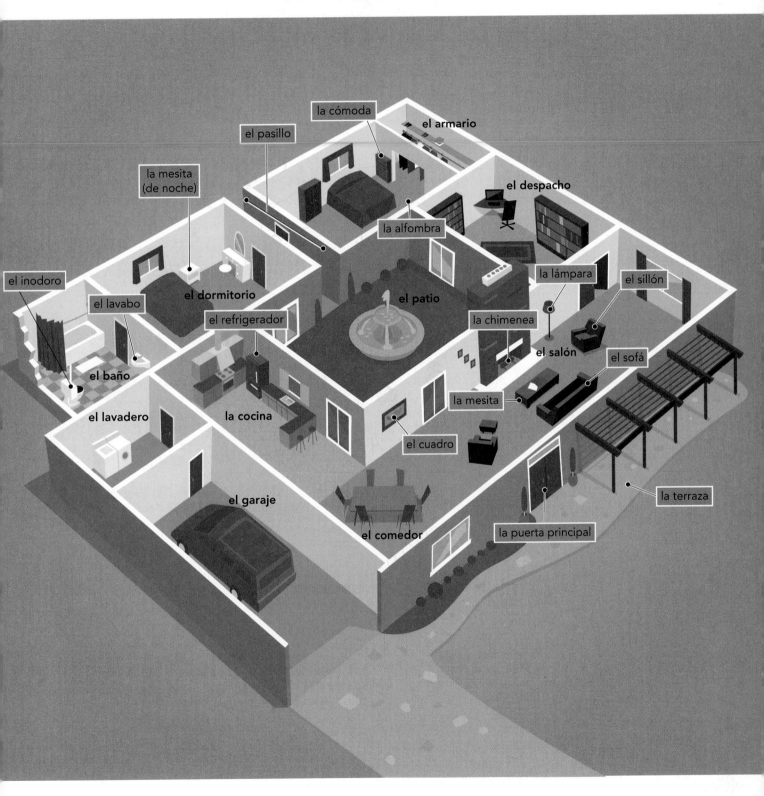

la cómoda

el armario

el pasillo

el despacho

la mesita (de noche)

la alfombra

el inodoro

el patio

la lámpara

el sillón

el lavabo

el dormitorio

la chimenea

el refrigerador

el baño

el salón

el sofá

el lavadero

la cocina

la mesita

el cuadro

la terraza

el garaje

la puerta principal

el comedor

| la cafetera | coffee maker |
| la ducha | shower |
| el dormitorio principal | master bedroom |
| la estantería | shelves |
| el (horno de) microondas | microwave (oven) |

Repaso: la cama, el escritorio, la estufa, el horno, el jardín, la lavadora, el lavaplatos, la mesa, la piscina, la secadora, la silla

## Otras preposiciones de lugar

| al lado de | next to |
| delante de | in front of |
| dentro de | inside |
| enfrente de | across from |
| arriba | upstairs; up |
| abajo | downstairs; down |
| adentro | inside |
| afuera | outside |

Repaso: a la derecha/izquierda (de), debajo de, encima de, entre

**ACTIVIDADES**

A. Asociaciones

PASO 1.  Empareje las actividades con la cosa o el lugar más lógico. ¡OJO! A veces hay más de una respuesta posible.

**ACTIVIDADES**

1. _____ secar la ropa
2. _____ cortar el césped
3. _____ poner la mesa
4. _____ lavar los platos
5. _____ mirar la televisión
6. _____ tomar una siesta
7. _____ sacar la basura
8. _____ hacer la cama
9. _____ limpiar el inodoro
10. _____ tender la ropa
11. _____ estudiar y leer
12. _____ jugar a las cartas
13. _____ sacudir la mesita
14. _____ trapear
15. _____ pasar la aspiradora
16. _____ tomar una copa

**COSAS Y LUGARES**

a. el dormitorio
b. el despacho
c. el baño
d. la cocina
e. el comedor
f. el salón
g. el lavadero
h. el garaje
i. el jardín

PASO 2.  Indique las acciones del Paso 1 que son quehaceres. ¿Cuáles son las actividades que no son quehaceres?

PASO 3.  Ahora, escoja tres actividades que Ud. hace y diga dónde las hace.

MODELO  tomar una siesta → Tomo una siesta en el sofá del salón todas las tardes.

B. ¿Dónde está? Diga en qué parte de la casa está cada persona descrita. ¡OJO! Hay más de una respuesta posible para algunas oraciones.

MODELO  Antonio está bañando (bathing) el perro. → Está en el jardín / la terraza.

1. Elisa está poniendo su ropa en la cómoda.
2. Esta parte conecta los cuartos de la casa y Marta está pasando la aspiradora allí.
3. Hace buen tiempo y la familia está comiendo afuera.
4. Todos en la familia están juntos, hablando y mirando la televisión.
5. Ramón está completando un informe (report) en la computadora para su clase de historia.
6. Mamá está esperando en el coche.
7. Inés está limpiando la ducha.
8. Olga está buscando mi libro en la estantería.

**C. Los muebles**

**PASO 1.** Diga en qué cuartos típicamente tenemos estos muebles, aparatos y otras cosas. ¡OJO! Hay más de una respuesta para algunas cosas.

**MODELO** la lámpara → Está en el salón / el dormitorio / el despacho.

1. el sillón
2. la estantería
3. el microondas
4. la cómoda

5. la mesita
6. la chimenea
7. el cuadro
8. el inodoro

**PASO 2.** Diga cuáles son las cosas del **Paso 1** que Ud. tiene, y explique dónde las tiene. Incluya una breve descripción.

**MODELO** Tengo una lámpara en el dormitorio. La lámpara es pequeña y vieja.

**D. En mi casa**

**PASO 1.** Haga un dibujo de su casa y ponga una etiqueta (*label*) en por lo menos seis muebles, aparatos u otras cosas. Si quiere, puede dibujar la casa de su familia o una casa inventada.

**PASO 2.** Intercambie su dibujo por el de un compañero / una compañera de clase. Escriba por lo menos seis descripciones de la casa de él/ella. Use palabras de la lista en sus descripciones. Dos de sus descripciones deben ser falsas.

| a la derecha | adentro | al lado de | debajo de | dentro de | enfrente de |
| a la izquierda | afuera | arriba | delante de | encima de | entre |
| abajo | | | | | |

**MODELO** En el salón hay un sofá. A la izquierda del sofá hay una mesita.

**PASO 3.** En parejas, túrnense para describir el dibujo que tienen. Su compañero/a va a decir si es cierto o falso, según el dibujo. Sigan el modelo.

Communication

**MODELO** E1: Tienes un sofá en el salón. A la izquierda del sofá, tienes una mesita.
E2: Sí, es cierto. / No es cierto. A la izquierda del sofá hay un sillón. La mesita está enfrente del sofá.

**E. Mi cuarto favorito**

**PASO 1.** En parejas, describan su cuarto o favorito de su casa.

Communication

**MODELO** Mi cuarto favorito es el salón porque paso mucho tiempo allí con mis amigos y mi familia. En el salón tenemos una chimenea, dos sofás, dos sillones...

**PASO 2.** Describa el cuarto favorito de su compañero/a sin mencionar el nombre del cuarto. La clase debe adivinar qué cuarto es.

**MODELO** Maura pasa mucho tiempo con sus amigos y su familia en su cuarto favorito. Hay una chimenea, dos sofás, dos sillones...

# Gramática

## 5.3 Reflexive Verbs

**GRAMÁTICA EN CONTEXTO**

### Las quejas de Antonia

¡Mi clase de química es horrible! Mis compañeros de clase y yo **nos aburrimos**. **Me frustro** mucho porque es una clase importante, ¡pero es tan aburrida! El profesor **se irrita** cuando no lo escuchamos. También **se enoja** cuando mis compañeros hablan durante la clase. **Me preocupo** mucho porque tenemos un examen esta semana y **me confundo** con toda la información. **Me deprimo** cuando pienso en el resto del semestre.

**Comprensión.** Indique si las oraciones se refieren a Antonia (**A**), a Antonia y sus compañeros de clase (**AC**) o al profesor (**P**).

|   | A | AC | P |
|---|---|---|---|
| 1. Se enoja. | ☐ | ☐ | ☐ |
| 2. Se preocupa. | ☐ | ☐ | ☐ |
| 3. Se irrita. | ☐ | ☐ | ☐ |
| 4. Se deprime. | ☐ | ☐ | ☐ |
| 5. Se aburren. | ☐ | ☐ | ☐ |

Spanish has a special category of verbs called reflexive verbs, which are used when speakers talk about what they do to themselves or for themselves. A reflexive verb consists of two parts, a reflexive pronoun followed by a conjugated form of the verb. Unlike direct object pronouns, a reflexive pronoun and the subject of the sentence always refer to the same person.

| **bañarse** (*to bathe; to swim*) ||
|---|---|
| me **baño** | nos **bañamos** |
| te **bañas** | os **bañáis** |
| se **baña** | se **bañan** |

Just as you have seen with direct object pronouns, in the case of a conjugated verb followed by an infinitive, the reflexive pronoun may be placed either before the conjugated verb or it may be attached to the infinitive. The meaning of the sentence remains the same.

| **Me** voy a divertir. | *or* | Voy a **divertirme**. |
|---|---|---|
| *I'm going to have a good time.* | | |

| **Nos** vamos a relajar. | *or* | Vamos a **relajarnos**. |
|---|---|---|
| *We're going to relax.* | | |

**GRAMÁTICA EN CONTEXTO** *Antonia's Complaints / My chemistry class is horrible! My classmates and I get bored. I get really frustrated because it's an important class, but it's so boring! The professor gets irritated when we don't listen to him. He also gets mad when my classmates talk during class. I'm really worried because we have an exam this week and I get confused by all the information. I get depressed when I think about the rest of the semester.*

All personal-care-related verbs are reflexive in Spanish, as shown in the following list.

| | |
|---|---|
| **acostarse** | to lie down |
| **afeitarse** | to shave |
| **despertarse (ie)** | to wake up |
| **desvestirse (i)** | to get undressed |
| **dormirse (ue)** | to fall asleep |
| **ducharse** | to take a shower |
| **lavarse la cara / las manos /** **el pelo** | to wash one's face/hands/hair |
| **lavarse los dientes** | to brush one's teeth |
| **maquillarse** | to put on make up |
| **secarse** | to dry off |
| **vestirse (ie)** | to get dressed |

There are many other verbs in Spanish that can be used reflexively and that you will learn later in this book. For now, the following are some reflexive verbs not related to personal care that you see in this chapter:

| | |
|---|---|
| **divertirse (ie)** | to have a good time, have fun |
| **relajarse** | to relax |
| **sentirse (ie)** | to feel |

## ACTIVIDADES

**A. ¿Es lógico o no?** Indique si las actividades están en orden lógico (**Sí**) o no (**No**). Si no, póngalas en orden.

|   | SÍ | NO |
|---|----|----|
| 1. Me levanto, me despierto, me ducho. | ☐ | ☐ |
| 2. Te desvistes, regresas a casa, cenas. | ☐ | ☐ |
| 3. Ellas se duchan, se visten, van al trabajo. | ☐ | ☐ |
| 4. Nos dormimos, nos acostamos, nos lavamos los dientes. | ☐ | ☐ |
| 5. Mi esposo se desviste, se acuesta, se duerme. | ☐ | ☐ |
| 6. Me maquillo, me lavo la cara, me despierto. | ☐ | ☐ |
| 7. Uds. se levantan, se bañan, se secan. | ☐ | ☐ |
| 8. Te afeitas, te despiertas, vas al trabajo. | ☐ | ☐ |

**B. ¿Para qué?** Indique lo que hacen estas personas, según lo que necesitan.

**MODELO** Tú necesitas acondicionador (*conditioner*). → Te lavas el pelo.

1. Esteban necesita una navaja (*razor*).
2. Nosotros necesitamos toallas (*towels*).
3. Mis hermanas necesitan lápiz labial (*lipstick*) y rímel (*mascara*).
4. Yo necesito jabón (*soap*).
5. Nosotros necesitamos pasta de dientes (*toothpaste*).
6. Tú necesitas champú (*shampoo*).
7. Mis padres necesitan sus almohadas (*pillows*).
8. Necesito mi ropa.

**C. Entrevista.** Entreviste a un compañero / una compañera de clase con estas preguntas. Luego, cambien de papel.

Ⓒ Communication

1. ¿A qué hora te despiertas los días de clase?
2. Los sábados, ¿a qué hora te levantas?
3. ¿A qué hora te acuestas los viernes?
4. Generalmente, ¿te duchas o te bañas?
5. ¿Cuántas veces al día te lavas los dientes?

(Continúa.)

6. Cuando te despiertas, ¿te levantas inmediatamente o te quedas en la cama un rato?
7. ¿Te afeitas / Te maquillas todos los días? Explica.
8. ¿Cómo te relajas después de clase?

## Nota cultural

### EL CAMINO DE SANTIAGO

El Camino de Santiago[a] es una serie de rutas medievales de peregrinación[b] que cruzan Europa hasta la tumba del apóstol Santiago en la Catedral de Santiago de Compostela, España. Muchos peregrinos[c] siguen este itinerario, la mayoría de ellos por motivos religiosos, y otros, para evitar la cárcel.[d] La ruta más popular es el Camino Francés, que atraviesa casi 500 millas.

Hoy día, los peregrinos hacen el peregrinaje desde muchos lugares y por razones diferentes. Unas personas llegan caminando y otras en bicicleta. Como toma muchos días de camino, se quedan[e] en albergues o refugios[f] o acampan.

[a]El... *The Way of Saint James*  [b]serie... *series of medieval pilgrimage routes*  [c]*pilgrims*  [d]evitar... *avoid a prison sentence*  [e]se... *they stay*  [f]albergues... *hostels or refuges*

**D. Un día en el Camino de Santiago**

**PASO 1.** Complete la lectura con la forma correcta del verbo entre paréntesis. **¡OJO!** Cuando hay dos verbos entre paréntesis, escoja primero el verbo correcto.

Enfrente de la Catedral de Santiago de Compostela

Álvaro (estar/ser[1]) estudiante. Este verano, sigue el Camino de Santiago con dos amigos. Todos los días, Álvaro (despertarse[2]) temprano,[a] a las 5:00 de la mañana. (*Álvaro:* Levantarse[3]) inmediatamente, (vestirse[4]) y (lavarse[5]) la cara y los dientes. Después, Álvaro y sus amigos (desayunar[6]), (poner[7]) sus cosas en sus mochilas y (salir[8]) para seguir el camino.

PERIODISTA:[b]  ¿Qué le parece el peregrinaje a Santiago? ¿Qué (*Ud.:* pensar[9]) de esta experiencia?

ÁLVARO:  Es una experiencia magnífica. (*Nosotros:* Caminar[10]) mucho todos los días, y al final del día, siempre (*nosotros:* estar/ser[11]) muy cansados. Pero todos los días (*yo:* conocer/saber[12]) a muchas personas, y me gusta mucho porque es interesante escuchar sus experiencias en el Camino.

PERIODISTA:  ¿Cómo (*Ud.:* relajarse[13]) al final del día?

[a]*early*  [b]*journalist*

ÁLVARO: Primero, (*yo: bañarse*[14]) en el albergue. Después, (*yo: vestirse*[15]) con ropa cómoda[c] y charlo con los otros peregrinos mientras (*nosotros: cenar*[16]). A veces un peregrino (**tocar**[17]) la guitarra y (**cantar**[18]) o (*nosotros: hablar*[19]) de nuestras experiencias en el Camino. Finalmente, (*yo: acostarse*[20]) temprano porque (*yo: conocer/saber*[21]) que mañana (*yo: tener*[22]) que caminar más.

[c]*comfortable*

**PASO 2.** Conteste las preguntas, según el **Paso 1.**

1. ¿A qué hora se despierta Álvaro? ¿Cuándo se levanta?
2. ¿Cómo empieza el día de Álvaro en el Camino de Santiago? ¿Qué hace?
3. ¿Cómo describe Álvaro su experiencia como peregrino?
4. ¿Cómo se siente Álvaro al final del día?
5. ¿Qué le gusta mucho a Álvaro? ¿Por qué?
6. ¿Cómo se relaja Álvaro al final del día?
7. ¿A qué hora se acuesta Álvaro? ¿Por qué?

**PASO 3.** Busque más información en el Internet sobre el Camino de Santiago y la importancia de Santiago en la historia de España. Comparta sus resultados con la clase.

Communities

# 5.4 Indefinite and Negative Words

Expressing Negation

**GRAMÁTICA EN CONTEXTO**

## ¡No hay nadie en casa!

Jordi es de Valencia. Estudia en la Universidad Complutense en Madrid y alquila una habitación en el piso de una familia madrileña. **Siempre** vuelve a casa para comer con la familia a las 2:00, pero cuando llega hoy, **no** hay **nadie. No** encuentra a **nadie, ni** en el salón, **ni** en la cocina. De hecho, **tampoco** hay **ningún** mueble en el piso. ¡Y **no** hay **nada** en la cocina! Desorientado, Jordi sale al pasillo para ver si **alguien** está en el piso vecino. Antes de llamar a la puerta, Jordi ve el número del piso vecino: 9-A. ¡Su familia **no** vive en el piso 9 y **nadie** vive en el piso 9-B! Jordi baja al piso 8-B donde toda la familia lo está esperando.

Comprensión. Indique si cada oración describe el Piso 8-B, 9-A o 9-B.

| | 8-B | 9-A | 9-B |
|---|---|---|---|
| 1. No hay nadie. | ☐ | ☐ | ☐ |
| 2. Nadie vive en el piso vecino. | ☐ | ☐ | ☐ |
| 3. Alguien espera. | ☐ | ☐ | ☐ |
| 4. Todavía no comen nada. | ☐ | ☐ | ☐ |
| 5. No tiene ninguna silla. | ☐ | ☐ | ☐ |
| 6. Alguien va a llamar a la puerta. | ☐ | ☐ | ☐ |

GRAMÁTICA EN CONTEXTO / ***There's No One at Home!*** / *Jordi is from Valencia. He studies at the Complutense University in Madrid and rents a room in a Madrid family's flat. He always returns home to eat with the family at two, but when he arrives today, no one is there. He doesn't find anyone, not in the living room, nor in the kitchen. In fact, there is no furniture in the flat either. And there is nothing in the kitchen! Disoriented, Jordi goes out to the hall to see if anyone is in the neighboring flat. Before knocking on the door, Jordi sees the number of the neighboring flat: 9-A. His family doesn't live on floor 9 and no one lives in flat 9-B! Jordi goes down to flat 8-B where the whole family is waiting for him.*

The use of negative expressions in Spanish works somewhat differently than in English.

**A.** In Spanish, a sentence may contain two or more negative forms, unlike English.

| | |
|---|---|
| No encontré **ninguna** fruta en el refrigerador. | *I didn't find any fruit in the refrigerator.* |
| No va a ir **ni** María **ni** Olga a visitar a su abuela. | *Neither María nor Olga is going to visit her grandmother.* |

However, if a negative word other than **no** begins a sentence in Spanish, no other negative word is necessary.

| | |
|---|---|
| **Nadie** usa el ascensor para subir al primer piso. | *Nobody (No one) uses the elevator to go up to the second floor.* |
| **Nunca** entro en ese vecindario. | *I never go into that neighborhood.* |

**B.** Most affirmative expressions in Spanish have a negative counterpart. Here are the most common of these expressions.

| INDEFINITE AND NEGATIVE WORDS | | | |
|---|---|---|---|
| **algo** | something | **nada** | nothing |
| **alguien** | someone | **nadie** | no one |
| **algún, alguna/os/as** | some | **ningún, ninguna** | none, not any |
| **o... o...** | either . . . or . . . | **ni... ni...** | neither . . . nor . . . |
| **siempre** | always | **nunca, jamás** | never |
| **también** | also | **tampoco** | neither; nor |

As an adjective, **algún** has four forms that agree in number and gender with the nouns they modify. **Ningún** is also an adjective and agrees in gender with the noun it modifies. However, **ningún** is almost never used in the plural since there is no plural of *none*.

| | |
|---|---|
| —¿Necesitas **algo** para la cocina? | *Do you need something for the kitchen?* |
| —No, **no** necesito **nada**. | *No, I don't need anything.* |
| —¿Conocen Uds. a alguien de este pueblo? | *Do you know anyone from this town?* |
| —No, **no** conocemos a **nadie** de aquí. | *No, we don't know anyone from here.* |
| —¿Busca Ud. **algunos** muebles para la casa? | *Are you looking for furniture for the house?* |
| —No, **no** busco **ningún** mueble, gracias. | *No, I'm not looking for any furniture, thank you.* |

CAPÍTULO 5 ¡Hogar, dulce hogar!

## ACTIVIDADES

**A.** En la casa de los Mendoza. Empareje cada oración de la columna A con la respuesta más lógica de la columna B.

**A**

1. ¿Todos los platos están limpios? _____
2. ¿Quién cocina la cena? _____
3. ¿Siempre te duchas por mucho tiempo? _____
4. ¿Hay alguna lámpara que puedo usar? _____
5. ¿Hay sillones aquí? _____
6. ¿Hay algunos libros en la estantería? _____
7. ¿Hay algo diferente en la cocina? _____
8. ¿Hay alguien en el baño? _____

**B**

a. No hay ningún sillón; tampoco hay sofás.
b. No, no hay ninguna.
c. No, ninguno está limpio.
d. No, no hay ningún libro.
e. Nadie está allí.
f. No, no hay nada diferente.
g. Nunca me ducho por mucho tiempo.
h. Nadie cocina la cena.

**B.** Al contrario. Cambie las oraciones para que sean (*so that they are*) negativas.

**MODELO** Hay alguna lámpara prendida (*on*). → No hay ninguna lámpara prendida.

1. Hay muchos cuadros en el salón.
2. Alguien está en el baño.
3. Hay una chimenea en la nueva casa.
4. Hay mesas en el comedor; también hay sillas.
5. Alguien canta en la ducha.
6. ¡Hay algo raro (*strange*) en mi cama!
7. Hay algunos libros interesantes en la estantería.
8. Los niños siempre juegan en el jardín.

**C.** Entrevista. En parejas, contesten las preguntas con oraciones completas.

Communication

1. ¿Siempre escriben Uds. la tarea?
2. ¿Hay muchas actividades divertidas en la universidad hoy?
3. ¿Hay algún estudiante del Japón en la clase?
4. ¿Estudian francés y también portugués?
5. ¿Pasan (*Are they showing*) alguna película buena este fin de semana?
6. ¿Siempre cenan en casa?
7. ¿Tienen alguna revista en su mochila?

**D.** La tertulia española

Cultures   Recycle

**PASO 1.** Complete la narración con la palabra correcta o la forma correcta del verbo entre paréntesis. Cuando hay dos verbos entre paréntesis, escoja primero el verbo correcto.

La tertulia (**estar/ser**[1]) una reunión[a] informal de personas que (**tener**[2]) interés en un tema. Este tema (**poder**[3]) ser específico, por ejemplo, el arte, la política o la literatura. El enfoque[b] de (**algunas/ninguna**[4]) tertulias es el cine, y otras se enfocan[c] en el medio ambiente.[d] (**También/Tampoco**[5]) hay tertulias sobre temas generales.

Sea cual sea su tema,[e] el fin[f] de la tertulia (**nunca / casi siempre**[6]) es educativo. Los participantes (**hablar**[7]) de (**algo/**

*Una tertulia*

---
[a]*get-together*   [b]*focus*   [c]*se... focus on*   [d]*el... the environment*   [e]*Sea... Whatever the topic may be*   [f]*purpose*

**alguno**[8]) de interés entre ellos y comparten sus ideas. (**Nada/Nadie**[9]) se queda callado.[g] Muchas veces las tertulias tienen lugar en un café. El ambiente[h] es animado, lleno de[i] conversación, comida, y emoción. Todos (**divertirse**[10]) mucho. ¡Una tertulia no es (**nunca/siempre**[11]) aburrida!

Si (**alguien/alguno**[12]) que suele participar en una tertulia no (**asistir**[13]) a ella, los otros participantes no (**pensar**[14]) bien de esa persona. (**También/Tampoco**[15]) (*ellos:* **hablar**[16]) bien de él o ella. ¡No hay (**alguna/ninguna**[17]) buena excusa para perderse[j] una tertulia!

---

[g]*se... stays quiet*  [h]*atmosphere*  [i]*lleno... full of*  [j]*to miss*

**PASO 2.** Conteste las preguntas, según el **Paso 1.**

1. ¿Qué es una tertulia?
2. ¿Qué hacen los participantes en una tertulia?
3. ¿Cuáles son algunos de los temas de las tertulias?
4. ¿Cómo es el ambiente de una tertulia? Descríbalo.
5. ¿Qué pasa si alguien no asiste a la tertulia?

Communication

**PASO 3.** En parejas, contesten las preguntas.

1. Uds. van a organizar una tertulia. ¿Cuál es el tema? ¿A quiénes invitan?
2. ¿Dónde va a ser la tertulia que organizan? ¿Cómo es el lugar?
3. ¿Cómo es el ambiente de su tertulia? ¿Cómo están los participantes durante la tertulia?

# Lectura cultural

Cultures

Ud. va a leer algunos anuncios de viviendas cerca de la ciudad de Granada, España, publicados en *Puerta Elvira,* una revista gratuita de viviendas de Granada. Algunas viviendas están ubicadas dentro de Granada, otras en pueblos en las afueras de Granada.

### ANTES DE LEER

Conteste las preguntas. Después, comparta sus respuestas con la clase.

1. Piense en anuncios típicos de viviendas de los periódicos o revistas del lugar donde Ud. vive. ¿Qué tipo de información incluyen?
2. Haga una lista de las características que a Ud. le gustan en una vivienda.
3. Los anuncios de todo tipo no tienen mucho espacio ni en los periódicos ni en las revistas y es común usar abreviaturas (*abbreviations*). Empareje las abreviaturas con las palabras correspondientes.

1. _____ aprox.
2. _____ ptas.
3. _____ Urb.
4. _____ dorm.
5. _____ Indep.
6. _____ electrod.

a. Independiente
b. Urbanización
c. aproximadamente
d. pesetas (antigua moneda [*currency*] española)
e. electrodomésticos
f. dormitorio(s)

CAPÍTULO 5 ¡Hogar, dulce hogar!

## INTERESANTES OFERTAS DE SEGUNDA MANO

CASA CON 5.000m$^2$ DE TERRENO EN COGOLLOS VEGA, casa con 3 Dormitorios, Salón, Cocina, Baño y un bajo[a] de 100m$^2$ aprox., piscina de 15x7 con depuradora,[b] agua de manantial,[c] Abundantes árboles frutales.
372.627 Euros (62.000.000 ptas)

AMBROZ, casa pueblo perfecto estado en 2 plantas: 200 m$^2$ útiles. 2 salones (1 de ellos con chimenea), cochera, cocina amueblada, baño y aseo[d] con plato ducha, 4 dormitorios patio 40 m$^2$ en planta baja y 2 terrazas planta alta
184.510 Euros (30.700.000 ptas)

CÁJAR, adosada: Salón, cocina amueblada, despensa,[e] aseo y 2 baños, 3 dormitorios, 2 armarios empotrados,[f] torreón[g] con una habitación de 12 m$^2$, piscina 3'5 de gresite,[h] suelo de tarima flotante,[i] pintura lisa,[j] calefacción[k] y semisótano.[l] 208.551 Euros (34.700.000 ptas)

ZUBIA, TOTALMENTE AMUEBLADO. Piso 100 m$^2$, salón, cocina amueblada, aseo y baño, 3 dormitorios, plaza de garaje y trastero,[m] terraza comunitaria. 122.606 Euros (20.400.000 ptas)

PURCHIL, 2 Adosadas próxima entrega:[n] Salón 28 m$^2$, cocina 15 m$^2$, lavadero, 4 dormitorios, aseo y 2 baños, patio 36 m$^2$, semisótano 57 m$^2$ terminado, tarima flotante, pintura lisa, calefacción. Urb. Privada con piscina.
164.076 Euros (27.300.000 ptas)

URB. EL VENTORRILLO, Chalet Indep.: 375 m$^2$ de parcela. 220 m$^2$ construidos. Salón 40 m$^2$, cocina 16 m$^2$ amueblada, 2 baños, 3 dormitorios, calefacción, suelo gres imitación parqué.[ñ] 234.394 Euros (39.000.000 ptas)

GRANADA, Apartamento próxima entrega: Salón, cocina, lavadero, despensa, baño, 1 dormitorio, terraza 12 m$^2$, pintura lisa, doble acristalamiento,[o] preinstalación aire acondicionado y acumuladores de calor, plaza de garaje y ascensor. 195.328 Euros (32.500.000 ptas)

GRANADA, DUPLEX-PALACIO DEPORTES: Completamente reformado. Salón con chimenea y terraza, cocina amueblada con electrod., lavadero, despensa, baño y aseo, 2 dormitorios con armarios empotrados, calefacción, aire acondicionado, pintura lisa, doble acristalamiento, ascensor, 2 cocheras. 218.768 Euros (36.400.000 ptas)

BELICENA, Adosada: Salón 23 m$^2$, cocina amueblada con electrodomésticos, baño y aseo, 3 dormitorios, patio 47 m$^2$ con barbacoa,[p] 54 m$^2$ semisótano, pintura lisa.
159.268 Euros (26.500.000 ptas)

GRANADA, Estudio en zona Estadio Juventud: 42 m$^2$ útiles. Salón, cocina independiente amueblada, 1 dorm., baño, calefacción individual, preinstalación aire acondicionado, ascensor.
121.103 Euros (20.150.000 ptas)

HIJAR, Adosada: 180 m$^2$ construidos. Salón 30 m$^2$, cocina amueblada, lavadero, 50 m$^2$ patio solado[q] con barbacoa, 2 baños y aseo, 3 dorm, semisótano con chimenea y trastero.
174.293 Euros (29.000.000 ptas)

ALBOLOTE, Urb. Villas Blancas: Chalet independiente con 270 m$^2$ útiles. Salón 30 m$^2$ con chimenea, cocina, despensa, lavadero, 3 baños, 2 armarios empotrados, calefacción, piscina con barbacoa. 306.516 Euros (51.000.000 ptas)

---

[a]planta baja  [b]*filter system*  [c]*agua... spring/well water*  [d]*half bathroom*  [e]*pantry*  [f]*built-in*  [g]*tower-like room at the top of a house*  [h]*ceramic tile*  [i]*tarima... laminated wood*  [j]*smooth*  [k]*heating system*  [l]*level of building partially below ground level*  [m]*storage room*  [n]*próxima... joined with a common wall*  [ñ]*gres... inlaid with imitation stoneware*  [o]*window panes*  [p]*barbecue*  [q]*with tiled floor*

**A.** Comprensión. Conteste las preguntas.

1. ¿A qué se refiere la información en letra mayúscula (*capital letters*) al principio de los anuncios?
2. ¿Cuántos tipos de viviendas aparecen en el anuncio?
3. ¿Qué tienen en común el duplex de Granada y el chalet situado en Urbanización Villas Blancas de Albolote?
4. Indique tres características que el apartamento y el estudio ubicados en Granada no tienen en común.
5. ¿Qué anuncio(s) incluyen un cuarto en la planta más baja de la vivienda? ¿Cómo se llama este cuarto?
6. ¿Qué vivienda le gusta más a Ud.? ¿Por qué? ¿Tiene las mismas características de la vivienda que Ud. describió (*described*) en la pregunta 2 de **Antes de leer**? Explique.

**B.** ¿Qué les sugiere Ud.? ¿Qué vivienda(s) deben comprar estas personas? Explique por qué.

1. a un matrimonio que no tiene mucho dinero
2. a las personas que les gusta comer fuera, cuando hace buen tiempo
3. a una persona soltera que no necesita mucho espacio
4. a las personas mayores que tienen dificultad para caminar y subir o bajar escaleras
5. a las personas que les gusta mucho nadar en el verano

Communication

**C.** Compro casa. En parejas, imagínense que Uds. van a comprar la vivienda de los anuncios que más les gusta. Escriban cinco preguntas apropiadas para hacerle al propietario (*owner*).

## España: Ana

La vivienda en Granada

### ANTES DE VER

Conteste las preguntas.

1. ¿Cree Ud. que en las ciudades españolas normalmente los matrimonios jóvenes viven en una casa o en un piso? Explique.
2. ¿Cómo cree que la vivienda afecta a las relaciones familiares?
3. En su opinión, ¿qué otros factores importantes hay que (*should one*) considerar al buscar una vivienda?

### Vocabulario práctico

| | | | |
|---|---|---|---|
| **Palacio Arzobispal** | archbishop's residence | **revista de** | apartment guide |
| **podrías** | you could | **apartamentos** | |
| **me encanta** | I love (it) | **¡Ni pensarlo!** | No way! |
| **posibilidades económicas** | sufficient funds | **broma** | joke |

### DESPUÉS DE VER

**A. Comprensión.** Vuelva a ver el segmento y termine las oraciones.

1. En Albaycín vemos _____.
2. En la Plaza de Bibarrambla hay _____.
3. El Paseo del Salón es un lugar perfecto para _____.
4. El perro de Lorena tiene un nombre especial porque _____.
5. En la revista, Eugenio encuentra un lugar perfecto, pero _____.
6. Eugenio propone (*proposes*) que el perro viva (*live*) con su madre (la madre de él), pero ella _____.
7. En la ciudad, hay diferentes posibilidades de vivienda, entre ellas: _____.

**B. Tema de discusión.** En parejas, contesten las preguntas. Después, compartan sus ideas con la clase.

¿Quién controla normalmente la casa en este país, el hombre o la mujer? ¿Creen Uds. que es igual en el mundo hispano? Expliquen.

# Vocabulario

## Las viviendas / Housing

| | |
|---|---|
| las afueras | outskirts; suburbs |
| el ascensor | elevator |
| la avenida | avenue |
| el balcón | balcony |
| el barrio | neighborhood |
| el bloque de pisos | block apartment building |
| el bulevar | boulevard |
| el campo | country(side) |
| la casa adosada | townhouse |
| el centro | downtown |
| el coche | car |
| la cochera | carport |
| el edificio de apartamentos | apartment building |
| el estudio | studio apartment |
| el piso | apartment; floor (*of a building*) |
| el primer piso | second floor |
| el segundo piso | third floor |
| la planta baja | first (ground) floor |
| el vecindario | neighborhood |
| el/la vecino/a | neighbor |

Cognados: el apartamento, el chalet, el patio
Repaso: la calle, la casa, el jardín, la ventana

## Los adjetivos

| | |
|---|---|
| amueblado/a | furnished |
| céntrico/a | central, centrally located |
| de al lado | next-door |
| lleno/a de luz | bright; well-lit |
| oscuro/a | dark; dim |
| sin amueblar | unfurnished |

## La casa

| | |
|---|---|
| la chimenea | fireplace |
| la cocina | kitchen |
| el comedor | dining room |
| el baño | bathroom |
| el despacho | office, study |
| el dormitorio (principal) | (master) bedroom |
| el lavadero | laundry room |
| el pasillo | hallway |
| la puerta principal | front door |
| el salón | living room |
| la terraza | terrace |

Cognado: el garaje
Repaso: el jardín, la piscina

## Los muebles y los aparatos domésticos

| | |
|---|---|
| la alfombra | rug |
| el armario | closet |
| la cafetera | coffee maker |
| la cómoda | chest of drawers, dresser |
| el cuadro | painting |
| la ducha | shower |
| la estantería | shelves |
| el inodoro | toilet |
| la lámpara | lamp |
| el lavabo | sink |
| la mesita | coffee table |
| la mesita (de noche) | nightstand |
| el refrigerador | refrigerator |
| el sillón | armchair |

Cognado: el sofá
Repaso: la cama, el escritorio, la estufa, el horno (de microondas), la lavadora, el lavaplatos, la mesa, la secadora, la silla

## Otras preposiciones de lugar

| | |
|---|---|
| abajo | downstairs; down |
| adentro | inside |
| afuera | outside |
| al lado de | next to |
| arriba | upstairs; up |
| delante de | in front of |
| dentro de | inside |
| enfrente de | across from |

Repaso: a la derecha/izquierda (de), debajo de, encima de, entre

## Los verbos reflexivos / Reflexive Verbs

| | |
|---|---|
| acostarse (ue) | to lie down |
| afeitarse | to shave |
| bañarse | to bathe; to swim |
| despertarse (ie) | to wake up |
| desvestirse (i) | to get undressed |
| divertirse (ie) | to have a good time, have fun |
| dormirse (ue) | to fall asleep |
| ducharse | to take a shower |
| lavarse la cara / las manos / el pelo | to wash one's face/ hands/hair |
| lavarse los dientes | to brush one's teeth |
| maquillarse | to put on makeup |
| relajarse | to relax |
| secarse (el pelo) | to dry off (one's hair) |
| sentirse (ie) | to feel |
| vestirse (i) | to get dressed |

## Las palabras indefinidas y negativas / Indefinite and Negative Words

| | |
|---|---|
| algo | something |
| alguien | someone |
| algún, alguno/a/os/as | some |
| nada | nothing |
| nadie | no one |
| ni... ni... | neither . . . nor . . . |
| ningún, ninguno/a | none, not any |
| nunca, jamás | never |
| o... o... | either . . . or . . . |
| siempre | always |
| también | also |
| tampoco | neither; nor |

# La familia

Connections

## ANTES DE VER

¿Cómo es la familia hispana típica? Indique si Ud. está de acuerdo o no con las oraciones.

| | ESTOY DE ACUERDO. | NO ESTOY DE ACUERDO. |
|---|---|---|

La familia hispana típica...

1. tiene más de tres hijos. ☐ ☐
2. comparte la vivienda con miembros de su familia extendida. ☐ ☐
3. va a la iglesia todos los domingos. ☐ ☐
4. es tradicional: la madre cuida a (*takes care of*) los hijos mientras el padre trabaja. ☐ ☐
5. prefiere hacer actividades en casa en vez de hacerlas (*instead of doing them*) al aire libre. ☐ ☐

### Vocabulario práctico

| | | | |
|---|---|---|---|
| **el horario** | schedule | **la quinceañera** | *celebration in honor of a girl's 15th birthday* |
| **darse un beso** | to kiss each other | | |
| **el mate** | *bitter, tea-like drink popular in Argentina and Uruguay* | **se sienten más a gusto** | (they) feel more at home |

## DESPUÉS DE VER

¿Qué aprendió Ud. sobre la familia hispana «típica»? Indique si las oraciones son ciertas (C) o falsas (F), según el vídeo.

| | C | F |
|---|---|---|

1. La vida fuera de casa es muy importante para las familias hispanas. ☐ ☐
2. En una familia tradicional, es el padre quien se encarga de (*is in charge of*) los hijos. ☐ ☐
3. En Argentina está prohibido mostrar afecto (*affection*) en público. ☐ ☐
4. Los animales domésticos no tienen mucha importancia en la vida de los hispanos. ☐ ☐
5. En México la iglesia es muy importante en la vida familiar. ☐ ☐
6. Los adolescentes mexicanos prefieren estar con sus padres en vez de estar con sus amigos. ☐ ☐

183

## LA PLAZA MAYOR

La Plaza Mayor de Madrid, la capital de España, está ubicada[a] en el centro de la ciudad. Hoy día está rodeada de[b] pisos, cafés, restaurantes y edificios municipales. Pero antes fue[c] el sitio de corridas de toros[d] y «autos de fe», tribunales[e] públicos de la Inquisición española.

[a]located
[b]rodeada... *surrounded by*
[c]*it was*
[d]corridas... *bullfights*
[e]*trials*

## LA PLAZA DE MAYO

La Plaza de Mayo siempre ha sido[a] un eje[b] importante en la vida política de Buenos Aires y de Argentina. El nombre conmemora la revolución del 25 de mayo de 1810, que condujo a[c] la independencia de España. La Casa Rosada, que se ve detrás de la plaza en la foto, es la sede[d] del poder[e] ejecutivo del país.

[a]ha... *has been*  [b]*focal point*
[c]condujo... *led to*  [d]*seat*
[e]*power*

## ACTIVIDADES

**A. Comprensión.** Complete las oraciones con información de las páginas anteriores (*preceding*).

1. Muchas plazas hispanas tienen _____ oficiales y construcciones _____ importantes.
2. Un aspecto único (*unique*) que tiene la Plaza Mayor en Madrid son los _____, viviendas para algunos españoles.
3. El Zócalo era el centro _____ y _____ de la antigua (*former*) capital azteca.
4. El nombre de la Plaza de Mayo celebra la _____ argentina de España.
5. El Zócalo y la Plaza de Armas fueron construidos (*were built*) encima de _____ de culturas prehispánicas.
6. Como otras ciudades tejanas (de Texas), San Antonio —y el río que lleva el mismo nombre— tiene una larga historia _____.

**B. Conexiones.** En parejas, contesten las preguntas.

1. ¿En qué son semejantes las plazas en el mundo hispano?
2. ¿Qué función tienen las plazas donde Uds. viven? Indiquen algunas diferencias y semejanzas entre las plazas de su país y las plazas de los países hispanos.

Connections

**C. A investigar más.** Escoja *uno* de estos lugares y prepare un breve informe. En su informe, escriba por lo menos cinco datos (*facts*) interesantes que no se presentan en las páginas anteriores. Use el Internet o la biblioteca para hacer su investigación.

1. la Plaza Mayor (Madrid, España)
2. el Zócalo (México, D.F.)
3. la Plaza de Mayo (Buenos Aires, Argentina)
4. la Plaza de Armas (Cusco, Perú)
5. el Paseo del Río (San Antonio, Texas)

**D. Temas de discusión.** En grupos pequeños, comenten *uno* de estos temas y escriban algunas conclusiones breves en español. Luego, compartan sus conclusiones con la clase.

Communication    Comparisons

1. mi plaza favorita de este país (de nuestra región)
2. los lugares de encuentro más populares de nuestra región
3. un lugar de encuentro famoso de este país (por ejemplo: Central Park en Nueva York, Bourbon Street en Nueva Orleans, etcétera)

## LA PLAZA DE ARMAS

En el centro de Cusco, Perú, se encuentra la Plaza de Armas, una plaza hermosa donde las personas se reúnen,[a] pasean y descansan. Antes de la llegada[b] de los españoles, Cusco fue[c] el centro del Imperio inca, y la Plaza de Armas fue construida[d] encima de las ruinas incas.

[a]se... get together
[b]arrival [c]was [d]constructed

## EL PASEO DEL RÍO[a]

No es una plaza, pero el Paseo del Río de San Antonio, Texas, sí es un lugar de encuentro para muchas familias y turistas. Aunque el río y la ciudad comparten una larga historia, el Paseo del Río como centro económico y cultural de esta vibrante ciudad hispana tiene sus raíces[b] en los años 60.

[a]Paseo... River Walk [b]roots

# Entrada cultural

## El Caribe: Cuba, Puerto Rico, la República Dominicana y Venezuela

**Cultures**

**En Cuba**

**En la República Dominicana**

**En Ponce, Puerto Rico**

Los países caribeños de habla española incluyen Cuba, Puerto Rico, la República Dominicana y Venezuela. Aunque todos presentan características propias, los países del Caribe tienen muchos elementos en común. Por ejemplo, tienen una sociedad multicultural que es una mezcla[a] de la población indígena, los colonizadores españoles y los esclavos africanos. Esa mezcla étnica se nota en la gastronomía, la música, el baile, el arte, la literatura, la moda[b] y la forma de hablar de la gente de la región.

La República Dominicana atrae a miles de turistas de todo el mundo por sus preciosas playas, y hoy día se considera entre los principales destinos turísticos de Latinoamérica. También es conocida por el béisbol y por el número de sus jugadores que juegan en las Grandes Ligas de los Estados Unidos.

Cuba, como la República Dominicana, es un destino turístico. Muchos visitantes quedan encantados con la amabilidad[c] de la gente, sus playas, su pasado colonial, su comida y la calidad de su tabaco y su ron. Pero un reto[d] para Cuba sigue siendo el rechazo[e] de la comunidad internacional por su gobierno socialista tanto como por la falta[f] de libertades y de calidad de vida para sus ciudadanos.[g]

En Puerto Rico, la música forma parte de la vida diaria. Esta isla cuenta con[h] diferentes ritmos folclóricos como la bomba y la plena, la salsa y el reggaetón. Además del turismo, las compañías farmacéuticas, electrónicas, textiles, petroquímicas y biotecnológicas son su principal fuente de ingresos.[i]

Oficialmente Venezuela es parte de Sudamérica y tiene rasgos continentales. Pero, especialmente en las zonas de la costa y en la Isla Margarita, Venezuela comparte muchos aspectos culturales con los países caribeños como, por ejemplo, la forma de hablar, la comida, la música y el baile.

---

[a]*mixture* [b]*fashion* [c]*friendliness* [d]*challenge* [e]*rejection* [f]*lack* [g]*citizens* [h]*cuenta... has* [i]*fuente... source of income*

# La plaza

Muchos pueblos y ciudades hispanos tienen una plaza central con edificios oficiales y construcciones religiosas importantes. En algunas plazas hay bares, cafés y restaurantes donde las familias pueden comer y tomar algo al aire libre. Como[a] la vida fuera de casa es una parte integral de la cultura hispana, la plaza tiene una función social y representa un espacio de ocio[b] y un lugar de encuentro[c] muy importante entre los hispanos.

[a]*Since*   [b]*leisure time*   [c]*lugar... meeting place*

## EL ZÓCALO

El Zócalo está ubicado en el centro histórico de México, D.F., y es una de las plazas más grandes del mundo. En el Zócalo hay muchos edificios importantes como la Catedral Metropolitana, el Palacio Nacional y otros edificios gubernamentales.[a] Antes era[b] el centro político y religioso de Tenochtitlán, la capital azteca.

[a]*government*   [b]*it was*

## ASÍ SE DICE

el bar = la bodega, la cantina, la cervecería, el pub, la taberna

el café = la cafetería, el cafetín

el ocio = la diversión, los ratos libres, el recreo, el tiempo libre

la plaza = la glorieta, la plazuela, el zócalo (*Mex.*)

el restaurante = el comedor, la fonda, el mesón, el restorán/restaurán

# ¡A comer!

*En una cafetería callejera de La Habana, Cuba*

1. ¿Qué tipos de comidas le gustan más? ¿la comida mexicana? ¿la china? ¿la italiana? ¿la de otra nacionalidad?

2. ¿Qué tipos de restaurantes hay en la ciudad donde Ud. vive?

3. ¿Hay restaurantes hispanos en la ciudad donde vive? ¿Cómo se llaman? ¿Dónde están?

**connect** | SPANISH

www.connectspanish.com

## Vocabulario del tema

### La comida

FRUTAS Y VERDURAS

Carnes, pescados y mariscos

la banana

el coco

la clienta

el cliente

el pollo

la carne de res

la vendedora

el tomate

la vendedor

la lechuga

el cerdo

la piña

las papas

los camarones

la langosta

el maíz

la naranja

el pescado

la cebolla

las habichuelas

## Otras carnes y pescados

| | |
|---|---|
| el atún | tuna |
| el bistec | (beef) steak |
| la carne de cerdo | pork |
| la carne picada | ground beef |
| la chuleta (de cerdo) | (pork) chop |
| los huevos | eggs |
| el jamón | ham |
| el pavo | turkey |
| la salchicha | sausage |
| el tocino | bacon |

## Other Meats and Fish

## Otras frutas y verduras

| | |
|---|---|
| el aguacate | avocado |
| los champiñones | mushrooms |
| el durazno | peach |
| las espinacas | spinach |
| la fresa | strawberry |
| los frijoles | beans |
| los guisantes | peas |
| la manzana | apple |
| la toronja | grapefruit |
| las uvas | grapes |
| la zanahoria | carrot |

## Other Fruits and Vegetables

Cognados: el kiwi, el mango, el melón, la papaya, la pera

## Los granos

| | |
|---|---|
| el arroz | rice |
| la galleta | cookie; cracker |
| el pan (integral) | (whole wheat) bread |

## Grains

Cognados: el cereal, la pasta

## Los productos lácteos

| | |
|---|---|
| la leche | milk |
| la mantequilla | butter |
| el queso | cheese |

## Dairy Products

Cognado: el yogur

## Los postres

| | |
|---|---|
| los dulces | candies |
| el flan | caramel custard |
| el helado | ice cream |
| el pastel | pie; cake |

## Desserts

Cognados: el chocolate, la menta, la vainilla

## Las bebidas

| | |
|---|---|
| el agua | water |
| la cerveza | beer |
| el jugo | juice |
| el refresco | soft drink |
| el vino (blanco/tinto) | (white/red) wine |

## Drinks

Cognados: el champaña, el té

## Otras palabras y expresiones

| | |
|---|---|
| el aceite (de oliva) | (olive) oil |
| el ajo | garlic |
| el azúcar | sugar |
| el mercado | market |
| la pimienta roja/negra | red/black pepper |
| el supermercado | supermarket |
| la tienda (de comestibles) | (grocery) store |

Cognados: preparar; la sal, el vinagre

### ACTIVIDADES

**A.** Los productos

**PASO 1.** Empareje cada marca (*name brand*) con el producto correspondiente.

| MARCAS | PRODUCTOS |
|---|---|
| 1. _____ Chiquita y Dole | **a.** la leche |
| 2. _____ Green Giant y Del Monte | **b.** las galletas |
| 3. _____ Borden y Horizon | **c.** el yogur |
| 4. _____ Dannon y Yoplait | **d.** el azúcar |
| 5. _____ Kraft and Sargento | **e.** el queso |
| 6. _____ Imperial y Domino | **f.** el atún |
| 7. _____ Keebler y Nabisco | **g.** la banana |
| 8. _____ Chicken of the Sea y Starkist | **h.** las habichuelas |

**PASO 2.** Empareje cada comestible (*food item*) con la sección del supermercado donde se encuentra.

| COMESTIBLES | SECCIÓN DEL SUPERMERCADO |
|---|---|
| 1. _____ los champiñones | **a.** las aves (*poultry*) |
| 2. _____ la mantequilla | **b.** las carnes |
| 3. _____ la toronja | **c.** el pescado y los mariscos |
| 4. _____ los camarones | **d.** las verduras |
| 5. _____ las chuletas | **e.** las frutas |
| 6. _____ el jugo | **f.** las bebidas |
| 7. _____ el pavo | **g.** los productos lácteos |
| 8. _____ el aceite | **h.** los aderezos (*seasonings*) y condimentos |

**B.** ¿De quién es?

**PASO 1.** Lea las descripciones de estas compañeras de casa. Luego, indique para quién son las compras: para Alejandra (**A**), Cecilia (**C**) o Nancy (**N**). **¡OJO!** Hay cosas que pueden ser para más de una persona.

| | | ALEJANDRA: | Es vegetariana y nunca toma bebidas alcohólicas. Tiene alergias al gluten. |

ALEJANDRA: Es vegetariana y nunca toma bebidas alcohólicas. Tiene alergias al gluten.

CECILIA: Es carnívora, pero come mucha fruta. Tiene alergias a los productos lácteos.

NANCY: Es carnívora y no le gustan las verduras verdes. Tiene alergias a los mariscos.

| | A | C | N | | | A | C | N |
|---|---|---|---|---|---|---|---|---|
| **1.** pan integral | ☐ | ☐ | ☐ | **7.** leche | | ☐ | ☐ | ☐ |
| **2.** tocino | ☐ | ☐ | ☐ | **8.** lechuga | | ☐ | ☐ | ☐ |
| **3.** guisantes | ☐ | ☐ | ☐ | **9.** papas | | ☐ | ☐ | ☐ |
| **4.** galletas | ☐ | ☐ | ☐ | **10.** fresas | | ☐ | ☐ | ☐ |
| **5.** queso | ☐ | ☐ | ☐ | **11.** camarones | | ☐ | ☐ | ☐ |
| **6.** jugo de naranja | ☐ | ☐ | ☐ | **12.** carne picada | | ☐ | ☐ | ☐ |

**PASO 2.** En parejas, hagan una lista de los comestibles que las tres amigas del **Paso 1** pueden compartir.

## C. Mi lista de compras

**PASO 1.** Haga una lista de los comestibles que Ud. necesita comprar esta semana en las tiendas o en el supermercado. Puede inventar algunas cosas si prefiere.

**PASO 2.** En parejas, hablen de los comestibles que van a comprar y dónde y cuándo los van a comprar. **¡OJO!** Apunten las respuestas de su compañero/a para el Paso 3.

MODELO  E1: ¿Qué necesitas comprar esta semana?
E2: Necesito comprar leche, cereal, pan, jamón y uvas.
E1: ¿Adónde vas para hacer las compras?
E2: Voy al supermercado Kroger porque está cerca de mi casa.
E1: ¿Cuándo vas?
E2: Voy esta tarde después de clase porque no tengo nada de comer en casa.

**PASO 3.** Conteste las preguntas, según la lista de su compañero/a. Luego, escriba una breve descripción de los hábitos de su compañero/a que puede compartir con la clase.

| Mi compañero/a... | SÍ | NO |
|---|---|---|
| **1.** casi siempre cocina en casa. | ☐ | ☐ |
| **2.** come muchas frutas y verduras. | ☐ | ☐ |
| **3.** come mucha comida chatarra (*junk*). | ☐ | ☐ |
| **4.** come comidas sanas (*healthy*). | ☐ | ☐ |
| **5.** es vegetariano/a. | ☐ | ☐ |

## D. La nutrición

**PASO 1.** En parejas, clasifiquen los comestibles presentados en el **Vocabulario del tema** de acuerdo con los siguientes valores nutritivos: (1) Carbohidratos, (2) Proteínas, (3) Vitaminas, (4) Calcio, (5) Grasas (*Fats*), (6) Azúcar **¡OJO!** Algunos comestibles pueden pertenecer (*belong*) a más de una categoría.

**PASO 2.** Preparen un menú para el desayuno, almuerzo y cena de las siguientes personas: (1) un atleta que necesita mucha energía, (2) un niño de 8 años que está creciendo (*growing*) y (3) una persona vegetariana que no puede comer carne pero que debe consumir proteínas.

## Nota cultural

### EL LECHÓN EN PUERTO RICO

*Un lechón asado*

El lechón asado es el plato tradicional en Puerto Rico durante las fiestas de Navidad. Algunos historiadores dicen que la forma de asar el lechón en Puerto Rico procede[a] de los antiguos piratas del Caribe y no existe en otras partes del mundo. Primero, aderezan el cerdo con sal, pimienta y orégano y lo dejan reposar[b] durante siete u ocho horas. Al día siguiente, preparan dos palos de madera[c] que terminan en forma de **y,** y ponen una vara[d] encima. Finalmente, en esta vara asan el cerdo muy lentamente sobre el fuego. Las familias puertorriqueñas preparan el lechón en el patio y es motivo de fiesta y reunión de familiares y amigos.

[a]*comes from*   [b]*lo... let it marinate*   [c]*palos... wooden sticks*   [d]*thick stick*

**PREGUNTAS** En parejas, contesten las preguntas. Después, compartan sus ideas con la clase.

1. ¿Cómo se cocina el lechón en Puerto Rico?
2. ¿En qué época del año es más común comer lechón asado? ¿Dónde preparan los puertorriqueños su asado de lechón?

## Nota comunicativa

Communication

### EXCLAMATIONS

The basic formula for exclamations in Spanish is: **¡qué** + *adj.*! (Note the accent on **qué**.) Here are some common exclamations you may hear related to food.

| | |
|---|---|
| **¡Qué delicioso/rico/sabroso!** | *How delicious!* |
| **¡Qué rica** es la comida de aquí! | *My, how delicious the food is here!* |
| **¡Qué buena** está esta salsa! | *Wow, this salsa tastes good!* |
| **¡Fuchi! ¡Qué mala** está esta sopa! | *Yuck! This soup tastes bad!* |

# Gramática

Expressing *to/for Whom* Something Is Done

## 6.1 Indirect Object Pronouns

**GRAMÁTICA EN CONTEXTO**

*En un mercado de Puerto Rico*

### En el mercado

*[Paz habla de su mercado favorito en San Juan, Puerto Rico.]*

¡**Me** gusta mucho este mercado! Siempre vengo aquí con mi amiga Adela. El Sr. Olmos es nuestro vendedor favorito porque tiene las mejores frutas. A veces **nos** da un descuento y siempre es amable, **dándonos** consejos sobre cuáles son las frutas más

**GRAMÁTICA EN CONTEXTO** *At the Market / Paz talks about her favorite market in San Juan, Puerto Rico. / I really like this market! I always come here with my friend Adela. Mr. Olmos is our favorite vendor because he has the best fruit. Sometimes he gives us a discount and he's always nice, giving us advice about which are the sweetest and freshest fruits. At the market, I buy a lot of fruits and vegetables for my husband and children. This morning, I'm going to buy my husband a papaya because it's his favorite fruit. My children always ask me for fruit salad, so I'm going to buy apples, pears, and oranges.*

dulces y frescas. En el mercado, **les** compro muchas frutas y legumbres a mi esposo y a mis hijos. Esta mañana, voy a **comprarle** una papaya a mi esposo porque es la fruta que más **le** gusta. Mis hijos siempre **me** piden ensalada de frutas, por eso, voy a comprar manzanas, peras y naranjas.

Comprensión. ¿Probable (**P**) o improbable (**I**)?

|  | P | I |
|---|---|---|
| 1. Paz siempre visita al Sr. Olmos cuando va al mercado. | ☐ | ☐ |
| 2. Paz le prepara muchas comidas frescas a su familia. | ☐ | ☐ |
| 3. Adela no le compra fruta al Sr. Olmos. | ☐ | ☐ |
| 4. El Sr. Olmos les recomienda las carnes más frescas. | ☐ | ☐ |

An indirect object indirectly receives the action of the verb in a sentence and generally answers the question *to whom?* or *for whom?*

| El camarero le **sirve** el café a José María. | *The waiter serves coffee to José María.* |
|---|---|
| Yolanda nos **prepara** la cena. | *Yolanda prepares dinner for us.* |

| INDIRECT OBJECT PRONOUNS | | | |
|---|---|---|---|
| me | to/for me | nos | to/for us |
| te | to/for you | os | to/for you |
| le | to/for you, him/her, it | les | to/for you, them |

**A.** Placement of indirect object pronouns is the same as for direct object pronouns. They are placed immediately before a conjugated verb or attached to the end of an infinitive or gerund. If pronouns are attached to a gerund, a written accent is needed to indicate the original stressed syllable.

| ¿Le **sirvo** más café a Ud.? | *Shall I serve you more coffee?* |
|---|---|
| Voy a **servirte** el postre. | *I'm going to serve you dessert.* |
| Estoy **preparándoles** té a mis amigos. | *I'm preparing tea for my friends.* |

**B.** If an indirect object noun is used in a sentence, it must be accompanied by the corresponding indirect object pronoun. This may seem redundant, but is necessary in Spanish. You can leave out the indirect object noun (e.g., **a mis amigos**) if the context is clear, but you must always include the indirect object pronoun (**me, te, le, nos, os, les**). Any indirect object nouns are always preceded by the preposition **a.**

| —Joven, ¿le va a traer una ensalada a mi amiga también? | *Waiter, are you going to bring a salad for my friend as well?* (Indirect object noun needed to establish context.) |
|---|---|
| —En seguida, señor. Ahorita le traigo una. | *Right away, sir. I'll bring her one right now.* (Indirect object noun no longer needed.) |

## Nota comunicativa

Communication

### THE VERBS dar AND decir

The verbs **dar** (*to give*) and **decir** (*to say; to tell*) are almost always used in conjunction with indirect object pronouns, because we almost always give, say, or tell something to someone. Here are the forms of **dar** and **decir** in the present tense. Note that both have irregular **yo** forms and that **decir** is also an **e → i** stem changing verb.

| dar (irreg.) to give | |
|---|---|
| doy | damos |
| das | dais |
| da | dan |

| decir (irreg.) to say; to tell | |
|---|---|
| digo | decimos |
| dices | decís |
| dice | dicen |

—¿Cuánto **le das** al mesero de propina? — How much do you give the waiter as a tip?
—Generalmente **le doy** el 15 por ciento. — I usually give 15 percent.
—¿**Me** puede **decir** cuál es el menú del día? — Can you tell me what today's special is?

**C.** Here are some common verbs that take indirect objects. Some of them you already know. Note that some of them have stem changes.

### COMMON VERBS THAT TAKE INDIRECT OBJECTS

| | | | | | |
|---|---|---|---|---|---|
| **contar (ue)** | to count; to tell | **mandar** | to send | **prometer** | to promise |
| **entregar** | to deliver; to hand in | **mostrar (ue)** | to show | **recomendar (ie)** | to recommend |
| **escribir** | to write | **ofrecer (zc)** | to offer | **regalar** | to give (as a gift) |
| **explicar** | to explain | **pedir (i)** | to request; to order | | |
| **deber** | to owe | **preguntar** | to ask (a question) | **servir (i)** | to serve |
| **hablar** | to speak | **prestar** | to loan | **sugerir (ie)** | to suggest |

## Nota comunicativa

Communication

### OTHER VERBS LIKE gustar

You'll recall that **gustar** agrees with the subject (the thing or action being liked) and that the person that's doing the liking (*lit.* to whom the subject is pleasing) is expressed as in indirect object pronoun (**me, te, le, nos, os, les**). There are several other verbs that require this same basic construction as **gustar.** Here are some of those verbs and phrases.

| | | | |
|---|---|---|---|
| **aburrir** | to bore | **llamar la** | to sound interesting (*lit.* to call out for |
| **encantar** | to love (*lit.* to enchant) | **atención** | one's attention) |
| **fascinar** | to fascinate | **molestar** | to bother |
| **interesar** | to interest | **preocupar** | to worry |

A mí **me encantan** las frutas tropicales. — I love tropical fruit (lit. Tropical fruit enchants me.)
Ay, este restaurante **me aburre.** Vamos a otro lugar. — Man, this restaurant bores me. Let's go somewhere else.
Mmm. Esa receta **me llama** mucho **la atención.** — Mmm. That recipe sounds interesting (lit. calls out for my attention).

## ACTIVIDADES

**A. Para la fiesta.** Forme oraciones usando las pistas. **¡OJO!** Dé (*Give*) la forma correcta de los verbos y adjetivos, y añada (*add*) las palabras necesarias.

MODELO  Pilar / (a nosotros) / comprar / fruta / para / fiesta
        Pilar nos compra fruta para la fiesta.

1. ¿(a ti) / (yo) poder / traer / algo / para / fiesta?
2. Leonor y su madre / (a mí) / ir / preparar / tamales
3. Uds. / (a ellas) / deber / explicar / direcciones / ir / a mi casa
4. no / (tú) necesitar / decir / (a ellos) / nada / sobre / fiesta
5. ¿cuánto / cebollas / (a ella) / (yo) tener que / comprar?
6. Paco / (a nosotros) / ir / tocar / música / en / fiesta

**B. ¿Quién te… ?** En parejas, háganse preguntas, usando palabras de la lista.

Communication

MODELO  ¿Quién te da… ? →
        E1: ¿Quién te da dinero para la comida?
        E2: Mis padres me dan dinero para la comida, pero yo también trabajo.

| ayuda | copas | favores | lecciones | problemas | secretos |
|-------|-------|---------|-----------|-----------|----------|
| comida | dinero | fiestas | preguntas | regalos | tarea |

1. ¿Quién te da… ?
2. ¿Quién te dice… ?
3. ¿Quién te trae… ?
4. ¿Quién te hace… ?
5. ¿Quién te pide… ?

6. ¿A quién le das… ?
7. ¿A quién le dices… ?
8. ¿A quién le pides… ?
9. ¿A quién le preparas… ?
10. ¿A quién le explicas… ?

**C. Entrevista.** Entreviste a un compañero / una compañera de clase sobre las fiestas con estas preguntas. Luego, cambien de papel.

Communication

1. ¿Con qué frecuencia haces fiestas? ¿A quién invitas? ¿a tus compañeros de clase? ¿a tus compañeros de trabajo? ¿a tus familiares? ¿a tus amigos?
2. ¿Qué comidas y bebidas les sirves a tus invitados?
3. ¿Haces fiestas grandes o prefieres hacer fiestas más íntimas?
4. En tus fiestas, ¿qué hacen los invitados? ¿bailan? ¿conversan? ¿otra cosa?

**D. El café cubano**

Cultures   Recycle

PASO 1.  Complete la conversación entre Lisa y Andy y su amigo cubano Emilio. Dé la forma correcta de las palabras entre paréntesis. Cuando aparece un verbo con una pista para un pronombre de objeto indirecto, dé la forma correcta del verbo y del pronombre. **¡OJO!** Coloque (*Place*) correctamente el pronombre.

LISA:   ¡Me encanta la comida cubana! ¡Es tan rica!

ANDY:   ¡A mí también! Gracias por (**preparar / a nosotros**[1]) esta cena deliciosa.

EMILIO: ¡(*Yo:* **Alegrarse**[2]) de que les guste! ¿(*Yo:* **traer / a Uds.**[3]) un café? También tengo café cubano.

LISA:   ¿A (**este**[4]) hora de la noche?

EMILIO: Sí, nosotros los cubanos (**tomar**[5]) café a todas horas. Es un ritual, un evento social para nosotros.

LISA:   Pues, entonces, ¡café cubano! ¿(*Yo:* **poder / a ti**[6]) ayudar?

EMILIO: No, gracias. (*Yo:* **ir / a Uds.**[7]) a preparar una espumita. ¿O (*Uds.:* **preferir**[8]) un cortado?

ANDY:   ¿Una espumita? ¿Un cortado? No (*yo:* **entender / a ti**[9]).

(Continúa.)

*Un cafecito cubano*

EMILIO: Ah, (*yo: explicar / a Uds.*[10]). Nosotros típicamente tomamos un cafecito, que es un café expreso con azúcar. (*Nosotros: Decir*[11]) *cafecito* porque servimos el café en tacitas, es decir, en tazas[a] muy pequeñas. Creo que Uds. (decir[12]) *demitasse cups.* Como el café cubano (ser[13]) muy fuerte,[b] lo tomamos con mucho azúcar.

ANDY: Pero tú nos dijiste[c] una espumita o un cortado.

EMILIO: Ah, sí. Para preparar una espumita, mezclamos[d] un poco de café con azúcar para formar una espuma dulce[e] y después, (*nosotros: poner*[14]) la espuma en un cafecito. Por eso, (*ese café: llamarse*[15]) espumita. Es un cafecito más elegante.

LISA: Y más dulce.

EMILIO: Sí. Y si la espumita es todavía demasiado[f] fuerte para ti, Lisa, (*yo: poder / a ti*[16]) preparar un cortado, que es un cafecito con un poco de leche.

LISA: ¡(*Tú: estar / a nosotros*[17]) dando una lección cultural sobre el café cubano!

EMILIO: ¡Ja, ja! Es que me encanta el café. (*Yo: Ser*[18]), como decimos en Cuba, muy cafetero.[g] ¿Qué tal si (*yo: preparar / a Uds.*[19]) una colada?

ANDY: ¿Una colada?

EMILIO: Sí. Es una taza grande de café con azúcar, con tres tacitas para compartir.

ANDY: ¿Por qué no? ¡Estás (*hacer / a nosotros*[20]) una fiesta de café! ¡Qué rico!

---

[a]*cups*  [b]*strong*  [c]*told*  [d]*we mix*  [e]*espuma... sweet foam*  [f]*todavía... still too*  [g]*muy... coffee addict*

**PASO 2.** Empareje cada palabra con la definición correcta.

1. ____ el cafecito
2. ____ la espumita
3. ____ la colada
4. ____ el cortado
5. ____ el cafetero

a. cafecito con leche
b. expreso con azúcar
c. adicto al café
d. cafecito con espuma de azúcar y café
e. tres o más tacitas de cafecito

Communication

**PASO 3.** Entreviste a un compañero / una compañera con estas preguntas. Luego, cambien de papel.

1. ¿Tienes amigos que te preparan comida? ¿Qué tipo de comida te preparan? ¿Te gustan los platos que te preparan?
2. ¿Qué comidas les preparas a tus amigos? ¿Les sirves café después de una cena?
3. ¿Dónde y cuándo te gusta tomar café? ¿Qué tipo de café te gusta? ¿Te gusta el café expreso? ¿Qué tipo de café sabes preparar?

# 6.2 Double Object Pronouns

## GRAMÁTICA EN CONTEXTO

### En la mesa

| | |
|---|---|
| MANUELA: | Mamá, ¿me pasas las tortillas, por favor? |
| ABUELA: | Con gusto **te las** paso, mi hija. Querido, ¿le sirves vino a Manuela, por favor? |
| ABUELO: | Sí, **se lo** sirvo en un momento. Manuela, ¿me pasas el maíz? |
| MANUELA: | Sí, papá. **Te lo** paso en un segundo. |
| ABUELO: | Gracias, mi hija. Querida, ¿cuándo nos vas a traer el postre? |
| ABUELA: | Paciencia, mi amor. Después de la comida, **se lo** traigo a todos. |

### ¿CIERTO O FALSO?

|   |   |   | C | F |
|---|---|---|---|---|
| 1. | ¿Las tortillas? Abuela se las pasa a su hija Manuela. | | ☐ | ☐ |
| 2. | ¿El vino? Abuelo está sirviéndoselo a Manuela en este momento. | | ☐ | ☐ |
| 3. | ¿El maíz? Abuelo se lo va a pasar a Manuela. | | ☐ | ☐ |
| 4. | ¿El postre? Abuela va a traérselo a todos después de la comida. | | ☐ | ☐ |

**A.** When a direct and an indirect object pronoun are found in the same clause, they always appear together, and the indirect object pronoun always precedes the direct object pronoun.

| | |
|---|---|
| —Papá, ¿**me** vuelves a contar <u>esa historia</u>? | *Papá, will you tell me that story again?* |
| —Sí, mi hija, te la vuelvo a contar. | *Yes, my child, I'll tell it to you again.* |

**B.** The indirect object pronouns **le** and **les** change to **se** when they precede the direct object pronouns **lo, la, los,** and **las.**

| | |
|---|---|
| —¿**Me** puede mostrar <u>la sandía</u>? | *Can you show me the watermelon?* |
| —Claro que sí, se la muestro en un momento. | *Of course, I'll show it to you in a moment.* |

**C.** Like individual object pronouns, double object pronouns can be attached to the end of an infinitive or gerund. In either case, a written accent is placed on the vowel of the syllable that receives the stress.

---

GRAMÁTICA EN CONTEXTO *At the Table / MANUELA: Mom, would you please pass me the tortillas?* **GRANDMA:** *I'll gladly pass them to you, my dear. Darling, would you please serve Manuela some wine?* **GRANDPA:** *Yes, I'll serve her some in a moment. Manuela, could you please pass me the corn?* **MANUELA:** *Yes, Dad. I'll pass it to you in a second.* **GRANDPA:** *Thank you, my dear. Darling, when are you going to bring us dessert?* **GRANDMA:** *Patience, my love. After dinner, I'll bring it out for everyone.*

| | |
|---|---|
| —¿Vas a pasar**me** <u>los platos</u>? | *Are you going to pass me the plates?* |
| —Sí, voy a **pasártelos.** | *Yes, I'm going to pass them to you.* |
| —¿**Nos** está explicando <u>el menú</u>? | *Is he explaining the menu to us?* |
| —Sí, está **explicándonoslo.** | *Yes, he's explaining it to us.* |

## ACTIVIDADES

**A. En el mercado.** Empareje las declaraciones con las respuestas para formar una secuencia lógica.

**DECLARACIONES**

1. Mamá, quiero uvas y manzanas. ____
2. Necesitamos un kilo de papas, por favor. ____
3. A papá no le gustan las espinacas. ____
4. ¿Puedo comer esta naranja? ____
5. Mis hermanos y yo les tenemos alergia a los camarones. ____
6. Esta bolsa (*bag*) de fruta es muy pesada (*heavy*). ____
7. Luis quiere pescado, pero no está fresco (*fresh*). ____

**RESPUESTAS**

a. Por eso tu madre nunca se los sirve.
b. Sí, pero voy a comprártela primero.
c. Entonces, no se lo voy a dar.
d. Ahora se lo traigo, señora.
e. Voy a comprártelas.
f. Por eso no se las compro.
g. Yo te la puedo llevar.

**B. Preparativos.** Amalia prepara una recepción grande. Conteste las preguntas que otras personas le hacen, según las pistas. **¡OJO!** Use dos pronombres en sus respuestas.

1. ¿Cuándo le debo mandar a Ud. las frutas? (mañana)
2. ¿Quién nos va a traer la langosta? (Ignacio)
3. Amalia, ¿puedo hacerte la lista de invitados? (sí)
4. Señora, ¿me va a escribir Ud. un cheque por los tomates? (sí)
5. ¿Adónde le tenemos que llevar las mesas? (al salón)
6. Amalia, ¿a quién les debo dar estas instrucciones? (a esos hombres)

**C. Vamos al mercado.** En parejas, imagínense que están en el mercado. Túrnense para pedir diferentes comidas, según el modelo. Usen palabras del **Vocabulario del tema.**

MODELO E1: Mmm. ¡Manzanas! ¿Me las compras?
E2: Sí, te las compro. ¡Me encantan las manzanas! / No, no te las voy a comprar porque están muy caras (*expensive*) hoy.

**D. Las frutas del Caribe**

PASO 1. Complete el texto sobre las frutas caribeñas con la forma correcta de las palabras entre paréntesis. Cuando aparecen dos opciones, escoja la correcta. Cuando aparecen **ser** y **estar** juntos, escoja el verbo correcto y dé la forma correcta.

Las frutas variadas del Caribe son un elemento clave[a] en los platos deliciosos de la región. Cuando Ud. visita un país del Caribe, (*Ud.:* tener[1]) la oportunidad de probar frutas (exótico[2]) que no (*nosotros:* poder[3]) comprar en este país. Y no (**te las / se las**[4]) puede traer a sus amigos como recuerdo.[b] (**Por/Para**[5]) eso, (**los/las**[6]) tiene que disfrutar mientras (*Ud.:* **ser/estar**[7]) en el Caribe.

El Caribe es una región de tierras[c] fértiles y generosas. Estas tierras (producir[8]) (rico[9]) frutas tropicales. Estas frutas desconocidas[d] les impresionaron[e] a los primeros

[a]*key* [b]*souvenir* [c]*lands* [d]*unknown* [e]*impressed*

exploradores,[f] pero se enfrentaron con[g] un problema: «¿Cómo (**se los / se las**[10]) vamos a llevar a los reyes españoles?» A lo largo de[h] los años, llevaron a Europa semillas[i] y plantas de tomate, maíz, aguacate, papas y (**otro**[11]) frutas y verduras.

Hoy en día, las frutas de las islas caribeñas (**ser/ estar**[12]) más variadas. Algunas frutas, como la guayaba,[j] (**ser/estar**[13]) originarias de[k] las islas. Otras frutas (**popular**[14]) del Caribe, como el aguacate y la piña, son de Centro o Sudamérica. Otras frutas (**venir**[15]) del sur de Asia, por ejemplo, la banana o plátano y el mango.

*Algunas frutas típicas del Caribe*

Una de las plantas (**caribeño**[16]) más importantes es la caña[l] de azúcar. Pero tampoco es originaria del Caribe; viene del oeste[m] de África. Los esclavos[n] (**africano**[17]) la trajeron[ñ] al Caribe con (**su**[18]) especias[o] y su música. La caña de azúcar floreció[p] en la tierra fértil del Caribe. Los caribeños todavía (**usar**[19]) el azúcar para endulzar[q] su comida y producir ron.[r] Y, aunque ya no (*ellos:* **ser/estar**[20]) los principales exportadores del azúcar, aún (**lo/la**[21]) (**vender**[22]) en el mercado europeo.

[f]*explorers* [g]*se... faced* [h]*A... Throughout* [i]*llevaron... took seeds to Europe* [j]*guava* [k]*originarias... native to* [l]*cane* [m]*west* [n]*slaves* [ñ]*brought* [o]*spices* [p]*flourished* [q]*sweeten* [r]*rum*

**PASO 2.** Indique las oraciones que son posibles, según el **Paso 1.**

1. ☐ Todas las frutas que asociamos con el Caribe son originarias del Caribe.
2. ☐ Es ilegal traer frutas del Caribe a este país como turista.
3. ☐ Muchas frutas exóticas florecen en el Caribe.
4. ☐ Los caribeños preparan comidas con frutas de las islas.
5. ☐ Los mangos son originarios del Caribe.
6. ☐ La piña es originaria de Cuba.
7. ☐ El Caribe exporta azúcar a Europa.

**PASO 3.** En parejas, busquen la región de origen de estas frutas u otras frutas tropicales que conocen. Luego, túrnense para pedir las frutas que desean. Su compañero/a va a decir de qué país se las va a traer.

Communication

**MODELO** E1: ¿Me puedes traer una banana?
E2: Sí, claro. Te la traigo de Asia.

| | |
|---|---|
| el aguacate, de ____ | el mango, de ____ |
| el marañón (*cashew*), de ____ | la papaya, de ____ |
| el coco, de ____ | la piña, de ____ |
| la mandarina (*tangerine*), de ____ | la toronja, de ____ |
| ¿ ?, de ____ | ¿ ?, de ____ |

# Palabra escrita

## A comenzar

> **Stating Your Topic Sentence.** The topic sentence is the central idea of a paragraph and any other information in that paragraph should simply support this main point. In this composition, you will be making comparisons. As you move from one comparative point to the next, the topic sentence can help you stay focused, and the reader will be able to follow and interpret your points clearly.

You are going to start the process of writing a brief composition that you will finalize in the **Palabra escrita: A finalizar** section of your *Manual de actividades*. The topic of this composition is **Las ventajas y desventajas de comprar comestibles en ciertos lugares.** The purpose of your composition will be to explain and compare the advantages and disadvantages of buying food in at least three of the following types of stores: superstores (e.g., Costco), large supermarket chains (e.g., Kroger), local grocery stores, convenience stores, and farmers markets.

**A. Lluvia de ideas.** En parejas, hagan una lluvia de ideas sobre estos temas relacionados con la compra de comestibles en diferentes tipos de tiendas, pensando en las comparaciones que pueden hacer.

1. la selección
2. los precios
3. la calidad
4. la economía local
5. ¿ ?

**B. A organizar sus ideas.** Repase sus ideas y organícelas en categorías. Mientras empieza a identificar los párrafos que va a escribir, forme una oración temática para cada párrafo. Comparta su información con la clase y apunte otras ideas que se le ocurran durante el proceso.

**C. A escribir.** Ahora, haga el borrador de su composición con las ideas y la información que recopiló (*collected*) en las actividades A y B. **¡OJO!** Guarde bien su trabajo. Va a necesitarlo otra vez para la sección de **Palabra escrita: A finalizar** en el *Manual de actividades*.

## Wilfredo Lam

La jungla, *1943*

El artista cubano Wilfredo Lam (1902–1982) es uno de los pintores surrealistas más originales de Latinoamérica. En sus obras se nota la influencia de Picasso, a quien Lam conoció[a] en París. Lam fusiona en sus obras su herencia afrocubana y las vanguardias europeas.

En *La jungla* se notan elementos primitivos africanos y elementos cubistas. De su herencia afrocubana vemos figuras enmascaradas,[b] caña de azúcar y bambú. Las figuras —mitad[c] animal y mitad humano bajo la luna[d]— sugieren la comunicación entre el espíritu y la naturaleza, un aspecto importante del misticismo afrocubano. Las perspectivas múltiples de estas figuras recuerdan el estilo cubista.

---

[a]*met*  [b]*masked*  [c]*half*  [d]*bajo... under the moon*

## Vocabulario del tema

### En la mesa y las comidas°

*meals*

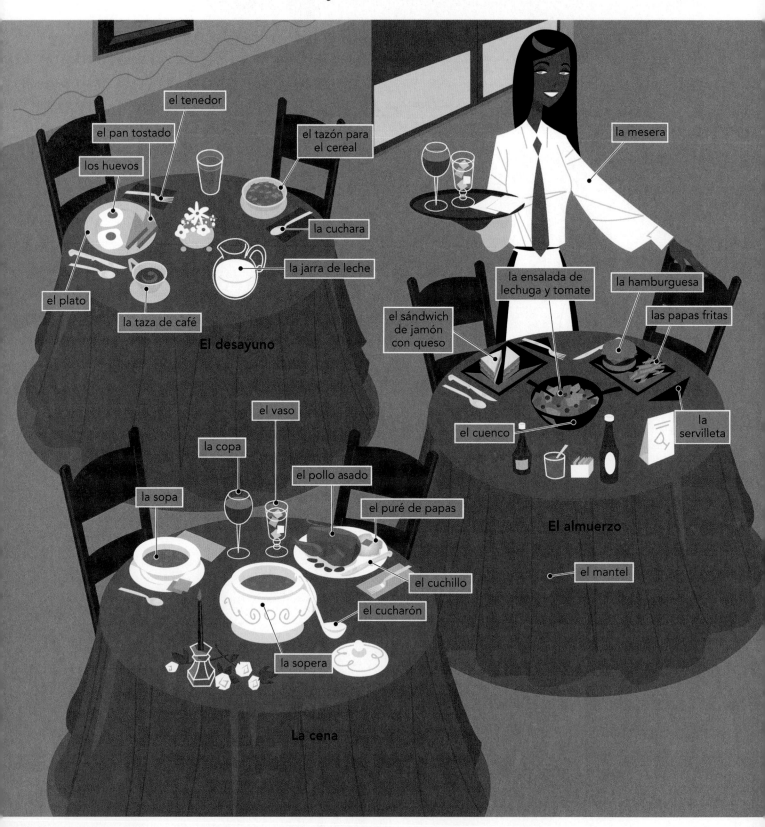

el tenedor

el pan tostado

el tazón para el cereal

la mesera

los huevos

la cuchara

la jarra de leche

el plato

la taza de café

la ensalada de lechuga y tomate

la hamburguesa

el sándwich de jamón con queso

las papas fritas

**El desayuno**

el vaso

la copa

el pollo asado

el cuenco

la servilleta

la sopa

el puré de papas

el cuchillo

el mantel

**El almuerzo**

el cucharón

la sopera

**La cena**

| contener (*like* tener) | to contain |
| cubrir | to cover |
| hervir (ie) | to boil |
| merendar (ie) | to snack |
| probar (ue) | to taste, try |
| el alimento | food; nourishment |

Cognados: los ingredientes, los utensilios; internacional, local, natural, orgánico/a, tradicional, tropical

## En el restaurante

| ordenar ⎫ | |
| pedir (i) ⎭ | to order |
| el/la cocinero/a | cook, chef |
| la cuenta | bill, check |
| el/la mesero/a | waiter/waitress |
| la propina | tip |
| la tarjeta de crédito | credit card |
| acogedor(a) | cozy; welcoming |
| relajante | relaxing |
| en efectivo | cash |

Cognados: aceptar; el menú, la reservación; romántico/a, variado/a

**ACTIVIDADES**

**A.** Un día típico

Communication

**PASO 1.** Haga una encuesta sobre lo que comen sus compañero/as en un día típico. Hágales preguntas a por lo menos cinco estudiantes para completar el cuadro (*chart*). Lleve las cuentas (*tallies*) del cuadro, según sus respuestas. Siga el modelo.

MODELO E1: ¿Qué comes para el desayuno?
E2: No desayuno nunca.
E1: [*Indique «no» en el cuadro.*] ¿Y qué comes para el almuerzo?
E2: Típicamente como un sándwich de jamón con queso y una manzana.
E1: [*Indique «proteínas», «frutas» y «granos» en el cuadro.*]

| | NO | PROTEÍNAS | VERDURAS | FRUTAS | GRANOS | DULCES |
|---|---|---|---|---|---|---|
| el desayuno | | | | | | |
| el almuerzo | | | | | | |
| la cena | | | | | | |

**PASO 2.** Ahora, la clase va a dibujar el cuadro en la pizarra. Deben apuntar en el cuadro todos los resultados. Digan si creen que los estudiantes de la clase comen bien o no, según los resultados.

**B.** Un restaurante

**PASO 1.** Escoja un restaurante local. Escriba una breve descripción del restaurante sin nombrarlo. Describa la comida que sirven, el ambiente (*atmosphere*), el servicio, etcétera.

MODELO Es un restaurante muy elegante con un ambiente relajante y acogedor. La comida es excelente pero un poco cara. Sirven...

**PASO 2.** Ahora, lea su descripción a la clase. Sus compañeros van a adivinar el nombre del restaurante.

**C.** El menú

**PASO 1.** En una hoja de papel aparte, invente un menú para un restaurante. En este restaurante sólo sirven una comida al día (desayuno, almuerzo o cena). Incluya los precios de cada cosa en el menú. Luego, escriba un breve anuncio para su restaurante que describa su ambiente y su comida.

**PASO 2.** Su profesor(a) va a dividir la clase en tres o cuatro grupos. Cada grupo va a recibir los menús y las descripciones de otro grupo. En su grupo, emparejen las descripciones con los menús. Luego con toda la clase, escojan su restaurante favorito.

**D.** Entrevista. Entreviste a un compañero / una compañera de clase con estas preguntas. Luego, cambien de papel.

1. ¿Qué utensilios tienes en casa? ¿Cocinas con frecuencia? ¿Qué sabes cocinar?
2. ¿Usas mantel en casa? Si lo usas, ¿para qué comidas o en qué ocasiones lo usas?
3. ¿A qué hora desayunas? ¿Qué prefieres comer para el desayuno? ¿Tomas café en la mañana?
4. ¿A qué hora almuerzas? ¿Qué prefieres comer para el almuerzo? ¿Dónde almuerzas?
5. ¿A qué hora cenas? ¿Cenas en casa o sales a cenar? ¿Cenas en la cafetería?
6. ¿Cuáles son tus restaurantes favoritos? ¿Cuántas veces a la semana comes en un restaurante? ¿Qué tipo de comida sirven en tus restaurantes favoritos?

---

## Nota interdisciplinaria

### CIENCIAS DE LA SALUD:[a] LA ALIMENTACIÓN

Una buena alimentación es la base principal de la salud. Sin embargo, hoy en día hay mucho debate sobre cuál es la dieta óptima para el ser humano. La Food and Drug Administration de los Estados Unidos hace las siguientes recomendaciones.

1. Comer productos variados de todos los grupos de alimentos y aumentar el consumo de los hidratos de carbono hasta un 57 por ciento en la dieta diaria. Es recomendable comer frutas, verduras y cereales integrales, y reducir el consumo de azúcar refinada.
2. Reducir las grasas hasta un 25 por ciento del consumo energético total para prevenir[b] las enfermedades[c] cardiovasculares.
3. Limitar las proteínas hasta un 15 por ciento de la dieta diaria. Comer aves y pescados y reducir el consumo de la carne de ternera[d] y otras carnes rojas.
4. Comer alimentos ricos en fibra, como las verduras, frutas, cereales integrales y legumbres enteras. La cantidad de fibra vegetal presente en la dieta no puede ser nunca inferior a los 22 gramos por día.
5. Consumir bebidas alcohólicas con moderación.
6. Evitar[e] los alimentos con alto contenido de sal, presente en alimentos procesados y comidas precocinadas,[f] para prevenir la hipertensión.

[a]*Health* [b]*to prevent* [c]*illnesses* [d]*veal* [e]*to avoid* [f]*precooked*

**PREGUNTAS** En parejas, contesten las preguntas. Después, compartan sus ideas con la clase.

1. ¿Qué alimentos son buenos para la salud y qué productos debemos evitar? Mencionen alimentos e ingredientes específicos.
2. Piensen en platos típicos de su cultura y en los ingredientes que llevan. De acuerdo con la información de la lectura, ¿creen que la dieta del lugar donde Uds. viven es, en general, saludable o no? Expliquen.

# Gramática

## 6.3 Formal Commands

### GRAMÁTICA EN CONTEXTO

Una receta para tostones

INGREDIENTES

2 bananas verdes
½ taza de aceite de maíz
sal (al gusto)

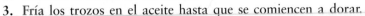

PREPARACIÓN

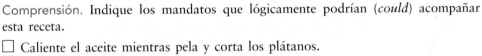

*Unos tostones*

1. Pele las bananas y **córtelas** en trozos gruesos.
2. Caliente el aceite en un sartén.
3. Fría los trozos en el aceite hasta que se comiencen a dorar.
4. **Retírelos** del sartén y **colóquelos** sobre toallas de papel para eliminar el exceso de grasa.
5. Aplaste los trozos uno por uno entre unas toallas de papel con la mano o con un vaso.
6. Fría los trozos aplastados en aceite caliente hasta que queden doraditos y crujientes.
7. Condimente con sal y **sirva** los tostones en un plato.

**Comprensión.** Indique los mandatos que lógicamente podrían (*could*) acompañar esta receta.

☐ Caliente el aceite mientras pela y corta los plátanos.
☐ Fría las bananas antes de cortarlas.
☐ Fría las bananas dos veces.
☐ Sirva las bananas con carne y arroz.

You've already been exposed to some commands in the activities of *Experience Spanish* and you've undoubtedly heard some from your professor in class. Which of the following commands do you recognize?

1. **Conteste** las preguntas.
2. **Empareje** las palabras...
3. **Escriba** una oración...
4. **Abran** los libros...
5. **Cierren** los libros.
6. **Hagan** las actividades A, B y C para mañana.

In this section, you will learn formal commands: those used to address people as **Ud.** or **Uds.** You'll learn about informal commands (**tú** and **vosotros/as**) in **Gramática 8.1.**

| FORMAL COMMANDS | | | | |
|---|---|---|---|---|
| INFINITIVE | PRESENT TENSE **yo** FORM | REMOVE **-o** | ADD "OPPOSITE VOWEL" ENDING | FORMAL COMMAND: **Ud., Uds.** |
| aplastar | aplasto | aplas- | -e, -en | aplaste, aplasten |
| comer | como | com- | -a, -an | coma, coman |
| vivir | vivo | viv- | -a, -an | viva, vivan |

GRAMÁTICA EN CONTEXTO *A recipe for Tostones / Ingredients: 2 green bananas; ½ cup of corn oil; salt (to taste) / Preparation:* **1.** *Peel the bananas and cut them in thick pieces.* **2.** *Heat the oil in a pan.* **3.** *Fry the pieces in oil until they begin to brown.* **4.** *Remove them from the pan and place them on paper towels to eliminate the excess oil.* **5.** *Mash the pieces one by one between the paper towels by hand or with a glass.* **6.** *Fry the mashed pieces in the hot oil until they become brown and crusty.* **7.** *Season with salt and serve the tostones on a plate.*

**A.** Most formal commands are formed by following these steps.

1. Take the **yo** form of the present tense: **cortar → corto**
2. Remove the -o ending of the yo form: **corto → cort-**
3. Add the "opposite vowel" ending.
   a. For **-ar** verbs, add **-e** for **Ud.** commands or **-en** for **Uds.** commands: **corte, corten**
   b. For **-er/-ir** verbs, add **-a** for **Ud.** commands or **-an** for **Uds.** commands: **coma, coman; viva, vivan**

**Pase** la sal y la pimienta, por favor.　　*Please pass the salt and pepper.*

**B.** If a verb has an irregular **yo** form in the present tense, whether it's due to a stem change (**duermo**) or some other irregularity (**tengo, conozco**), that same irregularity carries over to the formal command form.

**Pidan** el pollo asado. Es excelente.　　*Order the roast chicken. It's excellent.*
**Ponga** la botella de agua encima de la mesa, por favor.　　*Put the bottle of water on (top of) the table, please.*

**C.** There are five verbs whose formal command forms are not formed by following the preceding steps. Note the written accent on some of these forms.

| IRREGULAR FORMAL COMMANDS | | |
|---|---|---|
| INFINITIVE | **Ud.** COMMAND | **Uds.** COMMAND |
| dar | dé | den |
| estar | esté | estén |
| ir | vaya | vayan |
| saber | sepa | sepan |
| ser | sea | sean |

**Dé** algunos ejemplos de las comidas que le gustan.　　*Give some examples of the foods you like.*
**Vayan** a ese restaurante nuevo. Es muy bueno.　　*Go to that new restaurant. It's very good.*

**D.** To tell someone what *not* to do, put the word **no** in front of the affirmative formal command.

**No sirva** la comida antes de las bebidas.　　*Don't serve the food before the drinks.*

**E.** When using reflexive, indirect object, or direct object pronouns with an affirmative command form, the pronouns are always attached to the end of the command. Note that a written accent may have to be added to maintain the original stress pattern of the command form.

**Pruébenlo.** Les va a gustar.　　*Try it. You'll like it.*
**Denles** los platos.　　*Give them the plates. (No accent; stress on 2nd-to-last syllable)*

**Dénselos.**　　*Give them to them. (With accent; stress now on 3rd-to-last syllable)*

When using pronouns with a negative command, the pronouns always go between the **no** and command form.

**No se** sienten todavía. Van a
limpiar la mesa primero.
—¿Le pido la cuenta al mesero?
—Ay, amor. **No se la** pida todavía.
Quiero pedir algo de postre.

*Don't sit down yet. They're going to
clean the table first.*
*Shall I ask the waiter for the bill?*
*Oh, my dear. Don't ask him for it
yet. I want to order some dessert.*

**F.** Formal commands of verbs that end in **-car**, **-gar**, or **-zar** require an additional spelling change to maintain the original pronunciation pattern of the letters **c**, **g**, and **z**, as they're pronounced in the infinitive and present tense **yo** form.

### FORMAL COMMANDS OF -car, -gar, AND -zar VERBS

| INFINITIVE | PRESENT TENSE yo FORM | SPELLING CHANGE | FORMAL COMMAND |
|---|---|---|---|
| bus**c**ar | bus**c**o | c → qu | bus**que**(n) |
| pa**g**ar | pa**g**o | g → gu | pa**gue**(n) |
| almor**z**ar (ue) | almuer**z**o | z → c | almuer**ce**(n) |

**Paguen** la cuenta en la puerta,
por favor.
**No** almuercen con ellos, almuercen
con nosotros.

*Pay the bill at the door, please.*

*Don't eat lunch with them, eat lunch
with us.*

## Nota comunicativa

**Communication**

**Me gustaría... Quisiera...**

Spanish has two common ways of expressing *I would like:* **quisiera** and **me gustaría**. Both can be used to make a polite request, such as ordering in a restaurant.

> **Quisiera** la sopa de pollo, una ensalada y los camarones.
> De postre, **me gustaría** el pastel de chocolate con una taza de café.

Each can also be used to communicate a person's general wishes.

> **Me gustaría** viajar a Sudamérica algún día.
> **Quisiera** visitar el Morro durante mi viaje a Puerto Rico.

### ACTIVIDADES

**A. ¿En casa o en algún restaurante?** Indique dónde es más común escuchar estas oraciones: en casa (**C**), en algún restaurante (**R**) o en ambos (*both:* **A**).

|  | C | R | A |
|---|---|---|---|
| 1. ¡No pongan los pies en la mesa! | ☐ | ☐ | ☐ |
| 2. Tráiganos otra botella de vino, por favor. | ☐ | ☐ | ☐ |
| 3. Pongan la mesa. Ya es hora de comer. | ☐ | ☐ | ☐ |
| 4. No pidan las chuletas. No son buenas aquí. | ☐ | ☐ | ☐ |
| 5. Sírvanos el postre primero, por favor. | ☐ | ☐ | ☐ |
| 6. Llamen a su padre. La cena está lista. | ☐ | ☐ | ☐ |
| 7. Cierren la boca mientras están comiendo. | ☐ | ☐ | ☐ |
| 8. Dénos la cuenta, por favor. | ☐ | ☐ | ☐ |

**B.** ¡Mesero! Dé los mandatos que un cliente le da a su mesero.

MODELO traerme otro tenedor → Tráigame otro tenedor, por favor.

1. buscarnos otra mesa
2. darnos otra jarra de agua
3. no llevar se los menús todavía
4. explicarme dónde están las ensaladas
5. decirle al cocinero que el bistec está quemado (*burnt*)
6. servirnos más rápido
7. traernos la cuenta

Communication

**C.** Consejos. En parejas, denles por lo menos dos mandatos a estas personas.

MODELO una persona que tiene mucho estrés →
Haga ejercicio todos los días. No piense demasiado en sus problemas.

1. una persona que quiere perder peso
2. una persona anémica
3. los otros estudiantes de la clase
4. su profesor(a)
5. su jefe/a (*boss*)
6. todos sus amigos
7. el/la líder de este país
8. ¿ ?

Cultures  Recycle

**D.** Los paladares cubanos

PASO 1. Complete the conversation between Jorge and Sarita, tourists from Spain, and Norberto, the hotel concierge. Give the correct form of words in parentheses. Indicate the correct word or words when more than one choice is provided. ¡OJO! When choosing between **ser** and **estar,** you will also need to give the correct form. When the cue C appears, give the correct formal command with the pronouns indicated.

En un paladar cubano

JORGE: Disculpe, vamos a salir a comer y nos gustaría probar[a] la comida cubana auténtica.

NORBERTO: Muy bien. Hay muchas opciones y tengo una lista de restaurantes en la oficina. (*C, Uds.:* **Sentarse**[1]) un momento, por favor, y (**te la / se la**[2]) traigo.

JORGE: Gracias.

NORBERTO: Bueno, hay muchas consideraciones. La primera es la comida y Uds. quisieran comer comida (**cubano**[3]) o criolla, como (*nosotros:* **decir**[4]) aquí.

SARITA: Sí, comida criolla.

NORBERTO: Ahora, (*C, Uds.:* **decir / a mí**[5]) lo siguiente: ¿(*Uds.:* **Ir**[6]) a caminar o (*Uds.:* **preferir**[7]) ir en taxi? ¿Cuánto dinero (*Uds.:* **pensar**[8]) gastar? Y finalmente, ¿a qué tipo de restaurante (*Uds.:* **querer**[9]) ir: a un restaurante en un hotel, a un restaurante para turistas o a un restaurante local?

JORGE: Si hay un restaurante bueno cerca de aquí, (**nos / les**[10]) gustaría caminar, pero también (*nosotros:* **poder**[11]) ir en taxi. Lo más importante[b] para nosotros es probar comida auténtica en un lugar auténtico. (*C, Ud.:* **Decir / a nosotros**[12]) lo que recomienda.

NORBERTO: Si desean ir a un lugar auténtico, (*C, Uds.:* **ir**[13]) a un paladar.

SARITA: ¿A un paladar? ¿Qué (**ser/estar**[14]) eso?

NORBERTO: Bueno, los paladares (**ser/estar**[15]) restaurantes privados, no del gobierno. Las familias establecen[c] el paladar en (**su**[16]) casa. El límite oficial es de doce personas, pero en algunos paladares (*ellos:* **servir**[17]) a más clientes. Y yo (**te/les**[18]) puedo recomendar un paladar que (**ser/estar**[19]) muy cerca de aquí. La dueña prepara comida rica y auténtica y (**se la / se lo**[20]) sirve en el jardín de su casa, que es uno

---

[a]*to taste*   [b]*Lo... The most important thing*   [c]*establish*

de los jardines más (bonito[21]) de La Habana. Y sus precios (ser/estar[22]) muy razonables.

JORGE:    Ah, pues entonces, (*C, Ud.*: **explicar** / **a nosotros**[23]) cómo llegar.

**PASO 2.** Indique si las oraciones son ciertas (**C**) o falsas (**F**), según el **Paso 1.**

|  | C | F |
|---|---|---|
| **1.** Sarita y Jorge son cubanos. | ☐ | ☐ |
| **2.** Los hoteles de Cuba no tienen restaurantes. | ☐ | ☐ |
| **3.** Norberto les explica cómo es la comida auténtica cubana. | ☐ | ☐ |
| **4.** Los paladares son restaurantes grandes y elegantes. | ☐ | ☐ |
| **5.** Hay un paladar muy bueno cerca del hotel de Sarita y Jorge. | ☐ | ☐ |
| **6.** Sarita y Jorge probablemente van a caminar al restaurante. | ☐ | ☐ |

# 6.4 Preterite: Regular Verbs

Talking About Completed Past Actions (Part 1)

**GRAMÁTICA EN CONTEXTO**

## La Bodeguita del Medio

[*Loida visitó Cuba por primera vez el verano pasado. Viajó con dos amigos por un mes. Después de ocho días, visitó un cibercafé y le escribió su primer e-mail a su familia.*]

¡Saludos a todos!

¡Me encanta Cuba! Hoy, **comí** en la famosa Bodeguita del Medio en La Habana. No es como la Bodeguita del Medio de Miami. Este restaurante es muy bohemio y pequeño; no es nada elegante. Sirven platos típicos de Cuba y tiene una larga historia de personas famosas que han comido aquí. Cuando **llegamos, nos sentamos** en el bar por un rato. Jeff y Lynne **tomaron** mojitos. Luego, **comimos** en el

*En la Bodeguita del Medio, La Habana, Cuba*

patio. Los tres **compartimos** dos platos de comida típica. Lo **pasamos** muy bien, viendo a cientos de turistas entrar a sacar fotos y salir. ¡La pared está llena de nombres porque todo el mundo firma su nombre allí! **Busqué** un lugarcito limpio y **escribí** mi nombre y la fecha en la pared. **Leí** varios nombres, pero no **reconocí** a nadie famoso. Bueno, es todo por el momento.

Hablamos pronto.

Un beso,

Loida

**GRAMÁTICA EN CONTEXTO** *La Bodeguita del Medio* / Loida visited Cuba for the first time last summer. She traveled with two friends for one month. After a week, she visited a cybercafé and wrote her first e-mail to her family. / Greetings to everyone! I love Cuba! Today, I ate at the famous Bodeguita del Medio in Havana. It's not like Miami's Bodeguita del Medio. This restaurant is very Bohemian and small; it's not at all elegant. They serve typical Cuban dishes and it has a long history of famous people who have eaten here. When we arrived, we sat at the bar for a while. Jeff and Lynne drank mojitos. Later, we ate on the patio. The three of us shared two orders of typical food. We had a very good time, watching hundreds of tourists enter to take photos and leave. The wall is full of names because everyone signs their name there! I looked for a small empty place and I wrote my name and date on the wall. I read several names but I didn't recognize anyone famous. Well, that's all for now. We'll talk soon. Love (lit. A kiss), Loida

Comprensión. ¿Posible (P) o imposible (I)?

|  | P | I |
|---|---|---|
| 1. Loida estudió en Cuba. | ☐ | ☐ |
| 2. Jeff y Loida se conocieron en Cuba. | ☐ | ☐ |
| 3. En Cuba Loida visitó los cibercafés todos los días. | ☐ | ☐ |
| 4. Loida y sus amigos comieron en la Bodeguita. | ☐ | ☐ |
| 5. Loida y sus amigos sacaron fotos en la Bodeguita. | ☐ | ☐ |

So far in *Experience Spanish* you've only been talking about things in the present tense. In this section you will start to learn how to talk about things in the past. Spanish has two simple tenses to refer to past actions: *preterite* and *imperfect*. For now, we'll only focus on the preterite.

## FORMING THE PRETERITE

| PRETERITE OF **-ar** VERBS | |
|---|---|
| llevé | llevamos |
| llevaste | llevasteis |
| llevó | llevaron |

| PRETERITE OF **-er** VERBS | |
|---|---|
| comí | comimos |
| comiste | comisteis |
| comió | comieron |

| PRETERITE OF **-ir** VERBS | |
|---|---|
| salí | salimos |
| saliste | salisteis |
| salió | salieron |

**A.** The preterite is formed by removing the **-ar**, **-er**, or **-ir** from infinitives and adding the endings as shown in the preceding tables. Note the following points.

1. The **yo** and **Ud., él/ella** forms have an accent on the last letter: **llevé, llevó, comí, comió, salí, salió.**
2. The **-er** and **-ir** endings are the same: **-í, -iste, -ió, -imos, -isteis, -ieron.**
3. There are no accents on the **vosotros/as** forms.
4. The **nosotros/as** forms of **-ar** and **-ir** verbs are the same as the corresponding forms in the present tense. Context will determine the correct interpretation.

| | |
|---|---|
| Cenamos con nuestros padres **todos los domingos.** | *We eat dinner with our parents every Sunday.* |
| Cenamos con nuestros padres **el domingo pasado.** | *We ate dinner with our parents last Sunday.* |

**B.** The **yo** and **Ud., él/ella** forms of the verb **ver** do not have accents.

| | |
|---|---|
| vi | vimos |
| viste | visteis |
| vio | vieron |

**C.** **-ar** and **-er** verbs that have stem changes in the present tense do not have stem changes in the preterite.

| INFINITIVE | PRESENT TENSE | PRETERITE |
|---|---|---|
| pensar (ie) | pienso, piensas, piensa,... | pensé, pensaste, pensó,... |
| volver (ue) | vuelvo, vuelves, vuelve,... | volví, volviste, volvió,... |

**D.** The verbs **creer, leer,** and **oír** have a spelling change from -i- to -y- in the **Ud., él/ella** forms. Note also that the **tú, nosotros/as,** and **vosotros/as** forms have an accented -í-.

| PRETERITE OF creer, leer, AND oír | | | | | |
|---|---|---|---|---|---|
| **creer (y)** | | **leer (y)** | | **oír** (*irreg.*) | |
| creí | creímos | leí | leímos | oí | oímos |
| creíste | creísteis | leíste | leísteis | oíste | oísteis |
| creyó | creyeron | leyó | leyeron | oyó | oyeron |

**E.** The preterite **yo** forms of verbs that end in **-car, -gar,** and **-zar** undergo the same spelling changes that you learned for the formal commands of these verbs.

| | | |
|---|---|---|
| **buscar** | c → qu | **busqué** |
| **llegar** | g → gu | **llegué** |
| **empezar** (ie) | z → c | **empecé** |

## USING THE PRETERITE

**A.** The preterite is used to talk about specific actions that were completed over a limited time period, explicit or implied, in the past.

**Ayer** tomé un café con Julia.
*Yesterday I had a cup of coffee with Julia.* (completed past action that took place within the limited confines of *yesterday*)

Jaime y su novia **cenaron** en la Bodeguita del Medio **anoche.**
*Jaime and his girlfriend ate dinner at the Bodeguita del Medio last night.* (completed past action that took place within the limited confines of *last night*)

David **viajó** a la República Dominicana, **estudió** español **(por) un mes,** salió a bailar muchas veces y lo **pasó** muy bien.
*David traveled to the Dominican Republic, studied Spanish for one month, went out dancing many times, and had a great time.* (completed actions that took place within the limited confines of *one month*)

**B.** Due to the fact that actions expressed in the preterite are viewed as having been completed within the confines of a limited period of time, you will often see it used in conjunction with words and phrases that help establish that limited period of time. Note that **por** is optional in the last phrase of the list.

| COMMON WORDS AND PHRASES USED WITH THE PRETERITE | |
|---|---|
| anoche | la semana pasada |
| anteayer | la última vez que |
| ayer | a las + *specific time* |
| el lunes (martes, miércoles,... ) pasado | (por) + *specific time period* |
| el mes/año pasado | |

**Almorcé** con Esteban y Marcos anteayer.

*I ate lunch with Esteban and Marcos the day before yesterday.*

La última vez que **desayunamos** aquí, **comí** huevos revueltos con jamón.

*The last time we ate breakfast here, I ate scrambled eggs and ham.*

Mamá me **llamó** a las 7:00.
**Hablamos** (por) tres horas.

*Mom called me at 7:00.*
*We spoke for three hours.*

**ACTIVIDADES**

**A. Ayer.** Indique las oraciones que describen lo que Ud. hizo (*did*) ayer.

☐ Desayuné en casa.
☐ Asistí a todas mis clases.
☐ Comí fruta.
☐ Leí el periódico.

☐ Almorcé en la cafetería.
☐ Regresé a casa muy tarde.
☐ Miré la televisión.
☐ Cené en un restaurante.

Communication

**B. El viernes pasado.** En parejas, hablen de lo que hicieron (*you did*) el viernes pasado. Usen las ideas para hacer preguntas. Para saber qué hizo su compañero/a, pregúntenle: **¿Qué hiciste tú?** (*What did you do?*).

**MODELO** E1: El viernes pasado salí con mis amigos y vimos una película muy mala. ¿Qué hiciste tú?
E2: Salí con mi novia. Cenamos en un restaurante.

| | | |
|---|---|---|
| almorzar con... | descansar | mirar mucho la televisión |
| asistir a mis clases | escribir | pasar un rato con... |
| bailar con... | estudiar | salir con... |
| cenar en un restaurante | leer | ¿ ? |

Communication

**C. Entrevista.** Entreviste a un compañero / una compañera de clase sobre la última vez que comió en un restaurante elegante. Luego, cambien de papel.

1. ¿Quién te acompañó la última vez que comiste en un restaurante elegante?
2. ¿Qué ordenaron para comer? ¿Qué tipos de bebidas tomaron?
3. ¿Comieron postre al final de la comida? ¿Cuál? ¿Bebieron café?
4. ¿Se quedaron un rato en la mesa después de comer, o salieron inmediatamente? Si se quedaron en la mesa, ¿por cuánto tiempo se quedaron allí y qué hicieron?
5. ¿Cuánto les costó la comida? ¿Les gustó la experiencia?

Cultures

Recycle

**D. Colombia y el Caribe**

**PASO 1.** Complete la descripción de la región caribeña de Colombia con la forma correcta de las palabras entre paréntesis. Si un verbo aparece con la pista *pret.*, dé la forma correcta del pretérito. En otros casos, use el presente. Cuando aparecen **ser** y **estar** juntos, escoja el verbo correcto y dé la forma correcta.

¿Sabe Ud. que Colombia también es un país caribeño? Es verdad que Colombia (tener¹) una región andina (en las montañas^a), una costa en el Pacífico, una región de llanos^b y una zona amazónica. Pero la región que (ser/estar²) en el noreste,^c tiene una costa,^d una gente^e y un espíritu indudablemente^f caribeños.

Si Ud. (querer³) saber en qué aspectos es caribeña esta parte de Colombia, debe visitar la costa y probar la comida. Yo (*pret.*: viajar⁴) a Colombia el año pasado con la idea de que iba^g a visitar un bosque^h tropical y ver pájaros^i exóticos. Pues, sí, (yo,

---

^a*mountains* ^b*plains* ^c*northeast* ^d*coast* ^e*people* ^f*indisputably* ^g*was going* ^h*forest* ^i*birds*

*La Torre (Tower) del Reloj, Cartagena*

*pret.:* **visitar**[5]) una zona amazónica y (*yo, pret.:* **observar**[6]) varios pájaros y otros animales selváticos,[j] pero la segunda semana, nosotros (*pret.:* **viajar**[7]) al norte para conocer Cartagena. (*Ellos:* **Decir**[8]) que Cartagena es la ciudad colonial más preciosa de América. ¡Es verdad! Nosotros (*pret.:* **comer**[9]) (**mucho**[10]) platos de pescado y mariscos, (*pret.:* **caminar**[11]) por la Ciudad Amurallada,[k] el centro histórico de Cartagena, y (*pret.:* **disfrutar**[12]) de la arquitectura colonial. (*Nosotros, pret.:* **Tomar**[13]) el sol en la playa durante el día y (*nosotros, pret.:* **salir**[14]) a bailar (**todo**[15]) las noches. ¡Qué divertido! El aire, la gente, la comida, todo muy caribeño.

Colombia también (**tener**[16]) dos islas en el Caribe: San Andrés y Providencia. Nosotros sólo (*pret.:* **visitar**[17]) la primera, pero (*yo, pret.:* **leer**[18]) mucha información sobre las dos. Algunos historiadores (**decir**[19]) que Colón (*pret.:* **descubrir**[20]) San Andrés durante su cuarto viaje a América en 1502. Las islas se convirtieron en[l] una ruta de esclavos y contrabando. Los piratas también (*pret.:* **establecerse**[21])[m] en estas islas. Dicen que el pirata, Henry Morgan, (*pret.:* **planear**[22]) su ataque a Panamá en la isla de Providencia.

---

[j]*jungle*  [k]*Walled*  [l]*se... became*  [m]*to settle*

**PASO 2.** Empareje las frases de la columna A con las de la columna B para formar oraciones lógicas, según el **Paso 1.**

| A | B |
|---|---|
| 1. Henry Morgan atacó *e* | a. las islas para transportar contrabando. |
| 2. Cartagena está en *c* | b. varias regiones. |
| 3. Colón posiblemente visitó *f* | c. el noreste de Colombia. |
| 4. Colombia tiene *b* | d. el centro histórico de Cartagena. |
| 5. Los piratas usaron *a* | e. Panamá. |
| 6. La Ciudad Amurallada es *d* | f. la isla de San Andrés. |

# Lectura cultural

Ud. va a leer una receta de un postre delicioso: el flan de coco. Esta receta viene de la revista *Siempre mujer* y es parte de una serie de recetas en un artículo escrito por Doreen Colondres.

## ANTES DE LEER

**PASO 1.** En parejas, contesten las preguntas. Después, compartan sus respuestas con la clase.

1. ¿Cocinan Uds.? ¿En qué ocasiones? ¿Buscan recetas en las revistas o en el Internet, o prefieren crear sus propios platos? Expliquen.
2. ¿Hay algún miembro de su familia, o algún amigo / alguna amiga, que prepare un plato especial? ¿En qué ocasiones lo prepara? ¿Cuáles son los ingredientes?
3. Tengan en cuenta que la lectura es una receta, observen la imagen del flan y revisen los encabezados (*headings*). ¿Qué información esperan encontrar? ¿En qué forma están los verbos?

**PASO 2.** Repase el **Vocabulario práctico** y luego lea la receta del flan de coco. **¡OJO!** Trate de adivinar por el contexto las palabras que Ud. no sabe, sin usar el diccionario.

### Vocabulario práctico

| | | | |
|---|---|---|---|
| **último pedazo** | last piece | **dorado** | golden |
| **lata** | can | **quemado** | burnt |
| **agua de coco** | coconut milk | **verter (ie)** | to pour |
| **gotas** | drops | **nevera** | refrigerator |
| **hojuelas** | flakes | **tapar** | to cover |
| **olla** | sauce pan | **boca abajo** | upside down |

## Flan de coco

Esta receta es un éxito cuando tengo invitados en casa. Es fácil, todo el mundo quedará peleándose[a] por el último pedazo.

1 lata de leche condensada
1 lata de agua de coco
5 huevos
1 taza de azúcar
4-5 gotas de jugo de lima
4-5 gotas de agua
Hojuelas de coco para decorar

### Preparación

1. Primero... para disfrutar de esta receta ¡no puede estar a dieta!
2. Mezcle bien los huevos, luego les añade la leche condensada y el agua de coco. (Prefiero batir a mano que con batidora eléctrica.)
3. Una vez que todo esté mezclado,[b] proceda a hacer el caramelo, ¡que no muerde! Hacer caramelo no es difícil. En una olla pequeña caliente a fuego mediano el azúcar, el jugo de lima y el agua y revuelva hasta que el azúcar se disuelva totalmente y adquiera un color dorado oscuro (pero no quemado) Así el sabor del caramelo no será[c] más fuerte que el del flan.

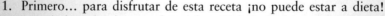

[a]quedará... *will end up fighting*  [b]Una... *Once everything is mixed*  [c]no... *won't be*

4. Vierta el caramelo en el molde y cubra bien todo el fondo. Una vez que el azúcar se haya secado[d] en el molde, añada la mezcla del flan.
5. Y ya está listo para ir al horno, pero lo va a poner en «Baño de María» (o sea, dentro de otro molde más grande con agua suficiente para cubrir al menos ¾ partes de la altura del flan).
   Hornee a 350° F por unos 45 minutos o hasta que le introduzca un cuchillo y éste salga limpio.[e]
6. Cuando se enfríe[f] por completo, póngalo en la nevera. Antes de sacarlo del molde, pásele un cuchillo por el borde. Después, tápelo con un plato grande boca abajo e inviértalo. Espere que salga todo el caramelo y decórelo a su gusto con las hojuelas de coco.

**Consejo**

Si lo prepara con ingredientes orgánicos, le quedará supercremoso y menos dulce. ¡Buen provecho!

---

[d]haya... *has dried*   [e]hasta... *until you can stick a knife in it and it comes out clean*   [f]se... *it has cooled down*

## DESPUÉS DE LEER

**A.** Sobre la lectura

**PASO 1.** Conteste las preguntas.

1. ¿Qué ingredientes contiene el flan de coco?
2. ¿Por qué dice la autora de la receta que no se puede estar a dieta y comer este flan?
3. ¿Cómo debe uno sacar el flan del molde al final del proceso?
4. ¿Qué cree Ud. que significa la última frase de la lectura: «¡Buen provecho!»?

**PASO 2.** En parejas, compartan sus respuestas del **Paso 1**.

Communication

**B.** Para comentar. En grupos de tres, comenten estos temas. Si necesitan más información, búsquenla en el Internet. Después, compartan sus ideas con la clase.

1. ¿Conocen Uds. el flan? ¿Dónde lo comieron? ¿Cuándo lo comieron? ¿Les gustó? Si no conocen el flan, ¿creen que les gustaría el flan de coco de la lectura? Expliquen.
2. ¿Cómo se compara el flan de coco con su postre favorito? Compárenlos en cuanto (*with regard*) al sabor, la cantidad de calorías, los ingredientes, el precio de sus ingredientes, la dificultad o facilidad (*ease*) de prepararlo, etcétera.
3. ¿Qué otros postres son comunes en la región donde Uds. viven? ¿Hay algún postre típico de su región? ¿Cuál es? ¿Cómo es? ¿En qué ocasiones lo comen? ¿Con qué frecuencia lo comen?

# Concurso de videoblogs

## República Dominicana: Merfry

### Santo Domingo y la comida dominicana

En este segmento, Merfry nos muestra la República Dominicana. En la capital, Santo Domingo, Merfry habla de la importancia de la historia en la ciudad. Allí conocemos la catedral, la Plaza de Colón y la Calle Las Damas.[a] Después, nuestra blogger busca un buen restaurante para almorzar y comer comida criolla. En el restaurante, Merfry pide dos platos típicos regionales: la bandera[b] dominicana y el sancocho.

[a]*Ladies*  [b]*flag*

### Vocabulario práctico

| | |
|---|---|
| **arena blanca** | white sand |
| **fortaleza** | fortress |
| **recuerdos** | memories |
| **explorador** | explorer |
| **clase alta** | upper class |
| **¡Qué rico huele!** | It smells so good! |
| **¡Buen provecho!** | *Bon appétit!* |

## ANTES DE VER

Conteste las preguntas.

1. ¿Es famosa por alguna razón en especial la ciudad o región donde Ud. vive? ¿Por qué? ¿Sabe quién la fundó (*founded*) o descubrió (*discovered*)? Explique.
2. ¿Hay algún plato típico de la región donde vive? ¿Cómo se llama? ¿Qué ingredientes contiene? ¿En qué lugar/restaurante recomienda comerlo?

## DESPUÉS DE VER

**A. Comprensión.** Vuelva a ver el segmento y termine las oraciones.

1. La República Dominicana es un pequeño país de aproximadamente _____.
2. Algunos recuerdos de la historia de la República Dominicana se ven (*are seen*) en _____.
3. La República Dominicana es un destino importante para _____.
4. La Calle Las Damas es famosa porque _____.
5. Para buscar un lugar donde almorzar, Merfry _____.
6. Las personas locales dicen que Merfry tiene que ir a _____.
7. En el restaurante, el plato de la bandera dominicana viene acompañado de _____.
8. El sancocho es _____.

**B. Temas de discusión.** En parejas, contesten las preguntas. Si es necesario, busquen información en la biblioteca o en el Internet. Después, compartan sus ideas con la clase.

1. ¿Cuál es la importancia de Cristóbal Colón en la historia del mundo hispano?
2. ¿En qué son semejantes y diferentes la comida caribeña y la comida hispana que Uds. ya conocen?
3. ¿En qué son semejantes y diferentes la comida caribeña y la comida de la región donde Uds. viven?

214

## Carnes, pescados y mariscos — Meats, Fish, and Shellfish

| | |
|---|---|
| el atún | tuna |
| el bistec | (beef) steak |
| los camarones | shrimp |
| la carne | |
| de cerdo | pork |
| de res | beef |
| picada | ground beef |
| la chuleta (de cerdo) | (pork) chop |
| la hamburguesa | hamburger |
| la langosta | lobster |
| el pavo | turkey |
| el pollo (asado) | (roast) chicken |
| los huevos | eggs |
| el jamón | ham |
| la salchicha | sausage |
| el tocino | bacon |

## Frutas y verduras — Fruits and Vegetables

| | |
|---|---|
| el aguacate | avocado |
| la cebolla | onion |
| los champiñones | mushrooms |
| el coco | coconut |
| el durazno | peach |
| las espinacas | spinach |
| la fresa | strawberry |
| los frijoles | beans |
| los guisantes | peas |
| las habichuelas | green beans |
| la lechuga | lettuce |
| el maíz | corn |
| la manzana | apple |
| la naranja | orange |
| las papas | potatoes (L.A.) |
| las papas fritas | French fries |
| el puré de papas | mashed potatoes |
| la piña | pineapple |
| la toronja | grapefruit |
| la zanahoria | carrot |

Cognados: la banana, el kiwi, el mango, el melón, la papaya, la pera, el tomate

## Los granos — Grains

| | |
|---|---|
| el arroz | rice |
| la galleta | cookie; cracker |
| el pan (integral) | (whole wheat) bread |
| el pan tostado | toast |

Cognados: el cereal, la pasta

## Los productos lácteos — Dairy Products

| | |
|---|---|
| la leche | milk |
| la mantequilla | butter |
| el queso | cheese |

Cognado: el yogur

## Los postres — Desserts

| | |
|---|---|
| los dulces | candies |
| el flan | caramel custard |
| el helado | ice cream |
| el pastel | pie; cake |

Cognados: el chocolate, la menta, la vainilla

## Las bebidas — Drinks

| | |
|---|---|
| el agua | water |
| la cerveza | beer |
| el jugo | juice |
| el refresco | soft drink |
| el vino (blanco/tinto) | (white/red) wine |

Cognados: el champaña, el té

## La comida y las comidas — Food and Meals

| | |
|---|---|
| contener (like tener) | to contain |
| cubrir | to cover |
| hervir (ie) | to boil |
| merendar (ie) | to snack |
| probar (ue) | to taste, try |
| el alimento | food; nourishment |
| el almuerzo | lunch |
| la cena | dinner |
| el comestible | food item; pl. groceries |
| el desayuno | breakfast |

Cognados: los ingredientes; internacional, local, natural, orgánico/a, tradicional, tropical

## Los utensilios

| | |
|---|---|
| la copa | (wine) glass |
| la cuchara | spoon |
| el cucharón | soup ladle |
| el cuchillo | knife |
| el cuenco | serving bowl |
| la jarra | pitcher |
| el mantel | tablecloth |
| el plato | plate; dish |
| la servilleta | napkin |
| la sopa | soup |
| la sopera | soup bowl (tureen) |
| la taza (de café) | cup (of coffee) |
| el tazón para el cereal | cereal bowl |
| el tenedor | fork |
| el vaso | (water) glass |

## En el restaurante

| | |
|---|---|
| ordenar / pedir (i) | to order |
| el/la cocinero/a | cook, chef |
| la cuenta | bill, check |
| el/la mesero/a | waiter/waitress |

| | |
|---|---|
| la propina | tip |
| la tarjeta de crédito | credit card |
| | |
| acogedor(a) | cozy; welcoming |
| relajante | relaxing |
| | |
| en efectivo | cash |

Cognados: aceptar; el menú, la reservación; romántico/a, variado/a

## Otras palabras y expresiones

| | |
|---|---|
| el aceite (de oliva) | (olive) oil |
| el ajo | garlic |
| el azúcar | sugar |
| la ensalada | salad |
| el mercado | market |
| la pimienta roja/negra | red/black pepper |
| el supermercado | supermarket |
| la tienda (de comestibles) | (grocery) store |
| el/la vendedor(a) | vendor |
| | |
| lo que | what, that which |

Cognados: el/la cliente/a, la sal, el sándwich, el vinagre

## Los pronombres de objeto indirecto — Indirect Object Pronouns

me, te, le, nos, os, les

## Los pronombres de objeto directo — Direct Object Pronouns

me, te, lo/la, nos, os, los/las

## Los verbos

| | |
|---|---|
| contar (ue) | to count; to tell |
| dar (irreg.) | to give |
| deber | to owe |
| decir (irreg.) | to say; to tell |
| entregar (gu) | to deliver; to hand in |
| explicar (qu) | to explain |
| mandar | to send |
| mostrar (ue) | to show |
| ofrecer (zc) | to offer |
| preguntar | to ask (a question) |
| prestar | to loan |
| prometer | to promise |
| regalar | to give (as a gift) |
| sugerir (ie) | to suggest |

Cognado: preparar, recomendar (ie)

## Otros verbos como gustar

| | |
|---|---|
| aburrir | to bore |
| encantar | to love (lit. to enchant) |
| llamar la atención | to sound interesting (lit. to call out for one's attention) |
| molestar | to bother |
| preocupar | to worry |

Cognados: fascinar, interesar

# ¡Vamos de compras!

*La moda (fashion) del diseñador venezolano Ángel Sánchez*

1. ¿Le gusta a Ud. ir de compras? ¿En dónde le gusta comprar ropa, en tiendas especializadas, en *boutiques* o prefiere ir a un centro comercial (*mall*)?

2. ¿Qué otros artículos (*items*), por ejemplo, artesanías, objetos para regalos (*gifts*), etcétera, le gusta comprar? ¿Cuáles son sus tiendas preferidas para comprar estos artículos?

www.connectspanish.com

## Vocabulario del tema

La ropa°

La... *Clothing*

¡GRAN VENTA HOY!

50% de descuento

¡REBAJAS!

el sombrero gris

la blusa blanca

la gorra roja

la chaqueta anaranjada

la camisa blanca

la corbata azul claro

el vestido de color fucsia

el bolso negro

el cinturón

el traje gris

la camiseta amarilla

el pantalón corto verde

la falda de color café

los calcetines blancos

los zapatos de tacón alto

las botas de color café

los zapatos de tenis

el pantalón

los zapatos negros

## Otra ropa y complementos

## Other Clothing and Accessories

| | |
|---|---|
| el abrigo | overcoat |
| los guantes | gloves |
| las medias | stockings |
| el polo | polo shirt |
| la ropa interior | lingerie, underwear |
| el traje (de baño) | (bathing) suit |
| los zapatos de tacón bajo | flats (*shoes*) |

Cognados: los jeans, el/la pijama, las sandalias, el suéter

## Las tallas

## Sizes

| | |
|---|---|
| chico/a | small |
| mediano/a | medium |
| (extra) grande | (extra) large |

## Las telas y los materiales

## Fabrics and Materials

| | |
|---|---|
| de algodón | cotton |
| de cuero/piel | leather |
| de lana | wool |
| de seda | silk |

## Los diseños y los colores

## Designs and Colors

| | |
|---|---|
| claro/a | light |
| liso/a | plain |
| metálico/a | metallic |
| oscuro/a | dark |
| vivo/a | brightly colored |
| de cuadros | plaid |
| de lunares | polka-dotted |
| de manga corta/larga | with short/long sleeves |
| de marca | name-brand |
| de rayas | striped |
| de última moda | fashionable |

Cognados: el beige; pastel

## Otras palabras y expresiones

| | |
|---|---|
| ir (*irreg.*) de compras | to go shopping |
| la calidad | quality |
| la moda | fashion |
| la prenda de ropa | piece/article of clothing |
| la rebaja | price reduction |
| el ropero | wardrobe |
| la venta | sale |
| actual | current |
| cómodo/a | comfortable |
| disponible | available |

Cognados: el estilo; moderno/a, unisex, vital

## ACTIVIDADES

**A. ¿Formal o informal?** Indique si Ud. cree que estas prendas de ropa son para ocasiones formales (**F**) o informales (**I**). **¡OJO!** Puede haber más de una respuesta. Explique su opinión.

MODELO  pantalones cortos → **I:** Los pantalones cortos son una prenda informal que llevamos en casa, a clase, al parque, para hacer ejercicio. No llevamos pantalones cortos a la oficina.

|  | F | I |  | F | I |
|---|---|---|---|---|---|
| **1.** una corbata | ☐ | ☐ | **5.** una camiseta | ☐ | ☐ |
| **2.** un traje de baño | ☐ | ☐ | **6.** unos zapatos de tenis | ☐ | ☐ |
| **3.** calcetines | ☐ | ☐ | **7.** un sombrero | ☐ | ☐ |
| **4.** unos zapatos de tacón alto | ☐ | ☐ | **8.** un traje | ☐ | ☐ |

**B. Llevo... para...** Indique cuándo lleva Ud. estas prendas de ropa: para estar en casa, para ir a clase o en una cena formal. Si hay algo que nunca lleva, diga: «Nunca me pongo... » y explique por qué. **¡OJO!** Puede haber más de una respuesta correcta.

MODELOS  jeans negros → Llevo jeans negros en casa y para ir a clase.
una blusa de seda → Llevo una blusa de seda a una cena formal.
una falda de cuero → Nunca me pongo una falda de cuero porque no me gusta el cuero / porque no llevo faldas.

1. zapatos de tenis
2. una chaqueta de colores metálicos
3. botas de piel
4. zapatos de tacón alto
5. pantalones de cuadros
6. un suéter de lana
7. una camisa de algodón
8. ¿ ?

**C. ¿Quién es?**

PASO 1.  Apunte lo que llevan tres o cuatro personas en la clase. Puede incluir a su profesor(a). Dé detalles del color y la tela si puede.

Communication

PASO 2.  Describa lo que lleva una persona de la clase sin indicarla. La clase va a adivinar quién es. Cuando Ud. adivine la persona descrita por otro/a estudiante, debe repetir lo que esa persona lleva. Siga el modelo.

MODELO  E1: Lleva zapatos de tenis, una camiseta verde y pantalones cortos negros.
E2: Es Greg.
E1: No, Greg lleva jeans.
E2: Es Lisa.
E1: Sí, es Lisa. ¿Qué lleva Lisa?
E2: Lisa lleva zapatos de tenis, una camiseta verde y pantalones cortos negros.

**D.** Búsqueda del tesoro (*Scavenger hunt*)

**PASO 1.** En una hoja de papel aparte, haga una lista de cinco prendas de ropa que en su opinión no son comunes.

**MODELO** un vestido rojo
una blusa azul de seda
¿ ?

**PASO 2.** Intercambie su lista del **Paso 1** con la de otro/a estudiante. Ahora, todos deben hacer una encuesta en la clase para saber quién tiene cada prenda de ropa de su lista. Después, compartan los resultados con la clase.

**MODELO** E1: ¿Tienes un vestido rojo?
E2: No, no tengo un vestido rojo.
E1: ¿Tienes una blusa azul de seda?
E2: Sí, tengo una blusa azul de seda. ¡Es mi favorita!

**E.** Mi ropero

**PASO 1.** Combine frases de cada columna para formar oraciones. Escriba por lo menos seis oraciones. **¡OJO!** Añada las palabras y haga los cambios necesarios.

**MODELO** En mi ropero tengo una falda negra y tres pares de botas.

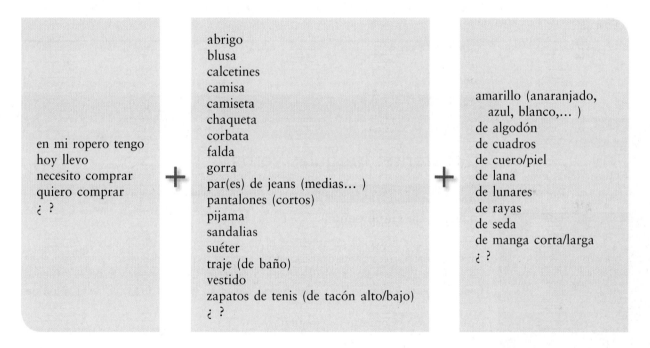

en mi ropero tengo
hoy llevo
necesito comprar
quiero comprar
¿ ?

**+**

abrigo
blusa
calcetines
camisa
camiseta
chaqueta
corbata
falda
gorra
par(es) de jeans (medias... )
pantalones (cortos)
pijama
sandalias
suéter
traje (de baño)
vestido
zapatos de tenis (de tacón alto/bajo)
¿ ?

**+**

amarillo (anaranjado, azul, blanco,... )
de algodón
de cuadros
de cuero/piel
de lana
de lunares
de rayas
de seda
de manga corta/larga
¿ ?

**PASO 2.** Entreviste a un compañero / una compañera con estas preguntas. Luego, cambien de papel.

1. ¿Qué ropa tienes en tu ropero? ¿Cuáles son tus prendas favoritas?
2. ¿Qué llevas hoy? ¿Normalmente llevas esto a clase?
3. ¿Qué necesitas comprar muy pronto? ¿Por qué?
4. ¿Qué ropa quieres comprar? ¿Dónde piensas comprarla?

**LA GUAYABERA: MODA DEL CARIBE**

*Una guayabera cubana*

La guayabera es una prenda de ropa típica del Caribe. Es un tipo de camisa que se lleva por encima de los pantalones, tiene varios bolsillos y es de tela ligera.[a] Según la historia y la tradición oral, los orígenes de la guayabera se remontan[b] al siglo XVIII, fecha de la llegada de los españoles a la ciudad cubana de Sancti Spiritus. El clima caribeño y la necesidad de vestir una camisa larga, de bolsillos amplios para cargar diversos objetos, inspiraron a los nuevos habitantes de Cuba a crear la guayabera. Originalmente fue confeccionada de algodón porque se adaptaba bien a las altas temperaturas de la isla. Esta prenda, tradicionalmente masculina, es famosa desde entonces en todo el Caribe y en las zonas cálidas[c] de Latinoamérica.

[a]*light*   [b]*se... date back*   [c]*hot*

**PREGUNTAS** En parejas, contesten las preguntas. Después, compartan sus ideas con la clase.

1. ¿Quiénes crearon las primeras guayaberas? ¿Por qué crearon esta prenda de ropa?

2. ¿Hay una prenda de ropa especial de la región donde Uds. viven? ¿Se la ponen con frecuencia o sólo en ocasiones especiales, por ejemplo, para una celebración especial o para hacer alguna actividad específica? Expliquen.

# Gramática

**Talking About Completed Past Actions (Part 2)**

## 7.1 Preterite: Irregular Verbs

**GRAMÁTICA EN CONTEXTO**

### La fiesta de cumpleaños

Carlos **dio** una fiesta de cumpleaños el fin de semana pasado. Muchos de sus amigos **fueron**, pero Santiago no **pudo** ir porque **estuvo** en Puerto Plata todo el fin de semana. Elena **trajo** la música. Patricio **puso** un CD de música bailable. Muchos bailaron, pero Jorge y Sofía no **quisieron** bailar. En general **fue** una fiesta divertida.

Comprensión. Conteste las preguntas.

1. ¿Quién dio la fiesta?
2. ¿Quiénes fueron a la fiesta?
3. ¿Quién trajo la música?
4. ¿Qué tipo de música puso Patricio?
5. ¿Quiénes no quisieron bailar?
6. ¿Cómo fue la fiesta?

**GRAMÁTICA EN CONTEXTO** / ***The Birthday Party*** / *Carlos threw a birthday party last weekend. A lot of his friends went, but Santiago couldn't go because he was in Puerto Plata all weekend. Elena brought the music. Patricio put on a CD of dance music. A lot of people danced, but Jorge and Sofía refused to dance. All in all, it was a fun party.*

There is a set of verbs that all have irregular stems and endings in the preterite. Note that there are no accents on the **yo** and **él/ella** forms.

| IRREGULAR PRETERITE VERBS | | | |
|---|---|---|---|
| INFINITIVE | STEM | ENDINGS | |
| andar | anduv- | -e | -imos |
| estar | estuv- | -iste | -isteis |
| hacer | hic-* | -o | -ieron |
| poder | pud- | | |
| poner | pus- | | |
| querer | quis- | | |
| saber | sup- | | |
| tener | tuv- | | |
| venir | vin- | | |

| | |
|---|---|
| **Anduve** en bicicleta por tres horas ayer. | *I went bike riding for three hours yesterday.* |
| Ay, Pablito, ¿por qué no te **pusiste** un suéter? | *Oh, Pablito, why didn't you put on a sweater.* |

**A.** The verbs **decir** and **traer** follow a pattern similar to that of the irregular verbs presented above with one difference: the **-i-** in the **ellos/as** ending is dropped.

| PRETERITE OF decir AND traer | | | |
|---|---|---|---|
| INFINITIVE | STEM | ENDINGS | |
| decir | dij- | -e | -imos |
| traer | traj- | -iste | -isteis |
| | | -o | -eron |

| | |
|---|---|
| Me **dijeron** que va a haber rebajas. | *They told me there are going to be price reductions.* |
| ¿**Trajiste** tu abrigo? Va a hacer frío. | *Did you bring your overcoat? It's going to get cold.* |

**B.** The verbs **ir** and **ser** have identical preterite forms. Context will determine meaning. Note that there are no accents on any of the forms and that there is no **-i-** in the **ellos/as** ending.

| PRETERITE OF ir AND ser | |
|---|---|
| fui | fuimos |
| fuiste | fuisteis |
| fue | fueron |

---

*The **él/ella** form of **hacer** in the preterite has a spelling change (-c- → -z-) to maintain the soft sound of the -c- in the infinitive and other preterite forms: **hacer** → **hice, hiciste, hizo, hicimos, hicisteis, hicieron.**

—¿Fueron Uds. al centro
comercial anoche?

*Did you go to the mall last night?*

—Sí, pero fuimos al cine primero.

*Yes, but we went to the movies first.*

—¿Cómo fue la película?

*How was the movie?*

**C.** The verb **dar** is conjugated like an **-er/-ir** verb in the preterite. Note that the written accents are dropped on forms with only one syllable.

Dimos una fiesta anoche, pero no
**vino** nadie.

*We threw a party last night, but nobody came.*

**D.** The preterite of **hay** is **hubo.**

Hubo un robo ayer en el mercado.

*There was a robbery yesterday in the market.*

| PRETERITE OF **dar** | |
|---|---|
| di | dimos |
| diste | disteis |
| dio | dieron |

## Nota comunicativa

Communication

### PRETERITE MEANING OF conocer, poder, querer, saber, AND tener

As you know, the preterite often signals the beginning or end of an action or situation. For that reason, certain verbs take on special meaning when expressed in the preterite. Compare the meaning of the following verbs in the present tense with their meaning expressed in the preterite.

| | PRESENT | PRETERITE |
|---|---|---|
| **conocer** | to know, to be familiar with | to meet (for the first time) |
| | —¿**Conoces** a Paula?<br>*Do you know Paula?* | —Sí, la **conocí** el año pasado.<br>*Yes, I met her last year.* |
| **poder** | to be able | to succeed |
| | ¿**Puedes** ir al mercado?<br>*Can you go to the market?* | **Pude** encontrar una camisa bonita.<br>*I succeeded in finding a pretty shirt.* |
| **no poder** | not to be able | to fail |
| | **No puede** vender nada.<br>*He can't sell anything.* | **No pudo** vender nada.<br>*He failed to sell anything.* |
| **querer** | to want | to try |
| | **Quiero** ir de compras esta tarde.<br>*I want to go shopping this afternoon.* | **Quise** ir de compras ayer.<br>*I tried to go shopping yesterday.* |
| **no querer** | not to want | to refuse |
| | **No quiero** ir de compras esta tarde.<br>*I don't want to go shopping this afternoon.* | **No quise** ir de compras ayer.<br>*I refused to go shopping yesterday.* |
| **saber** | to know | to find out |
| | —¿**Sabes** que hay rebajas?<br>*Do you know there are price reductions?* | —Sí, lo **supe** ayer.<br>*Yes, I found out (all about it) yesterday.* |
| **tener** | to have | to get, obtain, receive |
| | —¿**Tienes** una corbata azul?<br>*Do you have a blue tie?* | —**Tuve** la oportunidad de comprar una, pero no me gustó.<br>*I got the chance to buy one, but I didn't like it.* |

**A.** La última vez. Indique cuáles de estas cosas hizo Ud. la última vez que fue de compras.

|  | SÍ, LO HICE | NO, NO LO HICE |
|---|---|---|
| 1. Me puse ropa cómoda antes de salir. | ☐ | ☐ |
| 2. Mis amigos/as vinieron a mi casa y fuimos juntos/as. | ☐ | ☐ |
| 3. Fuimos a un almacén. | ☐ | ☐ |
| 4. No pude encontrar mi talla. | ☐ | ☐ |
| 5. Quise comprar ropa nueva, pero no encontré nada. | ☐ | ☐ |
| 6. No traje suficiente dinero conmigo. | ☐ | ☐ |
| 7. Tuve que hacer cola (*stand in line*) para pagar. | ☐ | ☐ |
| 8. No quise gastar mucho dinero ese día. | ☐ | ☐ |

**B.** La fiesta. Haga oraciones completas en el pretérito con las palabras indicadas.

1. mis compañeras de cuarto y yo / dar / fiesta / viernes / pasado
2. (nosotras) / tener / que / comprar / comida / y / decorar / casa
3. yo / ir / supermercado / y / compañeras / escribir / las invitaciones
4. (nosotras) / invitar / a Juan / pero / no / poder / venir
5. amigos / venir / y traer / música
6. Rebeca / no / querer / bailar
7. todos / decir / que / fiesta / ser / chévere (*cool*)

**C.** Descripciones. En parejas, tomen un elemento de cada columna para formar oraciones completas. **¡OJO!** Usen el pretérito de los verbos.

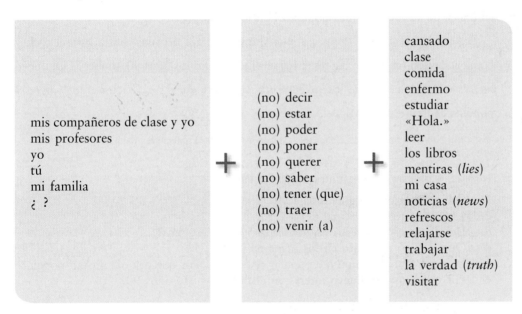

mis compañeros de clase y yo
mis profesores
yo
tú
mi familia
¿ ?

+

(no) decir
(no) estar
(no) poder
(no) poner
(no) querer
(no) saber
(no) tener (que)
(no) traer
(no) venir (a)

+

cansado
clase
comida
enfermo
estudiar
«Hola.»
leer
los libros
mentiras (*lies*)
mi casa
noticias (*news*)
refrescos
relajarse
trabajar
la verdad (*truth*)
visitar

Cultures   Recycle

## D. El bolero

**PASO 1.** Complete la narración con la forma correcta del verbo entre paréntesis en el pretérito. Cuando hay dos palabras entre paréntesis, escoja la palabra correcta, luego úsela en su forma correcta.

Un trío bolero

La cultura cubana es (**un/una**[1]) mezcla[a] de elementos (**africano**[2]) y (**europeo**[3]). Una forma musical, el bolero, (**tener**[4]) sus orígenes en Cuba y refleja esta mezcla. El bolero nació[b] en Cuba en el siglo XIX, y desde ese país caribeño (**pasar**[5]) a México; de allí, su influencia (**llegar**[6]) a extenderse por toda Latinoamérica, y más tarde, por el mundo.

El tema principal de los boleros (**estar/ser**[7]) el amor, y por eso, los boleros (**cruzar**[8]) fácilmente las fronteras.[c] Además de su letra[d] universal, el ritmo bailable del bolero (**contribuir**[9]) a su popularidad.

Todos los países le (**hacer**[10]) cambios al bolero para incluir sus ritmos individuales. Los músicos[e] de diferentes países (**cantar**[11]) los mismos boleros pero con variaciones. (**Mucho**[12]) películas también (**incluir**[13]) boleros, aumentando[f] así su popularidad aún más. En los Estados Unidos, artistas populares como Bing Crosby grabaron[g] versiones en inglés de los boleros más populares en los años 40.

El bolero (**estar/ser**[14]) muy popular durante varias décadas[h] hasta que[i] el rock y la música disco (**empezar**[15]) a tener más influencia. En los años 90, (**haber**[16]) un nuevo interés en el bolero entre los jóvenes gracias a las nuevas grabaciones[j] del joven y popular cantante, Luis Miguel.

[a]*mix*  [b]*was born*  [c]*borders*  [d]*lyrics*  [e]*musicians*  [f]*increasing*  [g]*recorded*  [h]*durante... for several decades*
[i]*hasta... until*  [j]*recordings*

**PASO 2.** Conteste las preguntas, según el **Paso 1.**

1. ¿Qué mezcla de culturas refleja el bolero?
2. ¿Cuál es el tema principal del bolero?
3. ¿Dónde nació el bolero? ¿Adónde pasó desde ese país?
4. ¿Qué le pasó al bolero en los otros países?
5. ¿Durante cuanto tiempo fue popular el bolero? ¿Por qué dejó de ser tan popular?
6. ¿Por qué hubo un nuevo interés en el bolero en los años 90?

Communication

**PASO 3.** En parejas, contesten las preguntas.

1. ¿Qué canciones o cantantes de otros países conocen Uds.? ¿Cómo es su música?
2. En su opinión, ¿qué forma musical mejor representa la región donde viven? Expliquen.
3. ¿Qué tipo de música les gusta escuchar? ¿Quién es su cantante favorito/a? ¿Por qué?
4. ¿Son semejantes los intereses musicales de Uds. a los de sus padres o son diferentes? Expliquen.

## 7.2 Preterite: Stem Changing Verbs

**GRAMÁTICA EN CONTEXTO**

### En la Avenida Duarte

BEGOÑA: ¿**Te divertiste** ayer, Paula?

PAULA: Sí, **me divertí** mucho. Diana y yo decidimos ir de compras en la Avenida Duarte en la Zona Colonial. Llegamos por la tarde, porque, como todos los sábados, Diana **durmió** hasta las 11:00. Cuando llegué a su casa a mediodía, Diana **se vistió** rápidamente y salimos para la Zona Colonial. Llegamos a la hora del almuerzo, cuando hay mucha gente, pero **conseguimos** sentarnos en un café cerca de la plaza. **Pedimos** una ensalada, comimos rápido y después paseamos por la Avenida.

BEGOÑA: ¿Compraste algo interesante?

PAULA: Yo no compré nada, pero toda la tarde **seguí** a Diana en busca del vestido perfecto para la boda de su sobrina. Visitamos diez o doce tiendas, y, por fin, Diana **consiguió** un vestido morado elegante.

**Comprensión.** ¿Cierto o falso?

|  | C | F |
|---|---|---|
| 1. Diana y Paula salieron ayer por la mañana. | ☐ | ☐ |
| 2. Paula durmió hasta muy tarde ayer. | ☐ | ☐ |
| 3. En la Zona Colonial, les sirvieron ensalada a Diana y Paula. | ☐ | ☐ |
| 4. Paula prefirió visitar las zapaterías. | ☐ | ☐ |

There are some verbs in Spanish that have stem changes in the preterite.

| PRETERITE OF **servir (i, i)*** ||
|---|---|
| serví | servimos |
| serviste | servisteis |
| sirvió | sirvieron |

| PRETERITE OF **dormir (ue, u)*** ||
|---|---|
| dormí | dormimos |
| dormiste | dormisteis |
| durmió | durmieron |

Nos **sirvieron** la cena en el patio.
Eugenio **durmió** doce horas anoche.

*They served us the dinner on the patio.
Eugenio slept for twelve hours last night.*

---

*Throughout *Experience Spanish*, whenever you see multiple stem changes in parentheses following an infinitive, the first stem change refers to the present tense and the second one to the preterite.

---

**GRAMÁTICA EN CONTEXTO** ***On Duarte Avenue* / BEGOÑA:** *Did you have fun yesterday, Paula? /* ***PAULA:*** *Yes, I had a lot of fun. Diana and I decided to go shopping on Duarte Avenue, in the Colonial District. We arrived in the afternoon, because, as always on Saturdays, Diana slept until eleven. When I arrived at her house at noon, Diana got dressed quickly and we left for the Colonial District. We arrived at lunchtime, when there are a lot of people, but we were able to sit at a café close to the plaza. We ordered salads, we ate quickly, and later we strolled along the Avenue. /* ***BEGOÑA:*** *Did you buy anything interesting? /* ***PAULA:*** *I didn't buy anything, but I followed Diana all afternoon in search of the perfect dress for her niece's wedding. We visited ten or twelve stores, and, at last, Diana got an elegant purple dress.*

**A.** There are two types of stem change in the preterite, **e → i** and **o → u**, and they only occur in **-ir** verbs that have a stem change in the present tense as well. Note that these preterite stem changes only affect third person forms. Here is a list of common stem changing verbs in the preterite.

| COMMON STEM CHANGING VERBS IN THE PRETERITE | | | |
|---|---|---|---|
| **e → i (i, i)** | | **o → u (ue, u)** | |
| INFINITIVE | THIRD PERSON FORMS | INFINITIVE | THIRD PERSON FORMS |
| conseguir | consiguió, consiguieron | morir(se) *(to die)* | (se) murió, (se) murieron |
| divertirse | se divirtió, se divirtieron | | |
| pedir | pidió, pidieron | | |
| preferir | prefirió, prefirieron | | |
| seguir | siguió, siguieron | | |
| sentir(se) | (se) sintió, (se) sintieron | | |
| vestir(se) | (se) vistió, (se) vistieron | | |

Susana y Alberto **pidieron** ayuda en la tienda, pero nadie los atendió.

Ana María **se divirtió** mucho en el mercado.

*Susana and Alberto asked for help in the store, but no one waited on them.*

*Ana María had a great time in the market.*

**B.** All preterite stem changing verbs have a similar stem change in the gerund form.

| STEM CHANGING GERUNDS | |
|---|---|
| INFINITIVE | GERUND |
| servir (i, i) | sirviendo |
| divertirse (i, i) | divirtiéndose |
| dormir (ue, u) | durmiendo |

Ay, estoy **muriéndome** de hambre.

Amor, ¿ya **te** estás **vistiendo**? Tenemos que salir en unos quince minutos.

*Oh, I'm dying of hunger.*

*Darling, are you getting dressed already? We have to leave in about fifteen minutes.*

**ACTIVIDADES**

**A.** ¿Qué pasó la semana pasada? Entreviste a sus compañeros/as de clase y apunte el nombre de una persona que hizo estas cosas la semana pasada. Si nadie las hizo, conteste: **Nadie.**

1. _____ se divirtió mucho en clase.
2. _____ se durmió mirando la tele.
3. _____ prefirió quedarse en casa y no salir.
4. _____ no pidió café antes de ir a clase.
5. _____ se vistió con ropa muy cómoda para ir a clase.
6. _____ siguió trabajando después de las 5:00.
7. _____ consiguió entradas (*tickets*) para un evento especial.

**B.** ¿Qué hicieron esta semana? En grupos de tres, tomen un elemento de cada columna para formar oraciones completas. **¡OJO!** Usen el pretérito de los verbos.

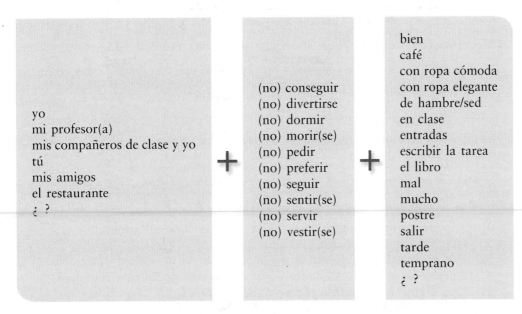

| | | |
|---|---|---|
| yo | (no) conseguir | bien |
| mi profesor(a) | (no) divertirse | café |
| mis compañeros de clase y yo | (no) dormir | con ropa cómoda |
| tú | (no) morir(se) | con ropa elegante |
| mis amigos | (no) pedir | de hambre/sed |
| el restaurante | (no) preferir | en clase |
| ¿ ? | (no) seguir | entradas |
| | (no) sentir(se) | escribir la tarea |
| | (no) servir | el libro |
| | (no) vestir(se) | mal |
| | | mucho |
| | | postre |
| | | salir |
| | | tarde |
| | | temprano |
| | | ¿ ? |

**C.** ¿Qué hicieron Uds.? En parejas, contesten las preguntas.

1. ¿A qué hora se durmieron Uds. anoche?
2. ¿Cómo se vistieron hoy para ir a clase?
3. ¿Cuándo fue la última vez que se divirtieron mucho con sus amigos? ¿Qué hicieron?
4. ¿Qué pidieron la última vez que comieron en un restaurante?
5. ¿Cómo se sintieron la última vez que tomaron un examen?

**D.** El Carnaval de La Vega, República Dominicana

**PASO 1.** Complete la descripción de Alejandro con la forma correcta del verbo entre paréntesis en el pretérito. Cuando hay dos palabras entre paréntesis, escoja la palabra correcta, luego úsela en su forma correcta.

El año pasado, mis amigos y yo (**ir**[1]) [*fuimos*] a La Vega, República Dominicana, para celebrar el Carnaval. (*Nosotros:* **Hacer**[2]) [*hicimos*] las reservaciones y (**conseguir**[3]) [*conseguimos*] los boletos de avión[a] con mucha anticipación[b] cuando (**conocer/saber**[4]) [*supimos*] que siempre va mucha gente a La Vega para el Carnaval.

El primer día, (*nosotros:* **desayunar**[5]) [*desayunamos*] temprano en el restaurante del hotel. Nos (*ellos:* **servir**[6]) [*sirvieron*] un desayuno dominicano típico: mangú[c] con un huevo frito, queso frito y café con leche. El desayuno (**estar**[7]) [*estuvo*] muy rico, y yo (**pedir**[8]) [*pedí*] otro café para llevar antes de salir a la calle.

Yo (**oír**[9]) [*oí*] la música y los gritos[d] del desfile y (**empezar**[10]) [*empecé*] a caminar hacia el ruido.[e] Mis amigos me (**seguir**[11]) [*siguieron*]. Pronto (**ver**[12]) [*vieron*] el desfile con todo su movimiento, sus colores y sus sonidos[f] alegres.

[a]*boletos... airplane tickets* [b]*con... well in advance* [c]*boiled, mashed, and seasoned plantains* [d]*shouts* [e]*hacia... toward the noise* [f]*sounds*

*Un diablo cojuelo*

De repente,[g] yo (sentir[13]) *sentió* un golpe fuerte.[h] Di la vuelta[i] y (ver[14]) *vió* al personaje principal del Carnaval vegano,[j] el diablo cojuelo,[k] con una vejiga[l]* en la mano. El diablo (querer[15]) *quiso* pegarme[m] otra vez, pero no (*él*: poder[16]) *pudo* porque yo (irse[17]) *me fui* corriendo. Más tarde, (conocer/saber[18]) *supe* que los vejigazos[n] son una tradición del Carnaval vegano.

Esa noche mis amigos (dormir[19]) *durmieron* bien, pero yo no. (*Yo*: Tener[20]) *tuve* que encontrar una manera de sobrevivir los vejigazos.

Al día siguiente, mis amigos y yo (vestirse[21]) *nos vestimos* de diablos cojuelos y ¡(defenderse[22]) *nos defendieron* de los vejigazos con nuestras propias vejigas!

---

[g]De... *Suddenly*  [h]un... *a hard blow*  [i]Di... *I turned around*  [j]*of or related to La Vega*  [k]el... *typical figure of La Vega's Carnival representing a mischievous, playful devil*  [l]*bladder*  [m]*to hit me*  [n]*blows with the vejiga*

**PASO 2.**  Conteste las preguntas, según el **Paso 1.**

1. ¿Adónde fueron Alejandro y sus amigos para celebrar el Carnaval?
2. ¿Qué hicieron con anticipación? ¿Por qué?
3. ¿Qué desayunaron? ¿Qué tal estuvo?
4. ¿Qué oyeron y vieron Alejandro y sus amigos cuando salieron del hotel?
5. ¿Qué le pasó a Alejandro? ¿Cómo respondió él?
6. ¿Qué hicieron Alejandro y sus amigos al día siguiente?

**PASO 3.**  En parejas, contesten las preguntas.

1. ¿Hay algún desfile o celebración especial en la región donde Uds. viven? ¿Cómo se llama? ¿Cómo es ese evento?
2. ¿En qué es semejante o diferente el Carnaval de La Vega de las celebraciones que Uds. conocen en este país? Expliquen.
3. Cuando Uds. celebran un día festivo, ¿prefieren quedarse en casa o salir a la calle? Expliquen.

**PASO 4.**  Busque más información en el Internet sobre las celebraciones del Carnaval en otros lugares y compárenlas con el Carnaval de La Vega. Compartan sus resultados con la clase.

---

*A **vejiga** is the dried out bladder of an animal that is normally used as a musical instrument.

# Palabra escrita

## A comenzar

Communication

> **Identifying the Purpose and Audience of Your Composition.** A writing task should have a purpose that is closely related to its function. For example, narrating a story is a very different task than trying to persuade the reader of the validity of something. The task should also address a likely need of your audience. The written format you choose and the audience you address will determine the content, style, tone, and level of formality of your composition. For example, if your task were to describe to your classmates what you did last weekend, what do you think your classmates would like to know? What tone and level of formality would you use in your composition? How would your composition be different if your parents, professor, priest, reverend, rabbi, and so on were the audience? How would things change if your purpose were not to describe what you did last weekend, but rather to convince your audience that what you did was a good use of your time?

You are going to start the process of writing a brief composition that you will finalize in the **Palabra escrita: A finalizar** section of your *Manual de actividades*. The topic of this composition is **Lo que hice el fin de semana pasado.** The purpose of your composition will be to tell the reader about what you did last weekend.

**A. Lluvia de ideas.** En parejas, hagan una lluvia de ideas sobre estas preguntas.

1. ¿Qué hicieron el fin de semana pasado para divertirse?
2. ¿Qué hicieron con sus amigos? ¿Fueron al cine? ¿Fueron de compras? ¿Dieron una fiesta? ¿Salieron a bailar? ¿Hicieron otra cosa?
3. ¿Qué ropa se pusieron durante el fin de semana? ¿Se vistieron con ropa de todos los días o tuvieron que llevar ropa especial para ir al trabajo o a algún evento especial?

**B.** A organizar sus ideas. Repase sus ideas y organícelas en categorías. Escoja el propósito (*purpose*) de su composición. ¿Es una comparación de las cosas que hizo? ¿Es una breve descripción de su fin de semana? Comparta su información con la clase y apunte otras ideas que se le ocurran durante el proceso.

**C.** A escribir. Ahora, haga el borrador de su composición con las ideas y la información que recopiló en las actividades A y B. **¡OJO!** Guarde bien su trabajo. Va a necesitarlo otra vez para la sección de **Palabra escrita: A finalizar** en el *Manual de actividades*.

## Dionisio Blanco

*Pintura de la serie* El Sembrador (Sower), *1986*

Dionisio Blanco (1953– ), profesor de dibujo en la Universidad Autónoma de Santo Domingo, es un pintor dominicano importante, cuyas[a] pinturas reflejan los brillantes colores del Caribe. Casi todos sus cuadros se centran en el personaje del Sembrador, representado sin rostro[b] y en mundos idílicos y fantásticos. Los personajes, sencillos y escondidos bajo[c] enormes sombreros sugieren una identidad colectiva: el campesino[d] universal.

En este cuadro, una singular figura femenina siembra[e] nubes en un mundo celestial, con una luna[f] en el fondo.[g] Los colores cálidos[h] de la figura contrastan con los colores frescos del cielo.

---

[a]*whose*   [b]*sin... faceless*   [c]*personajes... simple characters, hidden under*   [d]*farm worker*   [e]*is seeding*   [f]*moon*
[g]*en... in the background*   [h]*warm*

### De compras°

De... *Shopping*

## Otros artículos y tiendas

| | |
|---|---|
| las artesanías | arts and crafts |
| el centro comercial | mall |
| la cerámica | pottery |
| la floristería | flower shop |
| las joyas | jewelry |
| la joyería | jewelry (store) |
| la juguetería | toy store |
| el maquillaje | makeup |
| la máscara de carnaval | carnival mask |
| la papelería | stationery store |
| la perfumería | perfume shop |
| el puesto | stall (in a market) |
| la zapatería | shoe store |
| de arcilla | clay |
| de madera | wooden |
| de oro | gold |
| de paja | straw |
| de plata | silver |

## More Goods and Stores

Cognados: la *boutique*, los cosméticos, la hamaca, el perfume; de ámbar

## Para regatear

| | |
|---|---|
| el descuento | discount |
| el precio (alto, bajo, fijo) | (high, low, fixed) price |
| barato/a | cheap; inexpensive |
| caro/a | expensive |
| demasiado | too much |
| ¿Cuánto cuesta(n)? | How much does it (do they) cost? |
| ¿Cuánto vale(n)? | How much is it (are they) worth? |
| ¿En cuánto sale(n)? | How much is it (are they)? |

## Haggling

### ACTIVIDADES

**A. Asociaciones**

PASO 1. Empareje los materiales de la derecha con los artículos de la izquierda. ¡OJO! Puede haber más de una respuesta correcta.

1. _____ una canasta
2. _____ un collar
3. _____ un reloj
4. _____ unos aretes
5. _____ una máscara
6. _____ una escultura

a. de arcilla
b. de oro
c. de paja
d. de perlas
e. de plata
f. de madera

PASO 2. Diga en qué tienda de la lista puede comprar estos objetos.

la floristería  la juguetería  el mercado de artesanías
la joyería  la perfumería

1. un brazalete de oro
2. un collar de plástico
3. flores de seda
4. una hamaca de lana
5. aretes de plata
6. algún perfume de marca famosa
7. una escultura de madera
8. una máscara de carnaval
9. una cartera de piel
10. aretes de oro

**B. De compras.** En parejas, combinen frases de cada columna para formar oraciones lógicas. **¡OJO!** Añadan las palabras y hagan los cambios necesarios.

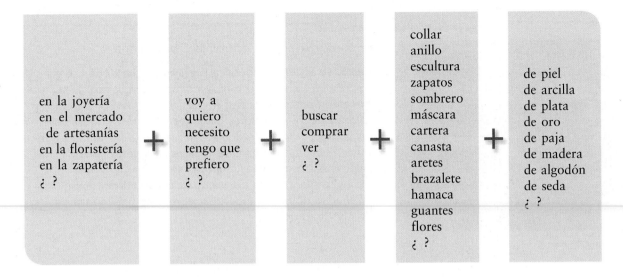

| en la joyería<br>en el mercado<br>de artesanías<br>en la floristería<br>en la zapatería<br>¿ ? | **+** | voy a<br>quiero<br>necesito<br>tengo que<br>prefiero<br>¿ ? | **+** | buscar<br>comprar<br>ver<br>¿ ? | **+** | collar<br>anillo<br>escultura<br>zapatos<br>sombrero<br>máscara<br>cartera<br>canasta<br>aretes<br>brazalete<br>hamaca<br>guantes<br>flores<br>¿ ? | **+** | de piel<br>de arcilla<br>de plata<br>de oro<br>de paja<br>de madera<br>de algodón<br>de seda<br>¿ ? |

**C. ¿Adónde fue?**

**PASO 1.** Haga una lista de cinco cosas que Ud. compró durante las últimas dos semanas.

**PASO 2.** En parejas, túrnense para decir qué compraron recientemente mientras su compañero/a adivina a qué lugar fue a comprarlo. Sigan el modelo.

Communication

**MODELO** E1: La semana pasada compré unos guantes de piel para mi hermana.
E2: ¿Fuiste a Macy's?
E1: No, los compré en una tienda pequeña, en la Boutique Alejandra.

**D. Sus tiendas favoritas**

**PASO 1.** En parejas, nombren sus tiendas y centros comerciales favoritos. Descríbanlos y digan por qué les gustan. Sigan el modelo.

Communication

**MODELO** la floristería → Mi floristería favorita es Flores Annabelle. Es una tienda pequeña pero tienen mucha variedad de flores y son frescas. También está cerca de mi casa y los precios son muy buenos.

1. la floristería
2. el centro comercial
3. la juguetería
4. la perfumería
5. la papelería
6. la zapatería
7. la joyería
8. la *boutique*
9. el mercado
10. ¿ ?

**PASO 2.** Digan cuándo fueron a sus tiendas y centros comerciales favoritos recientemente. ¿Qué compraron? ¿Para quién(es) lo compraron? Sigan el modelo.

**MODELO** Fui a Flores Annabelle la semana pasada. Compré flores para mi mamá el día de su cumpleaños. / No compré nada.

# Gramática

## 7.3 Impersonal and Passive **se**

**GRAMÁTICA EN CONTEXTO**

*Unos cuadros en una calle dominicana*

### De compras en la República Dominicana

Cuando **se visita** la República Dominicana, **se debe** ir de compras. En las tiendas, mercados y hasta en las calles **se ofrecen** productos típicos y artesanías bonitas. Por ejemplo, **se venden** cuadros de colores brillantes y máscaras de Carnaval. **Se puede** comprar café dominicano o joyería de ámbar o de larimar.* También, en muchos lugares **se ven** las famosas muñecas sin rostro. Estas muñecas **se hacen** de arcilla. Por todo el país la muñeca sin rostro **se considera** un símbolo de la identidad dominicana porque representa una mezcla de culturas y tradiciones.

### ¿CIERTO O FALSO?

|  | C | F |
|---|---|---|
| 1. Las artesanías se venden en las tiendas, mercados y calles. | ☐ | ☐ |
| 2. Se puede comprar joyería de ámbar. | ☐ | ☐ |
| 3. Las muñecas sin rostro se hacen de tela. | ☐ | ☐ |
| 4. Los cuadros se consideran un símbolo nacional. | ☐ | ☐ |

You already know that the pronoun **se** has many uses in Spanish. One use of this pronoun is to express ideas in an impersonal manner. In other words, speakers can use **se** as a grammatical subject to indicate that an action applies equally to everyone, not just you, me, or any person we specifically identify. The impersonal **se** has a number of different translations in English, but all of them share the idea of a non-specific subject doing the action. The impersonal **se** is always used with a verb in the third person singular.

| | |
|---|---|
| Hoy en día en muchos lugares públicos no **se permite** fumar. | *Nowadays in many public places one is not permitted to smoke.* |
| En ese mercado **se vende** ropa usada. | *In that market people sell second-hand clothing.* |

When the impersonal subject is plural, the verb can also become plural. This usage is commonly called the passive **se** because the same meaning can be expressed with a passive construction in English. The passive **se** uses a verb in third person singular or plural.

| | |
|---|---|
| En esa panadería **se prepara** un pastel delicioso. | *A delicious cake is made at that bakery.* |
| Aquí **se venden** cuadros muy bonitos. | *Very beautiful paintings are sold here.* |

---

*a rare blue variety of pectolite found only in the Dominican Republic

---

**GRAMÁTICA EN CONTEXTO** *Shopping in the Dominican Republic / When one visits the Dominican Republic, one should go shopping. Typical products and beautiful handcrafts are offered in the stores, markets, and even on the streets. For example, brightly colored paintings and Carnival masks are sold. One can buy Dominican coffee, or jewelry made of amber or larimar. Also, in many places one sees the famous faceless dolls. These dolls are made of clay. Throughout the country the faceless doll is considered a symbol of Dominican identity because it represents a mixture of cultures and traditions.*

## ACTIVIDADES

**A. ¿Dónde?** Indique dónde se hacen estas cosas en la ciudad donde Ud. vive. Si algo no se hace, conteste: **No se hace en ninguna parte.**

1. Se venden joyas.
2. Se regatea.
3. Se come bien.
4. Se habla español.
5. Se pide café.
6. Se reparan relojes.
7. Se compran zapatos.
8. Se encuentra ropa buena.

**B. ¿Qué pasa aquí?** Indique qué se hace en cada lugar. **¡OJO!** Use el **se** pasivo.

**MODELO** el supermercado: comprar comida → En el supermercado se compra comida.

1. la juguetería: comprar juguetes
2. ese restaurante: comer bien
3. el cine: poner películas
4. el centro comercial: vender maquillaje
5. el mercado: regatear
6. el parque: pasear
7. la zapatería: buscar zapatos nuevos
8. la joyería: vender joyas

**C. En nuestra ciudad.** En parejas, contesten las preguntas.

Communication

1. En nuestra ciudad, ¿cuándo se pide un taxi?
2. ¿Adónde se va para comer comida china?
3. ¿Dónde se ponen las películas más recientes?
4. ¿Cómo se va a la universidad?
5. ¿Dónde se toma el mejor café?
6. ¿Dónde se encuentra el almuerzo más económico?
7. ¿En qué emisora (*station*) de radio se escuchan las canciones más populares?
8. ¿Dónde se puede pasear?

**D. El coquí**

Cultures

Recycle

**PASO 1.** Complete el texto con el **se** pasivo del verbo entre paréntesis.

Es de noche en Puerto Rico y (escuchar[1]) claramente un sonido mágico. Este sonido misterioso (reconocer[2]) inmediatamente en la Isla del Encanto:[a] es el canto[b] del coquí.

Esta pequeña rana[c] de color café —cuyo[d] nombre onomatopéyico[e] imita su canto— (considerar[3]) un símbolo importante de la Isla. Todas las noches las notas melódicas (oír[4]), prestándole un toque romántico[f] a la noche. Los árboles (llenar[5]) de estas ranas diminutas cuya voz[g] llena el aire después del atardecer.[h]

Según una leyenda[i] puertorriqueña, el coquí hizo un papel importante en la creación de la Isla de Puerto Rico. (Decir[6]) que durante la creación del universo, Dios[j] se siente cansado y crea Puerto Rico como una almohada[k] para descansar antes de terminar. Dios duerme profundamente cuando de repente oye un canto insistente pero bonito. Dios se despierta y termina su creación. Como agradecimiento por su ayuda, Dios le permite al coquí vivir en Puerto Rico para siempre.

(Identificar[7]) setecientas especies[m] de coquí por todo el mundo, aunque la mayoría de las especies que cantan vive en Puerto Rico. Por eso, (creer[8]) en Puerto Rico que el coquí se muere de tristeza[n] si (llevar[9]) fuera de la Isla, y (oír[10]) dichos como «Soy más

*Un coquí*

---

[a]Isla... *Island of Enchantment (Puerto Rico's nickname)*  [b]*song*  [c]*frog*  [d]*whose*  [e]*onomatopoeic*
[f]prestándole... *lending a romantic touch*  [g]*voice*  [h]*dusk*  [i]*legend*  [j]*God*  [k]*pillow*  [m]*species*  [n]*sadness*

puertorriqueño que el coquí» para expresar el nacionalismo. Por su fuerte conexión con ese sentido de nacionalismo, el coquí sigue siendo un símbolo importante de Borinquén.[ñ]

[ñ]*indigenous name for the island of Puerto Rico*

**PASO 2.** Conteste las preguntas, según el **Paso 1.**

1. ¿Cuándo se oye el canto del coquí en Puerto Rico? ¿Cómo es su canto? Descríbalo.
2. ¿Cómo es el coquí? Descríbalo.
3. ¿Cuál es la importancia del nombre del coquí?
4. Según la leyenda, ¿qué papel hizo el coquí en la creación del universo?
5. ¿Por qué se considera el coquí un símbolo importante de la identidad puertorriqueña?

Communities

**PASO 3.** En parejas, contesten las preguntas.

1. ¿Qué sonidos asocian Uds. con el lugar en donde viven? ¿Cómo los/las hacen sentir?
2. ¿Qué elemento o fenómeno de la naturaleza mejor representa la región donde viven Uds.? Expliquen.
3. ¿Con qué símbolo de su región, estado/provincia o país se identifican más Uds.? Expliquen.

---

## Nota interdisciplinaria

Connections

### ARTE: LA ARTESANÍA EN EL CARIBE

*Unas máscaras de diablos*

Las artesanías en el Caribe, como todos los aspectos de su cultura, son una mezcla de elementos indígenas, africanos y españoles. Entre la gran variedad de productos artesanos de las islas, destacan los objetos tallados[a] en madera típicos de Puerto Rico y de la República Dominicana. Las máscaras de diablos de la República Dominicana son muy famosas y responden a una tradición que viene de los tiempos de los taínos, indígenas originarios de las islas. Desde la llegada de los españoles al Caribe en el siglo XVI, estas máscaras empezaron a usarse en la época de carnaval y su uso aún continúa hasta hoy.

[a]*carved*

PREGUNTAS En parejas, contesten las preguntas. Después, compartan sus ideas con la clase.

1. ¿Cuáles son los objetos tallados en madera más representativos de las islas caribeñas? ¿De dónde viene la tradición?
2. Las máscaras han sido (*have been*) también un elemento importante en la cultura de las tribus indígenas de Norteamérica desde tiempos remotos. Busquen información en el Internet sobre una tribu indígena de la región donde viven o de este país. ¿Qué material usan para sus máscaras? ¿En qué ocasiones se usan esas máscaras? ¿Qué semejanzas hay entre los objetos tallados en madera del Caribe y las máscaras de los grupos indígenas norteamericanos?

## 7.4 **Se** for Unplanned Occurrences

¡Ayer fue un día fatal!

1. A Pedro se le cayó el café.

2. Al coche de Alejandro se le acabó la gasolina.

3. A Lupe se le perdieron los lentes.

¿Y Ud.? ¿Cómo fue el día de ayer para Ud.? ¿Cierto o falso?

|  | C | F |
|---|---|---|
| 1. Se me perdieron las llaves (*keys*). | ☐ | ☐ |
| 2. Se me olvidó hacer la tarea. | ☐ | ☐ |
| 3. Se me rompieron los lentes. | ☐ | ☐ |
| 4. Se me acabó la leche. | ☐ | ☐ |

Another use of the pronoun **se** is in a special reflexive construction that expresses accidental or unplanned occurrences. Compare the following sentences and their English equivalents.

| | |
|---|---|
| Rompí la ventana. | *I broke the window.* |
| **Se me** rompió la ventana. | *The window broke (on me).* |

In the first construction, the speaker is the subject of the sentence and assumes direct responsibility for breaking the window (**rompí**). In the second sentence, the thing that broke is the subject in a reflexive construction (**se rompió**) and the speaker (identified by the indirect object pronoun **me**) was the innocent victim that just happened to be standing there. Here is the basic formula for this construction.

| **se** FOR UNPLANNED OCCURRENCES | | | | |
|---|---|---|---|---|
| **a** + *indir. obj. noun*<br>(person affected, optional) | **se** | *indir. obj. pron.*<br>**me, te, le, nos, os, les**<br>(innocent victim) | *third person verb*<br>(agrees with thing affected) | *subject*<br>(thing affected) |

**A.** The reflexive verb expresses the unplanned occurrence and always agrees with the subject, which always follows the verb.

| | |
|---|---|
| Uy, se nos olvidaron **los guantes.** | *Oops, we forgot our gloves.* |
| Ay, se me **quedó la tarea** en casa. | *Oh, I left my homework at home.* |

**B.** The innocent victim of the unplanned occurrence is denoted by an indirect object pronoun and it always separates the reflexive pronoun **se** from the verb.

| | |
|---|---|
| **Se me cayeron** los platos. | *I dropped the plates.* |
| **Se nos descompuso** el coche. | *Our car broke down.* |

**C.** Use the optional **a** + *indirect object noun* phrase to avoid confusion if necessary when the person affected by the unplanned occurrence is denoted by the indirect object pronouns **le** or **les.**

| | |
|---|---|
| A **Juan** se **le** perdieron las llaves. | *Juan lost the keys.* |
| A mis padres se **les** acabó la paciencia. | *My parents ran out of patience.* |

**D.** Here is a list of common verbs and their translations when used in this construction. Note that some of these verbs have other translations when used in other ways.

| | | | |
|---|---|---|---|
| **acabar** | to run out of | **olvidar** | to forget |
| **caer** | to drop | **perder (ie)** | to lose |
| **descomponer** | to break down | **quedar** | to leave (behind) |
| (*like* **poner**) | | **romper** | to break |

**A. ¡Qué semana!** Empareje las acciones de la columna A con las consecuencias de la columna B.

A

1. Se me perdieron las llaves del coche. __d__
2. A Juan se le olvidaron los lentes. __g__
3. Se te cayó el vaso de agua. __f__
4. A ellos se les olvidó la tarea. __c__
5. Al profesor se le descompuso la computadora. __h__ *fixing*
6. Se me cayeron los libros. __a__
7. A papá se le perdió la cartera. __b__ *wallet*
8. Se te olvidó comprar leche. __e__

B

a. Tengo que recogerlos (*pick them up*).
b. No tiene dinero.
c. No pueden entregarla.
d. Tengo que tomar el autobús.
e. Tienes que ir al supermercado.
f. Tienes que secar el piso.
g. No puede leer.
h. Tiene que comprar una nueva.

**B. Una día fatal.** Haga oraciones completas con las palabras indicadas, usando el **se** accidental y el pretérito del verbo.

MODELO  A los niños: caer / el plato → Se les cayó el plato.

1. A Pedro: olvidar / el celular
2. A ti: descomponer / el reloj
3. A mí: perder / el iPod
4. A nosotras: caer / los papeles
5. A mis papás: romper / la lámpara
6. A la profesora: olvidar / su bolígrafo
7. A ti: perder / la tarea
8. A mis compañeros de cuarto y a mí / olvidar / pagar la renta

**C. Entrevista.** Entreviste a un compañero / una compañera de clase con estas preguntas. Luego, cambien de papel.

Communication

1. ¿Qué se te olvida con frecuencia?
2. ¿Qué se te rompió recientemente?
3. ¿Qué aparato se te olvida apagar (*turn off*) con frecuencia?
4. A tus amigos, ¿qué se les olvida hacer con frecuencia?
5. ¿Se te perdió algo importante alguna vez? ¿Qué fue? ¿Lo encontraste?
6. ¿Se te cayó algo de valor (*valuable*) alguna vez? ¿Qué fue? ¿Qué pasó?

## Nota cultural

Cultures

### EL FESTIVAL DEL MERENGUE

El Festival del Merengue se celebra en Santo Domingo, República Dominicana, desde 1967. Cada año, durante la última semana de julio y la primera semana de agosto, miles de personas, tanto turistas como residentes de la ciudad, se juntan[a] en la capital dominicana para festejar[b] la música nacional: el merengue.

El festival comienza con un desfile por el Malecón[c] y comprende[d] una variedad de actividades y cosas diferentes: comida, artesanías y juegos, por ejemplo. Claro,[e] la atracción principal es el merengue que tocan grupos locales y también los artistas más conocidos. Con su ritmo fuerte y juguetón,[f] el merengue crea un ambiente animado y alegre. Sin lugar a dudas,[g] el Festival del Merengue es un evento perfecto para pasarlo bien.

[a]*tanto... both tourists as well as residents of the city gather*  [b]*celebrate*  [c]*waterfront avenue*
[d]*it includes*  [e]*Of course*  [f]*playful*  [g]*Sin... Without a doubt*

Cultures   Recycle

**D.** El Festival del Merengue

**PASO 1.** Complete el texto con la forma correcta del verbo entre paréntesis en el pretérito. ¡OJO! Use el **se** accidental cuando se indica con *se:*.

*Bailando merengue*

*Carlos escribe un blog sobre sus experiencias con su mejor amigo, Jacinto, en el Festival del Merengue.*

Nuestro viaje a Santo Domingo para el Festival del Merengue (**estar**¹) repleto^a de [*se estuvo*]

problemas... O así nos parecía al principio.

Jacinto y yo (**acostarse**²) muy tarde, pero con la intención de levantarnos temprano [*se nos acostamos*]

para no perder ningún momento de las festividades. Sin embargo, a mí (*se:* **olvidar**³) [*se olvido*]

poner el despertador.^b Por eso, (*nosotros:* **levantarse**⁴) tarde. Nos apuramos^c pero a [*nos levantamos*]

Jacinto (*se:* **perder**⁵) los lentes de sol^d y él (**pasar**⁶) más de media hora buscándolos. [*se perdió*] [*pasó*]

Por fin (*nosotros:* **salir**⁷), pero a Jacinto (*se:* **caer**⁸) la cámara y (*se:* **romper**⁹). Yo [*nos salimos*] [*se caió*] [*se rompió*]

le (**decir**¹⁰): «No te preocupes.^e Podemos usar mi cámara». [*se dijo*]

(*Nosotros:* **Empezar**¹¹) a caminar, pero no sabíamos^f adónde ir. Después de pedir [*nos empezamos*]

ayuda, por fin (*nosotros:* **llegar**¹²) al Malecón para ver el desfile. (*Yo:* **Sacar**¹³) varias [*nos llegamos*] [*me saqué*]

fotos, pero entonces (a mí) (*se:* **acabar**¹⁴) la pila^g de la cámara. [*se acabó*]

Después del desfile, (*nosotros:* **ir**¹⁵) a buscar comida. De repente, Jacinto (**gritar**¹⁶): [*nos fuimos*] [*se gritó*]

«¡Ay! ¡No puede ser!^h»

—¿Qué te pasa?

—(A mí) (*se:* **Olvidar**¹⁷) la cartera en el hotel. [*se olvidó*]

—¿Cómo? Pues, te presto^i algo, pero yo tampoco (**traer**¹⁸) mucho dinero. [*me traí*]

---

^a*full*  ^b*alarm clock*  ^c*We hurried*  ^d*lentes... sunglasses*  ^e*No... Don't worry*  ^f*we didn't know*  ^g*battery*
^h*¡No... It can't be!*  ^i*I'll loan you*

Bueno, como se pueden imaginar, (a nosotros) (*se:* **acabar**[19]) los pesos muy

pronto. Pero justo cuando (*yo:* **empezar**[20]) a pensar que todo iba a salir mal,[j] (**oír**[21])

la música de un merengue muy alegre. Todos (**bailar**[22]) y muchos (**cantar**[23]). Al escu-

char esa música animada y en medio de[k] tanta alegría, (a nosotros) (*se:* **olvidar**[24]) los

problemas inmediatamente.

*[handwritten: se acabó]*
*[handwritten: me empezé]*
*[handwritten: oí]*
*[handwritten: bailaron]*
*[handwritten: cantaron]*
*[handwritten: se olvidó]*

---

[j]*iba... was going to turn out badly* [k]*in the midst of*

**PASO 2.** Conteste las preguntas, según el **Paso 1.**

1. ¿Dónde y cuándo se celebra el Festival del Merengue?
2. ¿Qué cosas se les olvidaron a Carlos y a Jacinto? ¿Cómo los afectó?
3. ¿Qué le pasó a Jacinto con su cámara? ¿Y a Carlos?
4. ¿Cómo es el ambiente del festival? ¿Cómo influye el ambiente en el ánimo (*mood*) de Carlos y Jacinto?

**PASO 3.** En parejas, contesten las preguntas.

Communication

1. ¿Qué festivales se celebran en la región donde Uds. viven? ¿Cómo son? ¿Participan en estos festivales?
2. ¿Qué cosas se les pierden con frecuencia? ¿Qué hacen para encontrarlas?
3. ¿Qué clase de música los pone de buen humor (*in a good mood*)? ¿Con qué frecuencia escuchan esta música?

# Lectura cultural

Cultures

Ud. va a leer un artículo del periódico en línea de *El País* sobre la industria de la moda y el uso del Internet como medio de compartir los nuevos diseños con el público.

## ANTES DE LEER

Revise rápido el título y las primeras líneas del artículo. Luego en parejas, contesten las preguntas y después compartan sus ideas con la clase.

1. ¿Qué herramientas (*tools*) o redes (*networks*) sociales del Internet creen Uds. que los diseñadores de moda usan para promocionar sus desfiles (*fashion shows*)?
2. En su opinión, ¿qué ventajas tiene para los diseñadores usar el Internet de esta manera?

### La moda se convierte al fin a la religión de Internet

*Las firmas explotan[a] todas las herramientas de la Red[b]*

CARMEN MAÑANA - Madrid - 06/02/2010

Las firmas de moda siempre han visto el lujo[c] como algo incompatible con Internet, un mundo basado en la inmediatez, la accesibilidad y la democracia, frente a sus valores tradicionales de exclusividad y misterio», explica Susana Campuzano, directora de la consultora Luxury Advise. Sin embargo, en las últimas temporadas, la industria de la moda, a la vanguardia[d] por definición de casi todo ha decidido colocarse también a la cabeza[e] en Internet.

[a]*exploit* [b]*Internet* [c]*han... have viewed luxury* [d]*a... on the cutting edge* [e]*ha... has decided also to take the lead*

---

*Diseñador John Galliano y bloguera Tavi en el Paris Fashion Week*

Para hacerlo, en 2010, no basta con tener una web pintona[f] o una tienda online. Hermés, la pionera, abrió su propio portal de ventas en 2002, y aunque algunas firmas, como Loewe, acaban de inaugurar el suyo,[g] son mayoría las que buscan ir un paso más allá[h] y explotar todas las herramientas de la Red. Alexander McQueen, por ejemplo, emitió[i] en directo a través de Facebook su desfile para la primavera-verano de 2010. Hubo tanta gente que intentó entrar al mismo tiempo en su página que esta se colapsó. Dolce & Gabbana colgaron vídeos de todo el montaje[j] y preparación de sus presentaciones en Milán; Marc Jacobs de sus desfiles el mismo día en que tuvieron[k] lugar. A través de la web artofthetrench. com, Burberry ha pedido[l] a los internautas que cuenten[m] cómo es su gabardina[n] perfecta. Ya han recibido[ñ] casi cuatro millones de fotografías. El diseñador Henry Holland y la firma Dior publican en la web de mensajes Twitter sus noticias, impresiones, inquietudes…

«Por fin se han dado cuenta de[o] que Internet y las redes sociales pueden serles muy útiles», apunta Campuzano. Mejor tarde que nunca. A través de la Red, las firmas consiguen un contacto directo con sus consumidores, un estudio de mercado constante que les permite saber mejor lo que estos buscan. Además, pueden ampliar su clientela hacia un público joven, que sería[p] muy difícil de captar fuera de Internet.

La asesora cree que «la Red ha cambiado[q] el mundo del lujo». La prueba está en los desfiles. Antes, sólo unos pocos cientos de escogidos podían[r] disfrutar de ellos en su totalidad. Ahora, cualquier español puede ver desde su sofá y en

---

[f]*flashy*  [g]*theirs*  [h]*más… beyond*  [i]*broadcast*  [j]*assembly*  [k]*took*  [l]*ha… has asked*  [m]*they tell*  [n]*raincoat*
[ñ]*han… they have received*  [o]*se… they have realized*  [p]*would be*  [q]*ha… has changed*  [r]*were able*

tiempo real la presentación de Alexander McQueen en París. Incluso conocer las impresiones del diseñador entre bastidores[s] a través de Twitter. A los[t] pocos minutos, páginas especializadas como Style.com habrán colgado[u] fotos de todos los diseños que han subido a la pasarela.[v] Sin olvidar a blogueros como The Sartorialist, el filipino Bryanboy o la niña Tavi (de tan sólo 13 años), que los diseñadores sientan en primera fila,[w] junto a los editores de las grandes revistas y los compradores más poderosos, dándoles el lugar que les corresponde en la aristocracia de la moda. Desde sus portátiles comentan casi al instante cada salida, y sus cientos de miles de seguidores reciben ávidos[x] la información en sus ordenadores y móviles. Campuzano, que también es directora del Programa Superior de Dirección y Gestión Estratégica del Universo del lujo del IE Bussiness School, asegura que estar al alcance[y] de una audiencia global no tiene porqué hacer perder a una firma su exclusividad. «Una gran exposición al público no significa que todo el mundo pueda acceder a[z] tu marca. Sólo que más gente puede desearla, y eso es influencia».

[s]entre... *behind the scenes*  [t]A... *Within*  [u]habrán... *had probably uploaded*  [v]han... *had gone up on the runway*  [w]*row*  [x]*greedily*  [y]al... *within reach*  [z]pueda... *can access*

## DESPUÉS DE LEER

**A. Comprensión.** Indique si estas oraciones son ciertas (**C**) o falsas (**F**), según el artículo. Para las oraciones falsas, dé la información correcta.

|  | C | F |
|---|---|---|
| 1. Para las firmas de moda, usar el Internet significa ir más allá de tener una página Web o una tienda en línea. | ☐ | ☐ |
| 2. Hermés y Loewe fueron pioneras en presentar sus desfiles en Internet. | ☐ | ☐ |
| 3. Presentar la moda en el Internet puede ser favorable para las firmas. | ☐ | ☐ |
| 4. Emitir los desfiles en las redes sociales tiene un impacto en la clientela. | ☐ | ☐ |
| 5. La moda pierde exclusividad y misterio cuando se presentan los desfiles en línea y en tiempo real. | ☐ | ☐ |
| 6. El acceso fácil a los desfiles de moda significa que todo el mundo va a comprar diseños de marca famosos. | ☐ | ☐ |

**B. Temas de discusión.** En parejas, contesten las preguntas. Después, compartan sus ideas con la clase.

Communication

1. ¿Cuáles son tres ventajas que el uso del Internet puede tener para las firmas de moda?
2. ¿Qué aparatos electrónicos pueden usar las personas para tener acceso a las exposiciones en línea?
3. ¿Por qué creen Uds. que los blogueros son invitados a los desfiles y se sientan en la primera fila?
4. Cuando Uds. van a comprar ropa, zapatos o complementos, ¿se fijan en las marcas? ¿O prefieren comprar prendas de ropa más económicas e ir a las tiendas cuando hay rebajas? Expliquen.

# Concurso de videoblogs

## República Dominicana: Merfry
### De compras en San Pedro de Macorís

En este segmento, Merfry va a San Pedro de Macorís, en la costa. Primero, nos habla de la ciudad y después va de compras. Va a un mercado y entra en una tienda de arte, cerca del Parque Central. Allí compra un cuadro y, finalmente, en la playa de Juan Dolio, Merfry nos cuenta de la vida marítima de este maravilloso país caribeño.

### Vocabulario práctico

| | |
|---|---|
| libra | pound |
| edificio de los bomberos | fire station |
| güira, tambora, maraca | *musical instruments* |
| ballenas | whales |
| buscar pareja | look for a mate |
| dan saltos al aire | they jump into the air |

### ANTES DE VER

Conteste las preguntas y revise el **Vocabulario práctico.**

1. Cuando piensa en la posibilidad de viajar al Caribe, ¿cuáles de las siguientes ideas o imágenes se le ocurren? Explique.

   a. playas hermosas
   b. centros comerciales
   c. música alegre
   d. mercados típicos
   e. ciudades grandes
   f. restaurantes originales
   g. oportunidad de ir de compras
   h. ¿ ?

2. ¿Qué supone Ud. que Merfry va a presentar en su segundo videoblog de la República Dominicana, según el contenido de este capítulo?

### DESPUÉS DE VER

**A. Comprensión.** Conteste las preguntas, según el videoblog de Merfry.

1. ¿Cómo es San Pedro de Macorís y por qué es importante?
2. ¿Qué productos hay en el mercado? Mencione algunos de los productos que se muestran.
3. ¿Por qué entra Merfry en una pequeña tienda de arte?
4. ¿Qué aspectos de la vida local se mencionan en la tienda de arte?
5. ¿Qué opina Ud. de la forma de comprar y vender en la escena de la tienda?
6. ¿Por qué es famosa la vida marítima en la República Dominicana?

**B. Temas de discusión.** En parejas comenten los temas y preparen un breve informe para intercambiarlo con otras parejas. Después, compartan sus ideas con la clase.

1. El Caribe no es solamente un lugar turístico.
2. la vida diaria en San Pedro de Macorís
3. ir de compras en el Caribe: Las diferencias y semejanzas entre estas compras y las de la zona donde Uds. viven. ¿Qué opinan del regateo (*haggling*) después de ver el videoblog?

# Vocabulario

| La ropa | Clothing |
|---|---|
| el abrigo | coat |
| la blusa | blouse |
| las botas | boots |
| los calcetines | socks |
| la camisa | shirt |
| la camiseta | T-shirt |
| la chaqueta | jacket |
| la corbata | tie |
| la falda | skirt |
| las medias | stockings |
| el pantalón | pants |
| el pantalón corto | shorts |
| el polo | polo shirt |
| la prenda de ropa | piece/article of clothing |
| la ropa interior | lingerie, underwear |
| el ropero | wardrobe |
| el sombrero | hat |
| el traje (de baño) | (bathing) suit |
| el vestido | dress |
| los zapatos | shoes |
| de tacón alto/bajo | high-heeled shoes / flats |
| de tenis | tennis shoes |

Cognados: los jeans, el/la pijama, las sandalias, el suéter

| Los complementos | Accessories |
|---|---|
| el bolso | handbag |
| la cartera | wallet |
| el cinturón | belt |
| la gorra | cap |
| los guantes | gloves |
| el maquillaje | makeup |

Cognado: los cosméticos, el perfume

| Las tallas | Sizes |
|---|---|
| chico/a | small |
| mediano/a | medium |
| (extra) grande | (extra) large |

| Las telas y los materiales | Fabrics and Materials |
|---|---|
| de algodón | cotton |
| de arcilla | clay |
| de cuero/piel | leather |
| de diamantes | diamond |
| de lana | wool |
| de madera | wooden |
| de oro | gold |
| de paja | straw |
| de perlas | pearl |
| de plata | silver |
| de seda | silk |
| tallado/a en madera | wood-carved |

Cognado: de ámbar

| Los diseños y los colores | Designs and Colors |
|---|---|
| claro/a | light |
| de cuadros | plaid |
| de lunares | polka-dotted |
| de manga corta/larga | with short/long-sleeves |
| de marca | name-brand |
| de rayas | striped |
| de última moda | fashionable |
| liso/a | plain |
| metálico/a | metallic |
| oscuro/a | dark |
| vivo/a | brightly colored |

Cognados: el beige, el color fucsia; pastel
Repaso: el amarillo, el anaranjado, el azul, el blanco, el color café, el gris, el morado, el negro, el rojo, el rosado, el verde

| Las tiendas | |
|---|---|
| el centro comercial | mall |
| la floristería | flower shop |
| la joyería | jewelry (store) |
| la juguetería | toy store |
| la papelería | stationery store |
| la perfumería | perfume shop |
| el puesto | stall (in a market) |
| la zapatería | shoe store |

Cognados: la *boutique*
Repaso: el almacén, el mercado

| Las joyas | Jewelry |
|---|---|
| el anillo | ring |
| los aretes | earrings |
| el brazalete | bracelet |
| el collar | necklace |

| Las artesanías | Arts and Crafts |
|---|---|
| la canasta | basket |
| la cerámica | pottery |
| la escultura | sculpture |
| la hamaca | hammock |
| la máscara de carnaval | carnival mask |
| los tejidos | woven goods |

| Para regatear | Haggling |
|---|---|
| el precio (alto/bajo/fijo) | (high/low/fixed) price |
| barato/a | cheap; inexpensive |
| caro/a | expensive |
| demasiado | too much |
| ¿Cuánto cuesta(n)? | How much does it (do they) cost? |

| | | | |
|---|---|---|---|
| ¿Cuánto vale(n)? | How much is it (are they) worth? | | |
| ¿En cuánto sale(n)? | How much is it (are they)? | | |

Repaso: conseguir (i, i), divertirse (i, i), dormir (ue, u), pedir (i, i), perder (ie), preferir (i, i), seguir (i, i), sentir(se) (i, i), servir (i, i), vestir(se) (i, i)

## Los verbos

| | |
|---|---|
| acabar* | to run out of |
| caer* (*irreg.*) | to drop |
| descomponer (*like* **poner**) | to break down |
| conseguir (*like* **seguir**) + *inf.* | to manage to (*do something*) |
| hubo (*pret. of* **hay**) | there was/were |
| ir (*irreg.*) de compras | to go shopping |
| morir(se) (ue, u) | to die |
| olvidar | to forget |
| quedar* | to leave (behind) |
| regatear | to haggle |
| romper | to break |

## Otras palabras y expresiones

| | |
|---|---|
| la calidad | quality |
| el descuento | discount |
| la moda | fashion |
| la rebaja | price reduction |
| la venta | sale |
| | |
| actual | current |
| cómodo/a | comfortable |
| disponible | available |

Cognados: el estilo; moderno/a, unisex, vital

---

*The translations shown here for the verbs **acabar**, **caer**, and **quedar** only apply when used with the **se** for unplanned occurrences construction presented in **Gramática 7.4.** They have alternate meanings when used in different contexts.

# La comida

Connections

## ANTES DE VER

La comida mexicana es muy popular en este país. ¿Pero sabía Ud. (*did you know*) que hay tanta variedad gastronómica (*food*) en los países hispanos? ¿Cuánto sabe de la cocina (*cuisine*) hispana? Indique si está de acuerdo o no con estas oraciones.

|  | SÍ | NO |
|---|---|---|
| 1. Toda la comida hispana es picante (*spicy*). | ☐ | ☐ |
| 2. No se encuentran frutas tropicales como bananas y piñas en los países hispanos. | ☐ | ☐ |
| 3. La paella es un plato que tradicionalmente se sirve en muchos países hispanos. | ☐ | ☐ |
| 4. Algunos ejemplos de la cocina hispana llevan influencias de otros países y de otras culturas. | ☐ | ☐ |
| 5. Se sirven tortillas de maíz en cada país hispano. | ☐ | ☐ |
| 6. Los hispanos no suelen tomar café y chocolate caliente (*hot*). | ☐ | ☐ |

### Vocabulario práctico

| | | | |
|---|---|---|---|
| **la gastronomía** | food (*general*) | **un toquecito** | just a pinch |
| **sabrosa** | tasty | **el aceite verde** | olive oil |
| **tica** | **costarricense** | **se destaca** | is known |
| **el adobo** | sauce | **los bocadillos** | sandwiches |
| **a vapor** | steamed | **la madrugada** | early morning, |
| **el ají** | *type of chili pepper* | | pre-dawn |

## DESPUÉS DE VER

¿Indique a qué país se refieren estas frases, según el vídeo: a Costa Rica (**CR**), a la República Dominicana (**RD**) o a España (**E**).

|  | CR | RD | E |
|---|---|---|---|
| 1. la dieta mediterránea | ☐ | ☐ | ☐ |
| 2. las tortillas de maíz | ☑ | ☐ | ☐ |
| 3. un productor importante de café | ☐ | ☐ | ☐ |
| 4. los churros y chocolate | ☐ | ☐ | ☐ |
| 5. las influencias indígenas y africanas | ☐ | ☐ | ☐ |
| 6. las frutas tropicales exóticas | ☐ | ☐ | ☐ |

## MOROS Y CRISTIANOS

¡Es difícil encontrar un plato sin arroz en Cuba! Moros y cristianos es un plato delicioso que combina frijoles negros con arroz blanco. Otros ingredientes son agua, sal, aceite de oliva y varias verduras y especias.[a] Su nombre hace referencia a los moros[b] y los cristianos de la España medieval.

[a]spices  [b]Moors (name given to refer to various ethnic and cultural groups of Northern Africa)

## EL ARROZ CON GANDULES[a]

El plato nacional de Puerto Rico es arroz con gandules. Es un plato muy saludable[b] que se come en las reuniones familiares y en Navidad.[c] Lleva como ingredientes principales arroz, verduras, agua, aceite, sal y otros condimentos. Algunas recetas le añaden jamón en cubos. ¡Buen provecho!

[a]pigeon peas  [b]healthy  [c]Christmas

## ASÍ SE DICE: MÁS SOBRE LA COMIDA

**la banana** = **el plátano, el guineo** (*Carib.*)

**los camarones** (*L.A.*) = **las gambas** (*Sp.*)

**el durazno** (*L.A.*) = **el melocotón** (*Sp.*)

**los guisantes** = **los chícharos**

**las habichuelas** (*L.A.*) = **las judías verdes** (*Sp.*)

**el jugo** (*L.A.*) = **el zumo** (*Sp.*)

**el menú** = **la carta**

**el/la mesero/a** = **el/la camarero/a**

**la papa** (*L.A.*) = **la patata** (*Sp.*)

**la toronja** = **el pomelo**

**ACTIVIDADES**

**A. Comprensión.** Indique el plato que se describe. Si Ud. sabe el país de dónde viene, indique cuál es.

1. Lleva arroz blanco y frijoles negros. Su nombre se relaciona con la historia medieval.
2. Se toma en las reuniones familiares y en Navidad. A veces lleva jamón en cubos.
3. Es un postre con leche, limón y canela. Se sirve frío y a veces con otros ingredientes.
4. Es una bebida popular en los restaurantes mexicanos de los Estados Unidos.
5. Es amarilla por las especias que lleva: pimentón dulce y azafrán.

**B. Conexiones.** En parejas, contesten las preguntas.

Connections

1. ¿Han probado Uds. (*Have you tried*) otros ejemplos de la comida hispana? ¿Cuáles? ¿Les gustaron?
2. ¿Hay platos de arroz típicos en este país? ¿Cuáles son?
3. El arroz es un alimento básico en los países hispanos. ¿Qué alimentos son básicos en este país?

**C. A investigar más.** Escoja uno de los platos mencionados en las páginas anteriores. Use el Internet o la biblioteca para encontrar una receta de este plato y compártala con la clase.

**D. Temas de discusión.** En grupos pequeños, comenten *uno* de estos temas y escriban algunas conclusiones breves en español. Luego, compartan sus conclusiones con la clase.

Communication

1. los aportes (*contributions*) importantes de la gastronomía hispana a la cultura de este país
2. el plato nacional de este país (en su opinión) y lo que revela de nuestra cultura

## LA HORCHATA

La horchata es una bebida que se puede hacer con arroz u otro tipo de grano. Al arroz se le añaden[a] leche, azúcar y vainilla. Se puede pedir una horchata en muchos restaurantes mexicanos de los Estados Unidos. También se puede comprar en tiendas y mercados locales en los barrios hispanos de este país.

[a]se... are added

## EL ARROZ CON LECHE

El arroz con leche es un postre hispano muy popular. Sus ingredientes principales son el arroz de grano medio, leche y azúcar. También lleva cáscara de limón[a] y canela.[b] Se hierve la leche antes de añadir[c] el arroz, pero se toma frío. En algunos países también se hace con vainilla, coco o pasas.[d] ¡Riquísimo!

[a]cáscara... lemon zest  [b]cinnamon  [c]adding  [d]raisins

En las ruinas mayas de Tikal, Guatemala

# Entrada cultural

## Centroamérica

Cultures

Óscar Arias Sánchez

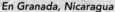
En Granada, Nicaragua

En una plantación de bananas

Centroamérica comprende[a] Guatemala, Honduras, El Salvador, Nicaragua, Costa Rica, Panamá y Belice (donde la lengua oficial es el inglés). Son países pequeños cuya población[b] se distribuye entre zonas urbanas muy habitadas y zonas rurales generalmente despobladas.[c] La población actual está formada por una mayoría mestiza[d] (60%), población indígena y blanca (19% y 17%, respectivamente) y una minoría de origen africano (4%).

Cuando Cristóbal Colón llegó a estas tierras en 1502, Centroamérica gozaba de[e] la importante presencia e influencia del pueblo maya, con una rica historia de unos 3.000 años. Millones de sus descendientes aún[f] viven en la región y muchos de ellos aún hablan alguna de las variantes de este idioma. Bajo la influencia de los movimientos independentistas del resto del continente americano, el último país centroamericano declaró su independencia de España en 1821 y abolió de manera definitiva la esclavitud en la región.

Esta región lo tiene todo para atraer al turismo internacional: playas hermosas, selvas[g] exuberantes, montañas, volcanes, lagos apacibles[h] y ruinas de antiguas civilizaciones. Es una región montañosa con una intensa actividad volcánica y sísmica. Por ser una zona de tránsito entre dos continentes, la flora y fauna de Centroamérica es particularmente rica.

La economía de Centroamérica se basa principalmente en la agricultura (café, bananas, caña de azúcar y algodón) que se destina a la exportación, en el turismo y en algunas industrias pequeñas. El canal de Panamá es su principal conexión con el resto del mundo y la principal vía de comunicación para el comercio. Pero la región enfrenta tres duros desafíos:[i] vencer la pobreza,[j] consolidar sus débiles[k] democracias y apagar los odios[l] que dejaron los largos años de guerras civiles en algunos de sus países. El costarricense Óscar Arias Sánchez recibió en 1987 el Premio Nóbel de la Paz por su participación en los procesos de paz en los conflictos armados de Centroamérica. La guatemalteca Rigoberta Menchú recibió el mismo premio en 1992 por su trabajo en el reconocimiento de los derechos de los pueblos indígenas.

[a]*includes*  [b]cuya... *whose population*  [c]generalmente... *scarcely populated*  [d]*racially mixed*  [e]*enjoyed*  [f]*still*  [g]*jungles*  [h]*calm*  [i]*challenges*  [j]vencer... *to defeat poverty*  [k]*weak*  [l]apagar los odios... *to snuff out hatred*

# El arroz

El arroz es un alimento fundamental en la gastronomía mundial. Hay muchos tipos de arroz y se usa de varias maneras: en platos principales, en postres y ¡hasta en bebidas! Es rico en almidón[a] y calorías, pero bajo en proteínas. Los árabes lo introdujeron en España durante la Edad Media[b] y hoy día es esencial en la cocina hispana.

[a]*starch*  [b]*Edad... Middle Ages*

## LA PAELLA

Hay muchas variedades de paella, un plato popular de España. La esencia de una sabrosa paella está en controlar los ingredientes fundamentales: agua, aceite de oliva, arroz, sal y verduras frescas. A veces también lleva carne y mariscos. El color amarillo del arroz viene de las especias: pimentón dulce[a] y azafrán,[b] la especia más cara del mundo.

[a]*pimentón... sweet paprika*  [b]*saffron*

# En la comunidad

Capítulo 8

Vista de San Antonio de Oriente (1957), por José Antonio Velásquez (Honduras, 1906–1983)

1. Observe el cuadro de José Antonio Velásquez. ¿Qué hacen las personas?
2. Piense en las zonas rurales y urbanas del lugar donde Ud. vive. ¿Cuáles son algunas de las semejanzas y diferencias entre las dos zonas?
3. ¿Prefiere Ud. vivir en una comunidad pequeña o en una ciudad grande? Explique.

McGraw Hill **connect**™
|SPANISH
www.connectspanish.com

### La comunidad urbana y las afueras

el avión

el rascacielos

la autopista

el tren

el edificio de oficinas

la cantina / el bar

la comisaría de policía

el puente

el carro / el coche

la fuente

la acera

la escuela

la plaza

la iglesia

la estatua

el camión

la oficina de correos

el taller de reparaciones

la gasolinera

el centro de salud

el banco

el autobús

la camioneta

la parada de autobuses

el cine

| | |
|---|---|
| el centro de salud | health center |
| la comisaría de policía | police station |
| el edificio de oficinas | office building |
| el estacionamiento | parking lot/place |

Cognados: el banco, la catedral, el palacio

## Las direcciones

| | |
|---|---|
| cruzar (c) | to cross |
| doblar | to turn |
| estacionar | to park |
| parar | to stop |
| seguir (*irreg.*) | to go; to keep going |
| la cuadra | block |
| el plano | city map |
| el semáforo | traffic light |
| ubicado/a | located |
| (al) norte (sur, este, oeste) | (to the) north (south, east, west) |
| (todo) derecho | straight ahead |

## Los medios de transporte

## Modes of Transportation

| | |
|---|---|
| conducir (zc) | to drive (*Sp.*) |
| manejar | to drive (*L.A.*) |
| montar en | to ride |
| viajar | to travel |
| el aeropuerto | airport |
| la autopista | freeway; (four-lane) highway |
| el barco | boat |
| el carnet de conducir | driver's license |
| la carretera | (two-lane) highway |
| la circulación | traffic |
| la estación de autobuses | bus station |
| el ferrocarril | railway |
| el metro | subway |
| la parada | (bus/subway) stop |

Cognados: la motocicleta, el taxi, el tráfico

## Otras palabras y expresiones

| | |
|---|---|
| el árbol | tree |
| el arbusto | bush |

**A. Asociaciones.** Empareje las palabras y frases de la columna A con las palabras correspondientes de la columna B.

| A | | B | |
|---|---|---|---|
| **1.** _____ doblar | | **a.** la fuente | |
| **2.** _____ el avión | | **b.** el ferrocarril | |
| **3.** _____ el taller de reparaciones | | **c.** el puente | |
| **4.** _____ seguir | | **d.** a la izquierda | |
| **5.** _____ parar | | **e.** el mecánico | |
| **6.** _____ el tren | | **f.** todo derecho | |
| **7.** _____ cruzar | | **g.** el aeropuerto | |
| **8.** _____ la plaza | | **h.** el semáforo | |

**B. Identificaciones.** Indique con qué asocia Ud. estas cosas: ¿con un negocio particular (*private business*), una institución social (gubernamental o académica), una ruta, un medio de transporte o un lugar público? Luego, nombre o diga dónde está una de las cosas que Ud. conoce. Siga el modelo.

**MODELOS** una cantina → Una cantina es un negocio particular. La cantina George's está cerca de la universidad.

una plaza → Una plaza es un lugar público. Mi plaza favorita está en el centro.

| | | |
|---|---|---|
| **1.** una escuela | **6.** un taller de reparaciones | **11.** una carretera |
| **2.** un avión | **7.** un semáforo | **12.** una oficina de correos |
| **3.** una fuente | **8.** un camión | **13.** una acera |
| **4.** un puente | **9.** un centro de salud | **14.** una gasolinera |
| **5.** una estatua | **10.** un tren | |

Communication

**C. Definiciones**

**PASO 1.** Dé la palabra definida.

1. Es un camino (*road*) grande entre ciudades, estados y provincias. No tiene semáforos.
2. Es un documento que necesitamos para manejar un vehículo legalmente.
3. Es una ruta para los peatones (*pedestrians*).
4. Es un negocio que visitamos cuando necesitamos reparar el coche.
5. Es cambiar de dirección mientras se camina o se maneja un vehículo.

**PASO 2.** Defina las palabras y frases.

| | | |
|---|---|---|
| **1.** una estatua | **3.** un rascacielos | **5.** cruzar |
| **2.** un puente | **4.** un centro de salud | **6.** un plano |

**D. Direcciones.** En parejas, túrnense para explicar cómo llegar a algún lugar desde este edificio. Su compañero/a va a adivinar el lugar. Sigan el modelo.

**MODELO** E1: Sales de aquí y doblas a la izquierda. Luego, sigues todo derecho por tres cuadras. Cruzas la calle y allí está el lugar.
E2: Es la Oficina de Correos.

**E.** Entrevista. Entreviste a un compañero / una compañera de clase con estas preguntas. Luego, cambien de papel.

1. ¿Qué medio de transporte prefieres usar? ¿Cuáles son los transportes públicos de esta ciudad? ¿Son buenos? ¿Cuáles usas?
2. ¿Hay alguna plaza con fuentes en esta ciudad? ¿Dónde está? ¿Pasas por allí con frecuencia?
3. ¿Qué calles, bulevares, avenidas, carreteras, etcétera, tienes que tomar para llegar a la universidad?

---

## Nota cultural

### EL TEATRO NACIONAL DE SAN JOSÉ DE COSTA RICA

El Teatro Nacional de San José, Costa Rica, es uno de los edificios más emblemáticos del país. Su construcción se inició a finales del siglo XIX como respuesta al interés cultural de sus ciudadanos.

Las presentaciones que se celebran son seleccionadas atendiendo a la calidad y el prestigio de las compañías de ópera y teatro, y es uno de los teatros más exigentes de Centroamérica. También hay funciones de la Orquesta Sinfónica Nacional de Costa Rica y de otros compositores extranjeros de renombre.[a]

El Teatro Nacional, además de su valor cultural, es un edificio de gran belleza. El frente del teatro es formidable, con estatuas que representan la Música, la Fama y la Danza. A los lados de la entrada están las estatuas del músico alemán Beethoven y del dramaturgo[b] español Pedro Calderón de la Barca. La riqueza[c] interior del teatro es impresionante. Las columnas, el mobiliario[d] ricamente decorado, las pinturas en paredes y techos[e] y las enormes lámparas de araña[f] son de estilo neoclásico y contribuyen a que la experiencia cultural sea[g] inolvidable.

[a]de... *renowned*  [b]*playwright*  [c]*beauty*  [d]*furniture*  [e]*ceilings*  [f]lámparas... *chandeliers*  [g]*(will) be*

**PREGUNTAS** En parejas, contesten las preguntas. Después, compartan sus ideas con la clase.

1. ¿Quiénes pueden actuar en el Teatro Nacional? ¿Por qué? ¿Qué significado tiene esto para la ciudad de San José?
2. ¿Creen Uds. que es importante ofrecer diversas presentaciones culturales en una ciudad? En la ciudad donde viven, ¿qué presentaciones culturales se ofrecen? ¿Qué tipos de espectáculos les gustan? ¿Con qué frecuencia asisten a estos espectáculos? Expliquen.

# Gramática

## 8.1 **Tú** Commands

**GRAMÁTICA EN CONTEXTO**

### ¿Cómo llego al Mercado Central?

[*Mark está en la Ciudad de Guatemala por
un mes y hoy quiere hacer unas compras en
el Mercado Central.*]

MARK: Ramón, **hazme** un favor. No
entiendo este plano.

RAMÓN: Cómo no. **Dime** qué necesitas.

MARK: **Explícame** cómo llegar al
Mercado Central. Quiero
caminar.

RAMÓN: Pues, queda un poco lejos, en la Zona 1. Pero, bueno, **sal** de aquí y
**dobla** a la izquierda. **Sigue** todo derecho por unas veinte cuadras.

MARK: ¡Veinte cuadras! ¡**No me digas**!

RAMÓN: Pues, sí, te dije, queda lejos. **Toma** el autobús si no quieres caminar,
porque hay unas veinte cuadras más.

MARK: ¡Dios mío! **Dime**, entonces, qué autobús debo tomar.

RAMÓN: Bueno, **no te enojes**, pero tienes que tomar tres autobuses desde aquí.
¿Te hago un plano?

MARK: Ay... sí, **hazme** uno, por favor.

Comprensión. Indique quién daría (*would give*) cada mandato: Ramón (**R**) o Mark (**M**).

|  | R | M |
|---|---|---|
| **1.** No camines porque queda lejos. | ☐ | ☐ |
| **2.** Dime dónde está el mercado. | ☐ | ☐ |
| **3.** ¡No me digas más! | ☐ | ☐ |
| **4.** Cruza esta avenida. | ☐ | ☐ |
| **5.** Diviértete en el mercado. | ☐ | ☐ |

You learned about formal commands (**Ud.** and **Uds.**) in **Gramática 6.3.** Now you
will learn about **tú** commands. **Tú,** or informal commands, have different forms in
the affirmative and negative.

GRAMÁTICA EN CONTEXTO *How Do I Get to the Central Market? / Mark is in Guatemala City for a
month and today he wants to do some shopping in the Central Market. / MARK: Ramón, do me a favor.
I don't understand this map. / RAMÓN: Of course. Tell me what you need. / MARK: Explain to me how
to get to the Central Market. I want to walk. / RAMÓN: Well, it's a little far, in Zone 1. But, okay, leave
here and turn to the left. Go straight for about twenty blocks. / MARK: Twenty blocks! No way! (lit. Don't
tell me!) / RAMÓN: Well, yes, I told you, it's far away. Take the bus if you don't want to walk, because
there's another twenty blocks. / MARK: Goodness! Tell me, then, what bus I should take. / RAMÓN: Well,
don't get angry, but you have to take three busses from here. Should I draw you a map? / MARK: Oh . . .
yes, draw me one, please.*

# AFFIRMATIVE **tú** COMMANDS

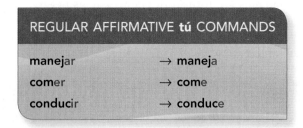

| REGULAR AFFIRMATIVE **tú** COMMANDS | |
|---|---|
| manejar | → maneja |
| comer | → come |
| conducir | → conduce |

**A.** To form regular affirmative **tú** commands, simply use the **Ud., él/ella** form of the present tense.

Toma la camioneta número 2.  *Take the number 2 minibus.*
Conduce con precaución.  *Drive safely.*

**B.** Any stem changes or other irregularities in the **Ud., él/ella** present tense forms are carried over into the **tú** command.

**Duerme** bien.  *Sleep well.*

**C.** When using reflexive, indirect object, and direct object pronouns with affirmative **tú** commands, they are attached to the end of the command and an accent is added to maintain the stress pattern that the command would have if there were no pronouns.

¡**Diviértete** mucho!  *Have a great time!*
**Pregúntale** al taxista cuánto  *Ask the taxi driver how much he's*
  nos va a cobrar.  *going to charge us.*
**Llámalo** después. Necesitamos  *Call him later. We need to take the*
  tomar el metro.  *subway.*

**D.** There are eight verbs that have irregular affirmative **tú** commands.

| IRREGULAR AFFIRMATIVE **tú** COMMANDS | | | |
|---|---|---|---|
| decir | → di | salir | → sal |
| hacer | → haz | ser | → sé |
| ir | → ve | tener | → ten |
| poner | → pon | venir | → ven |

Pon esto dentro del carro. Salimos  *Put this in the car. We're leaving in*
  en un momento.  *a moment*
Ven con nosotros. Vamos al centro.  *Come with us. We're going downtown.*

When using just one pronoun with these irregular affirmative commands, no accent is needed because the stress falls on the second-to-last syllable, which is the normal stress pattern for words ending in a vowel. If you use two pronouns, an accent is needed.

**Dime** a qué hora llega el autobús.  *Tell me what time the bus arrives.*
**Vete.** Ya no te quiero hablar.  *Go away. I don't want to talk to you*
  *anymore.*
**Díselo.**  *Tell it to him.*

## NEGATIVE tú COMMANDS

**A.** Negative **tú** commands are formed the same way as negative formal commands. The only difference is that they end with an **-s** like most **tú** forms. Note that when using pronouns with a negative **tú** command, the pronouns always go between the **no** and verb form.

| NEGATIVE tú COMMANDS | | | | |
|---|---|---|---|---|
| INFINITIVE | PRESENT TENSE **yo** FORM | REMOVE **-o** | ADD "OPPOSITE VOWEL" ENDING | NEGATIVE **tú** COMMAND |
| doblar | doblo | dobl- | -es | no dobles |
| comer | como | com- | -as | no comas |
| salir | salgo | salg- | -as | no salgas |
| volver | vuelvo | vuelv- | -as | no vuelvas |
| servir (i, i) | sirvo | sirv- | -as | no sirvas |
| conducir (zc) | conduzco | conduzc- | -as | no conduzcas |
| decir (*irreg.*) | digo | dig- | -as | no digas |

No dobles a la izquierda. Sigue derecho.

*Don't turn left. Keep going straight.*

¡No me digas!

*No way!* (lit. *Don't tell me!*)

**B.** Infinitives that end in **-car**, **-gar**, and **-zar** also have a spelling change in their negative **tú** commands.

| NEGATIVE tú COMMANDS OF -car, -gar, AND -zar VERBS | | | |
|---|---|---|---|
| INFINITIVE | PRESENT TENSE **yo** FORM | SPELLING CHANGE | NEGATIVE **tú** COMMAND |
| bus**c**ar | bus**c**o | c → qu | no bus**qu**es |
| pa**g**ar | pa**g**o | g → gu | no pa**gu**es |
| almor**z**ar (ue) | almuer**z**o | z → c | no almuer**c**es |

No pagues esa multa. No hiciste nada mal.

*Don't pay that fine. You didn't do anything wrong.*

**C.** The verbs that have irregular formal commands have similar irregular negative **tú** commands.

| IRREGULAR NEGATIVE **tú** COMMANDS | | |
|---|---|---|
| INFINITIVE | **Ud.** COMMAND | NEGATIVE **tú** COMMAND |
| dar | dé | no des |
| estar | esté | no estés |
| ir | vaya | no vayas |
| saber | sepa | no sepas |
| ser | sea | no seas |

No **vayas** por esa calle. Tiene muchos topes.
No le **des** esto a nadie. Guárdalo bien.

*Don't go down that street. It has a lot of speed bumps.*
*Don't give this to anyone. Keep it in a safe place.*

## Nota comunicativa

Communication

### Vosotros COMMANDS

If you plan to travel in Spain, it is worthwhile to learn the **vosotros** commands, at least for recognition purposes. To form affirmative **vosotros** commands, the **-r** at the end of the infinitive is replaced by a **-d.** To form negative **vosotros** commands, add **-éis** to the stem of the **Ud.** command for **-ar** verbs and **-áis** for **-er/-ir** verbs, and place the word **no** before the conjugated verb.

| INFINITIVE | AFFIRMATIVE **vosotros** COMMAND | NEGATIVE **vosotros** COMMAND |
|---|---|---|
| hablar | hablad | no habléis |
| comer | comed | no comáis |
| abrir | abrid | no abráis |
| volver | volved | no volváis |
| pedir | pedid | no pidáis |
| ir | id | no vayáis |

As with other command forms, pronouns are placed at the end of affirmative commands or between the **no** and the verb of negative commands.

(Continúa.)

| | |
|---|---|
| **Preguntadle** a qué hora nos vamos. Y ese tren, **no lo toméis** por la mañana porque siempre está muy lleno y hace muchas paradas. | Ask him what time we're leaving. And that train, don't take it in the morning, because it's always packed and it makes a lot of stops. |

The exception to this rule is with reflexive verbs. When the reflexive pronoun **os** is attached to the end of an affirmative **vosotros** command, the final **-d** of command form is dropped. Additionally, for **-ir** verbs, an accent must be added to the final **-i** of the command stem to maintain the original stress pattern. (Exception: When **os** is attached to the affirmative **vosotros** command of the verb **ir,** the **-d** is not dropped.)

| | |
|---|---|
| No os vayáis todavía. **Quedaos** un rato más. | Don't leave yet. Stay a while longer. |
| **¡Divertíos** mucho! | Have a great time! |
| **Idos** mañana. Hay una fiesta esta noche. | Leave tomorrow. There's a party tonight. |

## ACTIVIDADES

**A. En la ciudad.** Indique el verbo que completa correctamente cada mandato. ¡OJO! No se usan todos los verbos.

1. No _____ en la acera. Está prohibido.
2. _____ todo derecho.
3. No _____ la calle sin mirar.
4. _____ a la derecha.
5. No _____ estas direcciones. No son buenas.
6. _____ enfrente del centro de salud. Voy a esperarte allí.
7. _____ la avenida con cuidado. Hay mucho tráfico.
8. No _____ a la izquierda en esa esquina.

a. conduces
b. conduzcas
c. cruces
d. Cruza
e. Dobla
f. dobles
g. Para
h. pares
i. sigas
j. Sigue

**B. Una fiesta.** Complete el diálogo usando la forma correcta del mandato informal de los verbos entre paréntesis.

ROBERTO: Sara, ¿qué haces esta noche?

SARA: Pues, no sé, Roberto. No tengo planes.

ROBERTO: Pues, (**venir**[1]) a mi casa. Vamos a hacer una fiesta.

SARA: ¿De veras?[a]

ROBERTO: Sí. A las 8:00. (**Traer**[2]) a tu amiga Lisa.

SARA: ¿Cómo llego a tu casa?

ROBERTO: (**Tomar**[3]) el autobús número 433 y (**bajar**[4]) en la calle Girasol. Nuestro edificio es el número 212. (**Subir**[5]) al quinto piso, apartamento 504. Pero no (**tomar**[6]) el ascensor porque no funciona. (**Usar**[7]) las escaleras.[b]

SARA: ¡Uf! Mucho ejercicio, pero está bien. (**Oír**[8]), creo que prefiero conducir. (**Decirme**[9]) cómo llegar desde la universidad.

ROBERTO: Saliendo de la universidad, (**seguir**[10]) todo derecho en la calle León por cuatro cuadras. (**Doblar**[11]) a la derecha en la avenida Remedios. Después de seis cuadras, (**doblar**[12]) a la izquierda en la calle Girasol y (**seguir**[13]) derecho dos cuadras. Nuestro edificio está a la izquierda, es el número 212. ¡Ah! Y no (**estacionar**[14]) en la calle. El estacionamiento en el garaje del edificio es gratis.

---

[a]*Really?* [b]*stairs*

**CAPÍTULO 8** En la comunidad

SARA: ¿Necesitan algo para la fiesta?

ROBERTO: No (traer[15]) [*traigas*] comida. Ya tenemos mucha. Pero, tu música, (traerla[16]) [*tráela*] si quieres. Tu colección es impresionante.

SARA: Está bien. A las 8:00, ¿verdad?

ROBERTO: Sí. Y ¡no (olvidar[17]) [*olvides*] a tu amiga Lisa!

SARA: ¡Ay! Estás obsesionado con Lisa. ¡No (ser[18]) [*seas*] pesado[c] con ella! Lisa no es muy paciente.

ROBERTO: No (preocuparse[19]) [*No te preocupes.*] Voy a ser todo un caballero.[d]

*[handwritten: Cannot attach IOP to negative command!]*

---

[c]*annoying*  [d]*todo... a complete gentleman*

**C. Para llegar a...** En parejas, túrnense para dar direcciones para llegar a diferentes lugares en la universidad o en la ciudad, usando mandatos informales. No digan el lugar. Su compañero/a debe adivinarlo.

**Communication**

MODELO  E1: Sal de este edificio. Dobla a la derecha y sigue derecho por dos cuadras. El edificio está a la izquierda.
E2: Es la Facultad de Ciencias.

**D. La Ciudad de Guatemala**

**Cultures**  **Recycle**

**PASO 1.** Complete el texto con la forma correcta de las palabras entre paréntesis. Cuando aparece *MI* con un verbo, dé el mandato informal. Dé el presente de los otros verbos. Si aparecen dos palabras, escoja la palabra correcta. Cuando los verbos son **ser** y **estar,** escoja el verbo correcto y luego dé la forma apropiada.

La Ciudad de Guatemala, o «Guate» como la llaman los habitantes locales, es la capital de Guatemala desde 1776. Esta capital —cosmopolita y antigua a la vez— (ser/estar[1]) [*es*] la ciudad más grande no sólo de Guatemala, sino también[a] de Centroamérica. Aunque Guate (ser/estar[2]) [*es*] una ciudad muy grande, es fácil orientarse[b] porque (ser/estar[3]) [*es*] organizada en veintiuna zonas. Si (*tú: querer*[4]) [*quiera*] ver la parte histórica de la ciudad, (*tú, MI: ir*[5]) [*ve*] a la Zona 1, el Centro Histórico y el mero[c] centro de la capital. En esta zona, (*tú, MI: visitar*[6]) [*visite*] el Palacio Nacional de Cultura y la Catedral Metropolitana. Dentro

*El Palacio Nacional de Cultura*

del Palacio (ser/estar[7]) [*está*] el Kilómetro Cero. Desde (ese[8]) punto salen (todo[9]) las carreteras principales del país. Detrás de la Catedral (ser/estar[10]) [*está*] el Mercado Central. (*Tú, MI: Hacer*[11]) [*haz*] tus compras allí. Venden artesanías típicas de todo el país, flores y comida.

Para ir a (otro[12]) partes de la ciudad sin pagar mucho, (*tú, MI: tomar*[13]) [*tome*] los autobuses. ¡Pero no (*tú, MI: subir*[14]) [*suba*] a los autobuses pintados de muchos colores! (Ese[15]) van a los pueblos y lugares rurales, fuera de la ciudad. (*Tú, MI: Buscar*[16]) [*busce*] los autobuses rojos. Los autobuses rojos (ser/estar[17]) [*son*] muy populares entre los capitalinos

---

[a]*sino... but also*  [b]*to find your way around*  [c]*very*

porque (ser/estar[18]) *esta* baratos. Pero antes de usarlos, (tú, MI: aprender[19]) *aprenda* las rutas de los autobuses. Los autobuses siempre van llenos de gente y si no (tú: saber[20]) *sepas* dónde tienes que bajar,[d] (tú: ir[21]) a perder tu parada.

Si no te gusta el caos de los autobuses, (tú, MI: tomar[22]) *tomes* un taxi. Es bueno saber cuánto debes pagar porque algunos taxistas te cobran[e] más que otros. Antes de subir al[f] taxi, (tú, MI: decirle[23]) *dile* al taxista adónde quieres ir y (tú, MI: preguntarle[24]) *preguntele* cuánto te va a cobrar. En el taxi, vas a ver el ritmo del tráfico en Guate y vas a saber por qué te decimos: «¡No (tú, MI: conducir[25]) *conduzcas* en Guate!» Tienes que tener mucho talento, paciencia y nervios de acero[g] para conducir en las ciudades grandes como la Ciudad de Guatemala.

[d]*get off* [e]*charge* [f]*antes... before getting into the* [g]*nervios... nerves of steel*

**PASO 2.** Indique las cosas que se puede hacer en Guate, según el **Paso 1.**

1. ☐ Ir al Centro Histórico o Zona 1.
2. ☐ Visitar el Kilómetro Cero, donde empiezan todas las carreteras del país.
3. ☐ Tomar los autobuses pintados para ir a las zonas modernas.
4. ☐ Hablar del precio con el taxista antes de subir al taxi.
5. ☐ Hacer compras en la Catedral Metropolitana.
6. ☐ Tomar los autobuses rojos dentro de la ciudad.
7. ☐ Aprender las rutas de los autobuses.
8. ☐ Al llegar al aeropuerto de Guate, alquilar (*rent*) un coche.

Communication

**PASO 3.** En parejas, túrnense para dar instrucciones sobre cómo orientarse en una ciudad que conocen o en una parte de la ciudad donde viven. Den consejos prácticos en sus instrucciones, usando mandatos informales.

**MODELO** En la capital, no conduzcas, porque las calles son complicadas. Toma los autobuses o el metro. El transporte público de la capital es muy bueno.

---

| Modifying Verbs and Adjectives | # 8.2 Adverbs |

## Una secretaria eficiente

Leticia es una secretaria eficiente. Contesta el teléfono **profesionalmente.** Escribe **rápidamente** en la computadora. Trabaja **cuidadosamente** en los proyectos que le dan. Y si sus compañeros de trabajo le piden ayuda, los ayuda **gustosa** e **inmediatamente.**

**¿Y UD.?**

1. ¿Cómo contesta Ud. el teléfono? ¿profesionalmente? ¿casualmente? ¿ ?
2. ¿Escribe lenta o rápidamente en la computadora?
3. Si un compañero de trabajo le pide ayuda, ¿lo ayuda gustosamente? ¿No lo ayuda? ¿Lo ayuda, pero quejándose?

---

**GRAMÁTICA EN CONTEXTO** *An Efficient Secretary / Leticia is an efficient secretary. She answers the phone professionally. She types quickly on the computer. She works carefully on the projects they give her. And if her co-workers ask her for help, she happily and immediately helps them.*

**A.** Adverbs answer the questions *how? when? how much?* or *to what extent?* They can modify a verb, an adjective, or another adverb. You have already heard and used many common adverbs in Spanish, including **así, bien, mal, mucho, muy, nunca, poco, siempre, sólo,** and **tanto.**

El coche funciona **mal.**        *The car is running badly.*

**Mal** answers the question *how is the car running?*

Antonio conduce **muy bien.**        *Antonio drives very well.*

**Bien** tells how well Antonio drives, and **muy** answers the question *to what extent?*

Viajo **mucho** por autobús, pero        *I travel a lot by bus, but I travel*
viajo **poco** por tren.        *little by train.*

**B.** Other adverbs can be formed by adding the suffix **-mente** to the end of the feminine singular form of adjectives.

rápida → rápidamente        triste → tristemente
sola → solamente        total → totalmente
inmediata → inmediatamente

**C.** Here are some common adverbs that you should learn.

| | |
|---|---|
| **actualmente** | currently |
| **(des)afortunadamente** | (un)fortunately |
| **desgraciadamente** | unfortunately |

## ACTIVIDADES

**A. ¿Lo hace Ud. así?**

**PASO 1.**   Indique las oraciones que describen sus actividades.

1. ☐ Estudio fácilmente con la televisión puesta.
2. ☐ Conduzco rápidamente en el campus de la universidad.
3. ☐ Como principalmente en la cafetería de la universidad.
4. ☐ Leo mi e-mail frecuentemente.
5. ☐ Participo activamente en la política.
6. ☐ Soy totalmente independiente. Mis padres no pagan mis estudios; los pago yo.
7. ☐ Conozco bien esta ciudad y nunca me pierdo.
8. ☐ Uso el transporte público solamente.

**PASO 2.**   Ahora, comparta sus respuestas del **Paso 1** con su compañero/a de clase y pregúntele cómo él/ella hace las cosas.

**C**
Communication

**B. Simplemente.** Complete lógicamente las oraciones con un adverbio. Use adverbios de la primera lista o forme adverbios usando los adjetivos de la segunda lista. **¡OJO!** Hay más de una respuesta posible en algunos casos.

**ADVERBIOS**

| | | | | | |
|---|---|---|---|---|---|
| bien | mal | mucho | nunca | poco | siempre |

**ADJETIVOS**

| | | | | |
|---|---|---|---|---|
| absoluto/a | difícil | terrible | total | triste |

1. _____, nuestro perro murió la semana pasada.
2. No uso _____ el transporte público.
3. Estamos _____ encantados con nuestro coche nuevo.
4. Mi abuelo camina _____, y _____ tiene que usar bastón (*cane*).
5. No sé dónde estamos. Estamos _____ perdidos.
6. Ese libro es _____ largo. ¡_____ lo voy a terminar!
7. Ese muchacho no se lleva _____ con nadie.

**C. Entreviste.** Entreviste a un compañero / una compañera de clase con estas preguntas. Luego, cambien de papel. **¡OJO!** Usen adverbios apropiados.

1. ¿Cuándo y cuánto manejas?
2. ¿Cómo conduces en el campus? ¿en el centro? ¿en las carreteras?
3. ¿Con qué frecuencia usas el transporte público?
4. ¿Cómo estudias cuando tienes un examen difícil?
5. ¿Cuándo hablas con tus padres y por cuánto tiempo?
6. ¿Cómo te llevas con tu familia? Explica.

**D. La Ciudad de Panamá**

**PASO 1.** Complete el texto sobre la Ciudad de Panamá con la forma correcta de las palabras entre paréntesis. Cuando aparecen dos palabras, escoja la palabra correcta. Cuando aparecen **ser** y **estar** juntos, escoja el verbo correcto y luego dé la forma apropiada. Si un verbo aparece con la pista *pret.*, dé la forma correcta del pretérito. Dé el presente de los otros verbos. Cuando aparece la pista *adv.* con un adjetivo, dé el adverbio correspondiente.

*La Ciudad de Panamá*

La capital de Panamá es la Ciudad de Panamá. Aunque es más pequeña (**que/como**[1]) la Ciudad de Guatemala, es (**mucho/muy**[2]) más difícil orientarse en la Ciudad de Panamá. (*Adv.:* **Frecuente**[3]) dicen que la Ciudad de Panamá (**ser/estar**[4]) tres ciudades en una: Panamá la Vieja, el Casco Viejo y la Ciudad de Panamá.

Panamá la Vieja es la Ciudad de Panamá original. Establecida en 1519, (*pret.:* **ser/estar**[5]) la (**primero**[6]) ciudad europea en la costa[a] del Océano Pacífico. Este activo punto de tránsito fue (*adv.:* **enorme**[7]) importante para los españoles. (**Por/Para**[8]) aquí pasaban[b] los tesoros,[c] como el oro y la plata, de las colonias de América antes de ser mandados para España. La ciudad también (*pret.:* **servir**[9]) como centro de exploración y conquista[d] de partes de Centro y Sudamérica.

---

[a]*coast*  [b]*would pass*  [c]*treasures*  [d]*conquest*

En 1671 el pirata Henry Morgan atacó y saqueó[e] este centro (*adv.:* **violento**[10]). La ciudad quedó[f] (*adv.:* **práctico**[11]) destruida por un incendio[g] misterioso, cuyo[h] origen (**siempre/nunca**[12]) determinaron. Los residentes que sobrevivieron al ataque reconstruyeron la ciudad en una península al oeste de la ciudad original. Hoy, las ruinas de la ciudad (**ser/estar**[13]) conservadas,[i] incluso parte de (**el**[14]) Catedral de Nuestra Señora.

La nueva Ciudad de Panamá que construyeron en 1673 hoy se llama el Casco Viejo. La arquitectura de los 800 edificios de esta parte de la ciudad es (*adv.:* **tremendo**[15]) variada, y refleja las diferentes influencias en esta región. Esta península se considera el centro histórico o colonial de la capital.

La parte más grande, y (*adv.:* **seguro**[16]) más cosmopolita, de la capital (**ser/estar**[17]) al otro lado de la bahía,[j] entre el Casco Viejo y Panamá la Vieja. Los rascacielos y edificios modernos (*adv.:* **visual**[18]) reflejan la importancia de esta ciudad como un centro financiero y empresarial internacional. También (**ser/estar**[19]) uno de los destinos más populares para jubilarse.[k]

La población de la Ciudad de Panamá está (*adv.:* **excesivo**[20]) concentrada. Para resolver el problema de la circulación, hay un (**bueno**[21]) sistema de transporte público. Los autobuses de este sistema (**ser/estar**[22]) pintados de colores brillantes, algunos con imágenes religiosas, otros, (*adv.:* **cómico**[23]) con figuras políticas. Algunos de estos «diablos rojos», como los llaman, también llevan luces centelleantes[l] de colores. Es una experiencia (*adv.:* **definitivo**[24]) divertida.

[e]*looted*  [f]*was left*  [g]*fire*  [h]*whose*  [i]*maintained*  [j]*bay*  [k]*retiring*  [l]*blinking*

**PASO 2.** Indique a qué o a quién se refieren estas oraciones. **¡OJO!** Algunas respuestas se usan más de una vez.

1. \_\_\_\_ Es el centro histórico.
2. \_\_\_\_ Es la capital original.
3. \_\_\_\_ Destruyó la Ciudad de Panamá
4. \_\_\_\_ Tienen colores brillantes y luces centelleantes.
5. \_\_\_\_ Es un pirata famoso.
6. \_\_\_\_ Fue centro de exploración y conquista.
7. \_\_\_\_ Es tres ciudades en una.
8. \_\_\_\_ Tiene arquitectura variada e interesante.
9. \_\_\_\_ Hay muchos rascacielos y bancos.
10. \_\_\_\_ Son parte del transporte público.

a. Henry Morgan
b. la Ciudad de Panamá
c. el Casco Viejo
d. Panamá la Vieja
e. los diablos rojos

**PASO 3.** En grupos pequeños, busquen información en el Internet sobre uno de estos temas y hagan una presentación breve para la clase.

Communities

1. Henry Morgan y el saqueo de Panamá
2. la Ciudad de Panamá y los residentes internacionales
3. el Casco Viejo y las atracciones turísticas
4. los diablos rojos

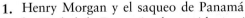

# Palabra escrita

## A comenzar

Communication

> **Developing Your Ideas: Collecting Information (Part 2).** As you may recall from **Capítulo 3,** collecting information is a pre-writing strategy that you need to use when you don't know enough about the subject of your composition. The resources you use to collect information may vary (Internet, library, questionnaires, interviews, and so on), depending on the topic of your composition. For this composition, you'll need to search reliable Internet sources or consult print materials at a library.

You are going to start the process of writing a brief composition that you will finalize in the **Palabra escrita: A finalizar** section of your *Manual de actividades.* The topic of this composition is **Guía práctica para conocer X** (X = city name) in a large city that you live in or are familiar with. The purpose of your composition will be to tell the reader about the things he/she should know when moving to or visiting that city.

**A.** Lluvia de ideas. En parejas, hagan una lluvia de ideas sobre algunos de estos temas relacionados con la vida urbana en su ciudad.

1. los barrios
2. los centros comerciales
3. las escuelas y universidades
4. el tráfico y el transporte público
5. los lugares de interés y diversión (parques, zoológicos,… )
6. los centros culturales (museos, teatros,… )
7. los restaurantes y los clubes
8. ¿ ?

**B.** A organizar sus ideas. Repase sus ideas y organícelas en categorías y en un orden lógico. Identifique las categorías en las que falta información y búsquela en el Internet. Comparta su información con la clase y apunte otras ideas que se le ocurran durante el proceso.

**C.** A escribir. Ahora, haga el borrador de su composición con las ideas y la información que recopiló en las actividades A y B. Use un tono familiar (**tú**) y busque oportunidades para usar los mandatos informales para explicarle a su lector(a) lo que puede ver, hacer o evitar en la ciudad que describe. **¡OJO!** Guarde bien su trabajo. Va a necesitarlo otra vez para la sección de **Palabra escrita: A finalizar** en el *Manual de actividades.*

# La mola

Cultures

*Una mujer kuna con su hija y unas molas*

La mola es una prenda de ropa representativa de la cultura y la identidad de los kunas, un grupo indígena de Panamá. La palabra «mola» significa «persona» en la lengua kuna. Su origen está en las tradiciones de los kunas de pintar sus cuerpos con dibujos geométricos, y durante la colonización española los dibujos empezaron a hacerse sobre telas. Las mujeres kunas crean obras de arte únicas en tela, con diseños geométricos y dibujos de animales y flores. Se hacen a mano y tienen varias capas[a] de tela de diferentes colores. Generalmente se venden en pares que sirven como la parte posterior y anterior[b] de una blusa. Algunas personas las usan para decoración en cojines[c] o se cuelgan[d] en la pared. En la foto se ve a una mujer kuna, con su hija, vestida de mola y otras ropas tradicionales de esta comunidad centroamericana donde la expresión artística es parte de la vida diaria.

---

[a]*layers*  [b]*posterior... back and front*  [c]*throw pillows*  [d]*se... they are hung*

## Vocabulario del tema

### La comunidad rural

el bosque

la montaña

la colina

el ganado

la aldea

la posada

la cerca

el lago

el pez (*pl.* los peces)

el camino

el río

el comedor

la oveja

la huerta

las aves de corral

el agricultor

la agricultora

el gallo

el conejo

el caballo

el burro

el buey

el toro

el pavo

la vaca

el cerdo

el chivo

la gallina

| las aves de corral | farm birds |
| el comedor | cafeteria style / roadside restaurant |
| la finca | farm |
| el ganado | livestock |
| la posada | inn |
| la propiedad | property |
| el pueblo | town |
| el sendero | path |
| la tierra | land; soil |
| el valle | valley |
| agrícola (*m., f.*) | agricultural |

Cognado: los animales domésticos; rural

## Otras palabras y expresiones

| la población | population |

Cognados: la agricultura

### ACTIVIDADES

**A.** Asociaciones

**PASO 1.** Indique con qué asocia Ud. estas cosas: con el agua, las montañas, los animales domésticos, una finca o un establecimiento. ¡OJO! Puede haber más de una respuesta.

MODELO el ganado → ANIMALES DOMÉSTICOS

|  | AGUA | MONTAÑAS | ANIMALES DOMÉSTICOS | FINCA | ESTABLECIMIENTO |
|---|---|---|---|---|---|
| **1.** el río | ☐ | ☐ | ☐ | ☐ | ☐ |
| **2.** la posada | ☐ | ☐ | ☐ | ☐ | ☐ |
| **3.** el bosque | ☐ | ☐ | ☐ | ☐ | ☐ |
| **4.** la oveja | ☐ | ☐ | ☐ | ☐ | ☐ |
| **5.** la huerta | ☐ | ☐ | ☐ | ☐ | ☐ |
| **6.** el comedor | ☐ | ☐ | ☐ | ☐ | ☐ |
| **7.** el agricultor | ☐ | ☐ | ☐ | ☐ | ☐ |
| **8.** el buey | ☐ | ☐ | ☐ | ☐ | ☐ |
| **9.** la cerca | ☐ | ☐ | ☐ | ☐ | ☐ |
| **10.** el lago | ☐ | ☐ | ☐ | ☐ | ☐ |

**PASO 2.** En parejas, túrnense para definir palabras del **Paso 1.** Su compañero/a debe adivinar la palabra definida.

Communication

MODELO E1: Es un grupo de vacas en una finca.
E2: Es el ganado.

**B.** Los animales

**PASO 1.** Empareje cada animal de la columna A con una palabra o frase de la columna B.

| A | B |
|---|---|
| **1.** _____ el conejo | **a.** el ganado |
| **2.** _____ la vaca | **b.** el lago |
| **3.** _____ el pez | **c.** el pollo |
| **4.** _____ el pavo | **d.** las Pascuas (*Easter*) |
| **5.** _____ el caballo | **e.** el Día de Acción de Gracias (*Thanksgiving*) |
| **6.** _____ la oveja | **f.** el tocino |
| **7.** _____ la gallina | **g.** árabe, mustang, palomino, andaluz, albino |
| **8.** _____ el cerdo | **h.** la lana |

**PASO 2.** Haga una lista de los animales que pueden servir de mascotas. Luego, en parejas, comparen sus listas y hablen de las mascotas que tienen. ¿Quién tiene la mascota más rara (*unusual*)?

**C. La utilidad.** En parejas, expliquen los usos o ventajas de estos animales, lugares y cosas.

**MODELO** la oveja → La oveja es un animal doméstico que nos da leche, lana, cuero y carne.

| | | | |
|---|---|---|---|
| **1.** una posada | **3.** una cerca | **5.** un burro | **7.** un comedor |
| **2.** una huerta | **4.** un sendero | **6.** una gallina | **8.** un cerdo |

**D.** ¿La ciudad o el campo?

**PASO 1.** Lea las explicaciones y diga si las personas que las dan viven en la ciudad o en el campo. Explique.

**MODELO** Tenemos una casa adosada con un pequeño jardín. → Vive en la ciudad, porque en la ciudad hay muchos barrios de casas adosadas.

**1.** Hay mucho tráfico a la hora en que voy al trabajo.
**2.** Tengo que levantarme temprano para darles de comer (*feed*) al ganado y a las aves.
**3.** Los viernes llevamos las verduras de nuestra huerta al mercado.
**4.** Tomo el metro para ir a la universidad.
**5.** Al fondo (*At the far end*) de la propiedad hay un lago con muchos peces.

**PASO 2.** Escriba tres oraciones que describan personas que viven en la ciudad o en el campo. Use las oraciones del **Paso 1** como modelo.

**PASO 3.** Comparta con la clase las oraciones que escribió para el **Paso 2.** Sus compañeros/as deben adivinar si las personas descritas viven en la ciudad o en el campo.

**E. Entrevista: En el campo.** Entreviste a un compañero / una compañera de clase con estas preguntas. Luego, cambien de papel.

**1.** ¿A quién conoces que vive en el campo? ¿Cómo es su casa? ¿Qué te gusta de su casa o propiedad? (Si Uds. no tienen ni amigos ni parientes que viven en el campo, describan alguna propiedad que han visto [*you have seen*] en el campo.)
**2.** ¿Es grande o pequeña la propiedad que tienen? ¿Es herencia (*inheritance*) de familia?
**3.** ¿Qué hacen con la propiedad? Por ejemplo, ¿es una finca? ¿Tienen animales? ¿Qué tipo de animales y cuántos tienen? ¿Tienen huerta? ¿Qué cultivan en la huerta? ¿Es la propiedad un negocio o sólo es una residencia? Explica.
**4.** ¿Cómo es el paisaje y qué características tiene? Por ejemplo, ¿hay un lago o estanque (*pond*)? ¿Se puede pescar (*fish*) allí?

# Nota cultural

## EL ÉXODO CAMPESINO

*En Solola, Guatemala*

Casi el 80 por ciento de la población de Latinoamérica vive actualmente en centros urbanos. El «éxodo» del campo a la ciudad tuvo su *boom* a lo largo del[a] siglo XX y ahora se mantiene como tendencia estable. La industrialización de las ciudades atrajo[b] a muchos hombres jóvenes, quienes decidieron emigrar del campo a la ciudad. Esto produjo un gran cambio en la forma de vida de los hogares rurales, en las aspiraciones de los jóvenes y en sus actitudes hacia[c] el trabajo rural.

Por tradición, los hombres y niños mayores se ocupan de los trabajos agrícolas y ganaderos,[d] mientras que las mujeres se dedican al trabajo del hogar y al cuidado de los animales domésticos. Sin embargo, la emigración de hombres está generando nuevos roles para los distintos miembros de la familia, especialmente para las mujeres, que muchas veces asumen el papel de jefas del hogar. Los jóvenes, a su vez, tienen cada vez menos[e] interés en los trabajos agrícolas y desean continuar sus estudios en núcleos urbanos para poder tener la opción de un mejor medio de vida.

Algunas de las consecuencias negativas de este éxodo son que los pueblos se están quedando sin habitantes y los cultivos[f] se reducen. Además, los gobiernos invierten[g] cada vez menos en asistencia sanitaria,[h] educación y transporte en estas áreas, para concentrarse en las necesidades de las ciudades.

---

[a]a... *throughout the* [b]*appealed* [c]*toward* [d]*livestock* [e]*cada... less and less* [f]*crops* [g]*invest*
[h]asistencia... *health (medical) care*

PREGUNTAS En parejas, contesten las preguntas. Después, compartan sus ideas con la clase.

1. ¿Dónde vive la mayoría de la población en Latinoamérica? ¿Por qué emigran los jóvenes del campo a la ciudad? ¿Qué atractivos presenta la ciudad?
2. ¿Qué problemas causa en los pueblos y en las ciudades la despoblación de las zonas rurales?
3. Si Uds. viven en una comunidad rural o pequeña, ¿les gustaría vivir en una ciudad grande? Expliquen.
4. Si viven en un núcleo urbano, ¿les gustaría vivir en una comunidad rural? Expliquen.

## Nota interdisciplinaria

### AGRICULTURA: LA AGRICULTURA EN CENTROAMÉRICA

*En una plantación de café nicaragüense*

La agricultura es la actividad económica más importante de Centroamérica, sobre todo en Nicaragua, Guatemala y Honduras. Esta zona geográfica tiene el suelo[a] y el clima ideales para el cultivo de productos tropicales.

El maíz, el arroz, los frijoles y otros productos se destinan al consumo interno de la población y se cultivan en pequeñas propiedades agrícolas, normalmente familiares. Sin embargo, hay otro tipo de agricultura, denominada agricultura de plantación, que se destina a la exportación. Estos productos se cultivan en grandes extensiones de tierra. Los cultivos más importantes de este tipo son el café, la banana, el cacao y la piña.

El café es el principal cultivo en El Salvador, Guatemala, Costa Rica, Honduras y Nicaragua, donde las cenizas[b] de los volcanes enriquecen[c] el suelo de cultivo. El cacao es el segundo producto en importancia en Costa Rica. La banana es la principal riqueza de Panamá, cuyo principal mercado son los Estados Unidos.

---

[a]*soil*  [b]*ashes*  [c]*enrich*

PREGUNTAS En parejas, contesten las preguntas. Después, compartan sus ideas con la clase.

1. ¿Qué tipos de agricultura existen? ¿Cuáles son los cultivos más importantes para cada tipo de agricultura?
2. ¿Qué diferencias hay entre la agricultura para consumo interno y para la exportación?
3. En el lugar donde Uds. viven, ¿es importante la agricultura? ¿Cuáles son los cultivos principales?
4. ¿Saben Uds. de dónde vienen las bananas, la piña, el cacao y el café que consumen? ¿De dónde vienen otros productos agrícolas que compran en el supermercado? (La próxima vez que visiten su supermercado, fíjense en el origen y compartan la información con la clase.)

# Gramática

## 8.3 Imperfect

**GRAMÁTICA EN CONTEXTO**

### Cuando mi papá era niño

En esta foto, mi papá **tenía** 8 años. **Eran** las 7:00 de la mañana y él y sus hermanos **esperaban** el autobús. Mi papá **tenía** un hermano mayor y un hermano menor. Todos **tenían** el pelo moreno y **llevaban** su uniforme escolar.

Mi papá y su familia **vivían** en el campo en una finca. Todos los días, mi papá y sus hermanos **se levantaban** temprano para ayudar con los animales. Después, **iban** a la escuela. Papá siempre **llevaba** su almuerzo y **comía** con sus amigos. Después de clase, papá **trabajaba** en la finca. **Cenaba** con su familia a las 6:00, **hacía** la tarea y **se acostaba** temprano. La vida no **era** fácil, pero mi papá **era** feliz.

¿Y Ud.? Escoja la mejor respuesta, según su propia experiencia. ¡OJO! Puede haber más de una respuesta correcta en algunos casos.

1. Cuando yo era niño/a, vivía en _____.
   a. el campo      b. una ciudad      c. un pueblo
2. Cuando yo era niño/a, mi familia y yo teníamos _____.
   a. un perro      b. un gato      c. una vaca      d. varios animales
3. Cuando yo era niño/a, siempre _____ la escuela.
   a. llevaba mi almuerzo a      b. comía en otro lugar o en la cafetería de
4. Cuando era niño/a, _____ temprano.
   a. me levantaba      b. me acostaba      c. mi mamá me despertaba

**GRAMÁTICA EN CONTEXTO** *When My Father Was a Boy* / *In this photo, my father was 8 years old. It was 7:00 A.M. and he and his brothers were waiting for the bus. My father had an older brother and a younger brother. They all had dark hair and were wearing their school uniforms.*
*My father and his family lived in the country on a farm. Every day my father and his brothers got up early to help with the animals. Then, they went to school. Dad always took his lunch and ate with his friends. After class, Dad worked on the farm. He had dinner with his family at 6:00, did his homework, and went to bed early. Life wasn't easy, but my father was happy.*

**A.** To form the imperfect, drop **-ar** infinitive endings and replace them with **-aba, -abas, -aba, -ábamos, -abais, -aban.** For **-er/-ir** verbs, drop the infinitive endings and replace them with **-ía, -ías, -ía, íamos, íais, -ían.** Note the written accent marks on all **-er/-ir** forms. With **-ar** verbs only the **nosotros** form carries a written accent.

| IMPERFECT: REGULAR VERBS | | |
|---|---|---|
| estudiar | comer | asistir |
| estudiaba | comía | asistía |
| estudiabas | comías | asistías |
| estudiaba | comía | asistía |
| estudiábamos | comíamos | asistíamos |
| estudiabais | comíais | asistíais |
| estudiaban | comían | asistían |

Only three verbs are irregular in the imperfect: **ir, ser,** and **ver.**

| IMPERFECT: IRREGULAR VERBS | | |
|---|---|---|
| ir | ser | ver |
| iba | era | veía |
| ibas | eras | veías |
| iba | era | veía |
| íbamos | éramos | veíamos |
| ibais | erais | veíais |
| iban | eran | veían |

**B.** In general, the imperfect is used to describe actions or states in the past that do not have any clear beginning or ending.

**1.** The imperfect describes actions that were habitual or that were ongoing but without limiting the time being referred to.

Cuando yo **vivía** en la ciudad **paseaba** por el centro todos los días.

*When I was living* (ongoing action) *in the city, I used to take* (habitual action) *a walk through downtown every day.* (no limiting time period mentioned)

2. Imperfect describes characteristics of people and things.

| | |
|---|---|
| Miguel **era** alto y **tenía** el pelo moreno y corto. | *Miguel was tall and had short dark hair.* |
| Siempre **estaba** alegre. | *He was happy all the time.* |
| **Tenía** 11 años cuando vino a vivir aquí. | *He was 11 when he came to live here.* |

3. Imperfect is used for dates, times, seasons, and weather conditions in the past.

| | |
|---|---|
| **Hacía** frío, **estaba** nublado y **llovía** mucho cuando llegamos. | *It was cold, it was cloudy, and it was raining a lot when we arrived.* |
| **Eran** las 3:00 de la tarde, pero **parecía** de noche. | *It was 3:00 in the afternoon, but it felt like nighttime.* |
| **Era** invierno, pero no **hacía** mucho frío. | *It was winter, but it wasn't very cold.* |

4. Imperfect describes two or more actions that were happening at the same time in the past.

| | |
|---|---|
| Mientras Marcos les **daba** de comer a los cerdos, María **preparaba** la cena. | *While Marcos was feeding the pigs, María was preparing supper.* |

5. Imperfect describes background information of a situation.

| | |
|---|---|
| **Era** un día bonito en Tegucigalpa. **Estaba** soleado, pero no **hacía** demasiado calor. No **había** nubes en el cielo... | *It was a beautiful day in Tegucigalpa. It was sunny, but it wasn't too hot. There were no clouds in the sky . . .* |
| Anoche a las 11:30 yo **dormía**, Óscar **estudiaba** para un examen y María y Jaime **bailaban** en un club de salsa. | *Last night at 11:30 I was sleeping, Óscar was studying for a test, and María and Jaime were dancing in a salsa club.* |

## ACTIVIDADES

**A. Cuando tenía 10 años...** Complete las oraciones con información personal.

Cuando yo tenía 10 años...

1. vivía en...
2. mi mejor amigo/a era...
3. mi padre/madre trabajaba en...
4. iba al parque...
5. mi maestro/a se llamaba...
6. me levantaba a las... para ir a la escuela.
7. pasaba los veranos con/en...
8. mi programa de televisión favorito era...

**B. La casa de mi tío abuelo** (*great uncle*). Complete la descripción con el imperfecto de los verbos entre paréntesis.

Mi tío abuelo, tío Mario, era el hermano menor de mi abuela materna. (*Él:* Ser[1]) un hombre excéntrico que, después de pasar cuarenta años viajando y conociendo el mundo, se compró una finca en el campo y ¡se casó a los 60 años con su amiga y compañera, Gabriela! El tío Mario siempre nos (contar[2]) cosas interesantes de sus viajes y aventuras y nos (enseñar[3]) fotos y vídeos de otros países. La tía Gabriela (ser[4]) muy divertida también y, como (ser[5]) antropóloga, (saber[6]) muchas cosas de otras culturas.

Me (gustar[7]) visitar a mi tío abuelo y a su esposa porque (tener[8]) muchos animales en su finca, algunos exóticos, como los cinco pavos reales.[a] (Ser[9]) hermosos ¡pero (hacer[10]) mucho ruido[b]! Mi pavo real favorito (ser[11]) blanco y me (fascinar[12]). Cerca de la finca, (haber[13]) un bosque y un lago. A veces (*nosotros:* ir[14]) a pescar[c] allí y casi siempre (*nosotros:* ver[15]) animales salvajes.[d]

---

[a]pavos... *peacocks*  [b]*noise*  [c]a... *fishing*  [d]*wild*

**C. Entrevista: La escuela secundaria.** Entreviste a un compañero / una compañera de clase con estas preguntas. Luego, cambien de papel.

1. ¿Cuántos estudiantes había en tu escuela secundaria? ¿y en tu clase cuando te graduaste?
2. ¿Qué tipo de escuela era? ¿Era una escuela urbana? ¿Estaba en las afueras? ¿Era rural?
3. ¿Cuál era la mascota de tu escuela? ¿y los colores?
4. ¿Qué deportes había en tu escuela? ¿Jugabas a algún deporte?
5. ¿Cuántos cursos tomaban los estudiantes al (*per*) año? ¿Cuántas clases tomaban al día?
6. ¿Cómo se llamaba el director / la directora de tu escuela? ¿Cómo era? ¿Era muy estricto/a? ¿exigente (*demanding*)?

**D. Las ciudades perdidas**

**PASO 1.** Complete el diálogo con la forma correcta de las palabras entre paréntesis. Si aparece la pista *MI* con un verbo, use el mandato informal. Si la pista es *PP,* use el participio presente. Dé los otros verbos en el imperfecto. Si aparece la pista *adv.* con un adjetivo, dé el adverbio correspondiente.

*Unas ruinas mayas de Copán, Honduras*

ÓSCAR:    Hola, Susana. ¿Qué tal?

SUSANA:    ¡Ay! ¡Qué susto!ᵃ (*Yo: Estar*¹) (*adv.: completo*²) metida enᵇ esta lectura.

ÓSCAR:    ¡Debe ser muy interesante!

SUSANA:    Sí, es para mi clase de arqueología. Estamos (*PP: estudiar*³) las ciudades perdidas. ¿Sabías que la arqueología, como ciencia, surgióᶜ del interés por encontrar ciudades perdidas?

ÓSCAR:    ¿Cómo?

---

ᵃ¡Qué... *You startled me!*   ᵇmetida... *absorbed by*   ᶜ*emerged*

SUSANA: Sí, (*PP:* empezar[4]) en el siglo XVI, los exploradores y aventureros (buscar[5]) ciudades perdidas, míticas, legendarias, en Asia, África y el Nuevo Mundo. Estas búsquedas dieron como resultado[d] la creación de esta ciencia social, la arqueología. Algunos de los exploradores (querer[6]) encontrar ciertas ciudades aunque todo el mundo les (decir[7]) que no (ser[8]) más que leyendas, pero en algunos casos llegaron a descubrir esas ciudades míticas. Por ejemplo, muchos (*ellos:* creer[9]) que Troya (ser[10]) una ciudad inventada. Pero, excavaciones del siglo XIX probaron[e] que Troya no (ser[11]) un mito.

ÓSCAR: Estás (*adv.:* total[12]) fascinada, ¿verdad?

SUSANA: Pues, sí. Me parece increíble cómo una ciudad tan enorme, un centro económico y político, puede desaparecer. Tikal, la ciudad maya en Guatemala, tiene una historia de unos 14.000 años. ¿Te imaginas? Durante parte de su larga historia, fue una de las ciudades mayas más grandes. Pero en el siglo X, fue abandonada y quedó oculta[f] debajo de la selva por otros 800 años.

ÓSCAR: Muchas de las ciudades mayas (estar[13]) escondidas así, casi olvidadas, por muchos años.

SUSANA: Es verdad. Copán, que (florecer[14]) al este de Tikal, en Honduras, también (ser[15]) un centro grande e importante. Esa ciudad (tener[16]) fama por las estelas[g] y otras esculturas en piedra.[h] Las estelas (crearse[17]) para honrar a los líderes de la ciudad.

ÓSCAR: ¡Ay! ¡Ya son las tres! Cuando te vi, (*yo:* ir[18]) para el laboratorio de lenguas para ver la película *Apocalypto.*

SUSANA: ¡No (*MI:* decirme[19])! ¡Increíble! Pero esa película es muy fuerte. Yo la vi, y durante muchas escenas, (tener[20]) que cerrar los ojos. Pues, ¡(*MI:* irte[21])! ¡No (*MI:* llegar[22]) tarde!

---

[d]Estas... *These searches resulted in* [e]*proved* [f]quedó... *remained hidden* [g]*carved stone columns* [h]*stone*

**PASO 2.** Indique la respuesta correcta para completar cada oración, según el **Paso 1.**

1. La arqueología se originó por ____.
   a. Centroamérica
   b. la ciudad de Troya
   c. las búsquedas de ciudades perdidas

2. La ciudad de Troya ____.
   a. era un lugar legendario
   b. nunca existió
   c. está en Guatemala

3. Los exploradores que buscaban ciudades perdidas siempre tenían que ____ su expedición.
   a. creer lo que todos decían de
   b. tener mucha fe (*faith*) en
   c. tener pruebas antes de

4. Tikal era una ciudad maya ____.
   a. conocida por sus estelas
   b. y un centro político importante
   c. en Honduras

5. Las estelas representan ____.
   a. a líderes mayas
   b. períodos históricos
   c. planos de ciudades mayas

6. Tikal fue ____ en el siglo X.
   a. construida
   b. descubierta
   c. abandonada

7. *Apocalypto* es ____.
   a. una ciudad maya
   b. una ciudad perdida
   c. una película

**PASO 3.** En parejas, busquen información en el Internet sobre una ciudad perdida en el mundo hispano y preparen una breve presentación para la clase.

Communities

# Lectura cultural

Cultures

**PASO 1.** Revise el título y la primera oración del artículo e indique cuál de estas opciones Ud. cree que resume mejor la idea general.

1. ☐ El artículo da consejos a los conductores para evitar accidentes de tráfico en las carreteras.
2. ☐ El artículo resume diez recomendaciones para evitar el uso innecesario de la gasolina y proteger el medio ambiente (*environment*)

**PASO 2.** Haga una lista de algunas cosas que Ud. cree que los conductores pueden hacer para ahorrar gasolina. Después, comparta sus ideas con la clase.

| Vocabulario práctico | |
| --- | --- |
| **acelerones** | sudden accelerations |
| **arrancar** | to start (*a car*) |
| **frenazos** | sudden stops |
| **maletero** | trunk |
| **mantenimiento** | maintenance |
| **neumáticos** | tires |
| **nivel de aceite** | oil level |

## Los operadores petrolíferos recomiendan medidas[a] para ahorrar combustible

*Se debe verificar la presión de los neumáticos con frecuencia.*

Madrid. (EUROPA PRESS). — La Asociación Española de Operadores de Productos Petrolíferos (AOP) publicó hoy un decálogo[b] con consejos para ahorrar combustible en tiempos de crisis y contribuir a un estilo de vida «más limpio, seguro y eficiente».

Entre los 10 consejos de la asociación, figura el de considerar la posibilidad de compartir el coche para ir a trabajar o durante el tiempo libre, lo que contribuirá[c] no sólo a reducir el consumo de combustible, sino también a aligerar[d] el tráfico. Otras de las medidas de conducción eficiente son las de observar las instrucciones de mantenimiento del coche, incluidas las referidas a la revisión periódica del nivel de aceite, o retirar peso[e] innecesario del maletero y de los asientos traseros.[f]

Junto a esto, recomienda revisar mensualmente la presión de los neumáticos, cerrar la ventanilla especialmente cuando se circula a gran velocidad, utilizar el aire acondicionado cuando sea necesario o iniciar la marcha nada más arrancar,[g] así como parar el motor cuando el vehículo lleve más de un minuto retenido.[h]

[a]*measures* [b]*top ten list* [c]*will contribute* [d]*lighten* [e]*weight* [f]*asientos... back seats* [g]*iniciar... start moving immediately, don't just start the car and sit there* [h]*lleve... has been motionless for more than a minute*

AOP aconseja también conducir con suavidad y a velocidades razonables, así como subir de marcha lo antes[i] posible, ya que las marchas largas como la cuarta, quinta o sexta son las que menos combustible consumen. Por último, considera conveniente anticiparse al tráfico, y como parte de esta medida insiste en la importancia de mantener la distancia de seguridad y buscar el campo visual[i] lo más amplio posible con el objeto de evitar frenazos y acelerones innecesarios.

[i]subir... *get up to the higher gears as soon as*   [i]campo... *field of vision*

## DESPUÉS DE LEER

**A.** Comprensión. Indique si estas oraciones son ciertas (**C**) o falsas (**F**), según el artículo. Corrija cada una de las afirmaciones falsas.

Para ahorrar gasolina y proteger el medio ambiente se debe...

|  | C | F |
|---|---|---|
| 1. viajar con otras personas para ir al trabajo o a cualquier otro lugar. | ☐ | ☐ |
| 2. dar frenazos y acelerones. | ☐ | ☐ |
| 3. controlar el nivel de aceite del coche. | ☐ | ☐ |
| 4. poner muchas maletas y paquetes en el maletero del coche. | ☐ | ☐ |
| 5. verificar la presión de los neumáticos periódicamente. | ☐ | ☐ |
| 6. esperar unos minutos después de arrancar el coche. | ☐ | ☐ |
| 7. usar el aire acondicionado sólo cuando es necesario. | ☐ | ☐ |
| 8. arrancar el coche mientras se espera a alguien. | ☐ | ☐ |
| 9. correr mucho en la segunda o la tercera marcha. | ☐ | ☐ |
| 10. mantener una distancia razonable del coche que está delante de Ud. | ☐ | ☐ |

**B.** Temas de discusión. En parejas, contesten las preguntas. Después, compartan sus ideas con la clase.

1. ¿Qué grupo publicó el decálogo? ¿Por qué? ¿Cuáles fueron sus objetivos fundamentales?
2. ¿Cómo es el tráfico en el lugar donde Uds. viven? ¿Qué impactos tiene en el lugar?
3. Den recomendaciones sobre cómo ahorrar gasolina y controlar la contaminación en una ciudad. Usen las recomendaciones de la lectura y usen los mandatos informales en sus respuestas. Deben dar dos recomendaciones más que no se incluyen en el texto.

## Costa Rica: Juan Carlos

Una excursión a Sarchí

En este segmento, Juan Carlos y sus amigos Catarina y Pedro visitan un lugar muy especial, Sarchí, donde vemos el arte tradicional de Costa Rica en una fábrica de carretas.[a] En camino a Sarchí nuestros amigos hablan de la vida rural y paran en un comedor para disfrutar de la gastronomía local.

[a]*Oxcarts*

### Vocabulario práctico

| | |
|---|---|
| **fábrica** | factory |
| **¡Pura vida!*** | Great! |
| **Pascua** | Easter |
| **cultivos** | agricultural products |
| **un pedido** | an order |
| **de cualquier modo** | in any case |

### ANTES DE VER

Conteste las preguntas. Después, comparta sus respuestas con la clase.

1. ¿Hay tradiciones propias (*unique*), como artesanías, costumbres, etcétera, de su región o país? Explique.
2. Haga una lista de por lo menos tres diferencias entre la manera de vivir en las zonas rurales y la manera de vivir en las grandes ciudades en este país.

### DESPUÉS DE VER

**A.** ¿Cierto o falso? Indique si las oraciones son ciertas (**C**) o falsas (**F**), según el videoblog de Juan Carlos. Corrija las oraciones falsas.

| | C | F |
|---|---|---|
| 1. Catarina es de Guatemala. | ☐ | ☐ |
| 2. Juan Carlos y sus amigos van a una fábrica de cerámica. | ☐ | ☐ |
| 3. El gallo pinto es una comida típica de Costa Rica. | ☐ | ☐ |
| 4. El casado tiene ese nombre porque se come en las bodas. | ☐ | ☐ |
| 5. Don Carlos lleva veinte años pintando carretas. | ☐ | ☐ |
| 6. En el siglo XIX las carretas eran un medio de transporte común. | ☐ | ☐ |
| 7. En los concursos de carretas se selecciona al artista más creativo. | ☐ | ☐ |

**B.** Temas de discusión. En parejas, contesten las preguntas. Después, compartan sus ideas con la clase.

1. ¿Por qué creen Uds. que Don Carlos todavía pinta carretas después de tantos años de trabajo?
2. ¿Qué impresión tienen de la fábrica de carretas? ¿Les gusta? ¿No les gusta? ¿Les fascina? ¿Les sorprende? Expliquen.

---

*¡Pura vida! is also used to greet and say good-bye to someone in a familiar setting.

# Vocabulario

## La comunidad urbana

| | |
|---|---|
| la acera | sidewalk |
| las afueras | suburbs; outskirts |
| la cantina | bar |
| el centro de salud | health center |
| la comisaría de policía | police station |
| el edificio de oficinas | office building |
| la escuela | school |
| el estacionamiento | parking lot/place |
| la estatua | statue |
| la fuente | fountain |
| la gasolinera | gas station |
| la oficina de correos | post office |
| el parque | park |
| el rascacielos | skyscraper |
| el taller de reparaciones | repair shop |

**Cognados:** el banco, el bar, la catedral, el palacio
**Repaso:** el barrio, el bloque de pisos, el cine, el edificio de apartamentos, la iglesia, la mezquita, el museo, el parque, la plaza, la sinagoga, el vecindario

## Las direcciones

| | |
|---|---|
| la cuadra | block |
| el plano | city map |
| el semáforo | traffic light |
| ubicado/a | located |
| (al) norte (sur, este, oeste) | (to the) north (south, east, west) |
| (todo) derecho | straight ahead |

**Repaso:** el lugar, el mapa; a la derecha, a la izquierda

## Los medios de transporte — Modes of Transportation

| | |
|---|---|
| el aeropuerto | airport |
| el autobús | bus |
| la autopista | freeway; (four-lane) highway |
| el avión | airplane |
| el barco | boat |
| el camino | road |
| el camión | truck |
| la camioneta | minibus |
| el carnet de conducir | driver's license |
| la carretera | (two-lane) highway |
| el carro | car |

| | |
|---|---|
| la circulación | traffic |
| la estación de autobuses | bus station |
| el ferrocarril | railway |
| el metro | subway |
| la parada | (bus/subway) stop |
| el puente | bridge |
| el tren | train |

**Cognados:** el coche, la motocicleta, el taxi, el tráfico
**Repaso:** la avenida, la bicicleta, el bulevar, la calle

## La comunidad rural

| | |
|---|---|
| el/la agricultor(a) | farmer |
| la aldea | village |
| el bosque | forest |
| la cerca | fence |
| la colina | hill |
| el comedor | cafeteria style / roadside restaurant |
| la finca | farm |
| la huerta | farmer's field; orchard |
| el lago | lake |
| la montaña | mountain |
| la posada | inn |
| la propiedad | property |
| el pueblo | town |
| el río | river |
| el sendero | path |
| la tierra | land; soil |
| el valle | valley |

## Los animales domésticos

| | |
|---|---|
| las aves de corral | farm birds |
| el buey | ox |
| el burro | donkey |
| el caballo | horse |
| el cerdo | pig |
| el chivo | goat |
| el conejo | rabbit |
| la gallina | hen |
| el gallo | rooster |
| el ganado | cattle |
| la oveja | sheep |
| el pez (*pl.* los peces) | fish |
| la vaca | cow |

**Repaso:** el gato, la mascota, el perro

## Los verbos

| | |
|---|---|
| conducir (zc) | to drive (*Sp.*) |
| cruzar (c) | to cross |
| doblar | to turn |
| estacionar | to park |
| manejar | to drive (*L.A.*) |
| montar en | to ride |
| parar | to stop |
| seguir (i, i) | to go; to keep going |
| viajar | to travel |

Repaso: tomar

## Los adverbios

| | |
|---|---|
| actualmente | currently |
| (des)afortunadamente | (un)fortunately |
| desgraciadamente | unfortunately |

Repaso: así, bien, mal, mucho, muy, nunca, poco, siempre, sólo, tanto

## Otras palabras y expresiones

| | |
|---|---|
| el árbol | tree |
| el arbusto | bush |
| la población | population |
| agrícola (*m., f.*) | agricultural |

Cognados: la agricultura; rural, urbano/a

# Capítulo 9

# Recuerdos del pasado

### EN ESTE CAPÍTULO
**Centroamérica**

**TEMA I**
Vocabulario
- Political World History **284**
- Natural Disasters **286**

Gramática
- More on **por** and **para** **288**
- Reciprocal Verbs **292**

**TEMA II**
Vocabulario
- Stages of Life **299**
- More Pastimes and Activities **300**

Gramática
- Preterite vs. Imperfect **302**

*¿Así te veías cuando eras joven, abuelo?*

1. ¿Qué buenos recuerdos tiene Ud. de su niñez? ¿Dónde vivía? ¿Qué hacía con sus amigos?
2. ¿Adónde viajaba con su familia cuando iban de vacaciones (*on vacation*)?

**connect**
**|SPANISH**

www.connectspanish.com

283

## Vocabulario del tema

### La historia política y mundial°

*World*

**1.** Durante la **época colonial,** los frailes españoles **establecieron** misiones y **convirtieron** a muchos **indígenas** al cristianismo. También, según algunas **crónicas** que tenemos hoy en día, los frailes les enseñaron a los indígenas varias formas de artesanía como, por ejemplo, tallados en madera, cerámicas finas y tejidos.

**2.** Los conquistadores españoles **exploraron** y **descubrieron** muchas partes de América, pero también **invadieron** y **conquistaron** muchas **civilizaciones precolombinas.** En algunos casos, los **guerreros** indígenas resistieron los **ataques** españoles pero, a fin de cuentas (*when all was said and done*), sin éxito.

**3.** Durante el **siglo** XIX, muchas **colonias** latinoamericanas les **declararon la guerra** a los **reinos** europeos. Las **fuerzas revolucionarias alcanzaron a independizarse** y luego establecer nuevas patrias (*nations*).

**4.** ...Repito: Un **terremoto** de 8,2 grados en la escala Richter **destruyó** el centro de la ciudad. Como pueden ver detrás de mí, la Cruz Roja y otras **organizaciones** de **rescate** ya siguen con sus esfuerzos para encontrar y **rescatar** a los **sobrevivientes...**

## Los verbos

| | |
|---|---|
| alcanzar (c) | to achieve; to reach |
|   alcanzar a + *inf.* |   to manage to (*do something*) |
| asesinar | to murder, assassinate |
| datar de + *time* | to date from + *time* |
| desintegrar(se) | to disintegrate, break up |
| florecer (zc) | to flourish; to thrive |
| independizarse (c) | to gain independence; to become independent |
| pertenecer (zc) (a) | to belong (to) |
| superar | to overcome |
| tener (*irreg.*) lugar | to take place |

Cognados: colonizar (c), disolver (ue), extender (ie), ocupar

## Las personas y las organizaciones

| | |
|---|---|
| la crónica | chronicle; report |
| la dictadura | dictatorship |
| el ejército | army |
| el/la esclavo/a | slave |
| el/la gobernador(a) | governor |
| el gobierno | government |
| el imperio | empire |
| la reina | queen |
| el rey | king |
| el virrey | viceroy |

Cognados: la autoridad, el/la conquistador(a), la república, el territorio, la unión

## Los conflictos y las relaciones internacionales

| | |
|---|---|
| la bandera | flag |
| la batalla | battle |
| el desfile | parade |
| la estabilidad | stability |
| la llegada | arrival |
| la paz | peace |
| el tratado | treaty |
| descubierto/a | discovered |

Cognados: las armas, la conquista, la independencia, la intervención, el nacionalismo, la procesión, el regionalismo, la sucesión; conservador(a), corrupto/a, federal, liberal

## Las épocas      Time Periods

| | |
|---|---|
| el siglo | century |

Cognados: la década, el milenio

# Los desastres naturales

| | |
|---|---|
| sobrevivir (a) | to survive |
| el cielo | sky |
| el incendio | fire |
| la inundación | flood |
| el maremoto | tsunami |
| la niebla | fog |
| el relámpago | lightning |
| la tormenta | storm |

Cognados: el huracán, el tornado

## ACTIVIDADES

**A.** Definiciones

**PASO 1.** Dé la palabra definida.

1. Son las fuerzas militares de una nación.
2. Son personas que están bajo el dominio absoluto de un dueño (*owner*). No tienen libertad.
3. Es declararse libre del poder y tiranía de otra nación o persona.
4. Son los monarcas de un país.
5. Son los años anteriores al nacimiento de Jesucristo.
6. Es un desastre natural que mueve la tierra violentamente.
7. Es una persona que gobierna en nombre y con la autoridad del rey en un lugar colonizado.
8. Es una descarga eléctrica que se presenta durante una tormenta.

**PASO 2.** Ahora, escriba la definición de dos palabras o frases del **Vocabulario del tema.** Va a leérselas a la clase y sus compañeros/as deben adivinar qué palabra o frase define.

**B.** ¿Qué pasó?

**PASO 1.** Empareje los verbos de la izquierda con el sustantivo correspondiente de la derecha. **¡OJO!** Puede haber más de una respuesta correcta.

| | |
|---|---|
| 1. asesinar _____ | a. a los indígenas |
| 2. descubrir _____ | b. la guerra |
| 3. sobrevivir _____ | c. colonias |
| 4. establecer _____ | d. al huracán |
| 5. declarar _____ | e. al dictador |
| 6. conquistar _____ | f. un nuevo continente |

**PASO 2.** Use los sustantivos y la forma correcta del pretérito de los verbos del **Paso 1** para completar las oraciones.

1. En 1941, después de los ataques de Pearl Harbor, los Estados Unidos, Inglaterra, Australia y otros aliados le _____ a Japón.
2. Después del descubrimiento del continente americano, los ingleses, los españoles y los portugueses _____.
3. Muchas personas que _____ Katrina en 2005 se mudaron a otras ciudades.
4. En 1492, Colón salió de España para las Indias, pero en vez de encontrar la ruta comercial que buscaba, _____.
5. Muchos _____, como Augusto Pinochet, para ganar poder, _____ a los líderes legítimos del país.
6. Después de los exploradores, llegaron otros grupos que _____ colonias en el Nuevo Mundo. San Agustín fue la primera colonia que se estableció en lo que hoy es Florida.

**C. Preguntas.** En parejas, contesten las preguntas. Si quieren, pueden buscar información en el Internet.

1. ¿Cuál fue la primera colonia inglesa?
2. ¿Cómo se llaman los reyes actuales de España?
3. ¿Cuándo terminó el período precolombino?
4. ¿Qué civilización indígena descubrió el cero?
5. ¿Cuáles eran las tres civilizaciones indígenas más grandes de Latinoamérica?
6. ¿Qué tipo de gobierno tiene Cuba?
7. ¿Cuándo tuvo lugar la Segunda Guerra Mundial?

## Nota cultural

### EL TERREMOTO DE MANAGUA DE 1972

*En Managua, después del terremoto*

En diciembre de 1972, hubo un terremoto en Managua, Nicaragua, de 7,2 grados de magnitud en la escala de Richter. Destruyó completamente la capital de Nicaragua, aunque no los alrededores, y causó cerca de 10.000 muertos y 20.000 heridos.[a]

El movimiento sísmico destruyó, no sólo los cimientos[b] de los edificios, sino también la economía de Managua. El 80 por ciento de la producción industrial del país se encontraba en la capital, y las fábricas y talleres quedaron destruidos también, así como hospitales, depósitos de agua, almacenes y escuelas. El gobierno incluso ordenó evacuar la ciudad para evitar una epidemia.

El desarrollo de Managua después del terremoto fue bastante desigual. La economía nunca volvió a recuperarse, ya que prácticamente todo el tejido económico fue destruido. Con la inmigración del campo a la ciudad, los habitantes de Managua construyeron casas alejadas de la antigua zona urbana. De hecho,[c] el antiguo centro de la ciudad aún sigue muy deteriorado.

---

[a]*wounded*  [b]*foundations*  [c]*De... In fact*

**PREGUNTA** En parejas, contesten la pregunta.

¿Qué impacto tuvo el terremoto en las personas, las casas y los negocios?

## 9.1 More on **por** and **para**

### Mis antepasados

[*Julián habla de sus antepasados.*]

Algunos de mis antepasados españoles salieron **para** el Nuevo Mundo en los siglos XVI y XVII. Tengo un bis-bis-bis-bis-bis-bis-bis-bisabuelo que primero llegó a Santo Domingo **para** buscar fortuna. Era muy joven y viajó **por** todo el Caribe y Centroamérica trabajando como marinero **para** diferentes tripulaciones. Hizo varios viajes **por** barco entre España y el Nuevo Mundo antes de establecerse en lo que hoy es Panamá. Otro de mis bis-bis-bis-bis-bis-bis-bis-bisabuelos españoles se estableció en el área de Honduras. Ese lado de la familia vivió allí **por** doscientos años, antes de mudarse a Panamá. En Panamá, había gente de muchas otras partes, **por** eso tengo antepasados españoles, franceses, africanos e indígenas. Es **por** mi madre que puedo contarles la historia de mi familia, porque **por** tres años ella hizo investigaciones **para** documentar nuestro árbol genealógico.

Comprensión. Empareje las frases para completar oraciones verdaderas sobre la familia de Julián.

1. Sus antepasados españoles probablemente llegaron al Nuevo Mundo ____.
2. En los siglos XVI y XVII, sus antepasados españoles salieron ____.
3. Algunos de sus antepasados vivieron en lo que hoy es Honduras ____.
4. Uno de sus antepasados trabajó ____.
5. Su madre trabajó mucho ____.

a. para documentar la historia de la familia
b. para el Nuevo Mundo
c. por 200 años
d. por barco
e. para tripulaciones que viajaban entre España y el Nuevo Mundo

---

The most common uses of **por** and **para** were presented in **Gramática 4.1.** This section reviews those uses and presents some new ones.

### A. Por

1. **Por** expresses *in the morning, in the afternoon,* and *in the evening.*

   por la mañana          por la tarde          por la noche

2. **Por** means *by* or *by means of* when used with modes of transportation or communication.

   por avión          por barco          por teléfono

---

**My Ancestors** / Julián talks about his ancestors. / Some of my Spanish ancestors left for the New World in the 16th and 17th centuries. I have a great-great-great-great-great-great-great-great-grandfather who first arrived in Santo Domingo to seek his fortune. He was very young and traveled throughout the Caribbean and Central America working as a sailor for different crews. He made several trips by boat between Spain and the New World before settling in what is today Panama. Another one of my Spanish great-great-great-great-great-great-great-great-great-grandfathers settled in the Honduras area. That side of the family lived there for two hundred years, before moving to Panama. In Panama, there were people from many places, therefore I have Spanish, French, African, and indigenous ancestors. It's because of my mother that I can tell you the story of my family, because for three years, she did research in order to document our family tree.

3. **Por** expresses movement through or along.

por la calle          por la puerta

4. **Por** means *because of* or *due to.*

| | |
|---|---|
| Estoy preocupado por la falta de seguridad de los reyes. | *I'm worried because of the lack of security for the king and queen.* |
| Por ser los reyes muy accesibles, hay más problemas con su seguridad. | *Due to the king and queen being very accessible, there are more security problems.* |

5. **Por** expresses *in exchange for.*

| | |
|---|---|
| El gobierno de los Estados Unidos compró Alaska por unos pocos millones de dólares. | *The U.S. government bought Alaska for a few million dollars.* |
| Gracias por la invitación. | *Thanks for the invitation.* |

6. **Por** means *for the sake of* or *on behalf of.*

| | |
|---|---|
| Los dictadores siempre dicen que hacen todo por el pueblo. | *Dictators always say that they do everything for the sake of the people.* |

7. **Por** expresses duration of time, but is often omitted.

| | |
|---|---|
| Francisco Franco gobernó (por) casi cuarenta años en España. | *Francisco Franco governed (for) almost forty years in Spain.* |

8. **Por** is used in many fixed expressions. Here are several new ones.

| | |
|---|---|
| ¡Por Dios! | *For heaven's sake!* |
| por primera/última vez | *for the first/last time* |
| por si acaso | *just in case* |
| por supuesto | *of course* |
| por todas partes | *everywhere* |

### B. Para

1. **Para** + *inf.* means *in order to* (*do something*). Note that in English we often mean *in order to* but only say *to.*

2. **Para** indicates who or what something is destined for or to be given to.

| | |
|---|---|
| Quería comprar algo para mi mamá. | *I wanted to buy something for my mom.* |

3. **Para** is used to express *toward* or *in the direction of.*

| | |
|---|---|
| Salimos para la capital anteayer. | *We left for the capital the day before yesterday.* |

4. **Para** is used to express deadlines.

| | |
|---|---|
| Tenemos que entregar el informe para el viernes. | *We have to turn in the report by Friday.* |

5. **Para** means *to be used for* when explaining what something does.

| | |
|---|---|
| Una crónica es para documentar los eventos históricos. | *A chronicle is for recording historic events.* |

6. **Para** is used to compare with others.

| | |
|---|---|
| Para (ser) presidente, no sabe mucho de la política extranjera. | *For (being) president, he doesn't know much about foreign politics.* |

7. **Para** expresses *in the employ of.*

| | |
|---|---|
| Trabajamos para la universidad. | *We work for the university.* |

## ACTIVIDADES

**A. Situaciones.** Empareje la primera parte de las oraciones de la columna A con la segunda parte más lógica de la columna B.

| A | B |
|---|---|
| 1. Estoy en la biblioteca _____ | a. salimos para la playa a las 4:00. |
| 2. Ayer trabajé _____ | b. es para mañana. |
| 3. La composición _____ | c. y por fin supimos qué iba a pasar. |
| 4. Juan está enfermo y yo _____ | d. por ese coche. |
| 5. El viernes _____ | e. tengo que trabajar por él. |
| 6. Ayer vimos a Margarita _____ | f. para estudiar. |
| 7. Anoche llamaron _____ | g. por diez horas. |
| 8. Pagaste demasiado _____ | h. caminando por el parque. |

**B. La fiesta.** Complete las oraciones con **por** o **para**.

1. Mis amigos y yo hacemos ejercicio _____ la mañana.
2. ¿_____ qué quieres estudiar otras lenguas?
3. Necesito escribir la tarea _____ mañana.
4. León tiene una computadora nueva. No sé cuánto pagó _____ ella.
5. Trabajas _____ una compañía panameña.
6. Tenía 17 años cuando fui a Costa Rica _____ primera vez.
7. ¿Te vas _____ las montañas durante las vacaciones?

**C. Entrevista.** Entreviste a un compañero / una compañera de clase con las preguntas. Luego, cambien de papel.

1. ¿Por cuántas horas estudias/trabajas cada semana?
2. ¿Para qué clase estudias más?
3. ¿Cuánto pagaste por tus libros este semestre?
4. ¿Cómo te comunicas más con tu familia, por teléfono o por e-mail?
5. ¿Cuándo y cómo conociste a tu mejor amigo/a por primera vez?
6. ¿Para quién trabajas?
7. ¿Por dónde pasas para llegar a la universidad?

**D. La carrera (race) de caballos de Todos Santos Cuchumatán**

**PASO 1.** Complete el texto con **por** o **para** o con la forma correcta de las palabras entre paréntesis. Use el presente de los verbos, y cuando hay dos palabras entre paréntesis, escoja la palabra correcta.

En el pueblo guatemalteco de Todos Santos Cuchumatán, en las montañas del noroeste de Guatemala, se celebra una fiesta (**único**[1]). La fiesta (**tener**[2]) lugar a finales de octubre y continúa (**por/para**[3]) varios días. La celebración conmemora el día festivo cuyo nombre lleva la ciudad.

Los habitantes mames[a] de Todos Santos de Cuchumatán, pueblo que (**estar/ser**[4]) a más de 3.000 metros de altura, se han aferrado a[b] su legado[c] maya. De hecho, para los españoles fue difícil someter[d] a los mam. (**Por/Para**[5]) eso, todavía hay mucha influencia precolombina y la cultura actual refleja un fuerte sincretismo.[e]

Las mujeres indígenas (**vestir**[6]) la ropa típica: una blusa bordada[f] y una falda, ambas de color violeta. Los hombres también llevan su ropa tradicional: una camisa de rayas moradas, un pantalón de rayas rojas y blancas y un sobrepantalón[g] negro.

---

[a]*Mayan indigenous people (pl. adj.)*   [b]*se... have clung to*   [c]*legacy*   [d]*conquer*   [e]*syncretism*   [f]*embroidered*
[g]*overpants*

*En una carrera de Todos Santos*

Esta ropa (estar/ser[7]) importante (por/para[8]) los mames porque sus colores se relacionan con la cosmovisión[h] del calendario maya. (Por/Para[9]) supuesto, algunos jóvenes ya empiezan a alejarse de estas tradiciones con las influencias de afuera.

La celebración de Todos Santos Cuchumatán (comenzar[10]) durante los últimos días de octubre cuando la gente (empezar[11]) a tomar mucho. En esta época, también se (presentar[12]) el baile del torito (por/para[13]) representar la historia de un conquistador del siglo XVI. Según la historia, el conquistador (establecer[14]) la corrida de toros y luego muere cuando lo hiere un toro.[i] El baile (estar/ser[15]) grotesco y es una burla de los conquistadores.

El evento principal de las festividades es el *skach koyl*, la carrera de caballos salvajes,[j] un rito antiguo[k] en Todos Santos. Según (algo/algún[16]) personas, la carrera representa el escape de un grupo de mames de los invasores españoles, mientras que otras (decir[17]) que es una forma de purificar la tierra. Sea cual sea su origen,[l] la carrera es un evento solemne. La noche antes de la carrera, los hombres participantes (tomar[18]) mucho, pero no (dormir[19]) y prestan un juramento.[m]

(Por/Para[20]) la mañana, todos (ir[21]) al cementerio donde la carrera (tener[22]) su comienzo. Suben a sus caballos y (*ellos:* correr[23]) de un extremo al otro de una ruta de unos 100 metros, dan la vuelta[n] y (volver[24]). Así continúa la carrera (por/para[25]) horas. (Por/Para[26]) entonces, los jinetes[ñ] (estar/ser[27]) cansados y embriagados[o] y muchos se tambalean[p] mientras otros se caen. Ganan los que (poder[28]) quedarse en su caballo. A veces, (alguno/algo[29]) de ellos se muere, lo cual, según la tradición, significa que el próximo año será un año de mucha suerte.[q]

---

[h]*understanding of the universe* [i]*lo… when he is wounded by a bull* [j]*wild* [k]*un… an ancient ritual* [l]*Sea… Whatever its orgin may be* [m]*prestan… they take an oath* [n]*dan… they turn around* [ñ]*horsemen* [o]*intoxicated* [p]*se… wobble* [q]*será… will be a very lucky year*

**PASO 2.** Conteste las preguntas, según el **Paso 1.**

1. ¿Dónde está la ciudad de Todos Santos Cuchumatán?
2. ¿Cómo es la ropa tradicional de los indígenas mames de Todos Santos?
3. ¿Cuándo se celebra la fiesta de la ciudad? ¿Cómo se celebra?
4. ¿Qué hacen los jinetes la noche antes de la carrera de caballos?
5. ¿Cómo es la carrera de caballos? ¿Quién gana?

**PASO 3.** En parejas, contesten las preguntas.

1. ¿Hay una fiesta o celebración única en la región donde Uds. viven? ¿Qué se conmemora o festeja (*celebrate*)? ¿Cuándo y cómo se celebra?
2. ¿Cuáles son las comidas y bebidas tradicionales en las celebraciones de su región? ¿Cuándo se consumen?
3. ¿Cuáles son los eventos más populares de su región? ¿Se observa algún rito (*ritual*) especial para asistir a estos eventos? Por ejemplo, ¿cuándo tienen lugar? ¿Qué ropa se usa? ¿Qué se come o se bebe? Expliquen.

# 9.2 Reciprocal Verbs

Expressing *each other*

## GRAMÁTICA EN CONTEXTO

### ¿Nos vemos en el museo?

*El Museo Nacional de Nicaragua, en Managua*

Nuncio y Olga **se conocieron** en una clase de historia colonial. Tienen muchos intereses en común y **se llevan** muy bien. Casi siempre **se reúnen** después de clase para tomar café. **Se hablan** por teléfono casi todos los días. Hoy, Nuncio invita a Olga al Museo Nacional de Nicaragua.

NUNCIO: ¿Quieres ir conmigo al Museo Nacional esta tarde? Tienen una nueva exposición.

OLGA: Sí, claro. Me encantan los museos. Podemos **reunirnos** en un café de la plaza y desde allí caminar juntos al museo.

NUNCIO: No salgo del trabajo hasta la 1:00. Pero, voy directo del trabajo al museo y podemos **juntarnos** allí a la 1:30. ¿Te parece?

OLGA: Perfecto. Entonces, **nos vemos** en unas horas.

**Comprensión.** Indique si Nuncio y Olga probablemente hacen (**Sí**) o no hacen (**No**) estas cosas.

| | SÍ | NO |
|---|---|---|
| 1. Se escriben cartas todos los días. | ☐ | ☐ |
| 2. Se abrazan cuando se ven. | ☐ | ☐ |
| 3. Se besan a veces. | ☐ | ☐ |
| 4. Se ven en el trabajo. | ☐ | ☐ |
| 5. Se gritan (*They yell at each other*) mucho. | ☐ | ☐ |

GRAMÁTICA EN CONTEXTO *Shall We Meet at the Museum?* / *Nuncio and Olga met each other in a colonial history class. They have many interests in common and they get along well. They almost always get together after class for coffee. They talk to each other on the phone almost every day. Today, Nuncio invites Olga to the National Museum of Nicaragua.* / **NUNCIO:** *Do you want to go with me to the National Museum this afternoon? They have a new exhibit.* / **OLGA:** *Yes, of course. I love museums. We can meet at a café in the plaza and from there walk together to the museum.* / **NUNCIO:** *I don't leave work until 1:00. But I'll go straight from work to the museum and we can get together at the museum at 1:30. How does that sound?* / **OLGA:** *Perfect. Then we'll see each other in a few hours.*

**A.** Most reciprocal verbs express the idea of "each other." This concept is expressed in Spanish with the reflexive pronouns that you have already studied: **nos, os,** and **se.** Only the plural pronouns are used because reciprocal actions require at least two people. Reciprocal verbs function the same way as reflexive verbs. That is, the verb is accompanied by a reflexive pronoun that matches the subject of the sentence. The main difference between reciprocal verbs and reflexive verbs is that reciprocal verbs can only occur in the plural forms. However, just about any verb, including a reflexive verb, can be used in a reciprocal context. Common reciprocal actions in Spanish include:

| | |
|---|---|
| **abrazarse** | *to hug each other* |
| **besarse** | *to kiss each other* |
| **comunicarse** | *to communicate (with each other)* |
| **darse la mano** | *to shake hands with each other* |
| **despedirse** (*like* **pedir**) | *to say good-bye to each other* |
| **llevarse bien/mal** | *to get along well/poorly (with each other)* |
| **parecerse** | *to look alike (like each other)* |
| **saludarse** | *to greet each other* |
| **verse** | *to see each other* |

| | |
|---|---|
| Pablo y Yolanda **se abrazan** y **se besan.** | *Pablo and Yolanda hug and kiss each other.* |
| **Nos vemos** esta tarde. | *I'll see you (lit. We see each other) this afternoon.* |
| Mi papá y yo **nos parecemos.** | *My father and I look alike.* |

**B.** In the rare case where the meaning could be either reflexive or reciprocal, or if one wants to emphasize the reciprocal nature of the action, the clarifying phrase **el uno al otro** (changed to appropriate forms for gender and number) may be added. For example, the expression **Ellos se miran** can be interpreted as *They look at each other* or *They look at themselves.* The addition of the phrase **el uno al otro** clarifies the speaker's intent.

| | |
|---|---|
| Ellos se miran **el uno al otro.** | *They look at each other.* |

### ACTIVIDADES

**A. Mis amigos y yo.** Indique las oraciones que describen la amistad entre Ud. y su mejor amigo/a.

1. ☐ Nos conocemos muy bien.
2. ☐ Nunca nos peleamos.
3. ☐ Nos abrazamos cuando nos vemos.
4. ☐ Nos hablamos por teléfono con frecuencia.
5. ☐ Nos comunicamos por e-mail todos los días.
6. ☐ Nos queremos mucho, aunque no nos vemos con frecuencia.
7. ☐ Nos ayudamos sin pensarlo dos veces (*without a second thought*).
8. ☐ Nos damos la mano cuando nos vemos.

**B. Las relaciones.** En parejas, describan lo que (no) hacen las personas, combinando un elemento de cada columna para formar oraciones completas.

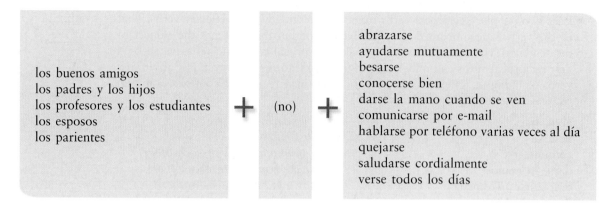

los buenos amigos
los padres y los hijos
los profesores y los estudiantes
los esposos
los parientes

**+** (no) **+**

abrazarse
ayudarse mutuamente
besarse
conocerse bien
darse la mano cuando se ven
comunicarse por e-mail
hablarse por teléfono varias veces al día
quejarse
saludarse cordialmente
verse todos los días

**C. ¿Y Ud.?**

**PASO 1.** Escriba por lo menos una pregunta con cada verbo. **¡OJO!** En el **Paso 2,** va a usar sus preguntas para entrevistar a su compañero/a de clase.

**MODELO** abrazarse → ¿Se abrazan tus amigos y tú en público?

1. comunicarse
2. saludarse
3. llevarse bien/mal
4. hablarse por teléfono

5. besarse
6. verse
7. ayudarse
8. visitarse

**PASO 2.** En parejas, entrevístense, usando sus preguntas del **Paso 1.**

**D. Mi juventud en Nicaragua**

**PASO 1.** Complete el texto con la forma correcta del verbo entre paréntesis en el imperfecto (**I**) o el pretérito (**P**). Cuando hay dos verbos, escoja el verbo correcto.

*El Lago de Managua*

Me llamo Armando. Cuando mi hermano y yo (*I: estar/ser*[1]) jóvenes, (*I: vivir*[2]) en Managua, Nicaragua. Él (*I: estar/ser*[3]) mayor que yo, pero (*nosotros: I: pasar*[4]) mucho tiempo juntos. Más tarde, cuando él (*P: casarse*[a5]) y (*P: mudarse*[b6]) al otro lado de la ciudad, todavía (*nosotros: I: verse*[7]) con frecuencia y (*I: seguir*[8]) siendo buenos amigos.

Mi hermano y yo (*I: quererse*[9]) mucho. Siempre (*I: saludarse*[10]) con una gran sonrisa.[c] (*I: Darse*[11]) la mano y (*I: abrazarse*[12]). Muchas veces (*yo: I: pasar*[13]) el domingo con su familia. (*Nosotros: I: Ir*[14]) al Lago de Managua o (*I: caminar*[15]) por la Plaza de la República y (*I: divertirse*[16]). Cuando era hora de volver a casa, (*I: despedirse*[17]) con mucho cariño[d] y con la promesa[e] de volver a vernos pronto.

Pero todo (*P: cambiar*[18]) cuando yo (*P: meterse*[f 19]) en las fuerzas que (*I: luchar*[20]) contra el gobierno sandinista. Alguien me (*P: identificar*[21]) y yo (*P: tener*[22]) que huir[g] del país. (*Yo: P: Ir*[23]) a los Estados Unidos donde el gobierno me (*P: dar*[24]) asilo[h] político. Ahora extraño[i] mucho a mi hermano mayor y espero volver a verlo algún día.

---

[a]*to get married*  [b]*to move*  [c]*smile*  [d]*affection*  [e]*con... promising*  [f]*to become involved*  [g]*flee*  [h]*asylum*  [i]*I miss*

**PASO 2.**  Conteste las preguntas, según el **Paso 1.**

1. ¿Dónde vivían Armando y su hermano cuando eran jóvenes?
2. ¿Quién era el mayor? ¿Y quién era el menor?
3. ¿Cómo se saludaban Armando y su hermano?
4. ¿Qué hacían Armando, su hermano y la familia de su hermano los domingos?
5. ¿Cuándo cambió todo? ¿Por qué cambió?
6. ¿Adónde fue Armando cuando huyó de su país? ¿Por qué razón huyó?

**PASO 3.**  En parejas, contesten las preguntas.

Communication

1. ¿Cómo se saludan Ud. y su familia? ¿Ud. y sus amigos? ¿Cómo se despiden?
2. ¿Adónde va la gente en su ciudad para pasar un rato en familia? ¿Qué hacen las familias? ¿Cambian según la estación las actividades en familia en su ciudad?
3. ¿Vive Ud. lejos de algún pariente o amigo querido (*dear*)? ¿Se comunican con frecuencia? ¿Con qué frecuencia se ven? ¿Qué hacen cuando se ven?

**PASO 4.**  Busque más información sobre el gobierno sandinista en el Internet. Comparta su información con la clase.

Communities

## Nota interdisciplinaria

### HISTORIA: NICARAGUA

*En una manifestación* (demonstration) *del FSLN*

Desde comienzos del siglo XX, Nicaragua sufría de la inestabilidad política y las intervenciones militares de los Estados Unidos. Esta situación dio origen a una resistencia liderada por Augusto C. Sandino, un general campesino que luchó contra la ocupación estadounidense en Nicaragua entre 1912 y 1933 y que fue asesinado en 1934 por la familia Somoza cuando los Estados Unidos abandonaron el país. Los Somoza, con ayuda estadounidense, instituyeron una dictadura en Nicaragua que duró varias décadas, pero las ideas de Sandino permanecían vivas. Como resultado, en 1979 estalló[a] la Revolución Sandinista.

Este conflicto armado duro relativamente poco tiempo, pero provocó la muerte de más de 50.000 personas. Finalmente, Somoza fue derrocado[b] y el Frente Sandinista de Liberación Nacional (FSLN), apoyado por Cuba y la Unión Soviética, tomó el control del país. Se realizaron grandes cambios sociales, como la expropiación de la propiedad privada, pero los conflictos continuaron.

Por fin, en 1990, se celebraron elecciones generales en el país, después de largos años de tiranía. Violeta Chamorro, candidata antisandinista, ganó esas elecciones. Inmediatamente inició un programa de reformas sociales y la situación mejoró, pero los problemas económicos continuaron y el desempleo, la pobreza y el hambre[c] aún se sufren hoy en todo el país. La situación se ha agravado debido a[d] los desastres naturales que ha tenido[e] Nicaragua y que han empobrecido[f] aún más a la población.

---

[a]*broke out*  [b]*overthrown*  [c]desempleo... *unemployment, poverty, and hunger*  [d]se... *has gotten worse due to*  [e]ha... *has had*  [f]han... *have impoverished*

**PREGUNTAS** En parejas, contesten las preguntas y compartan sus ideas con la clase.

**1.** ¿Cuáles son los problemas más serios que enfrenta Nicaragua desde los comienzos del siglo XX?

**2.** ¿Quiénes son los personajes más importantes de la historia nicaragüense?

**3.** ¿Por qué es muy significativo el año 1990 en Nicaragua?

# Palabra escrita

## A comenzar

Communication

> **Developing Your Ideas: Questions and Answers.** One way to generate ideas is to ask the six journalist questions: *Who?*, *What?*, *Where?*, *When?*, *Why?*, and *How?* Your answers to these questions may help you think of additional questions about the themes and thus help you to explore your topic in greater depth. As a result, your composition may present richer and more substantial content.

You are going to start the process of writing a brief composition that you will finalize in the **Palabra escrita: A finalizar** section of your *Manual de actividades*. The topic of this composition is **Un evento histórico.** The purpose of your composition will be to tell the reader about a historical event that interests you.

**A.** Lluvia de ideas. En este capítulo, como en el **Capítulo 4,** Ud. va a escoger el tema, esta vez, un tema histórico que le interese o que le parezca (*seems*) importante. En parejas, hagan una lluvia de ideas sobre diferentes tipos de eventos históricos y diferentes épocas para ayudarlos a escoger un tema. Usen las preguntas periodísticas (¿**quién**? ¿**qué**? ¿**dónde**? ¿**cuándo**? ¿**por qué**? y ¿**cómo**?) para empezar a formar ideas.

1. eventos históricos relacionados con la política o la economía
2. eventos históricos y sociales
3. una personalidad histórica interesante o importante para Uds.
4. ¿ ?

**B.** A organizar sus ideas. Repase sus ideas e indique las que más le interesen. Luego, escoja un tema. Identifique las partes en las que falta información (hágase las preguntas periodísticas) y busque más detalles en el Internet. Organice sus ideas, compártalas con la clase y apunte otras ideas que se le ocurran durante el proceso.

**C.** A escribir. Ahora, haga el borrador de su composición con las ideas y la información que recopiló en las actividades A y B. ¡**OJO!** Guarde bien su trabajo. Va a necesitarlo otra vez para la sección de **Palabra escrita: A finalizar** en el *Manual de actividades*.

## Los mayas: Pacal el Grande

La civilización maya se extendió por toda la península de Yucatán, partes de Honduras, Guatemala, El Salvador y Belice durante 3.000 años hasta el siglo XVI, cuando llegaron los españoles al continente americano. Los mayas tenían una economía fundamentalmente agrícola, cuyo producto principal era el maíz. También cultivaban el algodón, el tomate, el cacao, el frijol, el chile y otros productos. Tenían un sistema de ciudades basado en construcciones piramidales.

En una de las pirámides de Palenque, el Templo de las Inscripciones, se encuentra la tumba del rey Pacal, o Pacal el Grande. Su ajuar[a] funerario muestra la riqueza de la civilización maya. Su máscara está hecha de 340 piezas de jade que recuerdan[b] el ciclo anual agrícola. Según la leyenda, el rey Pacal se transformaría[c] así en un joven Dios del Maíz que regresaba a la naturaleza y que volvería[d] durante el ciclo anual agrícola.

La máscara del rey Pacal el Grande, cultura maya

[a]furnishings  [b]recall  [c]se... would be transformed  [d]would return

## Vocabulario del tema

### Las etapas° de la vida

Las... *Stages*

**1. La infancia**

Isabel

jugar (ue) (gu) con las muñecas

**2. La niñez**

**3. La adolescencia**

**4. La juventud**

tomar helado

Miguel

**5. La madurez**

Miguel

Isabel

**6. La vejez**

# Otros pasatiempos y diversiones

| | |
|---|---|
| acampar | to camp; to go camping |
| ayudar | to help |
| leer (y) cuentos | to read stories |
| ir (*irreg.*) de vacaciones | to go on vacation |
| pasear en barco | to go boating |
| pintar | to paint |
| practicar (qu) el ala delta | to hang glide |
| recitar poesía | to recite poetry |
| ver (*irreg.*) dibujos animados | to watch cartoons |
| | |
| el alpinismo | mountain climbing |
| la caminata | hike |
| el ciclismo | cycling |
| la equitación | horseback riding |
| la feria | festival; fair |
| el juguete | toy |
| la observación de pájaros | bird watching |
| la pesca | fishing |
| el senderismo | hiking |
| el parque zoológico | zoo |

**Repaso:** andar (*irreg.*) en bicicleta, bailar, hablar por teléfono, hacer (*irreg.*) ejercicio, jugar (ue) (gu), manejar, nadar, navegar (gu) en Internet, pasear, practicar (qu), sacar (qu) fotos, tomar el sol, ver (*irreg.*) películas, viajar; el cine, los deportes, la playa

## ACTIVIDADES

**A.** Las etapas de la vida y las actividades

**PASO 1.** Indique con qué etapa de la vida asocia Ud. las actividades de la columna A.

A

1. ____ Voy a visitar a Santa Claus en el centro comercial.
2. ____ Mis padres me cambian los pañales (*diapers*).
3. ____ Me gusta mucho cuando mis nietos vienen a visitarme.
4. ____ Mis amigos y yo andamos en bicicleta para ir a la tienda de la esquina a comprar refrescos.
5. ____ Después de clase, voy al gimnasio a hacer ejercicio y luego voy al trabajo.
6. ____ Trabajo en una oficina grande en el centro de la ciudad pero tengo una entrevista con una compañía en otra provincia.

B

a. la infancia
b. la niñez
c. la adolescencia
d. la juventud
e. la madurez
f. la vejez

Communication

**PASO 2.** Haga una lista de cosas o actividades que Ud. asocia con diferentes etapas de la vida. Luego, comparta su lista con su compañero/a de clase para ver si él/ella asocia la actividad con la misma etapa de la vida.

**B.** ¿Solo/a, con los amigos o con la familia?

**PASO 1.** Indique si Ud. hacía estas cosas solo/a (**S**), con sus amigos (**A**) o con su familia (**F**). Si nunca las hacía, indique nunca (**N**).

|  | S | A | F | N |
|---|---|---|---|---|
| **1.** Iba al parque zoológico. | ☐ | ☐ | ☐ | ☐ |
| **2.** Dibujaba y pintaba. | ☐ | ☐ | ☐ | ☐ |
| **3.** Hacía ciclismo. | ☐ | ☐ | ☐ | ☐ |
| **4.** Jugaba con las muñecas. | ☐ | ☐ | ☐ | ☐ |
| **5.** Daba caminatas. | ☐ | ☐ | ☐ | ☐ |
| **6.** Jugaba a los videojuegos. | ☐ | ☐ | ☐ | ☐ |
| **7.** Leía cuentos. | ☐ | ☐ | ☐ | ☐ |
| **8.** Pescaba. | ☐ | ☐ | ☐ | ☐ |
| **9.** Tomaba helado. | ☐ | ☐ | ☐ | ☐ |
| **10.** Veía dibujos animados. | ☐ | ☐ | ☐ | ☐ |
| **11.** Acampaba. | ☐ | ☐ | ☐ | ☐ |
| **12.** Recitaba poesía. | ☐ | ☐ | ☐ | ☐ |

**PASO 2.** En parejas, hablen de las actividades del **Paso 1** que hacían de jóvenes. ¿Cuáles eran sus favoritas? ¿Qué tienen Uds. en común? Nombren una actividad que les gustaba hacer, pero que no está en el **Paso 1**.

**C.** ¿Qué hacían? En parejas, formen oraciones lógicas, usando las palabras y frases de las columnas. Usen el imperfecto de los verbos y hagan los otros cambios necesarios. Adivinen si las oraciones de su compañero/a de clase son ciertas o falsas.

MODELO E1: Practicaba el ala delta con mis amigos.
E2: No, no es cierto.
E1: Sí, es cierto. Mis amigos y yo practicábamos en un club de ala delta.

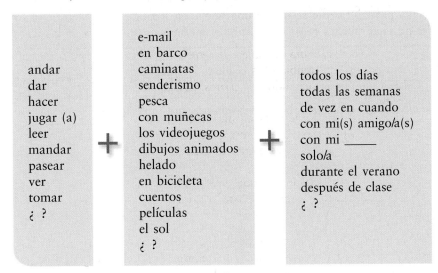

**D.** Entrevista. Entreviste a un compañero / una compañera de clase con las preguntas. Luego, cambien de papel.

1. ¿Qué hacías después de salir de la escuela cuando eras niño/a?
2. Cuando eras niño/a, ¿cuáles eran tus dibujos animados favoritos? ¿Y cuáles eran tus películas favoritas?
3. ¿Qué actividades creativas hacías? ¿Te gustaba dibujar? ¿pintar? ¿escribir poesía?
4. ¿Qué actividades al aire libre te gustaba hacer? ¿Te gustaba acampar? ¿hacer senderismo? ¿ciclismo? ¿alpinismo? ¿Cuándo lo hacías y con quién?
5. ¿A qué ferias asistías cuando eras joven? ¿Con quién ibas? ¿Qué tipo de ferias eran? ¿de la provincia o del condado (*county*)?

# Gramática

## 9.3 Preterite vs. Imperfect

### GRAMÁTICA EN CONTEXTO

*La Isla de Roatán*

### Una excursión a la Isla de Roatán

[*Cecilia habla de su viaje a Honduras.*]

Cuando **fuimos** a Honduras, yo **quería** visitar las islas del país, porque tienen historias interesantes. **Leí** que Roatán, la isla más grande de la Bahía de Honduras, **fue** un refugio preferido para los piratas ingleses, franceses y holandeses. Casi nadie **vivía** en las islas y los piratas las **usaban** como un centro de ataque. Desde sus escondites en las islas, **saqueaban** los grandes barcos españoles que **llevaban** los tesoros del Nuevo Mundo a España y a veces **atacaban** poblados del continente. Cuando le **dije** a mi esposo que **quería** ir a Roatán, él **buscó** una excursión de dos días. **Visitamos** toda la isla. Aunque, por su manera de vivir, los piratas no **dejaron** ningún monumento ni edificio histórico que ver, **fue** una excursión interesante y **resultó** divertido imaginar a los piratas en la isla.

Comprensión. ¿Cierto (**C**), falso (**F**) o no se sabe (**NSS**)?

|  | C | F | NSS |
|---|---|---|---|
| 1. Cecilia estaba casada cuando fue a Honduras. | ☐ | ☐ | ☐ |
| 2. Cecilia fue a Honduras el año pasado. | ☐ | ☐ | ☐ |
| 3. Los piratas establecieron grandes ciudades en Roatán. | ☐ | ☐ | ☐ |
| 4. Cecilia probablemente se quedó una noche en Roatán. | ☐ | ☐ | ☐ |
| 5. Cecilia sacó muchas fotos de estatuas y monumentos. | ☐ | ☐ | ☐ |

In this section you'll learn how to use the preterite and imperfect in conjunction to narrate, tell a story, or relate a personal anecdote to someone. However, let's first review what you've learned about the preterite and imperfect.

---

**GRAMÁTICA EN CONTEXTO** *An Excursion to Roatan Island / Cecilia talks about her trip to Honduras. / When we went to Honduras, I wanted to visit the islands of the country, because they have an interesting history. I read that Roatan, the largest island of the Bay of Honduras, was a preferred haven for English, French, and Dutch pirates. Almost no one lived on the islands and the pirates used them as a center of attack. From their hideaways on the islands, they could pillage the large Spanish vessels that carried treasures from the New World to Spain and sometimes they attacked settlements on the mainland. When I told my husband that I wanted to go to Roatan, he looked for a two-day excursion. We visited the whole island. Although, due to their way of life, the pirates didn't leave behind any monuments or historical buildings to see, it was an interesting tour and it ended up being fun to imagine the pirates on the island.*

## REVIEW: USES OF THE PRETERITE AND IMPERFECT

| PRETERITE | IMPERFECT |
|---|---|
| **1.** Preterite expresses actions completed in the past within an implied or stated specific time period.<br><br>El año pasado mis amigos y yo **acampamos** (por) una semana en las montañas.<br><br>*Last year my friends and I went camping for a week in the mountains.* | **a.** Imperfect describes background information in the past, including time, weather, age, mental and physical conditions.<br><br>**Era** verano y **hacía** calor. **Teníamos** 20 años y **estábamos** listos para una aventura.<br><br>*It was summer and it was hot. We were 20 years old and we were ready for an adventure.* |
| **2.** Preterite can express a series of sequential completed actions.<br><br>La primera mañana **nos levantamos, desayunamos, bajamos** la tienda y **salimos** caminando hacia una montaña lejana.<br><br>*That first morning, we got up, ate breakfast, took down the tent, and took off walking toward a distant mountain.* | **b.** Imperfect can express actions that were taking place simultaneously (usually in the background).<br><br>Mientras yo **sacaba** fotos, mi amigo Raúl **admiraba** la vista.<br><br>*While I was taking photos, my friend Raúl was admiring the view.* |
|  | **c.** Imperfect describes habitual actions that used to take place in the past.<br><br>Cuando era niño, mi familia y yo **dábamos** una caminata cada fin de semana.<br><br>*When I was a child, my family and I used to go for a hike every weekend.* |
| **3.** Preterite expresses an action that interrupted another action that was already in progress.<br><br>**Caminábamos** tranquilamente cuando un oso **cruzó** el sendero.<br><br>*We were walking along peacefully when a bear crossed the trail.* | **d.** Imperfect describes an action that was in progress when another action interrupted.<br><br>**Poníamos** la tienda cuando de repente **empezó** a llover.<br><br>*We were putting up the tent when all of a sudden it started to rain.* |
| **4.** The preterite of certain verbs has a different base meaning than the present tense meaning.<br><br>**conocer** — to meet (for the first time)<br>**poder** — to succeed<br>**no poder** — to fail<br>**querer** — to try<br>**no querer** — to refuse<br>**saber** — to find out<br>**tener** — to get, obtain, receive | **e.** The imperfect of all verbs has the same base meaning as the present tense meaning.<br><br>**conocer** — to know, be familiar with<br>**poder** — to be able<br>**querer** — to want<br>**saber** — to know (a fact)<br>**tener** — to have |

# USING THE PRETERITE AND IMPERFECT TO NARRATE

**A.** When telling a story or relating a past event, use the imperfect to set the stage and provide background details. In the following example, everything is background information that is setting the stage for our story. Nothing has actually happened yet, and no time has passed within the scene. It's as if we were looking at a snapshot of the scene.

| | |
|---|---|
| **Eran** las 2:00 de la tarde, **llovía** y no **había** nada que ver en la televisión. Mi hermana **miraba** la lluvia por la ventana mientras yo **trataba** de leer una novela, pero no me **gustaba**. **Estábamos** aburridos y no **sabíamos** qué hacer... | *It was 2:00 p.m., it was raining and there wasn't anything to watch on the television. My sister was watching the rain through the window while I tried to read a novel, but I didn't like it. We were bored and we didn't know what to do . . .* |

**B.** In a narration, the preterite expresses concrete events and actions that move the storyline forward in time. Here we see some specific actions taking place on the stage set up by the imperfect earlier.

| | |
|---|---|
| ...De repente, **sonó** el timbre. Mi hermana y yo **corrimos** a la puerta, la **abrimos** y... | *. . . All of a sudden, the doorbell rang. Mi sister and I ran to the door, opened it, and . . .* |

**C.** As you continue to tell your story, you may find it necessary to switch back and forth between preterite and imperfect, depending on whether you're expressing specific actions that move the storyline forward in time (preterite) or whether you pause to add background details about the scene or about what the characters in your story were thinking, feeling, or doing (imperfect). Notice how in the remainder of our story the preterite verbs (in purple text) do indeed move the storyline along and how imperfect verbs (in boldface) fill in the background details.

| | |
|---|---|
| ...**vimos** a nuestro tío Federico. Federico **era** el hermano de nuestra mamá y siempre nos **llevábamos** bien con él. Federico nos **dijo** que **iba** a llevarnos al cine porque **estaba** lloviendo y **sabía** que no **había** nada que hacer dentro de la casa. Le **dijimos** a nuestra mamá adonde **íbamos** y **salimos**.

Cuando **llegamos** al cine, **había** una larga cola de gente esperando comprar entradas. Mi hermana **gritó**: «Ay, por favor... ». Pero nuestro tío **sonrió** y le **dijo** a mi hermana: «tranquila, **compré** las entradas antes de recogerlos». Mi hermana **sonrió**, y así **pasamos** directo por la entrada. Luego, Federico nos **compró** palomitas, **fuimos** al baño y **vimos** la película. | *. . . we saw our uncle Federico. Federico was our mother's brother and we always got along well with him. Federico told us that he was going to take us to the movies because it was raining and he knew that there wasn't anything to do in the house. We told our mother where we were going and we left.*

*When we arrived at the movie theater, there was a long line of people waiting to buy tickets. My sister yelled, "Oh, please . . . ." But our uncle smiled and said to my sister, "Relax, I bought the tickets before picking you up." My sister smiled, and thus we went straight through to the entrance. Then Federico bought us popcorn, we went to the bathroom, and we saw the movie.* |

**A.** Cuando era niña. Escuche la descripción de lo que hacía Manuela en su niñez y termine las oraciones.

| Vocabulario práctico | |
| --- | --- |
| **no le prestaba atención a** | I wasn't paying attention to |
| **sentí un olor** | I noticed a smell |
| **di la vuelta** | I turned around |
| **se quemaba** | was burning |
| **nos reímos** | we laughed |

1. Cuando Manuela era niña ____.
   **a.** pasaba mucho tiempo con sus amigas
   **b.** pasaba mucho tiempo con sus primas
2. Ellas ____.
   **a.** jugaban con las muñecas
   **b.** jugaban a los videojuegos
3. Las muchachas también ____.
   **a.** iban al cine
   **b.** veían dibujos animados
4. A Manuela ____.
   **a.** le gustaba leer
   **b.** no le gustaba leer
5. En casa, Manuela ____.
   **a.** ayudaba a su papá a cortar el césped
   **b.** ayudaba a su mamá en la cocina
6. Un día, cuando Manuela tenía 10 años ____.
   **a.** su papá le preparó la cena
   **b.** su mamá la llamó para decirle que iba a llegar tarde a casa
7. Manuela empezó a preparar la cena. Mientras se cocinaba todo, ella ____.
   **a.** leía
   **b.** miraba la tele
8. Pero Manuela no le prestaba atención a la comida y ____.
   **a.** todo se quemó
   **b.** todo salió muy rico

**B.** ¿Qué pasa aquí? Complete el párrafo con la forma correcta de los verbos entre paréntesis en el pretérito o el imperfecto, según el contexto.

Rafael (**escuchar**[1]) la radio mientras (**estudiar**[2]) en su habitación. A las 4:45, Antonio (**entrar**[3]) y le (**preguntar**[4]) si (*él:* **querer**[5]) ir al cine. Rafael (**decir**[6]) que sí y los dos (**salir**[7]). (**Hacer**[8]) muy buen tiempo y mientras (*ellos:* **caminar**[9]), (**hablar**[10]) de sus clases. Por fin (*ellos:* **llegar**[11]) al cine, pero entonces (**saber**[12]) que se habían vendido todas las entradas.[a] Por eso, (**ir**[13]) a tomar un café y (**quedarse**[14]) allí charlando por dos horas.

_____
[a]se... *all the tickets had been sold*

**C.** Entrevista: Algo que me gustaba hacer. Piense Ud. en su niñez y en una actividad que le gustaba hacer cuando era joven. Mientras su compañero/a de clase le hace preguntas, trate de contestar sin mencionar la actividad. **¡OJO!** Para el número 6, su compañero/a debe hacerle más preguntas para poder adivinar la actividad de Ud.

1. ¿Lo hacías solo/a o con otras personas? ¿Lo hacías con una persona específica?
2. ¿Podías hacerlo en cualquier lugar, o tenías que hacerlo en un lugar específico? ¿Dónde lo hacías?
3. ¿Lo hacías frecuentemente o sólo en ocasiones especiales?
4. ¿Costaba mucho dinero hacerlo?
5. ¿Cuándo fue la última vez que lo hiciste?
6. ¿ ?
7. Tu actividad es/era...

**D.** Los garífunas de Centroamérica

**PASO 1.** Complete la narración con la forma correcta de los verbos entre paréntesis en el pretérito o el imperfecto, según el contexto.

Una bailarina garífuna

La cultura garífuna de Centroamérica tiene una larga y rica historia que muchos no conocen. Hace mucho tiempo, los indígenas arawacos (vivir[1]) en la isla de San Vicente. Pero, la tribu[a] kalipuna los (invadir[2]) y los kalipunas (ocupar[3]) la isla. La fusión de las dos tribus ocurrió poco después.

En 1635, un barco de esclavos de Nigeria naufragó[b] en el Caribe. Los nigerianos (sobrevivir[4]), pero (tener[5]) conflictos constantes con los kalipunas. Por fin, los dos grupos (empezar[6]) a vivir en paz y a casarse entre sí.[c] Los españoles en la región caribeña (llamar[7]) «Caribes» a los habitantes de la isla, pero ellos (llamarse[8]) «garífunas», nombre que significa «gente que come yuca».

La isla (ser[9]) colonia británica y en el siglo XVIII los garífunas (querer[11]) establecer una colonia independiente. Con el apoyo[d] de los franceses, los garífunas lucharon contra las fuerzas británicas, pero no (poder[11]) alcanzar su meta[e] de libertad. Como San Vicente (pertenecer[12]) a los europeos que (tener[13]) esclavos africanos y los garífunas (ser[14]) negros libres, los gobernantes (decidir[15]) trasladarlos[f] a otros lugares. En 1797, (enviar[16]) a los garífunas sobrevivientes a la isla de Roatán, en Honduras. Mientras los barcos (cruzar[17]) el mar, los españoles (capturar[18]) uno y lo (llevar[19]) a Trujillo. Más tarde, los españoles (conquistar[20]) Roatán y (llevar[21]) a los garífunas que (vivir[22]) allí a Trujillo.

A través de los años, las comunidades garífunas (extenderse[23]) por toda la costa caribeña desde Belice hasta Nicaragua. Los garífunas siempre han mantenido[g] su lengua y su cultura. Su música, una mezcla de ritmos africanos y bailes en forma de círculos que se llama «punta», se considera un elemento fundamental de su cultura. En 1978, una nueva variación de punta (darse[24]) a conocer,[h] la punta rock. Esta forma (florecer[25]) inmediatamente y hoy día, aún sigue siendo muy popular y representativa de una cultura única y rica de Centroamérica.

---

[a]*tribe*  [b]*shipwrecked*  [c]casarse... *to intermarry*  [d]*support*  [e]*goal*  [f]*move them*  [g]han... *have maintained*
[h]darse... *came out*

PASO 2.  Conteste las preguntas, según el **Paso 1.**

1. ¿Qué grupo indígena vivía en la isla de San Vicente? ¿Qué tribu invadió y ocupó la isla?
2. ¿Cómo llegaron los nigerianos a la isla? ¿Cómo era su relación con los indígenas?
3. ¿A quiénes pertenecía la colonia de San Vicente? ¿Qué querían hacer los garífunas con respecto a su situación política? ¿Alcanzaron su meta?
4. ¿Qué decidieron hacer los gobernantes británicos de San Vicente con los garífunas? ¿Qué pasó mientras los barcos cruzaban el mar?
5. ¿Por dónde se extendieron las comunidades garífunas a través de los años?
6. ¿Qué es la punta y cómo es?
7. ¿Qué forma musical se dio a conocer en los años 70? ¿Cómo fue recibida por la gente?

## Nota cultural

Cultures

### COSTA RICA: PAÍS DESMILITARIZADO

*Unos agentes de la Fuerza Pública*

Todos los años, el primero de diciembre, Costa Rica celebra uno de los acontecimientos[a] más significativos de su historia: la abolición del ejército como institución permanente en 1948 tras la finalización de la guerra civil. Costa Rica fue el primer país del mundo que abolió su ejército con el objetivo de impedir posibles influencias militares y asegurar la democracia en el país. En la actualidad sólo cuenta con la policía llamada Fuerza Pública, con unos 12.000 miembros que protegen a los 4,5 millones de habitantes de este pequeño país centroamericano. Los recursos económicos que se ahorran en defensa son destinados al mejoramiento[b] de la educación, la salud pública y la situación social de sus habitantes.

Los costarricenses se sienten orgullosos de no tener ejército y de emplear sus recursos económicos en mejoras[c] sociales y en el mantenimiento de las instituciones democráticas. Sin embargo, no están desprotegidos, pues Costa Rica tiene convenios[d] de defensa con sus países vecinos.

[a]*events*  [b]*improvement*  [c]*improvements*  [d]*treaties*

**PREGUNTAS** En parejas, contesten las preguntas. Después, compartan sus ideas con la clase.

1. ¿Por qué abolió Costa Rica su ejército? ¿En qué año lo eliminó?
2. ¿Qué sistemas de protección social tiene Costa Rica?
3. ¿Qué ventajas tiene para Costa Rica el hecho de no tener ejército? ¿En qué emplea el gobierno el dinero?

Ud. va a leer un artículo publicado en el periódico español *El País*, sobre los daños causados por la tormenta tropical Agatha, a finales de mayo de 2010, en algunos países centroamericanos.

**Cultures**

## ANTES DE LEER

**PASO 1.** Teniendo en cuenta el tema general del artículo, ¿qué información espera encontrar en la lectura? Haga una lista de tres ideas verosímiles (*likely*) y comparta su lista con un compañero / una compañera de clase. ¿Son similares sus ideas?

**Communication**

**PASO 2.** Revise el artículo rápidamente, sin leerlo y sin preocuparse por las palabras que no conoce. ¿Qué países centroamericanos sufrieron los efectos de la tormenta?

## La tormenta tropical Agatha causa varias decenas[a] de víctimas en Centroamérica

*En Quetzatenango, Guatemala, después de la tormenta Agatha*

---

[a]*tens*

*Los efectos de la tempestad en Guatemala, donde han muerto[b] más de 80 personas, se agravan al unirse a los de la erupción del volcán Pacaya. —En El Salvador hay nueve muertos y otros tres en Honduras por el mismo fenómeno meteorológico, que se ha degradado[c] a la categoría de depresión tropical.*

## Guatemala - 30/05/2010

Más de 80 personas han muerto en Guatemala, nueve en El Salvador y otras tres en Honduras como consecuencia de las lluvias producidas por la tormenta tropical Agatha, la primera de la temporada,[d] que se ha degradado a la categoría de depresión tropical tras entrar[e] en territorio guatemalteco. Cientos de personas ya han sido[f] evacuadas en previsión de[g] que se produzcan inundaciones. En Guatemala, los efectos devastadores de la tormenta se unen a los que desde el jueves está teniendo la erupción del volcán Pacaya.

Las autoridades de Guatemala han confirmado[h] la muerte de 63 personas, y siguen en búsqueda de otras 24. Erik de León, gobernador del departamento de Chimaltenango, situado a unos 60 kilómetros al oeste de la capital, ha confirmado que sólo en su región hay 50 fallecidos,[i] que sumados[j] al último recuento oficial del Gobierno deja un total de 63 víctimas de la tormenta tropical.

Además de las víctimas mortales, al menos once personas han desaparecido[k] en Guatemala, donde dos adultos y dos menores murieron en Alomonga (a 200 kilómetros al oeste de Ciudad de Guatemala), después de que un deslave de tierra sepultara[l] su casa, informaron los servicios de emergencia. Otros cuatro niños y cuatro adultos murieron en diferentes incidentes en la capital del país, donde los derrumbamientos[m] y las lluvias paralizaron el tráfico y provocaron cortes en el suministro[n] eléctrico de varios vecindarios.

El Gobierno de Guatemala, que esperaba que lo peor de la tormenta se viviera[ñ] este domingo sobre las nueve de la mañana (las cinco de la tarde, hora peninsular española), declaró el sábado el estado de alerta ante la proximidad de la tormenta tropical, que se formó en aguas del océano Pacífico. Las advertencias[o] se extendieron al sur de México y a El Salvador.

Tras expresar su solidaridad con los familiares de los fallecidos, el presidente de El Salvador, Mauricio Funes, también ha declarado[p] el estado de emergencia en el país. «En la actualidad, el 90 por ciento del territorio nacional está en riesgo, porque Agatha ha dejado un promedio[q] diario de precipitaciones mayores incluso que las registradas con los huracanes Mitch y Stan y la tormenta Ida», ha asegurado.[r] Una medida también decretada por Porfirio Lobo, presidente de Honduras, en un Consejo de Ministros que también ha convocado[s] a los representantes de la comunidad internacional para coordinar un programa de ayuda para hacer frente a[t] la situación que vive el país centroamericano.

---

[b]han... *have died*  [c]se... *has been downgraded*  [d]*season*  [e]tras... *after entering*  [f]han... *have been* [g]en... *as a precaution against*  [h]han... *have confirmed*  [h]*deceased*  [i]*muertos*  [j]*added*  [k]han... *have disappeared*  [l]un... *a landslide buried*  [m]*collapses*  [n]*supply*  [ñ]se... *would be experienced*  [o]*warnings* [p]ha... *has declared*  [q]ha... *has left an average*  [r]ha... *he has assured*  [s]ha... *has convened*  [t]hacer... *confront*

**A. Comprensión.** Escoja la opción correcta para completar las oraciones.

1. Los países afectados por la tormenta Agatha fueron ____.
   a. México, Guatemala y El Salvador
   b. Honduras, México y Guatemala
   c. Guatemala, El Salvador y Honduras
2. La tormenta no produjo ____ en el territorio afectado.
   a. derrumbamientos
   b. inundaciones
   c. lluvias fuertes
3. En Guatemala, la situación fue más severa ____.
   a. por la erupción de un volcán
   b. por su proximidad al Pacífico
   c. porque hubo muchos muertos
4. La región guatemalteca que registró más fallecidos fue ____.
   a. la Ciudad de Guatemala
   b. Alomonga
   c. Chimaltenango
5. El promedio diario de lluvias registradas por Agatha fue menor que las lluvias provocadas por ____.
   a. los huracanes Mitch y Stan
   b. la tormenta Ida
   c. los huracanes Mitch y Stan y la tormenta Ida

**B. Temas de discusión.** En parejas, contesten las preguntas. Después, compartan sus respuestas con la clase.

Communication

1. ¿Qué medidas adoptaron los presidentes de los tres países para evitar más desastres?
2. ¿Qué tipo de desastres naturales ocurren en este país? ¿Cuáles son las zonas geográficas más afectadas? ¿Qué tipo de desastres naturales ocurren con más frecuencia en la zona donde Uds. viven?
3. Piensen en un desastre natural reciente de su país y expliquen
   a. qué ocurrió.
   b. cuáles fueron las consecuencias del desastre.
   c. qué medidas tomaron el gobierno y la comunidad para ayudar a los afectados.

## Costa Rica: Juan Carlos

San José

En este blog, Juan Carlos nos muestra parte de la capital de Costa Rica, San José. Va acompañado por su amiga Catarina y su tía Leticia. Empiezan en el Parque Morazán, pasan por el Paseo Colón y visitan el Teatro Nacional y otros lugares.

## ANTES DE VER

**PASO 1.** En parejas contesten las preguntas. Después, compartan sus ideas con la clase.

1. ¿Cómo es la ciudad donde viven Uds.?
2. ¿Qué edificios o lugares de interés hay para los turistas que visitan su ciudad?
3. ¿Adónde va la gente de su ciudad a descansar o a pasar el tiempo libre? ¿Qué se puede hacer allí?

**PASO 2.** Repase el **Vocabulario práctico.**

| Vocabulario práctico | | | |
|---|---|---|---|
| **lindo** | pretty | **platican** | they talk |
| **ubicados** | located | **incómodo** | uncomfortable |

## DESPUÉS DE VER

**A.** Comprensión. Conteste las preguntas.

1. ¿Qué hay en el Parque Morazán en estos días?
2. ¿Qué fue antiguamente el Museo Nacional?
3. ¿Por qué le gusta el museo a Juan Carlos?
4. ¿Qué dice Juan Carlos que se puede comprar en el Mercado Central?
5. ¿Se puede comer en el mercado? Explique.

**B.** Temas de discusión. En parejas, comenten los temas y preparen un breve informe para intercambiar con otras parejas. Después, compartan sus ideas con la clase.

1. San José es una ciudad con lugares atractivos y una historia interesante.
2. El transporte en autobús es fundamental en la vida de Centroamérica.
3. Mencionen algunas diferencias y semejanzas entre San José y alguna ciudad importante de la región donde viven.

## Los verbos

| | |
|---|---|
| alcanzar (c) | to achieve; to reach |
| alcanzar a + *inf.* | to manage to (*do something*) |
| asesinar | to murder, assassinate |
| conquistar | to conquer |
| convertir (i, i) | to convert |
| datar de + *time* | to date from + *time* |
| descubrir (*like* cubrir) | to discover |
| desintegrar(se) | to disintegrate, break up |
| establecer(se) (zc) | to establish (oneself); *ref.* to settle |
| florecer (zc) | to flourish; to thrive |
| independizarse (c) | to gain independence; to become independent |
| pertenecer (zc) (a) | to belong (to) |
| superar | to overcome |
| tener (*irreg.*) lugar | to take place |

Cognados: colonizar (c), declarar, disolver (ue), explorar, extender (ie), invadir, ocupar, resistir

## La historia política y mundial — Political and World History

| | |
|---|---|
| el ataque | attack |
| la bandera | flag |
| la batalla | battle |
| la crónica | chronicle; report |
| el desfile | parade |
| la dictadura | dictatorship |
| el ejército | army |
| el/la esclavo/a | slave |
| la estabilidad | stability |
| la fuerza | force; power |
| el/la gobernador(a) | governor |
| el gobierno | government |
| la guerra (civil) | (civil) war |
| el/la guerrero/a | warrior |
| el imperio | empire |
| el/la indígena | native (*person*) |
| la llegada | arrival |
| la paz | peace |
| la reina | queen |
| el reino | kingdom |
| el rey | king |
| el tratado | treaty |
| el virrey | viceroy |
| descubierto/a | discovered |

Cognados: las armas, la autoridad, la civilización, la colonia, la conquista, el/la conquistador(a), la independencia, la intervención, el nacionalismo, la procesión, el regionalismo, la república, la sucesión, el territorio, la unión; colonial, conservador(a), corrupto/a, federal, liberal, precolombino/a

## Las épocas — Time Periods

| | |
|---|---|
| el siglo | century |

Cognados: la década, el milenio

## Los desastres naturales

| | |
|---|---|
| destruir (y) | to destroy |
| rescatar | to rescue |
| sobrevivir (a) | to survive |
| el cielo | sky |
| el incendio | fire |
| la inundación | flood |
| el maremoto | tsunami |
| la niebla | fog |
| el relámpago | lightning bolt |
| el rescate | rescue |
| el/la sobreviviente | survivor |
| el terremoto | earthquake |
| la tormenta | storm |

Cognados: el huracán, el tornado

## Las etapas de la vida — Stages of Life

| | |
|---|---|
| la adolescencia | adolescence |
| la infancia | infancy |
| la juventud | youth |
| la madurez | maturity |
| la niñez | childhood |
| la vejez | old age |

## Otros pasatiempos y diversiones

| | |
|---|---|
| acampar | to camp; to go camping |
| ayudar | to help |
| dibujar | to draw |
| ir (*irreg.*) de vacaciones | to go on vacation |
| pasear en barco | to go boating |
| pintar | to paint |
| practicar (qu) el ala delta | to hang glide |
| recitar poesía | to recite poetry |
| tomar helado | to eat ice cream |
| el alpinismo | mountain climbing |
| la caminata | hike |
| el ciclismo | cycling |
| el cuento | story |
| los dibujos animados | cartoons |
| la discoteca | disco, dance club |
| la equitación | horseback riding |
| la feria | festival; fair |
| la fotografía | photography |
| el juguete | toy |
| la muñeca | doll |
| la observación de pájaros | bird watching |
| la pesca | fishing |
| el senderismo | hiking |
| el parque zoológico | zoo |

Repaso: andar (*irreg.*) en bicicleta, bailar, hablar por teléfono, hacer (*irreg.*) ejercicio, jugar (ue) (gu), manejar, nadar, navegar en Internet, pasear, practicar (qu), sacar (qu) fotos, tomar el sol, ver (*irreg.*) películas, viajar; el cine, los deportes, la playa

## Expresiones con *por*

| | |
|---|---|
| ¡Por Dios! | For heaven's sake! |
| por primera/última vez | for the first/last time |
| por si acaso | just in case |
| por supuesto | of course |
| por todas partes | everywhere |

## Algunos verbos recíprocos

| | |
|---|---|
| abrazarse (c) | to hug each other |
| besarse | to kiss each other |
| comunicarse (qu) | to communicate (with each other) |

| | |
|---|---|
| darse (*irreg.*) la mano | to shake hands with each other |
| despedirse (*like* pedir) | to say good-bye to each other |
| llevarse bien/mal | to get along well/poorly (with each other) |
| parecerse (zc) | to look alike |
| saludarse | to greet each other |
| verse (*irreg.*) | to see each other |

# La naturaleza

Connections

## ANTES DE VER

¿Cuánto sabe Ud. de la geografía de la región donde vive? ¿Tiene su región algunas de estos elementos geográficos? ¿Cómo se llaman?

1. una cascada (*waterfall*) pintoresca (*picturesque*)
2. un volcán famoso
3. un parque nacional
4. un bosque tropical (*tropical rainforest*)
5. un desierto grande
6. una cordillera (*mountain range*) impresionante
7. un río largo
8. una playa hermosa

### Vocabulario práctico

| | | | |
|---|---|---|---|
| **la belleza** | beauty | **se destaca una** | one stands out |
| **los tamaños** | sizes | **magníficos** | magnificent |
| **los amantes** | lovers | **arcoíris** | rainbows |
| **las maravillas** | marvels, wonders | **goza de** | enjoys |

## DESPUÉS DE VER

Indique en qué país se mencionan estos lugares o elementos geográficos, según el vídeo: Costa Rica (**CR**), Argentina (**A**) o España (**E**).

| | CR | A | E |
|---|---|---|---|
| 1. las Cataratas del Iguazú | ☐ | ☐ | ☐ |
| 2. el Volcán Arenal | ☐ | ☐ | ☐ |
| 3. los Pueblos Blancos | ☐ | ☐ | ☐ |
| 4. los arcoíris | ☐ | ☐ | ☐ |
| 5. La Alpujarra | ☐ | ☐ | ☐ |
| 6. las montañas, costas y selvas | ☑ | ☐ | ☐ |

## EL YUNQUE

El Bosque Nacional El Yunque se encuentra en el norte de Puerto Rico. En El Yunque hay bosques tropicales preciosos y una gran variedad de árboles, plantas y animales. Esta reserva forestal federal pertenece al sistema de Bosques Nacionales de los Estados Unidos.

## EL PARQUE NACIONAL TORTUGUERO

El Parque Nacional Tortuguero está en Costa Rica. Aunque tiene muchas especies de animales, es famoso por ser un lugar importante para el desove[a] de tortugas baulas.[b] No se sabe por qué siempre vuelven a este lugar las tortugas, pero con el estatus del parque, están bajo protección del gobierno costarricense.

[a]egg laying  [b]tortugas... *leatherback sea turtles*

## ACTIVIDADES

**A. Comprensión.** Indique si estas oraciones son ciertas of falsas, según las páginas anteriores.

|  | C | F |
|---|---|---|
| 1. La preservación de lugares, animales y plantas es un fenómeno del siglo XX. | ☐ | ☐ |
| 2. El *U.S. Forest Service* es la organización que mantiene El Yunque en Puerto Rico. | ☐ | ☐ |
| 3. El nombre de las Islas Galápagos viene de las tortugas baulas que vuelven cada año a poner sus huevos allí. | ☐ | ☐ |
| 4. La protección de las Torres del Paine prohíbe el turismo. | ☐ | ☐ |
| 5. En la Sierra Nevada española, es posible esquiar y hacer *snowboard*. | ☐ | ☐ |

**B. Conexiones.** En parejas, contesten las preguntas.

1. ¿A Uds. les gusta visitar los parques nacionales? ¿Cuáles son sus favoritos y por qué?
2. Escojan un lugar presentado en esta sección y compárenlo con un lugar de su país. ¿Cuáles son algunas semejanzas entre los dos lugares? ¿Cuáles son algunas diferencias?

**C. A investigar más.** Escoja *uno* de estos lugares y prepare un folleto (*brochure*) turístico para atraer a más turistas a ese lugar. Use el Internet o la biblioteca para encontrar por lo menos tres datos interesantes que no se presentan en las páginas anteriores. Debe incluir fotos o dibujos para darle un elemento visual al folleto. ¡Sea creativo/a!

1. El Yunque
2. el Parque Nacional Tortuguero
3. el Parque Nacional Torres del Paine
4. las Islas Galápagos
5. la Sierra Nevada española

**D. Temas de discusión.** En grupos pequeños, comenten *uno* de estos temas y escriban algunas conclusiones breves en español. Luego, compartan sus conclusiones con la clase.

1. los aspectos positivos y negativos de los parques nacionales como instituciones gubernamentales
2. si la preservación de las maravillas naturales del mundo es un asunto (*matter*) de suma (*utmost*) importancia o no

## LA SIERRA NEVADA

La Sierra Nevada es una cordillera en el sureste de España y forma parte del Parque Nacional Sierra Nevada. Este lugar es famoso por los deportes de invierno que se puede hacer allí y por la biodiversidad de su ecosistema. En América, hay cordilleras del mismo nombre en Argentina y los Estados Unidos y un parque nacional en Venezuela que se llama Sierra Nevada también.

## ASÍ SE DICE

el bosque = la arboleda, la selva

el campo = el llano, la llanura, la pampa, el prado, la pradera

la cascada = la catarata, el salto, el torrente

la cordillera = la cadena, la serranía, la sierra

el lago = el embalse, la laguna

la montaña = el macizo, la mesa, el monte, el pico

el río = el arroyo, el riachuelo, el tributario

## LAS ISLAS GALÁPAGOS

Las Islas Galápagos, un archipiélago[a] y provincia de Ecuador, son un parque nacional y reserva marina. Las islas son muy conocidas por las tortugas terrestres[b] gigantes —o galápagos— y por su variedad de animales y aves únicos. Las islas también influyeron mucho en la obra *El origen de las especies* de Charles Darwin.

[a]*archipelago, chain of islands*   [b]*land*

# Entrada cultural

## Los países andinos: Bolivia, Colombia, Ecuador y Perú

Cultures

El Rodadero, Santa Marta, Colombia

La cosecha (harvest) de algodón, en Perú

**Una boliviana con su sombrero hongo (bowler hat)**

Los países andinos son aquellos que, por su posición geográfica, están en contacto directo con la cordillera de los Andes, el sistema montañoso más largo del mundo. Los Andes se extienden desde Venezuela hasta el sur del continente, y sirven de frontera natural entre Chile y Argentina hasta llegar al Océano Antártico. Venezuela, Colombia, Ecuador, Perú y Bolivia componen la Comunidad Andina. Estos países tienen en común muchos aspectos culturales, aunque conservan características individuales debido a las influencias culturales de otras comunidades de esta región. Por ejemplo, Venezuela y Colombia también comparten mucho con el Caribe. Por su parte, Argentina y Chile también poseen gran riqueza cultural y natural en sus zonas andinas. En resumen, las fronteras políticas no reflejan necesariamente las fronteras geográficas o culturales. Por eso algunos países pertenecen a más de una región.

En los países andinos hay un marcado contraste entre la vida de la costa y la vida de las montañas. La cordillera es como una gran pared que complica las comunicaciones dentro de los países y es por eso que la manera de vivir y las costumbres dependen de la zona del país. Este tipo de geografía también hace que haya[a] climas variados, con gran diversidad en la flora y la fauna y en la producción agrícola.

Cada país tiene productos representativos: Colombia es famosa por su exquisito café; Perú produce caña de azúcar y algodón; Bolivia es muy rica en gas natural, estaño y cobre;[b] Ecuador exporta bananas y petróleo junto con Venezuela, que es uno de los países productores de petróleo más importantes del mundo. A pesar de[c] esta abundancia de recursos naturales, existen grandes problemas económicos y sociales, resultado de una injusta distribución de la riqueza y de numerosos conflictos políticos.

Los países andinos poseen también una enorme riqueza cultural debido a los grandes contrastes en su variedad étnica. Los indígenas de cada región, especialmente los quechuas y los descendientes de europeos y africanos componen la diversa población del mundo andino. Esta variedad observa en diferentes modos de vivir, en la música y numerosos instrumentos musicales nativos, en la ropa y productos textiles y en las celebraciones y festividades.

[a]*there are*  [b]estaño... *tin and copper*  [c]A... *In spite of*

# Los parques nacionales

Hay muchos ejemplos de parques nacionales en el mundo hispano. En ellos se preservan especies de plantas, animales y lugares de interés geológico, histórico y visual. También permiten al público disfrutar de[a] estas maravillas naturales. La idea de este tipo de reserva es muy antigua. De hecho,[b] antes de la llegada de los españoles a América, el emperador azteca Moctezuma II había creado[c] reservas botánicas y zoológicas.

[a]disfrutar... *to enjoy* [b]De... *In fact* [c]había... *had created*

**LAS TORRES[a] DEL PAINE**

El Parque Nacional Torres del Paine es un lugar famoso y pintoresco en el sur de Chile. En este parque hay montañas altas, glaciares, ríos y lagos. Sus senderos y montañas hacen de él un lugar especial para el alpinismo y el turismo. En este parque son famosos los Cuernos[b] del Paine, unas torres inmensas de granito.

[a]*Towers* [b]*Horns*

# ¡Salgamos a explorar!

*En la Cordillera (Mountain Range) Blanca, cerca de Huaraz, Perú*

1. ¿Cuándo fue la última vez que Ud. viajó en avión? ¿Adónde fue? ¿Qué hizo allí?

2. ¿Qué planes tiene para las próximas vacaciones? ¿Piensa viajar a alguna parte (*somewhere*) o quedarse aquí? Si va a viajar, ¿adónde va?

connect™
**|SPANISH**
www.connectspanish.com

## Vocabulario del tema

### En el aeropuerto

① hacer (*irreg.*) una reservación

Eduardo

Vuelo 301 a Barranquilla

el maletero ②

el mostrador

③ pasar por el control de seguridad

④

Salida 23

embarcar (qu) en el avión

revisar el equipaje

la tarjeta de embarque

el maletín

⑤ la pasajera

el pasajero

la azafata

recoger (j) el equipaje

la maleta

⑥

pasar por la aduana

el pasaporte

ADUANA

# Los viajes

| | |
|---|---|
| bajarse (de) | to get off (of) (*a vehicle*) |
| facturar el equipaje | to check luggage |
| hacer (*irreg.*) cola | to stand in line |
| hacer escalas | to make stops (*layover*) |
| hacer las maletas | to pack one's suitcase(s) |
| pasar por inmigración | to pass through immigration |
| subir (a) | to get on/in (*a vehicle*) |
| volar (ue) | to fly |
| | |
| la aduana | customs |
| el asiento (de pasillo/ventanilla) | (aisle/window) seat |
| el billete | ticket (*Sp.*) |
| el boleto | ticket (*L.A.*) |
| el cheque de viajero | traveler's check |
| la clase económica | coach (class) |
| el crucero | cruise (ship) |
| el destino | destination |
| el equipaje | luggage |
| el/la extranjero/a | foreigner; *m.* abroad |
| la primera clase | first class |
| el reclamo de equipaje | baggage claim |
| la sala de espera | waiting room |
| la salida | departure; gate |
| el viaje | trip |
|   de ida |   one-way trip |
|   de ida y vuelta |   round trip |
| el visado | visa |
| el vuelo | flight |
| | |
| de viaje | on a trip |

**Cognados:** la inmigración, el/la turista

## ACTIVIDADES

**A.** Identificaciones

**PASO 1.** Indique si las palabras se refieren a una persona (**P**), a un artículo para viajar (**A**) o a un lugar (**L**).

| | P | A | L |
|---|---|---|---|
| **1.** el destino | ☐ | ☐ | ☐ |
| **2.** el extranjero | ☐ | ☐ | ☐ |
| **3.** el mostrador | ☐ | ☐ | ☐ |
| **4.** la pasajera | ☐ | ☐ | ☐ |
| **5.** la aduana | ☐ | ☐ | ☐ |
| **6.** el visado | ☐ | ☐ | ☐ |
| **7.** el boleto | ☐ | ☐ | ☐ |
| **8.** el maletero | ☐ | ☐ | ☐ |
| **9.** la maleta | ☐ | ☐ | ☐ |
| **10.** el reclamo de equipaje | ☐ | ☐ | ☐ |

**PASO 2.** En parejas, túrnense para dar una definición de una palabra del **Paso 1**, sin decir la palabra. Su compañero/a de clase debe adivinar la palabra definida.

Communication

**B.** Voy de viaje.

**PASO 1.** Empareje las oraciones de la columna A con la frase más lógica de la columna B. ¡**OJO**! Puede haber más de una respuesta, y algunas respuestas se repiten.

**A**

1. Hago las maletas _____.
2. Hago las reservaciones _____.
3. Facturo mi maleta _____.
4. Hacemos cola _____.
5. Hacemos escalas _____.
6. Saco la tarjeta de embarque _____.
7. Revisan mi equipaje _____.
8. Esperamos a embarcar en el avión _____.

**B**

a. en el control de seguridad
b. en la sala de espera
c. en el mostrador
d. en el avión
e. en casa
f. en la aduana
g. con el agente de viajes
h. en el Internet

**PASO 2.** En parejas, pongan las oraciones del **Paso 1** en orden cronológico.

**C.** Situaciones. En parejas, denles una buena sugerencia a estas personas.

**MODELO** Quiero hacer una reservación para un vuelo a Miami, pero no tengo computadora. → Ud. debe ir a una agencia de viajes.

1. Mi prima se casa en España y quiero ir a la boda, pero tengo miedo de viajar en avión.
2. Quiero ir a Nueva York para visitar a mis amigas, pero no tengo coche y tengo poco dinero.
3. Acabo de bajar del avión y necesito recoger mis maletas.
4. Quiero hacer un viaje romántico con mi esposa, pero no quiero preocuparme por las comidas, ni por el transporte… ni nada.
5. Necesito facturar mi equipaje antes de embarcar en el avión.
6. Vamos a hacer un viaje a India y China con los hijos y no estamos seguros de qué documentos vamos a necesitar.
7. Mi hija va a viajar a Perú para hacer un semestre de estudios en el extranjero. Va a necesitar dinero durante su estadía (*stay*) pero no quiero darle una tarjeta de crédito.
8. ¿Adónde debo ir después de llegar al aeropuerto en Ecuador?

**D.** Su último viaje

**PASO 1.** Describa el último viaje que Ud. hizo. Use las preguntas como guía.

1. ¿Adónde viajó Ud.?
2. ¿Cuándo fue?
3. ¿Con quién(es) hizo el viaje?
4. ¿Cómo viajó?
5. ¿Por cuánto tiempo estuvo de viaje?

**PASO 2.** En parejas, describan su último viaje.

## Nota cultural

Cultures

### VIAJAR A ECUADOR

*Un piquero de patas azules, en las Islas Galápagos*

Los precios en Ecuador se encuentran entre los más bajos de Latinoamérica, lo que convierte a este país en un destino turístico muy atractivo para los bolsillos[a] más pequeños. Los visitantes de casi todo el mundo pueden permanecer en Ecuador por un máximo de noventa días por año sin necesidad de visado. Además, desde el año 2000, el dólar estadounidense es la moneda[b] oficial del país. Los viajeros que no disponen de mucho dinero pueden disfrutar del centro histórico de Quito, las playas de Guayaquil o la biodiversidad de las Islas Galápagos con sólo unos veinte dólares al día.

Otra curiosidad es que Ecuador tiene un doble sistema de precios mediante el cual[c] los extranjeros pagan mucho más que los ecuatorianos por algunos servicios, principalmente el transporte y los hoteles más exclusivos. Esta regulación se conoce como el «impuesto gringo» y se puede evitar, alojándose[d] en hoteles económicos y tomando autobuses en lugar de trenes o aviones.

---

[a]*budgets*  [b]*currency*  [c]mediante... *through which*  [d]se... *it can be avoided by staying*

PREGUNTAS  En parejas, contesten las preguntas. Después, compartan sus ideas con la clase.

1. ¿Por qué es Ecuador un destino turístico atractivo? Mencione tres de las razones, según el texto.
2. ¿Qué es el «impuesto gringo»? ¿Qué servicios implementan este tipo de impuesto?

Talking About What
Has Happened
Recently

## 10.1 Present Perfect

**GRAMÁTICA EN CONTEXTO**

El monumento Mitad del Mundo,
Ecuador

### Un viaje especial

Virginia **ha viajado** mucho porque escribe guías turísticas. **Ha escrito** guías sobre más de cien lugares. **Ha planeado** un viaje a Ecuador y este viaje es especial por dos razones. Primero, nunca **ha estado** en el ecuador, o sea, la línea imaginaria que divide los hemisferios norte y sur de la Tierra. Segundo, nunca **ha hecho** un viaje tan largo con su hijo, Seve. En este momento, Seve está quejándose porque **se ha cansado** de hacer cola.

SEVE:    ¡Otra cola! ¿Cuántas colas **hemos hecho** en este viaje, mamá?

VIRGINIA:    Ay, no te quejes tanto, mi hijo. Esto es normal y en realidad no **hemos tenido** que esperar demasiado.

SEVE:    ¡Huy, mamá! **Te has acostumbrado** porque **has viajado** mucho. Tienes mucha paciencia con las colas, el control de seguridad y la aduana.

VIRGINIA:    Pero nunca **he hecho** un viaje al Ecuador. Por eso, es muy interesante para mí, especialmente porque lo estoy haciendo contigo, querido. Y mañana, vamos a la Mitad del Mundo.

Comprensión.  ¿Cierto o falso?

|  |  | C | F |
|---|---|---|---|
| **1.** | Seve ha viajado mucho. | ☐ | ☐ |
| **2.** | Virginia nunca ha ido a Ecuador. | ☐ | ☐ |
| **3.** | Virginia ha pasado por muchas aduanas. | ☐ | ☐ |
| **4.** | Seve no se ha quejado hoy. | ☐ | ☐ |
| **5.** | Virginia ha escrito mucho sobre otros países. | ☐ | ☐ |

GRAMÁTICA EN CONTEXTO *A Special Trip / Virginia has traveled a lot because she writes travel guides. She has written guides about more than a hundred places. She has planned a trip to Ecuador and this trip is special for two reasons. First, she has never been to the equator, that is, the imaginary line that divides the northern and southern hemispheres of the Earth. Second, she has never made such a long trip with her son, Seve. At this moment, Seve is complaining because he has gotten tired of standing in line. / **SEVE:** Another line! How many lines have we stood in on this trip, Mom? / **VIRGINIA:** Oh, don't complain so much, son. This is normal and we really haven't had to wait too much. / **SEVE:** Ghee wiz, Mom! You have gotten used to it, because you've traveled a lot. You have a lot of patience for lines, security checks, and customs. / **VIRGINIA:** But I've never taken a trip to Ecuador. That's why, it's very interesting for me, especially because I'm taking it with you, my dear. And tomorrow, we're going to the Middle of the World.*

**A.** The *present perfect* is a compound tense in both Spanish and English. Compound tenses include two parts: an *auxiliary verb* and a *past participle*. In Spanish, the verb **haber** serves as the auxiliary verb and is conjugated in the present tense to form the first element of the present perfect. The past participle of regular verbs is formed by removing the infinitive ending (-**ar**, -**er**, or -**ir**) and adding -**ado** for -**ar** verbs and -**ido** for -**er** and -**ir** verbs.

PRESENT PERFECT OF REGULAR VERBS

| he | | |
|----|---|---|
| has | | estudiado |
| ha | + | comido |
| hemos | | vivido |
| habéis | | |
| han | | |

**B.** Several verbs have irregular past participles.

IRREGULAR PAST PARTICIPLES

| | | |
|---|---|---|
| abrir | → | abierto |
| cubrir | → | cubierto |
| decir | → | dicho |
| describir | → | descrito |
| descubrir | → | descubierto |
| devolver | → | devuelto |
| escribir | → | escrito |
| hacer | → | hecho |
| imprimir | → | impreso |
| morir | → | muerto |
| poner | → | puesto |
| resolver | → | resuelto |
| romper | → | roto |
| ver | → | visto |
| volver | → | vuelto |

**C.** The present perfect is used to talk about actions that occurred in the past but that continue to affect the present. The words and phrases **alguna vez, nunca, ya, hasta ahora, recientemente, todavía,** and **últimamente** are frequently used in conjunction with the present perfect.

—¿Ya **has hecho** las reservaciones?  
*Have you already made the reservations?*

—Todavía no, pero sí **he comprado** los billetes de avión.  
*Not yet, but I have bought the airplane tickets.*

Últimamente **han ido** a muchas bodas.  
*Lately they've gone to a lot of weddings.*

**D.** The **haber** and the *past participle* are never separated. If a sentence is negative or if a sentence contains pronouns, the negative element and the pronouns are placed before the auxiliary verb.

—¿Nunca **has visitado** Perú?　　　*You've never visited Peru?*
—Sí, lo **he visitado** varias veces.　*Yes, I've visited it several times.*
—¿**Han visto** Uds. los Andes　　　*Have you ever seen the Andes?*
　alguna vez?
—No, nunca los **hemos visto**.　　　*No, we've never seen them.*

## Nota comunicativa

**Acabar de** + *inf.*

If you want to express *to have just* (*done something*), use **acabar de** + *inf.* with **acabar** conjugated in the present tense.

**Acabamos de asistir** a un festival　　*We have just been to an Andean*
　de música andina.　　　　　　　　*music festival.*
—¿Qué haces aquí? Yo pensaba que　*What are you doing here? I*
　estabas de vacaciones.　　　　　　*thought you were on vacation.*
—**Acabo de regresar** hoy.　　　　　*I just returned today.*

### ACTIVIDADES

**A. Este año.** Complete las oraciones para describir lo que Ud. y otras personas han hecho este año.

1. He leído _____.
2. Mis amigos y yo hemos visto _____.
3. He comido mucho/a _____.
4. Mis profesores han explicado _____.
5. Mi mejor amigo/a me ha dicho _____.
6. He hecho _____.
7. Mis amigos y yo hemos ido a _____.
8. Afortunadamente, he terminado _____.

**B. Mi viaje.** Complete las oraciones con el presente perfecto de los verbos entre paréntesis para describir lo que Ramón y Teresa han hecho (o no) hasta ahora durante su viaje por Sudamérica.

1. Ramón (**enfermarse**) de soroche (*altitude sickness*) dos veces.
2. Yo (**hablar**) mucho en español.
3. Ramón y yo (**visitar**) la Mitad del Mundo cerca de Quito.
4. Ramón (**comprar**) tres sombreros Panamá en Ecuador.
5. Ramón y yo (**viajar**) en tren a Machu Picchu.
6. Ramón y yo no (**ver**) el Lago Titicaca.
7. Nuestros amigos (**dar**) un paseo en balsa de totora en el Lago Titicaca.
8. ¡Ramón! ¿No encuentras las tarjetas de embarque? ¿(*Tú:* **Perderlas**)?

**C.** Entrevista: ¿Adónde ha viajado Ud.? Entreviste a un compañero / una compañera de clase con las preguntas. Luego, cambien de papel.

1. ¿Qué viajes has hecho durante el último año? ¿Qué lugares has visitado? ¿Con quién viajaste y cuándo hiciste los viajes?
2. ¿Cuántas veces has salido de este país? ¿Qué países has visitado en el extranjero?
3. ¿Cuántas veces has hecho un viaje largo en tren? ¿y en autobús? ¿Por qué viajaste en tren/autobús? ¿Adónde fuiste?
4. ¿Cuántas veces has perdido (*missed*) un vuelo? ¿Qué otros problemas has tenido durante un viaje? Por ejemplo, ¿has perdido tu pasaporte alguna vez?
5. ¿Qué excursiones has hecho en este estado / esta provincia?

**D.** Los caminos y puentes incas

**PASO 1.** Complete la conversación sobre la presentación de Julio. Cuando aparecen **por** y **para** entre paréntesis, escoja la preposición correcta. Dé la forma correcta de los verbos entre paréntesis. Dé el presente perfecto cuando un verbo aparece con *PP*. Cuando un verbo aparece con *P/I*, escoja entre el pretérito y el imperfecto y use la forma correcta.

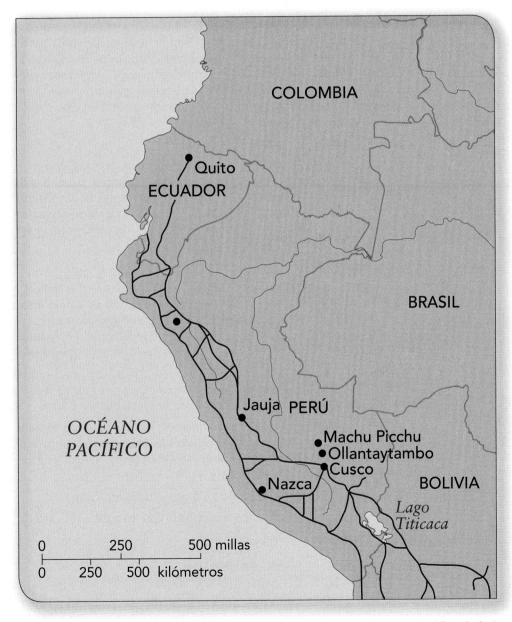

(Continúa.)

IRMA: ¿Qué tal, Julio? ¿Qué haces?

JULIO: Acabo de terminar el cartel para mi presentación sobre los incas (por/para[1]) la clase de antropología.

IRMA: Ah, sí, los incas, la gran civilización de Sudamérica, adoradores[a] del sol.

JULIO: Sí, David (PP: hacer[2]) una presentación sobre Inti, el dios del sol y varios estudiantes (PP: hablar[3]) de la política, del gobierno y de las guerras civiles.

IRMA: ¿Toda la clase tiene que hacer una presentación sobre los incas?

JULIO: Algunos. La profesora (PP: darnos[4]) opciones para los temas. Los estudiantes que (P/I: escoger[5]) un tema sobre los incas (PP: hacer[6]) sus presentaciones esta semana. Hoy por la tarde es mi presentación. Es la última.

IRMA: Pues, ¿qué tema sobre los incas (tú, PP: preparar[7])?

JULIO: Sobre los caminos y puentes. ¿Sabes que, aunque los incas nunca (P/I: inventar[8]) la rueda,[b] (P/I: tener[9]) más de 23.000 kilómetros de caminos? Muchos de ellos pavimentados.[c]

IRMA: 23.000 kilómetros en millas son…

JULIO: ¡Más de 15.000 millas! (Yo, PP: Incluir[10]) un mapa e imágenes de partes que todavía existen. Entonces, había dos caminos principales de orientación norte a sur: uno cerca de la costa y el otro (por/para[11]) los Andes. Por estos caminos, (P/I: transportar[12]) comida, fuerzas militares, todo. Pero no eran vías públicas. Sólo podías usar los caminos si trabajabas para el gobierno o tenías permiso especial.

IRMA: ¡Pero sin ruedas!

JULIO: (Por/Para[13]) transportar comida, (por/para[14]) ejemplo, (ellos, P/I: usar[15]) «trenes» de llamas. (Ellos, P/I: Tener[16]) también un sistema elaborado de comunicación. (Ellos, P/I: Mandar[17]) mensajes por medio de un sistema de cuerdas y nudos[d] que se llama quipu. Sus propios «mercurios» corrían en relevos[e] de una estación a otra (por/para[18]) unos diez kilómetros para llevar el mensaje al destinatario.

IRMA: ¡Qué complicado!

JULIO: ¡Y no (yo, PP: decirte[19]) ni la mitad[f]! En estos caminos (P/I: haber[20]) posadas donde los viajeros podían descansar, comer, dar de comer a sus animales y grandes almacenes[g] donde guardaban[h] provisiones (por/para[22]) 25.000 hombres. Los almacenes eran importantes (por/para[23]) los ejércitos que (P/I: usar[24]) estos caminos (por/para[25]) defender el imperio.

IRMA: Pero no (tú, PP: explicar[26]) cómo pudieron hacer caminos por los Andes. Son montañas peligrosas[i] y difíciles, con muchos precipicios[j] y ríos.

JULIO: Los incas (P/I: diseñar[27]) tres tipos de puentes. Los puentes suspendidos cruzaban cañones y valles estrechos.[k] A veces, usaban cestos con poleas[l] en estas situaciones. (Por/Para[28]) cruzar ríos y arroyos,[m] tenían puentes pontón con balsas.[n]

IRMA: ¡En cinco minutos (yo, PP: aprender[29]) mucho hablando contigo!

JULIO: Y yo (PP: practicar[30]) para mi presentación. ¿Qué te parece mi cartel[ñ]?

IRMA: ¡Perfecto! ¡Bien hecho, Julio!

---

[a]worshippers  [b]wheel  [c]paved  [d]cuerdas… ropes and knots  [e]relays  [f]ni… the half of it  [g]storehouses
[h]would store  [i]dangerous  [j]cliffs  [k]narrow  [l]cestos… baskets with pullies  [m]streams  [n]rafts  [ñ]poster

**PASO 2.** Indique si las oraciones son ciertas (**C**) o falsas (**F**), según el **Paso 1.**

|  | C | F |
|---|---|---|
| **1.** Julio acaba de dar su presentación a la clase. | ☐ | ☐ |
| **2.** Todos los estudiantes han hecho presentaciones sobre los incas. | ☐ | ☐ |
| **3.** David ha hecho su presentación sobre el dios Inti de la cultura inca. | ☐ | ☐ |
| **4.** Julio ha terminado su cartel, pero todavía no ha hecho su presentación. | ☐ | ☐ |
| **5.** Los caminos incas eran públicos. | ☐ | ☐ |
| **6.** Los caminos se extendían por unas 23.000 millas. | ☐ | ☐ |
| **7.** Para cruzar ríos y arroyos, los incas tenían puentes pontón. | ☐ | ☐ |
| **8.** Los quipus eran un tipo de puente para cruzar precipicios peligrosos. | ☐ | ☐ |

**PASO 3.** En parejas, corrijan las oraciones falsas del **Paso 2.** Luego, escriban tres oraciones más, algunas de ellas falsas. Uds. van a leer sus oraciones a la clase y los otros estudiantes van a decir si son ciertas o falsas.

Communication

*En el Camino Inca, cerca de Cusco, Perú*

# Nota interdisciplinaria

Connections

## LENGUAS EXTRANJERAS: EL QUECHUA

En los países andinos, el español es el idioma de más extensión, pero no es el único. El quechua, lengua que tiene sus raíces en las culturas indígenas de los Andes, tiene hoy en día, en Bolivia y Perú, el estatus de lengua oficial, junto con el español, además de que lo hablan millones de habitantes de Ecuador y de la zona andina de Argentina, Chile y Colombia. De hecho, un gran número de personas son bilingües: hablan quechua y español, aunque el español es generalmente su segundo idioma. Y para muchos peruanos y bolivianos, el quechua es el único idioma que hablan.

En español hay muchas palabras que vienen del quechua, lo cual[a] refleja la fusión cultural y lingüística entre ambos continentes. Por ejemplo, **chompa**[b] y **choclo**[c] son dos de esas palabras, también se nota su influencia en el inglés. ¿Sabía Ud. que las palabras inglesas *condor, llama, puma* y *quinine* tienen raíces en el quechua?

A continuación se presenta una lista de palabras y frases en quechua traducidas al español. Observe que muchos de los nombres de lugares de la región andina son de origen quechua y hacen alusión a la naturaleza y la geografía.

---

### Nombres de lugares en quechua

| | | |
|---|---|---|
| **Acomayo** | = | Llanura (*Plain*) de arena |
| **Arequipa** | = | Detrás del volcán |
| **Cajamarca** | = | Región de rocas |
| **Cochamarca** | = | Región de lagunas |
| **Pariamarca** | = | Región de flamencos |
| **Piscobamba** | = | Llanura de aves |
| **Yurajmayo** | = | Río blanco |

---

[a]lo... *which*   [b]*suéter*   [c]corn(cob)

PREGUNTAS En parejas, contesten las preguntas. Después, compartan sus ideas con la clase.

1. ¿Cuál es la situación lingüística en los países andinos? ¿Cuál es la lengua que más se habla en la zona de los Andes? ¿Qué comunidades son bilingües? ¿En qué comunidades no se habla español?
2. ¿Cuáles son algunas palabras en inglés que vienen de otra lengua? ¿De qué lengua vienen?
3. ¿Hay comunidades bilingües en este país? ¿Dónde están? ¿Qué idiomas hablan las personas que viven allí?

## 10.2 Hace + *time* + que

**GRAMÁTICA EN CONTEXTO**

### Un viaje a Perú

Antonio y su esposa Nuria van a Perú de vacaciones. Antonio **hizo** un viaje a Perú **hace diez años**, cuando era estudiante, y quería volver con Nuria porque sabe que le van a encantar todas las atracciones culturales. Pero **hace muchas horas que salieron** de México, y Nuria está impaciente porque nunca ha hecho un viaje tan largo.

NURIA: ¿Qué pasa, amor? **Hace casi una hora que esperamos** aquí.

ANTONIO: Apenas **hace veinte minutos que llegamos** a la aduana. Pero esto tarda un poco porque revisan el equipaje de todos. Como **hace sólo unas semanas que tuvieron** ese problema en el aeropuerto de Madrid, todos los aeropuertos toman precauciones especiales.

NURIA: Parece que nunca vamos a llegar a Lima.

ANTONIO: Pero, querida,... ya estamos en Lima. Pronto vamos a estar en nuestro hotel cerca de la Plaza de Armas. Y en dos días visitamos Cusco y el Valle Sagrado de los Incas. ¡**Quiero** compartir estas maravillas contigo **desde hace tanto tiempo**!

*La Plaza de Armas, en Lima*

**Comprensión.** ¿Quién lo diría (*would say it*)? ¿Antonio (**A**) o Nuria (**N**) o los dos (**D**)?

| | A | N | D |
|---|---|---|---|
| 1. Hace una hora que hacemos cola. | ☐ | ☐ | ☐ |
| 2. Hace un día que salí de México. | ☐ | ☐ | ☐ |
| 3. Hace diez años que estuve en Lima. | ☐ | ☐ | ☐ |
| 4. No hace mucho tiempo que llegamos a Lima. | ☐ | ☐ | ☐ |

English uses the present perfect to express that an action has been in progress for a specific length of time.

> ***We have been*** *in line for three hours.*
> ***He has wanted*** *to go to Bolivia for five years.*

However, to express similar ideas, standard Spanish requires a special construction with the verb **hacer.**

| | |
|---|---|
| **Hace** tres horas **que hacemos** cola. | *We have been standing in line for three hours.* |
| **Hace** cinco años que **quiere** ir a Bolivia. | *He has wanted to go to Bolivia for five years.* |

This construction is commonly referred to as the **hace** + *time* + **que** construction and it has a few variations, depending on the meaning you want to express.

---

**GRAMÁTICA EN CONTEXTO** / ***A Trip to Peru*** / *Antonio and his wife Nuria are going to Peru on vacation. Antonio took a trip to Peru ten years ago, when he was a student, and he wanted to return with Nuria because he knows she will love all the cultural attractions. But they left Mexico several hours ago, and Nuria is impatient because she has never taken such a long trip. /* **NURIA:** *What's happening, darling? We've been waiting here for an hour. /* **ANTONIO:** *It's barely been twenty minutes since we got to customs. But this takes awhile because they inspect everyone's luggage. Since it's only been a few weeks since they had that problem in the Madrid airport, all airports are taking special precautions. /* **NURIA:** *It seems like we're never going to get to Lima. /* **ANTONIO:** *But, my dear . . . We're already in Lima. Soon we'll be at our hotel close to the Plaza de Armas. And in two days, we're going to Cuzco and the Sacred Valley of the Incas. I have wanted to share these wonders with you for so long!*

**A.** Use the following structure with a present tense verb to express how long something has been in progress. (The action started in the past and is still going on.)

> **Hace** + *length of time* + **que** + *verb in present tense*

**Hace** dos años **que** vivo en Quito.
**Hace** mucho (tiempo) **que** esperamos el avión. Todavía no ha llegado.

*I have lived in Quito for two years.*
*We've waited a long time for the plane. It still hasn't arrived.*

You can switch the order of the clauses by removing the **que** and inserting **desde.**

> *verb in present tense* + **desde hace** + *length of time*

Vivo en Quito desde **hace** dos años.
Esperamos el avión desde **hace** mucho (tiempo). Todavía no ha llegado.

*I have lived in Quito for two years.*
*We've waited a long time for the plane. It still hasn't arrived.*

To ask (for) how long someone has been doing something, use the following construction. Note that the verb is in the present tense.

**¿Cuánto tiempo hace que** quieren viajar a Bolivia?

*How long have you wanted to travel to Bolivia?*

**B.** To express how long it's been since something (has) happened, use the following construction. (The action is no longer in progress.) Note that the verb **hace** does not change.

> **Hace** + *length of time* + **que** + *verb in preterite*

**Hace** seis meses **que** fui a Bogotá.

**Hace** tres minutos **que** cancelaron el vuelo.

*It's been six months since I went to Bogotá.*
*It's been three minutes since they cancelled the flight.*

You can switch the order of the clauses by dropping **que.** In this case, the underlying meaning is the same, but the sentences translate better into English as *ago.*

> *verb in preterite* + **hace** + *length of time*

Fui a Bogotá **hace** seis meses.
Cancelaron el vuelo **hace** tres minutos.

*I went to Bogotá six months ago.*
*They cancelled the flight three minutes ago.*

To ask how long it's been since (or how long ago) someone did something, use the following construction. Note that the verb is in the preterite and that the verb **hace** does not change.

**¿Cuánto tiempo hace que** fueron al Lago Titicaca?

*How long has it been since you went to Lake Titicaca? (How long ago did you go to Lake Titicaca?)*

## ACTIVIDADES

**A.** ¿Cuánto tiempo hace? Complete las oraciones con información personal verdadera. Si Ud. no ha hecho alguna de las cosas, conteste: «No he hecho eso».

1. Hace _____ meses/años que estudio español.
2. Hace _____ semanas/meses/años que vivo en _____.
3. No veo a mis padres desde hace _____.
4. Tengo pasaporte desde hace _____.
5. Hace _____ horas que me desperté.
6. Hace _____ que hice un viaje en avión.
7. Subí a un autobús hace _____.
8. Salí de la casa de mis padres hace _____.

**B.** Rubén y Rebeca. Use su imaginación para formar oraciones sobre las experiencias de Rubén y Rebeca. **¡OJO!** Tiene que añadir el nombre correcto. Siga el modelo.

MODELO  Hace casi seis horas que Rubén está en la oficina hoy.

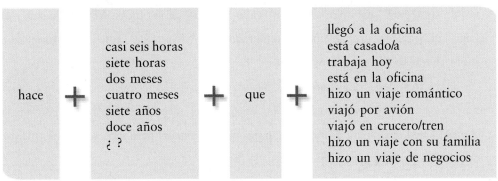

hace + 
casi seis horas
siete horas
dos meses
cuatro meses
siete años
doce años
¿ ?
+ que +
llegó a la oficina
está casado/a
trabaja hoy
está en la oficina
hizo un viaje romántico
viajó por avión
viajó en crucero/tren
hizo un viaje con su familia
hizo un viaje de negocios

**C.** Los viajes de Rubén y Rebeca. En parejas, contesten las preguntas sobre los viajes de Rubén y Rebeca según la actividad B. Deben inventar detalles.

1. ¿Cuánto tiempo hace que Rubén hizo un viaje romántico? ¿Adónde fue? ¿Con quién fue? ¿Por cuánto tiempo fueron?
2. ¿Cuánto tiempo hace que Rebeca hizo un viaje en avión? ¿Fue un viaje romántico? ¿Cómo viajó? ¿Adónde fue? ¿Qué hizo allí?
3. ¿Cuánto tiempo hace que Rubén hizo un viaje con sus hijos? ¿Qué tipo de viaje hizo? ¿Cómo lo pasó?
4. ¿Cuánto tiempo hace que Rebeca hizo un viaje en tren? ¿Qué tipo de viaje hizo? ¿Con quién fue? ¿Adónde fueron?

**D.** PeruRail

**PASO 1.** Complete el artículo sobre los trenes de PeruRail con las palabras correctas entre paréntesis.

*El tren Hiram Bingham, en Ollantaytambo*

Si Ud. piensa viajar a Perú, seguramente hay varios lugares interesantes que desea visitar, (por/para[1]) ejemplo: Cusco, el Valle Sagrado de los Incas, Machu Picchu y el Lago Titicaca. Pero, probablemente no ha (encontrar/encontrado[2]) suficiente información sobre el transporte entre esos lugares.

Hace tres meses que (hace/hice[3]) un viaje a Perú. Decidí aventurarme un poco y no (hice/hacía[4]) reservaciones para las excursiones antes de llegar. Me quedé[a] en la capital, Lima, (por/para[5]) unos días para hablar con los peruanos sobre las (mejor/mejores[6]) opciones para viajar dentro del país.

[a]Me... *I stayed*

Perú tiene muchas carreteras, pero si Ud. no está (acostumbrar/acostumbrado[7]) a los diferentes terrenos que necesita cruzar, va a ser un viaje estresante y difícil en coche. Aún los limeños[b] optan por el transporte público (por/para[8]) algunas excursiones.

La última vez que fui a Sudamérica, hice algunas excursiones (típico/típicas[9]), incluso el viaje a Machu Picchu (por/para[10]) autobús. ¡Qué placer[c] fue descubrir que a principios de este siglo, PeruRail renovó varias líneas entre los destinos más populares! (Hace/Hacen[11]) unos años que consiguieron unos vagones[d] clásicos de Singapur y (los/las[12]) renovaron al estilo de los años 20, con toques lujosos[e] y divertidos. Estas líneas turísticas incluyen cuatro servicios ferroviarios[f] distintos: el Backpacker, el Vistadome, el Andean Explorer y el Hiram Bingham. Las rutas incluyen viajes (entre/enfrente de[13]) Cusco y Machu Picchu, el Valle Sagrado (Ollantaytambo) y Machu Picchu, y Cusco y el Lago Titicaca (Puno). La última ruta, que se hace en el Andean Explorer, pasa (por/para[14]) el punto ferroviario más alto del mundo, después de Tibet: La Raya, entre Cusco y el Lago Titicaca. Estas líneas también (son/están[15]) la vía más rápida para llegar a Machu Picchu.

(Hace/Hacen[16]) casi 150 años que PeruRail (opera/operó[17]) trenes en Perú, pero estas líneas lujosas son nuevas y atraen a muchos turistas. La línea más económica es el Backpacker, y las más lujosas son el Andean Explorer y el Hiram Bingham. Si hace mucho tiempo (que/como[18]) Ud. no hace un viaje en tren y desea tener una experiencia especial, (busque/busca[19]) más información sobre los trenes de PeruRail. Es una experiencia romántica, pintoresca y nostálgica.

[b]personas de Lima, Perú  [c]*pleasure*  [d]*coaches*  [e]toques... *luxurious touches*  [f]*railway*

**PASO 2.**   Dé información, según el **Paso 1.**
1. cuatro destinos populares de Perú
2. los cuatro trenes turísticos de PeruRail
3. tres rutas de los trenes de PeruRail
4. el punto más alto de trenes de Sudamérica
5. el tren más económico de PeruRail
6. la capital de Perú y el adjetivo por el que se conocen sus habitantes

**PASO 3.**   En parejas, escojan uno de los trenes y rutas de PeruRail. Preparen una presentación, con un mapa de la ruta y una descripción del tren y de los lugares que se puede visitar en ese tren.

Communication

# Palabra escrita

## A comenzar

Communication

> **Exploring Your Ideas Through Narration.** A narrative text tells a story, fictional or experiential. Unlike strictly descriptive pieces of writing, narrative texts include details about the background descriptions that set the context, describe the characters, and so on and the specific actions that move a storyline along. When a story is narrated in the past, you should be aware of these two distinctions, because as you learned in **Capítulo 9,** Spanish uses different verb forms to express these elements: imperfect for descriptive background information, preterite for the specific actions that move the storyline along.

You are going to start the process of writing a brief composition that you will finalize in the **Palabra escrita: A finalizar** section of your *Manual de actividades*. The topic of this composition is **Un viaje.** The purpose of your composition will be to tell the reader about a significant trip that you took sometime in the past.

**A. Lluvia de ideas.** En parejas, hagan una lluvia de ideas sobre estas preguntas.

1. ¿Qué adjetivo han escogido Uds. para describir su viaje? ¿Por qué lo escogieron?
2. ¿Cuánto tiempo hace que hicieron ese viaje?
3. ¿Adónde y con quién(es) fueron?
4. ¿Cómo viajaron? ¿Fueron en tren? ¿en avión? ¿en carro? ¿Cómo fue el viaje? ¿largo? ¿difícil? ¿aburrido?
5. ¿Cómo era el lugar de destino cuando llegaron? (Descríbanlo.) ¿Qué tiempo hacía allí? ¿Qué planes tenían Uds.? ¿Qué iban a hacer? ¿Qué querían hacer?
6. ¿Qué hicieron allí? ¿Pasó algo? ¿Qué pasó?

**B. A organizar sus ideas.** Repase sus ideas y organícelas para escoger el enfoque de su composición. Haga dos listas: una lista de detalles descriptivos que puede incluir y otra lista de las acciones que desea narrar. Comparta su información con la clase y apunte otras ideas que se le ocurran durante el proceso.

**C. A escribir.** Ahora, haga el borrador de su composición con las ideas y la información que recopiló en las actividades A y B. **¡OJO!** Guarde bien su trabajo. Va a necesitarlo otra vez para la sección de **Palabra escrita: A finalizar** en el *Manual de actividades*.

## Fernando Botero

La calle, 1987

Al pintor y escultor Fernando Botero (1932– ) le gusta declarar que es el más colombiano de los artistas colombianos, y es uno de los artistas latino-americanos más conocidos. Es famoso por sus figuras gruesas,[a] tanto en su pintura como en su escultura. Esta redondez[b] se extiende más allá de[c] la figura humana. Sus animales, plantas, frutas y objetos inanimados también son redondos.[d] Sus obras incluyen naturalezas muertas[e] y paisajes, pero la mayoría de su obra se enfoca en retratos[f] de la figura humana. Muchos de sus retratos también son comentarios culturales, políticos, históricos o sociales.

En *La calle*, Botero muestra la vida diaria en Colombia. También es una escena de cualquier pueblo hispano. Como en otras obras, las figuras están desproporcionadas: puertas enormes, balcones pequeños y mujeres y hombres con cuerpos gruesos. Esta característica de la desproporción distingue la obra de Botero.

[a]*thick* [b]*roundness* [c]*más… beyond* [d]*round* [e]*naturalezas… still lifes* [f]*portraits*

# TEMA II: Las vacaciones
## Vocabulario del tema

### De vacaciones°

De… *On Vacation*

① el hotel de lujo

la recepción

el botones

el huésped

Maricarmen

la huéspeda

Antonio

② la cabaña rústica

Reserva Biológica la Neblina

③ hacer (*irreg.*) una excursión

Paco

Luis

Marcela

Lupe

Carlos

pasear en canoa

la mariposa

| | |
|---|---|
| alojarse<br>hospedarse | to stay (*in a hotel*) |
| quedarse | to stay (*in a place*) |
| recorrer | to travel around (*a town/city*) |
| registrarse | to check in |
| el alojamiento | lodging |
| la estadía | stay |
| la excursión | tour, daytrip |
| el/la gerente | manager |
| la habitación doble/sencilla | double/single room |
| la (tarjeta) postal | postcard |
| el recuerdo | souvenir |

Cognado: el hotel

## Los tipos de turismo

| | |
|---|---|
| el recorrido | tour; trip |
| las ruinas arqueológicas | archeological ruins |
| la ruta | route |
| la tirolina | zipline |
| acuático/a | water, aquatic |

Cognados: el agroturismo, el ecoturismo, la reserva biológica, el/la turista

## Otras palabras y expresiones

| | |
|---|---|
| disfrutar (de) | to enjoy |
| de lujo | luxury (*hotel*) |

**ACTIVIDADES**

**A.** Definiciones

**PASO 1.** Diga la palabra del **Vocabulario del tema,** según la definición.

1. Es hacer una pequeña excursión sobre el agua, típicamente en un lago o en un río.
2. Es la persona que está a cargo (*in charge*) de un hotel u oficina.
3. Es pasear por un sendero en el bosque o en las montañas.
4. Es un lugar adonde va la gente que quiere ser muy bien atendida (*taken care of*).
5. Es una región natural protegida por el gobierno.

**PASO 2.** En parejas, den definiciones de otras palabras del **Vocabulario del tema.** Una persona da la definición y otra adivina el significado. Luego, cambien de papel.

Communication

**B.** Un buen agente de viajes

**PASO 1.** En parejas, describan un plan de viaje para estas personas, de acuerdo con sus preferencias.

1. Héctor está jubilado y desea hacer un viaje especial de dos semanas con su esposa. Son muy activos para su edad, pero no practican deportes. A su esposa le encantan los museos y el teatro.
2. Carolina tiene 25 años y trabaja mucho. Aunque le gustan las actividades al aire libre, desea hacer un viaje cómodo, sin preocupaciones. Como no tiene novio y sus amigas no pueden ir con ella, va a viajar sola.
3. Susana y Wilbur tienen mucho interés en las civilizaciones precolombinas. Han ahorrado mucho dinero para hacer un viaje muy especial. No están en muy buenas condiciones físicas, pero les encanta ver sitios interesantes.
4. Carl y Pedro piensan pasar sus vacaciones de primavera en un lugar exótico. Les gustan los deportes y les encantan las actividades físicas y nuevas.

**PASO 2.** Comparen sus planes con los de otros estudiantes y escojan a los mejores agentes de viaje.

**C.** Una encuesta

**PASO 1.** Haga una encuesta entre sus compañeros de clase. Hágales las dos preguntas del modelo a por lo menos cinco estudiantes. Apunte sus respuestas en una tabla como la siguiente. **¡OJO!** La cuarta columna de la tabla es para el **Paso 2.**

MODELO  E1: ¿Cuál es tu actividad favorita durante las vacaciones?
          E2: Mi actividad favorita es tomar el sol.
          E1: ¿Qué actividad nunca te gusta hacer durante las vacaciones?
          E2: Nunca me gusta dar caminatas.

| ESTUDIANTE | FAVORITA | NUNCA | ¿SEDENTARIO O ACTIVO? |
|---|---|---|---|
| Kay | tomar el sol | dar caminatas | |
| | | | |
| | | | |
| | | | |

**PASO 2.** Indique en la cuarta columna de su tabla si cada estudiante es sedentario o activo, según sus respuestas. Si no está claro, escriba: «No sé».

**PASO 3.** Comparen los resultados con toda la clase. Por lo general, ¿son activos o sedentarios los estudiantes de la clase cuando están de vacaciones?

**D.** Entrevista. Entreviste a un compañero / una compañera de clase con estas preguntas. Luego, cambien de papel.

1. ¿Qué viajes interesantes has hecho? ¿Qué actividades hiciste allí?
2. Cuando vas de vacaciones, ¿qué tipo de cosas compras? ¿Mandas tarjetas postales durante tus viajes? ¿Compras artesanías típicas como recuerdos? ¿Compras camisetas para tus amigos o familia?
3. ¿Qué es el ecoturismo?
4. ¿Qué tipo de turismo te interesa más? Explica.

# Nota cultural

## El ECOTURISMO

*El Parque Nacional Sama, Bolivia*

El ecoturismo es una forma de turismo que se enfoca en conservar los recursos naturales[a] y la cultura local. Latino-américa tiene muchas regiones naturales protegidas que se puede visitar, pero se pide al turista que ejerza[b] un «turismo responsable», es decir, que cause el menor impacto posible. La biodiversidad de los países andinos hace de esta región un lugar privilegiado para el turismo, pero también es un ambiente frágil que necesita conservarse con cuidado. El ecoturismo es una alternativa ideal para disfrutar de las maravillas naturales de los Andes y contribuir a su preservación.

Bolivia está entre los ocho países con mayor biodiversidad del mundo y cuenta con[c] treinta y una áreas protegidas. Sus numerosas rutas ecoturísticas permiten apreciar toda su diversidad, como el altiplano,[d] marcado por la Cordillera de los Andes y el Lago Titicaca; la Amazonia,[e] caracterizada por los bosques tropicales[f] y las sabanas.[g]

Los Grandes Parques Naturales de Bolivia son áreas especialmente diseñadas para la protección de la biodiversidad, pero al mismo tiempo permiten el ejercicio de deportes de aventura, el senderismo, la apreciación de la riqueza de fauna y flora, y el contacto con sus pobladores de origen aymará e inca, todo en equilibrio con el medioambiente.[h]

---

[a]recursos... *natural resources*   [b]*exercise*   [c]cuenta... *it has*   [d]*high plateau*   [e]*Amazon region*   [f]bosques... *rain forests*   [g]*plains*   [h]*environment*

**PREGUNTAS** En parejas, contesten las preguntas. Después, compartan sus ideas con la clase.

1. ¿Creen Uds. que los países andinos promocionan (*promote*) el ecoturismo? ¿Qué les ofrece Bolivia a los amantes del ecoturismo? ¿Qué actividades turísticas se pueden practicar allí?
2. ¿Han practicado el ecoturismo alguna vez? ¿cuándo? ¿dónde? ¿En qué actividades participaron Uds.?
3. ¿Existe el ecoturismo en la comunidad o en el país donde Uds. viven? ¿dónde? ¿Qué actividades se puede hacer allí?

### Telling Other People What You Want Them to Do

# 10.3 Introduction to the Subjunctive

**GRAMÁTICA EN CONTEXTO**

*Un perezoso, en el Parque Nacional Madidi*

### Nuestro viaje a Bolivia

[*Rogelio quiere que su amigo Fernando le explique algunos detalles del viaje que Marta y Fernando van a hacer a Bolivia.*]

**ROGELIO:** ¿Cuándo salen Marta y tú para Bolivia?

**FERNANDO:** Salimos a principios de febrero. Queremos llegar durante el verano y antes de los carnavales. Nuestros amigos allí **quieren que vayamos** al Carnaval de Oruro que es a finales de febrero.

**ROGELIO:** ¿Y se van a alojar con sus amigos durante todo el viaje?

**FERNANDO:** Ay, no. Aunque Justo y Clemencia **quieren que nos quedemos** con ellos el mes entero, queremos hacer varias excursiones arqueológicas y naturales. Durante las excursiones, queremos alojarnos en cabañas rústicas o alojamientos muy básicos.

**ROGELIO:** ¿Van a los parques nacionales?

**FERNANDO:** Por supuesto, vamos a Madidi y al Parque Nacional Noel Kempff Mercado, pero primero **quiero que visitemos** Ulla Ulla y el Lago Titicaca. Quiero conocer a un kallawaya, un curandero indígena.

**ROGELIO:** Bueno, **quiero que** me **manden** muchas tarjetas postales, **que saquen** muchas fotos y **que se diviertan** muchísimo. Un mes entero en Bolivia: ¡qué envidia les tengo!

Comprensión. ¿Quién lo dice? ¿Fernando (**F**), Rogelio (**R**) o uno de los amigos bolivianos (**B**)?

|  | F | R | B |
|---|---|---|---|
| **1.** Quiero que se queden con nosotros. | ☐ | ☐ | ☐ |
| **2.** Quiero que me explique sus prácticas médicas. | ☐ | ☐ | ☐ |
| **3.** Quiero que me escriban. | ☐ | ☐ | ☐ |
| **4.** Quiero que vean nuestro carnaval. | ☐ | ☐ | ☐ |
| **5.** Quiero que hagamos muchos recorridos interesantes. | ☐ | ☐ | ☐ |

GRAMÁTICA EN CONTEXTO / *Our Trip to Bolivia* / *Rogelio wants his friend Fernando to explain to him some details about the trip that Marta and Fernando are taking to Bolivia.* / *ROGELIO: When do you Marta and you leave for Bolivia?* / *FERNANDO: We leave at the beginning of February. We want to arrive during the summer and before the carnival celebrations. Our friends there want us to go to the Oruro Carnival that is at the end of February.* / *ROGELIO: And you're going to stay with your friends during the whole trip?* / *FERNANDO: Oh, no. Although Justo and Clemencia want us to stay with them the whole month, we want to make several archeological and nature day trips. During the trips, we want to stay in rustic cabins or very basic lodgings.* / *ROGELIO: Are you going to the national parks?* / *FERNANDO: Of course, we're going to Madidi and the Noel Kempff Mercado National Park, but first I want us to visit Ulla Ulla and Lake Titicaca. I want to meet a Kallawaya, an indigenous medicine man.* / *ROGELIO: Well, I want you to send me a lot of postcards, to take a lot of photos, and to have a great time. A whole month in Bolivia: I'm so jealous of you!*

One way to ask someone to do something, or to express a request or desire that another person do something, is to use the construction: **querer** + **que** + *present subjunctive.*

**Quiero que** me hagas un favor.
Mi madre **quiere que** mi hermano la lleve al mercado.

*I want you to do me a favor.*
*My mother wants my brother to take her to the market.*

You'll notice that the verbs in purple text are expressed in a form you may not have seen before. These verbs are conjugated in the present subjunctive. For now, all you need to remember is that when the first clause of a sentence contains the **querer que** structure, it will be followed by a clause with a verb or verbs in the present subjunctive.

**A.** You have already learned most of the present subjunctive forms as formal commands. (See **Gramática 6.3** [p. 203] to review formal commands.) Remember that these forms are based on the **yo** form of the present indicative but with the "opposite" vowel ending. This means that -**ar** verbs will have an -**e** in the present subjunctive endings and -**er** and -**ir** verbs will have an -**a** in the present subjunctive endings.

| -ar | |
|---|---|
| hablar → hablø | |
| hable | hablemos |
| hables | habléis |
| hable | hablen |

| -er | |
|---|---|
| comer → comø | |
| coma | comamos |
| comas | comáis |
| coma | coman |

| -ir | |
|---|---|
| vivir → vivø | |
| viva | vivamos |
| vivas | viváis |
| viva | vivan |

Mi esposa **quiere que** nos hospedemos en un hotel de lujo.
**¿Quieres que** te diga la verdad?
Luis, Sandra, **quiero que** piensen en lo que van a hacer durante las vacaciones.
Chicos, después del viaje, **quiero que** suban las maletas, **que** las vacíen y luego **que** les escriban una carta a sus tíos, agradeciéndoles por invitarnos a su casa.

*My wife wants us to stay in a luxury hotel.*
*Do you want me to tell you the truth?*
*Luis, Sandra, I want you to think about what you're going to do during vacation.*
*Kids, after the trip, I want you to take your bags upstairs, empty them, and then write a letter to your aunt and uncle, thanking them for inviting us to their house.*

**B.** The present subjunctive of stem changing verbs that end with -**ir** have an extra stem change in the **nosotros/as** and **vosotros/as** forms, in addition to the usual stem change in the other forms.

| servir (i, i) | |
|---|---|
| sirva | sirvamos |
| sirvas | sirváis |
| sirva | sirvan |

| dormir (ue, u) | |
|---|---|
| duerma | durmamos |
| duermas | durmáis |
| duerma | duerman |

| Nuestros abuelos **quieren que** nos divirtamos mucho. | *Our grandparents want us to have great time.* |
| Papá **quiere que** manejemos con cuidado. No **quiere que** muramos en algún accidente. | *Dad wants us to drive carefully. He doesn't want us to die in an accident.* |

**C.** There are only six irregular verbs in the present subjunctive. Note that the first letter of each verb spells out the acronym DISHES.

**dar** → dé, des, dé, demos, deis, den
**ir** → vaya, vayas, vaya, vayamos, vayáis, vayan
**saber** → sepa, sepas, sepa, sepamos, sepáis, sepan
**haber** → haya, hayas, haya,* hayamos, hayáis, hayan
**estar** → esté, estés, esté, estemos, estéis, estén
**ser** → sea, seas, sea, seamos, seáis, sean

| ¿Quieres hacer tirolina? Bueno, **quiero que** vayas tú primero. | *You want to zipline? OK, I want you to go first.* |
| No **quiero que** haya mucha gente en esa excursión porque quiero explorar las ruinas arqueológicas en paz. | *I don't want there to be a lot of people on that tour because I want to explore the archeological ruins in peace.* |

## ACTIVIDADES

**A. ¿Qué quieren?** Indique las oraciones que son ciertas para Ud.

1. ☐ Mis padres/hijos quieren que yo los visite más.
2. ☐ Mi mejor amigo/a quiere que vayamos al cine el fin de semana que viene.
3. ☐ Mis amigos quieren que yo salga todos los viernes a bailar.
4. ☐ Mi profesor(a) de español quiere que yo sepa las formas verbales de memoria.
5. ☐ Quiero que mis padres me den más dinero este semestre.
6. ☐ Quiero que mi novio/a me llame esta noche.
7. ☐ Quiero que mis amigos hagan una fiesta el fin de semana que viene.

**B. En el hotel.** Describa lo que quieren las personas, según los dibujos en la página siguiente. Use las palabras de la lista para formar dos oraciones para cada dibujo. Si quiere, puede inventar otras ideas.

| | |
| contestar el teléfono | mandar unos sándwiches |
| hacer la cama | venir a la habitación |
| trabajar más | volver al trabajo / a la habitación |
| limpiar el baño / la habitación | la camarera (*maid*) |
| llevar el equipaje a las habitaciones | el servicio a habitaciones |

MODELOS  El gerente quiere que sus empleados vuelvan al trabajo.
El gerente quiere que sus empleados hagan más trabajo.

---

*The present subjunctive of **hay** is **haya**. You'll learn more about the subjunctive forms of **haber** in later chapters.

**1.**

**2.**

**3.**

**4.**

**C. ¿Qué quieren?** En parejas, hablen de las vacaciones típicas entre familia o con amigos. Pueden inventar situaciones si quieren, pero deben completar las oraciones para describir lo que quieren esas personas que hagan otras durante las vacaciones.

**MODELOS** Mis padres (no) quieren que... →
Mis padres quieren que mis hermanos y yo durmamos durante el viaje en coche.
Mis padres no quieren que mis hermanos y yo peleemos durante el viaje.

1. Yo (no) quiero que...
2. Mi hermano/a (no) quiere que...
3. Mi padre/madre/hijo/hija (no) quiere que...
4. Mis padres (no) quieren que...
5. Mis hermanos y yo (no) queremos que...
6. Los otros pasajeros (no) quieren que...
7. El gerente del hotel (no) quiere que...
8. ¿ ? (no) quiere(n) que...

**D.** Runa Tupari y el turismo comunitario

**PASO 1.** Complete la descripción. Cuando aparecen dos palabras, escoja la palabra correcta. Dé la forma correcta del subjuntivo de los verbos que aparecen con *S*. Dé el presente de indicativo de los otros verbos.

En 2001 se organizó un nuevo turismo en Ecuador, un turismo comunitario y rural, de desarrollo sostenible. El programa se centra en las comunidades del cantón[a] de Cotacachi. Cotacachi queda a dos horas al norte de Quito y (**es/está**[1]) muy cerca de Otavalo, un pueblo famoso por su pintoresco mercado.

---

[a]*administrative district of a province*

(Continúa.)

*La Catedral y el convento de Cotacachi, Ecuador*

Esta idea empezó (**hace/hacen**[2]) unos años con la Unión de Organizaciones Campesinas Indígenas de Cotacachi (UNORCAC), una organización intercultural que representa a cuarenta y cuatro comunidades indígenas, mestizas y afroecuatorianas del cantón. El propósito[b] de (**este/esta**[3]) organización es mejorar el nivel de vida[c] de las comunidades a través de[d] diferentes programas, como la reforestación, la conservación medioambiental, servicios y ayuda legales y de salud, educación bilingüe, renacimiento[e] cultural y turismo rural.

Para cumplir con la última meta, UNORCAC (**formó/formaba**[4]) una agencia de servicios comunitarios que se llama Runa Tupari. Runa Tupari (**es/está**[5]) una frase que en quechua significa «encuentro con los indígenas». Esta agencia quiere que el turista (*S:* **tener**[6]) una experiencia rural y comunitaria auténtica. Ofrece al turista alojamientos rurales, (**situados/situada**[7]) en cuatro comunidades diferentes en Cotacachi. Estos alojamientos (**son/están**[8]) como las otras viviendas de la comunidad. Son cabañas con camas para tres personas, agua caliente y un baño, porque los turistas quieren que los alojamientos (*S:* **ofrecer**[9]) las comodidades[g] básicas. Las cabañas tienen acceso a la huerta familiar mantenido por la familia anfitriona.[h] Los huéspedes ayudan en la huerta y (**aprende/aprenden**[10]) los usos culinarios y medicinales de las plantas y vegetales de la región.

Con Runa Tupari, los turistas (**saben/conocen**[11]) la tranquilidad del campo y las costumbres de las familias indígenas. Es una de las experiencias culturales más auténticas e íntimas posibles. Runa Tupari quiere que sus huéspedes (*S:* **participar**[12]) en actividades agrícolas, artesanales y culinarias (de preparación y degustación[i]). También

---

[b]*purpose*  [c]*nivel... standard of living*  [d]*a... through*  [e]*revival*  [g]*comforts*  [h]*host*  [i]*tasting*

quiere que las comunidades visitadas (*S:* **beneficiarse**[13]) directamente del turismo. Las familias anfitrionas se benefician, compartiendo su cultura y vida diaria y ganando un poco de dinero por recibir a los huéspedes. Además, Runa Tupari (**entrenó/entrenaba**[14]) a veinticinco guías nativos profesionales que (**son/están**[15]) de Cotacachi y viven allí. Estos guías llevan a los huéspedes de Runa Tupari a lugares como la Reserva Ecológica Cotacachi Cayapas, al Lago Cuicocha y al Volcán Cotacachi. Están muy (**orgullosos/ orgullosa**[16]) de su herencia cultural y geográfica y quieren que los visitantes (*S:* **salir**[17]) de Ecuador con un aprecio profundo por la belleza del país. (**Por/Para**[18]) eso, sus excursiones son informativas, bien organizadas y divertidas.

Las comunidades de Cotacachi, los guías nativos y UNORCAC son copropietarios[j] de Runa Tupari. En otras palabras, los ingresos[k] de (**este/esta**[19]) programa se distribuyen de una manera justa y proporcionada en la comunidad. UNORCAC realmente quiere que las comunidades de Cotacachi (*S:* **participar**[20]) en la economía sin perder su identidad cultural.

[j]*co-owners*  [k]*income*

**PASO 2.** Empareje las descripciones de la columna A con la palabra o frase correspondiente de la columna B. ¡OJO! Se puede usar las palabras de la columna B más de una vez.

|  | **A** |  | **B** |
|---|---|---|---|
| 1. | ____ significa «encuentro con los indígenas» | a. | UNORCAC |
| 2. | ____ ofrecen excursiones informativas | b. | Runa Tupari |
| 3. | ____ aprenden costumbres indígenas | c. | los guías nativos profesionales |
| 4. | ____ comparten su vida diaria | d. | las familias anfitrionas |
| 5. | ____ apoya a cuarenta y cuatro grupos étnicos | e. | los huéspedes de Runa Tupari |
| 6. | ____ es una agencia con servicios de turismo rural |  |  |
| 7. | ____ mantienen huertas familiares |  |  |
| 8. | ____ se alojan en cabañas con agua caliente y un baño |  |  |
| 9. | ____ Es una organización con programas medioambientales, de salud, legales y turísticos. |  |  |

**PASO 3.** En parejas, formen oraciones para describir lo que las organizaciones y personas de la izquierda quieren que haga o experimente cada cosa o grupo de la derecha, según el **Paso 1.** ¡OJO! También pueden inventar oraciones probables.

Communication

**MODELO** Los huéspedes quieren que _____. → los alojamientos sean cómodos.

1. Los organizadores de UNORCAC quieren que _____.
2. Runa Tupari quiere que _____.
3. Las familias anfitrionas quieren que _____.
4. Los guías nativos quieren que _____.
5. Los huéspedes quieren que _____.

los alojamientos
los huéspedes
las comunidades de Cotacachi
las familias anfitrionas
los guías nativos
los turistas

Cultures

Ud. va a leer un artículo de la revista *Nexos,* escrito por Ana Cristina Reymundo y publicado por la American Airlines, sobre una visita de tres días que la autora hizo a la ciudad ecuatoriana de Guayaquil.

## ANTES DE LEER

**A. Preguntas.** Lea el título y las primeras líneas (*en letra cursiva*) del artículo. Después, conteste las preguntas.

1. ¿Con qué ciudad compara la autora Guayaquil?
2. Según el hecho de (*fact*) que este artículo se haya publicado (*was published*) en una revista turística, ¿qué tipos de información espera (*do you expect*) encontrar en el resto del artículo?

**B. A leer.** Ahora lea el artículo entero. Mientras lee, trate de adivinar el significado de las palabras <u>subrayadas</u> sin buscar su definición en el diccionario. Mire las palabras antes y después, determine el contexto (quién habla, con quién y de qué) y busque raíces (*roots*) de otras palabras que ya sabe o que son cognados del inglés.

## Guayaquil: Costeña carismática

*Es tan diferente a Quito, su hermana y rival, como el mar es de la tierra. Una es serrana,[a] fresca y conservadora mientras la candente[b] y costeña Guayaquil me invita a disfrutar abiertamente. Me envuelve en su húmeda brisa incitándome a bailar lánguidamente con el vaivén[c] de la corriente de su río Guayas.*

*El Cerro de Santa Ana, en Guayaquil, Ecuador*

Es la ciudad más poblada del Ecuador. Y aunque es la cuna[d] de algunos de los pueblos más antiguos de las Américas, luce[e] como una ciudad relativamente

[a]*set in the mountains* [b]*caliente* [c]*swaying* [d]*birthplace* [e]*it shines*

moderna, recién construida. Con una sola visita al excelente Museo Municipal de Guayaquil me entero de[f] su historia prehispánica, su turbulenta política, los grandes fuegos que acabaron con[g] grandes sectores de la ciudad en más de una ocasión, y de las <u>olas</u> de inmigrantes y piratas, ambos atraídos por su vibrante comercio gracias al río Guayas. Recorriendo el Parque Histórico de Guayaquil comienzo a ver la fluidez con que se mezclaron las culturas de los nativos, los conquistadores españoles, los esclavos africanos, y los demás inmigrantes: europeos, chinos y <u>libaneses</u>. Siglo <u>tras</u> siglo, cada uno, y todos juntos, transformaron esta ciudad diversa. Tras esas experiencias creo comprender algo del caracter guayaquileño que es alegre, desenfadado,[h] dispuesto,[i] abierto y perseverante pues fue <u>forjado</u> en gran parte por la tensión o dinámica entre el agua y el fuego.

En el Grand Hotel Guayaquil disfruto de un sabroso y económico desayuno. Ubicado cerca del malecón y el centro, el hotel es un buen punto de partida y por eso el desayunar ahí se convierte en mi rito matutino[j] durante mi visita. Después de desayunar me pongo el sombrero para protegerme del brillante sol ecuatoriano y me dirijo[k] al malecón. Ese paseo me llena de paz y tranquilidad. Observo la fuerte corriente del Guayas, arrastrando[l] entre sus lodosas[m] aguas millares de lechuguillas.[n] A pesar del[ñ] calor, las fuertes brisas, las docenas de sombrosos <u>escondites</u>, sus jardines y esculturas convierten mi sencilla caminata por el malecón en una agradable aventura.

A la hora del almuerzo me fuí al Red Crab donde disfruté de coquillas de Saint Jacques[o] de lo más deliciosas. De ahí al mercado de artesanos donde compré algunos regalitos y un sombrerito muy mono.[p] La cena esa noche en Ristorante Riviera fue toda una <u>delicia</u>. Además del excelente servicio, los suculentos langostinos me dejan maravillada y satisfecha. Ya es tarde cuando salgo del restaurante pero la brisa y la luna me llaman y decido sentarme en una <u>banca</u> en el malecón antes de regresar al hotel. La capilla[q] y el faro[r] del Cerro de Santa Ana se ven tan lindos en la distancia. Me prometo subir el cerro al día siguiente.

Después de explorar las plazas y el Museo de la Música Popular Guayaquileña Julio Jaramillo subo los 482 escalones del Cerro Santa Ana. Al llegar a la <u>cima</u> entro a su linda capillita. Unos escalones más y me encuentro en el <u>mirador</u> del faro donde puedo apreciar una vista panorámica del río y de la ciudad. Antes de que se haga[s] muy tarde visito el Parque del Seminario, mejor conocido como el parque de las iguanas. De ahí me paso la tarde en el Museo Nahim Isaías. Es un pequeño y excepcional museo que <u>me cautiva</u> con su singular presentación de arte religioso. Por la noche me voy a cenar en Portofino en el Hotel Hilton Colón. Las chuletas de carnero[t] son una delicia. Su bar está lleno de vida y gente interesante.

Visitando panteones yo aprendo mucho sobre la cultura y valores de un pueblo. Me doy un paseo por el Cementerio General de Guayaquil, el cual no tiene nada que envidiarle a[u] Père Lachaise de París. Es monumental y tres días no serán[v] suficientes para explorarlo como me gustaría hacerlo. Me tengo que <u>conformar</u> con una tarde. Esa noche decido cenar en Blu. Me encantó su innovadora cocina *nouvelle* y la combinación de sabores es una sorprendente maravilla. Converso un rato con el chef y dueño. Es obvio que su gran pasión por la cocina y su deseo de <u>deleitar</u> a sus comensales[w] hizo de mi última cena en Guayaquil una inolvidable experiencia.

<u>Me pesa</u> despedirme de esta carismática costeña y mejor me voy con un «hasta luego» en los labios y la esperanza de regresar muy pronto.

---

[f]me... *I get up to speed on*  [g]acabaron... *put an end to*  [h]*easygoing*  [i]*helpful*  [j]*morning*  [k]me... *I make my way*  [l]*pulling*  [m]*muddy*  [n]millares... *thousands of floating water hyacinth plants*  [ñ]A... *In spite of the*  [o]coquillas... *scallops*  [p]*cute*  [q]*chapel*  [r]*lighthouse*  [s]Antes... *Before it gets*  [t]*mutton*  [u]el... *that has no reason to be jealous of*  [v]no... *won't be*  [w]*dinner guests*

**A.** Comprensión. Conteste las preguntas, según el artículo.

1. ¿Cómo son los guayaquileños?
2. ¿Qué importancia histórica y recreativa tiene el río Guayas en Guayaquil?
3. ¿Cómo es la comida y el ambiente de los restaurantes mencionados en el artículo?
4. ¿Qué platos comió la autora?
5. ¿Cree Ud. que a la autora le gustaría visitar Guayaquil en el fututo? Explique.

**B.** Las palabras subrayadas. ¿Pudo Ud. adivinar el significado de las palabras subrayadas en el artículo mientras lo leía? Ahora, búsquelas en algún diccionario para ver si adivinó bien. Si se equivocó (*you were wrong*), vuelva a leer esa parte del artículo.

**C.** Un viaje a mi ciudad favorita. Relate (*Tell about*) unas experiencias que Ud. tuvo cuando visitó un lugar durante unas vacaciones. Comente la comida, la gente, las cosas que vio, lo que hizo, etcétera. También dé su opinión en general del lugar e indique si le gustaría volver allí o no y por qué.

*Unos mangles* (mangrove trees), *en la Bahía de Guayaquil*

## Perú: María Elena

Cultures

Un viaje a Machu Picchu

En este segmento María Elena nos lleva a Machu Picchu, la famosa Ciudad Perdida de los Incas que el estadounidense Hiram Bingham encontró en 1911. Durante el viaje, vamos a pasar por la ciudad colonial de Cusco, el Valle Sagrado de los Incas, el pueblo de Ollantaytambo y el pueblo de Aguas Calientes. En Machu Picchu vamos a ver las ruinas y unas vistas impresionantes. Después, volvemos a Cusco para ver la ciudad antes de regresar a Lima.

### ANTES DE VER

Conteste las preguntas.

1. ¿Prefiere Ud. viajar solo/a o con otras personas? Explique.
2. ¿Cuáles son las ventajas y desventajas de viajar en grupo?
3. ¿Qué sabe Ud. de Machu Picchu y la cultura precolombina de los incas?

### DESPUÉS DE VER

**A. Comprensión.** Empareje los elementos.

| **Vocabulario práctico** | |
|---|---|
| **orgullosa** | proud |
| **nos llevará** | will take us |
| **a lo largo de** | all around |
| **de mucho movimiento** | very crowded |
| **no hay duda** | there's no doubt |

**A**

1. una región fértil con ruinas arqueológicas interesantísimas _____
2. El nombre de este lugar significa «montaña vieja». _____
3. un lugar pintoresco con restaurantes y tiendas de productos textiles _____
4. Fue la capital del Imperio inca. _____
5. un pueblo en el Valle Sagrado de los Incas _____

**B**

a. Aguas Calientes
b. Cusco
c. Machu Picchu
d. Ollantaytambo
e. Valle Sagrado de los Incas

**B. Temas de discusión.** En grupos pequeños, comenten los temas.

Communication

1. **El mundo andino:** Vuelvan a mirar el segmento y comenten los aspectos de los lugares y las personas que les parecen más interesantes.
2. **Lugares especiales:** Pensando en la información, las imágenes y la música del blog de María Elena, ¿creen que Cusco y Machu Picchu son lugares muy especiales? Expliquen.

## Los verbos

| | |
|---|---|
| alojarse | to stay (in a hotel) |
| bajarse (de) | to get off (of) (a vehicle) |
| disfrutar (de) | to enjoy |
| embarcar (qu) (en) | to board |
| facturar el equipaje | to check luggage |
| hacer (irreg.) cola | to stand in line |
| hacer las maletas | to pack one's suitcase(s) |
| hospedarse | to stay (in a hotel) |
| pasar por la aduana | to go through customs |
| pasar por el control de seguridad | to go through security |
| pasarlo bien/ fenomenal/mal | to have a good/great/bad time |
| quedarse | to stay (in a place) |
| recoger (j) el equipaje | to pick up luggage |
| registrarse | to check in |
| recorrer | to travel around / go through (a town/city) |
| revisar | to inspect |
| subir (a) | to get on/in (a vehicle) |
| volar (ue) | to fly |

**Repaso:** declarar, divertirse (ie, i), sacar (qu) fotos, viajar

## El viaje — Trip

| | |
|---|---|
| la aduana | customs |
| la agencia de viajes | travel agency |
| el asiento (de pasillo/ ventanilla) | (aisle/window) seat |
| el/la azafata | flight attendant |
| el billete | ticket (Sp.) |
| el boleto | ticket (L.A.) |
| el cheque de viajero | traveler's check |
| la clase económica | coach (class) |
| el control de seguridad | security (check point) |
| el crucero | cruise (ship) |
| el destino | destination |
| el equipaje | luggage |
| la escala | stop (layover) |
| el/la extranjero/a | foreigner; m. abroad |
| la maleta | suitcase |
| el/la maletero/a | skycap |
| el maletín | carry-on (bag) |
| el mostrador | (check-in) counter |

| | |
|---|---|
| el/la pasajero/a | passenger |
| la primera clase | first class |
| el reclamo de equipaje | baggage claim |
| la sala de espera | waiting room |
| la salida | departure; gate |
| la tarjeta de embarque | boarding pass |
| el viaje | |
| de ida | one-way trip |
| de ida y vuelta | round trip |
| el visado | visa |
| el vuelo | flight |
| de viaje | on a trip |

**Cognados:** la inmigración, el pasaporte, el/la turista
**Repaso:** el autobús, el avión, el barco, la llegada, la mochila, la parada, la reservación, el transporte, el tren

## De vacaciones — On Vacation

| | |
|---|---|
| el alojamiento | lodging |
| el botones inv. | bellhop |
| la cabaña rústica | rustic cabin |
| la estadía | stay |
| la excursión | tour, daytrip |
| el/la gerente | manager |
| la habitación doble/sencilla | double/single room |
| el/la huésped(a) | hotel guest |
| la mariposa | butterfly |
| el recorrido | tour; trip |
| el recuerdo | souvenir |
| las ruinas arqueológicas | archeological ruins |
| la ruta | route |
| la tarjeta postal | postcard |
| la tirolina | zipline |
| acuático/a | water aquatic |
| de lujo | luxury (hotel) |

**Cognados:** el agroturismo, la canoa, el ecoturismo, el hotel, el pasaporte, la recepción, la reserva biológica, el turismo, el/la turista
**Repaso:** el ascensor, la caminata, el paisaje, el senderismo, el sendero; agrícola (m., f.)

# La música, el arte y las celebraciones

*En la Feria de las Flores, Medellín, Colombia*

1. En la Feria de las Flores de Medellín, se presentan grandes arreglos de flores. También hay desfiles (vea la foto), conciertos y otros eventos culturales. ¿Ha estado Ud. alguna vez en un festival como la Feria de las Flores de Medellín? ¿Cómo era?

2. ¿Hay algún otro festival parecido en su país? ¿Cómo es esa celebración? ¿Qué tipo de actividades se realizan?

3. ¿Qué diversiones hay en el lugar donde Ud. vive?

www.connectspanish.com

351

## Vocabulario del tema

### Los días festivos°

Los... *Holidays*

1. celebrar

el Año Nuevo / la Nochevieja, el 31 de diciembre

2. la carroza

la Semana Santa

3. los espectadores

el encierro

los Sanfermines, el 7 de julio

4. los fuegos artificiales

el conjunto musical

el Día de la Independencia

## Otros días festivos y celebraciones

| | |
|---|---|
| el Día de Acción de Gracias | Thanksgiving Day |
| el Día de Canadá | Canada Day |
| el Día de la Madre | Mother's Day |
| el Día de la Raza | Columbus Day |
| el Día de los Muertos | Day of the Dead |
| el Día de los Reyes Magos | Feast of the Three Kings (Epiphany) |
| el Día del Padre | Father's Day |
| el día del santo | one's saint day |
| la festividad | festivity; feast |
| la Navidad | Christmas |
| la fiesta de quinceañera | young woman's fifteenth birthday party |
| la Pascua | Easter |
| la Pascua judía | Passover |
| la Semana Santa | Holy Week |
| las vacaciones de primavera | spring break |

Cognados: el Carnaval, el Cinco de Mayo, el festival; nacional, religioso/a

## Para celebrar

| | |
|---|---|
| disfrazarse (c) | to disguise oneself |
| el árbol de Navidad | Christmas tree |
| la carroza | parade float |
| el conjunto musical | band, musical group |
| la corrida de toros | bullfight |
| el encierro | running of the bulls |
| el regalo | gift |

Cognados: el folclor, el santo patrón / la santa patrona; adornado/a

### ACTIVIDADES

**A. Los meses de los días festivos**

PASO 1.  Diga en qué mes se celebran estos días festivos. Busque la respuesta en el Internet si Ud. no está seguro/a.

1. el Día de la Madre, en los Estados Unidos y Canadá
2. el Día del Padre, en los Estados Unidos y Canadá
3. la Navidad
4. el Día de Acción de Gracias, en los Estados Unidos
5. el Día de Acción de Gracias, en Canadá
6. los Sanfermines
7. el Día de la Independencia, en los Estados Unidos
8. el Año Nuevo
9. el Día de la Raza
10. el Día de Canadá

PASO 2.  En parejas, nombren un día festivo para los meses no representados en el **Paso 1.** Pueden buscar días festivos en el Internet si quieren.

Communication

**B.** Asociaciones

**PASO 1.** Diga el día festivo que Ud. asocia con estas actividades.

1. Fuimos a ver fuegos artificiales y un desfile con muchas banderas.
2. Hicimos la cuenta atrás hasta (*we counted down to*) la medianoche.
3. Encontramos muchos dulces en las canastas.
4. Fuimos al cementerio en conmemoración de nuestros parientes muertos.
5. Comimos mucho pavo y otros platos fuertes (*heavy*) y vimos partidos de fútbol americano.
6. Abrimos regalos debajo del árbol.
7. Me hicieron un pastel, me cantaron una canción y me dieron muchos regalos.

**PASO 2.** En parejas, describan algo que hacen en un día festivo u otro día especial. Su compañero/a de clase debe adivinar qué día es.

MODELO E1: Paso el día con mi familia y le hago un regalo a mi mamá.
E2: Es el Día de la Madre.

**C.** Entrevista: Las vacaciones de primavera. Entreviste a un compañero / una compañera de clase con las preguntas. Luego, cambien de papel.

1. ¿Cuándo son las próximas vacaciones de primavera?
2. ¿Cuáles son los destinos más populares entre los estudiantes de esta universidad para pasar las vacaciones de primavera?
3. ¿Qué quieres hacer para las próximas vacaciones de primavera? ¿Quieres hacer un viaje con amigos o quieren tus padres que pases las vacaciones con tu familia?
4. ¿Qué hiciste para las últimas vacaciones de primavera?

**D.** Los días festivos

**PASO 1.** Use las preguntas para entrevistar a por lo menos tres compañeros/as de clase. En una hoja de papel aparte, apunte sus respuestas en una tabla como la siguiente.

| MÁS IMPORTANTE | DIVERTIRSE | DÍA FESTIVO FAVORITO | DISFRAZARSE | MÁS REGALOS |
|---|---|---|---|---|
| | | | | |

1. ¿Cuál es el día festivo o celebración más importante para tu familia?
2. ¿Cuál es el día festivo o celebración en que más te diviertes tú?
3. ¿Tienes algún día festivo favorito?
4. ¿Te disfrazas en algún día festivo o celebración?
5. ¿En qué día festivo o celebración recibes más regalos?

**PASO 2.** Comparen sus respuestas del **Paso 1** con la clase. ¿Qué días festivos se mencionan más? Por ejemplo, ¿hay un día festivo o celebración más importante para la familia? ¿un día festivo o celebración en que más se divierten? ¿un día festivo favorito?

## Nota cultural

### LAS CORRALEJAS DE COLOMBIA

Las corralejas son festividades populares de la costa caribeña de Colombia. Tienen su origen en la época colonial y consisten en desfiles ecuestres,[a] bailes populares y muchos otros eventos alegres y divertidos. El evento más importante es una versión local de una corrida de toros de origen español.

La fiesta taurina[b] dura varios días y se realiza en varios puntos de la ciudad, pero termina en una plaza de toros temporal,[c] que se construye cada año especialmente para el evento. Durante esta fase, las gradas[d] se llenan de gente, y se sueltan[e] en la plaza toros jóvenes. Cualquier persona valiente y arriesgada[f] puede saltar a[g] la plaza e intentar torearlos.[h] Al final de su tiempo en la plaza, ningún toro muere, a diferencia de otros lugares como en España, donde sí hay toreros[i] profesionales y todos los toros son sacrificados.

Las corralejas más famosas son las de la ciudad de Sincelejo, que se celebran la tercera semana de enero, pero se festejan corralejas en otros pueblos de la región caribeña también en enero.

---

[a]*equestrian*  [b]*related to bullfighting*  [c]plaza... *temporary bullfighting ring*  [d]*(stadium) stands*  [e]se... *are let loose*  [f]*daring*  [g]saltar... *jump into*  [h]intentar... *try to engage the bulls with a cape*  [i]*bullfighters*

**PREGUNTAS**  En parejas, contesten las preguntas y después compartan sus ideas con la clase.

1. ¿Qué son las corralejas? ¿Dónde se celebran? ¿Cuándo?
2. ¿Cuáles son las corralejas más famosas?
3. ¿Por qué son diferentes las corralejas de las corridas de toros de España?

**Expressing Desire That Somebody Do Something**

## 11.1 Present Subjunctive: Volition

**GRAMÁTICA EN CONTEXTO**

### El Carnaval de Oruro

[*Jane es una joven canadiense que está estudiando un año en Bolivia. Su «hermano» boliviano, Fernando, la invita al Carnaval de Oruro.*]

**FERNANDO:** ¿Qué haces el sábado que viene?

**JANE:** Necesito estudiar un poco, pero no tengo planes.

**FERNANDO:** Pues, **insisto** en que **vengas** con nosotros a Oruro.

**JANE:** ¿A Oruro? Pero… Oruro es un pueblo minero. No me parece muy interesante. Prefiero quedarme aquí, en La Paz.

**FERNANDO:** Pero **es importante** que **vayas** porque esta semana empieza el Carnaval de Oruro. **Quiero** que **veas** cómo cambia un pueblo pequeño para estas celebraciones, las más espectaculares de Bolivia.

**JANE:** Está bien. Voy con Uds. ¿Qué **recomiendas** que **lleve** a Oruro?

**FERNANDO:** Te **sugiero** que **lleves** la cámara, un poquito de dinero para los asientos en las gradas y ropa cómoda para cuatro días.

**JANE:** ¡Cuatro días! Pero mi novio **quiere** que **salgamos** a cenar el domingo, y ¡hay clases el lunes y el martes!

**FERNANDO:** No hay clases esos días porque son días festivos. Yo le puedo **decir** a tu novio que **venga** a Oruro también. Las festividades en Oruro son maravillosas y siguen hasta el Miércoles de Ceniza.

### ¿CIERTO O FALSO?

|  |  | C | F |
|---|---|---|---|
| **1.** | Fernando insiste en que Jane estudie este fin de semana. | ☐ | ☐ |
| **2.** | Jane le pide a Fernando que le describa los desfiles del Carnaval. | ☐ | ☐ |
| **3.** | Fernando le dice a Jane que lleve su cámara a Oruro. | ☐ | ☐ |
| **4.** | Fernando recomienda que hagan el viaje en autobús. | ☐ | ☐ |

GRAMÁTICA EN CONTEXTO *The Oruro Carnaval / Jane is a young Canadian woman who is studying for a year in Bolivia. Her Bolivian "brother," Fernando, invites her to the Oruro Carnaval. / FERNANDO: What are you doing this Saturday? JANE: I have to study a little, but I don't have plans. FERNANDO: Well, I insist that you come with us to Oruro. JANE: To Oruro? But . . . Oruro is a mining town. That doesn't seem very interesting to me. I prefer to stay here in La Paz. FERNANDO: But it's important for you to go because this week the Oruro Carnaval begins. I want you to see how a small town changes for these celebrations, the most spectacular in Bolivia. JANE: OK. I'll go with you. What do you recommend that I take to Oruro? FERNANDO: I suggest you take a camera, a little money for bleacher seats, and comfortable clothing for four days. JANE: Four days! But my boyfriend wants us to go out to dinner on Sunday, and there are classes on Monday and Tuesday! FERNANDO: There are no classes those days because it's a holiday. I can tell your boyfriend to come to Oruro too. The festivities in Oruro are marvelous and go on through Ash Wednesday.*

Earlier you learned to use the subjunctive in complex sentences, in which the first clause contains a form of the verb **querer,** and the second is introduced by the conjunction **que** and contains the present subjunctive. The subject of the first clause and that of the second clause are always different. These sentences communicate a wish on the part of one person for another person to do something. These structures can be illustrated by the following formula.

Subject 1 + *verb/expression of volition* (present indicative) + **que** + Subject 2 + *present subjunctive*

Jaime **prefiere que** nosotros no vayamos con él.

*Jaime prefers that we not go with him.*

Note that impersonal expressions that begin with **Es** have the implied subject *it.* Here are some verbs and expressions of volition that trigger the subjunctive.

## PRESENT SUBJUNCTIVE: VOLITION

| | | | |
|---|---|---|---|
| aconsejar que | to advise that | necesitar que | |
| decir (*irreg.*) que | to tell | pedir (i, i) que | |
| desear que | | preferir (ie, i) que | |
| es importante que | | prohibir (prohíbo) que | |
| es necesario que | | querer (*irreg.*) que | |
| es urgente que | | recomendar (ie) que | |
| insistir en que | | sugerir (ie, i) que | to suggest that |

Mis padres me **prohíben** que **salga** con Sergio.

*My parents prohibit that I go out with (prohibit me from going out with) Sergio.*

**Insisto** en que **vengas** conmigo.

*I insist that you come with me.*

Os **pido** que no **habléis** durante la película.

*I ask you not to talk during the movie.*

El médico me **dice** que **coma** menos carne y más frutas y verduras.

*The doctor tells me to eat less meat and more fruits and vegetables.*

**Es necesario** que los niños **hagan** ejercicio todos los días.

*It is necessary that children exercise daily.*

Le **recomiendo/aconsejo** que **busque** libros sobre el asunto si quiere saber más.

*I recommend/advise that you look for books on the subject if you want to learn more.*

**A. ¿Quién?** Complete las oraciones con el nombre de las personas que hacen estas cosas. Si nadie las hace, use **Nadie.**

1. _____ insiste en que yo me disfrace para el Día de las Brujas (*Halloween*).
2. _____ quiere que yo pase su cumpleaños con él/ella.
3. _____ prefiere que sus amigos celebren el Año Nuevo en su casa con él/ella.
4. _____ nos recomienda que visitemos un país hispano durante la Semana Santa.
5. _____ me prohíbe que yo le dé un regalo de Navidad.
6. _____ piensa que es importante que la familia pase la Pascua judía en casa.
7. _____ pide que pasemos las vacaciones de primavera juntos/as.
8. _____ sugiere que miremos los fuegos artificiales para el Día de la Independencia.

**B. Las celebraciones.** Haga oraciones completas con las palabras indicadas. Añada palabras cuando sea necesario.

1. los padres / insistir en / que / hijos / tener / cuidado / durante / desfile
2. la esposa de Raúl / decir / que / él / llegar / temprano / para / fiesta / de / hija
3. yo / pedir / que / tú / pasar / por / supermercado / y / que / comprar refrescos / para / fiesta
4. Juanita / aconsejar / que / nosotras / buscar / árbol de Navidad / alto
5. ser / necesario / que / tus amigos / traer / música / a / fiesta
6. (yo) / recomendar / que / los abuelos / no dar / tanto / regalo / a / nietos
7. ser / importante / que / Tomasa / estar / en / fiesta de quinceañera / de / Mariana
8. (nosotros) / querer / que / ellos / estar / aquí / para / Semana Santa

**C. Descripciones.** En parejas, expresen lo que quieren que hagan otras personas. Para hacer las preguntas y respuestas, combinen un elemento de cada columna para formar oraciones completas. Sigan el modelo.

MODELO E1: ¿Qué quieres que hagan tus amigos?
       E2: Quiero que me inviten a una fiesta.

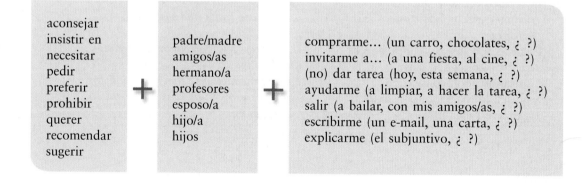

aconsejar
insistir en
necesitar
pedir
preferir
prohibir
querer
recomendar
sugerir

**+**

padre/madre
amigos/as
hermano/a
profesores
esposo/a
hijo/a
hijos

**+**

comprarme... (un carro, chocolates, ¿ ?)
invitarme a... (a una fiesta, al cine, ¿ ?)
(no) dar tarea (hoy, esta semana, ¿ ?)
ayudarme (a limpiar, a hacer la tarea, ¿ ?)
salir (a bailar, con mis amigos/as, ¿ ?)
escribirme (un e-mail, una carta, ¿ ?)
explicarme (el subjuntivo, ¿ ?)

**D.** La Feria de Alasitas

**PASO 1.** Llene los espacios en blanco con la forma correcta del verbo entre paréntesis en el presente de subjuntivo.

Si Ud. piensa visitar el altiplano de Bolivia, le recomiendo que (ir[1]) *vaya* a finales de enero para celebrar la Feria de Alasitas. Cada 24 de enero, los habitantes del altiplano celebran este festival que tiene sus raíces en la cultura aymará.

En la tradición aymará es importante que todos (hacer[2]) *hagan* una ofrenda[a] a la Pachamama, es decir,[b] a la Madre Tierra. En la celebración contemporánea es necesario que los creyentes[c] le (dar[3]) miniaturas de lo que más desean —un carro, dinero, casa y hasta títulos universitarios— a Ekeko, una deidad[d] de la abundancia, sonriente[e] y gorda. Así, los bolivianos le piden

En un mercado durante la Feria de Alasitas, en La Paz

a Ekeko que él (hacer[4]) realidad sus sueños y deseos.[f] ¿Pero cómo se hace? Le preguntamos a Javier Huayllani, vendedor de miniaturas, y así nos respondió:

—Si quieren participar en la feria, les recomiendo que (*Uds.*: ir[5]) al mercado de artesanías antes del 24 de enero. Les sugiero que (comprar[6]) la figura de Ekeko y todas las miniaturas de una vez.[g] Es necesario que (*Uds.*: poner[7]) las miniaturas en su Ekeko, ya que[h] él tiene que llevarlas en su persona.

Bueno, ya que Javier nos recomienda que no (*nosotros*: demorar[i8]), vamos al mercado. Allí hay una variedad increíble de miniaturas de todo. Le pido a un vendedor que él me (ayudar[9]) a seleccionar una figura de Ekeko. Insiste en que no (*yo*: llevar[10]) un Ekeko demasiado pequeño, ya que no va a poder cargar con[j] todos mis deseos, y me sugiere que (comprar[11]) uno muy grande. Prefiero que los vendedores me (dejar[12]) en paz,[k] y escojo rápidamente mis miniaturas: una moto nueva, una cámara nueva y mucho dinero.

En cambio, mi compañero de viaje no sabe qué pedirle a Ekeko. Necesita que los vendedores le (decir[13]) cuáles son los deseos más comunes antes de decidir. Por fin, le sugieren que (*él*: escoger[14]) varias miniaturas populares: un carro, una casa, dinero y comida. Llevamos nuestras compras[l] a casa, listos para el gran día.

El día 24, es urgente que le (*nosotros*: poner[15]) las miniaturas a Ekeko, y para hacerlo, nuestros amigos bolivianos nos recomiendan que se las (*nosotros*: coser[m16]). Pero antes, tenemos que rociarlas[n] con vino. También desean que (*nosotros*: encender[17]) velas[ñ] e incienso y que le (echar[18]) pétalos de flores a Ekeko. Así, nuestra ofrenda le va a ser agradable, y en un futuro que yo prefiero que (llegar[19]) *llegue* pronto, Ekeko va a convertir mis deseos en realidad.

---

[a]*offering*  [b]*es... that is*  [c]*believers*  [d]*deity*  [e]*smiling*  [f]*sueños... dreams and desires*  [g]*de... at once*  [h]*ya... since*
[i]*to delay*  [j]*cargar... to carry*  [k]*dejar... to leave alone*  [l]*purchases*  [m]*to sew*  [n]*sprinkle them*  [ñ]*candles*

**PASO 2.** Conteste las preguntas, según el **Paso 1.**

1. ¿Cuándo se celebra la Feria de Alasitas?
2. ¿Cuáles son las raíces de esta celebración?
3. ¿A quién es necesario que se le haga una ofrenda? ¿Cómo es este personaje?
4. ¿Cómo son las ofrendas? ¿Qué representan?
5. ¿Qué miniaturas selecciona el autor? ¿Y qué escoge su compañero de viaje?
6. Para hacer la ofrenda, ¿qué es necesario que hagan el autor y su compañero?

Communication

**PASO 3.** En parejas, contesten las preguntas.

1. ¿Qué celebraciones típicas hay en la ciudad o región donde Uds. viven? ¿Cómo son esas celebraciones? ¿Qué celebra la gente?
2. ¿Qué les recomiendan Uds. a los visitantes a esas festividades que hagan durante las celebraciones? ¿Adónde les sugieren que vayan?
3. ¿Cuáles son las artesanías típicas del lugar o región donde Uds. viven? ¿Cómo son? ¿Cuándo y dónde se venden?

---

**Expressing Emotions About a Situation**

# 11.2 Present Subjunctive: Emotion

**GRAMÁTICA EN CONTEXTO**

*Durante un desfile del Día de la Independencia, en Lima*

### El cambio de la guardia

[*Larry visita a su novia peruana, Gloria, a quien conoció mientras ella estudiaba en Detroit. Hoy visitan el Palacio de Gobierno en Lima.*]

GLORIA: **Espero** que **te guste** la arquitectura de mi ciudad. Aquí estamos en la Plaza Mayor, enfrente del Palacio de Gobierno.

LARRY: **Me sorprende** que **haya** tantos edificios coloniales en Lima. Cuando pienso en Perú, siempre pienso en las estructuras incas y precolombinas.

GLORIA: Nuestras ciudades tienen mucha influencia española. **Ojalá** que **podamos** ver el cambio de la guardia. **Es extraño** que aquí en Perú **tengamos** este toque tan europeo, pero es divertido. La guardia militar también participa en los desfiles del Día de la Independencia el 28 de julio.

LARRY: ¡Qué divertido! He visto el cambio de la guardia en Londres. **Es una lástima** que yo no **esté** aquí en julio para celebrar el Día de la Independencia de Perú contigo.

GLORIA: ¡Mira! ¡Ahora empieza el cambio! **Me alegro** de que lo **veas**.

---

GRAMÁTICA EN CONTEXTO *Changing of the Guard / Larry visits his Peruvian girlfriend, Gloria, whom he met while she studied in Detroit. Today they are visiting the Government Palace in Lima. / **GLORIA:** I hope you like the architecture of my city. Here we are in the Plaza Mayor, in front of the Government Palace. **LARRY:** I'm surprised there are so many colonial buildings in Lima. When I think of Peru, I always think of Incan and pre-Columbian structures. **GLORIA:** Our cities have a great deal of Spanish influence. Hopefully we can see the changing of the guard. It's strange that here in Peru we have this so very European touch, but it's fun. The military guard also participates in the Independence Day parades on July 28. **LARRY:** What fun! I have seen the changing of the guard in London. It's a pity that I won't be here in July to celebrate Peru's Independence Day with you. **GLORIA:** Look! The changing is starting! I'm happy that you are seeing this.*

Comprensión: ¿Probable (P) o improbable (I)?

|  | P | I |
|---|---|---|
| 1. Gloria se alegra de que Larry la visite en Perú. | ☐ | ☐ |
| 2. A la madre de Larry le preocupa que su hijo no vuelva a Detroit. | ☐ | ☐ |
| 3. Larry siente que tenga que irse antes de julio. | ☐ | ☐ |
| 4. La familia de Gloria tiene miedo de que ella y Larry se pierdan en Lima. | ☐ | ☐ |

The subjunctive is also used in Spanish after verbs of emotion in which speakers express their feelings about a subject. Remember that in a sentence that uses the subjunctive, the sentence will always have two clauses connected by **que,** and the two clauses will usually have different subjects. Here are some verbs and one expression of emotion that trigger the subjunctive. Note that **ojalá** is the only trigger after which **que** is optional.

## PRESENT SUBJUNCTIVE: EMOTION

| | | | |
|---|---|---|---|
| **alegrarse de que** | to be happy that | **gustar que** | |
| **es absurdo que** | | **ojalá (que)** | hopefully |
| **es bueno que** | | **preocupar que** | |
| **es extraño que** | it's strange that | **sentir (ie, i) que** | |
| **es increíble que** | | **sorprender que** | |
| **es malo que** | | **tener** (irreg.) **miedo** | |
| **es una lástima que** | it's a shame that | **de que** | |
| **esperar que** | to hope that | | |

| | |
|---|---|
| **Esperamos** que Uds. **puedan** visitarnos este verano. | *We hope that you all can visit us this summer.* |
| **Tengo** miedo de que Jorge **esté** muy enfermo. | *I'm afraid that Jorge is very ill.* |
| Es una lástima que **te sientas** mal hoy. | *It's a shame you feel sick today.* |
| La familia **se alegra** de que la **acompañes.** | *The family is happy that you are going with them.* |
| Me **gusta** que **tengas** más apetito que antes. | *I'm pleased that you have more appetite than before.* |
| **Ojalá** (que) **duermas** bien esta noche porque mañana vamos a tener un día largo. | *Hopefully you'll sleep well tonight because tomorrow we're going to have a long day.* |

### ACTIVIDADES

**A. Mis opiniones.** Diga si Ud. no está de acuerdo con las oraciones. Explique.

1. Es una lástima que la gente gaste tanto dinero en regalos de Navidad.
2. Es malo que los niños salgan a pedir dulces el Día de las Brujas (*Halloween*).
3. Siento que haya mucha gente que no tenga una buena comida el Día de Acción de Gracias.
4. Ojalá nadie se lastime con los fuegos artificiales.
5. Me preocupa que mucha gente tome bebidas alcohólicas y maneje en la Nochevieja.
6. Me sorprende que el Cinco de Mayo sea una fiesta tan reconocida en este país.
7. Es absurdo que las personas corran con los toros en los Sanfermines. ¡Es demasiado peligroso!
8. Me sorprende que haya tantas procesiones para celebrar la Semana Santa.

**B. La fiesta sorpresa.** Llene los espacios en blanco con la forma correcta del verbo en el presente de subjuntivo.

1. A mi mamá le sorprende que papá no _____ (**saber**) nada de su fiesta.
2. Le preocupa que mis hermanos y yo le _____ (**decir**) algo a papá.
3. Todos tenemos miedo de que la fiesta no _____ (**ser**) una sorpresa.
4. Me alegro de que mis hermanos _____ (**preparar**) la comida.
5. Pablito: a mamá le gusta que tú también _ayudes_ (**ayudar**) con los preparativos.
6. Siento mucho que mi tío _____ (**vivir**) demasiado lejos para venir a la fiesta.
7. Ojalá todos los otros invitados _____ (**venir**). _vengan_
8. ¡Espero que papá _____ (**divertirse**) en su fiesta!

**C. Mis opiniones.** En parejas, reaccionen ante las situaciones como en el modelo. ¡OJO! Usen los verbos y expresiones de emoción que aprendieron en esta sección.

MODELO  Muchas personas no pasan los días feriados en familia. →
Es una lástima que muchas personas no pasen los días feriados en familia.

1. Los niños reciben muchos regalos para su cumpleaños.
2. Muchas familias hispanas ponen altares para conmemorar el Día de los Muertos.
3. En el mundo hispano, los Reyes Magos les traen regalos a los niños.
4. En este país, muchas personas celebran el Cinco de Mayo.
5. Las familias pasan juntas la Pascua judía.
6. Los niños hispanos también celebran el día de su santo.
7. Las muchachas latinoamericanas tienen una gran fiesta cuando cumplen 15 años.
8. Muchos estudiantes norteamericanos viajan para las vacaciones de primavera.

**D. Inti Raymi: El Festival del Sol**

PASO 1. Complete el texto con la forma correcta del verbo entre paréntesis en el presente de subjuntivo, o en el pretérito o imperfecto cuando se indica con *P/I*. Cuando hay dos palabras entre paréntesis, escoja la palabra correcta y use su forma correcta.

*Un chamán baña a otro al comienzo del Festival del Sol*

Por su larga historia de convivencia,[a] no nos sorprende que en América Latina (**haber**[1]) tantas muestras[b] del sincretismo de tradiciones indígenas y europeas. Es increíble que estas tradiciones (**seguir**[2]) practicándose hoy día, a pesar de las muchas influencias del exterior.

El Festival del Sol, o el Inti Raymi en quechua, es un buen ejemplo de tal mezcla. En Ecuador, este festival se celebra principalmente en las provincias de Imbabura y Pichincha para festejar el solsticio de verano en junio. Sus orígenes se encuentran en la cosecha.[c] A la gente le preocupa que la Madre Tierra y el Padre Sol no (**saber**[3]) que todos están agradecidos[d] por la abundancia de la cosecha. Tienen miedo de que no (**haber**[4]) buenas cosechas en el futuro si no demuestran su agradecimiento.[e] Por eso, es importante que todos (**dar**[5]) las gracias.

En la ciudad de Otavalo, todo comienza con un baño ritual. Según la tradición, es bueno que uno (**bañarse**[6]) en un río o en la catarata[f] de Peguche, que está cerca. Los otavaleños[g] esperan que el baño les (**quitar**[7]) todo lo negativo. Se alegran de que (**comenzar**[8]) un nuevo ciclo desde ese momento.

---

[a]*coexistence*  [b]*examples*  [c]*harvest*  [d]*thankful*  [e]*thanks*  [f]*waterfall*  [g]*people of Otavalo*

CAPÍTULO 11  La música, el arte y las celebraciones

Después del baño, la celebración continúa con mucha música y mucho baile. Los bailarines bailan en un círculo para representar los dos solsticios y los dos equinoccios. Es interesante que el personaje central de esta celebración (**estar/ser**[9]) un diablo: el Diablo Huma. Este personaje lleva una máscara con dos caras que representan la noche y el día, y doce cuernos[h] que simbolizan los doces meses del año. La gente no tiene miedo de que este diablo les (**causar**[10]) problemas porque es el espíritu de la montaña y solamente viene a celebrar con los otavaleños. Por eso, se alegran de que el Diablo Huma (**estar/ser**[11]) allí. Es extraño que el Diablo Huma (**bailar**[12]) con todos como un invitado[i] más, pero es bueno que todos lo (**ver**[13]) como una presencia positiva.

Es interesante que el festival de Inti Raymi (**tener**[14]) lugar durante la misma época que la celebración del Día de San Juan, el 24 de junio. Los españoles introdujeron el festival de San Juan, el cual coincidía con el festival de Inti Raymi. Así, los indígenas (*P/I:* **poder**[15]) festejar a un santo europeo y no a dioses indígenas. No obstante, en los años 70, muchos (*P/I:* **volver**[16]) a llamar la fiesta por su nombre original, fortaleciendo así los lazos[j] con el pasado. Ojalá las nuevas generaciones no (**perder**[17]) el interés en este festival tan antiguo.

[h]*horns*  [i]*un… just another guest*  [j]*fortaleciendo… thus strengthening the ties*

**PASO 2.** Conteste las preguntas, según el **Paso 1.**

1. ¿Cuándo se celebra el festival de Inti Raymi? ¿En qué lugares de Ecuador se celebra principalmente?
2. ¿Qué significa «Inti Raymi»? ¿Qué celebra la gente en este festival? ¿De qué tiene miedo la gente?
3. ¿Quién es el personaje principal del Inti Raymi? Descríbalo. ¿Cómo se relacionan los otavaleños con este personaje?

**PASO 3.** En parejas, contesten las preguntas.

¿Qué días feriados celebrados en su región o en este país tienen vínculos (*links*) con otras culturas? ¿Cómo los celebran Uds.?

Connections

# Palabra escrita

## A comenzar

Communication

**Generating Ideas: Semantic Maps.** During your brainstorming process, you can organize your ideas visually in the shape of a semantic map. You have probably used semantic maps before, but if not, a semantic map is a diagram that links an encircled key word or concept in the middle of the map to encircled related ideas or secondary concepts on the edges of the map by means of arrows or lines. By organizing your ideas visually in such diagrams you can see how they all fit together and decide whether you need to add anything or not.

You are going to start the process of writing a brief composition that you will finalize in the **Palabra escrita: A finalizar** section of your *Manual de actividades*. The topic of this composition is **Un día especial**. The purpose of your composition will be to tell the reader about your plans, hopes, and expectations for a special holiday or celebration.

**A.** Lluvia de ideas

**PASO 1.**   En parejas, escojan un día festivo que se celebra o se observa en la región donde Uds. viven. En una hoja de papel aparte, creen (*create*) un mapa semántico, como en la siguiente figura, con el nombre del día festivo en el óvalo central. En los otros óvalos, pongan ideas relacionadas con su día festivo, por ejemplo, origen del día festivo, actividades y tradiciones importantes, actividades en las que a Uds. les gusta participar, etcétera. **¡OJO!** Pueden crear tantos óvalos en su mapa como necesiten.

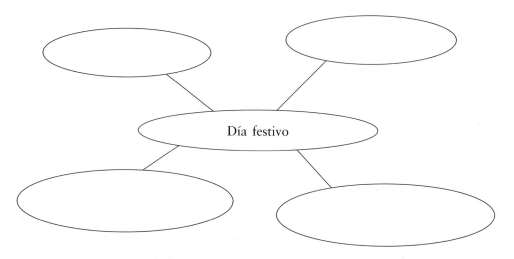

Día festivo

**PASO 2.**   Comparen su mapa con el de otra pareja para ver si han hecho todas las conexiones semánticas posibles. ¿Son muy diferentes los mapas semánticos de los diferentes días festivos? Añadan otras ideas (otros óvalos) si quieren.

**PASO 3.**   Imagínense que el día festivo que exploraron en los **Pasos 1** y **2** va a ser mañana. Usen su mapa semántico como referencia y estas frases como guía para hacer una lluvia de ideas sobre lo que Uds. piensan hacer y lo que esperan de ese día especial.

1. Pienso (+ *infinitive*)...
2. Espero que...
3. Ojalá (que)...
4. Tengo miedo de que...
5. ¿ ?

**B.** A organizar sus ideas. Repase todas sus ideas generadas en los pasos anteriores y organícelas para describir su día festivo ideal y lo que espera Ud. de ese día. Incluya también lo que espera de las personas que van a celebrarlo con Ud. Comparta su información con la clase y apunte otras ideas que se le ocurran durante el proceso.

**C.** A escribir. Ahora, haga el borrador de su composición con las ideas y la información que recopiló en las actividades A y B. **¡OJO!** Guarde bien su trabajo. Va a necesitarlo otra vez para la sección de **Palabra escrita: A finalizar** en el *Manual de actividades*.

## Rossmary Valverde

Feria, *2007*

La pintora peruana Rossmary Valverde (1969– ) nació en Lima y es una artista autodidacta[a] del arte *naïf*. Sus cuadros representan recuerdos de su niñez en colores brillantes e imágenes simplificadas. Este cuadro representa una feria en la Plaza Buenos Aires, en Lima, en un barrio llamado Barrios Altos. Barrios Altos es muy viejo, y durante la época colonial era el barrio más prestigioso de Lima. Hoy en día, Barrios Altos es muy bohemio, es decir, tiene muchos cafés al aire libre, bares, restaurantes, conciertos y otros eventos culturales, y se considera la cuna[b] del folclor afroperuano y de la música criolla en Perú.

[a]*self-taught*   [b]*cradle*

## Vocabulario del tema

### Las expresiones artísticas

① la pintura

② la escultura

el pintor — **Las artes plásticas** — la escultora

③ el artista — el dibujo

④ la música clásica

⑤ el ballet clásico — la bailarina — el bailarín — el escenario

⑥ el cine — el actor — la actriz

**Las artes escénicas**

| el baile folclórico | traditional/folkloric dance |
|---|---|
| la canción | song |
| el coro | choir, chorus |
| el escenario | stage |
| el espectáculo | show |
| la exposición | exhibition; art show |
| el grabado | print |
| el guión | script |
| la obra de arte | work of art |
| la obra maestra | masterpiece |
| el teatro | theater |

Cognados: el concierto, la danza, el jazz, el mural, la música pop, la música sinfónica, la ópera, la orquesta (sinfónica), el rock

## La literatura

| la obra de teatro | play |
|---|---|

Cognados: la comedia, el drama, la novela

## Los artistas y otras personas

| el/la aficionado/a | fan |
|---|---|
| el/la cantante | singer |
| el/la cineasta | film director |
| el/la compositor(a) | composer |
| el/la danzante | dancer |
| el/la dramaturgo | playwright |
| el/la escritor(a) | writer |
| el esculptor | sculptor |
| el/la espectador(a) | spectator |
| el/la fotógrafo/a | photographer |
| el/la músico/a | musician |
| la pintora | painter |

Cognados: el/la arquitecto/a, el/la director(a), el/la poeta

## Los verbos

| componer (*like* poner) | to compose |
|---|---|
| esculpir | to sculpt |
| tejer | to weave |

Cognado: crear

## ACTIVIDADES

### A. Obra, persona o evento

**PASO 1.** Indique si las palabras se refieren a una obra (**O**), a una persona (**P**) o a un evento (**E**). **¡OJO!** Puede haber más de una respuesta.

MODELOS

|  | O | P | E |
|---|---|---|---|
| el cantante | ☐ | ☑ | ☐ |
| la ópera | ☑ | ☐ | ☑ |

|  | O | P | E |  |  | O | P | E |
|---|---|---|---|---|---|---|---|---|
| 1. la comedia | ☐ | ☐ | ☐ |  | 7. la exposición | ☐ | ☐ | ☐ |
| 2. la escultura | ☐ | ☐ | ☐ |  | 8. el guión | ☐ | ☐ | ☐ |
| 3. la actriz | ☐ | ☐ | ☐ |  | 9. el pintor | ☐ | ☐ | ☐ |
| 4. el coro | ☐ | ☐ | ☐ |  | 10. el espectáculo | ☐ | ☐ | ☐ |
| 5. el dibujo | ☐ | ☐ | ☐ |  | 11. la canción | ☐ | ☐ | ☐ |
| 6. el cineasta | ☐ | ☐ | ☐ |  | 12. el grabado | ☐ | ☐ | ☐ |

**PASO 2.** En parejas, den definiciones para las palabras del **Paso 1.** Sigan los modelos.

MODELOS El cantante es una persona que interpreta canciones.
La ópera es una obra de arte escénica cantada.

**PASO 3.** En parejas, escriban dos definiciones para otras palabras del **Vocabulario del tema.** Van a leer sus definiciones a la clase y sus compañeros/as van a adivinar las palabras definidas.

### B. ¿Qué hacen?

**PASO 1.** Explique qué hacen estas personas. Siga el modelo.

MODELO la actriz → La actriz hace papeles en el cine o en el teatro.

| | |
|---|---|
| 1. el escultor | 5. el compositor |
| 2. la bailarina | 6. la dramaturga |
| 3. el espectador | 7. el fotógrafo |
| 4. la arquitecta | 8. la poeta |

**PASO 2.** En parejas, den el nombre de personas específicas a las que se les aplican las profesiones del **Paso 1.**

MODELO Penélope Cruz es una famosa actriz española.

### C. Obras maestras

**PASO 1.** Indique a qué tipo de arte corresponden las obras maestras. **¡OJO!** Si no sabe qué es alguna de estas obras maestras, búsquela en el Internet.

| | |
|---|---|
| 1. _____ *Las Meninas* | **a.** arquitectura |
| 2. _____ «Annabel Lee» | **b.** ballet |
| 3. _____ La Alhambra | **c.** cine |
| 4. _____ *Las bodas de Fígaro* | **d.** escultura |
| 5. _____ *Hamlet* | **e.** mural |
| 6. _____ *Don Quijote de la Mancha* | **f.** novela |
| 7. _____ *El lago de los cisnes* (*swans*) | **g.** obra de teatro |
| 8. _____ *El Guernica* | **h.** ópera |
| 9. _____ *El laberinto del fauno* | **i.** pintura |
| 10. _____ *David* | **j.** poesía |

**PASO 2.** Con toda la clase, den más información sobre las obras del **Paso 1.**

MODELO *Las Meninas* es una *obra* del pintor español Diego Velázquez. Es del año 1656.

**D.** El arte en mi vida

**PASO 1.** Para determinar qué tipo de arte tiene preferencia en su vida, escriba el número de cada respuesta en la columna correspondiente.

|  | PLÁSTICO | ESCÉNICO | LITERARIO |
|---|---|---|---|
| **1.** ¿Cuántas veces ha ido Ud. al museo este año? | _____ | _____ | _____ |
| **2.** ¿Cuántos grabados (*reproductions*) de pinturas famosas tiene en su casa? | _____ | _____ | _____ |
| **3.** ¿Cuántos libros de fotografía tiene en su casa? | _____ | _____ | _____ |
| **4.** ¿Cuántas veces ha ido a un concierto este año? | _____ | _____ | _____ |
| **5.** ¿Cuántas veces ha asistido a la ópera? | _____ | _____ | _____ |
| **6.** ¿Cuántas obras de teatro ha visto este año? | _____ | _____ | _____ |
| **7.** ¿Cuántas novelas ha leído este año? | _____ | _____ | _____ |
| **8.** ¿Cuántos libros de poesía tiene en casa? | _____ | _____ | _____ |
| **9.** ¿Cuántas obras de teatro ha leído? | _____ | _____ | _____ |

**PASO 2.** En parejas, comparen sus listas y hagan un análisis. ¿Qué tipo de arte es más popular entre los estudiantes? Luego, hablen de sus artistas favoritos y las obras que prefieren.

Communication

---

## Nota cultural

Cultures

### LAS TELENOVELAS

La telenovela —o novela, telerromance, teleserie, teleteatro o seriado— es un programa de televisión transmitido en episodios diarios que narra una historia ficticia de alto contenido melodramático. Las telenovelas gozan de gran popularidad en toda Latinoamérica. México, Colombia, Argentina, Venezuela, Perú, Chile y Brasil son los principales productores de telenovelas. La telenovela colombiana «Yo soy Betty, la fea», uno de los éxitos más grandes de la historia de la televisión, ha sido exportada a numerosos países, y ahora, millones de personas en Europa, los Estados Unidos y Asia son fanáticos de las telenovelas.

El argumento[a] más común de una telenovela es una protagonista pobre que se enamora de[b] un hombre rico y tiene que luchar por lograr su amor. Uno de los personajes esenciales es la villana, que quiere impedir este amor.

Los actores y actrices de las telenovelas gozan de mucha fama en su país de origen y muchos de ellos utilizan la televisión como paso previo a su actuación en el cine.

---

[a]*plot* [b]*se... falls in love with*

**PREGUNTAS** En parejas, contesten las preguntas. Después, compartan sus ideas con la clase.

**1.** ¿Cuáles son las características generales de las telenovelas latinoamericanas? ¿Existen programas parecidos en su país? ¿Cuáles son? ¿De qué se tratan generalmente?

**2.** ¿Cuáles son otros programas de éxito en su país? ¿Por qué creen Uds. que tienen tanto éxito?

**3.** ¿Les gusta ver telenovelas o prefieren ver otros programas? ¿cuáles? Expliquen.

# Gramática

## 11.3 Present Subjunctive: Doubt, Denial, and Uncertainty

**GRAMÁTICA EN CONTEXTO**

### Los bailes folclóricos

*[Paula le manda un e-mail con una foto a su familia en México.]*

¡Hola! Espero que todos estén bien.

He visto muchos bailes folclóricos durante mi tiempo en Cusco. **Creo** que **hay** más de doce bailes folclóricos peruanos. **Dudo** que **pueda** nombrarlos todos, pero **estoy segura** de que los más importantes **son** el huayano y el kashua. En la foto adjunta pueden ver a unas mujeres bailando el huayno. Los trajes tradicionales que llevan son muy coloridos, ¿no?

**Dudo** que **vea** mucho más mañana porque **creo** que **vamos** a salir para Lima bastante temprano. **Es posible** que los **llame** la semana que viene. Escriban un e-mail para decirme cuándo van a estar todos en casa.

Un abrazo y muchos besos,

Paula

### ¿CIERTO O FALSO?

|  | C | F |
|---|---|---|
| 1. Es posible que Paula esté en Cusco sola. | ☐ | ☐ |
| 2. Es probable que a Paula le gusten los bailes folclóricos. | ☐ | ☐ |
| 3. Es dudoso que Paula saque muchas fotos. | ☐ | ☐ |
| 4. Es probable que Paula esté aburrida. | ☐ | ☐ |
| 5. Es cierto que Paula tiene familia en México. | ☐ | ☐ |

The subjunctive in Spanish is used after expressions in which speakers deny something, indicate they are uncertain about something, or don't believe that something is true. Remember that in sentences that use the subjunctive, the sentence will always have two clauses connected by **que**. In addition, the two clauses will *usually* have different subjects, although this is not always the case with verbs and expressions of doubt, denial, and uncertainty. This category of verbs and expressions is also unique in that there will generally be a verb or expression with opposite meaning that does *not* take the subjunctive. In other words, when expressing belief, affirmation, or certainty, the subjunctive is not used, but rather the indicative. The following charts show common verbs and expressions of doubt, denial, and uncertainty side-by-side with their opposites.

---

**GRAMÁTICA EN CONTEXTO** *Folkloric Dances / Paula sends an e-mail with a photo to her family in Mexico. / Hello! I hope you're all well. / I have seen many folkloric dances during my time in Cuzco. I think there are more than twelve Peruvian folkloric dances. I doubt that I can name them all, but I'm sure that the most important ones are the huayno and the kashua. In the attached photo, you can see women dancing the huayno. The traditional suits that the dancers wear are very colorful, aren't they? / I doubt that I will see much more tomorrow because I think we're leaving for Lima fairly early. It's possible that I'll call you next week. Write an e-mail to tell me when everyone will be at home. / A hug and lots of kisses, / Paula*

Pay attention to expressions of probability and possibility, with these expressions, all cases, both affirmative and negative, trigger the subjunctive.

| DOUBT, DENIAL, UNCERTAINTY | | |
|---|---|---|
| no creer que | | |
| dudar que | | |
| negar (ie) que | | |
| no es cierto que | + | subjunctive |
| no es verdad que | | |
| no estar (irreg.) seguro/a (de) que | | |
| (no) es (im)posible que | | |
| (no) es (im)probable que | | |

| BELIEF, AFFIRMATION, CERTAINTY | | |
|---|---|---|
| creer que | | |
| no dudar que | | |
| afirmar que | + | indicative |
| es cierto que | | |
| es verdad que | | |
| estar seguro/a (de) que | | |

**Dudo** que mucha gente considere las tiras cómicas una forma legítima de arte.

**No es posible** que lleguemos al museo a tiempo.

**No estoy segura de** que él comprenda el arte abstracto.

**Creemos** que la exposición de arte folclórico viene a nuestra ciudad.

*I doubt that many people consider comic books a legitimate form of art.*

*It's not possible that we will arrive at the museum on time.*

*I'm not sure that he understands abstract art.*

*We believe that the folk art exhibition is coming to our city.*

## ACTIVIDADES

**A. ¿Qué opina?**

**PASO 1.** Indique lo que Ud. opina de las declaraciones.

| | ES CIERTO | NO ES CIERTO |
|---|---|---|
| 1. Dan Brown es el mejor escritor del mundo. | ☐ | ☐ |
| 2. Mis amigos y yo preferimos una obra de teatro a una buena película. | ☐ | ☐ |
| 3. Me encanta bailar. | ☐ | ☐ |
| 4. Los estudiantes de esta universidad saben mucho de los compositores clásicos. | ☐ | ☐ |
| 5. Los músicos tienen que practicar mucho. | ☐ | ☐ |
| 6. Mis amigos tienen mucho talento artístico. | ☐ | ☐ |
| 7. Hay muchas exposiciones de arte en esta ciudad. | ☐ | ☐ |
| 8. En esta ciudad, se puede escuchar música sinfónica en vivo. | ☐ | ☐ |

**PASO 2.** Ahora, repita las declaraciones del **Paso 1,** empezando con **Es cierto que...** o **No es cierto que...,** según sus respuestas. **¡OJO!** ¿Cuándo se necesita usar el subjuntivo?

**B. Una fiesta sorpresa.** Llene los espacios en blanco con la forma correcta del verbo.

1. Es verdad que la zampoña (*panpipe*) _____ (**ser**) un instrumento importante de la música tradicional andina.
2. No creo que muchos estudiantes universitarios _____ (**preferir**) ir al teatro.
3. Es imposible que nosotros _____ (**poder**) comprar esa obra de arte. ¡Cuesta demasiado!
4. El dramaturgo está seguro de que muchas personas _____ (**asistir**) al estreno (*debut*) de su obra de teatro esta noche.
5. Dudo que tú _____ (**ir**) a encontrar una ganga (*deal*) en esa tienda.
6. Es verdad que yo _____ (**cantar**) bien, pero no es cierto que _____ (*yo:* **ser**) cantante profesional.
7. No dudamos que Uds. _____ (**sacar**) buenas fotos. No obstante, no estamos seguros de que _____ (*Uds:* **sacar**) mejores fotos que un fotógrafo profesional.
8. ¡Qué va! (*No way!*) No es verdad que tú _____ (**esculpir**) estatuas en tu tiempo libre.

**C. En el museo.** En parejas, digan lo que opinan dos amigos de lo que ven en el museo. Hagan oraciones completas con las palabras indicadas. Añadan palabras cuando sea necesario.

1. BEATRIZ: (yo) / creer / que / escultura / ser / muy / bonito
2. ESTEBAN: (yo) dudar / que / cuadro / ser / original
3. BEATRIZ: (yo) / estar / seguro de / que / cuadro / representar / creencias / indígenas
4. ESTEBAN: no / ser / cierto / que / fotógrafos / trabajar / independientemente
5. BEATRIZ: yo / conocer / a ellos / y / (yo) / afirmar / que / ellos / no trabajar / para / nadie
6. ESTEBAN: es cierto / fotos / salir / bonito
7. BEATRIZ: ¿(tú) / no / negar / que / fotos / ser / bueno?
8. ESTEBAN: ¿tú / no / creer / que / yo / tener / buen gusto (*good taste*)?

Cultures    Recycle

**D. La música andina**

**PASO 1.** Complete el texto con la forma correcta del verbo entre paréntesis en el presente de subjuntivo o indicativo, o en el pretérito o imperfecto cuando se indica con *P/I*. Cuando hay dos palabras entre paréntesis, escoja la palabra correcta y use su forma apropiada.

«¿En qué consiste la música andina?»

Esta (*P/I:* **ser**[1]) la pregunta que le (*P/I: nosotros:* **hacer**[2]) al guía que nos acompañaba por la Galería de Instrumentos Musicales en el Museo Nacional de Antropología, Arqueología e Historia de Lima.

Es cierto que los instrumentos típicos de la música folclórica andina (**estar/ser**[3]) el charango,[a] la quena[b] y el sicu.[c] Se afirma que la quena y el sicu (**estar/ser**[4]) instrumentos de viento[d] de origen precolombino», el guía nos (*P/I:* **responder**[5]).

Es verdad que estas dos flautas diferentes (**formar**[6]) parte de la herencia[e] musical de los habitantes de los Andes, ya que se han encontrado ejemplos arqueológicos de ellas. En el pasado, los indígenas (*P/I:* **hacer**[7]) las quenas de huesos[f] de animales, pero

---

[a]*10-stringed instrument of the Andes*  [b]*recorder-like Andean flute*  [c]*type of Andean panpipe*  [d]*de... wind*
[e]*heritage*  [f]*bones*

CAPÍTULO 11  La música, el arte y las celebraciones

después, (*P/I: ellos:* **empezar**[8]) a construirlas de madera y de bambú. También al principio (*P/I: ellos:* **fabricar**[9]) el sicu de huesos y cerámica, y más tarde, de un material natural, la caña. Hoy día, también es cierto que algunas personas innovadoras (**construir**[10]) los sicus de materiales tan modernos como los tubos de plástico. Cabe añadir que[g] hay diferentes sicus según su tamaño, lo cual afecta su sonido.[h]

Una quena

En contraste con estas flautas, el charango tiene otra historia. Aunque es imposible que los musicólogos (**identificar**[11]) el origen exacto del charango, dudan que este instrumento de cuerda[i] (**tener**[12]) su comienzo antes de la colonización europea. Están seguros de que los indígenas de esta región no (*P/I:* **tocar**[13]) instrumentos de cuerda antes de la llegada de los europeos. No hay duda de que el charango (**compartir**[14]) características con otros instrumentos de cuerda europeos como, por ejemplo, la guitarra y la mandolina. Originalmente, la gente (*P/I:* **hacer**[15]) la caja[j] del charango de la concha[k] del armadillo, y sólo más tarde, de madera. Sea cual sea su origen exacto,[l] es verdad que el charango (**desempeñar**[16]) un papel importante en la música andina de hoy.

Juntos, estos instrumentos le prestan[m] un sonido único a la música andina. En el museo, están seguros de que a Ud. le (**ir**[17]) a encantar saber más de su historia. Esperan que Ud. (**venir**[18]) pronto a conocerla.

---

[g]Cabe... *It should be added that* [h]*sound* [i]*de... stringed* [j]*box* [k]*shell* [l]Sea... *Whatever its exact origen may be* [m]*lend*

**PASO 2.** Conteste las preguntas, según el **Paso 1.**

1. ¿Cuáles son los instrumentos típicos de la música folclórica andina? ¿Cómo es la quena? ¿el sicu? ¿el charango?
2. ¿Cuál es el origen de la quena? ¿del sicu? ¿Por qué estamos seguros de que ese es su origen?

**PASO 3.** En parejas, contesten las preguntas.

Communication

1. ¿Qué música tradicional o folclórica se asocia con la ciudad o la región donde Uds. viven? ¿Cómo es esa música? ¿Cuáles son los instrumentos típicos de esa música? ¿Cuál es el origen de esta música?
2. ¿Qué música típica de otros países conocen Uds.? ¿Cómo es esa música? ¿Qué instrumentos se asocian comúnmente con esa música?

**PASO 4.** Busque más información sobre la música andina en el Internet. Si es posible, escuche un ejemplo de la música andina. Comparta sus impresiones y resultados con la clase.

Communities

## Nota interdisciplinaria

### LITERATURA: GABRIEL GARCÍA MÁRQUEZ Y EL REALISMO MÁGICO

*Gabriel García Márquez*

Gabriel García Márquez (1928– ) nació y se crió[a] en un pequeño pueblo de Colombia en la casa de sus abuelos maternos, personas que inspiraron el mundo literario del futuro autor. Su abuelo le contaba historias de las guerras civiles del siglo XIX, poniéndolo en contacto con la realidad histórica. Su abuela, por el contrario, le contaba leyendas del pueblo y organizaba la vida de la casa de acuerdo con las premoniciones que veía en sueños: ella le dio la visión mágica de la realidad. De este material histórico transformado por la magia y la ficción, el autor crea *Cien años de soledad*[b] (1967), novela del género literario del realismo mágico que coloca a García Márquez como primera figura de la narrativa hispanoamericana contemporánea.

*Cien años de soledad* narra la vida de siete generaciones de la familia Buendía en el pueblo imaginario de Macondo, desde la fundación del pueblo hasta la desaparición completa de la saga familiar. A través de la historia de los Buendía, el autor cuenta la historia de Colombia, comenzando después del Libertador Simón Bolívar hasta los años 30, fusionada con eventos fantásticos y extraordinarios que para los personajes no son anormales. Según el famoso poeta chileno, Pablo Neruda, *Cien años de soledad* es la segunda obra más importante en español después del *Quijote*. Es la obra maestra de García Márquez y uno de los libros que más traducciones tiene y que mayores ventas ha logrado. García Márquez es autor de muchas otras novelas inolvidables.[c] En 1982 recibió el Premio Nóbel de Literatura por su contribución a las artes.

[a]se... *grew up*  [b]*solitude*  [c]*unforgettable*

PREGUNTAS  Conteste las preguntas.

1. ¿De quiénes recibió la inspiración literaria García Márquez?
2. ¿Cuáles son dos elementos de la novela *Cien años de soledad*? ¿Qué historias se cuentan en esta novela?
3. ¿Qué información en el texto indica la importancia de García Márquez en la literatura?

# Lectura cultural

Ud. va a leer un artículo de la revista *Nexos*, escrito por Javier Solano y publicado por la American Airlines, sobre un festival internacional de música que tiene lugar cada año desde el 2007 en Cartagena, Colombia.

Cultures

## ANTES DE LEER

**A. A primera vista** (*glance*). 1. Lea el título y las primeras líneas *en letra cursiva* del artículo. Luego, indique qué información espera encontrar en el resto del artículo.

1. ☐ el éxito del festival
2. ☐ fecha y lugar(es) del festival
3. ☐ fundadores del festival
4. ☐ descripción de la ciudad de Cartagena
5. ☐ otros programas de actividades del festival
6. ☐ número de asistentes

**B. Sinónimos.** Estas frases aparecen en el artículo. Empareje las palabras **en negrita** con su sinónimo o definición.

1. _____ ...**emitir** (*broadcast*) por radio o televisión...
2. _____ ...contribuyen a hacer realidad el **lema** del festival: «La música es para todos».
3. _____ «La IV versión del festival tiene una **novedad**...
4. _____ ...conciertos de inauguración y **clausura**...
5. _____ ...las clases magistrales que estos músicos **dictan** durante el festival.
6. _____ ...un **taller** de Mantenimiento de Instrumentos de cuerda...

a. algo nuevo
b. final del festival
c. presentaciones
d. eslogan
e. curso, seminario
f. enseñan

## Festival musical que se consolida

*Con tan sólo cuatro años, el Festival Internacional de Música de Cartagena se ha arraigado[a] como uno de los eventos culturales de Colombia. Diez días de música y clases magistrales[b] llenan distintos escenarios de la ciudad amurallada[c] y algunos de los bellísimos barrios de la ciudad.*

El IV Festival Internacional de Música de Cartagena se realizará[d] del 9 al 16 de enero de 2010. El festival tiene una audiencia aproximada de 22.000 personas que asisten a los 25 conciertos y las transmisiones por radio y televisión contribuyen a hacer realidad el lema del festival: «La música es para todos».

La IV versión del festival tiene una novedad especial: la transmisión televisiva en directo[e] de los conciertos de inauguración y clausura en los teatros de Cine Colombia y Unicentro (Bogotá). También se televisarán[f] seis conciertos en directo y dos conciertos en diferido y, por supuesto, también serán[g] radiados.

El festival tiene también una vertiente[h] educativa y social muy importante; además de que reconocidos músicos internacionales, convocados por los maestros Charles Wadsworth y Stephen Prutsman, directores artísticos del certamen,[i] se presentan en más de 20 conciertos, cerca de 3.000 niños de la ciudad y más de 400 estudiantes de música de todo el país tienen la oportunidad de asistir a las clases magistrales que estos músicos dictan durante el festival.

---

[a]*se... has taken root* [b]*masterful* [c]*ciudad... walled city (old town Cartagena)* [d]*se... will be held* [e]*en... live* [f]*se... will be televised* [g]*will be* [h]*outpouring* [i]*concurso*

*En el Festival Internacional de Música de Cartagena*

Esto responde a los deseos de sus fundadores, Víctor y Julia Salvi y el maestro Charles Wadsworth, que desde el 2007, han considerado prioritario dar a conocer[j] el proyecto educativo de la Fundación Salvi, organizadora del evento.

Cada año se incrementa el número de estudiantes que llegan de todas las regiones de Colombia para asistir a estas clases. Adicionalmente, el festival es un espacio de aprendizaje e intercambio para los músicos colombianos invitados y de promoción del talento nacional con conciertos que destacan[k] su trabajo y trayectoria profesional y les presenta ante el público colombiano.

Desde el 2009, la Fundación Salvi Colombia inició dentro del festival un taller de Mantenimiento de Instrumentos de cuerda para contribuir a la formación y fortalecimiento de este tema en la región Caribe: el resultado fue todo un éxito: 70 horas de clases se dictaron a cerca de 20 jóvenes de proyectos musicales de Cartagena. El trabajo realizado permitió arreglar[l] cerca de cien instrumentos.

La edición de 2010 trae dos escenarios adicionales a los espacios utilizados por el festival en sus versiones anteriores: la Iglesia de la Santísima Trinidad, pequeña iglesia colonial construida en 1643, ubicada en la Plaza de la Trinidad en Getsemaní, recibirá[m] a los artistas en un nuevo concierto que complementa la serie de Conciertos Matutinos[n] del certamen. También, la Plaza de la Trinidad, en el barrio Getsemaní, llenará de[ñ] música las noches cartageneras incrementando en dos, la serie de conciertos en las plazas de la ciudad.

---

[j]dar... *to make known*   [k]*highlight*   [l]*to fix*   [m]*will receive*   [n]*Morning*   [ñ]llenará... *will fill with*

**A. Comprensión.** Indique si está Ud. de acuerdo, o no, con estas oraciones. Si Ud. no está de acuerdo, explique por qué.

|  | SÍ | NO |
|---|---|---|
| **1.** El festival ofrece conciertos en distintos lugares de la ciudad. | ☐ | ☐ |
| **2.** Todos los conciertos se pasan por televisión o radio. | ☐ | ☐ |
| **3.** El festival ofrece clases de música y cursos de reparación de instrumentos musicales. | ☐ | ☐ |
| **4.** El festival incluye clases de baile. | ☐ | ☐ |
| **5.** La orquesta está compuesta exclusivamente por músicos colombianos muy famosos. | ☐ | ☐ |
| **6.** El número de participantes en el festival aumenta cada año. | ☐ | ☐ |

**B. Temas de discusión.** En grupos pequeños, contesten las preguntas.

**1.** ¿Qué importancia tiene el festival para la carrera profesional de los músicos colombianos?

**2.** ¿Creen Uds. que el festival cumple (*fulfills*) el objetivo de «la música es para todos»? Expliquen.

**3.** ¿Qué otros tipos de eventos culturales hay en el lugar donde viven? ¿Cómo son? ¿Cuándo son? ¿Quiénes participan normalmente? ¿Participan Uds.? Expliquen.

*En la región donde Ud. vive, ¿hay festivales de música latina como este festival puertorriqueño en Chicago?*

# Concurso de videoblogs

## Perú: María Elena

### Lima en el Mes Morado

En este, su segundo videoblog, María Elena nos muestra Lima con la ayuda de su amiga Graciela. María Elena y Graciela nos llevan al centro histórico, a varios distritos de la ciudad y al Museo de Arte de Lima (MALI). También, como es el mes de octubre, que los peruanos llaman el «Mes Morado», María Elena nos explica esta importante tradición peruana.

### Vocabulario práctico

| | |
|---|---|
| **un ratón se ha comido la lengua** | the cat's got her tongue (*lit.* a mouse has eaten her tongue) |
| **Huaca Pucllana** | *ceremonial center of Lima* |
| **vitrinas** | window displays |
| **he grabado** | I filmed |
| **mantillas blancas** | white head scarves |
| **motivos religiosos** | religious symbols |

### ANTES DE VER

Repase el **Vocabulario práctico** y conteste las preguntas antes de ver el videoblog de María Elena.

1. ¿Qué partes o qué cosas del lugar donde Ud. vive debe conocer una persona que visita su región? Explique por qué son algo que ningún visitante debe perderse (*miss*).
2. ¿Hay algunas celebraciones famosas o tradiciones importantes en el lugar donde Ud. vive? ¿Cuáles son? ¿Cómo son?

### DESPUÉS DE VER

**A. Comprensión.** Conteste las preguntas, según el videoblog de María Elena.

1. ¿Qué estudia Graciela y cuánto tiempo hace que vive en Lima?
2. ¿Cómo es Lima, en general?
3. ¿Cómo son los distritos de San Isidro, Miraflores y Barranco? ¿Qué se puede hacer allí?
4. ¿Qué le llamó la atención a Ud. en el Museo de Arte de Lima? Explique.
5. ¿Por qué es famosa la cerámica inca? ¿Cuál era su función principal?
6. ¿Qué hacen los limeños (gente de Lima) durante el Mes Morado?
7. ¿Por qué celebran los limeños al Señor de los Milagros?

**B. Temas de discusión.** En grupos pequeños, comenten estos temas.

1. Mencionen los aspectos del segmento que creen que identifican a Lima como una ciudad moderna.
2. Expliquen cómo se celebran las fiestas religiosas o seculares donde Uds. viven. ¿Hay alguna celebración como las fiestas de Lima en su región?
3. Busquen la página Web del Museo de Arte de Lima para ver su colección permanente de arte y escriban un breve informe para explicar por qué María Elena dice que MALI tiene una excelente colección de arte peruano.

## Los verbos

| | |
|---|---|
| brindar (por) | to toast (to) |
| componer (like poner) | to compose |
| disfrazarse (c) | to disguise oneself |
| esculpir | to sculpt |
| tejer | to weave |

Cognados: celebrar, crear
Repaso: bailar, cantar, dibujar, escribir, pintar

## Los días festivos y las celebraciones — Holidays and Celebrations

| | |
|---|---|
| el Año Nuevo | New Year's Day |
| el Día de Acción de Gracias | Thanksgiving Day |
| el Día de Canadá | Canada Day |
| el Día de la Independencia | Independence Day |
| el Día de la Madre | Mother's Day |
| el Día de la Raza | Columbus Day |
| el Día de los Muertos | Day of the Dead |
| el Día de los Reyes Magos | Feast of the Three Kings (Epiphany) |
| el Día del Padre | Father's Day |
| el día del santo | one's saint day |
| la Navidad | Christmas |
| la Nochevieja | New Year's Eve |
| la Pascua | Easter |
| la Pascua judía | Passover |
| la fiesta de quinceañera | young woman's fifteenth birthday party |
| los Sanfermines | San Fermín Festival (Running of the Bulls) |
| la Semana Santa | Holy Week |
| las vacaciones de primavera | spring break |

Cognado: el Carnaval, el Cinco de Mayo
Repaso: el cumpleaños

## Para celebrar

| | |
|---|---|
| el árbol de Navidad | Christmas tree |
| la carroza | parade float |
| el conjunto musical | band, musical group |
| la corrida de toros | bullfight |
| el encierro | running of the bulls |
| la festividad | festivity; feast |
| los fuegos artificiales | fireworks |
| el regalo | gift |

Cognados: el festival, el folclor, el santo patrón / la santa patrona; adornado/a, nacional, religioso/a
Repaso: la bandera, el desfile, la feria, la fiesta, la máscara; tradicional

## Las expresiones artísticas — Artistic Expressions

| | |
|---|---|
| las artes escénicas | performing arts |
| las artes plásticas | visual arts |
| el baile folclórico | traditional/folkloric dance |
| la canción | song |
| el coro | choir, chorus |
| el dibujo | drawing |
| el escenario | stage |
| el espectáculo | show |
| la exposición | exhibition; art show |
| el grabado | print |
| el guión | script |
| la obra de arte | work of art |
| la obra maestra | masterpiece |
| la pintura | painting |

Cognados: el ballet clásico, el concierto, la danza, el jazz, el mural, la música clásica, la música pop, la música sinfónica, la ópera, la orquesta (sinfónica), el rock
Repaso: la arquitectura, las artesanías, el cine, el cuadro, la escultura, la fotografía, el instrumento musical, la música, la película, el teatro, los tejidos

## La literatura

| | |
|---|---|
| la obra de teatro | play |

Cognados: la comedia, el drama, la novela
Repaso: la poesía

## Los artistas y otras personas

| | |
|---|---|
| la actriz | actress |
| el/la aficionado/a | fan |
| el bailarín, la bailarina | (ballet) dancer |
| el/la cantante | singer |
| el/la cineasta | film director |
| el/la compositor(a) | composer |
| el/la danzante | dancer |
| el/la dramaturgo/a | playwright |
| el/la escritor(a) | writer |
| el/la escultor(a) | sculptor |
| el/la espectador(a) | spectator |
| el/la fotógrafo/a | photographer |
| el/la músico/a | musician |
| el/la pintor(a) | painter |

Cognados: el actor, el/la arquitecto/a, el/la director(a), el/la poeta

| Verbos de voluntad, emoción y duda | Verbs of Volition, Emotion, and Doubt |
|---|---|
| aconsejar | to advise |
| alegrarse (de) | to be happy (about) |
| decir (irreg.) | to tell |
| dudar | to doubt |
| esperar | to hope |
| estar (irreg.) seguro/a (de) | to be sure (of) |
| negar (ie) | to deny |
| sorprender | to surprise |

Cognados: afirmar, insistir (en), prohibir (prohíbo)
Repaso: creer (y), desear, gustar, necesitar, pedir (i, i), preferir (ie, i), preocupar, querer (irreg.), recomendar (ie), sentir (ie, i), sugerir (ie, i), tener (irreg.) miedo (de)

| Algunas expresiones impersonales | Some Impersonal Expressions |
|---|---|
| es | |
|   cierto que | it's certain that |
|   es verdad que | it's true that |
|   extraño que | it's strange that |
|   una lástima que | it's a shame that |
| ojalá (que) | hopefully |

Cognados: es absurdo que, es importante que, (no) es (im)posible que, (no) es (im)probable que, es increíble que, es necesario que, es urgente que
Repaso: es bueno/malo que

# La música y la danza

Connections

## ANTES DE VER

¿Cuánta experiencia tiene Ud. con la música y danza hispanas?

|  | SÍ | NO |
|---|---|---|
| 1. He escuchado la radio en español. | ☐ | ☐ |
| 2. He comprado un CD de música hispana. | ☐ | ☐ |
| 3. He cantado en español. | ☐ | ☐ |
| 4. He visto un espectáculo de baile hispano. | ☐ | ☐ |
| 5. He bailado salsa, merengue, flamenco o tango. | ☐ | ☐ |
| 6. He tocado algún instrumento de una cultura precolombina. | ☐ | ☐ |

### Vocabulario práctico

| | | | |
|---|---|---|---|
| **los cantos** | singing | **la cantaora** | flamenco singer |
| **de cuerda** | stringed | **las palmadas** | handclaps |

## DESPUÉS DE VER

Complete las oraciones con información verdadera, según el vídeo. Use palabras de la lista. ¡OJO! Algunas palabras no se usan.

| barrio | de percusión | palmadas |
|---|---|---|
| cara | de viento | público |
| cuevas | influencia | tango |

1. En Perú, se observa mucho la _____ de las culturas precolombinas.
2. La zampoña y la quena son ejemplos de instrumentos _____.
3. Hablar de la música argentina es recordar la pasión y los movimientos sensuales del _____.
4. Los que bailan flamenco transmiten sus emociones a través de (*through*) las manos, el cuerpo y la _____.
5. El flamenco es un arte de pasión, comunicada por la voz, la guitarra, las _____ y los zapatos.

## EL FLAMENCO

El flamenco es un grupo de bailes y cantes[a] típicos del sur de España que se originó hace más de 200 años en Andalucía. Aunque se asocia con los gitanos,[b] tiene influencias de cantos judíos, melodías árabes y otros ritmos. El flamenco se destaca por[c] la pasión de los **tocaores**,[d] la sensualidad de los **bailaores**[e] y la emoción de los **cantaores**.

[a]canciones del flamenco    [b]gypsies
[c]se... is distinguished by
[d]flamenco guitarists    [e]flamenco dancers

## LOS MARIACHIS

Los mariachis representan una rica tradición del folclor mexicano. Se dice que el nombre **mariachi** viene de la palabra francesa *mariage*. Los mariachis siempre visten con trajes coloridos y sombreros enormes. Sus canciones, tocadas con guitarra, guitarrón,[a] violín y trompeta, son una parte integral de muchas celebraciones mexicanas.

[a]*large guitar used primarily in* **mariachi** *bands*

## ACTIVIDADES

**A.** Comprensión. ¿Cierto o falso?

|  | C | F |
|---|---|---|
| **1.** Los mariachis son una parte de la rica tradición folclórica de Perú. | ☐ | ☐ |
| **2.** El flamenco se relaciona con los gitanos y con las culturas árabe y judía. | ☐ | ☐ |
| **3.** La guitarra clásica también se llama **guitarra hispana.** | ☐ | ☐ |
| **4.** Andrés Segovia es un mariachi muy conocido. | ☐ | ☐ |
| **5.** La música de Carlos Santana tiene influencias de rock, reggaetón y *country-western*. | ☐ | ☐ |
| **6.** El documental *Buena Vista Social Club* creó mucho interés en la música cubana. | ☐ | ☐ |
| **7.** Las maracas y los tambores son instrumentos de viento. | ☐ | ☐ |

**B.** Conexiónes. En parejas, contesten las preguntas.

**1.** ¿Qué tipo(s) de música son populares donde Uds. viven? ¿Qué influencias históricas tiene la música de esa región? ¿Les gusta(n) o no?

**2.** ¿Cuáles son algunas conexiones entre la música y danza de diferentes regiones o países hispanos? ¿Qué tienen en común?

Connections

**C.** A investigar más. Escoja *uno* de estos temas para escribir un breve informe. Use el Internet o la biblioteca para encontrar por lo menos cinco datos interesantes que no se presentaron en las páginas anteriores.

**1.** el flamenco
**2.** los mariachis
**3.** el tango
**4.** el Buena Vista Social Club

**D.** Temas de discusión. En grupos pequeños, comenten *uno* de estos temas y escriban algunas conclusiones breves en español. Luego, compartan sus conclusiones con la clase.

Communication

**1.** la música o baile nacional de este país
**2.** la música o baile más popular entre los estudiantes de hoy

## CARLOS SANTANA

El guitarrista Carlos Santana es un icono de la música hispana. Nació en México, pero de adolescente se mudó a San Francisco, California. Ha vendido más de 100 millones de álbumes y ha ganado diez premios Grammy, ocho de ellos en el año 2000. En su música mezcla[a] diferentes géneros como el rock, los blues y el jazz.

[a]he blends

## EL BUENA VISTA SOCIAL CLUB: COMPAY SEGUNDO

El Buena Vista Social Club es un grupo compuesto por músicos legendarios cubanos como el guitarrista Compay Segundo, ya difunto.[a] En 1999 salió un documental[b] del mismo nombre que relata la historia del grupo y que fue esencial para promover[c] los ritmos cubanos. Hoy día el grupo sigue dando actuaciones por todo el mundo.

[a]deceased    [b]documentary    [c]para... in promoting

## ASÍ SE DICE: LOS INSTRUMENTOS MUSICALES...

- **de cuerda: el arpa** (harp), **el bajo** (bass guitar), **el contrabajo** (upright bass), **la guitarra, la mandolina, el violín, el violonchelo** (cello)
- **de percusión: la batería** (drums, drum set), **el bongo, el címbalo, las maracas, la pandereta** (tambourine), **el tambor** (drum, gen.)
- **de teclado: el clavicordio, el órgano, el piano**
- **de viento: el clarinete, la flauta, el saxofón, el trombón, la trompeta, la tuba**

El Cerro (Mt.) Fitz Roy, en la Patagonia

# Entrada cultural

## El Cono Sur: Argentina, Chile, Paraguay y Uruguay

Cultures

En la Isla de Pascua, Chile

Punta del Este, Uruguay

El mate

El Cono Sur comprende Argentina, Chile, Paraguay y Uruguay. Con excepción de Paraguay, la mayoría de la población de esos países es de origen europeo, debido a la fuerte ola de inmigración que llegó a estos países en los primeros años del siglo XX. La población de Paraguay es principalmente mestiza, y el guaraní es idioma cooficial junto con el español.

Argentina es montañosa al oeste, dominada por los Andes. Al este, Argentina es plana[a] y forma las famosas pampas, inmensas llanuras[b] dedicadas al pasto[c] de ganado y territorio por excelencia del gaucho.[d] La región de la Patagonia, al sur, combina la terminación de los Andes con hermosas playas y glaciares.

Chile es un país alargado y estrecho. Su suelo[e] es espléndido para los vinos y el subsuelo es rico en cobre,[f] plata y oro. Miles de kilómetros al oeste, en el Océano Pacífico está la misteriosa Isla de Pascua con sus gigantescas estatuas monolíticas construidas hace miles de años por los rapanuis, primitivos habitantes de la isla.

Uruguay se caracteriza por la ausencia de montañas en su geografía y por la mezcla de mar y bosque en partes de su territorio, como en Punta del Este, lugar reconocido internacionalmente como el principal balneario de América.

Paraguay es el país más mestizo del Cono Sur y se enorgullece[g] de conservar su pasado guaraní. Este país no tiene acceso al mar y la agricultura y la ganadería son sus principales fuentes de riqueza.

Los habitantes del Cono Sur comparten su pasión por el fútbol, el mate y la parrillada, así como un interés elevado por la cultura.

[a]*flat*  [b]*plains*  [c]*grazing*  [d]*kind of cowboy*  [e]*soil*  [f]*copper*  [g]*se... is proud*

# La guitarra

La guitarra es un instrumento musical de cuerda muy importante en la música hispana. Hay guitarras de diferentes tipos, como la clásica, la acústica y la eléctrica. Se usa tanto en las actuaciones de música y baile tradicionales como en los conciertos de rockeros hispanos actuales. Hoy en día es difícil imaginar la música sin los tonos irresistibles de una guitarra, tocada con suave dulzura[a] o a todo volumen.

[a]suave... *gentle sweetness*

**LA GUITARRA CLÁSICA: ANDRÉS SEGOVIA**

La forma actual de la guitarra clásica —también llamada guitarra española— no ha cambiado mucho desde el siglo XVI. Por lo general tiene seis cuerdas de nilón y se toca a solas, con pequeños grupos de otros músicos o en orquesta. El español Andrés Segovia (1893-1987) es uno de los intérpretes[a] clásicos más conocidos del género.

[a]*performers*

# El bienestar*

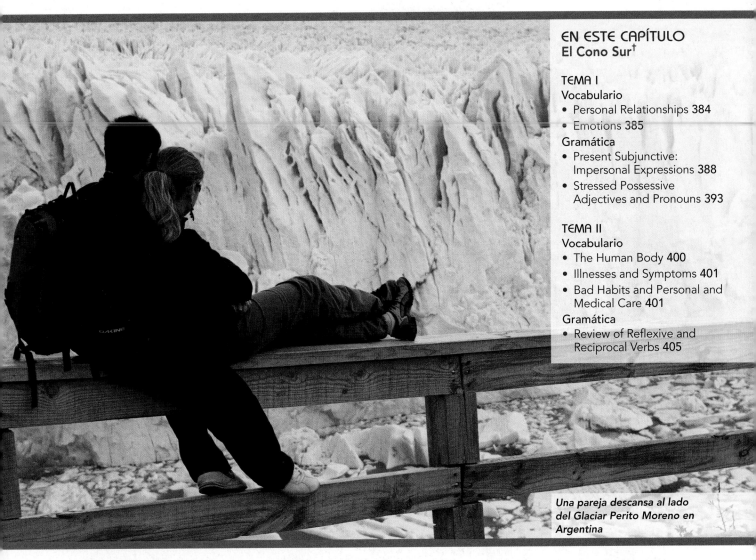

*Una pareja descansa al lado del Glaciar Perito Moreno en Argentina*

1. ¿Qué tipo de relación personal cree Ud. que existe entre las personas de la fotografía?

2. ¿Qué valora Ud. más en un amigo o amiga?

3. ¿Cree que los sentimientos de amor y amistad (*friendship*) **contribuyen al bienestar personal? ¿Cómo nos ayuda el cariño** (*affection*) **en nuestra vida? ¿Qué otros aspectos pueden contribuir al bienestar físico y mental de una persona?**

**connect**
|SPANISH
www.connectspanish.com

---

*El... Well-being
†Cono... Southern Cone (region of South America that includes Argentina, Chile, Paraguay, and Uruguay)

## Vocabulario del tema

### Las relaciones sentimentales

**La amistad**
①
reírse (i, i) (me río)
abrazarse (c)

**El amor**
②
la novia
sonreír (i, i) (sonrío)
enamorarse (de)
el novio

**El noviazgo**
③
el compromiso
el novio
la novia

**La boda**
④
casarse (con)
el novio
la novia

**El matrimonio**
⑤
el esposo
la esposa
llevarse bien (con)

**La separación**
⑥
discutir / pelear(se)
llevarse mal (con)
separarse (de)
divorciarse (de)

| | |
|---|---|
| gritar | to yell |
| llorar | to cry |
| quejarse | to complain |
| quererse (*irreg.*) | to love each other |
| romper con | to break up with |
| sentir (ie, i) cariño por | to be fond of |
| tenerle (*irreg.*) cariño a | to be fond of |
| la amistad | friendship |
| la cita | date |
| el compromiso | engagement |
| la luna de miel | honeymoon |
| la pareja | partner; couple |
| la pareja de hecho | common-law couple; domestic partner |

Repaso: besarse; el divorcio, el estado civil; casado/a, divorciado/a, separado/a

Observe

The word **novio/a** can have different meanings. It can mean *boyfriend/ girlfriend*, *fiancé(e)*, or *groom/bride*, depending on the context.

## Las emociones

| | |
|---|---|
| el amor | love |
| el cariño | affection |
| amable | friendly |
| celoso/a | jealous |
| enamorado/a (de) | in love (with) |

Repaso: alegre, cariñoso/a, contento/a, emocionado/a, enojado/a, irritado/a, nervioso/a, orgulloso/a, sereno/a, sorprendido/a, triste

### ACTIVIDADES

**A. Las etapas de las relaciones.** Indique qué tipo de pareja se describe en las oraciones: una pareja en su primera cita (**C**), novios comprometidos (**N**) o un matrimonio establecido (**M**). ¡OJO! En algunos casos, hay más de una respuesta posible.

| | C | N | M |
|---|---|---|---|
| 1. Hablan de todos los detalles de su boda. | ☐ | ☑ | ☐ |
| 2. Se sienten nerviosos en el restaurante durante la cita. | ☑ | ☐ | ☐ |
| 3. Se abrazan todas las mañanas antes de ir al trabajo. | ☐ | ☐ | ☑ |
| 4. Se queja de que su pareja no hace ciertos quehaceres. | ☐ | ☐ | ☑ |
| 5. Se besan tímidamente. | ☑ | ☐ | ☐ |
| 6. No se lleva bien con la futura suegra. | ☐ | ☑ | ☐ |
| 7. Se preocupan por el futuro de sus hijos. | ☐ | ☐ | ☑ |
| 8. Planean su luna de miel. | ☐ | ☑ | ☐ |
| 9. Exponen (*They explain*) sus intereses, estudios y planes para el futuro. | ☑ | ☐ | ☐ |
| 10. Se enamoran a primera vista (*at first sight*). | ☑ | ☐ | ☐ |

**B. Las relaciones buenas y malas**

**PASO 1.** Complete las oraciones con palabras de la lista.

| | | | |
|---|---|---|---|
| avergonzada | cita | me siento | pareja de hecho |
| casarse | enamorada | novio | se pelean |
| celosa | luna de miel | novios | se quieren |

1. La boda está planeada pero no creo que vayan a _____ *casarse* porque _____ *se pelean* y se gritan todo el tiempo.

2. Tengo una _____ *cita* con el amigo de Javier esta noche y _____ *me siento* muy nerviosa porque no lo conozco.

(Continúa.)

3. Marta se siente _____ *celosa* porque vio a su _____ *novio* con otra muchacha en el centro comercial.

4. Después de casarse, los _____ *novios* van a pasar la _____ *luna de miel* en un crucero que sale de Valparaíso.

5. Mariana se siente _____ porque está _____ del hermano de su novio.

6. Lourdes y Rolando viven juntos, pero no están casados. Son una _____, y después de quince años, todavía _____ mucho.

**PASO 2.** Diga si las relaciones que se describen en el **Paso 1** son buenas o malas. **¡OJO!** Si no hay suficiente información para calificar las relaciones, diga que es imposible saberlo y explique por qué.

**C. En mi familia**

**PASO 1.** Indique si cree que estas acciones y emociones son positivas o negativas y explique por qué.

**MODELO** sentirse celoso/a → Es una emoción negativa, porque está basada en la inseguridad.

1. besarse
2. casarse
3. romper con alguien
4. abrazarse
5. pelearse
6. divorciarse
7. discutir
8. amarse
9. reírse
10. llorar

Communication

**PASO 2.** En parejas, hablen de los miembros de su familia y digan quiénes han hecho o experimentado lo que aparece en la lista del **Paso 1.**

**MODELOS** Mis hermanos y yo hemos peleado mucho.
Mi madre le tiene mucho cariño a mi padre.

**D. Oraciones.** Forme oraciones usando las frases de las columnas. Complete cada idea con una explicación (**porque...**). Siga los modelos. **¡OJO!** En las oraciones va a hablar de sus sentimientos con relación a lo que podrían (*might*) hacer otras personas (en la segunda columna). Debe usar el subjuntivo del verbo.

**MODELOS** Temo que mi hermana y su esposo se divorcien porque se llevan muy mal y siempre se pelean enfrente de la familia.
Me alegro de que mi compañero de cuarto se case con su novia porque son una pareja perfecta y se llevan muy bien.

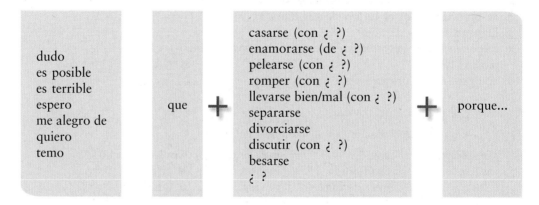

| dudo es posible es terrible espero me alegro de quiero temo | que **+** | casarse (con ¿ ?) enamorarse (de ¿ ?) pelearse (con ¿ ?) romper (con ¿ ?) llevarse bien/mal (con ¿ ?) separarse divorciarse discutir (con ¿ ?) besarse ¿ ? | **+** | porque... |

**E. ¿Qué forma una buena relación?**

**PASO 1.** Haga una lista de por lo menos seis cualidades que, en su opinión, debe tener una buena relación entre los amigos y entre las parejas. **¡OJO!** Debe hacer una lista para la amistad y otra para el amor.

**PASO 2.** Entreviste a un compañero / una compañera de clase con estas preguntas. Luego, cambien de papel.

1. ¿Es importante para ti la amistad? ¿Qué esperas de un buen amigo / una buena amiga?
2. ¿Tienes buenos amigos/as? ¿Quién es tu mejor amigo/a? ¿Por qué te llevas bien con esa persona? ¿Cuál es el secreto de su amistad?
3. ¿Qué comportamientos o acciones de tus amigos no te gustan? ¿Cómo te hacen sentir?
4. ¿Te gustaría casarte? (¿o estás casado/a ya?) ¿Qué comportamientos esperas de tu pareja?
5. Si no estás casado/a, ¿cómo ves tu futura boda? ¿Es una boda grande o pequeña e íntima?
6. Si estás casado/a, ¿cómo fue tu boda? ¿Fue una boda grande o no? ¿Cuántos invitados asistieron?

## Nota cultural

Cultures

### EL TANGO

*En Buenos Aires*

El tango, junto con la salsa, el merengue y la cumbia, es probablemente uno de los estilos musicales latinoamericanos de más fama internacional. El tango nació en Buenos Aires alrededor del año 1880. Se originó en una especie de casas grandes, llamadas «conventillos», en donde convivían[a] inmigrantes europeos y afroargentinos, como producto de la fusión de sus variadas culturas. En sus comienzos, el tango era considerado vulgar y atrevido,[b] pero con el tiempo se convirtió en el estilo de música más representativo de Argentina. De hecho, el tango es hoy la manifestación cultural más relevante de Argentina y signo de su identidad nacional.

Los principales instrumentos del tango son el bandoneón,[c] que se convirtió en el emblema de esta música, el piano y el violín. Al principio, sólo se representaba con instrumentos, pero con el tiempo se incorporaron los tangos cantados. El cantante y compositor de tango más famoso del mundo es Carlos Gardel. En Argentina aseguran que Gardel, aunque ya muerto... ¡cada día canta mejor!

[a]*coexisted* [b]*daring* [c]*type of accordion*

**PREGUNTAS** En parejas, contesten las preguntas. Después, compartan sus ideas con la clase.

1. ¿Cómo y cuándo nació el tango en Argentina? ¿Qué representa el tango en ese país?
2. ¿Qué instrumento es emblemático de este estilo de música? ¿Qué otros instrumentos se usan? ¿Quién ha sido su representante más famoso?
3. ¿Existe un tipo de música que represente a su país o a su comunidad? ¿Cuál es esa música? ¿Se baila? ¿Es una música alegre o melancólica? ¿De qué trata la letra de sus canciones? ¿Creen Uds. que esa música representa la identidad de su país o de su comunidad, o que manifiesta su cultura? Expliquen de qué forma.

## 12.1 Present Subjunctive: More About Impersonal Expressions

**GRAMÁTICA EN CONTEXTO**

### Para ser buenos amigos

Rita, David y Julio son buenos amigos y hablan francamente de su amistad. Los tres saben que **es importante** que **cultiven** su amistad. Según ellos, **es absurdo** que, desde el momento en que tienen novio o novia, algunas personas **desatiendan** a sus amistades. En su opinión, **es mejor** que los amigos **nutran** su amistad aunque tengan otras relaciones, porque cuando tienen problemas, los amigos se escuchan, se ayudan y se ofrecen consejos mutuamente. **Es una lástima** que algunos amigos **se peleen** por cosas insignificantes, pero cuando hay algún problema entre ellos, Rita, David y Julio dicen que **es necesario** que los amigos **sepan** comunicar sus sentimientos. **Es imposible** que **eviten** los celos y las mezquindades si no hay comunicación. Siempre **es bueno** que **compartan** su tiempo y que **se diviertan** juntos. **Es cierto** que estos tres amigos **hacen** muchas cosas juntas: les gusta salir a bailar, tomar café y asistir a partidos de los Albicelestes. ¿Qué hace Ud. para ser un buen amigo o una buena amiga?

**Comprensión.** ¿Qué dirían (*would say*) Rita, David y Julio sobre los buenos amigos?

1. ☐ Es importante que tengan algunos intereses en común.
2. ☐ Es preferible que les guste la misma comida.
3. ☐ Es malo que tengan novio o novia.
4. ☐ Es bueno que compartan su tiempo y que se diviertan juntos.
5. ☐ Es urgente que comuniquen sus sentimientos cuando tienen algún problema.
6. ☐ Es imposible que se peleen.

---

Impersonal expressions in Spanish take the form of **Es** + *adjective* and translate as *It is* + *adjective* in English. These types of generalizations trigger the subjunctive if they express volition, emotion, uncertainty, or doubt. In other words, if an impersonal expression fits any of the categories of subjunctive triggers that you have already seen, then the subjunctive should be used in the following clause. On the other hand, some impersonal expressions do not trigger the subjunctive because they express certainty, facts, observations, and so on. You saw several impersonal expressions in **Capítulo 11.** Those are repeated here as a review. For comparison, a few impersonal expressions that do not trigger the subjunctive are included as well.

---

GRAMÁTICA EN CONTEXTO | ***To Be Good Friends*** / *Rita, David, and Julio are good friends and they talk frankly about their friendship. The three of them know that it's important that they cultivate their friendship. According to them, it's absurd that, from the moment they get a boyfriend or girlfriend, some people neglect their friendships. In their opinion, it's better that friends maintain their friendships even though they have other relationships, because when they have problems, friends listen, help, and give each other advice. It's a shame that some friends fight over insignificant things, but when there's a problem between them, Rita, David, and Julio say that it's necessary for friends to know how to communicate their feelings. It's impossible for them to avoid jealousy and pettiness if there is no communication. It's always good for them to share their time and to have fun together. It's true that these three friends do a lot of things together: they like to go out dancing, have coffee, and go to Albicelestes games. What do you do to be a good friend?*

## IMPERSONAL EXPRESSIONS

| USED WITH THE SUBJUNCTIVE | USED WITH THE INDICATIVE |
|---|---|
| **es absurdo que**<br>**es bueno que**<br>**es importante que**<br>**es increíble que**<br>**es interesante que**<br>**es malo que**<br>**es mejor que**<br>**es necesario que**<br>**es una lástima que**<br>**es urgente que**<br>**no es cierto que**<br>**(no) es imposible que**<br>**(no) es improbable que**<br>**(no) es posible que**<br>**(no) es probable que**<br>**no es verdad que** | **es cierto que**<br>**es obvio que**<br>**es verdad que** |

| | |
|---|---|
| **Es mejor** que Silvia y Antonio se **casen.** | *It's best that Silvia and Antonio get married.* |
| **Es una lástima** que Rolando no tenga novia. | *It's a shame that Rolando doesn't have a girlfriend.* |
| **Es interesante** que Rolando no tenga novia. | *It's interesting that Rolando doesn't have a girlfriend.* |
| **Es verdad** que Anita y Víctor se **divorcian.** | *It's true that Anita and Victor are gettting divorced.* |

---

## Nota comunicativa

Communication

**Es** + *adj.* + *inf.*

Impersonal expressions may also be used to make generalizations about everyone rather than specific people. To express this type of generalization, simply use an infinitive (rather than **que** followed by the subjunctive). Compare the following pairs of sentences. The first in each pair is about specific people while the second is a pure generalization that could apply to anyone.

| | |
|---|---|
| **Es importante que entiendas** las responsabilidades del matrimonio. | *It's important that you understand the responsibilities of marriage.* |
| **Es importante entender** las responsabilidades del matrimonio. | *It's important to understand the responsibilities of marriage.* |
| ¿**Es posible que** ella **encuentre** por el Internet el esposo ideal? | *Is it possible for her to find the ideal husband on the Internet?* |
| ¿**Es posible encontrar** por el Internet el esposo ideal? | *Is it possible to find the ideal husband on the Internet?* |

## ACTIVIDADES

**A.** Las relaciones amorosas

**PASO 1.** ¿Cuáles de estas cosas debe observar una pareja para tener buenas relaciones? Enumere (*number*) las cosas de 1 (la más importante) a 8 (la menos importante), según su opinión.

Es importante que...

a. _____ cada persona exprese sus pensamientos o emociones cuando surgen problemas entre ellos.

b. _____ cada miembro de la pareja mantenga sus propias amistades.

c. _____ una pareja salga a bailar o a cenar todas las semanas.

d. _____ cada persona siempre escuche lo que la otra tiene que decir para que haya buena comunicación entre ellos.

e. _____ cada miembro de la pareja exprese sus emociones sin gritar o llorar.

f. _____ los dos pasen tiempo con otros amigos o personas.

g. _____ cuando uno de ellos se siente molesto o inseguro se lo diga al otro.

h. _____ cada persona cumpla con (*keep*) sus promesas.

**PASO 2.** Ahora escriba otras dos oraciones que expresen sus ideas personales sobre lo que es importante para tener buenas relaciones con un novio / una novia.

**PASO 3.** Comparta sus ideas con la clase. ¿Cómo comparan sus ideas con las de sus compañeros de la clase?

**B.** Unas opiniones sobre las relaciones. Complete las oraciones con la forma correcta de los verbos entre paréntesis.

1. Es imposible que (*nosotros:* **encontrar**) la pareja ideal.
2. Es absurdo que algunas personas (**casarse**) antes de graduarse.
3. Es malo que tantas parejas (**divorciarse**) en este país.
4. Es una lástima que la familia típica de hoy (**ser**) más pequeña que la del siglo pasado.
5. Es importante que los esposos no (**discutir**) enfrente de sus hijos.
6. Es mejor que las familias (**comer**) juntas todos los días.
7. Es cierto que (*tú:* **tener**) una novia cariñosa.
8. Es probable que (*yo:* **casarse**) en menos de un año.

*¿Qué opina Ud.? ¿Es bueno que los padres se peleen enfrente de los hijos?*

**C.** ¿Es verdad?

**PASO 1.** Forme oraciones usando palabras de cada columna. **¡OJO!** Algunas de ellas se pueden referirse a Ud. y otras no.

MODELOS  No es bueno que mi amiga se case este año.
Es verdad que mis padres se separan.

| (No) es | + | absurdo<br>bueno<br>cierto<br>importante<br>(im)posible<br>(im)probable<br>increíble<br>malo<br>mejor<br>necesario<br>una lástima<br>urgente<br>verdad | + | que | + | mi (mejor) amigo/a<br>mis padres<br>mi profesor(a)<br>mi novio/a<br>mi hermano/a<br>mi primo/a<br>mi esposo/a | + | casarse este año con…<br>enamorarse de…<br>tener una boda grande<br>pasar mucho tiempo<br>   con sus amigos<br>besar a…<br>romper con…<br>separarse<br>divorciarse<br>pelear con…<br>quejarse de…<br>sentir cariño por… |

**PASO 2.** En parejas, compartan sus oraciones del **Paso 1** y adivinen si son ciertas o falsas. Sigan los modelos.

Communication

MODELOS  E1: No es bueno que mi amiga se case este año.
E2: Es falso.
E1: Tienes razón. Es increíble que mi amiga se case este año. Tiene un novio fantástico.

E1: Es verdad que mis padres se separan.
E2: Es cierto.
E1: Es falso. No es verdad que mis padres se separen. Se quieren mucho.

**D.** Las bodas chilenas

Cultures

Recycle

**PASO 1.** Complete la descripción sobre cómo se celebran las bodas en Chile. Use el presente de indicativo o el subjuntivo de los verbos. Cuando hay dos palabras, escoja la palabra correcta.

Es verdad que las tradiciones de las bodas chilenas pueden ser semejantes a las de este país, pero hay algunos detalles que las distinguen. Por ejemplo, en Chile es posible que el novio le (dar[1]) un anillo de compromiso a la novia al pedirle la mano. Pero hay otra tradición acerca de los anillos. Los novios se dan anillos de boda al comienzo del noviazgo y (los/las[2]) llevan en la mano derecha durante el noviazgo. Es típico que los novios (tener[3]) una ceremonia civil unas semanas antes de la boda tradicional o religiosa. Durante la ceremonia civil, los novios transfieren los anillos a la mano izquierda.

(Continúa.)

*En una boda chilena tradicional*

Chile tiene fuertes raíces católicas y aunque es verdad que la mayoría de la población ya no (**practicar**[4]) su religión, la mayoría de los novios todavía celebra (**su/sus**[5]) boda en la iglesia, más o menos un mes después de la ceremonia civil. Pero esta ceremonia también (**tener**[6]) sus diferencias comparada con las ceremonias de este país. En una boda tradicional de este país, por ejemplo, es normal que los novios (**escoger**[7]) un padrino de boda[a] y una dama de honor[b] para acompañarlos durante la ceremonia. En muchos casos los novios norteamericanos quieren que entre seis y diez amigos (**formar**[8]) su séquito nupcial.[c] Pero en Chile, es raro que (**haber**[9]) un séquito nupcial. El padre de la novia (**lo/la**[10]) acompaña al altar, y la madre del novio acompaña a su hijo al altar. Sólo los padres y los novios, y a veces los compadres de los padres, (**quedarse**[11]) en el altar durante la ceremonia.

Después de la ceremonia religiosa, que se celebra con todos los detalles tradicionales, ¡hacen la fiesta! Son fiestas grandes y espectaculares porque las familias desean que todos sus parientes y amigos (**llegar**[12]) a celebrar la unión. Hay aperitivos, música, cena, baile y regalos para los invitados. Si Ud. va a una boda chilena, es probable que (**recibir**[13]) un regalo divertido de los novios a eso de la 1:00 ó 2:00 de la mañana. Pero no crea Ud. que la fiesta (**terminar**[14]) a esa hora. Es probable que los invitados (**seguir**[15]) bailando y festejando hasta las 5:00 ó 6:00 de la mañana.

[a]padrino... *best man*   [b]dama... *bridesmaid*   [c]séquito... *wedding party*

**PASO 2.**   Indique si cada oración describe tradiciones chilenas (**C**), de este país (**EP**) o de ambos países (**AP**), según el **Paso 1.**

|  | C | EP | AP |
|---|---|---|---|
| 1. El novio le da un anillo de compromiso a la novia. | ☐ | ☐ | ☐ |
| 2. Los novios llevan un anillo de boda en la mano derecha durante el noviazgo. | ☐ | ☐ | ☐ |
| 3. Los novios tienen una ceremonia civil. | ☐ | ☐ | ☐ |
| 4. Los novios se casan por la iglesia. | ☐ | ☐ | ☐ |
| 5. La ceremonia incluye los ritos católicos tradicionales. | ☐ | ☐ | ☐ |
| 6. Los mejores amigos acompañan a los novios al altar. | ☐ | ☐ | ☐ |
| 7. La madre del novio participa en la ceremonia. | ☐ | ☐ | ☐ |
| 8. Hay una fiesta o recepción después de la boda. | ☐ | ☐ | ☐ |

Communication

**PASO 3.**   En parejas, hablen de una de las bodas que han tenido, a las que han asistido o en las que han participado. ¿Dónde fue la boda? ¿Qué ritos se observaron en la ceremonia? ¿Cómo fue la fiesta después de la boda? ¿Sirvieron una gran cena? ¿Tocó un conjunto musical? ¿Hubo baile? ¿Qué más?

# 12.2 Stressed Possessives

**GRAMÁTICA EN CONTEXTO**

## Tus relaciones y las mías

[*Olga y Pilar comparan sus relaciones con sus parejas, Tomás y Mario.*]

*Una pareja en una playa uruguaya*

OLGA: Nuestra primera cita fue una invitación para ver una película. Vimos una película romántica.

PILAR: **La nuestra** fue para cenar en un restaurante y fue una cena romántica.

OLGA: Después de un año, Tomás me dio un anillo de compromiso.

PILAR: ¿De veras? **El anillo mío** me lo dio Mario después de sólo un mes.

OLGA: Nuestra boda fue romántica e íntima; sólo asistieron la familia y los amigos íntimos.

PILAR: **La boda nuestra** fue elegante y enorme; invitamos a todos nuestros parientes y conocidos.

OLGA: Pasamos nuestra luna de miel en Punta del Este, en el sur de Uruguay.

PILAR: Nosotros también pasamos **la nuestra** en el sur del Uruguay, pero en la Colonia del Sacramento. Allí también hay playas bonitas, pero pasamos más tiempo explorando ese precioso pueblo colonial.

OLGA: Los pasatiempos favoritos de Tomás son el patinaje y el ciclismo. ¿Cuáles son los de Mario?

PILAR: **Los suyos** son levantar pesas y jugar al ráquetbol. Pasamos todos los fines de semana en el gimnasio.

OLGA: Nosotros pasamos **los nuestros** en el parque.

Comprensión. ¿Olga (O) o Pilar (P)? ¡OJO! Puede haber más de una respuesta.

|  | O | P |
|---|---|---|
| **1.** Las primeras citas pueden ser importantes. Comió camarones al ajo en la suya. | ☐ | ☐ |
| **2.** Cuando una pareja escoge el cine para su primera cita, no puede hablar mucho. Habló muy poco en la suya. | ☐ | ☐ |
| **3.** Es una tradición darle un anillo de compromiso a la novia. Recibió el anillo suyo después de muy poco tiempo. | ☐ | ☐ |
| **4.** Muchas parejas discuten cuando planean la boda. Probablemente tuvo algunas discusiones con su novio porque la boda suya fue muy grande. | ☐ | ☐ |
| **5.** La luna de miel puede ser divertida y romántica. Pasó la suya en la playa. | ☐ | ☐ |
| **6.** Los esposos deben pasar juntos los fines de semana. Pasan los suyos en el parque. | ☐ | ☐ |

---

**GRAMÁTICA EN CONTEXTO** *Your Relationships and Mine / Olga and Pilar compare their relationships with their partners, Tomás and Mario. /* **OLGA:** *Our first date was an invitation to see a movie. We saw a romantic movie.* **PILAR:** *Ours was eating dinner in a restaurant and it was a romantic dinner.* **OLGA:** *After one year, Tomás gave me an engagement ring.* **PILAR:** *Really? Mario gave me my ring after only one month.* **OLGA:** *Our wedding was romantic and intimate; only family and close friends attended.* **PILAR:** *Our wedding was elegant and enormous; we invited all of our relatives and acquaintances.* **OLGA:** *We spent our honeymoon in Punta del Este, in the south of Uruguay.* **PILAR:** *We also spent ours in the south of Uruguay, but in Colonia del Sacramento. There are also nice beaches there, but we spent more time exploring that beautiful colonial town.* **OLGA:** *Tomás' favorite pastimes are skating and cycling. What are Mario's?* **PILAR:** *His are lifting weights and playing racquetball. We spend every weekend at the gym.* **OLGA:** *We spend ours in the park.*

**A.** You have already learned the unstressed possessive adjectives in **Gramática 1.2**: **mi(s)**, **tu(s)**, **su(s)**, **nuestro/a/os/as**, and **vuestro/a/os/as**. These are the most common possessive forms, but Spanish also has stressed forms that are used for emphasis. Here are the forms of the stressed possessive adjectives and pronouns.

| STRESSED POSSESSIVE ADJECTIVES AND PRONOUNS | | | |
|---|---|---|---|
| **mío/a/os/as** | my/mine | **nuestro/a/os/as** | our(s) |
| **tuyo/a/os/as** | your(s) | **vuestro/a/os/as** | your(s) |
| **suyo/a/os/as** | your(s), his, her(s), its | **suyo/a/os/as** | your(s), their(s) |

**B.** While the unstressed possessive adjectives precede the noun that they modify, the stressed possessive adjectives follow the noun they modify, and the noun must be preceded by a definite or indefinite article or a demonstrative adjective. The ending of each form will agree in both gender and number with the item that is possessed, not with the person who possesses it.

UNSTRESSED POSSESSIVES

Es **mi** libro.   *It's my book.*
Tengo **su** medicina.   *I have her medicine.*
Es **nuestro** primo.   *He's our cousin.*

STRESSED POSSESSIVES

Es **el** libro **mío**.   *It's my book.*
Tengo **la** medicina **suya**.   *I have her medicine.*
**Ese** primo es **nuestro**.   *That cousin is ours.*

### ACTIVIDADES

**A. Antes de la boda.** Empareje las oraciones de la columna A con las oraciones correspondientes de la columna B.

**A**

1. _____ La novia va a llevar rosas blancas.
2. _____ Nosotros vamos a llevar corbatas nuevas.
3. _____ El vestido de la novia va a ser tradicional.
4. _____ Va a haber muchas flores en su boda.
5. _____ Para su luna de miel van a ir a la Patagonia.
6. _____ ¿Uds. buscan vestidos también?
7. _____ Los padres de la novia van a vestirse muy elegantes. ¿Y los padres del novio?
8. _____ Tengo una cámara perfecta para sacar fotos en la boda.

**B**

a. Nosotros no. Las nuestras ya las hemos usado dos o tres veces.
b. Los suyos también.
c. No. Ya compramos los nuestros.
d. La nuestra no. No vamos a decorarla con flores.
e. La mía es mejor. Es digital.
f. La nuestra va a ser en Punta del Este, Uruguay.
g. Las mías van a ser rojas.
h. El mío no. El mío va a ser muy moderno.

**B. Las relaciones.** Complete las conversaciones con la forma correcta del pronombre posesivo.

[*Antes de la boda*]

MAURA:   ¿Cuándo es tu boda, Dulce? La boda de Inés fue el fin de semana pasado. Fue muy alegre. ¿Por qué no asististe?

DULCE:   No conozco bien a Inés y no me invitaron a la boda. Sí me dijeron que iban a celebrar la _____[1] en la playa.

MAURA: Sí. No se casaron en la iglesia. Hicieron la ceremonia y una fiesta en la playa. ¡Qué lástima que no fuiste!

DULCE: No importa. Miguel y yo pasamos el fin de semana planeando la _____.²

MAURA: ¡Qué emoción! La boda de Inés no fue religiosa, pero creo que la _____³ va a ser tradicional, ¿no?

DULCE: Sí. Adoro las ceremonias y las tradiciones. ¡Y nuestra fiesta va a ser espectacular!

[*Quince años después*]

MAURA: ¡Dios mío! ¡Qué complicado es el divorcio de Inés!

DULCE: Sí, el _____⁴ va a ser muy difícil porque su esposo no quiere hacerse responsable de los hijos. Pero el _____⁵ fue fácil. Miguel y yo todavía somos amigos.

MAURA: Pues, tu ex esposo es muy noble y responsable. Ayuda con los hijos y pasa tiempo con ellos. Contrariamente, los hijos de Inés nunca ven a su padre. Los _____⁶ hacen cosas con Miguel todas las semanas.

## C. Entrevista

Communication

**PASO 1.** Entreviste a un compañero / una compañera de clase con estas preguntas. Luego, cambien de papel. ¡OJO! Usen pronombres posesivos en sus respuestas. Si quieren, pueden usar nombres de personas famosas.

MODELO ¿Dónde han sido tus citas románticas favoritas? →
Las mías han sido en un parque o en un restaurante porque me gusta conversar.

1. ¿De dónde son tus mejores amigos/as?
2. ¿Dónde han sido tus citas románticas favoritas?
3. Por lo general, ¿cómo se llevan los miembros de tu familia?
4. ¿De qué se quejan tus padres/hijos?
5. ¿Cómo son tus hermanos/as?

**PASO 2.** Compartan sus respuestas al **Paso 1** con la clase. Después, todos van a votar. ¿Quién ha tenido las citas más románticas? ¿Quién tiene las familias más amables? ¿Se quejan todos los padres de la misma cosa?

## D. Nuestros ancianos (*elderly*) y el hogar

Cultures

Recycle

**PASO 1.** Complete la conversación entre dos muchachos chilenos que hablan de sus abuelos. Cuando se da un adjetivo posesivo entre paréntesis, dé Ud. la forma tónica (*stressed*) correcta. Cuando se dan dos palabras, escoja la palabra correcta.

BLAS: Sara, ¿quieres acompañarme a la biblioteca?

SARA: No puedo. (**Tengo/Debo**¹) que volver a casa dentro de media hora. Mis padres (**necesitan/tienen**²) que ir a una cena y necesito cuidar a mi abuelo y a mis hermanitos.

BLAS: ¿Tu abuelo vive con Uds.?

SARA: Pues, ¡claro!

BLAS: El (**mi**³) vive en un hogar de ancianos, en las afueras.

(Continúa.)

*Sara y su abuelo*

SARA: ¡Uf! Mi madre no permitiría[a] eso. Hace quince años que mi abuelo (**ha vivido / vive**[4]) con nosotros y ayudaba mucho en casa hasta que se enfermó de los pulmones.[b] No puede (**ser/estar**[5]) solo por mucho tiempo. Mis hermanos todavía (**son/están**[6]) muy jóvenes y no (**saben/conocen**[7]) darle las atenciones que necesita. Por eso, cuando mis padres (**necesitan/ tienen**[8]) salir, mi hermana mayor y yo tratamos de (**ser/estar**[9]) en casa.

BLAS: No creo que mi madre (**es/sea**[10]) tan tradicional como la (**tu**[11]).

SARA: A mi madre le daría mucha vergüenza instalar[c] a mi abuelo en un centro geriátrico porque él (**nos/les**[12]) cuidó a mí y a mis hermanos por tantos años. Mamá desea cuidar a su suegro como su madre cuidó al (**su**[13]).

BLAS: Nuestro país todavía sigue las tradiciones. (**Es/Está**[14]) natural, pues creo que (**son/sean**[15]) costumbres muy nobles, pero cada día es más y más difícil conservarlas.

---

[a]no... *would never allow*   [b]*lungs*   [c]le... *she would be very ashamed to place*

SARA: ¿Cómo decidieron Uds. instalar a su abuelo en un hogar de ancianos?

BLAS: Mi abuelo nunca vivió con nosotros como el (**tu**[16]). Después de que mi abuela se puso enferma, mi abuelo la cuidó por muchos años, vigilando[d] con mucho cariño su salud. Desafortunadamente, la salud (**su**[17]) declinó cuando mi abuela murió. Se dio cuenta de que[e] ya no podía vivir solo, y un día nos (**dijo/decía**[18]) que iba a mudarse al hogar de ancianos porque no quería ser un estorbo[f] para la familia.

SARA: ¿Y tu familia aceptó esa decisión (**su**[19])?

BLAS: Mi abuelo (**tenía/estaba**[20]) razón. (**Ninguno/Ningún**[21]) de mis tíos vive aquí en Santiago. Uno de mis tíos se mudó a México hace tres años. Es un problema típico ahora. Como mis padres trabajan largas horas y mi hermana y yo nunca (**somos/estamos**[22]) en casa durante el día, nadie podía cuidar a mi abuelo.

SARA: ¿Ves cómo las presiones modernas cambian las tradiciones nuestras?

BLAS: Es un juego de tira y afloja,[g] porque muchas familias como la (**tu**[23]) no aceptan estos cambios. Otras, enfrentadas con tantas dificultades, tienen que aceptarlos.

SARA: Es cierto que cada vez (**hay/haya**[24]) más hogares de ancianos en este país.

BLAS: Sí, pero parte del tira y afloja es que son caros. Muchas familias no pueden pagar los costos. Es más económico (**emplear/emplee**[25]) a una muchacha para que ayude con el anciano. Afortunadamente, mi abuelo tenía los fondos para pagar los (**su**[26]).

---

[d]*looking after*　[e]*Se... He realized that*　[f]*burden*　[g]*juego... tug of war*

**PASO 2.** Indique si las oraciones son probables (**P**) o improbables (**I**).

|  | P | I |
|---|---|---|
| 1. En Chile, la mayoría de los ancianos pasa sus últimos años en un hogar de ancianos. | ☐ | ☐ |
| 2. La familia de Sara es muy pequeña. | ☐ | ☐ |
| 3. Sara conoce bien a su abuelo. | ☐ | ☐ |
| 4. En Sudamérica, van a construir más hogares de ancianos en los próximos diez años. | ☐ | ☐ |
| 5. Muchos hijos jóvenes de familias chilenas trabajan en el extranjero. | ☐ | ☐ |
| 6. Hay presiones modernas en los países latinoamericanos. | ☐ | ☐ |
| 7. En Sudamérica, los hogares de ancianos son subvencionados (*subsidized*) por el gobierno. | ☐ | ☐ |
| 8. Los abuelos de Blas eran muy pobres. | ☐ | ☐ |

# Palabra escrita

## A comenzar

Communication

> **Stating Your Thesis.** The thesis statement is the central point of any composition or essay; everything else you write about supports this main idea. You should write your thesis statement in the first paragraph of your composition for three important reasons. First, it helps you select the information that best supports your thesis and disregard all other ideas that are not relevant. Second, it facilitates the overall organization of your composition. Finally, your thesis statement orients the reader, making it easier for him/her to follow your line of thought.

You are going to start the process of writing a brief composition that you will finalize in the **Palabra escrita: A finalizar** section of your *Manual de actividades*. The topic of this composition is **Para llevarse bien con alguien.** The purpose of your composition will be to tell the reader about how to get along well with someone. You can focus on getting along well with family members, friends, significant others, or even complete strangers.

**A.** Lluvia de ideas

**PASO 1.** En parejas, contesten las preguntas, pensando en una persona específica. Por ejemplo, en su pareja, en un amigo / una amiga, en un miembro de la familia, etcétera.

1. ¿Por qué es importante llevarse bien con alguien?
2. ¿Cómo contribuye al bienestar personal?

**PASO 2.** Ahora, cada persona debe escribir la tesis para su composición de acuerdo con sus respuestas a la pregunta 1 del **Paso 1.**

**PASO 3.** En parejas de nuevo, completen estas frases con todas las ideas que se les ocurran.

1. Es bueno/preferible que...
2. Es malo/absurdo que...
3. Es urgente/increíble que...
4. (No) Es cierto que...
5. (No) Es + *adj.* + *inf...*

**B. A organizar sus ideas.** Repase sus ideas y organícelas para escribir una serie coherente de consejos, según su tesis. Si es necesario, cambie o edite su tesis de acuerdo con las ideas que Ud. ha generado en la pregunta 2 de actividad A, **Paso 1.** Comparta su información con la clase y apunte otras ideas que se le ocurran durante el proceso.

**C. A escribir.** Ahora, haga el borrador de su composición con las ideas y la información que recopiló en las actividades A y B. **¡OJO!** Guarde bien su trabajo. Va a necesitarlo otra vez para la sección de **Palabra escrita: A finalizar** en el *Manual de actividades*.

## Marcela Donoso

Yuyito, *2000*

La pintora chilena Marcela Donoso (1961– ) estudió arte en la Universidad de Chile, y ahora es miembro del profesorado de la facultad de arte de esa universidad. Sus cuadros pertenecen al género artístico que se llama realismo mágico. Este género presenta mundos desde una perspectiva subjetiva, en que lo real y lo mágico coexisten al mismo nivel.

En este cuadro, «Yuyito» está en pose para meditar, en un campo cerca de un poblado[a] y, aparentemente, circundada[b] también de un segundo poblado celestial, mágico. Los tres pares de manos parecen representar tres fases de la meditación de esta joven.

———————————

[a]*populated area*  [b]*surrounded*

### El cuerpo° humano

*body*

los dedos

los ojos

la cabeza

la oreja

la nariz

los pulmones

el cuello

la boca

el hombro

la mano

el brazo

el pecho

los dientes

el estómago

la rodilla

la pierna

el corazón

el pie

| | |
|---|---|
| doler (ue) | to hurt, ache |
| resfriarse (me resfrío) | to catch a cold |
| toser | to cough |
| el cerebro | brain |
| el dedo del pie | toe |
| la espalda | back |
| la garganta | throat |
| el oído | inner ear |
| la sangre | blood |

## Las enfermedades y los síntomas°

Las... *Illnesses and Symptoms*

| | |
|---|---|
| el dolor | pain, ache |
| de cabeza | headache |
| de estómago | stomachache |
| de muela | toothache |
| el estrés | stress |
| la fiebre | fever |
| la gripe | flu |
| el resfriado | cold |
| la tos | cough |
| mareado/a | dizzy; nauseated |
| resfriado/a | congested |
| sano/a | healthy |

Repaso: enfermo/a

## Los vicios y el cuidado personal y médico°

Los... *Bad Habits and Personal and Medical Care*

| | |
|---|---|
| adelgazar (c) | to lose weight |
| cuidarse | to take care of oneself |
| dejar de + *inf.* | to stop/quit (*doing something*) |
| drogarse (gu) | to get high; to take drugs |
| fumar | to smoke |
| hacer (*irreg.*) ejercicio aeróbico | to do aerobics |
| ponerle (*irreg.*) una inyección | to give (*someone*) a shot |
| recetar | to prescribe |
| tomarle la temperatura | to take (*someone's*) temperature |
| el chequeo | check-up |
| el/la drogadicto/a | drug addict |
| el/la enfermero/a | nurse |
| el jarabe | cough syrup |
| el/la médico/a | doctor |
| la pastilla | pill |
| la receta | prescription |

Cognados: la adicción, el alcohol, el/la alcohólico/a, el/la dentista
Repaso: beber mucha agua, caminar, correr, hacer (*irreg.*) ejercicio, hacer (*irreg.*) meditación, hacer (*irreg.*) yoga, tocar (qu) un instrumento musical; el tratamiento

**A.** Asociaciones

**PASO 1.** Indique la(s) parte(s) del cuerpo que Ud. asocia con estas actividades. ¡OJO! Puede haber más de una respuesta correcta.

**MODELO** comer una manzana → la boca, los dientes, la garganta, el estómago

1. llevar una mochila
2. ponerse un anillo
3. escuchar música en el iPod
4. toser
5. leer una revista
6. jugar a los videojuegos
7. correr por el parque
8. fumar un cigarrillo
9. tocar el piano
10. cortarse un dedo de la mano
11. hablar por teléfono
12. tener miedo

**PASO 2.** Indique la(s) parte(s) del cuerpo que Ud. asocia con estas prendas de ropa. Luego, forme una oración usando la prenda de ropa y la parte del cuerpo. Siga el modelo.

**MODELO** los zapatos → los pies
　　　　Me pongo los zapatos en los pies.

1. los guantes
2. el sombrero
3. las medias
4. la corbata
5. los pantalones
6. los lentes
7. la camisa de manga larga
8. los calcetines

**B.** Explicaciones. Complete las oraciones con palabras lógicas. ¡OJO! Puede haber más de una respuesta correcta.

1. Tengo los _____ muy fuertes porque levanto pesas todos los días.
2. Tengo los _____ muy rojos porque he trabajado en la computadora por diez horas hoy.
3. Me duele la _____ porque me caí en la escalera.
4. Estoy _____ porque leía un libro en el autobús.
5. Tengo que tomar este _____ porque estoy tosiendo y me duele la _____.
6. La enfermera le toma la _____ al niño porque él tiene _____.
7. El médico me va a _____ un antibiótico para la infección.
8. No quiero comer nada porque tengo dolor de _____.

**C.** En el consultorio. En parejas, den recomendaciones médicas para estas situaciones. Sigan el modelo.

**MODELO** E1: Tengo dolor de cabeza. →
　　　　　E2: Quiero (Sugiero/Recomiendo) que tomes una aspirina y que descanses esta tarde.

1. Quiero adelgazar.
2. Tengo dolor de estómago.
3. Necesito dejar de fumar.
4. Sufro de mucho estrés en el trabajo y en mis estudios.
5. Temo que mi amigo sea drogadicto.
6. Me duele la garganta y tengo una tos muy fuerte.
7. Me gusta hacer ejercicio, pero me duelen las rodillas.
8. Estoy resfriado, pero tengo mucho trabajo.

**D. Malos hábitos.** Explique por qué estas actividades no son sanas y cómo afectan al cuerpo.

MODELO   Antes de tomar muchas bebidas alcohólicas con amigos, tomo aspirinas para evitar un dolor de cabeza. →
Es malo tomar aspirinas u otras pastillas para el dolor de cabeza cuando se toma mucho alcohol porque eso puede causar daño a los órganos.

1. Hago ejercicio aeróbico tres o cuatro veces al día todos los días.
2. Tomo jarabe dos o tres veces al día porque siempre me duele la garganta.
3. No me hago chequeos con el médico porque nunca me enfermo.
4. Fumo más o menos un paquete de cigarrillos al día.
5. Bebo más de veinte tazas de café al día.
6. Tomo una cerveza cuando estoy mareado/a.

**E. Entrevista.** Entreviste a un compañero / una compañera sobre sus hábitos y su cuerpo con estas preguntas. Luego, cambien de papel.

1. ¿Cuántas veces a la semana haces ejercicio? ¿Qué tipo de ejercicio te gusta hacer? ¿Dónde y con quién lo haces? Explica.
2. ¿Practicas algún deporte?
3. ¿Qué otras actividades haces para aliviar el estrés? ¿Por qué has elegido hacer esas actividades (en vez de otras)?
4. ¿Has tenido un accidente alguna vez? ¿Qué te pasó?
5. ¿Has tenido la gripe alguna vez? ¿Qué hiciste para curarte?
6. ¿Cuántas veces al año vas al médico? ¿Te haces un chequeo médico todos los años? Explica por qué te lo haces, o no.
7. ¿Con qué frecuencia faltas a (*do you miss*) clase porque estás enfermo/a? Generalmente, ¿por qué te sientes mal? ¿Es porque te resfrías? ¿Te da dolor de cabeza o de estómago?

---

## Nota comunicativa

**THE VERB doler (ue)**

To express the idea that something hurts or is painful to a person, Spanish uses the verb **doler.** It functions like the verb **gustar.** Usually the subject of the sentence with **doler** is a part of the body that is causing the pain. Remember that, like **gustar,** the verb **doler** will almost always be either third person singular or third person plural, depending on whether the thing that hurts is singular (e.g., **la cabeza**) or plural (e.g., **los ojos**). Also note that in Spanish, body parts are almost always referred to with the definite article **el/la/los/las** rather than the possessives.

Me caí y ahora **me duele la rodilla.**

A Ernesto **le dolía la cabeza** esta mañana y no asistió a clase.

*I fell down and now my knee hurts.*

*Ernesto had a headache (his head hurt) this morning and he didn't go to class.*

Connections

## EDUCACIÓN FÍSICA: EL EJERCICIO Y SUS BENEFICIOS

A nivel físico, los beneficios del ejercicio son muchos; ayuda a eliminar grasas y a prevenir la obesidad, aumenta la resistencia ante el agotamiento,[a] previene enfermedades cardiovasculares, mejora la capacidad respiratoria y estimula el sistema inmunológico, entre otros. Junto a esta dimensión biológica, existen además beneficios para la salud síquica, pues el ejercicio físico tiene efectos antidepresivos, elimina el estrés, previene el insomnio y regula el sueño.

Llevar un estilo de vida más activo y hábitos alimenticios saludables tiene también amplias repercusiones a nivel socio-afectivo o sociocultural. El ejercicio mejora la imagen corporal y, por tanto, favorece la autoestima y la relación personal del individuo con su entorno.[b]

Para lograr un estado completo de bienestar es importante, pues, incorporar en la rutina diaria un nivel de actividad mayor al que actualmente se tiene. Por ejemplo, realizar largas caminatas, correr, practicar algún deporte o ir a un gimnasio. Y si el horario no siempre lo permite, se pueden realizar pequeños cambios como subir o bajar las escaleras, pasear el perro, bajarse del autobús, aparcar[c] el carro unas cuadras antes del lugar de trabajo o realizar alguna actividad en casa.

---

[a]*exhaustion*  [b]*environment*  [c]*to park*

**PREGUNTAS** Conteste las preguntas. Después, comparta sus respuestas con la clase.

1. ¿Qué recomendaciones menciona la lectura para favorecer la actividad física?
2. Enumere algunos de los beneficios físicos, emocionales y sociales de la actividad física.
3. ¿Hace Ud. ejercicio con regularidad? ¿Qué tipo de ejercicio hace? ¿Tiene Ud. pequeñas estrategias para mantenerse (*stay*) activo/a cuando no puede ir al gimnasio, practicar un deporte o hacer ejercicios más intensos? ¿Cuáles son?

# Gramática

## 12.3 Review of Reflexive and Reciprocal Verbs

**GRAMÁTICA EN CONTEXTO**

### Nos cuidamos a nosotros mismos y el uno al otro

Miguel y Paulo son buenos amigos. Hacen algunas cosas para cuidarse a sí mismos y otras para cuidarse el uno al otro. Miguel explica:

Nuestra amistad nos importa mucho y **nos hablamos** por teléfono todos los días. **Nos vemos** casi todos los días también. Para **saludarnos**, **nos damos** la mano y **nos abrazamos**. **Nos contamos** los problemas, **nos escuchamos** bien y **nos damos** buenos consejos **el uno al otro**. También nos importa nuestra salud, por eso, **nos cuidamos a nosotros mismos**. Comemos bien y solemos hacer ejercicio. Para aliviar el estrés, hacemos yoga y **nos relajamos** escuchando música y viendo a los amigos. Pero lo más divertido son las excursiones que hacemos juntos. Hemos dado caminatas y hemos hecho excursiones a caballo por muchas partes de Chile. Nos encanta explorar las regiones de Chile y **nos divertimos** mucho en las excursiones.

*En el Parque Nacional Torres del Paine, Chile*

Comprensión. ¿A sí mismos o el uno al otro? ¡OJO! Puede haber más de una respuesta.

|  | A SÍ MISMOS | EL UNO AL OTRO |
|---|---|---|
| 1. Se cuidan. | ☐ | ☐ |
| 2. Se abrazan. | ☐ | ☐ |
| 3. Se cuentan los problemas. | ☐ | ☐ |
| 4. Se dan consejos. | ☐ | ☐ |
| 5. Se hablan mucho por teléfono. | ☐ | ☐ |
| 6. Se relajan. | ☐ | ☐ |
| 7. Se dan la mano. | ☐ | ☐ |
| 8. Se conocen. | ☐ | ☐ |

You have seen both reflexive and reciprocal verbs in previous chapters. Both types of verbs are used with reflexive pronouns but their meanings are different. While reflexive verbs generally express what people do to themselves, reciprocal verbs refer to what people do to each other. Complete conjugations of a reflexive verb and a reciprocal verb with their English equivalents are shown here to illustrate the difference. Remember that reciprocal verbs can only be used in the plural while reflexive verbs occur in all forms.

**GRAMÁTICA EN CONTEXTO** *We Take Care of Ourselves and of Each Other.* / *Miguel and Paulo are good friends. They do some things to take care of themselves and some to take care of each other. Miguel explains: / "Our friendship is very important to us and we talk every day on the phone. We see each other almost every day, too. To greet each other, we shake hands and we hug. We tell each other our problems, we listen to each other well, and we give each other good advice. Our health is also important to us, so we take care of ourselves. We eat well and we usually exercise. To alleviate stress, we do yoga and we relax by listening to music and seeing our friends. But what's most fun are the excursions that we take together. We have been on hikes and have made trips on horseback through many parts of Chile. We love to explore the regions of Chile and we have lots of fun on the excursions.*

| REFLEXIVE VERB | | RECIPROCAL VERB |
|---|---|---|
| **lavarse** (*to wash oneself*) | | **besarse** (*to kiss each other*) |
| **me lavo** (*I wash myself*) | **nos lavamos** (*we wash ourselves*) | **nos besamos** (*we kiss each other*) |
| **te lavas** (*you wash yourself*) | **os laváis** (*you wash yourselves*) | **os besáis** (*you kiss each other*) |
| **se lava** (*he washes himself, she washes herself, you wash yourself*) | **se lavan** (*they wash themselves, you wash yourselves*) | **se besan** (*they kiss each other, you kiss each other*) |

Remember that it is possible to interpret certain verbs as either reflexive or reciprocal, depending on the context. For example, **Ellos se conocen bien** would normally be interpreted as *They know each other well*, but could also mean *They know themselves well*. Typically, context will make the meaning clear but it may be necessary to include a clarifying phrase. To clarify a reflexive meaning, use: **a ellos mismos, a ellas mismas, a nosotros mismos, a nosotras mismas, a vosotros mismos, a vosotras mismas,** or **a Uds. mismos/as.** To clarify a reciprocal meaning, use the expression **el uno al otro,** with appropriate changes to agree with the number and gender of those involved.

CLARIFICATION OF REFLEXIVE
MEANING

**Se conocen** bien **a ellos mismos.**
*They know themselves well.*
**Nos vemos** en el espejo **a nosotros mismos.**
*We see ourselves in the mirror.*

CLARIFICATION OF RECIPROCAL
MEANING

**Se conocen** bien **el uno al otro.**
*They know each other well.*
**Nos vemos** en el espejo **el uno al otro.**

*We see each other in the mirror.*

---

### Nota comunicativa

Communication

**Volverse (ue)** + *adj.*

One way to express *to become* in Spanish is with the construction **volverse** + *adj.* It is used to refer to mental or psychological changes that are involuntary, and to changes that are more permanent in nature. It is most often heard with the adjective **loco/a.**

El hombre **se volvió loco** cuando murió su esposa.

**¡Me voy a volver loca** si ella no me deja de llamar!

*The man went (became) crazy when his wife died.*

*I'm going to go crazy if she doesn't stop calling me!*

---

**ACTIVIDADES**

**A.** Entre amigos

**PASO 1.** Indique lo que Ud. y sus amigos suelen hacer.

1. ☐ Nos besamos en las mejillas (*cheek*) al saludarnos.
2. ☐ Nos vemos todos los fines de semana.
3. ☐ Nos ayudamos en la tarea y proyectos para las clases.
4. ☐ Nos contamos los problemas que tenemos con los novios o la familia.
5. ☐ Nos llamamos por teléfono celular todos los días.

6. ☐ Nos abrazamos al despedirnos.
7. ☐ Nos entendemos bien.
8. ☐ Nos peleamos, a veces.
9. ☐ Nos respetamos.
10. ☐ Nos llevamos bien.

**PASO 2.** Compare sus resultados del **Paso 1** con la clase. ¿Quién tiene los amigos más íntimos? ¿Por qué?

**B. Mis amigos y yo.** Dé cinco oraciones para describir lo que Ud. y sus amigos hacen entre Uds. Use las frases de la actividad A. Puede modificar las frases para dar información correcta.

**MODELO** Mis amigos y yo no nos besamos en las mejillas al saludarnos, sino que (*but rather*) nos abrazamos.

Mis amigos y yo...

1. ...   2. ...   3. ...   4. ...   5. ...

**C. ¿Sus amigos y Ud.?** En parejas, háganse preguntas sobre lo que hacen Uds. con sus amigos. Usen las frases de la actividad A para formar preguntas. Pueden responder usando las oraciones que dieron en la actividad B.

Communication

**MODELO** E1: ¿Se besan en las mejillas tú y tus amigos al saludarse?
E2: No, no nos besamos, sino que nos abrazamos.

**D.** La Fundación Isabel Allende

Cultures

Recycle

**PASO 1.** Complete el texto de la cronología de la vida de Isabel Allende y la descripción del origen de la Fundación Isabel Allende con la forma correcta de las palabras entre paréntesis. Cuando se dan dos palabras, escoja la palabra correcta. Dé la forma apropiada del pretérito de los verbos entre paréntesis. **¡OJO!** Use el pronombre reflexivo o recíproco cuando sea necesario.

**1985** Isabel publicó *La casa de los espíritus,* una novela que empezó a escribir cuando (**supo/conoció**[1]) que su abuelo moría.

**1987** Isabel y su primer esposo (**divorciar**[2]). Allende publicó la novela *Eva Luna.*

**1988** Isabel y Willie Gordon (**casar**[3]).

**1989** Isabel publicó una colección de cuentos, *Cuentos de Eva Luna.*

**1991** Paula, la hija de Isabel, (**enfermar**[4]) de porfiria[a] en España. Isabel (**empezar**[5]) a escribir *El plan infinito.*

**1992** Paula murió en la casa de Isabel y Willie en California.

**1994** Isabel publicó la novela *Paula.*

**1996** Isabel (**establecer**[6]) la Fundación Isabel Allende.

Isabel Allende, novelista y cuentista chilena, también (**es/está**[7]) hija, esposa y madre. Como madre (**sufrir**[8]) lo peor cuando su hija Paula, de 28 años de edad, después de pasar un año en estado comatoso, murió de porfiria. Dos frutos[b] surgieron[c] directamente de esta tragedia: *Paula,* la novela de memorias que Isabel (**comenzar**[9]) a escribir cuando su hija (**era/estaba**[10]) en coma en el hospital, y la Fundación Isabel Allende.

---

[a]*Porphyria (a group of rare genetic disorders)*   [b]*benefits, results*   [c]*came out of*

(Continúa.)

*Isabel Allende*

Isabel (**crear**[11]) la Fundación Isabel Allende cuatro años después de la muerte de Paula. Paula (**dedicarse**[12]) al servicio comunitario, y la Fundación es un homenaje al espíritu que Paula cultivó y una extensión de su trabajo. Según Isabel, Paula (**hacer**[13]) de voluntaria[d] en comunidades pobres de España y Venezuela. La misión de la Fundación (**es/está**[14]) capacitar[e] y proteger a las mujeres y a las niñas. Para realizar (**esto/esta**[15]), la fundación da becas[f] y apoya a otras organizaciones que proveen[g] educación, cuidado médico, capacitación[h] y protección contra la violencia, la explotación y la discriminación. Las becas y donaciones (**son/están**[16]) distribuidas en tres programas: Donaciones Esperanza (para las organizaciones sin lucro[i]), Becas Paula (para la educación superior[j] de mujeres jóvenes) y Premios Espíritu (para honrar y reconocer logros[k] de servicio comunitario).

La misma escritora dice que los logros más importantes de su vida no (**son/están**[17]) sus libros, (**pero/sino**[18]) el amor compartido con su familia y amigos y la ayuda dirigida a los necesitados. La Fundación es un producto y reflejo de ese amor y espíritu magnánimo; es un reflejo del amor que Isabel y su hija (**sienten/sentían**[19]) la una por la otra.

---

[d]*hacer… to volunteer* [e]*to empower* [f]*grants, scholarships* [g]*provide* [h]*training* [i]*sin… nonprofit* [j]*advanced* [k]*achievements*

**PASO 2.** Indique la respuesta correcta. ¡OJO! Puede haber más de una respuesta.

1. Isabel Allende es _____.
   a. chilena    b. política       c. viuda       d. novelista
2. La hija de Allende murió _____.
   a. en España   b. en los Estados Unidos   c. en una casa   d. de una enfermedad rara
3. Lo más importante para Isabel son _____.
   a. sus libros   b. sus logros literarios   c. su familia y amigos   d. la fama

4. Paula trabajaba en comunidades marginales de _____.
   a. Chile        b. California        c. Venezuela        d. España
5. La Fundación Isabel Allende se estableció _____.
   a. para honrar el trabajo de Paula
   b. para capacitar y apoyar a las mujeres y las niñas
   c. para ayudar a los hospitales de España
   d. para combatir la violencia contra las mujeres
6. La Fundación Isabel Allende distribuye becas a _____.
   a. individuos    b. a otras organizaciones    c. a empresas    d. a novelistas
7. Premios Espíritu es un programa de la Fundación que _____.
   a. da becas a las mujeres
   b. ayuda a organizaciones sin lucro
   c. reconoce el trabajo de otros
   d. honra a los que sirven a la comundidad
8. Las mujeres que necesitan ayuda para pagar la matrícula universitaria deben solicitar _____.
   a. Donaciones Esperanza
   b. una beca de la Fundación Isabel Allende
   c. Becas Paula
   d. Premios Espíritu

## Nota cultural

Cultures

### DIEGO ARMANDO MARADONA

*Diego Armando Maradona*

El argentino Diego Armando Maradona es considerado uno de los mejores jugadores de la historia del fútbol mundial. Sus logros deportivos con la selección de su país y con los clubes europeos en los que[a] jugó, sobre todo con el Nápoles, todavía son aclamados por miles de *fans* de todo el mundo. Entre muchos e importantes galardones,[b] Maradona cuenta con la Copa Mundial en 1986, la Copa de la UEFA en 1989 y el subcampeonato de la Copa Mundial de 1990.

Sin embargo, la carrera profesional de este brillante jugador empezó a declinar en 1994 cuando tuvo que ser expulsado[c] de la Copa Mundial, celebrada en los Estados Unidos, por haber consumido drogas no reglamentarias. Su adicción a las drogas se hizo más severa, afectando seriamente su salud. Por fin, la obesidad y graves problemas cardíacos lo obligaron a concluir su exitosa carrera deportiva prematuramente. Tras ser hospitalizado en numerosas ocasiones, Maradona buscó ayuda profesional en reconocidas instituciones cubanas y europeas y hoy en día se considera recuperado de su adicción, aunque él mismo declara que es una enfermedad sin cura.

Maradona se retiró oficialmente del fútbol en 1998, pero desde su recuperación se ha mantenido activo. Ha realizado programas de televisión en Argentina y en Italia, y ha sido protagonista de varios documentales y películas de ficción. También ha sido entrenador de equipos importantes y el seleccionador de fútbol de su país. Por su origen humilde, Maradona es muy admirado en los sectores más populares de la sociedad y se ha convertido en el héroe deportivo de todo el mundo y en un icono de la cultura popular de Argentina.

[a] *en... in which*  [b] *accolades*  [c] *expelled*

**PREGUNTAS** En parejas, contesten las preguntas. Después, compartan sus ideas con la clase.

1. ¿Qué elementos del texto justifican que Maradona fue una gran figura del fútbol?
2. Existen problemas de adicción a las drogas entre los deportistas de su país? ¿Qué tipo de sustancias consumen? ¿Por qué creen Uds. que es tan común?

Ud. va a leer un artículo de la revista *Nexos,* escrito por María del Mar Cerdas y publicado por la American Airlines, sobre la meditación.

## ANTES DE LEER

Communication

**A.** La meditación. En parejas, contesten las preguntas. Después, compartan sus ideas con la clase.

1. ¿Cuál(es) de las siguientes cosas o actividades asocian Uds. con la meditación?
   a. ☐ el canto (*chanting*)
   b. ☐ el incienso
   c. ☐ los movimientos específicos del cuerpo
   d. ☐ la música tranquila
   e. ☐ las piedras lisas (*smooth stones*)
   f. ☐ el silencio
   g. ☐ las velas (*candles*)
   h. ☐ el yoga
   i. ☐ ciertas posturas corporales
   j. ☐ ¿ ?
2. ¿Han hecho meditación alguna vez? ¿Les gustó la experiencia? ¿Les fue útil (*useful*)? Expliquen. Si no la han hecho, ¿les parece interesante practicarla? Expliquen.

**B.** A primera vista. Lea el título y la introducción a la lectura *en letra cursiva.* ¿Cuál de estas oraciones cree Ud. que va a resumir mejor el contenido del artículo?

1. ☐ La meditación es una buena alternativa para mantenerse en forma cuando es imposible hacer ejercicio o practicar deportes.
2. ☐ Se ha demostrado científicamente que la meditación tiene efectos positivos en la salud mental y física.
3. ☐ La meditación no tiene base científica. Sirve solamente para relajarse y, además, está de moda.

**C.** Anticipación. Con la ayuda de sus respuestas a las actividades A y B y la foto que acompaña el artículo, ¿qué información espera encontrar Ud. en este artículo?

1. ☐ un resumen de algunos estudios sobre la relación entre la meditación y la salud
2. ☐ algunas técnicas para meditar
3. ☐ el papel de la meditación en las religiones orientales
4. ☐ una explicación de los problemas físicos o sicológicos que se pueden curar con la meditación
5. ☐ ¿ ?

## Meditar es sanar

*La meditación es una forma de mantener la mente en reposo,[a] para inducir un estado de relajación, profunda armonía interna y despertar de la conciencia. La medicina occidental la veía como algo esotérico, más del lado de la fe[b] que de la ciencia, pero las nuevas tecnologías en salud han cambiado esa percepción.*

La meditación tiene base científica: El neurólogo Álvaro Pascual-Leone (Universidad de Harvard), desarrolló hace unos años la hipótesis pionera de que el entrenamiento mental tiene el poder para modificar nuestra materia gris. De allí surgió[c] el concepto de «neuroplasticidad», la impresionante capacidad del cerebro

---

[a]en... *at rest*   [b]*faith*   [c]*arose*

**CAPÍTULO 12** El bienestar

de cambiar su estructura y funcionamiento como respuesta a la experiencia, física y mental. Su colega Herbert Benson concluyó que la práctica de la meditación contrarresta[d] los mecanismos cerebrales asociados al estrés.

Nuevos hallazgos han comprobado[e] lo anterior y lo han superado. Richard Davidson (Universidad de Wisconsin) reveló que la meditación fortalece[f] el sistema inmunológico, baja niveles de cortisol (hormona asociada con el estrés) y previene recaídas[g] en personas depresivas. Esto último lo comprobó también John Teasdale, de la Unidad de Ciencias Cognitivas y del Cerebro en Cambridge (Reino Unido), mediante[h] la combinación de meditación introspectiva con terapia cognitiva.

*Si Ud. practica la meditación o hace yoga, como esta mujer, ¿dónde lo hace?*

David Haaga (American University) sostiene que la meditación trascendental redujo la presión sanguínea y mejoró la salud mental de adultos jóvenes en peligro[i] de sufrir hipertensión.

Investigaciones del 2009 son positivas también. El Northwestern Memorial Hospital de Illinois advirtió[j] que la meditación puede ser un remedio efectivo contra el insomnio. Robert Schneider, de la Universidad de Administración de Empresas Maharishi (Iowa) presentó a la American Heart Association un estudio de nueve años de duración, con afroamericanos, que reportó disminución[k] de cerca del 50% en ataques del corazón y derrames[l] cerebrales entre practicantes de la meditación trascendental.

---

[d]*counteracts*  [e]*hallazgos... findings have confirmed*  [f]*strengthens*  [g]*previene... prevents relapses*  [h]*through*
[i]*danger*  [j]*advised*  [k]*decrease*  [l]*strokes*

## DESPUÉS DE LEER

**A. Los beneficios de la meditación.** En términos fisiológicos, ¿cómo se benefician las personas que practican la meditación, según el artículo? Indique todas las respuestas correctas.

La meditación...

1. ☐ fortalece el sistema inmunológico.
2. ☐ elimina las jaquecas (*migraines*).
3. ☐ puede mejorar la salud mental.
4. ☐ puede prevenir el insomnio.
5. ☐ elimina la hipertensión.
6. ☐ disminuye (*reduces*) la posibilidad de sufrir un ataque del corazón.
7. ☐ baja niveles de cortisol.
8. ☐ previene por completo los derrames cerebrales.
9. ☐ disminuye los efectos de la gripe.
10. ☐ reduce la presión sanguínea.

**B.** Otras maneras de mejorar la salud física y mental. Lea la información sobre algunas otras técnicas terapéuticas y conteste las preguntas. Después, comparta sus respuestas con la clase.

Además de la meditación, existen otras técnicas muy beneficiosas para mejorar la salud física y mental. El yoga es una terapia que combina ciertas posturas corporales con la respiración. Algunos estudios han demostrado las propiedades curativas del yoga en pacientes con anemia, ansiedad, colesterol alto, ciertos tipos de cáncer, hipertensión, problemas cardíacos y otras enfermedades.

El tai chi consiste en realizar movimientos lentos y armoniosos prestando especial atención a la respiración. También se ha demostrado que el tai chi ayuda en la prevención y curación de enfermedades cardíacas, tuberculosis pulmonar, reumatismo articular, anemia, obesidad y otros dolores crónicos. Además, mejora la circulación de la sangre y baja la presión sanguínea.

¿Cómo es posible esto? Se sabe que el cerebro controla todos los órganos del cuerpo, y mantener el cerebro relajado permite controlar todas las enfermedades que él provoca.

*El tai chi en un parque de Buenos Aires*

1. ¿Qué características tienen en común la meditación, el yoga y el tai chi?
2. ¿Cree Ud. que la meditación, el yoga, el tai chi y otras técnicas similares pueden curar por sí solas (*by themselves*) enfermedades como el cáncer o los problemas cardíacos, o es necesario combinarlas con tratamientos médicos tradicionales? Explique.
3. ¿Qué enfermedades mencionadas en el artículo de *Nexos* o en la selección que acaba de leer cree Ud. que estas técnicas pueden curar?
4. En su opinión, ¿cuáles son los mayores beneficios de estas prácticas terapéuticas?
5. Según la selección anterior, ¿cuál es la causa de muchas enfermedades físicas y sicológicas? ¿Está Ud. de acuerdo con esta idea? Explique.

Communication

**C.** Temas de discusión. En parejas, contesten las preguntas. Después, compartan sus respuestas con la clase.

1. ¿Hacen Uds. meditación o practican yoga o tai chi? Si su respuesta es, «sí», ¿cómo se sienten después? Si no lo hacen, ¿qué otras estrategias tienen Uds. para mantenerse sanos? ¿Cómo los ayudan estas estrategias? ¿Cómo se benefician Uds. al hacerlas (*by doing them*)?
2. Piensen en otras actividades que una persona puede hacer para mantenerse sana. Expliquen en qué consiste la actividad y los efectos que tiene en la salud mental y física. Busque información en el Internet o en la biblioteca si es necesario.
3. Creen que tiene sentido la expresión «meditar es sanar». Expliquen.

## Argentina: Federico

Cultures

Un viaje a las Cataratas
del Iguazú

En este segmento Federico nos presenta a su compañera Sol y ambos viajan con un grupo de estudiantes internacionales de Buenos Aires a las Cataratas del Iguazú. En el camino a Iguazú paran en Posadas para ver las ruinas de una misión jesuita y comen comida típica en una estancia (*ranch*) en la que se cultiva mate.

### ANTES DE VER

Conteste las preguntas antes de ver el videoblog de Federico.

1. ¿Por qué cree Ud. que Federico viaja con un grupo de estudiantes internacionales?
2. De los lugares que se mencionan en la introducción, ¿cuál piensa Ud. que será el más interesante? Explique.
3. ¿Qué sabe Ud. de las Cataratas del Niágara?

### DESPUÉS DE VER

**A. Comprensión.** Conteste las preguntas, según el videoblog de Federico.

1. ¿Con cuál se relaciona La Chacra, con la misión de San Ignacio o con una plantación de mate? Explique.
2. ¿Qué importancia tiene el mate en la cultura argentina?
3. ¿Recuerda algunos detalles sobre la variedad de animales y plantas del Parque Iguazú?
4. ¿Cuál es la parte favorita de todo el viaje para Federico?
5. ¿Qué es la Garganta del Diablo?
6. Según las palabras de Federico y Sol, ¿cuál cree que era el tema del concurso?
7. ¿Qué foto gana el concurso al final? ¿Por qué gana?

**B. Temas de discusión.** En grupos pequeños, comenten los temas.

1. ¿Qué es lo que más les ha llamado la atención del segmento? Expliquen.
2. Comenten las fotos que Sol y Federico han seleccionado. ¿Qué les parece su elección (*choice*)?

Communication

### Vocabulario práctico

| | |
|---|---|
| **a la vuelta** | after they return |
| **estancia** | hacienda, ranch |
| **parrilla** | grill |
| **dueños** | owners |
| **empate** | tie |

## Los verbos

| | |
|---|---|
| adelgazar (c) | to lose weight |
| amarse | to love each other |
| casarse (con) | to get married (to) |
| cuidarse | to take care of oneself |
| dejar de + inf. | to stop/quit (doing something) |
| discutir | to argue |
| doler (ue) | to hurt |
| drogarse (gu) | to get high; to take drugs |
| enamorarse (de) | to fall in love (with) |
| fumar | to smoke |
| gritar | to yell |
| hacer (irreg.) ejercicio aeróbico | to do aerobics |
| llorar | to cry |
| pelear(se) | to fight |
| ponerle (irreg.) una inyección | to give (someone) a shot |
| quejarse | to complain |
| quererse (irreg.) | to love each other |
| recetar | to prescribe |
| reírse (i, i) (me río) | to laugh |
| resfriarse (me resfrío) | to catch a cold |
| romper con | to break up with |
| sentir (ie, i) cariño por | to be fond of (someone) |
| sonreír (i, i) (sonrío) | to smile |
| tenerle (irreg.) cariño a | to be fond of (someone) |
| tomarle la temperatura | to take (someone's) temperature |
| toser | to cough |
| volverse (ue) + adj. | to become + adj. |

Cognados: divorciarse (de), separarse (de)

## Las relaciones sentimentales

| | |
|---|---|
| la amistad | friendship |
| la cita | date |
| el compromiso | engagement |
| la luna de miel | honeymoon |
| la novia | girlfriend; fiancée; bride |
| el noviazgo | courtship; engagement |
| el novio | boyfriend; fiancé; groom |
| la pareja (de hecho) | (common-law) couple; (domestic) partner |

Cognados: la separación

## Las emociones — Emotions

| | |
|---|---|
| el amor | love |
| el cariño | affection |
| amable | friendly |
| celoso/a | jealous |
| enamorado/a (de) | in love (with) |

## El cuerpo humano — The Human Body

| | |
|---|---|
| la boca | mouth |
| el brazo | arm |
| la cabeza | head |
| el cerebro | brain |
| el corazón | heart |
| el cuello | neck |
| el dedo | finger |
| el dedo del pie | toe |
| el diente | tooth |
| la espalda | back |
| el estómago | stomach |
| la garganta | throat |
| el hombro | shoulder |
| la nariz | nose |
| el oído | inner ear |
| los ojos | eyes |
| la oreja | ear |
| el pecho | chest |
| el pie | foot |
| la pierna | leg |
| los pulmones | lungs |
| la rodilla | knee |
| la sangre | blood |

## Las enfermedades y los síntomas — Illnesses and Symptoms

| | |
|---|---|
| el dolor | pain, ache |
| de cabeza | headache |
| de estómago | stomachache |
| de muela | toothache |
| el estrés | stress |
| la fiebre | fever |
| la gripe | flu |
| el resfriado | cold |
| la tos | cough |
| mareado/a | dizzy; nauseated |
| resfriado/a | congested |
| sano/a | healthy |

## Los vicios y el cuidado personal y médico — Bad Habits and Personal and Medical Care

| | |
|---|---|
| el chequeo | check-up |
| el/la drogadicto/a | drug addict |
| el/la enfermero/a | nurse |
| el jarabe | cough syrup |
| el/la médico/a | doctor |
| la pastilla | pill |
| la receta | prescription |

Cognados: la adicción, el alcohol, el/la alcohólico/a, el/la dentista

## Otras expresiones impersonales

Cognados: es interesante/mejor/obvio que

## Los posesivos tónicos — Stressed Possessives

mío/a(s), tuyo/a(s), suyo/a(s), nuestro/a(s), vuestro/a(s), suyo/a(s)

# Nuestro futuro

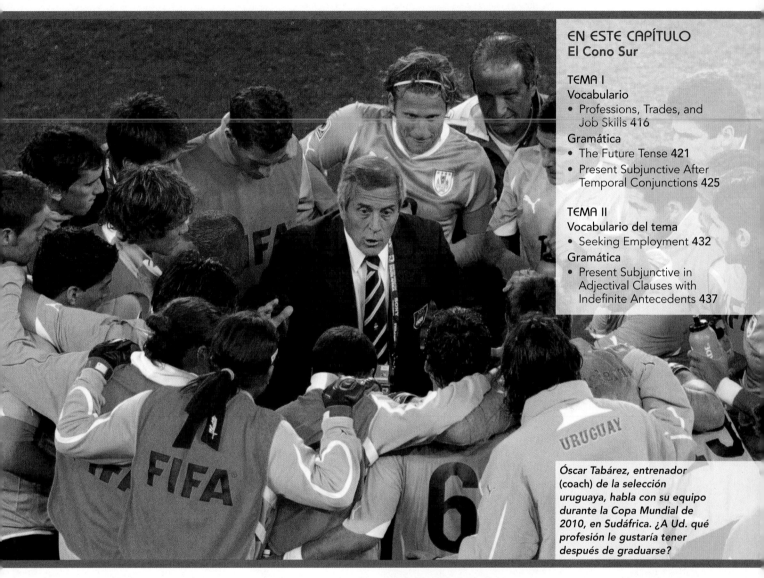

*Óscar Tabárez, entrenador (coach) de la selección uruguaya, habla con su equipo durante la Copa Mundial de 2010, en Sudáfrica. ¿A Ud. qué profesión le gustaría tener después de graduarse?*

1. ¿Qué planes tiene Ud. para después de la graduación? ¿Piensa buscar trabajo o prefiere continuar sus estudios en la escuela graduada?

2. ¿Tiene Ud. trabajo en la actualidad, además de sus estudios? ¿Qué tipo de trabajo? ¿A Ud. le gusta o no? ¿Por qué?

**connect**
**|SPANISH**
www.connectspanish.com

415

### Las profesiones y los oficios°

*Trades*

**① Los negocios y la contabilidad**

- el hombre de negocios
- el banquero (la banquera)
- la mujer de negocios
- el contador (la contadora)

**② La medicina y sicología**

- el sicólogo (la sicóloga)
- la enfermera (el enfermero)
- el farmacéutico (la farmacéutica)
- el médico (la médica)
- la veterinaria (el veterinario)

**③ El derecho**

- el abogado (la abogada)
- la jueza (el juez)

**④ Los oficios**

- la peluquera (el peluquero)
- la plomera (el plomero)
- el cocinero (la cocinera)
- el barbero (la barbera)
- el soldado (la mujer soldado)

| | |
|---|---|
| el/la albañil | bricklayer |
| el/la biólogo/a | biologist |
| el/la científico/a | scientist |
| el/la consejero/a | advisor; counselor |
| el/la diseñador(a) (de modas) | (fashion) designer |
| el/la electricista | electrician |
| el/la entrenador(a) | trainer; coach |
| el/la físico/a | physicist |
| el/la ingeniero/a | engineer |
| el/la intérprete | interpreter |
| el/la maestro/a | teacher |
| el/la periodista | journalist |
| el/la químico/a | chemist |
| el/la técnico/a | technician |
| el/la traductor(a) | translator |

Cognados: el/la atleta, el/la modelo, el/la programador(a), el/la recepcionista, el/la secretario/a

## Las habilidades y destrezas
## Abilities and Skills

| | |
|---|---|
| tener (*irreg.*) don de gentes | to get along well with others |
| el conocimiento | knowledge |
| emprendedor(a) | enterprising |
| fuerte físicamente | physically strong |
| íntegro/a | honest; upright |
| valiente | brave |

Cognados: la compasión, las relaciones públicas; bilingüe, carismático/a, honesto/a, organizado/a, puntual

### ACTIVIDADES

**A. Asociaciones.** Empareje cada definición de la columna A con la profesión correspondiente de la columna B.

A

1. _____ curar animales
2. _____ ayudar a las personas con problemas emocionales
3. _____ enseñar en la universidad
4. _____ dar las noticias en periódicos o en la televisión
5. _____ hacer planos para la construcción de edificios
6. _____ ayudar a los médicos y atender a los pacientes
7. _____ defender a las personas acusadas de crímenes
8. _____ preparar medicamentos

B

a. el/la enfermero/a
b. el/la arquitecto/a
c. el/la farmacéutico/a
d. el/la abogado/a
e. el/la veterinario/a
f. el/la sicólogo/a
g. el/la periodista
h. el/la profesor(a)

**B.** ¿Cuál es la respuesta correcta? Indique si las oraciones son lógicas (**L**) o ilógicas (**I**). Corrija las oraciones ilógicas.

|  | L | I |
|---|---|---|
| 1. Un cocinero trabaja en la recepción de un hotel. | ☐ | ☐ |
| 2. Un albañil construye o repara edificios. | ☐ | ☐ |
| 3. Una escultora pinta cuadros. | ☐ | ☐ |
| 4. Un biólogo usa el microscopio en su trabajo. | ☐ | ☐ |
| 5. Una diseñadora de modas modela prendas de ropa. | ☐ | ☐ |
| 6. Una jueza diseña sistemas para la computadora. | ☐ | ☐ |
| 7. Un contable trabaja en un banco. | ☐ | ☐ |
| 8. Una secretaria resuelve asuntos administrativos. | ☐ | ☐ |

**C.** Definiciones. Escriba una definición, para cuatro de las profesiones del **Vocabulario del tema.** Luego, en grupos de tres, lean sus definiciones sin nombrar las profesiones. Sus compañeros/as deben adivinar la profesión definida.

MODELO   E1: Esta persona cura a los enfermos. Trabaja en hospitales.
         E2: Es médico o médica.

**D.** ¿A quién debo llamar? Lea las situaciones y diga a quién(es) debe llamar y por qué.

MODELO   Las luces de la cocina no funcionan. → Debe llamar a un electricista porque él sabe arreglar problemas con la electricidad.

1. Tengo muchas presiones en el trabajo y estoy deprimido.
2. El médico me recetó tres medicinas y ahora necesito comprarlas.
3. Tengo un negocio pequeño que ha crecido mucho y necesito consejos financieros.
4. Tenemos que emplear a dos o tres profesionales para que nos ayuden en los diseños de los puentes de esta carretera.
5. Quiero divorciarme de mi esposo, pero él se niega a (*refuses*) darme el divorcio.

**E.** Cualidades profesionales

PASO 1.   Primero, indique las cualidades que cree que tiene Ud. mismo. Luego, indique qué profesiones requieren estas cualidades. **¡OJO!** Puede haber más de una respuesta.

1. ☐ tener don de gentes
2. ☐ ser carismático/a
3. ☐ ser emprendedor(a)
4. ☐ tener habilidad manual
5. ☐ ser íntegro/a
6. ☐ tener compasión
7. ☐ ser valiente
8. ☐ hablar otro idioma

PASO 2.   En parejas, comparen sus respuestas al **Paso 1.** Luego, digan qué profesiones les interesan a Uds. y qué cualidades tienen para dedicarse a esas profesiones.

**F.** Ofertas de empleo

PASO 1.   Lea las ofertas de trabajo en Buenos Aires y luego conteste las preguntas.

| | | |
|---|---|---|
| Recepcionista | Importante laboratorio se encuentra en la búsqueda de una Recepcionista, sexo femenino, hasta 45 años. Con experiencia en central telefónica. Es por un reemplazo de un mes. Trabajo temporal. | Flores (Capital Federal) |
| Ingeniero Químico | Importante fábrica de pintura busca Ingeniero Químico con experiencia en laboratorio. Sexo masculino, entre 30 y 45 años. | Escobar (Buenos Aires) |
| Oficial Electricista | Importante empresa de mantenimiento de hospitales busca Oficiales Electricistas para reemplazo de vacaciones. | Palermo / Caballito (Capital Federal) |
| Secretarias | Importante empresa central nuclear selecciona Secretarias con conocimiento PC y experiencia en Administración. Idiomas: inglés – alemán. | Zárate (Buenos Aires) |
| Administrativo | Buscamos Administrativo con experiencia en tareas administrativas y trámites bancarios. Requisitos: Poseer título de la secundaria completo y buen dominio de PC. Se valoran personas dinámicas con muy buena predisposición para trabajar. | Fcio. Varela (Buenos Aires) |
| Enfermeros/as | Se busca Enfermeros/as con sólida experiencia en enfermería laboral. Se requiere título profesional. Edad: 21 a 40 años. Amplia disponibilidad horaria. Residir en zonas cercanas a Lanús. | Lanús (Buenos Aires) |
| Oficial y Ayudante de Albañil | Obra en Zona Sur busca Oficiales Albañiles y Ayudantes. Presentarse el jueves 25/09 en Carlos Morel 22, Quilmes. | Burzaco (Buenos Aires) |
| Gerente Comercial | Importante empresa de ropa femenina busca una Gerente Comercial para la zona de Mendoza, capital. Sexo femenino, hasta 45 años. Con experiencia en el sector y disponibilidad horaria. | Mendoza (Mendoza) |
| Cocineros | Importante cadena de hipermercados busca Cocineros con experiencia gastronómica. Se requiere secundaria completa. Amplia disponibilidad horaria. Zona de trabajo: Capital Federal y Zona Norte. | Buenos Aires |

1. ¿Qué anuncios requieren experiencia para realizar el trabajo? Incluya el tipo de experiencia que se exige.
2. ¿Qué anuncios buscan mujeres para los puestos?
3. ¿Qué anuncios requieren explícitamente un título académico?
4. ¿Qué anuncios ofrecen puestos temporales?

**PASO 2.** En parejas, compartan sus respuestas al **Paso 1.**

**PASO 3.** En grupos de tres, comenten los temas.

Communication

1. La mayoría de los anuncios requiere que los aspirantes tengan cierta edad. ¿Es común este requisito en las ofertas de trabajo de su país? ¿Creen Uds. que es aceptable indicar la edad? ¿O creen que este requisito puede ser discriminatorio? Expliquen.

Communication

(Continúa.)

2. En el número 2 del **Paso 1,** Uds. indicaron las profesiones que se les ofrecen a las mujeres. Compárenlas con las ocupaciones que se les ofrecen a los hombres. ¿Creen que estos anuncios reflejan una división tradicional entre el papel del hombre y la mujer en el mundo del trabajo? ¿o no creen que sea así? ¿Es semejante a lo que ocurre en su país de origen? Si no está seguro/a de la respuesta, busquen ofertas de trabajo de su comunidad y compárenlas con las ofertas del **Paso 1.**

**G.** Mis metas (*goals*) personales

**PASO 1.** Conteste las preguntas.

1. ¿Qué quería ser cuando era pequeño/a?
2. Y ahora, ¿para qué estudia?
3. ¿Cómo han cambiado sus metas profesionales o sueños para el futuro?

Communication

**PASO 2.** Comparta sus respuestas con la clase. ¿Cuántos tienen las mismas metas que tenían de pequeños? ¿Cuántos han cambiado sus metas? Hagan una lista de las profesiones para las que (*for which*) Uds. se preparan. ¿Cuáles son las profesiones más populares entre la clase?

---

## Nota cultural

Cultures

### LOS GAUCHOS

*Un gaucho*

El gaucho es un jinete[a] sudamericano que se dedica generalmente a cuidar el ganado. Tiene algunas semejanzas con el charro mexicano y el vaquero estadounidense.

La figura del gaucho surgió durante la época colonial en la pampa argentina, territorio que se extendía desde el Río de la Plata hasta los Andes, y desde la Patagonia hasta partes de suelo brasileño. Se dice que fue en la inmensidad de esta llanura, con la sola compañía de su caballo, donde formó su carácter nómada e independiente, adquirió sus costumbres sencillas y aprendió el arte de la ganadería con gran destreza.

La imagen del gaucho ha estado tradicionalmente asociada a su cuchillo, su poncho y su mate, una especie de té típico de Sudamérica. Consumido por los indios guaraníes, los gauchos lo adoptaron como un hábito casi religioso y, desde entonces, el mate es un símbolo del país, incorporado a las costumbres de la mayoría de los argentinos. Quizá por su vida nómada y su trabajo con el ganado, el asado fue la dieta fundamental del gaucho, quien convirtió la técnica de asar la carne en puro arte. Al igual que el mate, el asado se extendió a todas las mesas argentinas, convirtiéndose en el plato por excelencia del país.

La modernización de la cría de ganado de finales del siglo XIX marcó el fin del modo de vida tradicional de los gauchos, muchos de los cuales[b] se convirtieron en trabajadores del campo a sueldo.[c] En la actualidad se conocen como gauchos los ganaderos de las zonas rurales en Argentina, Uruguay, Paraguay y algunas zonas de Bolivia, Chile y Brasil. El gaucho ha sido una figura heroica en el folclor, la música y la literatura sudamericanas, y aún sigue siéndola en nuestros días.

---
[a]*horseman*  [b]*de... of which*  [c]*a... for a salary*

**PREGUNTAS** En parejas, contesten las preguntas. Después, compartan sus ideas con la clase.

1. ¿Cuál es la profesión del gaucho sudamericano? ¿A qué territorios pertenece históricamente?
2. ¿Cómo es la personalidad del gaucho?
3. ¿Cómo era su estilo de vida hasta finales del siglo XIX? ¿Cómo vive el gaucho en estos tiempos?
4. ¿En qué aspectos de la cultura o historia de la Argentina actual ha influido el gaucho?
5. Expliquen las semejanzas entre el gaucho de hoy día y el vaquero norteamericano.

# Gramática

## 13.1 The Future Tense

**GRAMÁTICA EN CONTEXTO**

### Las computadoras y el Plan Ceibal

Los estudiantes de Rincón de Vignoli* han recibido sus computadoras portátiles como parte del Plan Ceibal. El Plan Ceibal **pondrá** computadoras en manos de todos los estudiantes de escuelas públicas de Uruguay. Todas las computadoras **tendrán** funciones para escribir documentos, grabar audio, sacar fotos y conectar al Internet, entre otras cosas. Uruguay es el primer país en implementar un plan como este.

Los estudiantes de Rincón de Vignoli se cuentan entre los primeros en recibir sus computadoras. ¿Qué **harán** estos estudiantes con sus computadoras? ¿Cómo las **usarán**? ¿Cómo **cambiarán** los maestros sus planes de clases?

**Comprensión.** ¿Probable o improbable?

|  | P | I |
|---|---|---|
| 1. El Plan Ceibal no tendrá mucho impacto en la vida académica de Uruguay. | ☐ | ☐ |
| 2. Todos los estudiantes recibirán sus computadoras al mismo tiempo. | ☐ | ☐ |
| 3. Algunos de los estudiantes no estudiarán en la universidad. | ☐ | ☐ |
| 4. Los maestros de las escuelas harán algunos cambios en sus clases. | ☐ | ☐ |

You have already learned two ways to express the future in Spanish: the present tense to talk about actions that will occur shortly, and **ir a** + *inf.* to talk about actions to occur in the more distant future. Now you'll learn the *future tense.*

**A.** The future tense is formed by adding the same future ending to the infinitive of **-ar, -er,** and **-ir** verbs.

| hablar | |
|---|---|
| hablar**é** | hablar**emos** |
| hablar**ás** | hablar**éis** |
| habar**á** | hablar**án** |

| volver | |
|---|---|
| volver**é** | volver**emos** |
| volver**ás** | volver**éis** |
| volver**á** | volver**án** |

| vivir | |
|---|---|
| vivir**é** | vivir**emos** |
| vivir**ás** | vivir**éis** |
| vivir**á** | vivir**án** |

*Rincón de Vignoli is a community in Uruguay, about 50 miles north of Montevideo. The grade school there was one of the first to be part of the Plan Ceibal computer distribution program.

**GRAMÁTICA EN CONTEXTO** *Computers and the Ceibal Plan* / *The students of Rincón de Vignoli have received their laptop computers as part of the Ceibal Plan. The Ceibal Plan will put computers in the hands of all of the public school students of Uruguay. All of the computers will have functions for writing documents, recording audio, taking photos, and connecting to the Internet, among other things. Uruguay is the first country to implement a plan like this one. / The students of Rincón de Vignoli are among the first to receive their computers. What will these students do with their computers? How will they use them? How will the teachers change their class plans?*

| Algún día Patricia **será** presidente de los Estados Unidos. | *Some day Patricia will be president of the United States.* |
| **Me graduaré** de la universidad en 2015. | *I will graduate from college in 2015.* |

**B.** Some common verbs use an irregular future stem rather than the infinitive.

## FUTURE TENSE: IRREGULAR VERBS

| decir → dir- | | |
| haber → habr-* | | |
| hacer → har- | -é | |
| poder → podr- | -ás | |
| poner → pondr- | -á | |
| querer → querr- | + -emos | |
| saber → sabr- | -éis | |
| salir → saldr- | -án | |
| tener → tendr- | | |
| venir → vendr- | | |

| Un día te **diré** la verdad acerca de tu padre. | *Someday I will tell you the truth about your father.* |
| **Habrá** menos problemas económicos en el futuro. | *There will be fewer economic problems in the future.* |

**C.** Another common use of the future tense in Spanish is to express what is called the *future of probability*. This use of the future tense expresses conjecture about the present. English speakers use *can, could,* or some similar phrase to express the equivalent.

| ¿Quién **será**? | *Who can that be?* |
| ¿Dónde **estará** Ana? | *Where could Ana be?* |
| ¿Cuántos años **tendrá** ella? | *How old do you suppose she is?* |

**D.** English speakers often use the future tense to ask people to do something for them. Spanish speakers do not use the future tense in that context. Instead they'll use the present indicative as a polite way of asking for something.

| ¿Me **ayudas**? | *Will you help me?* |
| ¿Me **trae** otro café? | *Will you bring me another coffee?* |

---

*The future of **hay** is **habrá** (*there will be*).

**A.** Un futuro brillante. Escuche la descripción que hace Ricardo del futuro que él se imagina para él y sus amigos. Después, indique a quién se refiere cada oración. **¡OJO!** Una oración puede referirse a más de una persona.

Carlos    Marisela    Raquel    Ricardo

1. Será cocinero en un restaurante elegante.
2. Construirán edificios importantes.
3. Tendrá en su clase los estudiantes más inteligentes.
4. Entrevistará al presidente de la república.
5. Se graduarán en dos años.
6. Invitará a sus amigos y les cocinará comidas deliciosas.
7. Ganará un premio.
8. Tendrán mucho éxito.

**B.** En diez años. Complete las oraciones con la forma correcta del verbo en el futuro.

1. Los científicos (**tener**) un remedio (*cure*) para el resfriado común.
2. Mis amigos y yo (**viajar**) por todo el mundo por motivos de trabajo.
3. Yo (**poder**) comprar un carro nuevo todos los años.
4. Tú (**trabajar**) para una compañía multinacional.
5. Los profesores ya no nos (**dar**) tarea por escrito porque los estudiantes (**hacer**) la tarea en computadora.
6. Los diseñadores (**volver**) a la moda de los años 70 para inspirarse.
7. Mi familia y yo (**vivir**) en una casa diseñada por el mejor arquitecto.
8. Un profesor (**ganar**) tanto dinero como un atleta.

**C.** Descripciones. En parejas, inventen detalles sobre los dibujos. ¿Quiénes serán estas personas? ¿Dónde estarán? ¿Qué harán?

Communication

1.

2.

3.

4.

**D.** El futuro de la ingeniería

**PASO 1.** Complete lo que dice el Ingeniero Ordóñez con la forma correcta del verbo entre paréntesis, según el contexto. Cuando se indica con *P/I*, escoja entre el pretérito y el imperfecto y use su forma correcta. Cuando hay dos verbos, seleccione el verbo apropiado y póngalo en la forma correcta.

*Unos paneles solares*

INGENIERO MIGUEL ORDÓÑEZ: Cuando yo (*P/I:* **estar/ser**[1]) estudiante universitario, mis compañeros de clase y yo solamente (*P/I:* **tomar**[2]) clases relacionadas con la ingeniería. No (*P/I:* **estar/ser**[3]) importante saber otras lenguas ni estudiar ecología. No (*nosotros: P/I:* **tener**[4]) que preocuparnos por esas materias. Ahora, las cosas (**estar/ser**[5]) cambiando.

En el futuro, la ingeniería (**estar/ser**[6]) muy diferente. Los ingenieros (**tener**[7]) que estudiar y utilizar fuentes[a] alternativas de energía. (*Nosotros:* **Usar**[8]) más la energía solar para generar electricidad tanto en las casas como en los negocios. En los lugares con mucho viento, los ingenieros (**poner**[9]) aerogeneradores y molinos de viento[b] para generar energía eólica[c] y la (*ellos:* **distribuir**[10]) a muchas partes. También (*nosotros:* **hacer**[11]) uso de la energía hidroeléctrica y la energía undimotriz[d] para aprovechar el poder del agua y de las olas.[e]

Además, un(a) estudiante de ingeniería (**estudiar**[12]) otras lenguas en la universidad porque (**querer**[13]) comunicarse directamente con sus clientes y colegas en otros países, ya que la cooperación internacional (**ser**[14]) imprescindible[f] para llegar a las mejores soluciones. Además de la lengua misma, un ingeniero (**conocer/saber**[15]) a fondo la cultura de las lenguas que habla. Así, (*él/ella:* **poder**[16]) relacionarse mejor con sus clientes y colegas de otros países.

Las computadoras y la tecnología (**desempeñar**[17]) un papel aún más importante. Los teléfonos celulares (**ser**[18]) tan poderosos que (*ellos:* **poder**[19]) cargar con[g] todos los programas necesarios para los ingenieros. No (*nosotros:* **necesitar**[20]) llevar una computadora portátil, solamente el celular y (*nosotros:* **estar/ser**[21]) listos para todo.

Algunos aspectos de esta profesión no (**cambiar**[22]). Por ejemplo, los ingenieros siempre (**tener**[23]) que poner a prueba[h] sus innovaciones, pues muchas veces estas[i] no (**funcionar**[24]) la primera vez. (*Nosotros:* **Seguir**[25]) trabajando en equipo para compartir ideas y así crear el mejor producto. Y sobre todo, siempre (*nosotros:* **buscar**[26]) la manera de mejorar todo lo que hacemos.

[a]*sources* [b]*molinos... windmills* [c]*energía... wind energy* [d]*energía... wave energy* [e]*waves* [f]*essential* [g]*cargar... take charge of* [h]*poner... test* [i]*the latter*

**PASO 2.** Conteste las preguntas, según el **Paso 1.**

1. ¿Qué materias estudiaban los estudiantes de ingeniería cuando el Ingeniero Ordóñez asistía a la universidad? ¿Qué materias no estudiaban?
2. ¿Cómo será la ingeniería en el futuro? ¿Qué tendrán que estudiar y utilizar los ingenieros?
3. ¿Cuáles serán algunas fuentes alternativas de energía? ¿Qué elementos de la naturaleza aprovecharán los ingenieros?
4. ¿Por qué estudiarán otras lenguas los estudiantes de ingeniería? Además de las lenguas, ¿qué más conocerán a fondo? ¿Cómo los ayudarán estos conocimientos?
5. ¿Qué papel harán las computadoras y la tecnología en la ingeniería del futuro? ¿Cómo ayudarán los teléfonos celulares a los ingenieros?
6. ¿Qué aspectos de la ingeniería no cambiarán? ¿Por qué?

**PASO 3.** En parejas, háganse y contesten las preguntas.

Communication

1. ¿Qué profesión estudias? ¿Qué materias estudias actualmente para prepararte para esa profesión? ¿Cómo serán diferentes los estudios para esta profesión en el año 2060?
2. ¿Cómo es la profesión para la que te preparas en la actualidad? ¿Cómo será diferente en el año 2100?
3. En tu profesión, ¿es necesario hablar otra lengua y conocer otra cultura? ¿Por qué? ¿Continuará esta necesidad para el año 2100? Explica.
4. En tu profesión, ¿qué papel desempeñan las computadoras y la tecnología? ¿Cómo cambiará ese papel para el año 2100? Explica.

## 13.2 Present Subjunctive After Temporal Conjunctions

Expressing Pending Future Situations

### GRAMÁTICA EN CONTEXTO

#### Un obrero en Chuquicamanta

*En la refinería Chuquicamanta*

Rodrigo es un obrero cualificado en la refinería Chuquicamanta en Chile. Sus jornadas son largas y físicamente desafiantes. Normalmente vuelve directamente a casa **en cuanto termina** su trabajo, pero hoy, **cuando se acabe** su turno, saldrá con algunos amigos a tomar una cerveza. No cenará **hasta que vuelva** a casa, donde su familia lo espera. **Tan pronto como llegue** a casa, se duchará y se cambiará de ropa. Siempre se siente a gusto y alegre **después de que** sus hijos le **cuentan** las historias de su día durante la cena.

Comprensión. ¿Típicamente (**T**) o sólo a veces (**AV**)?

|  | T | AV |
|---|---|---|
| 1. Rodrigo y su familia cenan juntos después de que él llega del trabajo. | ☐ | ☐ |
| 2. Rodrigo y sus amigos vuelven a casa tan pronto como salen del trabajo. | ☐ | ☐ |
| 3. La esposa y los hijos de Rodrigo no cenan hasta que Rodrigo se duche. | ☐ | ☐ |

GRAMÁTICA EN CONTEXTO *A Chuquicamanta Laborer / Rodrigo is a skilled worker at the Chuquicamanta refinery in Chile. His days are long and physically challenging. Normally he goes directly home when he finishes work, but today, when his shift is over, he will go out with friends to have a beer. He won't eat dinner until he returns home, where his family is waiting for him. As soon as he gets home, he will take a shower and change clothes. He always feels comfortable and happy after his children tell him the stories of their day during dinner.*

**A.** The present subjunctive is used after certain conjunctions of time when the clause that follows the conjunction refers to a future action. Here are some of the most common temporal conjunctions.

| TEMPORAL CONJUNCTIONS | | | |
|---|---|---|---|
| **cuando** | when | **hasta que** | until |
| **después de que** | after | **tan pronto como** | as soon as |
| **en cuanto** | as soon as | | |

| | |
|---|---|
| Mi hermano piensa hacerse maestro **cuando** termine los estudios. | *My brother plans to become a teacher when he finishes his studies.* |
| Va a mudarse **en cuanto** encuentre un buen trabajo. | *He's going to move as soon as he finds a good job.* |

**B.** Unlike the other uses of the subjunctive that you have studied up to now, sentences with adverbial clauses may have a different order to the clauses. However, the important thing to remember is that the subjunctive will always follow the adverbial conjunction of time, no matter if it is in the first clause or second clause.

| | |
|---|---|
| Nuestro jefe nos dará un aumento de sueldo **cuando** consigamos el nuevo contrato. | *Our boss will give us a raise when we get the new contract.* |
| **Cuando** consigamos el nuevo contrato, nuestro jefe nos dará un aumento de sueldo. | *When we get the new contract, our boss will give us a raise.* |

**C.** In contexts where the action following the conjunction is not in the future, the present indicative is used if the statement refers to a habitual action, and a past tense is used if the statement refers to something that already happened.

| | |
|---|---|
| **Todos los viernes salgo** con mis compañeros **cuando** recibimos nuestros cheques. | *Every Friday I go out with my friends when we receive our paychecks.* |
| **El año pasado tuve** que comprar un carro **cuando** cambié de trabajo. | *Last year I had to buy a car when I changed jobs.* |

### ACTIVIDADES

**A. Prácticas profesionales.** Lea las oraciones y determine si se trata de una acción habitual o de una acción que todavía no ha ocurrido. Luego, indique la palabra que mejor completa cada oración.

1. El contador siempre prepara un informe en cuanto sus clientes le (**dan/den**) toda su información financiera.
2. La veterinaria va a examinar al perro después de que su asistente le (**pone/ponga**) una inyección.
3. El público siempre tiene que levantarse tan pronto como la jueza (**entra/entre**).
4. La intérprete va a utilizar un micrófono cuando (**habla/hable**).
5. El electricista va a trabajar hasta que las luces (**funcionan/funcionen**) de nuevo.
6. El barbero barre el piso en cuanto (**termina/termine**) con cada cliente.
7. La farmacéutica habla con los pacientes cuando ellos le (**hacen/hagan**) preguntas.

**B. Un día.** Llene los espacios en blanco con la forma correcta del verbo.

1. Mis compañeros de trabajo y yo vamos a estar muy contentos cuando _____ (**tener**) los resultados del estudio.
2. Soy periodista y siempre trabajo en un artículo hasta que lo _____ (**terminar**).
3. Los programadores empiezan a escribir programas tan pronto como _____ (**saber**) lo que quiere el cliente.
4. La diseñadora de modas va a empezar el nuevo vestido en cuanto _____ (**llegar**) la tela.
5. El traductor escribirá la traducción después de que el técnico le _____ (**arreglar**) la computadora.
6. La dentista habla con sus nuevos pacientes hasta que _____ (**sentirse**) cómodos.
7. La secretaria va a hablar con su jefe cuando él _____ (**salir**) de su reunión.

**C. Descripciones.** Describa los dibujos, completando las oraciones, según el contexto de las escenas. Luego, describa su propia vida.

1.

a. Esta tarde, los amigos van a tomar un café cuando _____.
b. Siempre salgo con mis amigos cuando _____.
c. Este fin de semana, voy a _____ cuando _____.

2.

a. Esta tarde, Elena va a estudiar hasta que _____.
b. Siempre estudio hasta que _____.
c. Este fin de semana, pienso _____ hasta que _____.

(Continúa.)

**3.**

- **a.** El Sr. Pérez siempre vuelve a casa después de que _____.
- **b.** Siempre vuelvo a casa después de que _____.
- **c.** El verano que viene, voy a _____ después de que _____.

**4.**

- **a.** Los compañeros de trabajo van a almorzar tan pronto como _____.
- **b.** Siempre almuerzo tan pronto como _____.
- **c.** Mañana, voy a _____ tan pronto como _____.

**D.** Mi futura profesión

**PASO 1.** Complete lo que dice Felicia con la forma correcta del verbo entre paréntesis, según el contexto. Cuando se indica con *P/I*, escoja entre el pretérito y el imperfecto y use su forma correcta. Cuando hay dos verbos, seleccione el verbo apropiado y póngalo en la forma correcta.

Cuando yo (*P/I:* **estar/ser**[1]) niña, mi familia y yo (*P/I:* **vivir**[2]) en el campo. Siempre (*P/I: nosotros:* **tener**[3]) muchas mascotas y animales de todo tipo. Me (*P/I:* **encantar**[4]) los animales y (*P/I: yo:* **jugar**[5]) a ser veterinaria. Por eso, cuando (*yo: P/I:* **graduarme**[6]) de la secundaria, (*yo: P/I:* **decidir**[7]) estudiar para hacerme veterinaria.

Ahora, (*yo:* **estar/ser**[8]) estudiante universitaria y (**tomar**[9]) clases de veterinaria.[a] Mis compañeros de clase y yo siempre (**estudiar**[10]) hasta que cada uno (**entender**[11]) la lección. Después de que (*nosotros:* **terminar**[12]), siempre (*nosotros:* **salir**[13]) a tomar un café o a cenar juntos porque (**estar/ser**[14]) importante relajarse.

[a]*veterinary medicine*

A veces (**estar/ser**[15]) difícil estudiar tanto, pero (*yo:* **conocer/saber**[16]) que vale la pena.[b] Cuando yo (**estar/ser**[17]) veterinaria, podré ayudar a muchas personas y a sus mascotas. Tan pronto como (*yo:* **graduarse**[18]), voy a buscar un puesto con un veterinario con experiencia hasta que (*yo:* **poder**[19]) abrir mi propia[c] clínica. Pienso trabajar para ese veterinario hasta que me (*él:* **enseñar**[20]) todo lo posible. Entonces, en cuanto (*yo:* **sentirse**[21]) cómoda y preparada, voy a abrir mi propia clínica para atender a[d] toda clase de animales, desde los más pequeños hasta los más grandes.

Además de mi trabajo diario, voy a participar en otro proyecto que me interesa. Tan pronto como (*yo:* **tener**[22]) mi clínica, pienso colaborar con los sicólogos y médicos de la ciudad para ampliar[e] la terapia con mascotas. Según los estudios, no hay duda de que los animales (**poder**[23]) mejorar la salud de personas que padecen de[f] diversas condiciones, desde la depresión hasta la diabetes. Por eso, es importante que yo (**trabajar**[24]) con mis colegas en la medicina humana para concienciar a la gente acerca de[g] la terapia con mascotas.

Estoy segura de que mi vida como veterinaria (**ir**[25]) a ser muy activa, y dudo que (**haber**[26]) un solo día aburrido en mi futuro. Voy a estar muy contenta cuando (*yo:* **obtener**[27]) mi título y (**poder**[28]) empezar a trabajar como veterinaria.

[b]vale... *it's worth it* [c]*own* [d]atender... *care for* [e]*expand* [f]padecen... *suffer from* [g]concienciar... *make people aware of*

**PASO 2.** Conteste las preguntas, según el **Paso 1.**

1. ¿Cómo era la vida de Felicia cuando era niña? Descríbala.
2. ¿Por qué decidió estudiar veterinaria cuando se graduó de la secundaria?
3. ¿Hasta cuándo estudian Felicia y sus compañeros de clase? ¿Qué hacen después de que terminan de estudiar? ¿Por qué?
4. ¿Qué piensa hacer primero Felicia tan pronto como se gradúe? ¿Por cuánto tiempo piensa trabajar así? ¿Por qué? ¿Cuándo piensa Felicia abrir su propia clínica?
5. ¿En qué otro proyecto espera participar Felicia tan pronto como tenga su propia clínica? ¿Cuál es el efecto de los animales en la salud humana, según los estudios? ¿Por qué es importante que Felicia trabaje en este proyecto con sus colegas de otros campos?
6. ¿Cómo será la vida de Felicia como veterinaria, según ella? Explique.

**PASO 3.** En parejas, háganse y contesten las preguntas.

Communication

1. Cuando eras niño/a, ¿jugabas a alguna profesión? ¿Cuál era? ¿Con quién(es) jugabas? ¿Cómo jugabas? Explica.
2. ¿Qué piensas hacer tan pronto como te gradúes? Explica.
3. En tu opinión, ¿les proporcionan (*provide*) las mascotas a sus dueños (*owners*) algún beneficio en su salud física o emocional? Explica.

# Palabra escrita

## A comenzar

Communication

> **Selecting the Structure of Your Composition.** The way you organize a composition depends on your topic. Although this will vary depending on the purpose of your composition, a linear structure is normally best because it is straight-forward. Using this structure, first state your thesis in the introductory paragraph, thus preparing the reader to properly understand your point of view. Then, write a series of paragraphs supporting that thesis statement. Remember to include a topic sentence in each paragraph. Finally, write a conclusion in which you summarize the main points of your composition or reiterate your thesis statement.

You are going to start the process of writing a brief composition that you will finalize in the **Palabra escrita: A finalizar** section of your *Manual de actividades*. The topic of this composition is **Yo, y las profesiones del futuro.** The purpose of your composition will be to tell the reader about the professions in your field of study that will probably be in high demand when you graduate and what you will do to get a job in one of those professions.

**A.** Lluvia de ideas. En parejas, hagan una lluvia de ideas sobre estos temas relacionados con las profesiones y el futuro.

1. las posibles profesiones en su campo de estudio
2. las profesiones que tendrán demanda
3. lo que Uds. harán para conseguir trabajo en esos campos

**B.** A organizar sus ideas. Repase sus ideas y apunte oraciones que requieran el subjuntivo después de las conjunciones temporales que aprendió en el **Tema I: cuando, después de que, en cuanto, hasta que, tan pronto como.** Organice las oraciones en categorías y, cuando tiene sentido (*it makes sense*), en orden cronológico. Busque más información sobre las profesiones del futuro en el Internet y escoja un enfoque y una estructura para su composición. Comparta su información con la clase y apunte otras ideas que se le ocurran durante el proceso.

**C.** A escribir. Ahora, haga el borrador de su composición con las ideas y la información que recopiló en las actividades A y B. **¡OJO!** Guarde bien su trabajo. Va a necesitarlo otra vez para la sección de **Palabra escrita: A finalizar** en el *Manual de actividades*.

# Antonio Berni

La familia de Juanito emigra, *1970*

Antonio Berni (1905–1981) estudió primero en Argentina y luego en París, donde recibió la influencia del movimiento surrealista. Sus obras más famosas reflejan una conciencia social, ecológica y política. En algunas de sus obras creó dos arquetipos que representan a los sectores más explotados de la sociedad: Juanito Laguna y Ramona Montiel. Juanito simboliza todos los chicos pobres de la ciudad. Ramona Montiel representa a la muchacha de la aldea que se muda a la ciudad en busca de otra vida.

En este cuadro —un collage que mezcla el arte pop con el realismo social— parece que Juanito y su familia también se mudan por razones económicas.

## Vocabulario del tema

### La búsqueda° de trabajo

*Search*

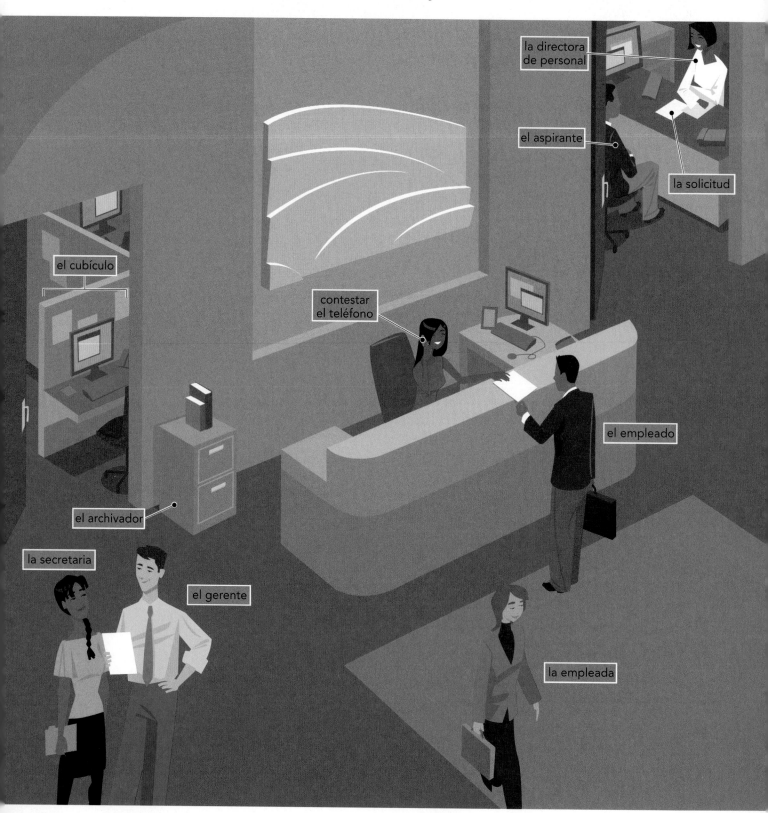

la directora de personal

el aspirante

la solicitud

el cubículo

contestar el teléfono

el empleado

el archivador

la secretaria

el gerente

la empleada

## El lugar de trabajo

| | |
|---|---|
| despedir (*like* pedir) | to fire |
| firmar | to sign |
| jubilarse | to retire |
| llenar | to fill out (*a form*) |
| renunciar (a) | to resign (from) (*a job*) |
| solicitar (trabajo) | to apply for (a job) |
| | |
| el/la administrativo/a | file clerk |
| el/la aspirante | applicant |
| el aumento | raise |
| el currículum | résumé, CV |
| el empleo a tiempo completo | full-time job |
| el empleo a tiempo parcial | part-time job |
| el horario de trabajo | work schedule |
| el/la jefe/a | boss |
| el plan de jubilación | retirement plan |
| el puesto | job; position |
| el salario (mínimo) | (minimum) wage; salary, pay |
| el seguro médico | health insurance |
| la solicitud | application |
| el sueldo | salary |
| las vacaciones pagadas | paid vacation |
| | |
| comprensivo/a | understanding |
| exigente | demanding |

Cognados: (in)flexible
Repaso: la entrevista, el/la gerente

## Las responsabilidades

| | |
|---|---|
| administrar | to manage; to administer |
| anotar datos | to enter data |
| archivar | to file |
| dirigir (j) | to manage (*people*) |
| escribir informes | to write reports |
| hacer (*irreg.*) copias | to make copies |
| manejar las cuentas | to manage accounts |
| supervisar | to supervise; to oversee |

## La tecnología en la oficina

| | |
|---|---|
| bajar | to download |
| guardar | to save (*a file*) |
| subir | to upload |
| | |
| el disco duro | hard disk |
| la página Web | webpage |

Cognados: el proyector, el software, la teleconferencia
Repaso: la computadora (portátil), el e-mail, el escritorio, el Internet

## ACTIVIDADES

**A. Definiciones.** Empareje las palabras o expresiones con sus definiciones correspondientes.

1. _____ salón donde trabaja un empleado
2. _____ persona que ayuda al personal a tomar decisiones laborales
3. _____ persona a cargo (*in charge*) de una empresa
4. _____ una reunión entre el aspirante a un puesto y el director de personal
5. _____ tiempo que un empleado debe trabajar cada día
6. _____ dinero que una persona recibe como pago por su trabajo
7. _____ programa que le sigue pagando a una persona cuando deja de trabajar por su edad
8. _____ este beneficio es importante cuando alguien se enferma

a. jefe
b. salario
c. plan de jubilación
d. oficina
e. consejero/a
f. seguro médico
g. horario de trabajo
h. entrevista

**B. Lo que hacemos en el trabajo**

**PASO 1.** Complete las oraciones con el verbo correspondiente del **Vocabulario del tema.**

1. Horacio no se lleva bien con sus colegas y tampoco le gusta su trabajo. Va a _____.
2. Leonor ha conseguido un nuevo puesto. El primer día de trabajo tiene que _____ varios documentos que describen sus responsabilidades y los beneficios.
3. Carlota cree que su hijo necesita _____ trabajo. Hace dos meses que se graduó y todavía vive en casa y no trabaja.
4. Necesito un software nuevo para la computadora y el jefe dice que lo puede _____ del Internet.
5. Mi disco duro falló (*failed*) y perdí algunos documentos que se me olvidó _____.

**PASO 2.** En parejas, formen oraciones con los verbos de la lista. Deben describir lo que Uds. hacen o han hecho (o no). Luego, su compañero/a va a adivinar si la oración es cierta o falsa.

**MODELO** supervisar →

    E1: En mi trabajo, superviso el trabajo de diez personas.
    E2: No es cierto. No creo que supervises a otros empleados.

| | | | |
|---|---|---|---|
| archivar | dirigir | hacer copias | llenar |
| despedir | escribir informes | jubilarse | manejar las cuentas |

**C.** Un anuncio de trabajo

**PASO 1.** Lea la oferta de trabajo y conteste las preguntas.

Profesionales o estudiantes de tecnología de la producción

Supervisor del área de producción

**EMPRESA:** Comfar S.A.E.C.A

**LOCALIDAD:** Asunción, Paraguay

**SECTOR:** Farmacéutica

**TIPO DE CONTRATO:** Indefinido; jornada completa

**EXPERIENCIA MÍNIMA:** 2 años

**SALARIO:** 5 millones de guaraníes* al mes

Envíe su currículum a esta oferta de trabajo.

1. ¿En qué lugar se ofrece el trabajo?
2. ¿Cuál es el sueldo que se ofrece?
3. ¿Qué tipo de contrato ofrece la empresa?

**PASO 2.** En parejas, modifiquen la oferta de trabajo para hacerla más atractiva a los posibles aspirantes. Incluyan detalles como el plan de jubilación, el ambiente laboral, el seguro médico, las vacaciones, el horario de trabajo o cualquier otra información que les parezca interesante.

Communication

**PASO 3.** Presenten su oferta a la clase. Comparen todas las ofertas y escojan la más atractiva.

Communication

**D.** En el trabajo

**PASO 1.** En parejas, escojan dos profesiones diferentes y describan las responsabilidades de las personas que las hacen y los recursos tecnológicos necesarios para su oficina o lugar de trabajo.

Communication

MODELO

PROFESIÓN: Profesor(a) de historia

RESPONSABILIDADES:
- enseñar tres cursos por semestre
- asistir a reuniones profesorales
- publicar artículos profesionales
- participar en congresos (*conferences*)

RECURSOS:
- computadora con acceso al Internet para hacer trabajos de investigación
- software que facilite subir información al Internet
- proyector para hacer presentaciones brillantes en PowerPoint
- cuenta de e-mail para tener comunicación rápida con los estudiantes
- reproductor (player) de DVD para mostrar documentales en clase

**PASO 2.** Compartan sus descripciones con la clase sin nombrar las profesiones. La clase debe adivinar la profesión que se describe.

---

*As of May, 2010: 5,000,000 guaranis = US $1,060.

**E.** Otras formas de trabajo

**PASO 1.** Lea el artículo.

## NUEVAS FORMAS DE TRABAJO

Con las nuevas tecnologías, aparecen nuevas formas de trabajo.

- **El teletrabajo:** El empleado que hace teletrabajo puede trabajar y vivir en casa lejos de la oficina central de la empresa o compañía. Algunas de las ventajas[a] para el empleador es que ahorra[b] algunos gastos (en locales, electricidad, limpieza, etcétera) para la empresa y reduce el absentismo. El empleado puede usar el tiempo más eficazmente, tiene mayor autonomía en su trabajo, mayor flexibilidad para adaptarse a las actividades familiares y de ocio[c]. Los inconvenientes incluyen: menos interacción social con los colegas, dificultades para coordinar actividades y lugares de trabajo (oficinas) con ambientes menos controlados y menos recursos tecnológicos.

- **Grupos de trabajo distribuidos:** Esta nueva forma de trabajo cooperativo se hace entre grupos geográficamente dispersos,[d] sin necesidad de mantener reuniones cara a cara. Las comunicaciones entre distintos lugares se hacen de varias maneras: por Internet, por teleconferencia, por videoconferencia, etcétera.

[a]*advantages*  [b]*saves*  [c]*leisure*  [d]*separated*

**PASO 2.** Indique si las oraciones son ciertas (**C**) o falsas (**F**), según el **Paso 1.**

|  | C | F |
|---|---|---|
| 1. El teletrabajo consiste en trabajar para una empresa pero desde otro lugar, generalmente desde la propia casa del empleado. | ☐ | ☐ |
| 2. Los grupos de trabajo colaboran en un proyecto común, pero los integrantes viven en lugares diferentes. | ☐ | ☐ |
| 3. Las computadoras y el Internet hacen posible la comunicación por teleconferencia y videoconferencia. | ☐ | ☐ |
| 4. El teletrabajo no tiene ventajas para la empresa. | ☐ | ☐ |

Communication

**PASO 3.** En parejas, hablen de las posibilidades de hacer teletrabajo o grupos de trabajo distribuidos. ¿Les gustaría trabajar en el futuro desde su casa o prefieren la idea de trabajar en una oficina? Justifiquen sus respuestas con detalles del texto y después compartan sus ideas con sus compañeros de clase. ¿Tiene la clase alguna tendencia en común?

## Nota cultural

### LA MUJER Y EL MERCADO LABORAL

En Latinoamérica, la mujer siempre ha sido importante para el mantenimiento de la economía familiar. Además de cuidar de la casa y de los hijos, la mujer desarrolla otras actividades laborales informales que ayudan a la principal fuente de ingresos, normalmente el hombre. Adicionalmente, en 1990, treinta y cuatro de cada cien mujeres trabajaban formalmente, mientras que en 2008, su tasa[a] de participación laboral era del 52%. Además, el nivel educativo de las mujeres es superior al de los hombres. Las cifras son aún mayores en los países del Cono Sur, especialmente en Argentina y Chile, cuyo desarrollo económico y social es superior a la media[b] en Latinoamérica.

Aunque hay más trabajo para las mujeres y están mejor preparadas que antes, todavía continúan los problemas en la calidad de su inserción laboral.[c] Por ejemplo, una mujer debe tener más años de estudio que un hombre para recibir un salario similar. Las mujeres siguen dominando en los sectores peores pagados y su presencia es mayoritariamente superior en el área de servicios y en el servicio doméstico, que absorbe el 17% del empleo femenino. Otro ejemplo de discriminación se ve en las posibilidades de promoción para la mujer en su lugar de trabajo, significativamente menores que las del hombre.

[a]*rate* [b]*mean* [c]*inserción… job placement*

PREGUNTAS En parejas, contesten las preguntas y después, compartan sus ideas con la clase.

1. En su opinión, ¿qué es un trabajo formal y qué es un trabajo informal?
2. ¿Qué problemas enfrenta la mujer latinoamericana en el mundo laboral?
3. ¿Cuáles son los trabajos realizados principalmente por las mujeres?
4. ¿Existe una situación similar en este país? Expliquen.

# Gramática

## 13.3 Present Subjunctive in Adjectival Clauses with Indefinite Antecedents

Describing Unknown or Non-existent Antecedents

### GRAMÁTICA EN CONTEXTO

La oficina de la fábrica Liebig

#### La oficina de la fábrica Liebig

Esta oficina de la fábrica Liebig, en Fray Bentos, Uruguay, se ha convertido en museo. ¿Por qué es museo ahora? Pues, probablemente **no hay** ninguna compañía moderna que **pueda** usarla. Esta oficina **no tiene** ningún cubículo que **separe** los escritorios. Un jefe moderno **va a querer** que todos sus empleados **tengan** computadoras con programas para escribir, documentar y

GRAMÁTICA EN CONTEXTO **The Office of the Liebig Factory** / This office at the Liebig factory in Fray Bentos, Uruguay, has been turned into a museum. Why is it a museum now? Well, there probably is no modern company that could use it. This office has no cubicles that separate the desks. A modern boss will want all of his employees to have computers with programs for writing, documenting, and connecting to the Internet, but this office only has typewriters and mechanical calculators.

conectarse al Internet, pero esta oficina sólo tiene máquinas de escribir y calculado-
ras mecánicas.

Comprensión. ¿Una oficina moderna (**M**) o antigua (**A**)?

|  | M | A |
|---|---|---|
| **1.** No hay ningún escritorio que tenga aparatos electrónicos. | ☐ | ☐ |
| **2.** La oficina tiene muchos cubículos. | ☐ | ☐ |
| **3.** Los empleados tienen aparatos modernos que conectan al Internet. | ☐ | ☐ |

You have already seen and used many examples of clauses in Spanish. One specific
kind of clause is an adjective clause, which is one that describes a noun or a pronoun,
and is introduced with the relative pronoun **que**. The noun or pronoun described is
referred to as the *antecedent*.

| Tengo un **amigo que trabaja en** **un banco.** | *I have a friend who works in a bank.* |
|---|---|

The adjective clause **que trabaja en un banco** describes **amigo**.

| Óscar encontró una **secretaria** **que hablaba español y japonés.** | *Óscar found a secretary who spoke* *Spanish and Japanese.* |
|---|---|

Here, the adjective clause **que hablaba español y japonés** describes **secretaria**.

In the preceding sample sentences, the verb in the adjective clause is in the indicative
(present indicative and imperfect) because the nouns (**un amigo** and **una secretaria**)
described exist from the speaker's point of view.

However, if the antecedent described by an adjective clause is either unknown (it
may exist but the speaker doesn't know) or is definitely nonexistent, the verb in the
adjective clause will be in the subjunctive.

| **Busco un trabajo** que **pague** el doble de lo que gano ahora. | *I'm looking for a job that pays double* *what I earn now.* (*unknown job.*) |
|---|---|
| **Quiero una computadora** que **cueste** menos de mil dólares. | *I want a computer that costs less than* *a thousand dollars.* (*unknown* *computer.*) |
| **No hay nadie aquí** que **hable** francés. | *There is no one here who speaks* *French.* (*No such person exists.*) |

### ACTIVIDADES

**A. La gente que conozco.** Indique cuáles de las oraciones describen a personas que
Ud. conoce.

1. ☐ Conozco a alguien que trabaja de recepcionista.
2. ☐ No conozco a nadie que se jubile pronto.
3. ☐ Hay alguien en la clase de español que también habla una tercera lengua.
4. ☐ En mi trabajo, no hay nadie que no sepa usar la computadora.
5. ☐ Hay una estudiante en la clase que trabaja a tiempo completo.
6. ☐ No hay nadie en la clase que sea jefe/a de su propio negocio.
7. ☐ En mi trabajo, hay un empleado que archiva todos los documentos.
8. ☐ Conozco a alguien que va a tener un aumento de sueldo muy pronto.

**B. Una jefa frustrada.** Dé la forma correcta del verbo entre paréntesis.

LICENCIADA DÁVILA: Hoy, mi asistente, Rolando, está enfermo. No hay otro
empleado que (saber[1]) ayudarme en todo y estoy desesperada.[a] Hay una recepcionista
que también (estar[2]) en la oficina de enfrente, pero ella tiene que atender a los clientes.

---

[a]*desperate*

Por eso, no hay nadie que (**contestar**[3]) los teléfonos. Además, tengo una computadora que siempre me (**causar**[4]) problemas y hoy tampoco funciona. ¡No sé qué hacer! Aparte de Rolando, no hay otro empleado que (**poder**[5]) arreglar[b] las computadoras. Sí, hay algunos técnicos que (**trabajar**[6]) para la empresa, pero ellos siempre tardan mucho.[c] Este día va a ser fatal. Pero he aprendido que necesito buscar otro asistente que (**colaborar**[7]) con Rolando en todos mis proyectos. También sé que hay alguien que (**ir**[8]) a recibir un aumento de sueldo: ¡Rolando!

[b]*fix* [c]*tardan... take a long time*

### C. Entrevista

**PASO 1.** Complete las oraciones con información personal.

1. Tengo un profesor / una profesora que...
2. El semestre que viene quiero tomar una clase que...
3. Cuando me gradúe, quiero tener un trabajo que...
4. Conozco a alguien que...
5. Tengo un(a) pariente que...
6. En mi clase no hay nadie que...
7. Actualmente tengo un trabajo que...
8. Este fin de semana no quiero hacer nada que...

**PASO 2.** Ahora, en parejas, háganse y contesten preguntas basadas en su oraciones del **Paso 1.**

Communication

### D. Los anuncios clasificados

**PASO 1.** Complete los anuncios con la forma correcta del verbo entre paréntesis, según el contexto.

Cultures    Recycle

Compañía internacional busca un vendedor[a] que (**hablar**[1]) chino y que (**tener**[2]) experiencia en ventas internacionales. Además de un buen sueldo, hay prestaciones[b] que (**incluir**[3]) seguro médico y dos semanas de vacaciones pagadas.

Pequeña empresa busca una recepcionista que (**saber**[4]) usar computadoras y (**poder**[5]) trabajar en múltiples proyectos a la vez. Ya tenemos una secretaria que (**archivar**[6]) los documentos y (**hacer**[7]) copias, pero necesitamos a alguien que (**contestar**[8]) el teléfono, que (**recibir**[9]) a los clientes y que (**organizar**[10]) reuniones.

Empresa nacional busca un supervisor de ventas. Ya tenemos una contadora que (**manejar**[11]) las cuentas y queremos encontrar a alguien que (**colaborar**[12]) con ella. Necesitamos a alguien que (**escribir**[13]) informes claros y concisos y que (**dirigir**[14]) a los otros empleados.

Empresa familiar busca un técnico que nos (**enseñar**[15]) a utilizar mejor la computadora. Queremos encontrar a alguien que (**diseñar**[16]) y (**manejar**[17]) una página Web para nuestra empresa, y que nos (**ayudar**[18]) a aprovechar todo el paquete de software que vino con la computadora portátil que (*nosotros:* **usar**[19]).

(Continúa.)

[a]*salesperson* [b]*benefits*

**PASO 2.** Conteste las preguntas, según el **Paso 1.**

1. ¿Qué busca la pequeña empresa? ¿Qué empleado/a tiene ya? ¿Qué hace esta persona? Según el anuncio, ¿qué necesita la empresa que haga el nuevo empleado / la nueva empleada?
2. ¿Qué busca la empresa familiar? ¿Qué necesitan que haga esta persona? ¿Qué tienen ya? ¿Qué clase de ayuda necesitan del nuevo empleado / de la nueva empleada?
3. ¿Qué busca la compañía internacional? ¿Qué le ofrecen al nuevo empleado / a la nueva empleada?
4. ¿Qué busca la empresa nacional? ¿Qué empleado/a tiene ya y qué hace esta persona? ¿Qué quiere encontrar la empresa? ¿Qué necesita que haga el nuevo empleado / la nueva empleada?

**PASO 3.** En parejas, escriban tres anuncios clasificados para estas empresas. Incluyan lo que ya tienen y lo que necesitan.

1. un nuevo negocio local
2. una empresa multinacional
3. una compañía que acaba de abrir su primera sucursal (*branch*)

---

## Nota interdisciplinaria

### LENGUAS EXTRANJERAS: LOS IDIOMAS EN EL MUNDO LABORAL

«Hola, Frank. How are you this morning?»

Con la creciente globalización de la economía mundial, saber varios idiomas es un requisito indispensable para encontrar trabajo. El conocimiento de idiomas es muy apreciado por las compañías y contribuye a la mejora de la propia carrera profesional. Puede ser la diferencia entre cerrar un negocio o no cerrarlo, conseguir un puesto laboral o no conseguirlo, obtener una promoción dentro de la compañía y así poder ganar un mejor salario o no ser considerado para ello.

El inglés es el idioma oficial en el mundo de los negocios y de la computación, y muchos de los estudios y textos científicos de importancia están escritos en este idioma, pero no es el único idioma importante. El alemán y el francés, por su importancia en Europa, son los que le siguen entre los idiomas con más demanda y, últimamente, se ha ido introduciendo otro idioma muy útil: el chino, debido al poder económico de China.

Latinoamérica está atravesando[a] por un momento de crecimiento económico, tecnológico e industrial. Con la creación de MERCOSUR (acuerdo comercial entre Brasil, Argentina, Uruguay y Paraguay, que se está ampliando a otros países), la región del Cono Sur aspira a ser una única zona comercial y económica. La presencia de Brasil, una de las potencias económicas latinoamericanas, convierte al portugués en un idioma importantísimo para tener éxito en esa región.

El español y el portugués harán un papel de suma[b] importancia para cualquier persona o compañía que quiera tener acceso al mayor mercado de Sudamérica. Por ello, son cada vez más[c] las universidades y escuelas que ofrecen español y portugués en sus currículos, y hay cada vez más compañías que les exigen[d] a sus empleados el conocimiento de un segundo o tercer idioma para tener acceso incluso al mercado europeo o asiático.

[a]está... *is going though*  [b]*tremendous*  [c]cada... *more and more*  [d]*demand*

**PREGUNTAS** En parejas, contesten las preguntas. Después, compartan sus ideas con la clase.

1. ¿Por qué es importante saber varios idiomas en el trabajo? ¿Qué beneficios aporta (*offer*) a la persona o a una empresa?
2. ¿Cuáles son los idiomas de mayor demanda? ¿Por qué?
3. ¿Qué importancia tiene saber español y portugués en Latinoamérica?
4. ¿Creen Uds. que hablar un segundo o tercer idioma puede ayudarlos/las en su futuro profesionalmente? ¿Qué idioma(s) les parece(n) indispensable(s)? Expliquen.

# Lectura cultural

Ud. va a leer un artículo de la revista argentina *Apertura*, escrito por Estefanía Giganti, sobre el teletrabajo en Argentina.

## ANTES DE LEER

**A. A primera vista.** Lea el título y las líneas *en letra cursiva* al principio y a mitad de la página 442. Luego, indique qué información espera encontrar en el resto del artículo.

1. ☐ datos (*data*) sobre un nuevo fenómeno laboral para las compañías grandes en Argentina
2. ☐ información sobre un nuevo sistema telefónico
3. ☐ información sobre las tareas domésticas de los argentinos
4. ☐ comentarios de algunas personas que trabajan desde la casa algunos días de la semana
5. ☐ comentarios de algunos jefes que manejan a empleados que trabajan desde la casa
6. ☐ información sobre las ventajas y desventajas del teletrabajo
7. ☐ comentarios sobre el viaje diario al trabajo en Argentina

**B. Sinónimos.** Las frases de la columna A aparecen en el artículo. Empareje las palabras **en negrita** con su sinónimo de la columna B.

| A | B |
|---|---|
| 1. _____ ...en lugar de **trasladarse** a los edificios corporativos. | a. añadir |
| 2. _____ ...tal como lo reveló un reciente **sondeo**... | b. el sector privado |
| 3. _____ ...hay que **sumarle** un 64% de ahorro... | c. encuesta |
| 4. _____ ...las encuestas... **arrojaron** un alto nivel de satisfacción... | d. es obvia |
| 5. _____ ...la evolución **salta a la vista**. | e. indicaron |
| 6. _____ ...el **trayecto** diario de ida y vuelta... | f. ir |
| 7. _____ ...el 6% de la población... que trabaja en **la actividad privada**... | g. viaje |

## El teletrabajo, el gran sueño de los argentinos

*El 70% de los empleados en relación de dependencia[a] asegura que podría[b] realizar sus tareas desde el hogar, al menos tres veces a la semana. Radiografía[c] de un fenómeno que no para de crecer.*

Si de utopías se trata, hay una que se multiplica en la mente de los trabajadores argentinos: trabajar desde su casa. Ya sea[d] en bata y pantuflas[e] o vestidos al mejor estilo oficina, una gran mayoría de los empleados preferiría[f] hacerlo desde su hogar, en lugar de trasladarse a los edificios corporativos.

Aunque es evidente que no cualquier trabajo es trasladable al hogar, el 70% de

*Una mujer trabaja desde la casa mientras su hija juega al fondo.*

[a]*en... under contract (that work for a company)* [b]*(they) could* [c]*A close look at (lit. x-ray)* [d]*Ya... Whether it be* [e]*bata... bathrobe and slippers* [f]*would prefer*

los trabajadores en relación de dependencia encuestados considera que su trabajo es teletrabajable, por lo menos tres días a la semana, tal como lo reveló un reciente sondeo de la consultora Jobing, sobre un total de 200 trabajadores activos.

De hecho, numerosas empresas comparten esta creencia, ya que[g] el teletrabajo está en pleno ascenso[h] en nuestro país y en el mundo. Como resultado de estas experiencias, surgieron[i] beneficios mutuos. Los empleados lograron evitar algunas de sus peores pesadillas:[j] los problemas de tránsito, la incomodidad del transporte público y las a veces extenuantes jornadas[k] fuera del hogar.

Pero no sólo los empleados que pudieron optar por esta modalidad resultaron satisfechos. Más bien se trató de un *win-win*, en el que las compañías también obtuvieron claras ventajas. «Hemos comprobado[l] que para las empresas que implementan el teletrabajo se genera un incremento[m] del 58% en la productividad de los empleados, a lo que hay que sumarle un 64% de ahorro[n] sobre el costo anual que un empleado implica para una compañía», explica Fabio Boggino, director de Jobing, consultora especializada en trabajo remoto.

Tal vez por todos estos beneficios el crecimiento del teletrabajo es incesante. Según datos oficiales, esta modalidad de empleo se incrementó en el último año un 20%. Actualmente, son 1,6 millones (el equivalente al 6% del total) las personas que trabajan bajo la modalidad del teletrabajo, aunque apenas[ñ] el 10% lo hace bajo relación de dependencia.

«Los resultados de las encuestas en empresas que aplicaron teletrabajo arrojaron un alto nivel de satisfacción de los empleados y sus jefes con este proyecto, mayor compromiso con la organización y mejores niveles de productividad», añadió Boggino.

Si se comparan estos datos con los de años anteriores, la evolución salta a la vista. En 2004, había sólo 300.000 teletrabajadores, cifra[o] que ascendió a 590.000 en 2007 y a 1.300.000 en 2008. «Con los datos expuestos, podemos inferir que actualmente aproximadamente el 6% de la población económicamente activa que trabaja en la actividad privada hace teletrabajo, en donde la Ciudad de Buenos Aires tiene la mayor proporción», analizó el consultor.

*El 26% de los argentinos invierte[p] más de 90 minutos en el viaje a la oficina.*

¿Lo desvela[q] el tiempo que pasa arriba del auto, el tren o el colectivo[r] para llegar al trabajo? No es el único. Según una encuesta de Regus, la operadora de espacios de trabajo, el 26% de los argentinos emplea más de 90 minutos en el trayecto diario de ida y vuelta al trabajo. Este promedio es bastante más alto que el de países como Canadá, Estados Unidos o España, donde el porcentaje de trabajadores que invierten este tiempo apenas supera el 10%. En las antípodas[s] se ubica China con 31% y Japón con 32%, superando ampliamente el promedio global del 20%.

Sin embargo, la media local se ubica en los 29 minutos y en el otro extremo se ubica un poco feliz grupo que asciende al 9% y que debe viajar más de una hora en este traslado.

Durante el traslado de la mañana, en Buenos Aires

[g]ya... *since*  [h]está... *is clearly on the rise*  [i]*became obvious*  [j]*nightmares*  [k]*periods of work*  [l]*confirmed*  [m]*increase*  [n]de... *in savings*  [ñ]*barely*  [o]*número*  [p]*invest*  [q]Lo... *Does (it) keep you up at night*  [r]*minibus*  [s]En... *On the opposite side of the coin*

El auto es el medio más utilizado. En Argentina alcanza al 54% de la población, por debajo del 64% mundial. Los otros medios de transporte más usados para ir a trabajar a nivel local son el tren (11% de los encuestados), la caminata (11%) y el colectivo (9%). El subte[t] y el taxi concentran un 6% adicional cada uno.

Una buena noticia para los argentinos es que el transporte es un poquito más barato acá que en el resto del mundo. Mientras que una media del 7% de los trabajadores de todo el mundo gasta[u] como mínimo el 10% de su salario en el transporte, en la Argentina este gasto[v] alcanza a sólo el 6% de los trabajadores. Para otro 17% de los empleados los viajes se sitúan localmente entre un 5 y un 10% de su sueldo.

---

[t]metro [u]*spend* [v]*expense*

## DESPUÉS DE LEER

**A. Comprensión.** Conteste las preguntas, según el artículo.

1. ¿Quiénes quieren trabajar desde la casa, la mayoría de los argentinos o sólo un grupo pequeño? ¿Les gustaría a los argentinos hacer el teletrabajo todos los días o sólo unos días a la semana? ¿Cuántos?

2. ¿Por qué quieren los argentinos hacer el teletrabajo? ¿Qué ventajas tiene el teletrabajo para las empresas?

3. ¿Qué tipos de empresas les ofrecen a sus empleados el teletrabajo? ¿Qué ciudad tiene la proporción más alta?

4. ¿Cuál es el promedio aproximado de minutos que los argentinos emplean todos los días para llegar a su trabajo? ¿Cuál es el medio de transporte que más utilizan?

**B. Temas de discusión.** En grupos pequeños, comenten estos temas. Después, compartan sus ideas con la clase.

Communication

1. La lectura informa sobre algunas de las ventajas del teletrabajo para el empleado y para la empresa. En su opinión, ¿qué otras ventajas hay? ¿Y las desventajas?

2. Piensen en su futuro profesional y personal después de que se gradúen de la universidad. ¿Les gustaría trabajar desde la casa o les gustaría ir todos los días a su lugar de trabajo? Expliquen.

3. ¿Qué tipo de trabajos creen Uds. que se pueden hacer de una manera eficiente sin ir al lugar de trabajo tradicional? Expliquen.

# Concurso de videoblogs

## Argentina: Federico

### Buenos Aires

**Cultures**

En este segmento, Federico nos enseña Buenos Aires con su amiga Sol, quien es una gran aficionada a la música moderna. La visita comienza en la Plaza de Mayo. Después, vemos la vida diaria de la capital y una variedad de barrios y lugares interesantes y pintorescos.

**Communication**

### Vocabulario práctico

| | |
|---|---|
| **discursos** | speeches |
| **manifestaciones** | demonstrations |
| **paseadores de perros** | dog walkers |
| **milongas** | traditional Argentinean dance |
| **porteños** | *inhabitants of Buenos Aires* |
| **La Boca** | *district in Buenos Aires* |

### ANTES DE VER

En parejas, contesten las preguntas. Luego, compartan sus ideas con la clase. Por fin, repasen el **Vocabulario útil** y vean el videoblog de Federico.

1. ¿Cómo son las ciudades grandes? Piensen en ciudades como Nueva York, Chicago o Los Ángeles. ¿Qué tienen con común?
2. ¿Cuáles son las ventajas de vivir en una ciudad grande? ¿y las desventajas?
3. ¿Prefieren Uds. vivir en una ciudad grande o pequeña? Expliquen.

### DESPUÉS DE VER

**A. Comprensión.** Resuma brevemente la información presentada en el segmento sobre estos temas o lugares.

1. la Plaza de Mayo
2. el centro de la ciudad
3. San Telmo, Mataderos, El Tigre
4. los porteños y la tecnología
5. La Boca
6. El Café Tortoni

**Communication**

**B. Temas de discusión.** En grupos pequeños, comenten los temas.

1. Después de ver el segmento, ¿por qué creen Uds. que algunas personas llaman a Buenos Aires «el París de Latinoamérica»?
2. Señalen los momentos y lugares del segmento que más les han gustado. Justifiquen su respuesta.
3. Busquen en Internet o en la biblioteca información sobre el Café Tortoni. Escriban un breve informe para presentar a la clase sobre este lugar emblemático en la historia de Buenos Aires.

## Los verbos

| | |
|---|---|
| administrar | to manage; to administer |
| anotar datos | to enter data |
| archivar | to file |
| bajar | to download |
| contestar el teléfono | to answer the phone |
| despedir (like pedir) | to fire |
| dirigir (j) | to manage (people) |
| escribir informes | to write reports |
| firmar | to sign |
| guardar | to save (a file) |
| hacer (irreg.) copias | to make copies |
| jubilarse | to retire |
| llenar | to fill out (a form) |
| manejar las cuentas | to manage accounts |
| renunciar (a) | to resign (from) (a job) |
| solicitar (trabajo) | to apply for (a job) |
| subir | to upload |
| supervisar | to supervise; to oversee |
| tener (irreg.) don de gentes | to get along well with others |

## Las profesiones y oficios — Professions and Trades

| | |
|---|---|
| el/la abogado/a | lawyer |
| el/la albañil | bricklayer |
| el/la banquero/a | banker |
| el/la barbero/a | barber |
| el/la biólogo/a | biologist |
| el/la científico/a | scientist |
| el/la consejero/a | advisor; counselor |
| el/la contador(a) | accountant |
| el/la diseñador(a) (de modas) | (fashion) designer |
| el/la electricista | electrician |
| el/la entrenador(a) | trainer; coach |
| el/la farmacéutico/a | pharmacist |
| el/la físico/a | physicist |
| el hombre / la mujer de negocios | businessman/ businesswoman |
| el/la ingeniero/a | engineer |
| el/la intérprete | interpreter |
| el/la juez(a) | judge |
| el/la maestro/a | teacher |
| el/la peluquero/a | hairdresser |
| el/la periodista | journalist |
| el/la plomero/a | plumber |
| el/la químico/a | chemist |
| el/la sicólogo/a | psychologist |
| el soldado (la mujer soldado) | soldier |
| el/la técnico/a | technician |
| el/la traductor(a) | translator |
| el/la veterinario/a | veterinarian |

Cognados: el/la atleta, el/la modelo, el/la programador(a), el/la secretario/a
Repaso: el/la arquitecto/a, el/la dentista, el/la enfermero/a, el/la escultor(a), el/la médico/a, el/la músico/a, el/la pintor(a), el/la profesor(a)

## El empleo — Job/Employment

| | |
|---|---|
| el derecho | law |
| el informe | report |
| los negocios | business |
| la sicología | psychology |
| comprensivo/a | understanding |
| exigente | demanding |

Cognados: la compasión, las relaciones públicas; (in)flexible
Repaso: la medicina

## Las habilidades y destrezas — Abilities and Skills

| | |
|---|---|
| el conocimiento | knowledge |
| emprendedor(a) | enterprising |
| fuerte físicamente | physically strong |
| íntegro/a | honest; upright |
| valiente | brave |

Cognados: bilingüe, carismático/a, honesto/a, organizado/a, puntual
Repaso: inteligente, trabajador(a)

## La búsqueda de trabajo — Job Search

| | |
|---|---|
| el/la aspirante | applicant |
| el currículum | résumé, CV |
| la solicitud | application |

Cognado: el/la director(a) de personal
Repaso: la entrevista

## El lugar de trabajo

| | |
|---|---|
| el/la administrativo/a | file clerk |
| el archivero | file cabinet |
| el aumento | raise |
| el/la empleado/a | employee |
| el empleo a tiempo completo | full-time job |
| el empleo a tiempo parcial | part-time job |
| el horario de trabajo | work schedule |
| el/la jefe/a | boss |
| el plan de jubilación | retirement plan |
| el puesto | job; position |
| el salario (mínimo) | (minimum) wage; salary, pay |
| el seguro médico | health insurance |
| el sueldo | salary |
| las vacaciones pagadas | paid vacation |

Cognados: el cubículo
Repaso: el/la gerente

| La tecnología en la oficina | |
| --- | --- |
| el disco duro | hard disk |
| la página Web | web page |

Cognados: el proyector, el software, la teleconferencia
Repaso: la computadora (portátil), el e-mail, el escritorio, el Internet

| Conjunciones temporales | Temporal Conjunctions |
| --- | --- |
| después de que | after |
| en cuanto | as soon as |
| hasta que | until |
| tan pronto como | as soon as |

Repaso: cuando

# La vida moderna

Connections

## ANTES DE VER

¿Cómo le afecta a Ud. la vida del siglo XXI? Indique si las oraciones son verdaderas para Ud. o no.

|  | SÍ | NO |
|---|---|---|
| 1. Vivo en una ciudad grande. | ☐ | ☐ |
| 2. La ciudad donde vivo tiene rascacielos. | ☐ | ☐ |
| 3. El tráfico es un problema para mí. | ☐ | ☐ |
| 4. Suelo navegar en Internet más de dos horas al día. | ☐ | ☐ |
| 5. Uso mi teléfono celular sólo para hablar. | ☐ | ☐ |
| 6. Aparte de mi teléfono celular, tengo una cámara digital. | ☐ | ☐ |
| 7. Prefiero escuchar música en mi iPod u otro reproductor (*player*) de MP3 (emepetrés). | ☐ | ☐ |
| 8. Cuando viajo, saco muchas fotos con una cámara digital. | ☐ | ☐ |

---

**Vocabulario práctico**

| | | | |
|---|---|---|---|
| **cada vez más** | more and more | **los porteños** | residents of Buenos Aires |
| **tardar** | to take (*time*) | | |
| **ancha** | wide | | |

---

## DESPUÉS DE VER

Complete las oraciones con información verdadera, según el vídeo. Use palabras de la lista. ¡OJO! Algunas palabras no se usan.

los adultos      moderna       Santiago Calatrava
antigua          mundial       el tráfico
colonial         Puerto Madero la vida moderna
los jóvenes

1. _____ es un gran problema en la ciudad de Buenos Aires.
2. _____ es el distrito más moderno de Buenos Aires.
3. Lima, la capital de Perú, es una ciudad _____ y _____.
4. Guanajuato es una ciudad _____ de México.
5. _____ mexicanos se visten como sus contemporáneos de otros países del mundo moderno.

## EL INTERNET

El Internet es un medio de comunicación usado por millones de hispanos. En muchas viviendas urbanas los hispanos usan el Internet, pero en las zonas rurales el acceso es más limitado. Además del uso privado del Internet en casa, los hispanos también lo usan en lugares públicos como las bibliotecas o los cibercafés.

## ASÍ SE DICE

**el blog** (*L.A.*) = **la bitácora** (*Sp.*)

**el celular** (*L.A.*) = **el móvil** (*Sp.*)

**la computadora** (*L.A.*) = **el ordenador** (*Sp.*)

**el Internet** = **el internet, la red**

**el periódico** = **el diario**

**la televisión** = **la tele, el televisor**

### Préstamos[a] del inglés

CD-ROM, chat, DVD, e-mail, módem, MP3, hardware, laptop, netbook, notebook, software, spam, USB

---

[a]*Borrowed words*

## LOS TELÉFONOS CELULARES

Los teléfonos celulares permiten que las personas se comuniquen casi sin límites. Algunos celulares son como computadoras de mano[a] con posibilidades técnicas maravillosas. Aunque en general se acepta su utilidad en la sociedad, hay usuarios que no respetan el espacio personal o privado de los demás.

---

[a]*de... hand-held*

## ACTIVIDADES

**A. Comprensión.** Indique el medio de comunicación o aparato que se describe. Use palabras de la lista. **¡OJO!** Hay más de una respuesta posible en muchos casos.

el Internet la prensa la televisión en español
los medios sociales los teléfonos celulares

1. *The New York Times, People en español*
2. Univisión, Telemundo, CNN en Español
3. Facebook, Twitter
4. BlackBerry, iPhone
5. Se vende en kioscos en la calle.
6. Es muy útil para la comunicación interpersonal.
7. Un hispano en Chicago puede informarse sobre los eventos actuales en Argentina.

**B. Conexiones.** En parejas, contesten las preguntas.

1. ¿Cuántas cadenas de televisión o emisoras (*stations*) de radio en español hay donde Uds. viven? ¿Qué tipo(s) de programación ofrecen? ¿Cuántas veces a la semana suelen mirar o escuchar los programas?
2. ¿Usan Uds. los medios sociales para estar en contacto con amigos o conocidos hispanos? ¿Con qué frecuencia se comunican con ellos? ¿Les escriben sólo en español o utilizan una mezcla de español e inglés?

**C. A investigar más.** Haga una investigación por el Internet para saber cuáles son los diez aparatos tecnológicos o medios sociales más populares entre los estudiantes. Luego, haga una encuesta entre cinco de sus compañeros de clase, haciéndoles preguntas como las siguientes u otras, si quiere. ¿Cómo se comparan los resultados de su encuesta con los resultados de su investigación?

- ¿Tienes teléfono celular? ¿Qué marca tienes? ¿Cómo lo usas, por lo general?
- ¿Tienes una cuenta (*account*) de Facebook u otro medio social? ¿Cuántas horas al día accedes a tu cuenta?

**D. Temas de discusión.** En grupos pequeños comenten *uno* de estos temas y escriban algunas conclusiones breves en español. Luego, compartan sus conclusiones con la clase.

1. los aspectos positivos y negativos de los teléfonos celulares en la vida moderna
2. el uso frecuente de los medios sociales por los estudiantes: lo positivo y lo negativo

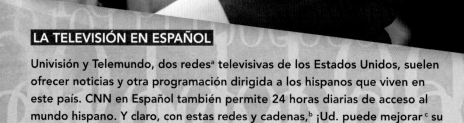

## LA TELEVISIÓN EN ESPAÑOL

Univisión y Telemundo, dos redes[a] televisivas de los Estados Unidos, suelen ofrecer noticias y otra programación dirigida a los hispanos que viven en este país. CNN en Español también permite 24 horas diarias de acceso al mundo hispano. Y claro, con estas redes y cadenas,[b] ¡Ud. puede mejorar[c] su español!

[a]*networks*  [b]*channels*  [c]*improve*

## LA PRENSA[a]

La prensa es un medio de comunicación muy popular en los países hispanos. Para las personas a quienes les gusta tocar el papel de los periódicos y revistas, estos se venden en librerías o kioscos en la calle. Y para los que prefieren leer las noticias en línea, también hay ediciones digitales a las que se puede acceder desde la computadora o el celular.

[a]*press*

En el Dominican Day Parade, en Nueva York

# Entrada cultural

## La cultura hispana global

Cultures

En una clase de salsa, en Canadá

Unos ecuatorianos, durante una celebración en España

Un restaurante mexicano, en Hong Kong

La comunidad hispana ha gozado de una presencia importante en los Estados Unidos desde hace muchas décadas. En su vecino del norte, Canadá, hay inmigrantes recientes de México, El Salvador, Chile, Colombia, Venezuela y algunos otros países latinoamericanos, también. La mayoría de los hispanos en Canadá es joven, vive en las ciudades y tiene cierto nivel educativo. Casi la mitad vive en Toronto, Montreal y Vancouver. Al igual que en los Estados Unidos, los hispanos en Canadá se integran en la nueva cultura sin perder sus propias tradiciones. Se celebran festivales, tienen emisoras[a] de radio, programas de televisión, periódicos y centros hispanos que ayudan a mantener la cultura y el idioma.

Pero la fuerte presencia de latinoamericanos no existe sólo en Norteamérica. En Europa, es cada vez más común encontrar comercios o emisoras de radio gestionados[b] por hispanos. La mayoría de ellos llega a Europa a través de España. Después de España, Italia es el país con mayor presencia de hispanos en el continente europeo.

Y, en un mundo cada vez más globalizado, no es extraño que haya también presencia hispana en el continente asiático y el africano. La cultura hispana es muy atractiva para las culturas orientales y es común encontrar virtuosos de la guitarra española en Japón, restaurantes especializados en gastronomía caribeña en China o seminarios de literatura española y latinoamericana en Australia. Indudablemente, los hispanos están contribuyendo en el cambio de la sociedad de los países receptores de inmigrantes, aportando una mayor diversidad étnica, lingüística, religiosa y cultural.

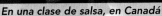

[a]stations  [b]managed

# Los medios de comunicación

La vida moderna en los países hispanos es como la de[a] este país: hay personas que adoran la nueva tecnología y otras que se sienten más cómodas con medios de comunicación más tradicionales. Mientras hay los que se afanan por[b] adquirir los celulares más recientes u otros aparatos como los iPads, hay otros que se sienten más a gusto con mirar la televisión o con leer periódicos[c] o revistas.[d] La verdad es que, sea cual sea[e] la preferencia tecnológica, ¡hay gustos para todos!

[a]la... that of  [b]se... strive to  [c]newspapers  [d]magazines  [e]sea... no matter what

### LOS MEDIOS SOCIALES

Los jóvenes hispanos son expertos en medios sociales como Facebook, Twitter y otros que amplían[a] el espacio de la comunicación con noticias de última hora.[b] Pero los medios sociales no están sólo en los ambientes juveniles—ahora muchos padres acceden a[c] estos espacios, ¡con resultados a veces no deseados por sus hijos!

[a]widen  [b]de... up-to-the-minute  [c]acceden... access

# Nosotros y el mundo natural

*En la Reserva Nacional Tambopata, Perú*

1. ¿Qué sabe Ud. de los problemas en los bosques de la Amazonia?
2. ¿Se preocupa Ud. por el medio ambiente? ¿Qué problema medioambiental cree Ud. que es el más grave en el mundo de hoy? ¿por qué?
3. ¿Qué medidas deben tomarse para proteger la Tierra? ¿Cree que la conservación del medio ambiente es responsabilidad de los gobiernos o de todos los ciudadanos? ¿por qué?
4. ¿Qué hace Ud. para proteger el entorno natural?

**connect** |SPANISH

www.connectspanish.com

449

# TEMA I: El mundo natural

## Vocabulario del tema

La geografía, la naturaleza
y el medio ambiente

① La zona ártica

el quetzal

El bosque tropical ②

el iceberg

el glaciar

la serpiente

la ballena

el papagayo

el hielo

el oso polar

el insecto

el jaguar

la foca

la rana

la gaviota

El archipiélago

el pelícano

③

el volcán

la palmera

el delfín

la roca

el océano

las olas

la medusa

el caballo marino

el arrecife (de coral)

la almeja

el tiburón

la tortuga

las conchas

el cangrejo

## Otros términos geográficos

| | |
|---|---|
| el altiplano | high plateau |
| la arena | sand |
| la bahía | bay |
| la llanura | plain |
| el mar | sea |
| la orilla | shore |
| el pantano | wetland; marsh |
| la selva | jungle |
| la sierra | mountain range |

Cognados: el desierto

## Otros animales (salvajes) / *Other (Wild) Animals*

| | |
|---|---|
| la abeja | bee |
| el águila (*pl.* las águilas) | eagle |
| la araña | spider |
| el mono | monkey |
| el oso | bear |

Cognados: el caribú, el cocodrilo, el elefante, el gorila, los insectos, el león, el panda, el pingüino, el puma, el reptil, el tigre

## Los recursos naturales

| | |
|---|---|
| el agua dulce/salada | fresh/salt water |
| la biodiversidad | biodiversity |

Cognados: el gas natural, los metales, los minerales, el petróleo

## Otras palabras y expresiones

| | |
|---|---|
| el cacto | cactus |
| el coco (tero) | coconut (tree) |
| la flor y fauna (silvestre) | (wild) plant and animal life |

### ACTIVIDADES

**A.** ¡Busque al intruso!

**PASO 1.** Indique la palabra que no pertenece a la serie.

1. ☐ la rana ☐ el quetzal ☐ el papagayo ☐ la gaviota
2. ☐ el cangrejo ☐ la almeja ☐ el coco ☐ el tiburón
3. ☐ la medusa ☐ el delfín ☐ el caballo marino ☐ el oso polar
4. ☐ la abeja ☐ la mariposa ☐ el mono ☐ la araña
5. ☐ la llanura ☐ el pantano ☐ la laguna ☐ el mar
6. ☐ el cocotero ☐ la roca ☐ la palmera ☐ el arbusto
7. ☐ el glaciar ☐ el ave ☐ el hielo ☐ la nieve
8. ☐ el oso ☐ el mono ☐ la foca ☐ la concha

**PASO 2.** Indique la palabra que no pertenece a la categoría y diga a qué categoría pertenece.

1. el agua: ☐ el mar ☐ las olas ☐ el pantano ☐ la sierra
2. las montañas: ☐ la sierra ☐ la gaviota ☐ el volcán ☐ el altiplano
3. los mamíferos (*mammals*): ☐ el oso polar ☐ la ballena ☐ la serpiente ☐ el mono
4. las aves: ☐ el mono ☐ la gaviota ☐ el águila ☐ el pelícano
5. la flora: ☐ el arbusto ☐ la palmera ☐ el cacto ☐ la bahía

## B. Definiciones

**PASO 1.** Indique la palabra definida del **Vocabulario del tema.** Luego, nombre un ejemplo que conoce.

**MODELO** Es una masa grande de agua salada. → el mar: El Mar Caribe está al este del Golfo de México.

1. Es una extensión de tierra con muchos árboles.
2. Es una extensión de agua más pequeña que un lago.
3. Es una montaña de donde sale lava.
4. Es una gran extensión de hielo.
5. Es una gran extensión de terreno llano (*flat*).
6. Es una región cubierta de barro y aguas poco profundas, estancadas (*stagnant*), pero ricas en hierbas y otra vegetación.

**PASO 2.** Dé la definición de las palabras.

1. la foca
2. la mariposa
3. la ola
4. el arrecife
5. la tortuga
6. el delfín
7. el mono
8. la isla

## C. Asociaciones. Diga qué asocia Ud. con estas cosas y explique por qué.

**MODELO** la isla → las playas, las palmeras, el mar u océano, las olas: Porque las islas están rodeadas de agua y siempre hay olas, playas y a veces palmeras.

1. el glaciar
2. el arrecife
3. la arena
4. el bosque tropical
5. la biodiversidad
6. el delfín
7. el águila
8. el iceberg

Communication

## D. Nuestra región

**PASO 1.** En grupos de tres, diseñen un folleto (*brochure*) sobre la región donde Uds. viven. Describan las características geográficas y la flora y fauna de su estado o provincia. Incluyan comentarios sobre el clima y las estaciones. Pueden incluir fotos o dibujos en su folleto.

**MODELO** En nuestra parte del estado, la característica geográfica predominante es la llanura. No hay ninguna montaña o colina. El animal silvestre más común es el coyote. Los inviernos aquí son muy difíciles. Hace mucho viento y frío…

**PASO 2.** Comparen su folleto con los de otros grupos. ¿Presentan todos información parecida?

**PASO 3.** Si alguno/a de Uds. es originario/a de otra región, describa esa región para compararla con esta. Si sus compañeros/as le hacen preguntas sobre esa región, contéstelas.

**E.** El ambiente ideal

**PASO 1.** Haga una lista de las cosas que le gusta hacer, del clima que prefiere, del ambiente más agradable para Ud., de la naturaleza que más le atrae y de cualquier otra cosa o cualidad que Ud. asocia con el ambiente ideal.

**PASO 2.** En parejas, describan las actividades que les gusta hacer, el clima, el ambiente, etcétera, ideales, según sus apuntes del **Paso 1.** Luego, háganse sugerencias sobre dónde deben vivir y qué tipo de vacaciones deben escoger cada año.

Communication

## Nota cultural
Cultures

### LAS ISLAS GALÁPAGOS

*Una tortuga gigante*

Las Islas Galápagos forman un archipiélago situado a unos mil kilómetros de la costa de Ecuador. El archipiélago está formado por trece grandes islas volcánicas, seis islas más pequeñas y 107 rocas e islotes.[a] Estas islas, como gran parte del territorio que hoy conocemos como la región andina, estaban habitadas por los incas y fueron descubiertas por los colonizadores españoles en 1535. Las Islas Galápagos fueron utilizadas por los piratas ingleses como escondite[b] de sus robos a barcos españoles que, en su ruta desde las Indias hacia España, iban cargados de[c] oro y plata. Los barcos balleneros también las usaron como puerto y, desde entonces, la caza[d] de ballenas, focas y tortugas ha sido muy significativa en esta parte del Pacífico.

Las Islas Galápagos son un tesoro de la historia natural por su biodiversidad, una región única por la flora y la fauna. Además de miles de especies de plantas, su hábitat se caracteriza por conservar especies endémicas, como tortugas gigantes, iguanas, focas y pingüinos que no se encuentran en otros lugares del planeta. En 1835, el barco británico *Beagle* desembarcó en las Galápagos con el propósito de realizar un estudio científico. Entre los investigadores estaba Charles Darwin, y los descubrimientos realizados en estas islas le sirvieron para formular su famosa teoría de la evolución.

Las Islas Galápagos son Patrimonio Natural de la Humanidad y Reserva de la Biosfera. Su hábitat, sin embargo, se encuentra actualmente en peligro debido a la acción humana.

[a]*small islands*  [b]*hiding place*  [c]*cargados... loaded with*  [d]*hunting*

**PREGUNTAS** En parejas, contesten las preguntas. Después, compartan sus ideas con la clase.

1. ¿Qué grupos de personas han habitado las Islas Galápagos a lo largo de la historia?
2. ¿Qué animales específicos se pueden encontrar en estas islas?
3. ¿Por qué son las Islas Galápagos un lugar único?
4. ¿Por qué están en peligro las Islas Galápagos? ¿Conocen Uds. algún otro hábitat en peligro? ¿Qué deben hacer los gobiernos para preservar los hábitats naturales?

# Gramática

## 14.1 Present Subjunctive After Conjunctions of Contingency and Purpose

### GRAMÁTICA EN CONTEXTO

**El Programa de Protección de la Biodiversidad de la Isla de Bioko (BBPP)**

El BBPP es parte de una asociación académica con la Universidad Nacional de Guinea Ecuatorial para proteger a los animales salvajes y la naturaleza de la isla. Bioko es uno de los lugares ecológicamente más diversos de África. En esta isla viven siete especies de primates raros y también es uno de los principales refugios de tortugas marinas. Pero estos animales están en peligro de extinción y **a menos que** los habitantes de la isla **cambien** algunas de sus prácticas, van a desaparecer. BBPP emplea a cincuenta personas locales que hacen guardia en los bosques tropicales **para que** los residentes no **cacen** o **maten** los animales.

*Unos miembros del BBPP observan una lombriz (earthworm).*

Comprensión. ¿Probable (**P**) o improbable (**I**)?

|  | P | I |
|---|---|---|
| 1. Algunos voluntarios hacen el censo de la población de primates para que el BBPP siga el progreso de sus programas. | ☐ | ☐ |
| 2. Las personas locales que hacen guardia llevan pistolas en caso de que tengan que matar a cazadores (*hunters*). | ☐ | ☐ |

When one action or situation depends on another, this is a relationship of contingency and is expressed with adverbial conjunctions of contingency. Other adverbial conjunctions indicate the purpose of an action. The subjunctive is *always* used in a clause following adverbial conjunctions of contingency or purpose. Adverbial conjunctions of contingency and purpose include the following:

### CONJUNCTIONS OF CONTINGENCY AND PURPOSE

| | | | |
|---|---|---|---|
| **a menos que** | unless | **en caso de que** | in case |
| **antes de que** | before | **para que** | so that |
| **con tal (de) que** | provided that | **sin que** | without |

| | |
|---|---|
| Me encanta ir a la playa **a menos que** esté lloviendo. | *I love to go to the beach unless it's raining.* |
| **Antes de que** se cierre, quiero visitar ese parque nacional. | *Before it closes, I want to visit that national park.* |

---

GRAMÁTICA EN CONTEXTO *The Bioko Biodiversity Protection Program (BBPP) / BBPP is part of an academic alliance with the National University of Equatorial Guinea to protect the wild animals and nature of the island. Bioko is one of the most ecologically diverse places in Africa. Seven species of rare primates live on the island and the island is also one of the primary havens for sea turtles. But these animals are endangered and unless the inhabitants of the island change some of their practices, they will disappear. BBPP employs fifty locals who guard the tropical forests so that residents don't hunt and kill the animals.*

**A. Mi mundo.** Indique las oraciones que son aplicables a su experiencia en la universidad o en su tiempo libre.

1. ☐ Siempre voy a clase antes de que llegue el profesor.
2. ☐ Siempre llevo un paraguas (*umbrella*) en el coche en caso de que llueva.
3. ☐ Uso el transporte público para que mis padres no tengan que recogerme (*pick me up*).
4. ☐ Participo en organizaciones medioambientales con tal de que tengan un impacto positivo en nuestro campus.
5. ☐ Me gusta pasar tiempo en la playa a menos que haga mucho calor.
6. ☐ Hago ciclismo de montaña con tal de que haya senderos seguros (*safe*).
7. ☐ Mis amigos y yo no acampamos en el bosque sin que nadie sepa adónde vamos ni por cuánto tiempo nos quedamos.
8. ☐ No podemos hacer alpinismo cerca de aquí a menos que hagamos un viaje largo a las montañas.

**B. Sucesos.** Empareje cada oración de la primera columna con la frase correspondiente de la segunda columna y dé la forma correcta del verbo para completar la oración.

1. Nuestros padres se mudan a las montañas _____ una casa a precio razonable.
2. Voy a la reserva biológica con estos niños _____ algunos animales salvajes de cerca (*up close*).
3. El parque ecológico no va a abrir este verano _____ la construcción de los caminos y cabañas para mayo.
4. No pueden extraer más minerales de esta cordillera _____ algunas de las minas.
5. Van a sembrar más hierbas en este pantano _____ suficientes hierbas después de esta sequía (*drought*).
6. _____ los osos polares, quiero ver uno en su hábitat natural.

a. para que / ver
b. en caso de que / no haber
c. con tal de / encontrar
d. a menos que / terminar
e. sin que / derrumbarse (*to cave in*)
f. antes de que / desaparecer

**C. ¿Qué podemos hacer?** En parejas, hablen de lo que podemos hacer para crear más áreas protegidas y por qué las debemos crear. Completen las oraciones, luego formen dos oraciones originales.

1. Debemos establecer más reservas biológicas para que...
2. Podemos proteger los peces en peligro de extinción sin que...
3. Es posible restaurar los pantanos que van desapareciendo a menos que...
4. El gobierno va a proteger más bosques tropicales del país con tal de que...
5. Debemos cerrar las minas a tajo abierto (*strip mines*) antes de que...
6. Es importante hacer donaciones a las organizaciones ambientales para que...
7. ¿ ?
8. ¿ ?

Ⓒ
Communication

(Continúa.)

**Cultures** **Recycle**

## D. Maravillas geográficas

**PASO 1.** Complete la narración sobre la geografía latinoamericana con la forma correcta de los adjetivos y verbos entre paréntesis. Dé el presente de indicativo o de subjuntivo de los verbos. Cuando aparecen dos palabras entre paréntesis, escoja la palabra correcta.

*El Lago Pehoe, en la Patagonia*

Ud. probablemente ya sabe que la geografía de Latinoamérica es maravillosa. Pero para que (*Ud.:* **entender**[1]) mejor esa grandeza, debe reflexionar sobre las primeras impresiones que esta naturaleza (**les/los**[2]) causó a los exploradores.

La naturaleza del Nuevo Mundo dejó pasmados[a] a los exploradores (**europeo**[3]). Europa tenía sus (**bello**[4]) características naturales, pero los exploradores se enfrentaron con una naturaleza gigantesca y, por consecuencia, más impresionante e inolvidable. (**Era/Estaba**[5]) un mundo creado en una escala más grande: una geografía vasta e imponente, aguas colosales, un clima poderoso y abrumador.[b] La naturaleza llegó a (**ser/estar**[6]) una entidad viva y un personaje en la vida de los colonizadores. (**Era/Estaba**[7]) presente en la literatura, en el arte y en la política de las colonias.

(**Es/Está**[8]) difícil comprender el sobrecogimiento[c] de los exploradores a menos que Ud. (**tener**[9]) en cuenta el contraste de este mundo con Europa. En el Caribe, Colón y sus marineros, impresionados por la vegetación exuberante, documentaban todas las (**nuevo**[10]) especies de flora y fauna. También documentaron un huracán, el primer huracán occidental documentado, en 1502 durante la cuarta expedición. Era más imponente y violento que cualquier tormenta que habían presenciado.[d] Esta exploración y documentación continuó por cientos de años. En caso de que Ud. (**tener**[11]) espíritu aventurero y le (**interesar**[12]) la naturaleza, queremos enumerar unas pocas características geográficas y acuáticas documentadas durante esas expediciones.

- Las Cataratas del Iguazú (**son/están**[13]) en la frontera de Argentina con Brasil y (**considerarse**[14]) una de las siete maravillas naturales del mundo. El conquistador Álvar Núñez Cabeza de Vaca fue el primer europeo en descubrir las cataratas. El explorador moderno puede admirar 275 saltos o cataratas que (**extenderse**[15]) por casi tres kilómetros.

- El Lago Titicaca en los altiplanos de Bolivia y Perú, el lago navegable más alto del mundo, (**es/está**[16]) como un océano. Los primeros europeos en ver este lago (**fueron/estuvieron**[17]) los soldados de Francisco Pizarro entre 1520 y 1530.

---

[a]*dazzled* [b]*overwhelming* [c]*awe* [d]*habían… had witnessed*

- La Patagonia es una región (**geológico**[18]) en el extremo sur de Argentina y Chile y tiene características extremas: glaciares, lagos y fiordos prístinos y montañas con picos[e] drásticos. Fernando de Magallanes descubrió (**este/esta**[19]) región durante una de sus expediciones en 1520. Los españoles (**tenían/necesitaban**[20]) que pasar por el Estrecho de Magallanes en la Patagonia para llegar al oeste de Sudamérica hasta que se construyó el Canal de Panamá en el siglo XX.

- La Selva Amazónica, el bosque tropical más grande del mundo, sobrepasó[f] la imaginación de los exploradores. Se extiende por más de 1.7 mil millones de[g] acres cuadrados y en un solo acre (**habitar**[21]) entre 300 y 400 especies de animales y plantas.

- Los Andes, la cordillera más larga del mundo, se extienden por 7.000 kilómetros desde Venezuela hasta el extremo sur de Chile y Argentina. Como (**formar**[22]) parte del Cinturón de Fuego del Pacífico,[h] entre sus picos (**haber**[23]) volcanes y por eso toda esta región es propensa[i] a actividad sísmica.

[e]peaks  [f]surpassed  [g]mil... billion  [h]Cinturón... Pacific Ring of Fire  [i]prone

**PASO 2.** Indique el lugar o evento que corresponde a cada frase o dato, según el **Paso 1.**

a. los Andes
b. las Cataratas del Iguazú
c. el Lago Titicaca
e. el primer huracán documentado
d. la Patagonia
f. la Selva Amazónica

1. _____ 1502
2. _____ Fernando de Magallanes
3. _____ 1,7 mil millones de acres cuadrados
4. _____ las expediciones de Pizarro
5. _____ el Cinturón de Fuego del Pacífico
6. _____ 275 saltos
7. _____ mas de 300 especies por acre
8. _____ cuarta expedición de Colón
9. _____ en la frontera de Argentina con Brasil
10. _____ volcanes y actividad sísmica
11. _____ el océano de los altiplanos
12. _____ 1520

**PASO 3.** En parejas, busquen más información en el Internet sobre una de las características climáticas o geográficas del mundo hispano. Hagan una presentación para la clase.

Communication

# Palabra escrita

## A comenzar

Communication

> **Organizing Your Ideas: Selecting Appropriate Content.** As you develop your composition, you should decide which ideas to include and which ones to disregard. Your decisions should be informed by your thesis statement, your goals as a writer, and the goals of your intended audience. Ask yourself the following questions:
>
> **1.** Does all the information illustrate the point I want to make?
> **2.** What information does the reader expect to find in my work?
> **3.** Will the information that I'm offering help the audience achieve a goal?

You are going to start the process of writing a brief composition that you will finalize in the **Palabra escrita: A finalizar** section of your *Manual de actividades*. The topic of this composition is **Nuestros recursos naturales.** The purpose of your composition will be to tell the reader about the natural resources in your area and how they are being wasted or used responsibly. Include ideas about what will or will not happen to those resources, based on community habits, actions, or programs that affect them.

**A. Lluvia de ideas.** En parejas, hagan una lluvia de ideas sobre estos temas y la región donde Uds. viven.

1. los recursos naturales que hay
2. las amenazas (*threats*) en contra de los recursos naturales
3. los programas para protegerlos
4. el futuro de los recursos naturales

**B. A organizar sus ideas.** Repase sus ideas y escoja uno o dos de los recursos naturales. Organice todo lo que afecta al recurso / a los recursos que escogió: amenazas, esperanzas, programas posibles, etcétera. Busque más información en el Internet. Según la información que encuentre, escriba la tesis de su ensayo y haga un bosquejo (*outline*) de sus párrafos. Apunte oraciones que requieran el subjuntivo después de las conjunciones de dependencia (*contingency*) y propósito (*purpose*) que aprendió en el **Tema I: antes de que, sin que, para que, a menos que, con tal (de) que, en caso de que.** Comparta su información con la clase y apunte otras ideas que se le ocurran durante el proceso.

**C. A escribir.** Ahora, haga el borrador de su composición con las ideas y la información que recopiló en las actividades A y B. **¡OJO!** Guarde bien su trabajo. Va a necesitarlo otra vez para la sección de **Palabra escrita: A finalizar** en el *Manual de actividades*.

## Remedios Varo

Naturaleza muerta (*Still Life*) resucitando, 1963

Remedios Varo (1908–1963), nacida en Gerona, España, formó parte, junto con Salvador Dalí, del grupo de pintores surrealistas españoles de los años 20. Debido a la Guerra Civil española en 1936, y luego la Segunda Guerra Mundial, Varo se exilió primero en París y más tarde en México, donde se involucró[a] en el movimiento surrealista mexicano.

Muchas de las obras de Varo reflejan sus huidas[b] de conflictos y casi siempre incluyen figuras humanas que representan la fuga[c] de una prisión figurativa. En *Naturaleza muerta resucitando,* su última obra, no son seres humanos los que se escapan, sino objetos: una mesa, ocho platos, fruta y una vela.[d] Los objetos sintetizan la vida de la artista, volando como pequeños planetas alrededor de la vela en preparación para la huida por una ventana pequeña.

[a]se... *she became involved*
[b]*escapes*  [c]*escape*  [d]*candle*

# TEMA II: Lo que podemos hacer nosotros

## Vocabulario del tema

### Los problemas ambientales

① La contaminación del aire

la atmósfera

② El desastre ambiental

el humo

el smog

la fábrica

el petrolero

el petróleo

la contaminación del agua

③ La deforestación

el aire puro

el bosque tropical

④ Los desechos urbanos

el basurero

la basura

la tala de árboles

la contaminación del suelo

| | |
|---|---|
| arrojar | to throw out, spew |
| contaminar | to pollute |
| desarrollar | to develop |
| desperdiciar | to waste |
| destruir (y) | to destroy |
| el basurero | landfill |
| la bolsa de plástico | plastic bag |
| el calentamiento global | global warming |
| el cambio climático | climate change |
| la capa de ozono | ozone layer |
| el cartón | cardboard |
| el envase de plástico/vidrio | plastic/glass container |
| la escasez | shortage |
| la especie en peligro de extinción | endangered species |
| la excavación minera | mining |
| la pila | battery |
| los pesticidas | pesticides |
| la población densa | dense population |
| los productos no reciclables | non-recyclable products |
| los productos del petróleo | petroleum products |
| los productos químicos | chemical products |
| los residuos peligrosos | hazardous waste |
| la sobrepoblación | overpopulation |
| contaminado/a | polluted |
| peligroso/a | dangerous |

Cognados: afectar, provocar (qu), la combustión, la destrucción

## Algunas soluciones

| | |
|---|---|
| cerrar (ie) el grifo | to turn off the faucet |
| conservar (agua) | to conserve (water) |
| evitar | to avoid |
| mejorar | to improve |
| proteger (j) | to protect |
| resolver (ue) | to solve; to resolve |
| reutilizar (c) (agua) | reuse (water) |
| el reciclaje | recycling |
| la reserva (natural) | (nature) reserve |
| anticontaminante | anti-pollution |
| (no) renovable | (non)renewable |
| terrestre | land (adj.) |

Cognados: conservar, reciclar; la conservación; ecológico/a

# Otras maneras de mejorar al medio ambiente

1. la energía nuclear

2. la energía solar

3. la energía eólica

4. la energía hidroeléctrica

5. el transporte público

6. el transporte anticontaminante

el carro/coche eléctrico/híbrido     electric/hybrid car
la presa                             dam
el tren ligero                       light rail

## ACTIVIDADES

**A.** ¿Desperdicio (*Waste*) o conservación? Indique si asocia Ud. estas cosas con el desperdicio (**D**) o la conservación (**C**). Explique sus respuestas.

|  | D | C |
|---|---|---|
| **1.** las fábricas | ☐ | ☐ |
| **2.** los pesticidas | ☐ | ☐ |
| **3.** la energía solar | ☐ | ☐ |
| **4.** la sobrepoblación | ☐ | ☐ |
| **5.** los productos reciclables | ☐ | ☐ |

6. la tala de árboles ☐ ☐
7. el petróleo ☐ ☐
8. el transporte público ☐ ☐
9. mejorar ☐ ☐
10. proteger ☐ ☐

## B. Asociaciones

**PASO 1.** Empareje las palabras de la columna A con las palabras correspondientes de la columna B.

**MODELO** reciclar → los envases de vidrio

| A | B |
|---|---|
| 1. _____ arrojar | a. los minerales |
| 2. _____ el cambio climático | b. el calentamiento global |
| 3. _____ conservar | c. los desechos |
| 4. _____ la deforestación | d. la sobrepoblación |
| 5. _____ los pesticidas | e. cerrar el grifo |
| 6. _____ la excavación minera | f. la tala de árboles |
| 7. _____ la población densa | g. el humo |
| 8. _____ la combustión | h. los residuos peligrosos |

**PASO 2.** Explique las asociaciones del **Paso 1.**

**MODELO** En mi ciudad, podemos reciclar envases de vidrio.

## C. Oraciones. Complete las oraciones con palabras del **Vocabulario del tema.**

1. La fábrica _____ el aire.
2. La _____ de árboles contribuye a la deforestación.
3. Desde mi casa, puedo reciclar envases de plástico y _____, y cajas (*boxes*) de _____.
4. Para conservar agua, debes cerrar el _____ mientras te cepillas (*brush*) los dientes.
5. No es necesario usar las _____ de plástico del supermercado si llevas unas de tela.
6. La _____ es un elemento integral de la energía hidroeléctrica.
7. Las turbinas de estas llanuras producen energía _____.
8. Los delfines y las ballenas no son animales _____.

## D. Su comunidad

**PASO 1.** En grupos pequeños, describan los problemas ambientales de su comunidad. ¿Hay fábricas que arrojan residuos a la atmósfera o al agua? ¿Hay especies en peligro de extinción? Escriban un breve párrafo sobre los problemas principales.

Ⓒ Communication

**PASO 2.** Ahora describan algunos programas o iniciativas dirigidos a resolver los problemas. Si no los hay, describan algunas soluciones posibles.

Ⓒ Communities

**PASO 3.** Compartan sus ideas con la clase. ¿Escribieron todos de los mismos problemas y soluciones?

## E. Los hábitos de la clase

**PASO 1.** Haga una encuesta entre cuatro o cinco estudiantes de la clase. Apunte sus respuestas a las preguntas en un cuadro como el de la siguiente página.

**MODELO** E1: ¿Qué productos reciclas?
E2: Reciclo papel y cartón.

(Continúa.)

| | LISA | | | | |
|---|---|---|---|---|---|
| **1.** ¿Qué productos reciclas? | *papel y cartón* | | | | |
| **2.** ¿Qué transporte público usas? | | | | | |
| **3.** ¿Qué transporte anticontaminante usas? | | | | | |
| **4.** ¿Qué evitas para conservar o no contaminar? | | | | | |
| **5.** ¿Qué haces para conservar agua? | | | | | |

**PASO 2.** Comparta sus resultados con la clase. Entre todos, hagan listas de sus resultados para saber cuáles son las tendencias de la clase.

## Nota cultural

### LA AGRICULTURA ORGÁNICA EN LATINOAMÉRICA

*En un mercado orgánico, en San Cayetano, Costa Rica*

Latinoamérica tiene una larga tradición de agricultura sostenible.[a] En el pasado, los agricultores trabajaban los productos agrícolas a mano, no usaban pesticidas ni fertilizantes artificiales y utilizaban productos y técnicas naturales en los cultivos. Esta cultura agrícola ha resurgido[b] en los últimos años. Muchos agricultores pequeños han decidido usar técnicas orgánicas, asegurando la conservación del suelo, del agua y la producción de alimentos saludables a un costo relativamente bajo.

Los países latinoamericanos que tienen los porcentajes más altos de su superficie agrícola dedicados al cultivo orgánico son Argentina, Costa Rica, El Salvador y Chile. Aunque a menor escala, Ecuador y Paraguay están adoptando también este tipo de labor agrícola. El café y las bananas son los productos de exportación más importantes en Centroamérica, el azúcar en Paraguay, los cereales[c] en Argentina y las frutas, hierbas y hortalizas[d] en Chile.

El movimiento agroecológico latinoamericano ha crecido mucho, especialmente con los pequeños productores. Con ello se espera una agricultura socialmente justa, económicamente realizable y ecológicamente sostenible.

[a]*sustainable* [b]*reappeared* [c]*grains* [d]*vegetales*

PREGUNTAS En parejas, contesten las preguntas. Después, compartan sus ideas con la clase.

**1.** ¿En qué consisten las técnicas orgánicas agrícolas?
**2.** ¿Qué beneficios aporta la agricultura orgánica? ¿Por qué están fomentando el cultivo agroecológico en Latinoamérica?
**3.** ¿Consumen Uds. productos orgánicos? ¿Con qué frecuencia? ¿Por qué?

# Gramática

## 14.2 Review of the Subjunctive

### Las ciclovías de Marikina

Los oficiales de Manila, Filipinas, lamentan que los contaminantes del aire **hayan llegado** a niveles peligrosos. Para combatir la contaminación del aire, la Brigada de Luciérnagas quería que la ciudad de Marikina, parte de la metrópolis de Manila, **sirviera** como prototipo para un sistema de ciclovías. Es increíble que **hayan construido** unos sesenta kilómetros de ciclovías en Marikina. Se espera que las ciclovías **animen** a los residentes a usar sus bicicletas para ir al trabajo. Para que **sea** más efectivo el programa, la Brigada llegó a un acuerdo con el sistema de trenes ligeros (LRT). Las líneas del LRT permiten que los ciclistas **suban** al tren. Hay un carro especial al final que se llama el «carro verde». Limitan el número de bicicletas en el carro y es preciso que las bicicletas **sean** plegables. En cualquier caso, esta cooperación hace posible que los ciclistas **lleguen** más rápido a la oficina.

*En el tren ligero de Manila*

**Comprensión.** Empareje las frases para formar oraciones sobre Marikina.

1. Es una lástima que ____
2. La Brigada de Luciérnagas quiere que ____
3. El LRT insiste en que ____
4. Es verdad que ____
5. Marikina es una ciudad que ____

a. los ciclistas tengan bicicletas plegables.
b. los marikeños usan más sus bicicletas ahora.
c. tiene unos sesenta kilómetros de ciclovías.
d. en Manila haya niveles peligrosos de contaminación del aire.
e. más gente llegue al trabajo en bicicleta.

You have now seen the subjunctive used in several different situations. This section will review the main functions that you have seen so far.

### SUBJUNCTIVE IN NOUN CLAUSES

**A.** In complex sentences of two clauses (or more), the subjunctive is required in the second, or subordinate clause, if all of the following conditions apply.

1. The verbal expression in the main clause expresses volition, emotion, doubt, or uncertainty.
2. The two clauses are separated by **que.**

---

GRAMÁTICA EN CONTEXTO *The Bikeways of Marikina* / *Officials of Manila, Philippines lament that the air pollution has reached dangerous levels. To fight air pollution, the Firefly Brigade wanted the city of Marikina, part of the Manila metropolitan area, to serve as a prototype for a system of bikeways. It's incredible that they have built some sixty kilometers of bikeways in Marikina. It's hoped that the bikeways will encourage residents to use their bikes to go to work. So that the program might be more effective, the Brigade came to an agreement with the light rail system (LRT). The LRT lines allow cyclists to board the train. There is a special car at the end that is called the "green car." They limit the number of bicycles in the car and it's necessary that the bikes be foldable. Nevertheless, this cooperation makes it possible for cyclists to arrive more quickly to the office.*

**3.** The subject in the second clause is different from the subject in the main clause.*

(subject 1) *verb/expression* + **que** + (subject 2) *subjunctive*

| | |
|---|---|
| **Queremos que** esta ciudad **aumente** los servicios de reciclaje. | *We want this city to increase recycling services.* |
| **Es increíble que** el petróleo **tenga** tanta influencia en la política del mundo. | *It's incredible that oil has so much inclucence on world politics.* |

If all three conditions listed above are not met, the subjunctive is not used.
No change of subject → use infinitive.

| | |
|---|---|
| No **quieren participar** en el programa de limpieza. | *They don't want to participate in the clean-up program.* |

No "triggering" expression in the main clause → use indicative.

| | |
|---|---|
| **Creo que** la contaminación está disminuyendo en muchas ciudades. | *I think that pollution is decreasing in many cities.* |

## SUBJUNCTIVE IN ADVERBIAL CLAUSES

The subjunctive is required in sentences with certain adverbial conjunctions.

**A.** Adverbial conjunctions of time trigger the subjunctive if the action of the subordinate clause is in the future. To review, here are some of the conjunctions of time.

| | |
|---|---|
| **cuando** | **hasta que** |
| **después de que** | **tan pronto como** |
| **en cuanto** | |

| | |
|---|---|
| No habrá grandes cambios **hasta que** haya soluciones prácticas al problema de la energía. | *There won't be big changes until there are practical energy solutions.* |

If the action of the subordinate clause is not in the future, the indicative (past or present) is used.

| | |
|---|---|
| Yo tenía mucha curiosidad **cuando** los primeros productos «verdes» salieron al mercado. | *I was very curious when the first "green" products entered the market.* |

**B.** Adverbial conjunctions of contingency and purpose are always followed by the subjunctive. Here are some examples.

| | |
|---|---|
| **a menos que** | **en caso de que** |
| **antes de que** | **para que** |
| **con tal (de) que** | **sin que** |

| | |
|---|---|
| Nos preocupamos tanto por el medio ambiente **para que** nuestros hijos tengan un mundo en que se pueda vivir. | *We worry so much about the environment so that our children have a world in which one can live.* |

---

*Ocassionally, sentences expressing doubt will have the same subject in both clauses. **Dudo que yo pueda ir.** *I doubt that I can go.*

## SUBJUNCTIVE IN ADJECTIVAL CLAUSES

As you have seen, adjective clauses function just like adjectives to describe nouns. In Spanish, any adjectival clause that describes a noun that is unknown to the speaker or nonexistent will require the subjunctive.

**Buscamos un carro que** no consuma mucha gasolina.

*We are looking for a car that doesn't use a lot of gas.*

**¿Conoces un taller de reparaciones donde** reciclen el aceite usado?

*You do know a repair shop where they recycle used oil?*

---

### Nota comunicativa

Communication

#### PAST SUBJUNCTIVE

The past subjunctive is used in past contexts in Spanish for many of the same reasons that the present subjunctive is used in present and future contexts. To form the past subjunctive, begin with the third person plural form of the preterite. The **-ron** ending is eliminated and the past subjunctive endings **-ra, -ras, -ra, -ramos, -rais,** and **-ran** are added. All **nosotros/as** forms have an accent mark on the vowel preceding the ending **-ramos.** Any spelling changes in the third person preterite forms will also appear in the corresponding past subjunctive forms.

|  | hablar | comer | vivir |
|---|---|---|---|
| THIRD PERSON PLURAL PRETERITE FORM | hablaron | comieron | vivieron |
| PAST SUBJUNCTIVE ENDINGS | hablara<br>hablaras<br>hablara<br>habláramos<br>hablarais<br>hablaran | comiera<br>comieras<br>comiera<br>comiéramos<br>comierais<br>comieran | viviera<br>vivieras<br>viviera<br>viviéramos<br>vivierais<br>vivieran |

Here are three sample sentences that include the past subjunctive in a noun clause, an adverbial clause, and an adjectival clause, respectively.

**Queríamos que** esta ciudad **aumentara** los servicios de reciclaje.

*We wanted this city to increase recycling services.*

**Protegían** el medio ambiente **para que** sus hijos **pudieran** vivir mejor.

*They protected the environment so that their children would live better.*

**Buscábamos un carro que** no **consumiera** mucha gasolina.

*We were looking for a car that wouldn't use a lot of gas.*

## Nota comunicativa

Communication

### PRESENT PERFECT SUBJUNCTIVE

You may have noticed the present perfect subjunctive forms used in the **Gramática en contexto** presentation on p. 465. As you may have guessed, the present perfect subjunctive is generally used in subjunctive contexts when you want to express a present perfect idea. The present perfect subjunctive is formed by combining the subjunctive of the auxiliary verb **haber** with the *past participle.*\*

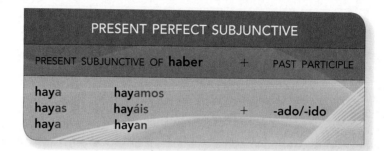

| PRESENT PERFECT SUBJUNCTIVE | | |
|---|---|---|
| PRESENT SUBJUNCTIVE OF **haber** | + | PAST PARTICIPLE |
| **hay**a **hay**amos | | |
| **hay**as **hay**áis | + | **-ado/-ido** |
| **hay**a **hay**an | | |

**Esperamos que** este programa de reciclaje ya **se haya aprobado.**

**Ojalá hayan dejado** de excavar en esa mina de cobre.

*We want this recycling program to have already been approved.*

*Hopefully they have stopped excavating in that copper mine.*

### ACTIVIDADES

**A. ¿Está de acuerdo?**

**PASO 1.**  Indique si está Ud. de acuerdo o no.

|  | SÍ | NO |
|---|---|---|
| 1. Es mejor que eliminemos el uso de combustibles fósiles por completo. | ☐ | ☐ |
| 2. Tenemos que desarrollar coches que usen tecnología de hidrógeno. | ☐ | ☐ |
| 3. El gobierno debe prohibir que las empresas e industrias desperdicien los recursos naturales. | ☐ | ☐ |
| 4. Deben ponerles multas a los hogares que consuman por día más de cincuenta galones de agua por persona. | ☐ | ☐ |
| 5. Creo que el reciclaje de productos plásticos debe ser obligatorio. | ☐ | ☐ |
| 6. Es urgente que el gobierno, no la industria privada, construya plantas de energía solar y eólica. | ☐ | ☐ |
| 7. Vamos a destruir el planeta dentro de cien años a menos que detengamos el calentamiento global. | ☐ | ☐ |
| 8. Muchas especies van a extinguirse antes de que resolvamos los problemas medioambientales que las ponen en peligro. | ☐ | ☐ |

**PASO 2.**  En parejas, compartan sus respuestas al **Paso 1.**

---

\*Review the irregular past participles that you learned on in **Gramática 10.1** (p. 323).

**468** cuatrocientos sesenta y ocho | **CAPÍTULO 14**  Nosotros y el mundo natural

**B. Oraciones incompletas.** Dé la forma correcta de los verbos entre paréntesis y termine las oraciones.

1. Necesitamos un gobierno que (**establecer**)...
2. Es una lástima que (**haber**)...
3. Las autoridades municipales deben requerir que todos (**reciclar**)...
4. No van a limitar el uso del agua en esta región a menos que (**haber**)...
5. Los ríos se contaminarán más y más hasta que las fábricas (**dejar**)...
6. Para tener un campus más verde, sugiero que nuestra universidad (**prohibir**)...
7. Necesitamos científicos que (**saber**)...
8. Tenemos que reducir el desperdicio del agua antes de que (*nosotros:* **perder**)...
9. ¿ ?

**C. ¿Qué opinan Uds.?**

Communication

**PASO 1.** En parejas, compartan las oraciones que crearon en la actividad B y expliquen el porqué de (*reason for*) sus ideas como en el modelo.

MODELO Necesitamos un gobierno que establezca iniciativas para la energía verde, porque si no lo hacemos, la contaminación del aire llegará a niveles más críticos cada día.

**PASO 2.** Compartan los resultados del **Paso 1** con la clase. ¿Están todos a favor o no? Expliquen.

**D. La moderación**

Cultures  Recycle

**PASO 1.** Complete la conversación con la forma correcta del presente de indicativo o de subjuntivo o con el infinitivo de los verbos entre paréntesis. Cuando aparecen dos palabras entre paréntesis, indique la palabra correcta.

HERNÁN: ¡Hola, chicas! ¿Qué tal?

SONIA: ¡Uf! Prefiero que no (**preguntar**[1]).

HERNÁN: Pero, ¿qué (**les/las**[2]) pasa?

SONIA: Acabamos de (**salir**[3]) de la clase del profesor Álvarez y...

NORA: ... y ¡ahora nos duele la cabeza! Ay, qué pesado. Ojalá no hubiera asistido[a] a clase hoy.

HERNÁN: Pero, hombre, ¿qué pasó en clase?

SONIA: Estamos (**estudiar/estudiando**[4]) el medio ambiente y la ecología en los países hispanos. Hoy el tema fue sobre (**los/las**[5]) problemas ambientales. Me da muchísima pena que (**haber**[6]) tantos problemas, problemas que nosotros mismos causamos.

*¿Cree Ud. que hay soluciones para los problemas de la sobrepoblación y contaminación del aire en ciudades como México, D.F.?*

NORA: El profesor sabe que el tema del medio ambiente y la contaminación nos (**aburrir**[7]), por eso le gusta (**personalizar**[8]) los temas. Quiere que (*nosotros:* **saber**[9]) qué impacto tienen nuestras acciones.

SONIA: Sí, el profesor sugiere que (*nosotros:* **analizar**[10]) nuestros hábitos. Es cierto que yo ya (**hacer**[11]) bastante, pero creo que (**poder**[12]) hacer más.

HERNÁN: ¿De qué problemas hablaron en clase hoy?

(Continúa.)

---

[a]Ojalá... *I wish I hadn't gone*

NORA: [*como en trance hipnótico*] De la sobrepoblación en ciudades como México, D.F., y Sao Paolo, Brasil; de la contaminación (**del / de la**[13]) aire en estas grandes ciudades; del agua, como en el río Coatzacoalcos en Oaxaca, México, en el río Riachuela en Buenos Aires, Argentina, y en el lago artificial Cerrón Grande, en El Salvador. (**También/Tampoco**[14]) hablamos del sobredesarrollo,[b] una práctica destructiva que contribuye a la deforestación y la destrucción de hábitats. Y en caso de que esos problemas no te (**deprimir**[15]), debemos mencionar la agricultura insostenible, un problema grande en África, Asia y varios países latinoamericanos. En países como Perú y Chile, la sobrepesca[c] ha causado problemas ecológicos y económicos. No hay ninguna rama[d] industrial o económica o ecológica que no (**sufrir**[16]) las consecuencias de nuestra... nuestra...

SONIA: ... de nuestra falta de moderación.

HERNÁN: Pero, esos (**ser**[17]) problemas enormes y no personales.

SONIA: El profesor empezó con problemas globales y grandes. Y nos preguntó: ¿Es posible que todos estos problemas (**tener**[18]) una cosa en común? ¿Puedes adivinarlo, Hernán?

NORA: [*hablándose a sí misma*] ... y la contaminación del suelo, los pesticidas y fertilizantes, los desperdicios...

HERNÁN: La moderación, o mejor dicho,[e] la falta de moderación. Pero, dudo que (**tener**[19]) sentido[f] deprimirse por estos problemas. La pobre de Nora está casi catatónica pensando en esto. Uds., o mejor dicho, nosotros, podemos ser más moderados.

SONIA: Ya es tarde, ¿no crees? Dudo que la moderación (**corregir**[20]) tantos años de excesos e indulgencias.

HERNÁN: Es mejor que (*nosotros:* **ser**[21]) optimistas, Sonia. En nuestro microcosmos, es importante que (*nosotros:* **reciclar**[22]) y que (**hacer**[23]) cosas que mejoren nuestro ambiente inmediato. Así no sólo mejoramos nuestro entorno,[g] sino también es posible que (*nosotros:* **servir**[24]) de ejemplo a otras personas.

SONIA: Posiblemente... Ay, mira, la pobre Nora. De verdad, esta clase la (**afectar**[25]) mucho. La voy a (**invitar**[26]) a un café aquí en la esquina. ¿Quieres acompañarnos? Sirven café orgánico de comercio libre.[h]

HERNÁN: Encantado. ¿Y ves? Vamos a (**apoyar**[27]) una buena práctica tomando café orgánico de comercio libre.

---

[b]*overdevelopment*  [c]*overfishing*  [d]*branch*  [e]*o... or rather*  [f]*tener... to make sense*  [g]*surroundings*  [h]*comercio... free trade*

**PASO 2.** Indique la palabra o frase correcta para completar cada oración. **¡OJO!** Puede haber más de una respuesta.

1. Sonia y Nora toman una clase _____ con el profesor Álvarez este semestre.
   **a.** de arqueología  **b.** medioambiental  **c.** sobre Latinoamérica
2. Al profesor Álvarez le gusta que sus estudiantes _____.
   **a.** piensen  **b.** se aburran  **c.** tomen apuntes
3. Los temas que menciona Nora *no* incluyen _____.
   **a.** los ríos contaminados  **b.** la contaminación del aire  **c.** el calentamiento global
4. Una ciudad sobrepoblada de Sudamérica es _____.
   **a.** México, D.F.  **b.** Oaxaca  **c.** Sao Paolo
5. Hay problemas con la sobrepesca en _____.
   **a.** Perú  **b.** Chile  **c.** Sudamérica

6. Una característica común entre los problemas que menciona Nora es _____.
   **a.** la contaminación    **b.** la falta de moderación    **c.** el agua
7. Hernán sugiere que tomen medidas (*take measures, do things*) dentro de _____.
   **a.** su microcosmos    **b.** casa    **c.** clase
8. Sonia quiere que Nora y Hernán _____.
   **a.** sean más «verdes»    **b.** reciclen más    **c.** tomen un café con ella

## Nota interdisciplinaria

Connections

### CIENCIAS AMBIENTALES: LOS EFECTOS DEL CAMBIO CLIMÁTICO

*Un glaciar en los Andes de Chile*

Los efectos del cambio climático, o calentamiento global, son variados y devastadores para la Tierra. En Latinoamérica, el aumento de las temperaturas ha modificado gran parte de los ecosistemas de la región, alterando los servicios para los que estaban destinados y comprometiendo, así, su futuro y su desarrollo económico. Las consecuencias de estos cambios son significativas y varían según las zonas.

En el Caribe ha habido[a] una destrucción casi total de los ecosistemas de coral y esto ha disminuido la actividad turística. En los Andes ocurren dos fenómenos opuestos: por un lado,[b] los glaciares están desapareciendo, lo cual puede causar graves inundaciones; por otro,[c] la disminución del nivel de los lagos de montaña puede provocar una importante escasez de agua en algunas ciudades. Los trópicos también se ven afectados. Es muy posible que los bosques tropicales desaparezcan, provocando la ausencia de lluvias y aumento de temperaturas que cambiarán los ecosistemas a regiones áridas y casi desérticas.[d] En países como Argentina y Uruguay, el cambio climático ha afectado las pampas y hoy en día las largas sequías arruinan los productos agrícolas y matan miles de animales, dejando a miles de personas sin trabajo y reduciendo las exportaciones.

Hasta ahora se ha hecho muy poco para contrarrestar[e] estos efectos, pero cada vez existen más fundaciones que se organizan para informar a la gente de la situación y para educarla en la prevención de estos males.

[a]ha... *there has been*    [b]por... *on one hand*    [c]por... *on the other hand*    [d]*desert-like*    [e]*counteract*

**PREGUNTAS**  En parejas, contesten las preguntas. Después, compartan sus respuestas con la clase.

**1.** ¿Qué consecuencias está teniendo el calentamiento global en los países latinoamericanos ¿Cuál le parece la más devastadora? ¿Por qué?
**2.** ¿Qué medidas se pueden tomar para solucionar este problema? Den por lo menos tres recomendaciones.

# Lectura cultural

Ud. va a leer un artículo de la revista *Nexos*, escrito por Guillermo de la Corte y publicado por la American Airlines, sobre el pez vela (*sailfish*).

Cultures

**ANTES DE LEER**

**A. A primera vista.** Mire la foto y lea el título, los encabezados y las primeras líneas *en letra cursiva*, y haga una lista de los temas que espera encontrar en el artículo. Luego, compare su lista con la de un compañero / una compañera de clase.

**B. Preguntas.** En parejas, contesten las preguntas. Después, compartan sus respuestas con la clase.

1. ¿Qué saben Uds. de la pesca deportiva (*sport fishing*)? ¿La han practicado alguna vez? ¿Dónde? ¿Cúando? ¿Qué pescaron (*did you catch*)?
2. Si nunca han practicado la pesca deportiva, ¿les gustaría hacerlo? Expliquen.
3. En términos de la pesca, ¿qué significa la frase «atrapar y soltar»?

**C. A leer.** Lea el artículo y trate de adivinar el significado de las palabras y frases <u>subrayadas</u> por el contexto, sin buscarlas en el diccionario.

## Guatemala y el pez vela

*En la costa del Pacífico de Guatemala se reúnen unas condiciones naturales únicas que combinadas con las adecuadas regulaciones gubernamentales y el <u>cumplimiento</u> de ellas, aseguran una fuente inagotable del pez vela, para deleite de los pescadores deportivos. Está considerada como la Capital Mundial del Pez Vela.*

*Un pez vela*

No hay nada más frustrante para un pescador deportivo que volver a su casa con las manos <u>vacías</u>, sin esa foto del pez capturado, para <u>presumir</u> con los amigos. En la costa del Pacífico de Guatemala, es prácticamente imposible que eso ocurra. En el 2006 un barco con cinco pescadores llegó a capturar 124 peces vela en un solo día. Eso es un récord, pero como <u>media</u> se puede esperar una captura de 15 a 20 peces por barco por día. La pesca es bastante consistente a lo largo del año, si bien[a] de noviembre a mayo es la época más <u>fructífera</u> cuando los peces emigran desde aguas más frías.

Las playas, de arena volcánica, imprimen al área las condiciones ideales para refugio de una gran variedad de vida silvestre y especies de animales. Las tortugas marinas, por ejemplo, eligen sus playas para la reproducción. En el mar adentro,[b] un cañón submarino profundo de 15 millas de anchura,[c] corrientes marinas de México a El Salvador, la temperatura del agua y algunos de los peces preferidos por el pez vela como la caballa,[d] el arenque[e] y el calamar,[f] conforman el hábitat ideal para su desarrollo. Por un lado la ausencia de especies <u>depredadoras</u> naturales y por otro, que las hembras[g] desovan varias veces al año, soltando un millón de huevos, contribuyen al mantenimiento y crecimiento de la especie.

El gobierno guatemalteco se encarga del otro depredador «natural»: el hombre que debe seguir dos reglas básicas: toda la pesca deportiva es de «atrapar y soltar» y el uso obligatorio de los <u>anzuelos</u> circulares que atrapan pero no dañan al pez.

### Criatura espectacular

Salimos a pescar con John Mills, el dueño de Pacific Fins, una compañía que ofrece paquetes de pesca y alojamiento. Mar adentro, los tripulantes prepararon los aparejos, señuelos, carnada[h] y el famoso anzuelo circular, y lo lanzaron al agua. No pasó media hora, y una de las cañas[i] <u>dio un tirón</u>. ¡Ya picó! Con tranquilidad

---

[a]si... *especially* [b]En... *At sea* [c]de... *in width* [d]*mackerel* [e]*herring* [f]*squid* [g]*females* [h]aparejos,... *tackle, lures, bait* [i]*fishing poles*

se le dio hilo[j] al pez y después poco a poco se procedió a recoger el hilo y traerlo. Como novato,[k] no me dieron la caña hasta que no supieron que el animal estaba bien <u>enganchado</u>. En ese momento, empecé a entender la pasión por ese tipo de pesca. El animal luchaba, <u>tiraba de mí</u> con una extraordinaria fuerza, que casi me sacaba por la borda.[l] Ya cerca del barco, saltaba al aire agitando la cabeza para intentar soltarse. ¡Qué belleza de animal! No puedo recordar cuánto tiempo pasó hasta que lo subimos al barco, pero me pareció una eternidad. Él <u>no se daba por vencido</u>, y yo ya no aguantaba[m] más del cansancio. Se procedió a cortar el hilo y devolverlo al mar.

El pez vela es la especie más rápida del planeta. Puede alcanzar una velocidad de 109 km/h. La cabeza es <u>puntiaguda</u> con un pico, como una espada,[n] en la punta,[ñ] que obviamente le sirve para abrirse paso en el agua a esa velocidad. Tiene la piel lisa,[o] sin <u>escamas</u>, y está recubierto de una gelatina que lo hace <u>resbaladizo</u> al tacto.[p] En el dorsal cuenta con una enorme <u>aleta</u> en forma de vela de barco. El más grande de tamaño puede llegar a los 2,5 m con un peso de 65 kg, si bien lo más normal es entre 32 y 45 kg.

## Conservar las especies

La pesca del pez vela es puro deporte, pues es un animal noble, rápido y luchador que pone la adrenalina del pescador a tope.[q] Pero no es un pescado comestible, así que el matarlo no tiene objeto. La práctica conjunta de «atrapar y soltar» y el anzuelo circular, permite la conservación del pez vela y otras especies, y como consecuencia, el desarrollo de la industria turística asociada con el deporte. Guatemala y Costa Rica lo ven así y emplean los controles necesarios para que se cumplan las regulaciones de pesca. <u>Lamentablemente</u>, otros países donde también se practica este tipo de pesca, no siempre ejercen los mismos controles.

[j]*line*  [k]*novice*  [l]*por... overboard*  [m]*no... couldn't put up with*  [n]*sword*  [ñ]*tip*  [o]*smooth*  [p]*al... to the touch*  [q]*a... to the limit*

## DESPUÉS DE LEER

**A. Comprensión.** En parejas, contesten las preguntas, según el artículo. Después, compartan sus respuestas con la clase.

1. ¿Es fácil o difícil capturar peces vela? ¿Cuántos peces puede capturar un barco diariamente?
2. ¿Cuál es la mejor época para pescar? ¿Por qué?
3. ¿Por qué razones no se permite atrapar y guardar (*keep*) el pez vela?
4. Además de Guatemala, ¿qué país tiene regulaciones para conservar este animal? ¿Qué hacen en otros países?

**B. Temas de discusión.** En grupos pequeños, contesten las preguntas. Después, compartan sus ideas con la clase.

1. ¿Están Uds. de acuerdo con los deportes como la pesca o la caza? Expliquen.
2. ¿Qué piensan Uds. de la regulación de capturar peces y devolverlos al mar? ¿Creen que estas acciones justifican la pesca como deporte? ¿O creen que los animales sufren en todo caso?
3. En su opinión, ¿hay casos en que la muerte de algún animal está justificada? Expliquen.

# Concurso de videoblogs

## Los Ángeles: Héctor

Final del concurso

En un café de Los Ángeles Héctor muestra algunos momentos especiales de los videoblogs y después selecciona al ganador del concurso.

### ANTES DE VER

En parejas, contesten las preguntas.

1. De todos los videoblogs que Uds. han visto desde el **Capítulo 1** hasta este **Capítulo 14**, ¿cuáles les gustaron más? Expliquen.
2. ¿Quién creen Uds. que va a ganar el concurso? Expliquen.

### DESPUÉS DE VER

**Fin del concurso**

**PASO 1.** En parejas, comenten los temas y contesten las preguntas. Luego, compartan sus ideas con la clase.

1. ¿Qué les parecieron los fragmentos que mostró Héctor en este segmento? ¿Creen que representan bien lo que Uds. recuerdan de los segmentos originales? Expliquen.
2. ¿Creen que Héctor escogió bien al ganador del concurso? Expliquen.
3. ¿Qué otros momentos recuerdan de los videoblogs que han visto este semestre/trimestre o de semestres/trimestres anteriores? Es decir, ¿qué más les impresionó? Expliquen.
4. ¿Cuáles de los lugares o países que vieron en los videoblogs les gustaría visitar algún día? Expliquen.

**PASO 2.** Con toda la clase, comparen sus ideas del **Paso 1.** Si alguien en la clase ya hay visitado uno de los lugares presentados en el concurso, ¿puede compartir sus impresiones de ese lugar con la clase? (La clase debe hacerle preguntas para saber más.)

**Vocabulario práctico**

| | |
|---|---|
| **¿Sale?** | OK? (Mex.) |
| **alfajores** | type of pastry popular in Argentina |

474

## Los verbos

| | |
|---|---|
| arrojar | to throw out, spew |
| cerrar (ie) el grifo | to turn off the faucet |
| desarrollar | to develop |
| desperdiciar | to waste |
| destruir (y) | to destroy |
| evitar | to avoid |
| mejorar | to improve |
| proteger (j) | to protect |
| resolver (ue) | to solve; to resolve |
| reutilizar (c) | reuse |

Cognados: afectar, conservar, contaminar, provocar (qu), reciclar

Repaso: destruir (y)

## La geografía

| | |
|---|---|
| el altiplano | high plateau |
| la arena | sand |
| el arrecife (de coral) | (coral) reef |
| la bahía | bay |
| el bosque tropical | tropical rain forest |
| el glaciar | glacier |
| el hielo | ice |
| el mar | sea |
| el pantano | wetlands; marsh |
| la llanura | plain |
| la nieve | snow |
| la orilla | shore |
| la selva | jungle |
| la sierra | mountain range |
| la zona ártica | arctic region |

Cognados: el archipiélago, la costa, el desierto, el iceberg, la laguna, el océano, la roca, el volcán

## Los animales y las plantas (salvajes) / (Wild) Animals and Plants

| | |
|---|---|
| la abeja | bee |
| el águila (pl. las águilas) | eagle |
| la almeja | clam |
| la araña | spider |
| la ballena | whale |
| el caballo marino | seahorse |
| el cacto | cactus |
| el cangrejo | crab |
| el cocotero | coconut tree |
| el delfín | dolphin |
| la foca | seal |
| la gaviota | seagull |
| el mono | monkey |
| el oso (polar) | (polar) bear |
| la medusa | jellyfish |
| la palmera | palm tree |
| el papagayo | parrot (macaw) |
| el quetzal | quetzal bird |

| | |
|---|---|
| la rana | frog |
| la serpiente | snake |
| el tiburón | shark |
| la tortuga | turtle |

Cognados: el caribú, el cocodrilo, el elefante, el gorila, el insecto, el jaguar, el león, el pelícano, el pingüino, el panda, el puma, el reptil, el tigre

## La naturaleza y los recursos naturales / Nature and Natural Resources

| | |
|---|---|
| el agua dulce/salada | fresh/salt water |
| la biodiversidad | biodiversity |
| la concha | (sea) shell |
| la flora y fauna (silvestre) | (wild) plant and animal life |
| la ola | wave |

Cognados: el gas natural, los metales, los minerales, el parque nacional, el petróleo, la vegetación

## Los problemas y soluciones ambientales / Environmental Problems and Solutions

| | |
|---|---|
| el aire puro | clean air |
| el basurero | landfill |
| la bolsa de plástico | plastic bag |
| el bosque tropical | tropical rainforest |
| el calentamiento global | global warming |
| el cambio climático | climate change |
| la capa de ozono | ozone layer |
| el carro/coche eléctrico/híbrido | electric/hybrid car |
| el cartón | cardboard |
| la contaminación | pollution |
| del agua | water pollution |
| del aire | air pollution |
| del suelo | soil pollution |
| el desastre ambiental | environmental disaster |
| los desechos urbanos | urban waste |
| la energía | power; energy |
| eólica | wind power |
| hidroeléctrica | hydroelectric power |
| nuclear | nuclear power |
| solar | solar power |
| el envase de plástico/vidrio | plastic/glass container |
| la escasez | shortage |
| la especie en peligro de extinción | endangered species |
| la excavación minera | mining |
| la fábrica | factory |
| el humo | smoke |
| los pesticidas | pesticides |
| el petróleo | crude oil |
| el petrolero | oil tanker |
| la pila | battery |
| la población densa | dense population |
| la presa | dam |

| los productos no reciclables | non-recyclable products |
|---|---|
| los productos del petróleo | petroleum products |
| los productos químicos | chemical products |
| el reciclaje | recycling |
| la reserva (natural) | nature reserve |
| los residuos peligrosos | hazardous waste |
| la sobrepoblación | overpopulation |
| la tala de árboles | tree felling |
| el tren ligero | light rail |
| la turbina eólica | wind turbine |
| | |
| anticontaminante | anti-pollution |
| contaminado/a | polluted |
| (no) renovable | (non)renewable |
| peligroso/a | dangerous |
| terrestre | land (*adj.*) |

**Cognados:** la atmósfera, la combustión, la conservación, la deforestación, la destrucción, los gases, el panel solar, el smog; ecológico/a, orgánico/a, reciclado/a

## Las conjunciones de dependencia y propósito

| | |
|---|---|
| **a menos que** + *subj.* | unless |
| **antes de que** + *subj.* | before |
| **con tal (de) que** + *subj.* | provided that |
| **en caso de que** + *subj.* | in case |
| **para que** + *subj.* | so that |
| **sin que** + *subj.* | without |

# La vida moderna

*En Chichicastenango, Guatemala*

1. ¿Qué impresiones le causa la imagen de la fotografía? ¿Cómo se imagina la manera de vivir de esas personas?

2. En su opinión, ¿cuáles son las mayores presiones de la vida moderna? ¿Se siente Ud. estresado/a a veces? ¿En qué situaciones se siente más estresado/a?

3. ¿Cree que los avances tecnológicos y la rapidez en las comunicaciones añaden más presión a la vida de las personas o no? ¿Por qué?

**connect** SPANISH
www.connectspanish.com

## Vocabulario del tema

### Los avances tecnológicos

1. el teléfono celular
   el auricular bluetooth
   VENTA PENDIENTE
   GARC...
   Bienes Ra...

2. el satélite
   la radio por satélite

3. la televisión de alta definición
   la televisión de pantalla ancha

4. los alimentos transgénicos

5. la clonación

6. manejar las cuentas por el Internet
   buscar (qu) novio/a por el Internet
   E-pareja
   Hola, Sofía
   BANCO VIRTUAL
   mandar un e-mail
   Cibermercado
   CINE EN LÍNEA
   comprar entradas de cine por el Internet
   hacer (irreg.) las compras por el Internet

| | |
|---|---|
| la agenda electrónica | PDA |
| la fibra óptica | fiber optics |
| leer (y) el e-mail | to read/check one's e-mail |
| llamar por el celular | to call someone on their cell phone |

Cognados: la cámara digital, el láser; acelerado/a, cibernético/a
Repaso: el carro/coche eléctrico/híbrido, la página Web.

## La computadora

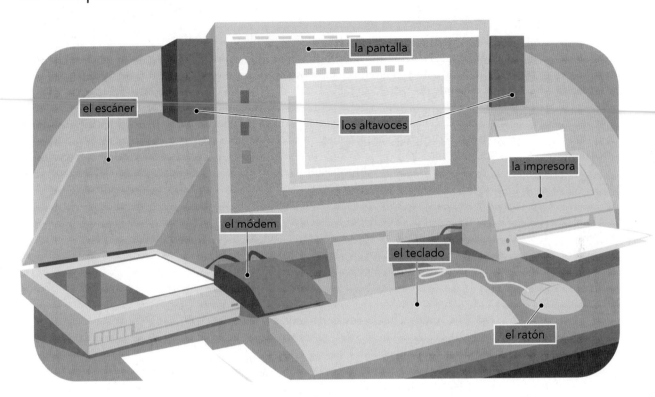

el escáner — los altavoces — la pantalla — la impresora — el módem — el teclado — el ratón

| | |
|---|---|
| almacenar | to backup |
| adjuntar | to attach |
| borrar | to delete |
| digitalizar (c) | to digitize |
| escanear | to scan |
| fallar | to crash |
| guardar (como) | to save (as) |
| imprimir | to print |
| el (documento) adjunto | attachment |
| el archivo | file |
| la conexión (WiFi) | (WiFi) connection |
| el lápiz de memoria | flash drive |
| inalámbrico/a | wireless |

Cognados: el CD-ROM, el DVD-ROM, el router
Repaso: abrir, bajar, cerrar (ie), mandar, recibir, subir; la computadora portátil, el disco duro

## Los medios de comunicación°

Los... *Mass Media*

| | |
|---|---|
| enterarse (de) | to find out, learn (about) |
| estar (*irreg.*) al día | to be up to date |

| las noticias | news |
| el noticiero | news report |
| el periódico (en línea) | (online) newspaper |
| la prensa | the press |
| la revista (en línea) | (online) magazine |
| la televisión de alta definición | HDTV |

**Cognado:** informar
**Repaso:** el Internet

### ACTIVIDADES

**A.** Definiciones. Indique la palabra definida.

1. _____ sistema de vídeo con mayor resolución
2. _____ se producen organismos genéticamente idénticos
3. _____ funciona con gasolina y electricidad
5. _____ comida modificada al nivel molecular
6. _____ fuente de información accesible por el Internet
7. _____ transmite información a gran velocidad y a gran distancia
8. _____ dispositivo (*device*) de emisión de luz
9. _____ receptor inalámbrico para el teléfono celular
10. _____ una computadora de mano para organizar calendarios, citas, direcciones, etcétera

a. los alimentos transgénicos
b. la agenda electrónica
c. la fibra óptica
d. la alta definición
e. el láser
f. la clonación
h. el auricular bluetooth
i. la página Web
j. el carro híbrido

**B.** ¿Qué usa Ud.?

**PASO 1.** Indique las cosas de la lista que Ud. tiene o usa.

☐ la impresora
☐ la conexión WiFi
☐ los altavoces
☐ el lápiz de memoria
☐ el celular
☐ la televisión de alta definición
☐ la agenda electrónica
☐ el auricular bluetooth
☐ el escáner
☐ la computadora portátil

**PASO 2.** Explique dónde tiene o cuándo usa Ud. las cosas que indicó en el **Paso 1.**

**MODELOS** la impresora → Tengo una impresora en casa (en mi habitación) y la uso para imprimir tareas, informes y otros trabajos para mis clases.

No tengo impresora en casa, pero uso la impresora de Kinko's cuando necesito imprimir algún informe o tarea.

**C.** ¿Son buenos hábitos o no?

**PASO 1.** Diga si estos hábitos son buenos para conservar el equipo (*equipment*) tecnológico que usamos o no.

**MODELO** Siempre llevo mi agenda electrónica, el celular y la computadora portátil a todas partes. → No es buen hábito. / Es buen hábito.

1. Limpio la pantalla de mi televisión con agua.
2. Siempre apago mi computadora antes de acostarme.
3. Nunca borro ningún e-mail.
4. Almaceno mis documentos una vez a la semana.
5. Bajo muchos programas, juegos, música y películas del Internet.
6. Limpio el teclado de mi computadora con la aspiradora.
7. Tengo el Internet gratis porque uso la conexión WiFi de algún vecino.
8. Imprimo todos mis e-mails porque es más fácil leerlos así.

**PASO 2.** En parejas, comparen sus respuestas del **Paso 1** y coméntenlas. Digan también si Uds. hacen esas cosas.

MODELOS No es buen hábito llevar la agenda, el celular y la computadora a todas partes porque a veces debemos separarnos de esos medios de comunicación.

Es buena práctica llevar la agenda, el celular y la computadora a todas partes para mantener contacto con la familia, los amigos y el trabajo a todas horas.

**D.** ¿Es Ud. moderno/a o anticuado/a (*old-fashioned*)?

**PASO 1.** Indique con qué frecuencia hace Ud. estas cosas.

| | MUCHO | TODAS LAS SEMANAS | UNA VEZ AL MES | DE VEZ EN CUANDO | NUNCA |
|---|---|---|---|---|---|
| PUNTOS | 5 | 4 | 3 | 2 | 1 |
| 1. Hago compras por el Internet. | ☐ | ☐ | ☐ | ☐ | ☐ |
| 2. Uso un auricular bluetooth. | ☐ | ☐ | ☐ | ☐ | ☐ |
| 3. Apunto mis citas y tareas en una agenda electrónica. | ☐ | ☐ | ☐ | ☐ | ☐ |
| 4. Me encanta escuchar la radio por satélite. | ☐ | ☐ | ☐ | ☐ | ☐ |
| 5. Pago mis cuentas por el Internet. | ☐ | ☐ | ☐ | ☐ | ☐ |
| 6. Compro entradas de cine y conciertos por el Internet. | ☐ | ☐ | ☐ | ☐ | ☐ |
| 7. Organizo mis fotos y documentos en archivos electrónicos. | ☐ | ☐ | ☐ | ☐ | ☐ |
| 8. Leo el periódico en línea en mi computadora. | ☐ | ☐ | ☐ | ☐ | ☐ |

**PASO 2.** En parejas, comparen sus respuestas del **Paso 1**. Si Ud. tiene cuarenta puntos, es muy moderno/a; si sólo tiene ocho puntos, es bastante anticuado/a. ¿Quién de los/las dos es más moderno/a? ¿Quién es más tradicional?

**E. Mi vida tecnológica.** Complete las oraciones con palabras y expresiones del **Vocabulario del tema.** Las oraciones deben ser lógicas y pueden relacionarse con su vida o no. Sus compañeros/as van a adivinar si lo que dice Ud. es cierto o falso.

1. No puedo vivir sin...
2. Necesito comprar...
3. No aguanto (*I can't put up with*)...
4. Siempre veo/escucho...
5. Nunca uso...
6. Cuando estudio, prefiero...
7. Para comunicarme con amigos prefiero...
8. Uso el Internet para...

**F. Para estar al día**

**PASO 1.** Entreviste a tres compañeros/as de clase para saber cómo se informan y qué tipo de información les interesa. **¡OJO!** Debe formar preguntas lógicas para averiguar (*find out*) la siguiente información sobre cada compañero/a.

1. el tipo de noticiero que ve: local, nacional, mundial, ¿ ?
2. el tipo de periódico que lee: (de papel) en casa, (de papel) en un café, en línea, ¿ ?

(Continúa.)

3. el tipo de revistas que lee: de actualidad, de moda, de la televisión y del cine, de personas famosas, ¿ ?

4. los tipos de noticias que prefiere: de su comunidad, del país, de espectáculos y personas famosas, de asuntos políticos, del mundo, ¿ ?

5. cómo prefiere enterarse de las noticias: por la televisión, por la radio, por un periódico (de papel), por el Internet, ¿ ?

**PASO 2.** Comparen sus respuestas al **Paso 1** con la clase. ¿Creen Uds. que todos están al día y que se informan bien? ¿Les interesan más las noticias de la actualidad o tienen más interés en los espectáculos y personas famosas? Expliquen.

Communication

**G.** La tecnología

**PASO 1.** En parejas, apunten tres aspectos positivos y tres negativos que la tecnología ha traído a la vida moderna.

**PASO 2.** Compartan sus ideas con la clase y hagan una lista completa de los aspectos positivos y otra de los aspectos negativos. **¡OJO!** Todos los estudiantes de la clase deben estar de acuerdo con el contenido de las listas.

**PASO 3.** Según las listas del **Paso 2,** ¿cuál es la opinión general de la clase? ¿Consideran que la tecnología tiene más aspectos positivos o negativos? Expliquen.

---

## Nota cultural

Cultures

### TE MANDO UN *TWEET*

Las tecnologías no sólo cambian nuestra forma de trabajar o divertirnos, también cambian la forma en la que hablamos. Por ejemplo, expresiones que en un principio pertenecían a un campo específico, el de la computación, han pasado a ser formas de expresión propias del lenguaje coloquial, y el uso del e-mail y el *chat* ha favorecido el nacimiento de nuevos verbos y palabras en español. Así, «cambiar el *chip*», es cambiar de tema o pensamiento, «estar formateado» significa quedarse en blanco, y cuando buscamos algo por el Internet, estamos «surfeando».

Los *chats* surgen como una alternativa de comunicación equivalente a una conversación informal y a menudo no se respetan las normas gramaticales y ortográficas. Su repercusión es mundial. El conocido diccionario Collins ha introducido algunos de los términos SMS[a] más populares entre sus páginas y los estudiantes neozelandeses,[b] desde 2008, pueden utilizar el idioma abreviado de los SMS en su examen de acceso a la universidad.

Las redes[c] sociales como Facebook, MySpace y Twitter han creado también su propio idioma y forma de vida. Ya no es necesario llamar por teléfono a los amigos para saber de ellos, organizar una fiesta o esperar hasta verlos para compartir las fotos del fin de semana pasado. Basta con *login* en la cuenta, subir las fotos, chatear o mandar un *tweet*. Y si alguno todavía no se ha enterado, siempre se puede hacer un *ping* a última hora.

---

[a]*text messaging (SMS = Short Message Service)*  [b]*from New Zealand*  [c]*networks*

PREGUNTAS En parejas, contesten las siguientes preguntas. Después, compartan sus ideas con la clase.

1. ¿Qué redes sociales y servicios de *chat* o mensajería (*messaging*) utilizan Uds.? ¿Cuáles están de moda? ¿Han cambiado su forma de relacionarse con otras personas? ¿Han modificado incluso su lenguaje?

2. ¿Qué les parece la idea de permitir este lenguaje de la computación en los exámenes?

3. ¿Creen que es posible prescindir de (*to do without*) estos servicios? ¿Cómo cambiaría su vida si no tuvieran acceso al Internet?

4. Busquen por el Internet una lista de las abreviaturas en español que se utilizan para enviar SMS e intenten usarlas y chatear con su compañero/a.

# Gramática

## 15.1 Conditional

**GRAMÁTICA EN CONTEXTO**

### Los cibercafés

No hay duda de que los avances tecnológicos han cambiado nuestro mundo, especialmente cómo nos comunicamos y cómo nos ponemos al día. Pero, ¿quién **se imaginaría** el impacto de estos avances en los países en desarrollo, especialmente en los lugares remotos? **Podríamos** citar muchos ejemplos de ese impacto, pero **nos gustaría** hablar de los cibercafés que ahora son popularísimos por toda Latinoamérica.

Muchas personas —tanto en las zonas urbanas como en las rurales— se aprovechan de los cibercafés. Los jóvenes y adultos que nunca **se comprarían** una computadora ni **tendrían** acceso al Internet, entran en los cibercafés, abren cuentas de e-mail, usan Skype para llamar a los amigos y la familia y navegan en Internet. Un joven que entra en este café de San Pedro de Atacama, Chile, **pagaría** 1.200 pesos* por hora por usar el Internet. Es obvio que la tecnología está cambiando el mundo.

*Un cibercafé en San Pedro de Atacama, Chile*

**Comprensión.** Empareje las frases para formar oraciones lógicas.

1. Sería muy diferente _____
2. Sería muy caro _____
3. Sería divertido _____

   a. comunicarse sin los cibercafés.
   b. visitar un cibercafé.
   c. vivir en Latinoamérica sin los avances tecnológicos.

**A.** The conditional is used to talk about what a person *would* do. English forms the conditional tense with the auxiliary verb *would* followed by the main verb. In Spanish, the conditional is formed by adding the conditional endings **-ía, -ías, -ía, -íamos, -íais, -ían** to the infinitive of **-ar, -er,** and **-ir** verbs.

| hablar | |
|---|---|
| hablaría | hablaríamos |
| hablarías | hablaríais |
| habaría | hablarían |

| volver | |
|---|---|
| volvería | volveríamos |
| volverías | volveríais |
| volvería | volverían |

| vivir | |
|---|---|
| viviría | viviríamos |
| vivirías | viviríais |
| viviría | vivirían |

**GRAMÁTICA EN CONTEXTO** *Cybercafés / There is no doubt that technological advances have changed our world, especially how we communicate and how we stay up to date. But, who would imagine the impact of those advances on developing countries, especially in remote regions? We could cite many examples of that impact, but we would like to talk about cybercafés that are now very popular throughout Latin America. / Many people, in urban as well as rural zones, also take advantage of cybercafés. Young people and adults who would never buy a computer nor have Internet access, go into cybercafés, open e-mail accounts, use Skype to call friends and family, and explore the Internet. A young person who goes into this cybercafé in San Pedro de Atacama, Chile, would pay 1,200 pesos per hour to use the Internet. It's obvious that technology is changing the world.*

*1,200 Chilean pesos is less than $3.00 U.S.

Preferiría tomar la foto con una cámara digital.

*I would prefer to take the picture with a digital camera.*

Trabajaría más eficazmente con una agenda electrónica.

*I would work more efficiently with a PDA.*

**B.** Several of the most common verbs do not use the infinitive as the stem for the conditional. These verbs, with their stems, are the same as those that are irregular in the future tense.

CONDITIONAL: IRREGULAR VERBS

| | |
|---|---|
| decir → dir- | |
| haber → habr-* | |
| hacer → har- | -ía |
| poder → podr- | -ías |
| poner → pondr- | -ía |
| querer → querr- | + -íamos |
| saber → sabr- | -íais |
| salir → saldr- | -ían |
| tener → tendr- | |
| venir → vendr- | |

¿**Tendrías** una videocámara para grabar el partido?

*Would you have a videocamera to record the game?*

No **podría** vivir sin mi teléfono celular.

*I would not be able to live without my cell phone.*

**C.** The verbs **poder** and **gustar** are frequently used in the conditional to soften requests and make suggestions politely.

¿**Podría** decirme cuánto cuesta esta impresora?

*Could you tell me how much this printer costs?*

Nos **gustaría** usar la computadora.

*We would like to use the computer.*

**D.** The conditional is also used to express the future from the point of view of the past, just as English does.

Mi papa me prometió que me **regalaría** un iPod para mi cumpleaños.

*My dad promised me that he would give me an iPod for my birthday.*

**ACTIVIDADES**

**A.** Con más dinero y tiempo

**PASO 1.** Indique cuáles de las oraciones describen lo que Ud. haría con más dinero y más tiempo.

1. ☐ Tendría una computadora portátil en cada cuarto de mi casa.
2. ☐ Usaría una agenda electrónica para recordar todas mis citas importantes.
3. ☐ Leería un periódico todos los días.
4. ☐ Compraría un carro híbrido.
5. ☐ Siempre estaría al día.
6. ☐ Miraría DVDs en una televisión de alta definición.
7. ☐ Prepararía y comería comida más sana.

---

*The conditional of **hay** is **habría** (*there would be*).

**PASO 2.** En parejas, compartan sus respuestas al **Paso 1.**

**B. En un mundo perfecto.** Complete el párrafo con la forma correcta de los verbos entre paréntesis en el condicional.

En un mundo perfecto, todos (*nosotros:* **llevarse**[1]) bien. Cada ciudadano (**respetar**[2]) las leyes y no (**haber**[3]) dictadores en ninguna parte. Los políticos siempre (**decir**[4]) nada más que la verdad. Los trabajadores no (**tener**[5]) que hacer huelgas porque siempre (**recibir**[6]) un trato justo. Sin duda, tú nunca (**perderse**[7]) las noticias porque las (**ver**[8]) por el Internet en tu celular. ¿Y yo? Pues, en el mundo de mis sueños, (**poder**[9]) hacer de voluntaria para ayudar a la gente… ¡pero nadie (**necesitar**[10]) mi ayuda!

Communication

**C. Entrevista: ¿Qué haría Ud.?** Entreviste a un compañero / una compañera de clase con estas preguntas. Luego, cambien de papel.

1. Con más tiempo, ¿qué harías todos los días que no haces ahora?
2. Con todo el dinero necesario, ¿qué clase de carro comprarías? ¿por qué?
3. ¿Participarías en una manifestación? ¿por qué sí o por qué no? De ser que (*If the answer is*) sí, ¿qué causa apoyarías?
4. ¿Postularías (*Would you apply for*) para algún puesto político? ¿por qué sí o por qué no? De ser que sí, ¿para qué puesto postularías?
5. ¿Utilizarías un auricular bluetooth al manejar tu auto? ¿por qué sí o por qué no?
6. ¿Escucharías la radio por satélite en español? ¿por qué sí o por qué no?
7. ¿Te gustaría tener un celular con agenda electrónica? Explica.
8. ¿Donarías dinero a alguna causa social? ¿por qué sí o por qué no? De ser que sí, ¿a qué causa donarías?

**D. ¿Cómo comunicarse?**

Cultures

Recycle

**PASO 1.** Complete el diálogo de la página siguiente con la forma correcta del verbo entre paréntesis en el presente, el condicional, el pretérito o el imperfecto, según el contexto. **¡OJO!** Cuando hay dos verbos, escoja el verbo correcto y úselo en su forma apropiado.

*Marta hace una videollamada por el Internet.*

(Continúa.)

Esteban Romero (**estar/ser** [1]) de Paraguay, pero desde hace un año (**vivir** [2]) y (**trabajar** [3]) en Montreal. Ahora Esteban (**hablar** [4]) con una compañera de trabajo hondureña, Marta Baldomero, sobre cómo comunicarse con sus familiares y amigos en su país.

ESTEBAN: Marta, ¿cómo (*tú:* **comunicarse** [5]) típicamente con tu familia y tus amigos en tu país?

MARTA: Pues, les (*yo:* **escribir** [6]) mucho e-mail y también (**tener** [7]) una página en Facebook. Así (**estar/ser** [8]) muy fácil compartir fotos y enviarnos mensajes.

ESTEBAN: ¿Facebook? Pero yo no (**conocer/saber** [9]) usarlo.

MARTA: Ay, Facebook te (**encantar** [10]). Con Facebook, tu familia y tú (**poder** [11]) enviar y dejar mensajes. También (*tú:* **poner** [12]) fotos de tu esposa y tus hijos, y todos tus parientes y amigos las (**ver** [13]). (**Estar/Ser** [14]) muy fácil comenzar, y yo te (**ayudar** [15]). Estoy segura que no (*tú:* **tener** [16]) ningún problema.

ESTEBAN: ¿(*Tú:* **Conocer/Saber** [17]) algo acerca de las videollamadas? Otro compañero me (*P/I:* **decir** [18]) recientemente que las utiliza para hablar con su familia en Puerto Rico.

MARTA: Claro que sí. Para hacer una videollamada, lo único que (*tú:* **necesitar** [19]) es una cámara Web en tu computadora y un micrófono. Uds. (**seleccionar** [20]) un paquete de software de videollamadas y en un día y a una hora acordados,[a] (**tener** [21]) su *chat*. Y ese *chat* no les (**costar** [22]) nada.

ESTEBAN: Así que mi familia y yo (**comprar** [23]) las cámaras y los micrófonos y (*nosotros:* **verse** [24]) y (*nosotros:* **hablarse** [25]) a través del Internet, ¿correcto?

MARTA: Correcto.

ESTEBAN: ¡Qué bueno! ¿Me (*tú:* **acompañar** [26]) a la tienda a buscar los accesorios?

MARTA: Claro que sí. ¿Te (**gustar** [27]) ir después del trabajo hoy?

ESTEBAN: Perfecto. Gracias por tu ayuda.

MARTA: De nada.

----

[a]*agreed upon*

**PASO 2.** Conteste las preguntas, según el **Paso 1.**

1. ¿De dónde es Esteban Romero? ¿y Marta Baldomero? ¿Dónde viven y trabajan Esteban y Marta? ¿De qué hablan?
2. ¿Cómo se comunica Marta con su familia y sus amigos en su país? ¿Qué sabe Esteban de estos medios de comunicación?
3. Según Marta, ¿cómo podría utilizar Esteban Facebook para comunicarse con su familia en Paraguay? ¿Le sería fácil o difícil a Esteban empezar a usar Facebook? ¿por qué?
4. Para hacer una videollamada, ¿qué necesitaría Esteban? ¿Qué harían Esteban y su familia en Paraguay para hablarse por medio de una videollamada?
5. ¿Qué hará Esteban primero para empezar a comunicarse con su familia?

**PASO 3.** En parejas, contesten las preguntas.

Communication

1. ¿Cómo se mantienen Uds. en contacto con sus amigos y familiares? ¿Por qué utilizan estos medios de comunicación? Expliquen.
2. ¿Prefieren Uds. hablar por teléfono o por el Internet con sus amigos y familiares, o prefieren escribir e-mail o mensajes SMS? Expliquen.
3. Si Uds. vivieran (*lived*) en un país lejos de sus amigos y familiares, ¿cómo se comunicarían con ellos? ¿Usarían diferentes medios de comunicación de los que ya utilizan? ¿Por qué? ¿Qué equipo o accesorios necesitarían para comunicarse? Expliquen.

## Nota interdisciplinaria

Connections

### INFORMÁTICA: EL LENGUAJE DE LA INFORMÁTICA

*Fuera de un cibercafé, en Barcelona*

El inglés es, indudablemente, el idioma de la computación, así se han ido adoptando en español (al igual que en todas las lenguas del mundo) muchos términos técnicos y científicos ingleses para cubrir las deficiencias del idioma en estas materias. Cuando en español no hay un equivalente exacto del concepto, se usan los términos en inglés, como por ejemplo, *software, hardware, multimedia, byte, chip* o *bit*. A veces, sin embargo, se adaptan los términos ingleses a las características particulares de la lengua española y hoy nuestro idioma cuenta con términos nuevos como *cursor, interfaz, disquete, formatear, computarizar, indexar, cederrón* y *devedé*, todos recogidos en el Diccionario de la Real Academia Española. Cuando el español tiene un equivalente exacto al inglés para expresar un concepto, esta palabra se traduce directamente a la lengua española. Es el caso de los términos usados en procesadores de datos y computadoras, como por ejemplo, *guardar, cortar, copiar* o *pegar*.

PREGUNTAS En parejas, contesten las preguntas. Después, compartan sus ideas con la clase.

1. ¿Por qué a veces el español utiliza términos directamente del inglés?
2. ¿Qué términos presentan una mezcla de las grafías (*spellings*) inglesa y española? ¿Reconocen Uds. su significado?
3. ¿Se les ocurren otros contextos en que el español usa términos del inglés? ¿Cuáles?

# Palabra escrita

## A comenzar

Communication

> **Developing a Persuasive Argument.** A persuasive argument should express the writer's personal opinion about an issue and attempt to convince the reader to adopt his/her point of view. To make your argument more persuasive, you should anticipate the reader's opposing viewpoints on the matter and let the reader know that you are aware of them. One way of doing this is to try to include in your composition as many potential opposing arguments as possible that the reader may consider, and then explain why your point of view is more valid. A good way to practice this skill is to choose a viewpoint that opposes your own, and then develop a persuasive argument in support of that viewpoint.

You are going to start the process of writing a brief composition that you will finalize in the **Palabra escrita: A finalizar** section of your *Manual de actividades*. The topic of this composition is **¿Conectarse o no?** The purpose of your composition will be to tell the reader about Generation Z, the most "connected" generation in history, and then argue why it is, or why it could be, good or bad to have, expect, and maintain that level of connectedness to people, media, the Internet, music, news, entertainment, and so on.

**A. Lluvia de ideas.** En parejas, hagan una lluvia de ideas sobre estas preguntas.

1. ¿Quiénes pertenecen a la Generación Z?
2. ¿Qué significa «estar conectado/a»?
3. ¿Cuáles son o podrían ser las ventajas de estar conectado/a?
4. ¿Cuáles son o podrían ser los peligros y las desventajas de estar conectado/a?
5. ¿Cómo podría afectar al resto del mundo esa conectividad de la Generación Z? ¿Qué podría cambiar? (Piensen en la economía, las normas sociales, la salud y otros factores.)

**B. A organizar sus ideas.** Repase sus ideas, busque más información en el Internet sobre la Generación Z, escoja su argumento y organice todas sus ideas. Comparta su información con la clase y apunte otras ideas que se le ocurran durante el proceso.

**C. A escribir.** Ahora, haga el borrador de su composición con las ideas y la información que recopiló en las actividades A y B. ¡OJO! Guarde bien su trabajo. Va a necesitarlo otra vez para la sección de **Palabra escrita: A finalizar** en el *Manual de actividades*.

## Salvador Dalí

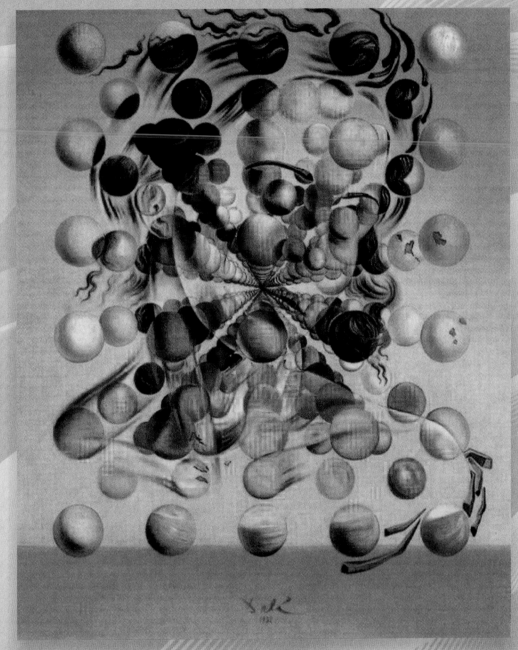

Galatea de las esferas, *1952*

El pintor y escultor español Salvador Dalí (1904–1989) es uno de los máximos representantes del surrealismo. Entre los amigos de su juventud se cuentan[a] el poeta y dramaturgo Federico García Lorca y el cineasta Luis Buñuel. Cuando Dalí se mudó a París, conoció también al pintor español Pablo Picasso y participó en el movimiento surrealista. La personalidad, el comportamiento y la apariencia de Dalí fueron tan famosos como sus obras, y eran otra proyección de su creatividad. Los meticulosos detalles de las obras de Dalí les dan a sus imágenes un ambiente fotográfico.

Una de sus musas favoritas fue su esposa Gala (Elena Ivanovna Diakonova, 1894–1982). Este retrato de ella, *Galatea de las esferas*, se forma a través de pequeñas esferas en un universo imaginado.

[a]se... *are included*

## Vocabulario del tema

### Los retos° de la vida moderna

*Challenges*

la salud

③

④ el dinero

⑤ el amor

⑥ el tiempo

la carrera

② el empleo

① la familia

⑦ la casa

casa en venta

⑧ la formación académica

| | |
|---|---|
| ahorrar dinero | to save money |
| buscar (qu) / encontrar (ue) empleo estable | to look for / to find stable employment |
| formar una familia | to start a family |
| formarse | to get educated |
| invertir (ie, i) en la bolsa | to invest in the stock market |
| manejar (bien/mal) el tiempo | to manage one's time (well/poorly) |
| mantener (*like* tener) una casa | to maintain a home |
| pagar (gu) las cuentas | to pay the bills |
| planear la jubilación | to plan one's retirement |
| tener (*irreg.*) una carrera | to have a career |

Repaso: casarse (con), cuidar (se), enamorarse (de)

## Las cuentas y los gastos°

Las... *Bills and Expenses*

| | |
|---|---|
| pagar (gu)... | to pay (the)... |
| el agua | water (bill) |
| el alquiler | rent |
| el cable | cable (bill) |
| el celular | cell phone (bill) |
| el coche | car (payment) |
| las cuentas médicas | medical bills |
| el Internet | Internet (bill) |
| el gas | (natural) gas (bill) |
| la hipoteca | mortgage |
| la luz | electric bill |
| la matrícula | tuition |
| el préstamo estudiantil | student loan |
| el satélite | satellite (bill) |
| el sistema de vigilancia | security system (bill) |
| el teléfono | telephone bill |
| la deuda | debt |
| el pago (anual, mensual, semanal) | (annual, monthly, weekly) payment |

## El bienestar físico y mental

Para quitarse el estrés...

1. Luis se estira y respira profundo.

2. Julia habla con una amiga íntima.

**3.** Penélope **medita** y **practica la aromaterapia.**

**4.** Alberto **hace de voluntario** con Hábitat para la Humanidad.

| | |
|---|---|
| emocionarse | to display emotion |
| expresarse | to express oneself |
| ser (*irreg.*) orgulloso/a | to be arrogant |
| sufrir de estrés | to suffer from stress |
| tenerle (*irreg.*) manía | to have it in (*for someone*) |
| el altruismo | unselfishness |
| la autoestima | self-esteem |
| el egoísmo | selfishness |
| la envidia | envy |
| el odio | hate |
| el orgullo | pride; arrogance |
| la presión | pressure |
| el ritmo de vida | pace of life |
| el sentimiento | feeling |
| altruista | unselfish |
| apasionado/a | passionate |
| egoísta | selfish |
| rencoroso/a | resentful |
| sentimental | sentimental; emotional |

**Cognados:** la ambición, la depresión, la pasión, el respeto, la terapia (de grupo); ambicioso/a, respetuoso/a
**Repaso:** hacer ejercicio, hacer (*irreg.*) yoga; el miedo

**ACTIVIDADES**

**A.** En haikú

**PASO 1.** Empareje cada haikú con la palabra correspondiente del dibujo en la página 490.

**1.** fuego de hogar (*hearth*)
abrigarse (*bundle up*) familiar
dulce descanso (*rest*)

**2.** peso pagado
honrar aves y héroes
quetzales colón

**3.** imaginado
calcular en fragmentos
vividas horas

**4.** profunda pasión
partir los corazones
emoción honda

**5.** buena o mala
respirar espiritual
corporal mental

**6.** lápiz y papel
escribir las palabras
sumar números

**PASO 2.** Escriba un haikú para describir otra palabra del **Vocabulario del tema.** Para escribir un haikú, siga lo siguiente: primera línea = cinco sílabas, segunda línea = siete sílabas, tercera línea = cinco sílabas. Comparta su haikú con la clase. Sus compañeros/as deben adivinar la palabra.

**B.** ¿**Lógico o ilógico?** Indique si las oraciones son lógicas (**L**) o ilógicas (**I**) y luego explique por qué.

|  | L | I |
|---|---|---|
| 1. Es peligroso ahorrar dinero para la formación académica de los hijos. | ☐ | ☐ |
| 2. Les recomiendo que formen una familia antes de graduarse. | ☐ | ☐ |
| 3. Cuando mis padres se pongan viejos, mi esposo y yo vamos a cuidarlos. | ☐ | ☐ |
| 4. Quiero encontrar empleo estable antes de tener hijos. | ☐ | ☐ |
| 5. Necesito planear mi jubilación antes de graduarme. | ☐ | ☐ |
| 6. No vamos a pagar las cuentas porque queremos invertir en la bolsa. | ☐ | ☐ |
| 7. Mi esposa y yo no tenemos hijos todavía porque nuestras carreras son muy exigentes. | ☐ | ☐ |
| 8. Nuestro gasto mensual más grande es la hipoteca. | ☐ | ☐ |
| 9. El sistema de vigilancia paga muchas de nuestras cuentas médicas. | ☐ | ☐ |
| 10. Después de graduarme, tengo que empezar a pagar mis préstamos estudiantiles. | ☐ | ☐ |

**C. Asociaciones**

**PASO 1.** Indique con qué asocia Ud. cada oración: la formación académica, la familia o la carrera. ¡**OJO!** Puede haber más de una respuesta. Luego, explique su respuesta.

1. mantener la casa
2. formarse
3. la jubilación
4. el empleo estable
5. manejar el tiempo

6. el sueldo
7. la matrícula
8. ahorrar dinero
9. pagar la hipoteca
10. la deuda

**PASO 2.** En parejas, comparen sus respuestas del **Paso 1.** Luego, formen oraciones con las expresiones.

Communication

**MODELO** mantener la casa → Mantenemos bien la casa por la familia porque es importante tener una casa tranquila y organizada.

**D. Definiciones.** Empareje las palabras con las definiciones correspondientes.

1. _____ valoración y aprecio de sí mismo
2. _____ sentimiento de aversión fuerte
3. _____ mover brazos y piernas para que no estén rígidos
4. _____ limpiar o dejar en blanco la mente
5. _____ una reunión para compartir problemas
6. _____ tensión, coerción que se siente
7. _____ tristeza profunda
8. _____ la emoción

a. la depresión
b. la terapia de grupo
c. la presión
d. la autoestima
e. el sentimiento
f. meditar
g. estirarse
h. el odio

**Communication**

**E. ¿Bueno o malo?**

**PASO 1.** En parejas, digan si estos conceptos son buenos o malos. **¡OJO!** Puede haber más de una respuesta, pero Uds. deben ponerse de acuerdo y explicar su opinión.

MODELO  el miedo → El miedo es malo porque es una emoción defensiva y negativa.

1. el orgullo
2. la ambición
3. el altruismo
4. la autoestima
5. la envidia
6. el odio
7. la pasión
8. la depresión
9. la presión
10. el egoísmo
11. emocionarse
12. tenerle manía a alguien
13. sufrir de estrés
14. meditar
15. estirarse

**PASO 2.** Ahora, escojan uno de los conceptos que dijeron que es malo y otro de los que dijeron que es bueno, y expliquen en qué situación o desde qué perspectiva pueden ser lo opuesto.

MODELO  el miedo → El miedo puede ser bueno en situaciones en que debemos tener más precaución para evitar algún peligro.

---

## Nota cultural

**Cultures**

### LAS YERBAS MEDICINALES

*En un mercado de Mendoza, Argentina*

Las plantas han sido usadas por el hombre desde los tiempos más remotos, tanto para alimentarse como para curarse. Las yerbas medicinales constituyen una fuente complementaria a la alimentación para mantener el buen funcionamiento del cuerpo y la buena salud. El uso de yerbas y otros remedios naturales tiene cada vez más aceptación en combinación con o en sustitución de la medicina occidental. La naturaleza ofrece medios para evitar y combatir enfermedades, siempre que se utilicen a tiempo y con sabiduría.

En Latinoamérica es muy típico el uso de las yerbas medicinales para aliviar malestares menores y estas plantas están disponibles en tiendas especializadas. Aquí tiene algunos remedios fáciles para malestares comunes.

Tomar infusiones de valeriana ayuda a dormir bien. La tila[a] y la melisa[b] son tranquilizantes naturales que pueden ayudar antes de un examen. Para los malestares del estómago o una digestión pesada: la manzanilla,[c] la menta[d] y el anís. El té de jengibre[e] alivia las náuseas. Si tiene dolor de cabeza, pruebe unas gotas de aceite de lavanda o de mejorana[f] sobre las sienes.[g] Para la resaca[h] tras una noche de fiesta, lo mejor es hervir hojas de ortiga[i] en agua durante cinco minutos, colar[j] el agua, añadir el jugo de un limón y tomarla en ayunas.[k]

[a]*linden flower*  [b]*lemon balm*  [c]*chamomile*  [d]*mint*  [e]*ginger*  [f]*sweet marjoram*  [g]*temples*  [h]*hangover*  [i]*stinging nettle*  [j]*strain off*
[k]*en... on an empty stomach*

**PREGUNTAS** En parejas, contesten las preguntas. Después, compartan sus ideas con la clase.

1. ¿Para qué sirven las yerbas medicinales?
2. ¿Qué malestares y remedios se citan como ejemplos? ¿Conocen Uds. alguna otra yerba con propiedades curativas?
3. ¿Han utilizado Uds. alguna vez yerbas medicinales para combatir algún malestar? ¿Cuál? ¿Se sintieron mejor después de tomar la yerba?
4. ¿Cuál es su opinión personal sobre el uso de las yerbas medicinales y otra medicina alternativa como la aromaterapia o la acupuntura? ¿Creen que son eficaces?

# Gramática

## 15.2 **Si** Clauses

### GRAMÁTICA EN CONTEXTO

#### Los programas de bienestar

Los programas para el bienestar de los empleados son cada vez más populares por todo el mundo. Los empleadores se han dado cuenta de que **si** les **ofrecen** programas de bienestar a sus empleados, la empresa **se beneficia** también.

En la mayoría de los países, **si** una compañía **ofrece** un programa de bienestar, **es** para aliviar el estrés en el empleado. La estrategia es esta: **si** los empleados **tuvieran** menos estrés, **se enfermarían** menos, **faltarían** menos días de trabajo y **serían** más productivos. Pero en los Estados Unidos y en Latinoamérica, **si** una empresa **tiene** un programa de bienestar, **es** para reducir los costos del seguro médico.

*Una empleada medita durante un descanso en el trabajo.*

**Comprensión.** Empareje las frases para formar oraciones lógicas.

1. Si siento mucho estrés _____
2. Si mi compañía ofreciera un programa de bienestar, _____

   a. habría menos absentismo.
   b. voy al gimnasio.

---

There are four possible situations involved with the use of **si.**

**A.** Present Habitual Situations: **Si** + *present* + *present*

To express what happens habitually if something else happens, both verbs are conjugated in the present tense.

> Si un amigo me deja un mensaje, lo llamo.
>
> *If a friend leaves me a message, I call him.*

**B.** Past Habitual Situations: **Si** + *imperfect* + *imperfect*

To express what used to happen habitually in the past if something else happened, both verbs are conjugated in the imperfect.

> Si un amigo me dejaba un mensaje, lo llamaba.
>
> *If a friend left me a message, I called him.*

**C.** Possible/Probable Situations: **Si** + *present* + *future*

To talk about possible or probable situations that may happen (in the future) if something else happens now, the verb in the **si** clause is conjugated in the present and the verb in the main clause is in some form of the future.

> Si tengo tiempo, voy a editar mi página de Facebook.
>
> *If I have time, I'm going to edit my Facebook page.*

---

GRAMÁTICA EN CONTEXTO *Wellness Programs / Wellness programs are increasingly popular throughout the world. Employers have realized that if they offer wellness programs to their employees, the company benefits, too. / In most countries, if a company offers a well-being program, it is to relieve employee stress. The strategy is this: if the employees were less stressed, they would get sick less, miss fewer days of work, and be more productive. But in the United States and Latin America, if a company provides a wellness program, it's to reduce health insurance costs.*

**D.** Present Hypothetical Situations: **Si** + *past subjunctive* + *conditional*

Present Hypothetical situations are expressed with the past subjunctive in the **si** clause and the conditional in the main clause. (See the **Nota comunicativa** on p. 467 to review the forms of the past subjunctive.)

Si **tuviera** tiempo, **editaría** mi          *If I had time, I would edit my*
    página de Facebook.              *Facebook page.*

## ACTIVIDADES

**A. En su niñez.** Complete las oraciones con la forma correcta del verbo entre paréntesis, según el contexto.

1. Cuando era niño, si yo no miraba *Plaza Sésamo* (Sesame Street) (**ponerse**) triste.
2. Mi abuelo y yo (**ir**) a comer un helado si él me visitaba los domingos.
3. Mis amigos (**dar**) fiestas de cumpleaños si sus mamás se lo permitían.
4. Si (*tú:* **jugar**) al escondite (*hide and seek*) con tus amigos, ¿dónde te escondías?
5. Si mis papás (**tener**) que trabajar, mis hermanos me cuidaban.
6. Mamá preparaba una cena especial si mis hermanos y yo (**sacar**) buenas notas.
7. Mi mamá me llevaba a la escuela si (**hacer**) mal tiempo.
8. Mi mamá no nos permitía ver la televisión si mis hermanos y yo (**pelearse**).

Communication

**B. Situaciones habituales.** En parejas, contesten las preguntas.

1. Si tienen tiempo libre después de las clases o después del trabajo, ¿qué hacen Uds.?
2. Cuando Uds. eran niños/as, ¿qué hacían si tenían tiempo libre después de la escuela?
3. Si Uds. necesitaban ayuda con su tarea cuando eran niños/as, ¿a quién se la pedían?
4. Hoy día, si su computadora o teléfono celular no funciona, ¿a quién le piden ayuda?
5. Si Uds. están muy frustrados/as con alguien, ¿cómo se expresan? ¿Qué le dicen?
6. Cuando eran niños/as, ¿cómo se expresaban si estaban enojados/as con alguien?
7. Si Uds. tienen mucho estrés, ¿cómo se relajan?
8. Cuando eran jóvenes, ¿cómo se relajaban Uds. si se sentían estresados/as?

**C. El fin de semana que viene.** Complete las oraciones con la forma correcta del verbo entre paréntesis, según el contexto.

1. El fin de semana que viene, voy a estudiar más si todavía no (**entender**) la lección.
2. ¿Vas a llamarme si (**salir**) a tomar un café? Me gustaría ir contigo.
3. Si ellos juegan a los videojuegos hoy, (**llamar**) a Mariana porque les encanta jugar con ella.
4. Vamos a grabar el programa de televisión si no (**poder**) estar en casa a esa hora.
5. Felipe va a comprar un televisor plasma de pantalla ancha si en la tienda (*ellos:* **tener**) todavía el modelo que le gusta.
6. Los Gómez pagarán su hipoteca este año si todo (**salir**) bien.
7. Si ellos nos invitan, nosotros (**hacer**) yoga por primera vez.

**D. Situaciones hipotéticas.** Complete las oraciones con la forma correcta del verbo entre paréntesis, según el contexto.

1. Yo pagaría la hipoteca si (**ganar**) la lotería.
2. Si mis papás tuvieran más dinero, (**invertir**) en la bolsa.
3. Martina haría de voluntaria si (**tener**) más tiempo.
4. Si tuviéramos un iPod, (**escuchar**) música todo el tiempo.
5. Si mi computadora (**fallar**) en este momento, estaría desesperado.

**E. Preguntas hipotéticas y probables.** En parejas, contesten las preguntas.

Communication

1. Si Uds. tienen tiempo, ¿qué van a hacer este fin de semana?
2. ¿Qué harían Uds. si tuvieran un millón de dólares?
3. ¿Qué harían Uds. si su computadora fallara mientras trabajaban en un proyecto importante?
4. Si Uds. no tienen que estudiar después de las clases hoy, ¿qué van a hacer?
5. Si un amigo íntimo / una amiga íntima les pidiera un préstamo (*loan*), ¿se lo darían? Expliquen.
6. ¿Qué van a hacer Uds. esta noche para relajarse si no tienen que hacer otra cosa?
7. Si Uds. compraran una computadora nueva, ¿qué características buscarían en ella? ¿Qué accesorios tendrían que tener?
8. ¿Dejarían Uds. un trabajo si no sintieran pasión por él, o seguirían aguantando la miseria? Expliquen.

**F. Mis raíces**

Cultures  Recycle

**PASO 1.** Complete el texto con la forma correcta del verbo entre paréntesis, según el contexto. Cuando hay dos verbos, escoja el verbo correcto y úsela en su forma apropiada.

JAIME: Cuando yo (*P/I:* **estar/ser**[1]) niño y (*yo:* **vivir**[2]) en Bolivia, siempre (*P/I:* **escuchar**[3]) la radio. Me (*P/I:* **encantar**[4]) toda clase de música: música andina, salsa, merengue, rock, boleros, y mucho más. Ponía un disco[a] si (*yo:* **escribir**[5]) la tarea y también si no (*yo:* **hacer**[6]) nada. Si de alguna manera (*yo:* **tener**[7]) un poco de dinero, siempre lo gastaba en discos. Para mí, la música (*P/I:* **estar/ser**[8]) una verdadera pasión.

Ahora, ya no (**estar/ser**[9]) en mi país sino en Japón por razones de trabajo. Aquí no (**tener**[10]) muchos amigos hispanos y extraño mucho mi cultura y mi país. Afortunadamente, la tecnología me (**ayudar**[11]) a mantenerme en contacto con mis raíces. Siempre leo un periódico boliviano en línea, antes del desayuno si (*yo:* **tener**[12]) tiempo, o por la tarde si no tengo tiempo. También (*yo:* **ver**[13]) la tele de mi país por el Internet si hay algo que me interesa.

Pero en mi opinión, lo mejor de todo es la música. Si (*yo:* **querer**[14]), puedo escuchar una de varias emisoras de radio en el Internet. Un día, escucho música andina si me (**interesar**[15]) y rock en español otro día si (*yo:* **tener**[16]) ganas. Además, un aficionado siempre (**poder**[17]) bajar música del Internet si le gusta mucho. Esta tarde, voy a bajar unas canciones nuevas si (*yo:* **terminar**[18]) temprano mi trabajo.

No sé qué haría si no (*yo:* **poder**[19]) leer o ver las noticias de mi país. Estoy seguro que (*yo:* **volverse**[20]) loco si no escuchara mi música todos los días. Además, me sentiría muy alejado de mis amigos que viven en Bolivia si no (*yo:* **saber**[21]) qué pasaba en mi país. Por eso, si cualquier inmigrante me (**preguntar**[22]) qué hacer para mantenerse en contacto con sus raíces, le diría que se aprovechara de la tecnología.

(Continúa.)

---
[a]*record*

**PASO 2.** Conteste las preguntas, según el **Paso 1.**

1. ¿Dónde vivía Jaime cuando era niño? ¿Cómo pasaba el tiempo? ¿Qué era lo que más le gustaba?
2. ¿Dónde vive Jaime ahora y por qué? ¿Cómo se siente en ese lugar?
3. ¿Cómo ayuda a Jaime la tecnología a mantenerse en contacto con su cultura y su país?
4. ¿Cómo ayuda a Jaime la tecnología a seguir cultivando su gran pasión por la música?
5. ¿Qué le diría Jaime a otro inmigrante si este le preguntara cómo mantenerse en contacto con su cultura y su país?

**PASO 3.** En parejas, contesten las preguntas.

1. Cuándo Uds. eran niños/as, ¿cómo pasaban su tiempo libre? ¿Qué pasatiempos eran verdaderas pasiones para Uds.?
2. Hoy día, si Uds. tienen tiempo libre, ¿cómo lo pasan? ¿Qué pasatiempos o actividades son pasiones para Uds.?
3. Si Uds. vivieran en otro país, ¿qué harían para mantenerse en contacto con su cultura y su propio país? ¿Qué aspectos de su cultura extrañarían más? Expliquen.
4. Si un(a) inmigrante le preguntara cómo conocer mejor la cultura de este país, ¿qué le dirían? Expliquen.

# Lectura cultural

Ud. va a leer un artículo de la revista *Nexos*, escrito por Julio César Rivas y publicado por la American Airlines, sobre el impacto que las redes (*networks*) sociales han tenido en la sociedad de hoy.

## ANTES DE LEER

**A. A primera vista.** Lea el título y las primeras líneas *en letra cursiva*. Luego en parejas, contesten las preguntas.

1. ¿Qué redes sociales conocen Uds.? ¿Cuáles son las redes sociales más populares entre Uds. y sus amigos?
2. ¿Qué tipos de servicios ofrecen estas redes? ¿Ofrecen todas los mismos servicios o cada una se especializa en un servicio específico? Expliquen.

**B. Vocabulario nuevo.** Empareje las palabras de la columna A con su significado correspondiente de la columna B.

| A | B |
|---|---|
| 1. _____ se dirigió | a. diseminar (información) |
| 2. _____ musulmana | b. exposición oral |
| 3. _____ afición | c. habló |
| 4. _____ usuarios | d. sigue la religión de Mahoma |
| 5. _____ discurso | e. personas que utilizan algún servicio |
| 6. _____ difundir | f. pasatiempo |

You already know that the past subjunctive is formed by taking the third person plural (**ellos/as**) form of the preterite, removing the **-ron** ending, and adding the endings **-ra, -ras, -ra, -ramos, -rais,** and **-ran.** However, there's another past subjective that you will see in the following reading. It's formed by following the same process but with the endings: **-se, -ses, -se, -semos, -seis,** and **-sen.**

| | |
|---|---|
| Me sorprendió que me **llamase** después de tanto tiempo. | *It surprised me that he would call after so much time.* |
| Querían que **fuésemos** a la fiesta, pero no fue posible. | *They wanted us to go to the party, but it wasn't possible.* |
| Si **tuviese** tiempo, descansaría un rato. | *If I had time, I'd relax a bit.* |

# El ABC de las redes sociales

*¿Cuánto tiempo pasa Ud. a diario en las redes sociales?*

*Cuando el presidente estadounidense Barack Obama se dirigió a la comunidad musulmana el pasado mes de junio con su histórico discurso en El Cairo, la capital egipcia, el dirigente norteamericano no se limitó a esperar a que las cadenas de televisión y los medios de comunicación de todo el mundo difundiesen su mensaje.*

*Al mismo tiempo que la imagen de Obama era contemplada por centenares[a] de millones de personas en todo el mundo, el gobierno* estadounidense lanzó una ofensiva en las llamadas «redes sociales» de Internet. Twitter, Facebook y YouTube fueron las herramientas elegidas por el gobierno más poderoso del mundo para que su mensaje llegase a todos los rincones[b] del planeta de la forma más efectiva posible.

Lo sucedido[c] el pasado 4 de junio es el perfecto ejemplo del poder que han adquirido en escaso tiempo las «redes sociales» de Internet. Su crecimiento ha sido tan rápido que hace sólo seis años Facebook, quizás la red social más conocida hoy en día, no existía. Y Twitter, el otro nombre que ahora domina la escena, fue creado sólo en el 2006. Se puede decir que el origen de las redes sociales en Internet comenzó con los Chat Rooms y los Bulletin Boards.

Una red social es un grupo de individuos conectados por Internet para compartir alguna afición, o comunicar información, que establecen múltiples conexiones con otros usuarios. La amplia utilización cotidiana de ordenadores e Intertnet ha hecho posible que estas redes sociales acumulasen la suficiente masa crítica como para crear un movimiento imparable. Pero la popularidad de los teléfonos móviles y el cada vez mayor número de estos aparatos que disponen de Internet, cámaras fotográficas y de vídeo y aplicaciones para colgar[d] texto, imagen y sonido en Internet, ha cimentado la dependencia de las redes sociales.

---

[a]*hundreds*  [b]*parts* (lit. *corners*)  [c]*Lo... What happened*  [d]*post*

Según un reciente estudio de la empresa Nielsen Online, los usuarios de Internet pasaron ¡14.000 millones de minutos en Facebook en abril del 2009. ¡14.000 millones de minutos! ¡El equivalente a 26.636 años!

La principal razón que justifica estas asombrosas cifras es que para jóvenes de 12 a 17 años, Facebook es una herramienta indispensable para sus relaciones sociales. A través de Facebook comparten pensamientos, actividades, fotografías, experiencias, buscan almas gemelas[e] y exploran relaciones. Los adultos y el sector empresarial, han aprendido el potencial de Facebook y sitios similares, y han empezado a utilizarlos de forma masiva.

Mientras, MySpace (que fue creada en el 2003 e inició la moda entre los jóvenes norteamericanos) ha perdido terreno. En abril del 2009, los usuarios sólo pasaron 7.200 millones de minutos (según la misma encuesta de Nielsen Online) en MySpace, un 31 por ciento menos que hace un año.

Pero MySpace se está convirtiendo en el rey del vídeo. Los usuarios de MySpace miraron a través del sitio más de 120 millones de emisiones de vídeo en abril y pasaron más de 384 millones de minutos mirándolas. En comparación, los números de Facebook se limitaron a 41,5 millones de transmisiones y 113 millones de minutos viendo clips.

Lo que estas cifras encierran[f] es otra de las características, quizás la más cruel, de los «nuevos medios»: su precariedad. Como explicó el vicepresidente para medios de Nielsen Online, Jon Gibs, «lo más claro sobre redes sociales es que no importa lo rápido que un sitio crezca o lo grande que sea, lo cierto es que pueden caer en el olvido rápidamente».

Ese es el caso de Friendster, un sitio similar a Facebook o MySpace que empezó con fuerza antes que estos dos pero que ahora ha sido superado por ellos, al menos entre los usuarios norteamericanos y europeos. MySpace es también un buen ejemplo de la fragilidad del éxito ya que hasta hace poco menos de dos años, era el líder indiscutible del sector.

Quizás la otra característica de las redes sociales es su especialización. Facebook, MySpace y Friendster son ideales para comunicarse con amistades o conocidos. Twitter se ha convertido en la herramienta perfecta para la inmediatez y los usuarios de teléfonos móviles. LinkedIn está orientado a los negocios y a profesionales que quieren ampliar sus oportunidades laborales. Para aquellos que quieren compartir fotografías, Flickr es una obligación. Y para los que prefieren el vídeo como forma de comunicación, YouTube.

Pero cualquiera que sea[g] la forma o contenido que adapten, los expertos consideran que las redes sociales serán claves para el futuro, tanto económicamente para el sector privado como socialmente para los individuos.

---

[e]almas... *soul mates*  [f]*include, imply*  [g]cualquiera... *no matter what may be*

## DESPUÉS DE LEER

**A. Comprensión.** En parejas, contesten las preguntas, según el artículo. Después, compartan sus respuestas con la clase.

1. ¿Cuál fue el origen de las redes sociales? ¿Qué aparato ha sido fundamental en el éxito de las redes sociales? ¿Por qué?
2. ¿Qué red social era la más popular o usada en el 2009? ¿Qué datos del texto lo indican?
3. ¿Qué red social perdió popularidad entre los usuarios en ese mismo año? ¿Se perdió completamente o lo reutilizaron para otros servicios? Expliquen.
4. ¿Cuáles son dos características de estos medios de información y comunicación? Expliquen.
5. ¿Qué contribuciones aportan estas redes a la sociedad?

**B. Temas de discusión.** En grupos pequeños, comenten estos temas. Después, compartan sus ideas con la clase.

1. ¿Qué prefieren Uds. para comunicarse con sus familiares o amigos, el teléfono celular, el e-mail, una red social u otro medio de comunicación? ¿Usan el mismo medio de comunicación para todas las ocasiones? ¿O varía el medio de comunicación según la persona con quien se comunican? Expliquen.

2. Comenten las opiniones de Verónica y Alberto. ¿Con quién están de acuerdo? Expliquen.

VERÓNICA: A mí me encantan las redes sociales. Me permiten mantener el contacto con todos mis amigos y familiares y realmente me siento más conectada con ellos. Podemos comunicarnos de relámpago[a] y organizar alguna fiesta u otro evento en pocos minutos.

ALBERTO: Odio[b] las redes sociales, los celulares, el SMS y todas esas cosas. Sí, es más fácil comunicarse a través de esos avances tecnológicos, pero ¿vale la pena? Quiero decir, ¿qué perdemos a cambio de[c] la rapidez? ¿Es auténtica la comunicación de relámpago? ¿Cuántos malentendidos[d] ha habido gracias a esta comunicación rápida? Prefiero *hablar* con mis amigos y familiares por teléfono, o mejor, cara a cara. La comunicación de este tipo, para mí, es real. Puedo ver a la persona con quien hablo. Puedo ver su sonrisa o si está deprimida. O sea, siento una mejor conexión con él/ella.

---

[a]de... *in a flash*   [b]*I hate*   [c]a... *in exchange for*   [d]*misunderstandings*

## Los avances tecnológicos

| | |
|---|---|
| buscar (qu) novio/a por el Internet | Internet dating |
| hacer (irreg.) las compras por el Internet | Internet shopping |
| manejar las cuentas por el Internet | Internet banking |
| la agenda electrónica | PDA |
| los alimentos transgénicos | genetically modified foods |
| el auricular bluetooth | Bluetooth earphone |
| la clonación | cloning |
| la fibra óptica | fiber optics |
| la radio por satélite | satellite radio |
| la televisión de alta definición | HD TV |
| la televisión de pantalla ancha | wide-screen TV |

Cognados: comprar entradas de cine por el Internet; la cámara digital, el láser; acelerado/a, cibernético/a el (teléfono) celular cell (phone)
Repaso: leer (y) el e-mail, llamar por el celular, mandar un e-mail; el carro/coche eléctrico/híbrido, la página Web

## La computadora

| | |
|---|---|
| almacenar | to backup |
| adjuntar | to attach |
| borrar | to delete |
| digitalizar (c) | to digitize |
| escanear | to scan |
| fallar | to crash |
| guardar (como) | to save (as) |
| imprimir | to print |
| los altavoces | speakers |
| el archivo | file |
| la conexión (WiFi) | (WiFi) connection |
| el (documento) adjunto | attachment |
| el escáner | scanner |
| la impresora | printer |
| el lápiz de memoria | flash drive |
| el módem | modem |
| la pantalla | (monitor) screen |
| el ratón | mouse |
| el teclado | keyboard |
| inalámbrico/a | wireless |

Cognados: el CD-ROM, el DVD-ROM, el router
Repaso: abrir, bajar, cerrar (ie), mandar, recibir, subir; la computadora portátil, el disco duro

## Los medios de comunicación — Mass Media

| | |
|---|---|
| enterarse (de) | to find out, learn (about) |
| estar (irreg.) al día | to be up to date |
| las noticias | news |
| el noticiero | news report |
| el periódico (en línea) | (online) newspaper |
| la prensa | the press |
| la revista (en línea) | (online) magazine |

Cognados: informar

## Los retos de la vida moderna — Challenges of Modern Life

| | |
|---|---|
| ahorrar dinero | to save money |
| buscar (qu) / encontrar (ue) empleo estable | to look for / find stable employment |
| formar una famila | to start a family |
| formarse | to get educated |
| invertir (ie, i) en la bolsa | to invest in the stock market |
| manejar (bien/mal) el tiempo | to manage one's time (well/poorly) |
| mantener (like tener) una casa | to maintain a home |
| pagar (gu) las cuentas | to pay the bills |
| planear la jubilación | to plan one's retirement |
| tener (irreg.) una carrera | to have a career |
| la carrera | career |
| la formación académica | education |

Repaso: casarse (con), cuidar (se), enamorarse (de); el amor, la casa, el dinero, el empleo, la familia, la salud, los hijos, el tiempo

## Las cuentas y los gastos — Bills and Expenses

| | |
|---|---|
| pagar (gu)... | to pay (the) . . . |
| el agua | water (bill) |
| el alquiler | rent |
| el cable | cable (bill) |
| el celular | cell phone (bill) |
| el coche | car (payment) |
| las cuentas médicas | medical bills |
| el Internet | Internet bill |
| el gas | (natural) gas (bill) |
| la hipoteca | mortgage |
| la luz | electric bill |
| la matrícula | tuition |
| el préstamo estudiantil | student loan |
| el satélite | satellite (bill) |
| el sistema de vigilancia | security system (bill) |
| el teléfono | telephone bill |
| la deuda | debt |
| el pago (anual, mensual, semanal) | (annual, monthly, weekly) payment |

## El bienestar físico y mental — Physical and Mental Well-Being

| | |
|---|---|
| emocionarse | to display emotion |
| estirarse | to stretch |
| expresarse | to express oneself |
| hacer (irreg.) de voluntario/a | to volunteer |
| quitarse el estrés | to remove stress |
| respirar profundo | to breathe deeply |
| ser (irreg.) orgulloso/a | to be arrogant |

| | |
|---|---|
| **sufrir de estrés** | to suffer from stress |
| **tenerle** (*irreg.*) **manía** | to have it in (*for someone*) |
| **el/la amigo/a íntimo/a** | close friend |
| **el altruismo** | unselfishness |
| **la autoestima** | self-esteem |
| **el egoísmo** | selfishness |
| **la envidia** | envy |
| **el odio** | hate |
| **el orgullo** | pride; arrogance |
| **la presión** | pressure |
| **el ritmo de vida** | pace of life |
| **el sentimiento** | feeling |

| | |
|---|---|
| **altruista** | unselfish |
| **apasionado/a** | passionate |
| **egoísta** | selfish |
| **rencoroso/a** | resentful |
| **sentimental** | emotional |

**Cognados: meditar, practicar (qu) la aromaterapia; la ambición, la depresión, la pasión, el respeto, la terapia (de grupo); ambicioso/a, respetuoso/a**
**Repaso: hacer ejercicio, hacer (*irreg.*) yoga; el miedo**

## C. Irregular Verbs

| INFINITIVE PRESENT PARTICIPLE PAST PARTICIPLE | INDICATIVE PRESENT | IMPERFECT | PRETERITE | FUTURE | CONDITIONAL | SUBJUNCTIVE PRESENT | PAST | IMPERATIVE |
|---|---|---|---|---|---|---|---|---|
| andar andando andado | ando andas anda andamos andáis andan | andaba andabas andaba andábamos andabais andaban | anduve anduviste anduvo anduvimos anduvisteis anduvieron | andaré andarás andará andaremos andaréis andarán | andaría andarías andaría andaríamos andaríais andarían | ande andes ande andemos andéis anden | anduviera anduvieras anduviera anduviéramos anduvierais anduvieran | anda / no andes ande andemos andad / no andéis anden |
| caber cabiendo cabido | quepo cabes cabe cabemos cabéis caben | cabía cabías cabía cabíamos cabíais cabían | cupe cupiste cupo cupimos cupisteis cupieron | cabré cabrás cabrá cabremos cabréis cabrán | cabría cabrías cabría cabríamos cabríais cabrían | quepa quepas quepa quepamos quepáis quepan | cupiera cupieras cupiera cupiéramos cupierais cupieran | cabe / no quepas quepa quepamos cabed / no quepáis quepan |
| caer cayendo caído | caigo caes cae caemos caéis caen | caía caías caía caíamos caíais caían | caí caíste cayó caímos caísteis cayeron | caeré caerás caerá caeremos caeréis caerán | caería caerías caería caeríamos caeríais caerían | caiga caigas caiga caigamos caigáis caigan | cayera cayeras cayera cayéramos cayerais cayeran | cae / no caigas caiga caigamos caed / no caigáis caigan |
| dar dando dado | doy das da damos dais dan | daba dabas daba dábamos dabais daban | di diste dio dimos disteis dieron | daré darás dará daremos daréis darán | daría darías daría daríamos daríais darían | dé des dé demos deis den | diera dieras diera diéramos dierais dieran | da / no des dé demos dad / no deis den |
| decir diciendo dicho | digo dices dice decimos decís dicen | decía decías decía decíamos decíais decían | dije dijiste dijo dijimos dijisteis dijeron | diré dirás dirá diremos diréis dirán | diría dirías diría diríamos diríais dirían | diga digas diga digamos digáis digan | dijera dijeras dijera dijéramos dijerais dijeran | di / no digas diga digamos decid / no digáis digan |
| estar estando estado | estoy estás está estamos estáis están | estaba estabas estaba estábamos estabais estaban | estuve estuviste estuvo estuvimos estuvisteis estuvieron | estaré estarás estará estaremos estaréis estarán | estaría estarías estaría estaríamos estaríais estarían | esté estés esté estemos estéis estén | estuviera estuvieras estuviera estuviéramos estuvierais estuvieran | está / no estés esté estemos estad / no estéis estén |
| haber habiendo habido | he has ha hemos habéis han | había habías había habíamos habíais habían | hube hubiste hubo hubimos hubisteis hubieron | habré habrás habrá habremos habréis habrán | habría habrías habría habríamos habríais habrían | haya hayas haya hayamos hayáis hayan | hubiera hubieras hubiera hubiéramos hubierais hubieran | |

Verb Charts

# Verb Charts

## A. Regular Verbs: Simple Tenses

| INFINITIVE / PRESENT PARTICIPLE / PAST PARTICIPLE | INDICATIVE | | | | | SUBJUNCTIVE | | IMPERATIVE |
|---|---|---|---|---|---|---|---|---|
| | PRESENT | IMPERFECT | PRETERITE | FUTURE | CONDITIONAL | PRESENT | PAST | |
| hablar<br>hablando<br>hablado | hablo<br>hablas<br>habla<br>hablamos<br>habláis<br>hablan | hablaba<br>hablabas<br>hablaba<br>hablábamos<br>hablabais<br>hablaban | hablé<br>hablaste<br>habló<br>hablamos<br>hablasteis<br>hablaron | hablaré<br>hablarás<br>hablará<br>hablaremos<br>hablaréis<br>hablarán | hablaría<br>hablarías<br>hablaría<br>hablaríamos<br>hablaríais<br>hablarían | hable<br>hables<br>hable<br>hablemos<br>habléis<br>hablen | hablara<br>hablaras<br>hablara<br>habláramos<br>hablarais<br>hablaran | habla / no hables<br>hable<br>hablemos<br>hablad / no habléis<br>hablen |
| comer<br>comiendo<br>comido | como<br>comes<br>come<br>comemos<br>coméis<br>comen | comía<br>comías<br>comía<br>comíamos<br>comíais<br>comían | comí<br>comiste<br>comió<br>comimos<br>comisteis<br>comieron | comeré<br>comerás<br>comerá<br>comeremos<br>comeréis<br>comerán | comería<br>comerías<br>comería<br>comeríamos<br>comeríais<br>comerían | coma<br>comas<br>coma<br>comamos<br>comáis<br>coman | comiera<br>comieras<br>comiera<br>comiéramos<br>comierais<br>comieran | come / no comas<br>coma<br>comamos<br>comed / no comáis<br>coman |
| vivir<br>viviendo<br>vivido | vivo<br>vives<br>vive<br>vivimos<br>vivís<br>viven | vivía<br>vivías<br>vivía<br>vivíamos<br>vivíais<br>vivían | viví<br>viviste<br>vivió<br>vivimos<br>vivisteis<br>vivieron | viviré<br>vivirás<br>vivirá<br>viviremos<br>viviréis<br>vivirán | viviría<br>vivirías<br>viviría<br>viviríamos<br>viviríais<br>vivirían | viva<br>vivas<br>viva<br>vivamos<br>viváis<br>vivan | viviera<br>vivieras<br>viviera<br>viviéramos<br>vivierais<br>vivieran | vive / no vivas<br>viva<br>vivamos<br>vivid / no viváis<br>vivan |

## B. Regular Verbs: Perfect Tenses

| INDICATIVE | | | | | | | | | | SUBJUNCTIVE | | | |
|---|---|---|---|---|---|---|---|---|---|---|---|---|---|
| PRESENT PERFECT | | PLUPERFECT | | PRETERITE PERFECT | | FUTURE PERFECT | | CONDITIONAL PERFECT | | PRESENT PERFECT | | PLUPERFECT | |
| he<br>has<br>ha<br>hemos<br>habéis<br>han | hablado<br>comido<br>vivido | había<br>habías<br>había<br>habíamos<br>habíais<br>habían | hablado<br>comido<br>vivido | hube<br>hubiste<br>hubo<br>hubimos<br>hubisteis<br>hubieron | hablado<br>comido<br>vivido | habré<br>habrás<br>habrá<br>habremos<br>habréis<br>habrán | hablado<br>comido<br>vivido | habría<br>habrías<br>habría<br>habríamos<br>habríais<br>habrían | hablado<br>comido<br>vivido | haya<br>hayas<br>haya<br>hayamos<br>hayáis<br>hayan | hablado<br>comido<br>vivido | hubiera<br>hubieras<br>hubiera<br>hubiéramos<br>hubierais<br>hubieran | hablado<br>comido<br>vivido |

## C. Irregular Verbs (continued)

| INFINITIVE / PRESENT PARTICIPLE / PAST PARTICIPLE | INDICATIVE | | | | | SUBJUNCTIVE | | IMPERATIVE |
| --- | --- | --- | --- | --- | --- | --- | --- | --- |
| | PRESENT | IMPERFECT | PRETERITE | FUTURE | CONDITIONAL | PRESENT | PAST | |
| hacer<br>haciendo<br>hecho | hago<br>haces<br>hace<br>hacemos<br>hacéis<br>hacen | hacía<br>hacías<br>hacía<br>hacíamos<br>hacíais<br>hacían | hice<br>hiciste<br>hizo<br>hicimos<br>hicisteis<br>hicieron | haré<br>harás<br>hará<br>haremos<br>haréis<br>harán | haría<br>harías<br>haría<br>haríamos<br>haríais<br>harían | haga<br>hagas<br>haga<br>hagamos<br>hagáis<br>hagan | hiciera<br>hicieras<br>hiciera<br>hiciéramos<br>hicierais<br>hicieran | haz / no hagas<br>haga<br>hagamos<br>haced / no hagáis<br>hagan |
| ir<br>yendo<br>ido | voy<br>vas<br>va<br>vamos<br>vais<br>van | iba<br>ibas<br>iba<br>íbamos<br>ibais<br>iban | fui<br>fuiste<br>fue<br>fuimos<br>fuisteis<br>fueron | iré<br>irás<br>irá<br>iremos<br>iréis<br>irán | iría<br>irías<br>iría<br>iríamos<br>iríais<br>irían | vaya<br>vayas<br>vaya<br>vayamos<br>vayáis<br>vayan | fuera<br>fueras<br>fuera<br>fuéramos<br>fuerais<br>fueran | ve / no vayas<br>vaya<br>vayamos<br>id / no vayáis<br>vayan |
| oír<br>oyendo<br>oído | oigo<br>oyes<br>oye<br>oímos<br>oís<br>oyen | oía<br>oías<br>oía<br>oíamos<br>oíais<br>oían | oí<br>oíste<br>oyó<br>oímos<br>oísteis<br>oyeron | oiré<br>oirás<br>oirá<br>oiremos<br>oiréis<br>oirán | oiría<br>oirías<br>oiría<br>oiríamos<br>oiríais<br>oirían | oiga<br>oigas<br>oiga<br>oigamos<br>oigáis<br>oigan | oyera<br>oyeras<br>oyera<br>oyéramos<br>oyerais<br>oyeran | oye / no oigas<br>oiga<br>oigamos<br>oíd / no oigáis<br>oigan |
| poder<br>pudiendo<br>podido | puedo<br>puedes<br>puede<br>podemos<br>podéis<br>pueden | podía<br>podías<br>podía<br>podíamos<br>podíais<br>podían | pude<br>pudiste<br>pudo<br>pudimos<br>pudisteis<br>pudieron | podré<br>podrás<br>podrá<br>podremos<br>podréis<br>podrán | podría<br>podrías<br>podría<br>podríamos<br>podríais<br>podrían | pueda<br>puedas<br>pueda<br>podamos<br>podáis<br>puedan | pudiera<br>pudieras<br>pudiera<br>pudiéramos<br>pudierais<br>pudieran | |
| poner<br>poniendo<br>puesto | pongo<br>pones<br>pone<br>ponemos<br>ponéis<br>ponen | ponía<br>ponías<br>ponía<br>poníamos<br>poníais<br>ponían | puse<br>pusiste<br>puso<br>pusimos<br>pusisteis<br>pusieron | pondré<br>pondrás<br>pondrá<br>pondremos<br>pondréis<br>pondrán | pondría<br>pondrías<br>pondría<br>pondríamos<br>pondríais<br>pondrían | ponga<br>pongas<br>ponga<br>pongamos<br>pongáis<br>pongan | pusiera<br>pusieras<br>pusiera<br>pusiéramos<br>pusierais<br>pusieran | pon / no pongas<br>ponga<br>pongamos<br>poned / no pongáis<br>pongan |
| predecir<br>prediciendo<br>predicho | predigo<br>predices<br>predice<br>predecimos<br>predecís<br>predicen | predecía<br>predecías<br>predecía<br>predecíamos<br>predecíais<br>predecían | predije<br>predijiste<br>predijo<br>predijimos<br>predijisteis<br>predijeron | predeciré<br>predecirás<br>predecirá<br>predeciremos<br>predeciréis<br>predecirán | predeciría<br>predecirías<br>predeciría<br>predeciríamos<br>predeciríais<br>predecirían | prediga<br>predigas<br>prediga<br>predigamos<br>predigáis<br>predigan | predijera<br>predijeras<br>predijera<br>predijéramos<br>predijerais<br>predijeran | predice / no predigas<br>prediga<br>predigamos<br>predecid / no predigáis<br>predigan |
| querer<br>queriendo<br>querido | quiero<br>quieres<br>quiere<br>queremos<br>queréis<br>quieren | quería<br>querías<br>quería<br>queríamos<br>queríais<br>querían | quise<br>quisiste<br>quiso<br>quisimos<br>quisisteis<br>quisieron | querré<br>querrás<br>querrá<br>querremos<br>querréis<br>querrán | querría<br>querrías<br>querría<br>querríamos<br>querríais<br>querrían | quiera<br>quieras<br>quiera<br>queramos<br>queráis<br>quieran | quisiera<br>quisieras<br>quisiera<br>quisiéramos<br>quisierais<br>quisieran | quiere / no quieras<br>quiera<br>queramos<br>quered / no queráis<br>quieran |

# C. Irregular Verbs (continued)

**INFINITIVE / PRESENT PARTICIPLE / PAST PARTICIPLE**

### saber / sabiendo / sabido

| | PRESENT | IMPERFECT | PRETERITE | FUTURE | CONDITIONAL | SUBJ. PRESENT | SUBJ. PAST | IMPERATIVE |
|---|---|---|---|---|---|---|---|---|
| | sé | sabía | supe | sabré | sabría | sepa | supiera | |
| | sabes | sabías | supiste | sabrás | sabrías | sepas | supieras | sabe / no sepas |
| | sabe | sabía | supo | sabrá | sabría | sepa | supiera | sepa |
| | sabemos | sabíamos | supimos | sabremos | sabríamos | sepamos | supiéramos | sepamos |
| | sabéis | sabíais | supisteis | sabréis | sabríais | sepáis | supierais | sabed / no sepáis |
| | saben | sabían | supieron | sabrán | sabrían | sepan | supieran | sepan |

### salir / saliendo / salido

| | PRESENT | IMPERFECT | PRETERITE | FUTURE | CONDITIONAL | SUBJ. PRESENT | SUBJ. PAST | IMPERATIVE |
|---|---|---|---|---|---|---|---|---|
| | salgo | salía | salí | saldré | saldría | salga | saliera | |
| | sales | salías | saliste | saldrás | saldrías | salgas | salieras | sal / no salgas |
| | sale | salía | salió | saldrá | saldría | salga | saliera | salga |
| | salimos | salíamos | salimos | saldremos | saldríamos | salgamos | saliéramos | salgamos |
| | salís | salíais | salisteis | saldréis | saldríais | salgáis | salierais | salid / no salgáis |
| | salen | salían | salieron | saldrán | saldrían | salgan | salieran | salgan |

### ser / siendo / sido

| | PRESENT | IMPERFECT | PRETERITE | FUTURE | CONDITIONAL | SUBJ. PRESENT | SUBJ. PAST | IMPERATIVE |
|---|---|---|---|---|---|---|---|---|
| | soy | era | fui | seré | sería | sea | fuera | |
| | eres | eras | fuiste | serás | serías | seas | fueras | sé / no seas |
| | es | era | fue | será | sería | sea | fuera | sea |
| | somos | éramos | fuimos | seremos | seríamos | seamos | fuéramos | seamos |
| | sois | erais | fuisteis | seréis | seríais | seáis | fuerais | sed / no seáis |
| | son | eran | fueron | serán | serían | sean | fueran | sean |

### tener / teniendo / tenido

| | PRESENT | IMPERFECT | PRETERITE | FUTURE | CONDITIONAL | SUBJ. PRESENT | SUBJ. PAST | IMPERATIVE |
|---|---|---|---|---|---|---|---|---|
| | tengo | tenía | tuve | tendré | tendría | tenga | tuviera | |
| | tienes | tenías | tuviste | tendrás | tendrías | tengas | tuvieras | ten / no tengas |
| | tiene | tenía | tuvo | tendrá | tendría | tenga | tuviera | tenga |
| | tenemos | teníamos | tuvimos | tendremos | tendríamos | tengamos | tuviéramos | tengamos |
| | tenéis | teníais | tuvisteis | tendréis | tendríais | tengáis | tuvierais | tened / no tengáis |
| | tienen | tenían | tuvieron | tendrán | tendrían | tengan | tuvieran | tengan |

### traer / trayendo / traído

| | PRESENT | IMPERFECT | PRETERITE | FUTURE | CONDITIONAL | SUBJ. PRESENT | SUBJ. PAST | IMPERATIVE |
|---|---|---|---|---|---|---|---|---|
| | traigo | traía | traje | traeré | traería | traiga | trajera | |
| | traes | traías | trajiste | traerás | traerías | traigas | trajeras | trae / no traigas |
| | trae | traía | trajo | traerá | traería | traiga | trajera | traiga |
| | traemos | traíamos | trajimos | traeremos | traeríamos | traigamos | trajéramos | traigamos |
| | traéis | traíais | trajisteis | traeréis | traeríais | traigáis | trajerais | traed / no traigáis |
| | traen | traían | trajeron | traerán | traerían | traigan | trajeran | traigan |

### valer / valiendo / valido

| | PRESENT | IMPERFECT | PRETERITE | FUTURE | CONDITIONAL | SUBJ. PRESENT | SUBJ. PAST | IMPERATIVE |
|---|---|---|---|---|---|---|---|---|
| | valgo | valía | valí | valdré | valdría | valga | valiera | |
| | vales | valías | valiste | valdrás | valdrías | valgas | valieras | vale / no valgas |
| | vale | valía | valió | valdrá | valdría | valga | valiera | valga |
| | valemos | valíamos | valimos | valdremos | valdríamos | valgamos | valiéramos | valgamos |
| | valéis | valíais | valisteis | valdréis | valdríais | valgáis | valierais | valed / no valgáis |
| | valen | valían | valieron | valdrán | valdrían | valgan | valieran | valgan |

### venir / viniendo / venido

| | PRESENT | IMPERFECT | PRETERITE | FUTURE | CONDITIONAL | SUBJ. PRESENT | SUBJ. PAST | IMPERATIVE |
|---|---|---|---|---|---|---|---|---|
| | vengo | venía | vine | vendré | vendría | venga | viniera | |
| | vienes | venías | viniste | vendrás | vendrías | vengas | vinieras | ven / no vengas |
| | viene | venía | vino | vendrá | vendría | venga | viniera | venga |
| | venimos | veníamos | vinimos | vendremos | vendríamos | vengamos | viniéramos | vengamos |
| | venís | veníais | vinisteis | vendréis | vendríais | vengáis | vinierais | venid / no vengáis |
| | vienen | venían | vinieron | vendrán | vendrían | vengan | vinieran | vengan |

# Verb Charts

## C. Irregular Verbs (continued)

| INFINITIVE / PRESENT PARTICIPLE / PAST PARTICIPLE | INDICATIVE | | | | | SUBJUNCTIVE | | IMPERATIVE |
|---|---|---|---|---|---|---|---|---|
| | PRESENT | IMPERFECT | PRETERITE | FUTURE | CONDITIONAL | PRESENT | PAST | |
| ver | veo | veía | vi | veré | vería | vea | viera | ve / no veas |
| viendo | ves | veías | viste | verás | verías | veas | vieras | vea |
| visto | ve | veía | vio | verá | vería | vea | viera | veamos |
| | vemos | veíamos | vimos | veremos | veríamos | veamos | viéramos | ved / no veáis |
| | veis | veíais | visteis | veréis | veríais | veáis | vierais | vean |
| | ven | veían | vieron | verán | verían | vean | vieran | |

## D. Stem Changing and Spelling Change Verbs

| INFINITIVE / PRESENT PARTICIPLE / PAST PARTICIPLE | INDICATIVE | | | | | SUBJUNCTIVE | | IMPERATIVE |
|---|---|---|---|---|---|---|---|---|
| | PRESENT | IMPERFECT | PRETERITE | FUTURE | CONDITIONAL | PRESENT | PAST | |
| construir (y) | construyo | construía | construí | construiré | construiría | construya | construyera | construye / no construyas |
| construyendo | construyes | construías | construiste | construirás | construirías | construyas | construyeras | construya |
| construido | construye | construía | construyó | construirá | construiría | construya | construyera | construyamos |
| | construimos | construíamos | construimos | construiremos | construiríamos | construyamos | construyéramos | construid / no construyáis |
| | construís | construíais | construisteis | construiréis | construiríais | construyáis | construyerais | construyan |
| | construyen | construían | construyeron | construirán | construirían | construyan | construyeran | |
| creer (y [3rd-pers. pret.]) | creo | creía | creí | creeré | creería | crea | creyera | cree / no creas |
| creyendo | crees | creías | creíste | creerás | creerías | creas | creyeras | crea |
| creído | cree | creía | creyó | creerá | creería | crea | creyera | creamos |
| | creemos | creíamos | creímos | creeremos | creeríamos | creamos | creyéramos | creed / no creáis |
| | creéis | creíais | creísteis | creeréis | creeríais | creáis | creyerais | crean |
| | creen | creían | creyeron | creerán | creerían | crean | creyeran | |
| dormir (ue, u) | duermo | dormía | dormí | dormiré | dormiría | duerma | durmiera | duerme / no duermas |
| durmiendo | duermes | dormías | dormiste | dormirás | dormirías | duermas | durmieras | duerma |
| dormido | duerme | dormía | durmió | dormirá | dormiría | duerma | durmiera | durmamos |
| | dormimos | dormíamos | dormimos | dormiremos | dormiríamos | durmamos | durmiéramos | dormid / no durmáis |
| | dormís | dormíais | dormisteis | dormiréis | dormiríais | durmáis | durmierais | duerman |
| | duermen | dormían | durmieron | dormirán | dormirían | duerman | durmieran | |
| pedir (i, i) | pido | pedía | pedí | pediré | pediría | pida | pidiera | pide / no pidas |
| pidiendo | pides | pedías | pediste | pedirás | pedirías | pidas | pidieras | pida |
| pedido | pide | pedía | pidió | pedirá | pediría | pida | pidiera | pidamos |
| | pedimos | pedíamos | pedimos | pediremos | pediríamos | pidamos | pidiéramos | pedid / no pidáis |
| | pedís | pedíais | pedisteis | pediréis | pediríais | pidáis | pidierais | pidan |
| | piden | pedían | pidieron | pedirán | pedirían | pidan | pidieran | |
| pensar (ie) | pienso | pensaba | pensé | pensaré | pensaría | piense | pensara | piensa / no pienses |
| pensando | piensas | pensabas | pensaste | pensarás | pensarías | pienses | pensaras | piense |
| pensado | piensa | pensaba | pensó | pensará | pensaría | piense | pensara | pensemos |
| | pensamos | pensábamos | pensamos | pensaremos | pensaríamos | pensemos | pensáramos | pensad / no penséis |
| | pensáis | pensabais | pensasteis | pensaréis | pensaríais | penséis | pensarais | piensen |
| | piensan | pensaban | pensaron | pensarán | pensarían | piensen | pensaran | |

## D. Stem Changing and Spelling Change Verbs (continued)

| INFINITIVE / PRESENT PARTICIPLE / PAST PARTICIPLE | INDICATIVE | | | | | SUBJUNCTIVE | | IMPERATIVE |
|---|---|---|---|---|---|---|---|---|
| | PRESENT | IMPERFECT | PRETERITE | FUTURE | CONDITIONAL | PRESENT | PAST | |
| producir (zc, j) produciendo producido | produzco produces produce producimos producís producen | producía producías producía producíamos producíais producían | produje produjiste produjo produjimos produjisteis produjeron | produciré producirás producirá produciremos produciréis producirán | produciría producirías produciría produciríamos produciríais producirían | produzca produzcas produzca produzcamos produzcáis produzcan | produjera produjeras produjera produjéramos produjerais produjeran | produce / no produzcas produzca produzcamos producid / no produzcáis produzcan |
| reír (i, i) riendo reído | río ríes ríe reímos reís ríen | reía reías reía reíamos reíais reían | reí reíste rio reímos reísteis rieron | reiré reirás reirá reiremos reiréis reirán | reiría reirías reiría reiríamos reiríais reirían | ría rías ría riamos riáis rían | riera rieras riera riéramos rierais rieran | ríe / no rías ría riamos reíd / no riáis rían |
| seguir (i, i) (g) siguiendo seguido | sigo sigues sigue seguimos seguís siguen | seguía seguías seguía seguíamos seguíais seguían | seguí seguiste siguió seguimos seguisteis siguieron | seguiré seguirás seguirá seguiremos seguiréis seguirán | seguiría seguirías seguiría seguiríamos seguiríais seguirían | siga sigas siga sigamos sigáis sigan | siguiera siguieras siguiera siguiéramos siguierais siguieran | sigue / no sigas siga sigamos seguid / no sigáis sigan |
| sentir (ie, i) sintiendo sentido | siento sientes siente sentimos sentís sienten | sentía sentías sentía sentíamos sentíais sentían | sentí sentiste sintió sentimos sentisteis sintieron | sentiré sentirás sentirá sentiremos sentiréis sentirán | sentiría sentirías sentiría sentiríamos sentiríais sentirían | sienta sientas sienta sintamos sintáis sientan | sintiera sintieras sintiera sintiéramos sintierais sintieran | siente / no sientas sienta sintamos sentid / no sintáis sientan |
| volver (ue) volviendo vuelto | vuelvo vuelves vuelve volvemos volvéis vuelven | volvía volvías volvía volvíamos volvíais volvían | volví volviste volvió volvimos volvisteis volvieron | volveré volverás volverá volveremos volveréis volverán | volvería volverías volvería volveríamos volveríais volverían | vuelva vuelvas vuelva volvamos volváis vuelvan | volviera volvieras volviera volviéramos volvierais volvieran | vuelve / no vuelvas vuelva volvamos volved / no volváis vuelvan |

# Vocabulario español-inglés

This Spanish-English Vocabulary contains all of the words that appear in the textbook, with the following exceptions: (1) most close or identical cognates that do not appear in the chapter vocabulary lists; (2) most conjugated verb forms; (3) most diminutives ending in -ito/a; (4) augmentatives ending in -ísimo/a; (5) most adverbs ending in -mente. Only meanings used in the text are given. Numbers following translations indicate the chapter in which that meaning of the word was first presented as active vocabulary. The English-Spanish Vocabulary (p. V-41) is based on the chapter lists of active vocabulary.

The letter **n** precedes **ñ** in alphabetical order.

The gender of nouns is indicated, except for masculine nouns ending in **-o** and feminine nouns ending in **-a**. Stem changes and spelling changes are indicated for verbs: **dormir (ue, u); llegar (gu); conocer (zc).**

The following abbreviations are used in this vocabulary.

| | | | |
|---|---|---|---|
| *adj.* | adjective | *lit.* | Literally |
| *adv.* | adverb | *m.* | masculine |
| *anat.* | anatomy | *Mex.* | Mexico |
| *Arg.* | Argentina | *n.* | noun |
| *coll.* | colloquial | *obj.* | object |
| *conj.* | conjunction | *p.p.* | past participle |
| *cont.* | continued | *pl.* | plural |
| *dir.* | direct | *P.R.* | Puerto Rico |
| *f.* | feminine | *prep.* | preposition |
| *fam.* | familiar | *pres.* | present |
| *form.* | formal | *pret.* | preterite |
| *gram.* | grammatical term | *pron.* | pronoun |
| *ind.* | indicative | *rel.* | relative |
| *indir.* | indirect | *s.* | singular |
| *inf.* | infinitive | *Sp.* | Spain |
| *interj.* | interjection | *sub.* | subject |
| *inv.* | invariable | *subj.* | subjunctive |
| *irreg.* | irregular | *v.* | verb |
| *L.A.* | Latin America | | |

## A

**a** at (1); to; **a cargo (de)** in charge (of); **a causa de** because of; **a continuación** following; **a finales de** at the end of; below; **a gusto** comfortable, at ease; **a la(s)** + *time* at + *time* (1); **a la derecha (de)** to the right (of) (2); **a la izquierda (de)** to the left (of) (2); **a la parrilla** grilled; **a la vez** at once; **a la vuelta** upon return(ing); **a mano** by hand; **a mediados de** halfway through; **a menos que** + *subj.* unless (14); **a menudo** often; **a partir de** beyond (4), as of; from (*point in time*) on; **a primera vista** at first sight; **a principios de** at the beginning of; **¿a qué hora?** at what time? (1); **a solas** alone; **a su vez** at the same time; **a tiempo** on time; **a tiempo completo** full-time (*job*); **a tiempo parcial** part-time; **a veces** sometimes (P), at times

**abajo** downstairs (5); down (5); **boca abajo** face-down

**abandonar** to abandon, leave

**abecedario** alphabet (P)

**abeja** bee (14)

**abierto/a** (*p.p. of* **abrir**) open

**abogado/a** lawyer (13)

**abolición** *f.* abolition

**abolir** to abolish

**abrazar (c)** to hug; **abrazarse** to hug each other (9)

**abrazo** *n.* hug

**abreviado/a** abridged, shortened

**abreviatura** abbreviation

**abrigarse (gu)** to cover up

**abrigo** coat (7); overcoat

**abril** April (2)

**abrir** (*p.p.* **abierto**) to open (1)

**absentismo** absenteeism

**absoluto/a** absolute

**absurdo/a: es absurdo que** it's absurd that (11)

**abuelo/a** grandfather/grandmother (4); *m. pl.* grandparents (4); **tío abuelo** great uncle

**abundancia** *n.* abundance, prosperity

**aburrido/a** bored (2); boring (1)

**aburrir** to bore (6); **aburrirse** to get/become bored

**abusar** to abuse; **abusar de** + *noun* to do/take (*something*) in excess

**acabar** to finish; to exhaust (*someone's* patience); to run out of (*in accidental* **se** *construction*) (7); **acabar de** + *inf.* to have just (*done something*) (10)

**academia** academy

**académico/a** academic; **formación** (*f.*) **académica** education (15)

**acampar** to camp; to go camping (9)

**acaso: por si acaso** just in case (9)

**acceder (a)** to access

**acceso** access, entry

**accesorio** accessory

**accidente** *m.* accident

**acción** *f.* action; **Día** (*m.*) **de Acción de Gracias** Thanksgiving Day (11)

**aceite** *m.* oil (6); **aceite de oliva** olive oil (6)

**acelerado/a** accelerated (15)

**acelerar** to accelerate

**aceptable** acceptable

**aceptación** *f.* acceptance

**aceptar** to accept (6)

**acera** sidewalk (8)

**acerca de** *prep.* about; concerning

**acero** steel; **nervios de acero** nerves of steel

**aclamado/a** acclaimed

**aclarar** to clarify

**acogedor(a)** cozy (6); welcoming (6)

**acomodar** to accommodate

**acompañar** to go with; to accompany

**acondicionado/a: aire** (*m.*) **acondicionado** air conditioning

**acondicionador** *m.* (hair) conditioner

**aconsejar** to advise (11)

**acontecer (zc)** to happen, take place

**acontecimiento** event

**acordado/a** agreed upon

**acostarse (ue)** to lie down (5)

**acostumbrado/a (a)** accustomed (to) / used to

**acre** *m.* acre

**acristalamiento: doble acristalamiento** double-paned (*windows*)

**actitud** *f.* attitude

**actividad** *f.* activity (1)

**activista** *m., f.* activist

**activo/a** active

**actor** *m.* actor (11)

**actriz** *f.* (*pl.* **actrices**) actress (11)

**actuación** *f.* performance

**actual** current (7); present-day, modern

**actualidad** *f.* present-time; **en la actualidad** currently, right now

**actualmente** currently (8)

**actuar (actúo)** to act

**acuático/a** water, aquatic (10)

**acueducto** aqueduct

**acuerdo** agreement; **de acuerdo** in agreement; **de acuerdo a** according to; **de acuerdo con** in accordance with; **estar** (*irreg.*) **de acuerdo** to agree

**acumulador** (*m.*) **de calor** heating system

**acupuntura** acupuncture

**acusado/a** *adj.* accused

**acústico/a** acoustic

**adaptar(se)** to adapt; to adjust (*to something*)

**adecuado/a** adequate

**adelgazar (c)** to lose weight (12)

**además** moreover; **además de** *prep.* besides

**adentro** *adv.* inside (5); within (5)

**aderezar (c)** to dress, season (*food*)

**aderezo** *s.* seasonings

**adicción** *f.* addiction (12)

**adicionalmente** additionally

**adicto/a** *n.* addict; **adicto/a a** addicted (to)

**adiós.** good-bye. (P)

**adivinar** to guess

**adjetivo** *gram.* adjective (1); **adjetivo posesivo** *gram.* possessive adjective (1)

**adjuntar** to attach (*a document*) (15)

**adjunto** attachment (15); **documento adjunto** attachment (15)

**administración** *f.* administration; **administración empresarial** business administration (1)

**administrar** to manage (13); to administer (13)

**administrativo/a** *n.* file clerk (13); *adj.* administrative

**admirar** to admire

**adobo** sauce, marinade (*for cooking*)

**adolescencia** adolescence (9)

**adolescente** *n. m., f.* adolescent

**¿adónde?** (to) where? (2)

**adoptar** to adopt

**adoptivo/a: hijo/a adoptivo/a** adopted son/daughter (4)

**adorador(a)** *n.* worshipper

**adorar** to adore

**adornado/a** adorned (11), decorated

**adosado/a: casa adosada** townhouse (5)

**adquirir (ie, i)** to acquire; to purchase

**aduana** customs (10); **pasar por la aduana** to go through customs (10)

**adulto/a** *n., adj.* adult

**adverbio** *gram.* adverb (8)

**aeróbico/a** aerobic; **hacer** (*irreg.*) **ejercicio aeróbico** to do aerobics (12)

**aerogenerador** *m.* wind generator

**aeropuerto** airport (8)

**afanarse por** to strive for

**afectar** to affect (14)

**afeitar(se)** to shave (oneself) (5)

**aferrar** to seize, grab hold of

**afición** *f.* interest, liking; hobby

**aficionado/a** fan (11)

**afirmación** *f.* statement

**afirmar** to affirm (11); to declare (11)

**afloja: tira y afloja** *m.* give and take

**afortunadamente** fortunately (8)

**africano/a** *n., adj.* African

**afroargentino/a** *adj.* Afro-Argentinean

**afrocubano/a** *adj.* Afro-Cuban

**afroecuatoriano/a** *adj.* Afro-Ecuadorian

**afuera** outside (5); **afueras** *pl.* outskirts (5); suburbs (5)

**agencia** agency; **agencia de viajes** travel agency (10)

**agenda electrónica** PDA (15)

**agente** *m., f.* agent; **agente de viajes** travel agent

**agosto** August (2)

**agotamiento** exhaustion

**agradable** pleasant

**agradecer (zc)** to thank

**agradecido/a** grateful

**agradecimiento** gratitude

**agravar** to make worse

**agrícola** *m., f.* agricultural (8)

**agricultor(a)** farmer (8)

**agricultura** agriculture (8), farming

**agroturismo** agricultural tourism (10)

**agua** *f.* (*but* **el agua**) water (6); **agua dulce/salada** fresh/salt water (14); **aguas termales** hot springs; **contaminación** (*f.*) **del agua** water pollution (14); **pagar (gu) el agua** to pay the water (bill) (15)

**aguacate** *m.* avocado (6)

**aguantar** to endure

**águila** *f.* (*but* **el águila**) eagle (14)

**ahijado/a** godson/goddaughter (4)

**ahora** now

**ahorita** right now

**ahorrar** to save; **ahorrar dinero** to save money (15)

**aire** *m.* air (14); **aire acondicionado** air conditioning; **aire puro** clean air (14); **al aire libre** outdoors; **contaminación** (*f.*) **del aire** air pollution (14)

**aislado/a** isolated

**ají** *m.* (bell) pepper

**ajo** garlic (6)

**ajuar** *n. m. s.* furnishings

**al** (*contraction of* **a** + **el**) to the; **al aire libre** outdoors; **al contrario** on the contrary; **al día** up to date; **al final** in the end; **al gusto** to one's liking; **al horno** baked; **al lado de** next to (5); **al principio** in the beginning, at first; **al principio de** at the beginning of; **al vapor** steamed; **de al lado** next-door (5); **estar** (*irreg.*) **al día** to be up to date (15); **ponerse** (*irreg.*) **al corriente** to catch up

**ala** (*f. but* **el ala**) **delta** hang gliding; **practicar (qu) el ala delta** to hang glide (9)

**alacena** cupboard

**alargado/a** long

**albañil** *m.* bricklayer (13)

**albergue** *m.* hostel

**álbum** *m.* record (music); **álbum de fotos** photo album

**alcanzar (c)** to achieve (9); to reach (9); **alcanzar a** + *inf.* to manage to (*do something*) (9)

**alcatraz** *m.* (*pl.* **alcatraces**) calla lily

**alcoba** bedroom

**alcohol** *m.* alcohol (12)

**alcohólico/a** *n.* alcoholic (12); **bebida alcohólica** alcoholic drink (6)

**aldea** village (8)

**alegrarse (de)** to be happy (about) (11)

**alegre** happy (2); **estar** (*irreg.*) **alegre** to be happy

**alegría** happiness, joy

**alejado/a (de)** distant, far away from

**alejarse (de)** to move away from

**alemán** *m.* German (*language*) (1)

**alergia** allergy

**alfabetización** *f.* literacy

**alfombra** rug (5)

**algo** something (5)

**algodón** *m.* cotton (7)

**alguien** someone (5), somebody

**algún, alguno/a(s)** some (5); any; **algún día** someday; **alguna vez** once; ever

**aliado/a** ally

**alimentación** *f.* diet

**alimentarse** to feed/nourish (oneself)

**alimenticio/a** nutritious

**alimento** food (6); nourishment (6); **alimentos transgénicos** genetically modified foods (15)

**aliviar** to relieve; to lessen

**allá** over there; **más allá** further, farther; **más allá de** beyond

**allí** there

**alma** *f.* (*but* **el alma**) soul

**almacén** *m.* market; grocery store

**almacenar** to backup (15)

**almeja** clam (14)

**almidón** *m.* starch (*food*)

**almohada** pillow

**almorzar (ue) (c)** to eat lunch (3)

**almuerzo** lunch (6)

**¿aló?** hello? (*when answering telephone*)

**alojamiento** lodging (10)

**alojarse** to stay (*in a hotel*) (10)

**alpinismo** mountain climbing (9)

**alquilar** to rent

**alquiler** *m.* rent; **pagar (gu) el alquiler** to pay the rent (15)

**alrededor: alrededor de** *prep.* around; **alrededores** *n. m. pl.* surroundings

**altar** *m.* altar

**altavoz** *m.* (*pl.* **altavoces**) loudspeaker; *pl.* speakers (15)

**alternativa** alternative, option

**altiplano** high plateau (14)

**alto/a** tall (1); high; **en voz alta** aloud; **precio alto** high price (7); **televisión** (*f.*) **de alta definición** HD TV (15); **zapatos de tacón alto** high-heeled shoes (7)

**altoparlante** *m.* loudspeaker

**altruismo** unselfishness (15)

**altruista** *m., f.* unselfish (15)

**altura: de altura** in height

**alusión** *f.* reference

**ama** (*f. but* **el ama**) **de casa** housewife

**amabilidad** *f.* kindness

**amable** friendly (12)

**amante** *m., f.* lover

**amar(se)** to love (each other)

**amarillo** *n.* yellow (2)

**amarillo/a** *adj.* yellow

**amarse** to love each other (12)

**amazónico/a** *adj.* Amazon

**ámbar** *m.* amber; **de ámbar** amber (7)

**ambición** *f.* ambition (15)

**ambicioso/a** ambitious (15)

**ambiental** environmental; **desastre** (*m.*) **ambiental** environmental disaster (14); **problema** (*m.*) **ambiental** environmental problem (14); **solución** (*f.*) **ambiental** environmental solution (14)

**ambiente** *m.* atmosphere, environment; **medio ambiente** environment (14)

**ambos/as** *pl.* both

**amenaza** threat

**americano/a** American; **fútbol** (*m.*) **americano** football (1); **jugar (ue) (gu) al fútbol americano** to play football (1)

**amigo/a** friend (1); **amigo/a íntimo/a** close friend (15); **mejor amigo/a** best friend (1)

**amistad** *f.* friendship (12)

**amor** *m.* love (12)

**ampliar (amplío)** to extend; to increase

**amplio/a** ample

**amueblado/a** furnished (5)

**amueblar** to furnish; **sin amueblar** unfurnished (5)

**amurallado/a** walled

**añadir** to add

**analizar (c)** to analyze

**anaranjado** *n.* orange (*color*) (2)

**anaranjado/a** *adj.* orange

**anatomía** anatomy (1)

**ancho/a** wide; **televisión** (*f.*) **de pantalla ancha** wide-screen TV (15)

**anciano/a** elderly person

**andaluz(a)** *adj.* Andalusian (*of or from Andalucía, region in southern Spain*)

**andante: caballero andante** knight-errant

**andar** *irreg.* to walk; **andar en bicicleta** to ride a bicycle (1)

**andino/a** Andean

**anémico/a** anemic

**anfitrión** *m.* host

**anfitriona** hostess

**anillo** ring (7)

**animado/a** cheerful; **dibujos animados** cartoons (9)

**animal** *m.* animal; **animal doméstico** domesticated (farm) animal (8); **animal salvaje** wild animal (14)

**ánimo** spirit; **estado de ánimo** state of mind

**anís** *m.* anise

**aniversario** anniversary

**año** year (3); **Año Nuevo** New Year's Day (11); **¿cuántos años tiene usted (Ud.)?** how old are you (*s. form.*)? (4); **¿cuántos años tienes?** how old are you (*s. fam.*)? (4); **cumplir años** to have a birthday; **el año pasado** last year (6); **los años setenta** the seventies; **por año** yearly; per year; **tener** (*irreg.*)... **años** to be... years old (3); **todo el año** all year; **todos los años** every year

**anoche** last night (6)

**anotar** to make a note of; **anotar datos** to enter data (13)

**antártico/a: Mar Antártico** Antarctic Sea

**ante** before; **ante todo** above all

**anteayer** the day before yesterday (6)

**antecedente** *m. gram.* antecedent

**antepasado/a** ancestor

**anterior** previous

**antes** before; **antes (de)** before (1); **antes de que** + *subj.* before (14)

**antibiótico** antibiotic

**anticipación** *f.*: **con anticipación** ahead of time

**anticontaminante** anti-pollution (14)

**anticuado/a** outdated

**antidepresivo** antidepressant

**antigüedad** *n. f.* antique

**antiguo/a** ancient, old

**antipático/a** mean (1), disagreeable (1)

**antropología** anthropology

**anual** annual; **pago anual** annual payment (15)

**anuncio** advertisement

**apacible** gentle; mild

**apagar (gu)** to turn off; to soften

**aparato** device; **aparato doméstico** appliance (3)

**aparcamiento** parking

**aparcar (qu)** to park

**aparecer (zc)** to appear

**aparentemente** *adv.* apparently

**apariencia** appearance

**apartamento** apartment (5); **edificio de apartamentos** apartment building (5)

**aparte** *adv.* separate; **aparte de** *prep.* apart from; as well as

**apasionado/a** passionate (15)

**apellido** last name

**apenas** hardly; barely

**aperitivo** appetizer

**apetito** appetite

**apio** celery

**aplastar** to mash, squash

**aplicar (qu)** to apply

**aportar** to provide

**aporte** *m.* contribution

**apóstol** *m.* apostle

**apoyar** to support

**apoyo** *n.* support

**apreciación** *f.* appreciation; evaluation, assessment

**apreciar** to appreciate

**aprecio** *n.* esteem; value

**aprender** to learn (1); **aprender a +** *inf.* to learn to (*do something*) (1)

**apretado/a** tight

**aprobar (ue)** to approve

**apropiado/a** appropriate; fitting

**aprovechar** to take advantage of

**aproximadamente** approximately

**apuntar** to note; to jot down

**apunte** *m.* note; **tomar apuntes** to take notes (1)

**apurar** to hurry

**aquel, aquella** *adj.* that (over there); *pron.* that one (over there) (4)

**aquello** that (over there) (*concept, unknown thing*) (4)

**aquellos/as** *adj.* those (over there); *pron.* those ones (over there) (4)

**aquí** here

**árabe** *n. m.* Arabic (*language*) (1); *n. m., f.* Arab; *adj.* Arabic

**araña** spider (14)

**arawaco/a** *adj.* of or from the Arawak tribes from the West Indies

**árbol** *m.* tree (8); **árbol de Navidad** Christmas tree (11); **tala de árboles** tree felling (14), deforestation

**arboleda** grove; woodland

**arbusto** bush (8)

**archipiélago** archipelago (14), chain of islands

**archivador** *m.* file cabinet (13)

**archivar** to file (13)

**archivo** file (15)

**arcilla: de arcilla** clay (7)

**arco** arch

**arcoíris** *m.* rainbow

**área** *f. (but* **el área***)* area; **área protegida** protected area

**arena** sand (14); arena, stadium

**aretes** *m.* earrings (7)

**argentino/a** Argentine (P)

**argot** *m.* slang, jargon

**argumento** argument; plot (*story*)

**árido/a** dry; **clima** (*m.*) **árido** dry climate

**arma** *f. (but* **el arma***)* arm, weapon (9)

**armado/a** *adj.* armed; **conflicto armado** armed conflict

**armario** closet (5)

**aro** ring; **aro de piedra** stone ring

**aromaterapia** aromatherapy; **practicar (qu) la aromaterapia** to do aromatherapy (15)

**arpa** *f. (but* **el arpa***)* harp; lyre

**arqueología** archeology

**arqueológico/a** archeological; **ruinas arqueológicas** archeological ruins (10)

**arqueólogo/a** archeologist

**arquero** archer; goalkeeper

**arquetipo** archetype

**arquitecto/a** architect (11)

**arquitectura** architecture (1)

**arrecife** *m.* reef (14); **arrecife de coral** coral reef (14)

**arreglar** to arrange; to tidy, clean up; **arreglar el cuarto** to tidy/clean up the room (3)

**arriba** upstairs (5); up (5)

**arriesgado/a** daring; dangerous

**arrogante** arrogant; **ser** (*irreg.*) **arrogante** to be arrogant

**arrojar** to throw out, spew (14)

**arroyo** stream

**arroz** *m.* rice (6)

**arte** *f. (but* **el arte***)* art (1); **artes escénicas** performing arts (11); **artes marciales** martial arts; **artes plásticas** visual arts (11); **bellas artes** fine arts (1); **Facultad** (*f.*) **de**

**Bellas Artes** School of Fine Arts (1); **obra de arte** work of art (11)

**artesanal** handmade

**artesanías** arts and crafts (7)

**artesano/a** *adj.* artisan, handmade

**ártico/a** arctic; **zona ártica** Arctic region (14)

**articulación** *f.* joint (*anat.*)

**artículo** article (7); good (*merchandise*) (7)

**artificial** artificial; **fuegos artificiales** fireworks (11)

**artista** *m., f.* artist (11)

**artístico/a** artistic

**arzobispal: Palacio Arzobispal** archbishop's residence

**asado/a** roasted (6)

**asar** to roast

**ascensor** *m.* elevator (5)

**asegurar** to assure; **asegurarse** to make sure

**asentamiento** settlement (*of a population*)

**aseo** toilet

**asesinar** to murder, assassinate (9)

**asesor(a)** adviser, counselor

**así** thus; so; like this/that; **así como** as well as; **así pues** so; **así que** therefore, consequently, so; **aun así** even so, still

**asiático/a** *adj.* Asian

**asiento** seat (10); **asiento de pasillo** aisle seat (10); **asiento de ventanilla** window seat (10)

**asilo** asylum

**asistencia** assistance

**asistir (a)** to attend, go to (*a class, event*) (1)

**asociación** *f.* association; relationship

**asociar** to associate

**asomar** to jut out

**aspecto** aspect; look, appearance

**aspiradora** vacuum cleaner (3); **pasar la aspiradora** to vacuum (3)

**aspirante** *m., f.* applicant (13)

**aspirar** to aspire (*to be something*)

**aspirina** aspirin

**astronomía** astronomy (1)

**asumir** to assume (*responsibility*)

**asunto** matter; subject; theme

**asustado/a** scared (2)

**atacar (qu)** to attack

**ataque** *m.* attack (9)

**atar** to tie

**atardecer** *m.* dusk

**atención** *f.* attention; **llamar la atención** to sound interesting (*lit.* to call out for one's attention) (6); **prestar atención** to pay attention

**atender (ie) (a)** to attend (to)

**atleta** *m., f.* athlete (13)

**atmósfera** atmosphere (14)

**atómico/a** atomic

**atracción** *f.* attraction

**atractivo/a** attractive

**atraer** (*like* **traer**) (*p.p.* **atraído**) to attract

**atrapar** to catch; to trap

**atrás: hacer** (*irreg.*) **la cuenta atrás** to count down (*to midnight*)

**atravesar (ie)** to go through; to cross

**atrevido/a** cheeky; daring

**atún** *m.* tuna (6)

**auditivo/a** *adj.* auditory

**aumentar** to increase, to rise

**aumento** *n.* raise (13); increase, rise; **aumento de sueldo** raise

**aun** *adv.* even

**aún** *adv.* still, yet

**aunque** *adv., conj.* although

**auricular** *m.* receiver; **auricular bluetooth** Bluetooth earphone (15)

**ausencia** absence

**auténtico/a** authentic

**auto** car

**autobús** *m.* bus (8); **estación** (*f.*) **de autobuses** bus station (8)

**autodidacto/a** *adj.* self-taught

**autoestima** self esteem (15)

**automático/a** automatic; **cajero automático** ATM, cash machine

**automóvil** *m.* car; automobile

**autonomía** autonomy; independence

**autónomo/a** autonomous

**autopista** freeway; (four-lane) highway (8)

**autor(a)** author

**autoridad** *f.* authority (9)

**autorretrato** self-portrait

**autosuficiente** *adj.* self-sufficient

**avance** *m.* advance; **avance** (*m.*) **tecnológico** technological advance (15)

**ave** *f.* (*but* **el ave**) bird; **ave de corral** farm bird (8)

**avenida** avenue (5)

**aventura** adventure

**aventurero/a** *n.* adventurer; *adj.* adventurous

**avergonzado/a** ashamed; embarrassed

**averiguar (ü)** to find out

**aversión** *f.* aversion

**avión** *m.* airplane (8)

**avisar** to warn

**¡ay!** *interj.* oh no!; ouch!

**ayer** yesterday (6)

**ayuda** *n.* help

**ayudante** *n. m., f.* assistant

**ayudar** to help (9)

**ayuna: en ayunas** before breakfast; fasting

**ayuntamiento** town council

**azafata** *m., f.* flight attendant (10)

**azafrán** *m.* saffron

**azteca** *n., adj. m., f.* Aztec

**azúcar** *m.* sugar (6); **caña de azúcar** (sugar) cane

**azul** blue (2)

# ß

**bahía** bay (14)

**bailador(a)** dancer

**bailar** to dance (1)

**bailarín, bailarina** (ballet) dancer (11)

**baile** *m.* dance; **baile folclórico** traditional/folkloric dance (11)

**bajar** to download (13); to get down; to lower; **bajarse (de)** to get off (of) (*a vehicle*) (10)

**bajo/a** short (1); **planta baja** first (ground) floor (5); **precio bajo** low price (7); **zapatos de tacón bajo** flats (7)

**balcón** *m.* balcony (5)

**ballena** whale (14)

**ballenero** *adj.* whaling; **barco ballenero** whaling ship

**ballet** (*m.*) **clásico** classical ballet (11)

**balneario** bathing resort; spa; water park

**balompié** *m.* soccer

**balón** *m.* ball

**baloncesto** basketball

**balsa** raft

**bambú** *m.* bamboo

**banana** banana (6)

**bañar** to bathe; **bañarse** to bathe (oneself); to swim (5)

**bancario/a** *adj.* banking

**banco** bank (8)

**banda** band (*musical*)

**bandera** flag (9)

**bandoneón** *m.* large concertina (*type of accordion used for Tango music*)

**bañera** bathtub

**baño** bathroom (5); **baño termal** hot bath; **traje** (*m.*) **de baño** bathing suit (7)

**banquero/a** banker (13)

**bar** *m.* bar (*drinking establishment*) (8)

**barato/a** cheap (7); inexpensive (7)

**barbacoa** barbecue

**barbero/a** barber (13)

**barco** boat (8); **barco ballenero** whaling ship; **pasear en barco** to go boating (9)

**barrer el piso** to sweep the floor (3)

**barrio** neighborhood (5)

**barro** mud

**barroco/a** Baroque

**basado/a (en)** (*p.p. of* **basar**) based (on)

**base** *f.* base, foundation

**básico/a** basic

**basquetbol** *m.* basketball (1); **jugar (ue) (gu) al basquetbol** to play basketball (1)

**basta** enough

**bastante** *adj.* enough; sufficient

**bastón** *m.* walking stick

**basura** trash, garbage (3); **sacar (qu) la basura** to take out the trash/garbage (3)

**basurero** landfill (14); garbage can

**batalla** battle (9)

**bate** *m.* bat (*sports*)

**batería** drums

**batidora** mixer; **batidora eléctrica** electric mixer

**batir** to beat

**baula: tortuga baula** leatherback sea turtle

**bautismo** baptism

**bautizo** baptism (*ceremony*) (4)

**beber** to drink (1)

**bebida** drink (6); **bebida alcohólica** alcoholic drink (6)

**beca** grant; scholarship

**béisbol** *m.* baseball (1); **jugar (ue) (gu) al béisbol** to play baseball (1)

**beisbolista** *m., f.* baseball player

**belleza** beauty

**bello/a** *adj.* beautiful; **bellas artes** fine arts (1); **Facultad** (*f.*) **de Bellas Artes** School of Fine Arts (1)

**beneficiarse (de)** to benefit (from)

**beneficio** benefit

**besar** to kiss; **besarse** to kiss each other (9)

**beso** kiss

**biblioteca** library (1)

**bibliotecario/a** librarian (1)

**bicicleta** bicycle, bike; **andar en bicicleta** to ride a bicycle (1)

**bien** *adv.* fine, well (2); **bien.** fine. (*response to greeting*) (P); **estar** (*irreg.*) **bien** to be well; **llevarse bien** to get along well (with each other) (9); **manejar bien el tiempo** to manage one's time well (15); **muy bien.** very well. (P); **no muy bien.** not very well. (P); **pasarlo bien** to have a good time (3); **salir** (*irreg.*) **bien** to turn out well

**bienestar** *m.* well-being; **bienestar físico/mental** physical/mental well-being (15)

**bienvenido/a** welcome

**bilingüe** bilingual (13)

**billar** *m.* pool, billiards (3); **jugar (ue) (gu) al billar** to play pool (3)

**billete** *m.* ticket (*Sp.*) (10)

**biodiversidad** *f.* biodiversity (14)

**biografía** biography

**biología** biology (1)

**biológico/a** biological; **reserva biológica** biological reserve (10)

**biólogo/a** biologist (13)

**biométrico/a** biometric

**bioquímica** biochemistry

**biosfera** biosphere

**biotecnológico/a** biotechnological

**bisabuelo/a** great-grandfather/great-grandmother

**bistec** *m.* steak (6)

**bitácora** blog

**blanco** *n.* white (2); **espacio en blanco** blank (space); **quedarse en blanco** to go blank (*mind*)

**blanco/a** *adj.* white; **pizarrón** (*m.*) **blanco** whiteboard (1); **vino blanco** white wine (6)

**bloque** *m.* block; **bloque de pisos** block apartment building (5)

**bluetooth: auricular** (*m.*) **bluetooth** Bluetooth earphone (15)

**blusa** blouse (7)

**boca** mouth (12); **boca abajo** face-down

**boda** wedding (4)

**bohemio/a** bohemian

**bola** ball

**bolero** love song; *a dance and musical rhythm typical of Cuba*

**boleto** ticket (*L.A.*) (10)

**bolígrafo** pen (1)

**boliviano/a** Bolivian (P)

**bolsa** bag; stock market (15); **bolsa de plástico** plastic bag (14); **invertir (ie, i) en la bolsa** to invest in the stock market (15)

**bolsillo** pocket

**bolso** handbag (7)

**bomba** bomb

**bombero/a** firefighter

**bongo** bongo drum

**bonito/a** pretty (1)

**bordado/a** embroidered

**borde** *m.* edge, border

**bordear** to border

**boricua** *adj. m., f.* Puerto Rican

**borrador** *m.* eraser (*for whiteboard*) (1); (*writing*) draft

**borrar** to delete (15)

**bosque** *m.* forest (8); **bosque tropical** tropical rainforest (14)

**botánico/a** botanic, botanical

**botas** boots (7)

**botella** bottle

**botones** *m. inv.* bellhop (10)

**boutique** *f.* boutique, specialty store (7)

**Brasil** Brazil

**brasileño/a** Brazilian

**brazalete** *m.* bracelet (7)

**brazo** arm (12)

**breve** brief; short

**brillante** brilliant; shining

**brindar (por)** to toast (to) (11)

**británico/a** British

**broma** joke

**bruja** witch

**buceo** underwater diving

**buen, bueno/a** good (1); **buen provecho** bon appétit; **buenos días.** good morning. (*until midday meal*) (P); **buenas noches.** good evening. (*after evening meal*) (P); **buenas tardes.** good afternoon. (*until evening meal*) (P); **bueno...** well . . .; **estar** (*irreg.*) **de buen humor** to be in a good mood; **hace (muy) buen tiempo.** it's (very) nice out. (2); **¡qué buena onda!** how cool!; **sacar (qu) buenas notas** to get good grades (1); **ser** (*irreg.*) **buena onda** to be (a) cool (person)

**buey** *m.* ox (8)

**bulevar** *m.* boulevard (5)

**burla** mockery

**burro** donkey (8)

**busca** search

**buscar (qu) (algo)** to look for (something) (1); **buscar empleo estable** to look for stable employment (15); **buscar novio/a por el Internet** to look for a boyfriend/girlfriend online, Internet dating (15)

**búsqueda de trabajo** job search (13)

## C

**caballeresco/a** *adj.* chivalresque

**caballería** chivalry; **libro de caballería** book of chivalry

**caballero** gentleman; **caballero andante** knight-errant

**caballo** horse (8); **caballo marino** seahorse (14); **montar a caballo** to ride a horse

**cabaña** cabin; **cabaña rústica** rustic cabin (10)

**caber** *irreg.* to fit

**cabeza** head (12); **dolor** (*m.*) **de cabeza** headache (12)

**cable** *m.* cable (*electric*); **pagar (gu) el cable** to pay the cable TV (bill) (15)

**cacao** cacao bean

**cacto** cactus (14)

**cada** *inv.* each, every; **cada vez** every time; **cada vez más** more and more; **cada vez menos** less and less

**cadena** chain; channel (*television*)

**caer** *irreg.* to drop (*in accidental* **se** *construction*) (7); to fall; **caerse** to fall down

**café** *m.* coffee (3); café; **color café** brown (2); **de color café** brown; **tomar un café** to have a cup of coffee (3)

**cafecito** espresso with sugar (*Cuba*)

**cafeína** caffeine

**cafetera** coffee maker (5); coffeepot

**cafetería** cafeteria (1)

**cafetero/a** coffee addict

**caja** box

**cajero automático** ATM, cash machine

**calabaza** pumpkin

**calcetines** *m.* socks (7)

**calcio** calcium

**calculadora** calculator

**calcular** to calculate

**cálculo** calculus

**calefacción** *f.* heating

**calendario** calendar (2)

**calentamiento global** global warming (14)

**calentar (ie)** to warm up

**calidad** *f.* quality (7)

**cálido/a** warm (*climate*)

**caliente** warm (*temperature*)

**calificar (qu)** to assess; to qualify

**callado/a** quiet

**calle** *f.* street (2)

**callejero/a** *adj.* street; **puesto callejero** street shop/stall

**calma** calm

**calor** *m.* heat; **hace (mucho) calor.** it's (very) hot. (2); **tener** (*irreg.*) **(mucho) calor** to be (very) hot (3)

**caloría** calorie

**cama** bed (3); **hacer** (*irreg.*) **la cama** to make the bed (3)

**cámara digital** digital camera (15)

**camarero/a** waiter; chambermaid

**camarones** *m. pl.* shrimp (6)

**cambiar** to change

**cambio** change; **cambio climático** climate change (14)

**caminar** to walk (1)

**caminata** hike (9); **dar** (*irreg.*) **una caminata** to go on a hike (9)

**camino** road (8)

**camión** *m.* truck (8)

**camioneta** minibus (8)

**camisa** shirt (7)

**camiseta** T-shirt (7)

**campeonato** championship

**campesino/a** farm worker

**campo** country(side) (5); playing field (*sports*)

**campus** *m.* campus (1)

**caña (de azúcar)** (sugar) cane

**Canadá** Canada; **Día** (*m.*) **de Canadá** Canada Day (11)

**canadiense** *n., adj. m., f.* Canadian

**canal** *m.* canal

**canasta** basket (7)

**cancelar** to cancel

**cancha** court; **cancha de tenis** tennis court

**canción** *f.* song (11)

**candidato/a** candidate

**canela** cinnamon

**cangrejo** crab (14)

**canoa** canoe (10)

**cansado/a** tired (2)

**cantante** *m., f.* singer (11)

**cantaora** *female flamenco singer*

**cantar** to sing (1)

**cantidad** *f.* amount, quantity; abundance

**cantina** bar (8)

**canto** song; singing

**cañón** *m.* canyon

**caos** *m. s.* chaos

**capa** cape; **capa de ozono** ozone layer (14)

**capacidad** *f.* ability, capacity

**capacitación** *f.* training

**capacitar** to prepare

**capital** *f.* capital (*city*)

**capitalino/a** *n.* inhabitant of the capital

**capitel** *m.* capital (*architecture*)

**capítulo** chapter

**capturar** to capture

**cara** face; **lavarse la cara** to wash one's face (5)

**carácter** *m.* personality

**característica** *n.* characteristic

**característico/a** *adj.* characteristic

**caracterizar(se) (c)** to characterize; to portray

**caramelo** caramel

**carbohidrato** carbohydrate

**carbono** carbon; **dióxido de carbono** carbon dioxide; **emisiones** (*f.*)

**de carbono** carbon emissions; **monóxido de carbono** carbon monoxide (CO)

**cárcel** *f.* prison, jail

**cardíaco/a** cardiac, involving the heart

**cargado/a** *adj.* full, loaded

**cargar (gu) (con)** to carry

**cargo: a cargo (de)** in charge (of)

**Caribe** *m.* Caribbean; **Mar** (*m.*) **Caribe** Caribbean Sea

**caribeño** *n., adj.* Caribbean

**caribú** *m.* caribou (14)

**cariño** affection (12); **sentir (ie, i) cariño por** to be fond of (12); **tenerle** (*irreg.*) **cariño a** to be fond of (12)

**cariñoso/a** affectionate (4)

**carismático/a** charismatic (13); charming (13)

**Carnaval** *m.* Carnival (11); **máscara de carnaval** carnival mask (7)

**carne** *f.* meat (6); **carne de cerdo** pork (6); **carne de res** beef (6); **carne de ternera** veal; **carne picada** ground beef (6)

**carnet** *m.* identification card; **carnet de conducir** driver's license (8)

**carnicería** butcher's shop

**carnívoro/a** carnivore

**caro/a** expensive (7)

**carrera** career (15); major (1); race; **tener** (*irreg.*) **una carrera** to have a career (15)

**carreta** (ox) cart

**carretera** (two-lane) highway (8); road

**carro** car (8); **carro eléctrico** electric car (14); **carro híbrido** hybrid car (14)

**carroza** parade float (11)

**carta** menu; letter; card; *pl.* playing cards (3); **jugar (ue) (gu) a las cartas** to play cards (3)

**cartel** *m.* poster

**cartera** wallet (7)

**cartón** *m.* cardboard (14)

**casa** home; house (3); **ama** (*f. but* **el ama**) **de casa** housewife; **casa adosada** townhouse (5); **limpiar la casa** to clean the house (3); **mantener** (*like* **tener**) **una casa** to maintain a home (15)

**casado/a** married (4); **recién casado/a** newlywed

**casarse (con)** to marry, get married (to) (12)

**cascada** waterfall

**cáscara** peel

**casco viejo** old quarter (*part of town*)

**casero/a** home-made

**casi** *adv.* almost

**caso** case; situation; **en caso de que** + *subj.* in case (14)

**castaño/a** chestnut (*color*)

**castellano** Spanish (*language*) (*Sp.*)

**castillo** castle

**casualmente** casually

**catalán** *m.* Catalan (*language*)

**catalán, catalana** *n., adj.* Catalan

**catalogar (gu)** to classify; to list

**catarata** waterfall

**catatónico/a** catatonic

**catedral** *f.* cathedral (8)

**categoría** category

**católico/a** *n., adj.* Catholic

**catorce** fourteen (P)

**causa** cause; **a causa de** because of

**causar** to cause

**cazador(a)** hunter

**cazar (c)** to hunt

**CD-ROM** *m.* CD-ROM (15)

**cebolla** onion (6)

**cederrón** *m.* CD-ROM

**celebración** *f.* celebration (11)

**celebrado/a** celebrated

**celebrar** to celebrate (11)

**celestial** *n.* sky; *adj.* heavenly

**celos** *m. pl.* jealousy

**celoso/a** jealous (12)

**celular** *m.* cell (phone) (1); **pagar (gu) el celular** to pay the cell phone (bill) (15); **teléfono celular** cell (phone) (1)

**cementerio** cemetery

**cena** dinner (6)

**cenar** to eat dinner (1)

**ceniza** ash

**censo** census

**centelleante** *adj.* twinkling

**central** *adj.* central

**centrar(se)** to focus (on)

**céntrico/a** central, centrally located (5)

**centro** downtown (5); **centro comercial** mall (7); **centro de salud** health center (8); **centro estudiantil** student union (1); **centro geriátrico** retirement home

**Centroamérica** Central America

**cepillar(se)** to brush; **cepillarse los dientes** to brush one's teeth

**cerámica** pottery (7)

**cerca** *n.* fence (8); *adv.* near; **cerca de** *prep.* close to (2)

**cercano/a** *adj.* near, close by

**cerdo** pig (8); **carne** (*f.*) **de cerdo** pork (6); **chuleta de cerdo** pork chop (6)

**cereal** *m.* cereal (6); grain

**cerebro** brain (12)

**ceremonia** ceremony; **ceremonia civil** civil ceremony (4)

**cero** zero (P)

**cerrar (ie)** to close (3); **cerrar (ie) el grifo** to turn off the faucet (14)

**cerveza** beer (6)

**césped** *m.* lawn, grass; **cortar el césped** to mow the lawn (cut the grass) (3)

**cesto/a** *n.* large basket

**chalet** *m.* chalet

**champán** *m.* champagne

**champaña** *m.* champagne (6)

**champiñones** *m.* mushrooms (6)

**champú** *m.* shampoo

**chaqueta** jacket (7)

**charango** ten-stringed instrument of the Andes

**charlar** to chat (1)

**charreada** rodeo (*Mex.*)

**charro** cowboy (*Mex.*)

**chatarra** *adj. inv.*: **comida chatarra** junk food

**chatear** to chat (*online*)

**cheque** *m.* check; **cheque (*m.*) de viajero** traveler's check (10)

**chequeo** check-up (12)

**chévere** cool; **¡qué chévere!** (how) cool!

**chícharo** pea

**chico/a** *n.* boy/girl; *adj.* small (7)

**chileno/a** Chilean (P)

**chimenea** fireplace (5)

**chino** *n.* Chinese (*language*) (1)

**chino/a** *adj.* Chinese

**chisme** *m.* gossip

**chivo** goat (8)

**choclo** corn

**chocolate** *m.* chocolate (6); hot chocolate

**chofer** *m.* chauffeur

**chompa** sweater

**chuleta** chop (6); **chuleta de cerdo** pork chop (6)

**churro** fritter

**cibercafé** *m.* cybercafé, Internet café

**cibernético/a** cybernetic (15); online (15)

**ciclismo** cycling (9)

**ciclista** *m., f.* cyclist

**ciclo** cycle, series

**ciclovía** cycle lane; bike path

**cielo** sky (9)

**cien** one hundred (2)

**ciencia** science (1); **ciencia social** social science; **ciencias políticas** political science (1); **Facultad (*f.*) de Ciencias** School of Science (1)

**científico/a** *n.* scientist (13); *adj.* science

**ciento...** one hundred . . . ; **ciento dos** one hundred two (4); **ciento noventa y nueve** one hundred ninety-nine (4); **ciento tres** one hundred three (4); **ciento uno** one hundred one (4); **por ciento** percent

**cierto/a** true; certain; **es cierto que** it's certain that (11)

**cifra** number; figure

**cigarrillo** cigarette

**címbalo** cymbal

**cimiento** base, foundation (*of a building*)

**cinco** five (P)

**cincuenta** fifty (2)

**cine** *m.* movie theatre (3); **comprar entradas de cine por el Internet** to buy movie tickets online (15); **ir (*irreg.*) al cine** to go to the movies (3)

**cineasta** *m., f.* film director (11)

**cinturón** *m.* belt (7)

**circulación** *f.* traffic (8)

**círculo** circle

**circuncisión** *f.* circumcision

**circundado/a** *adj.* surrounded

**cisne** *m.* swan

**cita** date (12); appointment

**ciudad** *f.* city

**ciudadano/a** citizen

**civil** civil (*of society*); **ceremonia civil** civil ceremony (4); **estado civil** marital status (4); **guerra civil** civil war (9)

**civilización** *f.* civilization (9)

**clarinete** *m.* clarinet

**claro/a** light (*color*) (7); *adv.* clearly; **¡claro que sí!** of course!

**clase** *f.* class (1); **clase económica** coach (class) (10); **compañero/a de clase** classmate; **primera clase** first class (10); **salón (*m.*) de clase** classroom (1); **tomar una clase** to take a class (1)

**clásico/a** classical; **ballet (*m.*) clásico** classical ballet (11); **música clásica** classical music (11)

**clasificado/a** classified

**clasificar (qu)** to classify

**claustro** cloister

**clave** *adj. inv.* key, fundamental

**clavicordio** clavichord

**clemencia** clemency, mercy

**cliente/a** client (6)

**clima** *m.* weather; climate; **clima árido** dry climate

**climático/a** *adj.* climatic; **cambio climático** climate change (14)

**clínica** clinic (1)

**clonación** *f.* cloning (15)

**club** *m.* club

**cobrar** charge

**cobre** *m.* copper

**coche** *m.* car (5); **coche eléctrico** electric car (14); **coche híbrido** hybrid car (14); **pagar (gu) el coche** to pay the car payment (15)

**cochera** carport (5)

**cocina** kitchen (5)

**cocinar** to cook (3)

**cocinero/a** cook (6); chef (6)

**coco** coconut (6)

**cocodrilo** crocodile (14)

**cocotero** coconut tree (14)

**coerción** *f.* coercion

**coexistir** to coexist

**cognado** cognate (1)

**cola** line; **hacer (*irreg.*) cola** to stand in line (10)

**colaborar** to collaborate, to assist

**colección** *f.* collection

**colectivo** bus; taxi

**colectivo/a** *adj.* collective

**colega** *m., f.* coworker, colleague

**colegio** high school

**colgar (ue) (gu)** to hang

**colina** hill (8)

**collage** *m.* collage

**collar** *m.* necklace (7)

**colocar (qu)** to place, put

**colombiano/a** Colombian (P)

**colonia** colony (9)

**colonial** colonial (9); **época colonial** colonial era (9)

**colonización** *f.* colonization

**colonizador(a)** colonist, colonizer

**colonizar (c)** to colonize (9)

**coloquial** colloquial

**color** *m.* color (2); **color café** brown (2); **de color violeta** violet, purple

**colorido/a** colorful

**colosal** colossal

**columna** column (*of text*)

**coma** *m.* coma (*medicine*); *f.* comma (*grammar*)

**comadre** *f.* godmother; friend

**comatoso/a** comatose

**combatir** to fight

**combinación** *f.* combination

**combinar** to combine; to mix

**combustible** *n. m.* fuel; **combustible fósil** fossil fuel

**combustión** *f.* combustion

**comedia** comedy

**comedor** *m.* dining room (5); cafeteria style / roadside restaurant (8)

**comentar** to comment on

**comentario** commentary; remark

**comenzar (ie) (c)** to begin, to start

**comer** to eat (1); **comerse** to eat (*something*) up; **dar (*irreg.*) de comer** to feed

**comercial** commercial; **centro comercial** mall (7); business center

**comercio** trade; **comercio libre** free trade

**comestible** *m.* food item (6); *pl.* groceries (6); **tienda de comestibles** grocery store (6)

**cómico/a** *n.* comedian; *adj.* funny; **tira cómica** comic, comic strip

**comida** food (6); meal (6); **comida chatarra** junk food

**comienzo** start, beginning

**comisaría de policía** police station (8)

**como** like, as; **así como** as well as; **guardar como** to save as (15); **tal como** just as; **tan... como** as . . . as (4); **tan pronto como** as soon as (13); **tanto como** as much as (4); **tanto/a(s)... como** as much/many . . . as (4)

**¿cómo?** how? (1); what?; **¿cómo eres?** what are you (s. fam.) like? (P); **¿cómo es usted (Ud.)?** what are you (s. form.) like? (P); **¿cómo está usted (Ud.)?** how are you (s. form.)? (P); **¿cómo estás?** how are you (s. fam.)? (P); **¿cómo se llama usted (Ud.)?** what's your (s. form.) name? (P); **¿cómo te llamas?** what's your (s. fam.) name? (P)

**cómoda** chest of drawers, dresser (5)

**comodidad** *f.* comfort, convenience

**cómodo/a** comfortable (7)

**compa** *m., f.* buddy

**compadrazgo** coparenthood

**compadre** *m.* godfather; friend; *pl. what a child's parents and godparents call each other*

**compañero/a** companion; **compañero/a de clase** classmate (1); **compañero/a de cuarto** roommate (1)

**compañía** company; business; performing group

**comparación** *f.* comparison (4)

**comparar** to compare

**compartir** to share

**compasión** *f.* compassion (13)

**complejo/a** complex

**complementario/a** complimentary

**complemento** (clothing) accessory (7)

**completar** to complete; finish

**completo/a** complete; **empleo a tiempo completo** full-time job (13)

**complicado/a** complicated

**complicar (qu)** to complicate

**componente** *m.* component

**componer** (*like* **poner**) (*p.p.* **compuesto**) to compose (11)

**comportamiento** behavior

**composición** *f.* essay; composition

**compositor(a)** composer (11)

**compra** purchase; **hacer** (*irreg.*) **las compras por el Internet** to shop online, Internet shopping (15); **ir** (*irreg.*) **de compras** to go shopping (7)

**comprar** to buy (1); **comprar entradas de cine por el Internet** to buy movie tickets online (15)

**comprender** to understand (1)

**comprensión** *f.* understanding

**comprensivo/a** understanding (13)

**comprometido/a** engaged to be married

**compromiso** engagement (12)

**computación** *f.* computer science

**computadora** computer (1); **computadora portátil** laptop (1); **laboratorio de computadoras** computer laboratory (1)

**computarizar (c)** to computerize

**común** *adj.* common; mutual

**comunicación** *f.* communication; **medios** (*pl.*) **de comunicación** mass media (15)

**comunicarse (qu)** to communicate (with each other) (9)

**comunicativo/a** communicative

**comunidad** *f.* community (8)

**comunitario/a** *adj.* community; **servicio comunitario** community service

**con** with (1); **con cuidado** carefully; **con frecuencia** often; **¿con qué frecuencia?** how often? (3); **¿con quién(es)?** with whom? (1); **con tal (de) que** + *subj.* provided that (14)

**concentrarse** to concentrate; to focus on

**concepto** concept; idea

**concha** (sea)shell (14)

**conciencia** conscience; awareness

**concienciar** to make aware

**concierto** concert (11)

**conciso/a** concise

**concluir (y)** to conclude, come to an end

**conclusión** *f.* conclusion, end

**concurso** competition

**condado** county

**condensado/a** condensed

**condición** *f.* condition

**condimento** seasoning

**cóndor** *m.* condor

**conducir** *irreg.* to drive (*Sp.*) (8); **carnet** (*m.*) **de conducir** driver's license (8)

**conectar** to connect

**conejo** rabbit (8)

**conexión** *f.* connection; **conexión WiFi** WiFi connection (15)

**confeccionar** to make

**confesar** to confess

**confirmación** *f.* confirmation

**conflicto** conflict, clash; **conflicto armado** armed conflict

**congelado/a** *adj.* frozen

**congregarse (gu)** to assemble

**congreso** conference

**conjunción** *f.* conjunction; **conjunción de dependencia y propósito** *gram.* conjunction of contingency and purpose (14); **conjunción temporal** *gram.* temporal conjunction (13)

**conjunto** group; collection; **conjunto musical** band, musical group (11)

**conjunto/a** *adj.* joint

**conmemoración** *f.* commemoration

**conmemorar** to commemorate

**conmigo** with me (2)

**cono** cone

**conocer (zc)** to know, to be familiar with (3)

**conocido/a** *n.* acquaintance; *adj.* well-known

**conocimiento** knowledge (13)

**conquista** conquest (9)

**conquistador(a)** conqueror, conquistador (9)

**conquistar** to conquer (9)

**conseguir** (*like* **seguir**) to get, obtain (3); **conseguir** + *inf.* to manage to (*do something*) (7)

**consejero/a** advisor, counselor (13)

**consejo** advice, council

**conservación** *f.* conservation (14)

**conservador(a)** conservative (9)

**conservar** to conserve (14), save

**consideración** *f.* consideration

**considerar** to consider; to think (*about*)

**consistir** to consist

**consolidar** to consolidate

**constante** constant

**constitución** *f.* constitution

**construcción** *f.* construction

**construir (y)** to build

**consultor(a)** counselor, consultant

**consultorio** office

**consumir** to consume

**contabilidad** *f.* accounting (1)

**contable** *m., f.* accountant

**contactar** to contact

**contacto** contact; **mantenerse** (*like* **tener**) **en contacto (con)** to stay in touch (with); **ponerse** (*irreg.*) **en contacto con** to get in touch with

**contador(a)** accountant (13)

**contaminación** *f.* pollution (14); **contaminación del agua** water pollution (14); **contaminación del aire** air pollution (14); **contaminación del suelo** soil pollution (14)

**contaminado/a** polluted (14)

**contaminante** *n. m.* pollutant; *adj.* contaminating, polluting

**contaminar** to pollute (14)

**contar (ue)** to count (6); to tell (6)

**contemporáneo/a** contemporary

**contener** (*like* **tener**) to contain (6)

**contenido** *n.* content

**contento/a** content, happy (2)

**contestar** to answer (1); **contestar el teléfono** to answer the phone (13)

**contexto** context

**contigo** with you (*s. fam.*) (2)

**continente** *m.* continent

**continuación** *f.* continuation; **a continuación** following; below

**continuar (continúo)** to continue

**contra** against

**contrabajo** double-bass

**contrabando** contraband; a prohibited commodity

**contrariamente** contrarily

**contrario/a** opposite; **al contrario** on the contrary; **por el contrario** on the contrary

**contraste** *m.* contrast

**contrato** contract

**contribución** *f.* contribution

**contribuir (y)** to contribute

**control** *m.* control; **control de seguridad** security; **pasar por el control de seguridad** to go through security (10)

**controlar** to control; to check

**convención** *f.* convention

**convencional** conventional

**convenio** contract; agreement

**conventillo** tenement

**convento** convent

**conversación** *f.* conversation

**conversar** to talk, to converse

**convertir (ie, i)** to convert (9); **convertirse en** to change, to become

**convivencia** living together

**convivir** to live together

**cooperación** *f.* cooperation

**cooperativo/a** cooperative

**coordinar** to coordinate, arrange

**copa** (alcoholic) drink (3); (wine) glass (6); **tomar una copa** to have a drink (*alcoholic*) (3)

**copia: hacer** (*irreg.*) **copias** to make copies (13)

**copiar** to copy

**copropietario/a** co-owner

**coquí** *m.* tree frog (*P.R.*)

**coral** *m.* coral; **arrecife** (*m.*) **de coral** coral reef (14)

**corazón** *m.* heart (12)

**corbata** tie (7)

**cordillera** mountain range

**coro** choir (11); chorus (11)

**corporal** *adj.* body; physical

**corral** *m.* yard; barnyard; **ave** (*f. but el ave*) **de corral** farm bird (8)

**corrala** *a type of community housing typical of Madrid*

**corraleja** *a type of bull-fighting festival in Colombia*

**correcto/a** correct

**corredor** *m.* corridor, passage

**corregir (i, i) (j)** to correct

**correo** post; **oficina de correos** post office (8)

**correr** to run (1); to jog (1)

**corresponder** to correspond; to be fitting

**correspondiente** *adj.* corresponding

**corrida** race; **corrida de toros** bullfight (11)

**corriente: ponerse** (*irreg.*) **al corriente** to catch up

**corrupción** *f.* corruption

**corrupto/a** corrupt (9)

**cortar** to cut; **cortar el césped** to mow the lawn (cut the grass) (3)

**corte** *n. m.* cut; **corte de pelo** haircut; *f.* court

**corteza** peel

**cortijo** farm

**cortina** curtain

**corto/a** short; **de manga corta** with short sleeves (7); **pantalón** (*m.*) **corto** shorts (7)

**cosa** thing (3)

**cosecha** harvest

**coser** to sew

**cosméticos** *pl.* cosmetics (7)

**cosmopolita** *adj. m., f.* cosmopolitan

**cosmovisión** *f.* understanding of the universe

**costa** coast (14)

**costar (ue)** to cost; **¿cuánto cuesta(n)?** how much does it (do they) cost? (7)

**costarricense** Costa Rican (P)

**costo** *n.* cost, price

**costumbre** *f.* custom

**cotidiano/a** daily

**coyote** *m.* coyote

**creación** *f.* creation

**crear** to create (11)

**creatividad** *f.* creativity

**creativo/a** *adj.* creative

**crecer (zc)** to grow

**crédito: tarjeta de crédito** credit card (6)

**creencia** belief

**creer (y)** (*p.p.* **creído**) to believe (2)

**cría** breeding (*of cattle*)

**crianza** raising

**crimen** *m.* crime

**criollo/a** *adj.* Creole

**crisis** *f.* crisis

**cristianismo** Christianity

**cristiano/a** Christian; **moros y cristianos** black beans and rice

**Cristo** Christ

**crítico/a** *n.* critic; *adj.* critical

**crónica** chronicle (9); report (9)

**cronología** chronology

**cronológico/a** chronological

**crucero** cruise (ship) (10)

**crujiente** crunchy

**cruz** *f.* (*pl.* **cruces**) cross

**cruzar (c)** to cross (8)

**cuaderno** notebook (1)

**cuadra** block (8)

**cuadrado/a** squared

**cuadro** painting (5); **de cuadros** plaid (7)

**cual: el/la cual** which; **lo cual** which; **sea cual sea** whatever

**¿cuál(es)?** what? (1); which? (1); **¿cuál es su nombre?** what's your (*form.*) name? (P); **¿cuál es tu nombre?** what's your (*fam.*) name? (P)

**cualidad** *f.* quality

**cualificado/a** *adj.* qualified

**cualquier** *adj.* any

**cuando** when (2); **de vez en cuando** from time to time

**¿cuándo?** when? (1)

**cuanto: en cuanto** *conj.* as soon as (13); **en cuanto a** regarding

**¿cuánto?** how much? (1); **¿cuánto cuesta(n)?** how much does it (do they) cost? (7); **¿cuánto tiempo hace que... ?** how long has it been since . . . ?; **¿cuánto vale(n)?** how much is it (are they) worth? (7); **¿en cuánto sale(n)?** how much is it (are they)? (7)

**¿cuántos/as?** how many? (P); **¿cuántos años tiene usted (Ud.)?** how old are you (*s. form.*)? (4); **¿cuántos años tienes?** how old are you (*s. fam.*)? (4)

**cuarenta** forty (2)

**cuarto** room (3); **arreglar el cuarto** to tidy/clean up the room (3); **compañero/a de cuarto** roommate (1)

**cuarto/a** fourth (5), quarter (*hour*); **menos cuarto** quarter to (1); **y cuarto** quarter past (1)

**cuate/a** *coll.* friend

**cuatro** four (P); **son las cuatro.** it's four o'clock. (1)

**cuatrocientos/as** four hundred (4)

**cubano/a** Cuban (P)

**cubículo** (office) cube (13), cubicle

**cubierto/a** (*p.p. of* **cubrir**) covered

**cubista** *m., f.* cubist

**cubrir** (*p.p.* **cubierto**) to cover (6)

**cuchara** spoon (6)

**cucharada** spoonful

**cucharadita** teaspoon

**cucharón** *m.* soup ladle (6)

**cuchillo** knife (6)

**cuello** neck (12)

**cuenco** serving bowl (6)

**cuenta** bill, check (6); **hacer** (*irreg.*) **la cuenta atrás** to count down (*to midnight*); **manejar las cuentas** to manage one's accounts (13); **manejar las cuentas por el Internet** to manage one's accounts online, Internet banking (15); **pagar (gu) las cuentas (médicas)** to pay the (medical) bills (15)

**cuentista** *m., f.* story writer; author

**cuento** story (9)

**cuerda** rope; cord

**cuerno** horn

**cuero** leather; **de cuero** leather (7)

**cuerpo** body; **cuerpo humano** human body (12)

**cuestión** *f.* question; issue

**cueva** cave

**cuidado** care; **con cuidado** carefully; **cuidado médico/personal** medical/personal care (12); **tener** (*irreg.*) **cuidado** to be careful (3)

**cuidadosamente** carefully

**cuidar a** to take care of (*someone*); **cuidarse** to take care of oneself (12)

**culinario/a** culinary

**cultivar** to cultivate; to grow, to develop

**cultivo** crop

**cultura** culture

**cumbia** *dance native to Colombia*

**cumpleaños** *m. inv.* birthday (4); **pastel de cumpleaños** birthday cake

**cumplir** to carry out; **cumplir años** to have a birthday

**cuñado/a** brother-in-law/sister-in-law (4)

**cura** treatment; cure

**curandero/a** folk healer

**curar** to cure

**curativo/a** *adj.* healing

**curiosidad** *f.* curiosity

**currículum** *m.* résumé, CV (13)

**curso** course

**cuyo/a** whose

# D

**dama** lady

**daño** harm, damage

**danza** dance (11)

**danzante** *m., f.* dancer (11)

**dar** *irreg.* to give (6); **dar de comer** to feed; **dar la vuelta** to turn around; **dar un paseo** to take a stroll; **dar una caminata** to go on a hike (9); **dar una fiesta** to throw a party; **darle pena** to make (*someone*) sad; **darle vergüenza** to embarrass (*someone*); **darse la mano** to shake hands with each other (9)

**datar de** + *time* to date from + *time* (9)

**dato** fact; **anotar datos** to enter data (13)

**de** *prep.* from (P); of (1); **de acuerdo** in agreement; **de acuerdo a** according to; **de acuerdo con** in accordance with; **de al lado** next-door (5); **de compras** shopping; **¿de dónde eres?** where are you (*s. fam.*) from? (P); **¿de dónde es usted (Ud.)?** where are you (*s. form.*) from? (P); **de enfrente** *adj.* front; **de habla española** Spanish-speaking; **de ida** one-way (trip); **de ida y vuelta** round (trip); **de la mañana** in the morning (1); A.M.; **de la noche** in the evening, at night (1); P.M.; **de la tarde** in the afternoon (1); P.M.; **de marca** name-brand; **de nada.** you're welcome. (P); **de todos modos** at any rate; **de última moda** fashionable; **de una vez** once and for all; **de vacaciones** on vacation; **¿de veras?** really?; **de vez en cuando** from time to time; **de viaje** on a trip; **de vuelta** again

**debajo** *adv.* below; **debajo de** *prep.* under (2)

**debate** *m.* debate

**deber** to owe (6); **deber** + *inf.* should, ought to (*do something*) (3)

**débil** *adj.* weak

**década** decade (9)

**decidir** to decide

**décimo/a** tenth (5)

**decir** *irreg.* (*p.p.* **dicho**) to say (6); to tell (6)

**decisión** *f.* decision; **tomar una decisión** to make a decision

**declaración** *f.* statement, declaration

**declarar** to declare (9); to state

**declinar** to decline

**decoración** *f.* decoration

**decorar** to decorate

**dedicar (qu)** to dedicate; to devote

**dedo** finger (12); **dedo del pie** toe (12)

**defender (ie)** to defend, to protect

**defensa** *n.* defense; defender; *adj.* defense

**defensivo/a** defensive

**deficiencia** deficiency, lack

**definición** *f.* definition; **televisión** (*f.*) **de alta definición** HD TV (15)

**definir** to define

**definitivo/a** definitive

**deforestación** *f.* deforestation (14)

**degustación** *f.* tasting

**deidad** *f.* deity

**dejar de** + *inf.* to stop/quit (*doing something*) (12)

**del** (*contraction of* **de** + **el**) from the (P); of the

**delante de** in front of (5)

**delantero** forward (*sports*)

**deletrear** to spell out

**delfín** *m.* dolphin (14)

**delgado/a** thin (4)

**delicadamente** *adv.* delicately

**delicioso/a** delicious

**delta: practicar (qu) el ala delta** to hang glide (9)

**demanda** *n.* demand; request

**demás: lo demás** the rest; **los/las demás** the rest, others

**demasiado** *adv.* too much (7)

**democracia** democracy

**democrático/a** democratic

**demorar** to delay

**demostrar (ue)** to demonstrate, show

**demostrativo** *gram.* demonstrative (4)

**denominado/a** named, called

**denso/a: población** (*f.*) **densa** dense population (14)

**dentista** *m., f.* dentist (12)

**dentro** *adv.* inside; **dentro de** *prep.* inside (5); within; **dentro de poco** in a little while

**departamento** department; apartment (*Mex.*)

**dependencia** dependence; **conjunción** (*f.*) **de dependencia y propósito** *gram.* conjunction of contingency and purpose (14)

**depender** to depend

**dependiente** *adj.* dependent

**deporte** *m.* sport; **practicar (qu) un deporte** to participate in a sport (1)

**deportivo/a** *adj.* sports, sport-related

**depresión** *f.* depression (15)

**deprimirse** to become depressed

**depuradora** filter

**derecha** *n.* right side; **a la derecha (de)** to the right (of) (2)

**derecho** law (*profession*) (1); right (*legal*); straight (ahead) (8); **seguir (i, i) derecho** to go straight; **todo derecho** straight ahead (8);

**derretir (i, i)** to melt

**derrocar (qu)** to overthrow; to topple

**derrota** *n.* defeat

**derrumbarse** to destroy, demolish

**desafiante** *adj.* challenging

**desafío** challenge

**desafortunadamente** unfortunately (8)

**desánimo** dejection, despondency

**desaparecer (zc)** to disappear

**desaparición** *f.* disappearance

**desarrollar** to develop (14)

**desarrollo** *n.* development

**desastre** *m.* disaster; **desastre natural** natural disaster (9); **desastre ambiental** environmental disaster (14)

**desastroso/a** disastrous

**desatender (ie)** to neglect

**desayunar** to eat breakfast (1)

**desayuno** breakfast (6)

**descansar (un rato)** to rest (a bit) (1)

**descanso** *n.* rest; break

**descargar (gu)** to download

**descendiente** *m., f.* descendent

**descomponer** (*like* **poner**) (*p.p.* **descompuesto**) to break down (*in accidental* **se** *construction*) (7)

**descomposición** *f.* breakdown, decomposition

**desconocido/a** *adj.* unknown

**descontado/a** *adj.* discounted

**describir** (*p.p.* **descrito**) to describe (1)

**descripción** *f.* description (P)

**descriptivo/a** descriptive

**descubierto/a** discovered (9)

**descubrir** (*like* **cubrir**) (*p.p.* **descubierto**) to discover (9)

**descuento** discount (7)

**desde** *prep.* from; **desde entonces** since then; **desde hace... años** for . . . years; **desde la(s)... hasta la(s)...** from . . . until . . . (*time*)

**desear** to want; **desear + inf.** to desire/want to (*do something*) (1)

**desecho** waste; **desechos urbanos** urban waste

**desechos urbanos** urban waste (14)

**desembarcar (qu)** to disembark

**desempleo** unemployment

**deseo** desire, wish

**desertificación** *f. process by which an area becomes a desert*

**desesperado/a** desperate

**desfile** *m.* parade (9)

**desgraciadamente** unfortunately (8)

**desierto** desert (14)

**designar** to appoint

**desigual** erratic; inconsistent

**desintegrar(se)** to disintegrate, break up (9)

**desmilitarizado/a** *adj.* demilitarized

**desorientado/a** lost

**desove** *m.* egg-laying

**despacho** (individual) office (1); study (5)

**despedida** good-bye, leave taking (P)

**despedir** (*like* **pedir**) to fire (13); **despedirse** to say good-bye to each other (9)

**despensa** pantry

**desperdiciar** to waste (14)

**despertador** *m.* alarm clock

**despertar (ie)** to wake; **despertarse** to wake up (5)

**despoblación** *f.* depopulation

**despoblado/a** unpopulated, deserted

**desproporción** *f.* disproportion

**desproporcionado/a** mismatched

**desprotegido/a** *adj.* unprotected

**después** *adv.* after (1); later; then; **después de** *prep.* after; **después de que** *conj.* after (13)

**destacar (qu)** to emphasize

**destinar** to appoint

**destino** destination (10)

**destreza** skill (13)

**destrucción** *f.* destruction (14)

**destructivo/a** destructive

**destruido/a** *adj.* destroyed

**destruir (y)** to destroy (9)

**desventaja** disadvantage

**desvestirse** (*like* **vestir**) to get undressed (5)

**detalle** *m.* detail

**detener** (*like* **tener**) to stop; to arrest

**deteriorado/a** *adj.* deteriorated; damaged

**determinación** *f.* determination

**determinar** to determine, to decide

**detrás de** *prep.* behind (2)

**deuda** debt (15)

**devolver** (*like* **volver**) (*p.p.* **devuelto**) to return (*something*); to give back (9)

**día** *m.* day (1); **algún día** someday; **buenos días.** good morning. (*until midday meal*) (P); **Día de Acción de Gracias** Thanksgiving Day (11); **Día de Canadá** Canada Day (11); **Día de la Independencia** Independence Day (11); **Día de la Madre** Mother's Day (11); **Día de la Raza** Columbus Day (11); **Día de los Muertos** Day of the Dead (11); **Día de los Reyes Magos** Feast of the Three Kings (Epiphany) (11); **Día de San Valentín** St. Valentine's Day; **Día de Todos los Santos** All Saints' Day; **Día del Padre** Father's Day (11); **día del santo** one's saint day (11); **Día del Trabajo** Labor Day; **día feriado** holiday; **día festivo** holiday (11); **días de entre semana** weekdays (1); **estar** (*irreg.*) **al día** to be up to date (15); **todos los días** every day (1)

**diabetes** *f. s.* diabetes

**diablito** little devil

**diablo** devil

**diagrama** *m.* diagram

**diálogo** conversation, dialogue

**diamante** *m.* diamond; **de diamantes** diamond (7)

**diario/a** daily (2)

**dibujar** to draw (9)

**dibujo** drawing (11); **dibujos animados** cartoons (9)

**diccionario** dictionary (1)

**dicho/a** (*p.p. of* **decir**) said; **mejor dicho** or rather, in other words

**diciembre** December (2)

**dictador(a)** dictator

**dictadura** dictatorship (9)

**diecinueve** nineteen (P)

**dieciocho** eighteen (P)

**dieciséis** sixteen (P)

**diecisiete** seventeen (P)

**diente** *m.* tooth (12); **cepillarse los dientes** to brush one's teeth; **lavarse los dientes** to brush one's teeth (5); **pasta de dientes** toothpaste

**diéresis** *f. s.* dieresis

**dieta** diet

**diez** ten (P)

**diferencia** difference

**diferenciarse** to distinguish; to differentiate

**diferente** different

**difícil** difficult (1)

**dificilísimo/a** very difficult

**dificultad** *f.* difficulty, problem

**difunto/a** *adj.* deceased, dead

**digestión** *f.* digestion

**digital: cámara digital** digital camera (15)

**digitalizar (c)** to digitize (15)

**dimensión** *f.* dimension

**diminuto/a** little, tiny

**dinámico/a** *adj.* dynamic

**dinero** money; **ahorrar dinero** to save money (15)

**dios** *m. s.* god; **¡por Dios!** for heaven's sake! (9)

**dióxido** dioxide; **dióxido de carbono** carbon dioxide

**dirección** *f.* address; direction; *pl.* directions (8)

**directo/a** direct, straight; **objeto directo** *gram.* direct object; **pronombre** (*m.*) **de objeto directo** *gram.* direct object pronoun (5)

**director(a)** director (11); **director(a) de personal** personnel director (13)

**dirigir (j)** to manage (*people*) (13)

**disco** disc, disk; **disco duro** hard disk (13)

**discoteca** dance club (9)

**discriminación** *f.* discrimination

**discriminatorio/a** discriminatory, discriminating

**disculpar** to excuse

**discutir** to argue (12)

**diseñador(a)** designer (13); **diseñador(a) de modas** fashion designer (13)

**diseñar** to design

**diseño** design (7)

**disfrazarse (c)** to disguise oneself (11)

**disfrutar (de)** to enjoy (10)

**disminuir (y)** to reduce, to decrease

**disolver (ue)** (*p.p.* **disuelto**) to dissolve (9)

**disperso/a** scattered

**disponer** (*like* **poner**) (*p.p.* **dispuesto**) to arrange

**disponibilidad** *f.* availability; readiness to help

**disponible** available (7)

**dispositivo** device

**disquete** *m.* floppy disk

**distancia** distance

**distinguir (g)** to distinguish, to differentiate

**distinto/a** different

**distracción** *f.* entertainment, hobby (3)

**distribución** *f.* distribution

**distribuir (y)** to distribute

**distrito** district

**diversidad** *f.* diversity, variety

**diversión** *f.* fun thing to do (9), amusement, entertainment

**diverso/a** different, diverse

**divertido/a** fun (1)

**divertirse (ie, i)** to have fun (7)

**dividir** to divide, split up

**división** *f.* division

**divorciado/a** divorced (4)

**divorciarse (de)** to get divorced (from) (12)

**divorcio** divorce (4); **divorcio exprés** *law in Spain that allows divorce without a separation period*

**doblar** to turn (8); **doblar la ropa** to fold clothes (3)

**doble** double; **doble acristalamiento** double-paned windows; **habitación** (*f.*) **doble** double room (10)

**doce** twelve (P)

**doctor(a)** doctor

**documental** *m.* documentary

**documentar** to document

**documento** document; **documento adjunto** attachment (15)

**dólar** *m.* dollar

**doler (ue)** to hurt (12)

**dolor** *m.* pain, ache (12); **dolor de cabeza** headache (12); **dolor de estómago** stomachache (12); **dolor de muela** toothache (12)

**doméstico/a** domestic; **animal** (*m.*) **doméstico** domesticated (farm) animal (8); **aparato doméstico** appliance (3); **quehacer** (*m.*) **doméstico** domestic chore (3)

**dominar** to control, dominate; to overlook

**domingo** Sunday (1)

**dominicano/a** Dominican (P)

**dominio** control; mastery

**dominó: jugar (ue) (gu) al dominó** to play dominos (2)

**don** *m. title of respect used with a man's first name;* **tener** (*irreg.*) **don de gentes** to get along well with others (13)

**doña** *title of respect used with a woman's first name*

**donación** *f.* donation

**donar** to donate

**donde** where

**¿dónde?** where? (1); **¿de dónde eres?** where are you (*s. fam.*) from? (P); **¿de dónde es usted (Ud.)?** where are you (*s. form.*) from? (P)

**doradito/a** browned, golden (*cooking*)

**dorado/a** golden

**dorar** to brown (*cooking*)

**dormir (ue, u)** to sleep (3); **dormir la siesta** to nap; **dormirse** to fall asleep (5)

**dormitorio** bedroom (5); **dormitorio principal** master bedroom (5)

**dos** two (P); **ciento dos** one hundred two (4); **dos mil** two thousand (4); **dos millones (de)** two million (4); **son las dos.** it's two o'clock. (1)

**doscientos/as** two hundred (4)

**drama** theater (11)

**dramaturgo/a** playwright (11)

**drástico/a** drastic

**droga** drug

**drogadicto/a** drug addict (12)

**drogarse (gu)** to get high (12); to take drugs (12)

**ducha** shower (5)

**ducharse** to take a shower (5)

**duda** doubt; **verbo de duda** *gram.* verb of doubt (11)

**dudar** to doubt (11)

**dueño/a** landlord/landlady; master

**dulce** *n. m.* candy; *adj.* sweet; **agua** (*f. but* **el agua**) **dulce** fresh water (14); *pl. m.* candies (6)

**dulzura** sweetness

**duración** *f.* length, duration

**durante** during

**durazno** peach (6)

**duro/a** hard; **disco duro** hard disk (13)

**DVD** *m.* DVD; **reproductor** (*m.*) **de DVD** DVD player; **sacar (qu) un DVD** to check out a DVD (1); **ver** (*irreg.*) **un DVD** to watch a DVD (3)

**DVD-ROM** *m.* DVD-ROM (15)

# E

**e** and (*used instead of* **y** *before words beginning with stressed* **i**- *or* **hi**-, *except* **hie**-)

**echar** to throw, cast

**eco** echo

**ecología** ecology

**ecológico/a** ecological (14)

**economía** economics (1)

**económico/a** economic; **clase** (*f.*) **económica** coach (class) (10); **recurso económico** financial resources

**ecosistema** *m.* ecosystem

**ecoturismo** ecotourism (10)

**ecoturístico/a** ecotour

**ecuador** *m.* equator

**ecuatoguineano/a** Equatoguinean, from Equatorial Guinea (P)

**ecuatorial** equatorial

**ecuatoriano/a** Ecuadorian

**ecuestre** equestrian

**edad** *f.* age; period (*historical*)

**edición** *f.* edition; publication

**edificio** building (1); **edificio de apartamentos** apartment building (5); **edificio de oficinas** office building (8)

**editar** to edit

**educación** *f.* education (1); **educación superior** higher education; **Facultad** (*f.*) **de Educación** School of Education (1)

**educativo/a** educational

**efectivo/a** effective; **en efectivo** cash (6)

**efecto** effect

**eficaz** (*pl.* **eficaces**) *adj.* effective

**eficiente** efficient

**egoísmo** selfishness (15)

**egoísta** selfish (15)

**eje** *m.* axis; focal point

**ejecutar** to carry out; to execute

**ejecutivo/a** *adj.* executive

**ejemplo** example; **por ejemplo** for example (4)

**ejercer (z)** to practice (*a profession*)

**ejercicio** exercise; **hacer** (*irreg.*) **ejercicio** to exercise (3); **hacer ejercicio aeróbico** to do aerobics (12)

**ejército** army (9)

**ekeko** *an indigenous deity of abundance*

**el** *def. art. m. s.* the (P); **el más/menos... de** the most/least . . . of/in (4); **el lunes (martes, miércoles,... )** on Monday (Tuesday, Wednesday, . . . ) (1); **el lunes (martes, miércoles,... ) pasado** last Monday (Tuesday, Wednesday, . . . ) (6); **el lunes (martes, miércoles,... ) que viene** next Monday (Tuesday, Wednesday, . . . ) (1)

**él** *sub. pron.* he (P); *obj.* (*of prep.*) him

**elaborado/a** (*p.p. of* **elaborar**) made

**elección** *f.* choice; election

**electricidad** *f.* electricity

**electricista** *m., f.* electrician (13)

**eléctrico/a** electric; **batidora eléctrica** electric mixer; **carro/coche** (*m.*) **eléctrico** electric car (14)

**electrodoméstico** electrical (household) appliance

**electrónico/a** electronic; **agenda electrónica** PDA (15)

**elefante** *m.* elephant (14)

**elegante** elegant; graceful

**elegido/a** *adj.* chosen; elected

**elegir (i, i) (j)** to choose; to elect

**elemento** element, factor

**elevado/a** *adj.* elevated, high

**eliminar** to eliminate

**elitista** *m., f.* elitist

**ella** *sub. pron.* she (P); *obj.* (*of prep.*) her

**ellos/as** *sub. pron.* they (P); *obj.* (*of prep.*) them

**elote** *m.* corn cob

**e-mail** *m.* e-mail (1); **leer (y) el e-mail** to read/check one's e-mail (1); **mandar un e-mail** to send an e-mail (6)

**embalse** *m.* reservoir

**embarcar (qu) (en)** to board (10)

**embargo: sin embargo** however; nevertheless

**embarque: tarjeta de embarque** boarding pass (10)

**emblema** *m.* emblem, symbol

**emblemático/a** emblematic, symbolic

**embriagado/a** drunk, intoxicated

**emergencia** emergency

**emigración** *f.* immigration

**emigrante** *m., f.* immigrant

**emigrar** to immigrate

**emisión** *f.* emission; **emisiones de carbono** carbon emissions

**emisora de radio** radio station

**emoción** *f.* emotion; **verbo de emoción** *gram.* verb of emotion (11)

**emocionado/a** excited (2)

**emocional** emotional (2)

**emocionante** *adj.* moving; exciting

**emocionarse** to display emotion (15)

**empanada** filled pastry, turnover

**emparejar** to match; to pair up

**empate** *m.* tie (*game score*)

**emperador(a)** emperor/empress

**empetrés** mp3; **reproductor** (*m.*) **de empetrés** mp3 player

**empezar (ie) (c)** to begin (3); **empezar + a + inf.** to begin to (*do something*) (3)

**empiezo** beginning

**empleado/a** employee (13)

**empleador(a)** employer

**emplear** to employ

**empleo** job (13); employment (15); **buscar (qu) / encontrar (ue) empleo estable** to look for / find stable employment (15); **empleo a tiempo completo/parcial** full-/ part-time job (13)

**empobrecer (zc)** to impoverish

**empotrado/a** built-in

**emprendedor(a)** enterprising (13)

**empresa** business, enterprise

**empresarial** pertaining to business; **administración** (*f.*) **empresarial** business administration (1)

**empresario/a** businessman/ businesswoman

**empujar** to push, press

**en** in; on; at; **en ayunas** before breakfast; fasting; **en casa** at home; **en caso de que + subj.** in case (14); **en cuanto** *conj.* as soon as (13); **en cuanto a** regarding; **¿en cuánto sale(n)?** how much is it (are they)? (7); **en efectivo** cash (6); **en general** generally; **en la actualidad** currently, right now; **en línea** online; **en ninguna parte** nowhere; **en parejas** in pairs; **en punto** sharp, exactly (*with time*) (1); **en seguida** right away; **en vivo** live; **en voz alta** aloud; **mantenerse** (*like* **tener**) **en contacto (con)** to stay in touch (with); **patinar en línea** to inline skate (2); **periódico en línea** online newspaper (15); **revista en línea** online magazine (15)

**enamorado/a (de)** in love (with) (12)

**enamorarse (de)** to fall in love (with) (12)

**encaje** *m.* lace

**encantado/a** delighted; **encantado/a.** it's a pleasure (to meet you). (P)

**encantar** to love (*lit.* to enchant) (6)

**encargarse (gu) (de)** to take charge (of)

**encender (ie)** to light

**encendido/a** *adj.* burning; switched on

**enchufe** *m.* connection

**encierro** running of the bulls (11)

**encima de** on top of (2)

**encontrar (ue)** to find (3); **encontrar empleo estable** to find stable employment (15)

**encuesta** survey

**encuestado/a** *adj.* polled

**endémico/a** endemic

**endulzar (c)** to sweeten

**energético/a** *adj.* energetic

**energía** power; energy (14); **energía eólica** wind power (14); **energía hidroeléctrica** hydroelectric power (14); **energía nuclear** nuclear power (14); **energía solar** solar power (14); **energía undimotriz** wave energy

**enero** January (2)

**enfermarse** to get sick

**enfermedad** *f.* illness (12)

**enfermería** hospital

**enfermero/a** nurse (12)

**enfermo/a** sick (2)

**enfocar (qu)** to focus

**enfrentar** to confront; to bring face to face

**enfrente** *adv.* opposite; facing; **de enfrente** *adj.* front; **enfrente de** *prep.* in front of (2); across from (5)

**enfriar (enfrío)** to cool

**engordar** to gain weight (12)

**enlatado/a** canned

**enloquecido/a** crazed, gone mad

**enmascarado/a** masked

**enojado/a** angry (2)

**enojar** to anger

**enorgullecer (zc) (de)** to be proud (of)

**enorme** huge

**enormemente** *adv.* enormously

**enriquecer (zc)** to enrich

**ensalada** salad (6)

**enseñar** to teach; to show

**entender (ie)** to understand (3)

**entendido/a** *adj.* understood

**enterarse (de)** to find out, learn (about) (15)

**entero/a** whole

**entidad** *f.* entity

**entonces** *adv.* then; **desde entonces** since then

**entorno** environment

**entrada** ticket; admission; inning (*baseball*); **comprar entradas de cine por el Internet** to buy movie tickets online (15)

**entrar (a/en)** to enter

**entre** *prep.* between (3); among; **días** (*m.*) **de entre semana** weekdays (1); **entre semana** during the week (1)

**entregar (gu)** to deliver (6); to hand in (6)

**entrenador(a)** trainer (6); coach (13)

**entrenamiento** training

**entrenar** to train

**entretener** (*like* **tener**) to entertain

**entretenimiento** entertainment

**entrevista** interview (13)

**entrevistador(a)** interviewer (13)

**entrevistar** to interview (13)

**enumerar** to count; to list

**enunciado** statement

**envase** *m.* container; **envase de plástico/vidrio** plastic/glass container (14)

**enviar (envío)** to send

**envidia** envy (15)

**eólico/a** *adj.* wind; **energía eólica** wind power (14); **turbina eólica** wind turbine (14)

**epidemia** epidemic

**episodio** episode; event

**época** time period (9); season (9); **época colonial** colonial era (9)

**equilibrio** balance

**equinoccio** equinox

**equipaje** *m.* luggage (10); **facturar el equipaje** to check luggage (10); **reclamo de equipaje** baggage claim (10); **recoger (j) el equipaje** to pick up luggage (10)

**equipo** team

**equitación** *f.* horseback riding (9)

**equivalente** *n. m.* equivalent

**eres** you (*s. fam.*) are (P)

**es** he/she is (P); you (*s. form.*) are (P)

**escala** stop (*layover*) (10); scale; **hacer** (*irreg.*) **escalas** to make stops

**escalera** staircase, stair

**escanear** to scan (15)

**escáner** *m.* scanner (15)

**escapar** to escape

**escaparate** *m.* shop window

**escape** *m.* escape

**escasez** *f.* (*pl.* **escaseces**) shortage (14)

**escena** scene

**escenario** stage (11)

**escénico/a** scenic; **artes** (*f. but* **el arte**) **escénicas** performing arts (11)

**esclavitud** *f.* slavery

**esclavo/a** slave (9)

**escoger (j)** to choose

**escolar** *adj.* school

**escondido/a** *adj.* hidden

**escondite** *m.* hiding place; **jugar (ue) (g) al escondite** to play hide-and-seek

**escribir** (*p.p.* **escrito**) to write (1); **escribir informes** to write reports; **máquina de escribir** typewriter

**escrito/a** (*p.p. of* **escribir**) written

**escritor(a)** writer (11)

**escritorio** desk (1)

**escuchar** to listen to (1); **escuchar música** to listen to music (1)

**escuela** school (8); **escuela primaria** elementary school; **escuela secundaria** high school

**esculpir** to sculpt (11)

**escultor(a)** sculptor (11)

**escultura** sculpture (7)

**ese/a** *adj.* that (4); *pron.* that one (4)

**esencia** essence

**esencial** essential

**esfera** sphere

**esférico/a** spherical

**esfuerzo** effort

**esmalte** *m.* enamel

**eso** that (*concept, unknown thing*) (4); **por eso** that's why (4)

**esos/as** *adj.* those (4); *pron.* those ones (4)

**espacio** space; **espacio en blanco** blank (space)

**espalda** back (12)

**español** *m.* Spanish (*language*) (1)

**español(a)** *adj.* Spanish (P)

**especia** spice

**especial** special

**especializado/a** specialized, skilled

**especie** *f. s.* species; **especie en peligro de extinción** endangered species (14)

**específico/a** specific

**espectacular** spectacular

**espectáculo** show (11)

**espectador(a)** spectator (11)

**espejo** mirror

**espera: sala de espera** waiting room (10)

**esperanza** hope, expectation

**esperar** to wait (11); to hope; to expect

**espinacas** *pl.* spinach (6)

**espíritu** *m.* spirit

**espiritual** spiritual

**espléndido/a** splendid

**esposo/a** husband/wife (1)

**espuma** foam

**espumita** espresso coffee with a sweet foam (*Cuba*)

**esquí** *m.* ski, skiing

**esquiar (esquío)** to ski

**esquina** corner

**estabilidad** *f.* stability (9)

**estable** *adj.* stable; **buscar (qu) / encontrar (ue) empleo estable** to look for / find stable employment (15)

**establecer (zc)** to establish (9); **establecerse** to settle (9)

**establecido/a** *adj.* established, set

**establecimiento** establishment

**estación** *f.* season (2); station; **estación de autobuses** bus station (8)

**estacionamiento** parking lot/place (8)

**estacionar** to park (8)

**estadía** stay (10)

**estadio** stadium (1)

**estadística** statistics (1)

**estado** state; **estado de ánimo** state of mind; **estado civil** marital status (4); **estado físico** physical state (2); **Estados Unidos** United States

**estadounidense** *n., adj.* American, of the United States of America

**estallo** crashing noise

**estancado/a** *adj.* stagnant

**estancia** stay (*in a hotel*)

**estándar** *m.* standard

**estaño** tin

**estanque** *m.* pond

**estantería** shelves (5)

**estar** *irreg.* to be (2); **¿cómo está usted (Ud.)?** how are you (*s. form.*)? (P); **¿cómo estás?** how are you (*s. fam.*)? (P); **está lloviendo.** it's raining. (2); **está (muy) nublado.** it's (very) cloudy. (2); **está nevando.** it's snowing. (2); **estar + gerund** to be (*doing something*) (2); **estar a cargo (de)** to be in charge (of); **estar al día** to be up to date (15); **estar bien** to be well; **estar de acuerdo** to agree; **estar de buen humor** to be in a good mood; **estar seguro/a (de)** to be sure (of) (11)

**estatua** statue (8)

**estatus** *m.* status; **estatus social** social status

**este** *m.* east; **al este** (to the) east (8)

**este/a** *adj.* this (4); *pron.* this (one) (4); **esta mañana** this morning (1); **esta noche** tonight (1); **esta tarde** this afternoon (1)

**estilo** style (7)

**estimulante** *m.* stimulant

**estimular** to encourage; to stimulate

**estiramiento** *n.* stretching

**estirarse** to stretch (15)

**esto** this (*concept, unknown thing*) (4)

**estómago** stomach (12); **dolor** (*m.*) **de estómago** stomachache (12)

**estorbo** nuisance

**estos/as** *adj.* these (4); *pron.* these ones (4)

**estrategia** strategy

**estrecho** *n.* strait; **Estrecho de Magallanes** Strait of Magellan

**estrecho/a** *adj.* narrow

**estreno** premiere

**estrés** *m.* stress (12); **quitarse el estrés** to remove stress (15); **sufrir de estrés** to suffer from stress (15)

**estresado/a** *adj.* stressed

**estresante** *adj.* stressful

**estricto/a** strict

**estructura** structure

**estudiante** *m., f.* student (1)

**estudiantil** *adj.* student; **centro estudiantil** student union (1); **pagar (gu) el préstamo estudiantil** to pay the student loan (15); **residencia estudiantil** student dorm (1)

**estudiar** to study (1)

**estudio** studio apartment (5); study (*room*)

**estufa** stove (3)

**estupendo/a** wonderful

**etapa** stage, period; **etapa de la vida** stage/period of life (9)

**etcétera** *adv.* et cetera

**eterno/a** eternal

**etiqueta** label

**étnico/a** ethnic

**euro** euro (*money*)

**Europa** Europe

**europeo/a** European

**evacuar** to evacuate

**evaluación** *f.* evaluation

**evento** event (4)

**evidencia** evidence

**evidente** evident, obvious

**evitar** to avoid (14)

**evolución** *f.* assessment; evaluation

**exacto/a** exact

**examen** *m.* exam, test

**examinar** to examine

**excavación** *f.* excavation; **excavación minera** mining (14)

**excavar** to dig; to excavate

**excelencia** excellence

**excelente** excellent

**excéntrico/a** eccentric

**excepción** *f.* exception

**excesivo/a** excessive

**exceso** excess

**exclusivo/a** exclusive

**excursión** *f.* tour, daytrip (10); excursion, expedition, trip

**excusa** excuse

**exhibir** to exhibit

**exigente** demanding (13)

**exigir (j)** to demand, require

**exilio** exile

**existir** to exist

**éxito** success; **tener** (*irreg.*) **éxito** to be successful (3)

**exitoso/a** successful

**éxodo** exodus

**exótico/a** exotic

**expansión** *f.* expansion

**expectación** *f.* expectation, anticipation

**expedición** *f.* expedition

**experiencia** experience

**experto/a** expert, authority

**explicación** *f.* explanation

**explicar (qu)** to explain (6)

**explícitamente** *adv.* explicitly

**exploración** *f.* exploration

**explorador(a)** explorer

**explorar** to explore (9)

**explotación** *f.* exploitation

**explotar** to exploit

**exponerse (like poner) (p.p. expuesto)** to expose oneself

**exportación** *f.* exportation

**exportador(a)** exporter

**exportar** to export

**exposición** *f.* exhibition (11); art show (11)

**exprés: divorcio exprés** *law in Spain that allows divorce without a separation period*

**expresar** to express; **expresarse** to express oneself (15)

**expresión** *f.* expression (P); **expresión impersonal** *gram.* impersonal expression (11)

**expreso** *n.* espresso (coffee)

**expropiación** *f.* expropriation

**expuesto/a** (*p.p. of* **exponer**) exposed

**expulsar** to throw out

**expulsión** *f.* expulsion

**exquisito/a** exquisite

**extender (ie)** to extend (9)

**extensión** *f.* extension

**exterior** *n. m., adj.* outside, exterior

**extinción** *f.* extinction; **especie** (*f.*) **en peligro de extinción** endangered species (14)

**extinguirse (g)** to die out, become extinct

**extra** extra; **extra grande** extra large (*clothing size*) (7)

**extracto** extract

**extraer** (*like* **traer**) (*p.p.* **extraído**) to extract

**extraescolar** *adj.* extracurricular

**extrañar** to miss

**extranjero/a** foreigner (10); *adj.* foreign; *m.* abroad (10); **lenguas extranjeras** foreign languages (1)

**extraño/a** strange; **es extraño que** it's strange that (11)

**extravagante** extravagant

**extremo/a** extreme

**extrovertido/a** outgoing (4)

**exuberante** exuberant

# F

**fábrica** factory (14)

**fabricar (qu)** to make, manufacture

**fachada** facade

**facial: tratamiento facial** facial treatment

**fácil** easy (1)

**facilidad** *f.* ease

**facilitar** to facilitate, make easy

**factor** *m.* factor

**facturar el equipaje** to check luggage (10)

**facultad** *f.* school; **Facultad de Bellas Artes** School of Fine Arts (1); **Facultad de Ciencias** School of Science (1); **Facultad de Educación** School of Education (1); **Facultad de Letras** School of Humanities (1); **Facultad de Leyes** School of Law (1); **Facultad de Medicina** School of Medicine (1)

**falda** skirt (7)

**fallar** to crash (*computer*) (15)

**falso/a** false

**falta** *n.* lack, absence

**faltar** to miss

**fama** fame

**familia** family (4); **familia política** in-laws (4)

**familiar** *adj.* family (4)

**famoso/a** famous

**fanático/a** *n.* fan

**fantasía** fantasy

**fantástico/a** fantastic

**farmacéutico/a** *n.* pharmacist (13); *adj.* pharmaceutical

**fascinar** to fascinate (6)

**fase** *f.* phase

**fatal** bad; awful

**fauna: flora y fauna (silvestre)** (wild) plant and animal life (14)

**fauno** satyr

**favor** *m.* favor; **por favor** please (4)

**favorecer (zc)** to favor

**favorito/a** *n., adj.* favorite

**fe** *f.* faith

**febrero** February (2)

**fecha** date (*calendar*) (2)

**federal** federal (9)

**feliz** (*pl.* **felices**) happy

**femenino/a** feminine

**fenicio/a** Phoenician

**fenomenal** great; **pasarlo fenomenal** to have a great time

**fenómeno** phenomenon

**feo/a** ugly (1)

**feria** festival (9); fair (9)

**feriado/a: día** (*m.*) **feriado** holiday

**ferrocarril** *m.* railway (8)

**ferroviario/a** *adj.* railroad; pertaining to a railroad

**fértil** fertile

**fertilidad** *f.* fertility

**fertilizante** *m.* fertilizer

**festejar** to celebrate

**festival** *m.* festival (11)

**festividad** *f.* festivity (11); feast (11)

**festivo/a** festive; **día** (*m.*) **festivo** holiday (11)

**fibra óptica** optical fiber (15); fiber optics

**ficción** *f.* fiction

**ficticio/a** fictitious

**fiebre** *f.* fever (12)

**fiesta** party (2); **dar** (*irreg.*) **una fiesta** to throw a party; **fiesta de sorpresa** surprise party; **fiesta de quinceañera** young woman's fifteenth birthday party (11); **hacer** (*irreg.*) **una fiesta** to throw a party (2)

**figura** figure; shape; statue

**figurativo/a** figurative

**fijarse (en)** to pay attention (to)

**fijo/a** fixed (7); permanent; **precio fijo** fixed price (7); **teléfono fijo** landline

**Filipinas: Islas Filipinas** Philippines

**filosofía** philosophy (1)

**fin** *m.* end; **el fin de semana pasado** last weekend; **fin de semana** weekend (1) **por fin** finally (4)

**final** *n. m.* end; *adj.* final; **a finales de** at the end of; **al final** in the end

**finalización** *f.* end

**finalizar (c)** to finish, complete

**financiamiento** financing

**financiero/a** *adj.* financial

**finca** farm (8)

**fino/a** fine; high-quality

**fiordo** fjord

**firma** signature

**firmar** to sign (13)

**física** physics (1)

**físicamente: fuerte físicamente** physically strong (13)

**físico/a** *n.* physicist (13); *adj.* physical; **bienestar** (*m.*) **físico** physical well-being (15); **estado físico** physical state (2)

**fisiología** physiology

**flamenco** *music and dance of Andalusia*

**flan** *m.* caramel custard (6); (baked) custard

**flauta** flute

**flexibilidad** *f.* flexibility

**flexible** flexible (13)

**flor** *f.* flower

**flora y fauna (silvestre)** (wild) plant and animal life (14)

**florecer (zc)** to flourish (9); to thrive (9); to flower

**floristería** flower shop (7)

**flotante** *adj.* floating

**foca** seal (14)

**folclor** *m.* folklore (11)

**folclórico/a** folkloric; **baile** (*m.*) **folclórico** traditional/folkloric dance (11)

**folleto** brochure, pamphlet

**fomentar** to encourage, foster

**fondo** background; bottom; depth; fund; **a fondo** deeply

**fontanero/a** plumber

**forestal** *adj.* forest

**forma** form; manner, way

**formación** (*f.*) **académica** education (15)

**formal** formal; **mandato formal** *gram.* formal command; **salón formal** living room

**formalmente** *adv.* formally; seriously

**formarse** to get educated (15)

**formatear** to format

**formidable** tremendous, fantastic

**formular** to formulate

**foro** forum

**fortalecer (zc)** to strengthen, fortify

**fortaleza** fort

**fortuna** fortune; fate

**fósil** *m.* fossil; **combustible** (*m.*) **fósil** fossil fuel

**foto(grafía)** photo(graph); **álbum** (*m.*) **de fotos** photo album; **sacar (qu) fotos** to take photos (2)

**fotografía** photography (9)

**fotográfico/a** photographic

**fotógrafo/a** photographer (11)

**foyer** *m.* sitting room

**frágil** fragile

**fragmento** fragment, piece; excerpt

**francamente** *adv.* frankly, openly

**francés, francesa** *n.* French person; *m.* French (*language*) (1); *adj.* French

**Francia** France

**frase** *f.* phrase

**fraude** *m.* fraud

**frecuencia** frequency; **con frecuencia** often; **¿con qué frecuencia?** how often? (3)

**frecuente** *adj.* common, frequent, often

**fregadero** kitchen sink

**fregar (gu)** to wash

**frente** *m.* front

**fresa** strawberry (6)

**fresco/a** fresh; cool; **hace fresco.** it's cool. (2)

**frijoles** *m.* beans (6)

**frío/a** cold; **hace (mucho) frío.** it's (very) cold. (2); **tener** (*irreg.*) **frío** to be cold (3)

**frito/a** fried; **papas fritas** French fries (6)

**frontera** border; frontier

**frustrado/a** frustrated

**fruta** fruit (6)

**frutal** *adj.* fruit

**frutería** fruit shop

**fruto** result

**fucsia** fuchsia; **de color** (*m.*) **fucsia** fuchsia; **de fucsia** fuchsia (7)

**fuego** fire; **fuegos artificiales** fireworks (11)

**fuente** *f.* fountain (8)

**fuerte** strong; **fuerte físicamente** physically strong (13)

**fuerza** force (9); power (9)

**fuga** escape

**fumar** to smoke (12)

**función** *f.* function

**funcionamiento** operation, functioning

**funcionar** to work, to function; to run (*a machine*)

**fundación** *f.* foundation

**fundado/a (en)** based (on)

**fundamental** *adj.* fundamental

**fundar** to found; to establish

**funeral** *m.* funeral

**funerario/a** funeral

**furgoneta** van

**furioso/a** furious (2)

**fusión** *f.* fusion, merging
**fusionar** to fuse, to merge
**futbito** indoor soccer (*Sp.*)
**fútbol** *m.* soccer (1); **fútbol americano** football (1); **jugar (ue) (gu) al fútbol** to play soccer (1); **jugar (ue) (gu) al fútbol americano** to play football (1)
**futbolista** *m., f.* soccer player
**futsal** *m.* indoor soccer
**futuro/a** *n., adj.* future

# G

**gafas** *f., pl.* glasses
**Galápagos: Islas Galápagos** Galapagos Islands
**galardón** *m.* award, prize
**galería** gallery
**gallego** Galician (*language*)
**galleta** cookie (6); cracker (6)
**gallina** hen (8)
**gallo** rooster (8)
**galón** *m.* gallon
**gamba** prawn, shrimp (*Sp.*)
**gamuza** suede
**ganadería** livestock farming
**ganadero/a** livestock farmer
**ganado** *n.* cattle (8)
**ganador(a)** winner
**ganar** to win
**ganas: tener** (*irreg.*) **ganas de** + *inf.* to feel like (*doing something*) (3)
**gandules** *m.* pigeon peas
**ganga** bargain
**garaje** *m.* garage (5)
**garganta** throat (12)
**garífuna** *indigenous group of Central America*
**gas** *m.* gas; **gas natural** natural gas (14); **pagar (gu) el gas** to pay the (natural) gas (bill) (15)
**gasolina** gasoline
**gasolinera** gas station (8)
**gastar** to spend
**gasto** expense (15)
**gastronomía** gastronomy
**gastronómico/a** gastronomic
**gato** cat (4)
**gaucho** Argentine cowboy
**gaviota** seagull (14)
**gemelo/a** twin (4)
**genealógico/a** genealogical
**generación** *f.* generation
**general** *adj.* general; **en general** generally; **por lo general** generally (4); in general
**general(a)** *n.* general (*military*)

**generar** to generate, to create
**genero** genre
**generoso/a** generous
**genética** *n., s.* genetics
**genéticamente** genetically
**gente** *f. s.* people (4); **tener** (*irreg.*) **don** (*m.*) **de gentes** to get along well with others (13)
**geografía** geography (1)
**geográfico/a** geographical
**geológico/a** geological
**geométrico/a** geometric, geometrical
**gerente** *m., f.* manager (10)
**geriátrico/a** geriatric; **centro geriátrico** retirement home
**gestionar** to manage
**gigante** *n. m.* giant; *adj.* enormous
**gigantesco/a** huge, gigantic
**gimnasio** gymnasium (1)
**girasol** *m.* sunflower
**gitano/a** *n., adj.* gypsy
**glaciar** *m.* glacier (14)
**global** global; **calentamiento global** global warming (14)
**globalización** *f.* globalization
**globalizado/a** *adj.* globalized
**gobernador(a)** governor (9)
**gobernante** *n. m., f.* leader, ruler
**gobernar (ie)** to govern
**gobierno** government (9)
**gol** *m.* goal
**golero/a** goalkeeper
**golf** *m.* golf (2); **palo de golf** golf club
**golfo** gulf
**golpe** *m.* blow, collision
**goma** eraser (*for pencil*) (1)
**gordo/a** fat (4)
**gorila** *m.* gorilla (14)
**gorra** cap (7)
**gota** drop
**gótico/a** gothic
**gozar (c)** to enjoy oneself
**grabación** *f.* recording
**grabado** print (11); engraving
**grabadora** (tape) recorder/player
**gracias** thanks; **gracias.** thank you. (P); **Día** (*m.*) **de Acción de Gracias** Thanksgiving Day (11); **gracias a** thanks to; **gracias por** thank you for; **muchas gracias** thank you very much
**grada** row; *pl.* stands (*of an sports arena*)
**grado** degree (*temperature*)
**graduación** *f.* graduation
**graduado/a** *adj.* graduated
**graduarse (me gradúo)** to graduate
**graffiti** graffiti

**grafía** *n.* spelling
**gramática** grammar
**gramatical** grammatical
**gramo** gram
**gran, grande** large (1), big; great; **extra grande** extra large (*clothing size*) (7); **gran velocidad** high speed; **grande** large (*clothing size*) (7)
**grandeza** grandeur, magnificence
**granito** granite
**granja** farmhouse
**grano** grain (6)
**grasa** grease
**gratis** *inv.* free (*of charge*)
**gratuita** free (*of charge*)
**grave** serious
**gres** *m.* stone (*flooring*)
**gresite** *m.* ceramic tile
**grifo** faucet (14); **cerrar (ie) el grifo** to turn off the faucet (14)
**gringo/a** *coll.:* **impuesto gringo** *a tax in Ecuador that only North Americans must pay*
**gripe** *f.* flu (12)
**gris** gray (2)
**gritar** to yell (12)
**grito** *n.* shout; **Grito (de la Independencia)** Mexican Independence Day
**grosor** *m.* thickness
**grotesco/a** grotesque
**grueso/a** thick
**grupo** group; **terapia de grupo** group therapy (15)
**guantes** *m.* gloves (7)
**guapo/a** handsome (1); pretty (1)
**guaraní** *m.* Guaraní (*indigenous language of Paraguay*); *m., f. Guaraní person*
**guardameta** *m., f.* goalkeeper
**guardar** to save (15); to save (*a file*) (13); **guardar como** to save as (15)
**guardia** guard
**Guate** *coll.* Guatemala City
**guatemalteco/a** Guatemalan (P)
**¡guau!** *interj.* wow!
**guayaba** guava
**guayabera** *typical style of shirt in the Caribbean*
**gubernamental** *adj.* government
**guerra** war (9); **guerra civil** civil war (9)
**guerrero/a** warrior (9)
**guía** *f.* guidebook; *m., f.* guide (*person*)
**guineo** banana
**guión** *m.* script (11)
**güira** *a percussion instrument commonly used for merengue, bachata, and cumbia music*

**guisantes** *m.* peas (6)

**guitarra** guitar

**guitarrista** *m., f.* guitar player

**guitarrón** *m. large guitar used in Mexico*

**gustar** "to like" (*lit.* to be pleasing) (1); **me gustaría** I would like (6)

**gusto** *n.* taste, preference, liking; **a gusto** comfortable, at ease; **al gusto** to one's liking; **mucho gusto.** it's a pleasure (to meet you). (P)

**gustosamente** *adv.* gladly

# H

**haber** *irreg.* to have (*auxiliary*); *infinitive form of* **hay**; **había** there was/were; **habrá** there will be; **hay** there is/are; **hay que** + *inf.* one has to (*do something*); **hubo** there was/were (*pret. of* **hay**) (7); **no hay paso** no entrance

**habichuelas** green beans (6)

**habilidad** *f.* ability (13)

**habitación** *f.* room; **habitación doble/sencilla** double/single room (10)

**habitado/a** inhabited

**habitante** *m., f.* inhabitant; resident

**habitar** to live in, to inhabit

**hábitat** *m.* (*pl.* **hábitats**) habitat

**hábito** habit

**habla** *f.* (*but* **el habla**) speech; **de habla española** Spanish-speaking

**hablar** to speak (1); to talk; **hablar por teléfono** to speak on the phone (1)

**hacer** *irreg.* (*p.p.* **hecho**) to do (2); to make (2); **desde hace... años** for . . . years; **hace** + *period of time* + **que** + *present tense* to have been (*doing something*) for (*a period of time*); **hace** + *time* ago; **hace fresco.** it's cool. (2); **hace (mucho) calor.** it's (very) hot. (2); **hace (mucho) frío.** it's (very) cold. (2); **hace (mucho) sol.** it's (very) sunny. (2); **hace (mucho) viento.** it's (very) windy. (2); **hace (muy) buen/mal tiempo.** it's (very) nice/bad out. (2); **hacer cola** to stand in line (10); **hacer copias** to make copies (13); **hacer de voluntario/a** to volunteer (15); **hacer ejercicio** to exercise (3); **hacer ejercicio aeróbico** to do aerobics (12); **hacer escalas** to make stops; **hacer la cama** to make the bed (3); **hacer la cuenta atrás** to count down (*to midnight*); **hacer las compras por el Internet** to shop online, Internet shopping (15); **hacer la(s) maleta(s)** to pack one's suitcase(s) (10); **hacer negocios** to do business; **hacer paradas** to make stops; **hacer preguntas** to ask questions; **hacer snowboarding** to snowboard; **hacer surfing** to surf; **hacer un pedido** to place an order; **hacer una fiesta** to throw a party (2); **hacer yoga** to do yoga (3); **hacerse** + *noun* to become (*a profession*); **¿qué tiempo hace?** what's the weather like? (2)

**hacienda** country house, property

**haikú** *m.* haiku

**hamaca** hammock (7)

**hambre** *f.* (*but* **el hambre**) hunger

**hamburguesa** hamburger (6)

**hasta** until; **desde la(s)... hasta la(s)...** from . . . until . . . (*time*); **hasta luego.** see you later. (P); **hasta mañana.** see you tomorrow. (P); **hasta pronto.** see you soon. (P); **hasta que** *conj.* until (13)

**hay** there is/are (P); **hay (muchas) nubes.** it's (very) cloudy. (2); **hay que** + *inf.* it's necessary to (*do something*); **no hay de qué.** don't mention it. (P)

**hecho** *n.* fact; event; **pareja de hecho** common-law couple; domestic partner

**hecho/a** (*p.p. of* **hacer**) done; made; **pareja de hecho** common-law couple (12); domestic partner (12); **trato hecho** it's a deal

**heladería** ice-cream shop/stand

**helado** ice cream (6); **tomar helado** to eat ice cream (9)

**hemisferio** hemisphere

**herencia** inheritance

**herido/a** *n.* wounded person

**herir** (**ie, i**) to wound

**hermanastro/a** stepbrother/stepsister (4)

**hermanito/a** little brother/sister

**hermano/a** brother/sister (4); *pl.* siblings (4); **medio/a hermano/a** half brother/sister (4)

**hermoso/a** pretty (4)

**héroe** *m.* hero

**heroico/a** *adj.* heroic

**hervir** (**ie, i**) to boil (6)

**híbrido/a** hybrid; **carro/coche** (*m.*) **híbrido** hybrid car (14)

**hidalgo** nobleman

**hidrato de carbono** carbohydrate

**hidráulico/a** hydraulic

**hidroeléctrico/a: energía hidroeléctrica** hydroelectric power (14)

**hidrógeno** hydrogen

**hielo** ice (14); **pista de hielo** ice-skating rink

**hierba** herb

**hierro** iron

**hijastro/a** stepson/stepdaughter (4)

**hijo/a** son/daughter (4); *pl.* children (4); **hijo/a adoptivo/a** adopted son/daughter (4); **hijo/a único/a** only child (4)

**hipermercado** supermarket

**hipertensión** *f.* high blood pressure

**hipnótico/a** hypnotic

**hipoteca** mortgage (15); **pagar (gu) la hipoteca** to pay the mortgage (15)

**hispánico/a** *adj.* Hispanic

**hispano/a** *n., adj.* Hispanic

**hispanoamericano/a** Spanish American; Latin American

**hispanohablante** *m., f.* Spanish speaker

**historia** history (1); **historia mundial** world history (9); **historia política** political history (9)

**historiador(a)** historian

**histórico/a** historic

**hogar** *m.* home; household

**hoja** sheet (of paper); leaf

**hojuela** flake

**hola.** hello. (P)

**holandés, holandesa** *adj.* Dutch

**hombre** *m.* man (1); **hombre de negocios** businessman (13)

**hombro** shoulder (12)

**homenaje** *m.* homage, tribute

**hondureño/a** Honduran (P)

**honesto/a** honest (13)

**honor** *m.* honor

**honrar** to honor

**hora** hour; **¿a qué hora?** at what time? (1); **¿qué hora es?** what time is it? (1); **ser hora de** + *inf.* to be time to (*do something*)

**horario** schedule; **horario de trabajo** work schedule (13)

**horchata** *cold drink made from ground rice, water and sugar*

**hornear** to bake

**horno** oven (3); **al horno** baked; **horno de microondas** microwave oven (3)

**hospedarse** to stay (*in a hotel*) (10)

**hospital** *m.* hospital (1)

**hospitalidad** *f.* hospitality

**hospitalizar (c)** to hospitalize

**hostil** *adj.* hostile

**hotel** *m.* hotel (10)

**hoy** today (1); **hoy (en) día** nowadays

**huayno** *folkloric music and dance of Peru*

**hubo** there was/were (*pret. of* **hay**) (7)

**huele** he/she, it smells (*pres. ind. of* **oler**)

**huelga** strike

**huerta** farmer's field (8); orchard (8)

**hueso** bone

**huésped(a)** hotel guest (10)

**huevo** egg (6); **huevos revueltos** scrambled eggs

**huir (y)** to flee

**humanidad** *f.* humanity; **Patrimonio Natural de la Humanidad** World Heritage Site (UNESCO)

**humano/a** human; **cuerpo humano** human body (12); **ser** (*m.*) **humano** human being

**humilde** humble

**humillación** *f.* humiliation

**humo** smoke (14)

**humor** *m.* mood; **estar** (*irreg.*) **de buen humor** to be in a good mood

**huracán** *m.* hurricane (9)

**¡huy!** *interj.* gosh!; gee whiz!

# I

**ibérico/a** Iberian; **Península Ibérica** Iberian Peninsula

**iberoamericano/a** Latin American

**iceberg** *m.* iceberg (14)

**icono** icon

**ida: viaje** (*m.*) **de ida** one-way trip (10); **viaje de ida y vuelta** round trip (10)

**idealismo** idealism

**idealista** *m., f.* idealistic

**idéntico/a** identical

**identidad** *f.* identity

**identificación** *f.* identification

**identificar (qu)** to identify

**idílico/a** idyllic

**idioma** *m.* language

**iglesia** church (3); **ir** (*irreg.*) **a la iglesia** to go to church (3)

**igual** equal

**igualmente.** likewise. (P)

**ilegal** illegal

**ilógico/a** illogical; unreasonable

**ilusión** *f.* illusion

**imagen** *f.* image

**imaginación** *f.* imagination

**imaginar(se)** to imagine

**imitación** *f.* imitation

**imitar** to imitate, to copy

**impaciente** impatient

**impacto** impact

**impedir** (*like* **pedir**) to prevent

**imperfecto** *gram.* imperfect

**imperio** empire (9)

**impersonal: expresión** (*f.*) **impersonal** *gram.* impersonal expression (11)

**implementar** to implement

**imponente** imposing; majestic

**imponer** (*like* **poner**) (*p.p.* **impuesto**) to impose

**importancia** importance

**importante** important; **es importante que** it's important that (11)

**importar** to amount; to come to

**imposible** impossible; **es imposible que** it's impossible that (11)

**imprescindible** indispensable; essential

**impresión** *f.* impression

**impresionado/a** impressed

**impresionante** amazing; impressive

**impresionar** to impress

**impreso/a** (*p.p. of* **imprimir**) printed

**impresora** printer (15)

**imprimir** (*p.p.* **impreso**) to print (15)

**improbable** improbable, unlikely; **es improbable que** it's improbable that (11)

**impuesto** *n.* tax; **impuesto gringo** *a tax in Ecuador that only North Americans must pay*

**inacabado/a** unfinished

**inaceptable** unacceptable

**inalámbrico/a** wireless (15); cordless

**inanimado/a** inanimate

**inauguración** *f.* inauguration

**inca** *n. m., f.* Inca; *adj. m., f.* Incan

**incaico/a** Incan

**incendio** fire (9)

**incienso** *n.* incense

**incluir (y)** to include

**incluso** including

**incómodo/a** uncomfortable

**incompetencia** incompetence

**incompleto/a** incomplete

**inconveniente** *n. m.* difficulty; drawback

**incorporación** *f.* incorporation

**incorporado/a** built-in

**incorporar** to incorporate

**increíble** incredible; **es increíble que** it's incredible that (11)

**indefinido/a** indefinite; vague; **palabra indefinida** *gram.* indefinite word (5)

**independencia** independence (9); **Día** (*m.*) **de la Independencia** Independence Day (11); **Grito de la Independencia** Mexican Independence Day

**independentista** *adj. m., f.* pro-independence

**independizarse (c)** to gain independence (9); to become independent (9)

**indexar** to index

**indicación** *f.* sign; instruction

**indicar (qu)** to indicate

**indicativo/a** *gram.* indicative

**índice** *m.* index

**indígena** *n. m., f.* native (*person*) (9); *adj.* indigenous

**indio/a** *n., adj.* Indian

**indirecto/a: objeto indirecto** *gram.* indirect object; **pronombre** (*m.*) **de objeto indirecto** *gram.* indirect object pronoun (6)

**indispensable** indispensable; essential

**individualidad** *f.* individuality

**individuo** *n.* individual

**indudablemente** undoubtedly

**indulgencia** indulgence

**industria** industry

**industrial** *adj.* industrial

**industrialización** *f.* industrialization

**inestabilidad** *f.* instability

**infancia** infancy (9)

**infanta** princess

**infección** *f.* infection

**inferior** inferior; lower

**inferir (ie, i)** to infer; to deduce

**infinitivo** *n. gram.* infinitive

**infinito/a** infinite

**inflexible** inflexible (13); rigid

**influencia** influence

**influir (y)** to influence

**influyente** influential

**información** *f.* information

**informal** informal; **mandato informal** *gram.* informal command

**informar** to inform (15); to report

**informática** computer science (1)

**informativo/a** instructive

**informe** *m.* report (13); **escribir informes** to write reports (13)

**infusión** *f.* infusion

**ingeniería** engineering (1)

**ingeniero/a** engineer (13)

**Inglaterra** England

**inglés, inglesa** *n.* English person; *m.* English (*language*) (1); *adj.* English

**ingrediente** *m.* ingredient; *pl.* ingredients (6)

**ingreso** entry; entrance

**iniciar** to initiate; to start

**iniciativa** initiative; proposal

**inicio** *n.* start; beginning

**injusticia** injustice

**injusto/a** unjust

**inmediato/a** immediate; next

**inmejorable** incapable of improvement

**inmensidad** *f.* immensity

**inmenso/a** immense

**inmigración** *f.* immigration

**inmigrante** *m., f.* immigrant

**inmobiliaria** real estate agency

**inmortalizar (c)** to immortalize

**inmunológico/a** *adj.* immune

**innovación** *f.* innovation

**innovador(a)** innovative

**inocente** innocent

**inodoro** toilet (5)

**inolvidable** unforgettable

**inquilino/a** tenant

**inquisición** *f.* investigation

**inscripción** *f.* inscription

**insecto** insect (14)

**inseguridad** *f.* insecurity; uncertainty

**inseguro/a** insecure; uncertain

**inserción** *f.* insertion

**insignificante** insignificant

**insistente** insistent

**insistir (en)** to insist (on) (11)

**insomnio** insomnia

**insostenible** unsustainable

**inspiración** *f.* inspiration

**inspirar** to inspire

**instalación** *f.* installation

**instalar** to install; to place

**institución** *f.* institution

**instituir (y)** to establish; to appoint

**instrucción** *f.* instruction; education

**instructor(a)** instructor; teacher

**instrumento** instrument; **instrumento musical** musical instrument

**intacto/a** intact

**integración** *f.* integration

**integral** complete; integral; **pan** (*m.*) **integral** whole wheat bread (6)

**integrante** *m., f.* member

**integrar** to integrate

**íntegro/a** honest (13); upright (*righteous*) (13); whole, entire

**inteligente** intelligent

**intención** *f.* intention

**intencionado/a** intentional, deliberate

**intenso/a** intense

**intentar** to try

**interacción** *f.* interaction

**interactuar (interactúo)** to interact

**intercambiar** to exchange, swap

**intercambio** exchange

**interdisciplinario/a** interdisciplinary

**interés** *m.* interest

**interesante** interesting (1); **es interesante que** it's interesting that (12)

**interesar** to interest (6)

**interfaz** *f.* interface

**interior** *n.* interior; inside; *adj.* inner; inside; **ropa interior** lingerie, underwear (7)

**intermedio** intermission

**internacional** international (6)

**Internet** *m.* Internet; **buscar (qu) novio/a por el Internet** to look for a boyfriend/girlfriend online, Internet dating (15); **comprar entradas de cine por el Internet** to buy movie tickets online (15); **hacer** (*irreg.*) **las compras por el Internet** to shop online, Internet shopping (15); **manejar las cuentas por el Internet** to manage one's accounts online, Internet banking (15); **navegar (gu) en Internet** to surf the Internet (1); **pagar (gu) el Internet** to pay the Internet bill (15)

**interno/a** internal

**intérprete** *m., f.* interpreter (13)

**interrogativo/a** *gram.* interrogative; **palabra interrogativa** *gram.* question word (1)

**intervención** *f.* intervention (9)

**íntimo/a** intimate, close; **amigo/a íntimo/a** close friend (15)

**introducción** *f.* introduction

**introducir** (*like* **conducir**) to introduce

**intruso/a** *n.* intruder

**inundación** *f.* flood (9)

**invadir** to invade (9)

**invasor(a)** *n.* invader

**inventado/a** made-up

**inventar** to invent; to make-up

**inversión** *f.* investment

**invertir (ie, i)** to invest; **invertir en la bolsa** to invest in the stock market (15)

**investigación** *f.* investigation

**investigador(a)** investigator

**investigar (gu)** to investigate

**invierno** winter (2)

**invitación** *f.* invitation

**invitado/a** guest

**invitar** to invite

**involucrar** to involve

**inyección** *f.* injection; **ponerle** (*irreg.*) **una inyección** to give (*someone*) a shot (12)

**ir** *irreg.* to go (2); **ir + a +** *inf.* to be going to (*do something*) (2); **ir a la iglesia** to go to church (3); **ir a la mezquita/sinagoga** to go to the mosque/synagogue (3); **ir al cine** to go to the movies (3); **ir de compras** to go shopping (7); **ir de vacaciones** to go on vacation (9); **irse** to leave, go away

**irresponsable** irresponsible

**irritado/a** irritated (2)

**irritarse** to become irritated

**isla** island (14); **Islas Galápagos** Galapagos Islands; **Islas Filipinas** Philippines

**islote** *m.* small island

**-ísimo** *suffix, adv.* very, very

**-ísimo/a** *suffix, adj.* very, very

**Italia** *n.* Italy

**italiano** *n.* Italian (*language*) (1)

**italiano/a** *adj.* Italian

**itinerario** route; itinerary

**izquierda** left; **a la izquierda (de)** to the left (of) (2)

## J

**jabón** *m.* soap

**jacuzzi** *m.* jacuzzi (3)

**jade** *m.* jade

**jaguar** *m.* jaguar (14)

**jamaicano/a** Jamaican

**jamás** *adv.* never (5); at no time

**jamón** *m.* ham (6)

**Japón** *m.* Japan

**japonés** *m.* Japanese (*language*) (1)

**japonés, japonesa** *adj.* Japanese

**jarabe** *m.* cough syrup (12)

**jardín** *m.* garden (3); yard (3); **trabajar en el jardín** to work in the garden/yard (3)

**jardinero/a** gardener

**jarra** pitcher (6)

**jarro** jug

**jazz** *m.* jazz (11)

**jeans** *m. pl.* (blue)jeans (7)

**jefe/a** boss (13)

**jengibre** *m.* ginger

**jerga** jargon

**Jesucristo** Jesus Christ

**jesuita** *adj.* Jesuit

**jinete** *m., f.* horseman, horsewoman

**jornada** workday

**joven** *m., f.* (*pl.* **jóvenes**) young person (2); *adj.* young

**joya** jewel; *pl.* jewelry (7)

**joyería** jewelry (store) (7)

**jubilación** *f.* retirement; **plan** (*m.*) **de jubilación** retirement plan (13); **planear la jubilación** to plan one's retirement (15)

**jubilado/a** retired (4)

**jubilarse** to retire (13)

**judía verde** green bean

**judío/a** *n.* Jew, Jewish person; *adj.* Jewish; **Pascua judía** Passover (11)

**juego** game

**jueves** *m. inv.* Thursday (1)

**juez(a)** judge (13)

**jugador(a)** player

**jugar (ue) (gu) (a)** to play (*a game, sport*) (1); **jugar a las cartas** to play cards (3); **jugar a los videojuegos**

**jugar** (*cont.*)
to play videogames (3); **jugar al basquetbol** to play basketball (1); **jugar al béisbol** to play baseball (1); **jugar al billar** to play pool (3); **jugar al dominó** to play dominos (2); **jugar al escondite** to play hide-and-seek; **jugar al fútbol** to play soccer (1); **jugar al fútbol americano** to play football (1); **jugar al tenis** to play tennis; **jugar al vólibol** to play volleyball (1)

**jugo** juice (6)

**juguete** *m.* toy (9)

**juguetería** toy store (7)

**juguetón, juguetona** *adj.* playful

**julio** July (2)

**jungla** jungle

**junio** June (2)

**juntar(se)** to put, bring together

**junto** *adv.*: **junto a** next to; **junto con** together with

**juntos/as** together

**juramento** judgment

**justificar (qu)** to justify

**justo/a** just; fair

**juvenil** juvenile; youthful

**juventud** *f.* youth (9)

**juzgar (gu)** to judge

# K

**kalipuna** *tribe indigenous to Central America*

**kilo** kilo(gram)

**kilómetro** kilometer

**kiosco** kiosk, newspaper stand

**kiwi** *m.* kiwi (6)

# L

**la** *def. art. f. s.* the (P); *dir. obj. pron. f. s.* her (5); you (*form.*) (5); it (5); **a la(s)** + *time* at + *time* (1); **la más/ menos… de** the most/least . . . of/in (4)

**laberinto** labyrinth; maze

**labial** *adj.* lip

**labio** lip

**laboral** *adj.* labor; working

**laboratorio** laboratory (1); **laboratorio de computadoras** computer laboratory (1)

**lácteo/a: producto lácteo** dairy product (6)

**lado** side; **al lado de** next to (5); **de al lado** next-door (5)

**ladrillo** brick

**lago** lake (8)

**laguna** lagoon (14)

**lamentar** to regret

**lámpara** lamp (5)

**lana** wool; **de lana** wool (7)

**langosta** lobster (6)

**lápiz** *m.* (*pl.* **lápices**) pencil (1); **lápiz de memoria** flash drive (15)

**largo/a** *adj.* long; **de manga larga** with long sleeves (7)

**larimar** *m. blue pectolite gemstone*

**las** *def. art. m. pl.* the (P); *dir. obj. pron. f. pl.* you (*form. Sp.; fam., form. elsewhere*) (5); them (5); **las más/ menos… de** the most/least . . . of/in (4)

**láser** *m.* laser (15)

**lástima** pity; shame; **es una lástima que** it's a shame that (11)

**lastimarse** to hurt (oneself)

**lata** can

**latín** *m.* Latin (*language*)

**latino/a** *adj.* Latino

**Latinoamérica** Latin America

**latinoamericano/a** Latin American

**lavabo** sink (5)

**lavadero** laundry room (5)

**lavadora** washer, washing machine (3)

**lavanda** lavender

**lavaplatos** *m. inv.* dishwasher (3)

**lavar** to wash; **lavar la ropa** to wash clothes (1); **lavar los platos** to wash the dishes (3); **lavarse la cara / las manos / el pelo** to wash one's face/hands/hair (5); **lavarse los dientes** to brush one's teeth (5)

**lazo** bond; tie

**le** *indir. obj. pron.* to/for him/her (6); to/ for you (*s. form.*) (6); to/for it (6)

**lección** *f.* lesson

**leche** *f.* milk (6)

**lechón** *m.* suckling pig

**lechuga** lettuce (6)

**lector(a)** reader (*person*)

**lectura** reading

**leer (y)** (*p.p.* **leído**) to read (1); **leer el e-mail** to read/check one's e-mail (1)

**legado** legacy

**legal** *adj.* legal

**legendario/a** legendary

**legítimo/a** legitimate

**legumbre** *f.* vegetable

**lejano/a** distant

**lejos (de)** far (from) (2)

**lema** *m.* motto; slogan

**lenguaje** *m.* language

**lenguas** languages (1); **lenguas extranjeras** foreign languages (1)

**lentejuela** sequin

**lentes** *m.* glasses

**lento/a** slow

**león** *m.* lion (14)

**les** *indir. obj. pron.* to/for you (*pl. form. Sp.; pl. fam., form. elsewhere*) (6); to/for them (6)

**letra** letter; *pl.* humanities (1); **Facultad** (*f.*) **de Letras** School of Humanities (1)

**levantar** to lift; to rise; **levantar pesas** to lift weights (3); *refl.* to get up

**ley** *f.* law; *pl.* law (1); **Facultad** (*f.*) **de Leyes** School of Law (1)

**leyenda** legend

**liberación** *f.* liberation

**liberal** liberal (9)

**libertad** *f.* freedom; liberty

**libertador(a)** *n.* liberator

**libra** pound

**libre** free; **comercio libre** free trade; **ratos libres** free time (2); **tiempo libre** free time (2)

**librería** bookstore (1)

**libro** book; **libro de caballería** book of chivalry; **libro de texto** textbook (1)

**licenciado/a** graduate

**licuada** milkshake

**licuadora** blender (3); juicer

**líder** *m., f.* leader

**liderado/a por** led by

**liga** league

**ligero/a** *adj.* light; **tren** (*m.*) **ligero** light rail (14)

**limeño/a** *person from Lima, Peru*

**limitado/a** *adj.* restricted

**limitar** to limit; to restrict

**límite** *m.* limit

**limón** *m.* lemon

**limonada** lemonade

**limpiar** to clean; **limpiar la casa** to clean the house (3)

**limpieza** cleaning

**limpio/a** clean (2)

**lindo/a** pretty, lovely

**línea** line; **patinar en línea** to inline skate (2); **periódico en línea** online newspaper (15); **revista en línea** online magazine (15)

**lingüístico/a** linguistic

**lino** linen

**lirio** iris

**liso/a** plain (7); smooth

**lista** *n.* list

**listo/a** smart (4); clever; ready

**literario/a** literary

**literatura** literature (1)

**llamar** to call (1); **¿cómo se llama usted (Ud.)?** what's your (*form.*) name? (P); **¿cómo te llamas?** what's your (*fam.*)

name? (P); **llamar la atención** to sound interesting (*lit.* to call out for one's attention) (6); **llamar por teléfono** to call on the phone (1); **me llamo…** my name is . . . (P)

**llanero/a** *adj.* in / of / pertaining to the plains

**llano** plain (*geography*), prairie

**llanura** plain (*geography*) (14); prairie

**llave** *f.* key

**llegada** arrival (9)

**llegar (gu)** to arrive (1)

**llenar** to fill; to fill out (*a form*) (13)

**lleno/a** full; **lleno/a de luz** bright (5); well-lit (5)

**llevar** to carry (1); to wear; **llevarse bien/mal** to get along well/poorly (with each other) (9)

**llorar** to cry (12)

**llover (ue)** to rain; **está lloviendo. / llueve.** it's raining. (2)

**lluvia** rain

**lo** *dir. obj. pron. m. s.* him (5); you (*s. form.*) (5); it (5); **lo cual** *rel. pron.* which; **lo demás** the rest; **lo que** *rel. pron.* what (6); that which (6); **lo siento** I'm sorry; **por lo general** generally (4); **por lo menos** at least (4)

**lobo** wolf

**local** *adj.* local (6)

**localidad** *f.* place; town

**loco/a** crazy (2)

**lógico/a** *adj.* logical

**lograr** to achieve; to obtain

**logro** achievement

**Londres** London

**longitud** *f.* length

**los** *def. art. m. pl.* the (P); *dir. obj. pron. m. pl.* you (*form. Sp.; fam., form. elsewhere*) (5); them (5); **los años setenta** the seventies; **los demás** the others, the rest; **los más/ menos… de** the most/least . . . of/in (4)

**lotería** lottery

**lucha** fight

**luchar** to fight

**luciérnaga** glowworm; firefly; **brigada de luciérnaga** the firefly brigade, *an activist group that promotes clean-air initiatives*

**lucrativo/a** lucrative

**lucro** profit; **organizaciones** (*f.*) **sin lucro** non-profit organizations

**luego** then, afterward, next; **hasta luego.** see you later. (P)

**lugar** place (1); **lugar de trabajo** workplace (13); **ningún lugar** nowhere; **preposición** (*f.*) **de lugar**

*gram.* preposition of location (2); **tener** (*irreg.*) **lugar** to take place (9)

**lujo** luxury; **de lujo** *adj.* luxury (*hotel*) (10)

**lujoso/a** luxurious

**luna** moon; **luna de miel** honeymoon (12)

**lunar** *m.*: **de lunares** polka-dotted (7)

**lunes** *m. inv.* Monday (1); **el lunes** on Monday (1); **el lunes pasado** last Monday (6); **el lunes que viene** next Monday (1); **los lunes** on Mondays (1)

**luz** *f.* (*pl.* **luces**) light; **lleno/a de luz** bright (5); well-lit (5); **pagar (gu) la luz** to pay the electric bill (15)

# M

**macizo** massif (*mountain*)

**madera** wood; **de madera** wooden (7); **tallado/a en madera** carved-wood (7)

**madrastra** stepmother (4)

**madre** *f.* mother (4); **Día** (*m.*) **de la Madre** Mother's Day (11); **Madre Tierra** Mother Earth

**madrileño/a** of/from Madrid, Spain

**madrina** godmother (4)

**madrugada** dawn; daybreak

**madurez** *f.* maturity (9)

**maestría** Master's (degree)

**maestro/a** *n.* teacher (13); *adj.* master; **obra maestra** masterpiece (11)

**Magallanes: Estrecho de Magallanes** Strait of Magellan

**magia** magic

**mágico/a** magical

**magnánimo/a** magnanimous

**magnífico/a** magnificent

**magnitud** *f.* magnitude

**mago** magus, wise man; **Día** (*m.*) **de los Reyes Magos** Feast of the Three Kings (Epiphany) (11)

**maíz** *m.* (*pl.* **maíces**) corn (6)

**mal** *adv.* bad, not well (2); sick (2); **llevarse mal** to get along poorly (with each other) (9); **manejar mal el tiempo** to manage one's time poorly (15); **pasarlo mal** to have a bad time (3); **salir** (*irreg.*) **mal** to turn out poorly

**mal, malo/a** *adj.* bad (1); **hace (muy) mal tiempo.** it's (very) bad out. (2); **¡qué mala onda!** what a bummer; **sacar (qu) malas notas** to get bad grades (1); **ser** (*irreg.*) **mala onda** to be a jerk

**malecón** seafront walkway

**malestar** *m.* discomfort; unease

**maleta** suitcase (10); **hacer** (*irreg.*) **la(s) maleta(s)** to pack one's suitcase(s) (10)

**maletero/a** skycap (10)

**maletín** *m.* carry-on (bag) (10)

**mamá** mom (1)

**mamífero** mammal

**manantial** *m.* spring (*water*)

**mandar** to send (6); to order (*someone to do something*); **mandar un e-mail** to send an e-mail (6)

**mandarina** tangerine

**mandato (formal/informal)** *gram.* (formal/informal) command

**mandolina** mandolin

**manejar** to drive (*L.A.*) (8); **manejar (bien/mal) el tiempo** to manage one's time (well/poorly) (15); **manejar las cuentas** to manage one's accounts (13); **manejar las cuentas por el Internet** to manage one's accounts online, Internet banking (15)

**manera** way; manner

**manga** sleeve; **de manga corta/larga** with short/long sleeves (7)

**mango** mango (6)

**manía: tenerle** (*irreg.*) **manía** to have it in (*for someone*) (15)

**manifestación** *f.* demonstration; expression (*artistic*)

**manifestar (ie)** to express; to show

**manito/a** *coll.* friend; buddy

**mano** *f.* hand; **a mano** by hand; **darse** (*irreg.*) **la mano** to shake hands with each other (9); **de segunda mano** second-hand; **lavarse las manos** to wash one's hands (5)

**mantel** *m.* tablecloth (6)

**mantener** (*like* **tener**) to maintain; to keep; **mantener una casa** to maintain a home (15); **mantenerse en contacto (con)** to stay in touch (with)

**mantenimiento** maintenance

**mantequilla** butter (6)

**manual** *n. m.* manual; workbook; *adj.* manual

**manzana** apple (6); (city) block

**manzanilla** chamomile tea

**mañana** *n.* morning; *adv.* tomorrow (1); **de la mañana** in the morning (1); A.M.; **esta mañana** this morning (1); **hasta mañana.** see you tomorrow. (P); **pasado mañana** the day after tomorrow (1); **por la mañana** in the morning (1)

**mapa** *m.* map

**maquillaje** *m.* makeup (7)

**maquillarse** to put on makeup (5)

**máquina** machine; **máquina de escribir** typewriter

**mar** *m.* sea (14); **Mar Antártico** Antarctic Sea; **Mar Caribe** Caribbean Sea

**maraca** maraca (*percussion instrument*)

**maravilla** *n.* marvel, wonder; **pasarlo de maravilla** to have a great time

**maravilloso/a** marvelous

**marca** brand (name); **de marca** name-brand (7)

**marcador** *m.* marker (1)

**marcar (qu)** to mark

**marcial: artes** (*f. but* **el arte**) **marciales** martial arts

**mareado/a** dizzy (12); nauseated (12)

**maremoto** tsunami (9)

**marginal** poor; peripheral

**marido** husband

**marinero/a** sailor

**marino/a** *adj.* sea, marine; **caballo marino** seahorse (14); **reserva marina** marine reserve; **tortuga marina** sea turtle

**mariposa** butterfly (10)

**mariscos** *pl.* shellfish (6)

**marítimo/a** *adj.* sea, maritime

**mármol** *m.* marble (*substance*)

**martes** *m. inv.* Tuesday (1); **el martes** on Tuesday (1); **el martes pasado** last Tuesday (6); **el martes que viene** next Tuesday (1); **los martes** on Tuesdays (1)

**marzo** March (2)

**más** more; most; plus; **el/la/los/las más... de** the most . . . of/in (4); **más allá** further, farther; **más allá de** beyond; **más de** + *number* more than + *number* (4); **más... que** more . . . than (4)

**masaje** *m.* massage (3)

**máscara** mask (7); **máscara de carnaval** carnival mask (7)

**mascota** pet (4)

**masculino/a** masculine

**matar** to kill

**mate** *m.* herbal tea

**matemáticas** *pl.* math (1)

**materia** class, subject (1)

**material** *m.* material (7)

**materialista** materialistic

**materno/a** maternal

**matrícula** tuition; **pagar (gu) la matrícula** to pay tuition (15)

**matrimonio** marriage (4); married couple (4)

**máximo** *n.* maximum

**máximo/a** *adj.* utmost; most important

**maya** *n., adj. m., f.* Mayan

**mayo** May (2)

**mayor** older; oldest; greater; greatest; **mayor que** older than (4); **plaza mayor** main square

**mayoría** majority

**mayoritariamente** primarily

**mayormente** mainly

**mayúscula** capital (letter)

**me** *dir. obj. pron.* me (5); *indir. obj. pron.* to/for me (6); *refl. pron.* myself; **me gustaría** I would like (6); **me llamo...** my name is . . . (P)

**mecánico/a** *n.* mechanic; *adj.* mechanical

**mediados: a mediados de** halfway through

**mediano/a** medium (7)

**medianoche** *f.* midnight (1)

**mediante** *adv.* by means of; through

**medias** *pl.* stockings (7)

**medicamento** medicine

**medicina** medicine (1); **Facultad** (*f.*) **de Medicina** School of Medicine (1)

**medicinal** medicinal; **yerba medicinal** medicinal herb

**médico/a** doctor (12); *adj.* medical; **cuidado médico** medical care (12); **pagar (gu) las cuentas médicas** to pay the medical bills (15); **seguro médico** health insurance (13)

**medida** measure

**medieval** *adj.* Medieval

**medio** *n.* medium; means; **medio ambiente** environment (14); **medio de transporte** mode of transportation (8); **medios de comunicación** mass media (15)

**medio/a** *adj.* half; **medio/a hermano/a** half brother/sister (4); **y media** half past (1)

**medioambiental** environmental

**mediodía** *m.* noon (1)

**medir (i, i)** to measure

**meditación** *f.* meditation (3)

**meditar** to meditate (15)

**mediterráneo/a** Mediterranean

**medusa** jellyfish (14)

**mejilla** cheek

**mejor** better; best; **es mejor que** it's better that (12); **mejor amigo/a** best friend (1); **mejor dicho** or rather, in other words

**mejoramiento** improvement

**mejorar** to improve (14)

**melancolía** melancholy

**melancólico/a** melancholic, moody

**melocotón** *m.* peach

**melodía** melody

**melódico/a**

**melodramático/a** melodramatic

**melón** *m.* melon (6)

**memoria** memory; **lápiz** (*m.*) **de memoria** flash drive (15); **saber** (*irreg.*) **de memoria** to know by heart

**mencionar** to mention

**menonita** *m., f.* Mennonite

**menor** minor; younger; youngest; less; least; **menor que** younger than (4)

**menos** less; least; minus; **a menos que** + *subj.* unless (14); **el/la/los/las menos... de** the least . . . of/in (4); **menos cuarto/quince** quarter to (1); **menos de** + *number* less than + *number* (4); **menos... que** less . . . than (4); **por lo menos** at least (4)

**mensaje** *m.* message

**mensajería** chat (messaging) service

**mensual** monthly; **pago mensual** monthly payment (15)

**menta** mint (6)

**mental** mental; **bienestar** (*m.*) **mental** mental well-being (15)

**mente** *f.* mind

**mentira** lie

**menú** *m.* menu (6)

**menudo: a menudo** often

**mercado** market (6)

**mercurio** courier

**merendar (ie)** to snack (6)

**merengue** *m.* Merengue (*Dominican dance and music*)

**meridional** southern

**mero/a** mere

**mes** *m.* month (2); **el mes** (*m.*) **pasado** last month (6); **una vez al mes** once a month (3)

**mesa** table (1); **poner** (*irreg.*) **la mesa** to set the table (3); **quitar la mesa** to clear the table (3)

**mesero/a** waiter/waitress (6)

**mesita** coffee table (5); nightstand (5); **mesita de noche** nightstand (5)

**mestizaje** *m.* cross-breeding, mixed races

**mestizo/a** of mixed race

**meta** goal

**metafórico/a** metaphorical

**metal** *m.* metal (14)

**metálico/a** metallic (7)

**meterse (en)** to meddle, get involved (in)

**meticuloso/a** meticulous

**método** method

**metro** subway (8)

**metrópolis** *f.* metropolis

**metropolitano/a** metropolitan

**mexicano/a** Mexican (P)

**mezclar** to mix

**mezquindad** *f.* pettiness

**mezquita** mosque; **ir** (*irreg.*) **a la mezquita** to go to the mosque (3)

**mí** *obj.* (*of prep.*) me

**mi(s)** *poss. adj.* my (1); **mi nombre es...** my name is . . . (P)

**microcosmos** *m. s.* microcosm

**micrófono** microphone

**microondas** *m. inv.* microwave (3); **horno de microondas** microwave oven (3)

**microscopio** microscope

**miedo** fear; **tener** (*irreg.*) **miedo (de)** to be afraid (of) (3)

**miel** *f.* honey; **luna de miel** honeymoon (12)

**miembro** member

**mientras** while

**miércoles** *m. inv.* Wednesday (1); **el miércoles** on Wednesday (1); **el miércoles pasado** last Wednesday (6); **el miércoles que viene** next Wednesday (1); **los miércoles** on Wednesdays (1)

**mil** thousand (4); one thousand (4); **dos mil** two thousand (4)

**milagro** miracle

**milagrosamente** miraculously

**milenio** millennium (9)

**militar** *n. m.* military person; *adj.* military

**milla** mile

**millón** *m.* million; **dos millones (de)** two million (4); **un millón (de)** one million (4)

**mimo** *m., f.* mime

**mina** mine

**mineral** *n. m.* mineral (14); *adj.* mineral

**minero/a** *adj.* mining; **excavación** (*f.*) **minera** mining (14)

**miniatura** miniature

**minibar** *m.* mini-bar

**mínimo/a** minimum; **salario mínimo** minimum wage (13)

**minoría** minority

**minuto** minute

**mío/a** *poss. adj.* my (12); *poss. pron.* mine (12)

**mirar** to look at; to watch; **mirar la televisión** to watch TV (1)

**misa** mass (*religion*)

**miseria** poverty

**misión** *f.* mission

**mismo** *adv.* same

**mismo/a** *adj.* same; self

**misterio** mystery

**misterioso/a** mysterious

**misticismo** mysticism

**mitad** *f.* half

**mítico/a** mythical

**mito** myth

**mobiliario** furniture; furnishings

**mochila** backpack (1)

**moda** fashion (7); **de última moda** fashionable (7); **diseñador(a) de modas** (fashion) designer (13)

**modelo** *m., f.* model (13)

**módem** *m.* modem (15)

**moderación** *f.* moderation

**modernidad** *f.* modernity

**modernismo** modernism

**modernización** *f.* modernization

**moderno/a** modern (7)

**modificar (qu)** to modify

**modo** mode; means; **de todos modos** at any rate; **ni modo** no way

**molde** *m.* mold (*pattern*)

**molestar** to bother (6)

**molesto/a** annoyed

**molino** windmill

**momento** moment

**momia** mummy

**monarca** *m.* monarch

**monasterio** monastery

**moneda** coin; currency

**monitor** *m.* monitor

**mono** monkey (14)

**monolítico/a** monolithic

**monótono/a** monotonous

**monóxido de carbono** carbon monoxide

**montaña** mountain (8)

**montañoso/a** mountainous

**montar** to ride; **montar a caballo** to ride a horse; **montar en** to ride (8); **montar en motocicleta** to ride a motorbike

**monte** *m.* mountain

**monumento** monument

**morado** *n.* purple (2)

**morado/a** *adj.* purple

**moreno/a** dark-haired (1); dark-skinned (1)

**morir(se) (ue, u)** (*p.p.* **muerto**) to die (7)

**moro/a** *n.* Moor; *adj.* Moorish; **moros y cristianos** black beans and rice

**mostrador** *m.* (*check-in*) counter (10)

**mostrar (ue)** to show (3)

**motivo** motive

**moto** *f.* motorcycle

**motocicleta** motorcycle (8); **montar en motocicleta** to ride a motorbike

**mover (ue)** to move

**móvil** *m.* cell phone; **teléfono móvil** cell phone

**movilidad** *f.* mobility

**movimiento** movement

**muchacho/a** boy/girl

**mucho** *adv.* a lot; much

**mucho/a** *adj.* a lot; *pl.* many; **muchas gracias** thank you very much; **mucho gusto.** it's a pleasure (to meet you). (P)

**mudarse** to move

**mueble** *m.* piece of furniture; *pl.* furniture (3); **sacudir los muebles** to dust the furniture (3)

**muela** molar, back tooth; **dolor** (*m.*) **de muela** toothache (12)

**muerde: que no muerde** it's not hard (*lit.* it doesn't bite)

**muerte** *f.* death

**muerto/a** (*p.p. of* **morir**) *n.* dead person; *adj.* dead; **Día** (*m.*) **de los Muertos** Day of the Dead (11); **naturaleza muerta** still life (*painting*)

**mujer** *f.* woman (1); **mujer de negocios** businesswoman (13); **mujer soldado** female soldier (13)

**multa** fine

**multinacional** multinational

**múltiple** many, numerous; multiple

**multitud** (*f.*) **de** numerous

**mundial** *adj.* world (9); **Copa Mundial** World Cup (*soccer*); **historia mundial** world history (9)

**mundo** world

**muñeca** doll (9)

**municipal** *adj.* local; municipal

**mural** *m.* mural (11)

**musa** muse

**museo** museum

**música** music (1); **escuchar música** to listen to music (1); **música clásica** classical music (11); **música pop** pop music (11); **música sinfónica** symphonic music (11)

**musical** musical; **conjunto musical** band, musical group (11); **instrumento musical** musical instrument

**músico/a** musician (11)

**musicólogo/a** musicologist

**musulmán, musulmana** *n., adj.* Muslim

**muy** *adv.* very; **muy bien.** very well. (P); **no muy bien.** not very well. (P)

# N

**nacer (zc)** to be born

**nacimiento** birth

**nación** *f.* nation; **Naciones Unidas** United Nations

**nacional** national (11); **parque** (*m.*) **nacional** national park (14)

**nacionalidad** *f.* nationality (P)

**nacionalismo** nationalism (9)

**nada** nothing (5), not anything; **de nada.** you're welcome. (P); **para nada** at all

**nadar** to swim (2); **nadar en la piscina** to swim in the swimming pool (2)

**nadie** no one (5), nobody, not anybody

**naranja** orange (*fruit*) (6)

**naranjo** orange tree

**nariz** *f.* (*pl.* **narices**) nose (12)

**narración** *f.* narration

**narrar** to narrate

**narrativa** narrative

**natación** *f.* swimming (2)

**natalidad** *f.* birthrate

**nativo/a** native

**natural** natural (6); **desastre** (*m.*) **natural** natural disaster (9); **gas** (*m.*) **natural** natural gas (14); **Patrimonio Natural de la Humanidad** World Heritage Site (UNESCO); **recurso natural** natural resource (14); **reserva natural** refuge; natural reserve (14)

**naturaleza** nature (10); **naturaleza muerta** still life (*painting*)

**naufragar** (**gu**) to sink; to be shipwrecked

**náusea** nausea; **tener** (*irreg.*) **náuseas** to be nauseous

**navaja** razor

**navegar** (**gu**) **en Internet** to surf the Internet (1)

**Navidad** *f.* Christmas (11); **árbol** (*m.*) **de Navidad** Christmas tree (11)

**neblina** mist

**necesario/a** necessary; **es necesario que** it's necessary that (11)

**necesidad** *f.* necessity

**necesitar** to need; **necesitar** + *inf.* to need to (*do something*) (1)

**negar** (**ie**) (**gu**) to deny (11); **negarse** to refuse

**negativo/a** negative; **palabra negativa** *gram.* negative word (5)

**negociación** *f.* negotiation

**negociar** to negotiate; to do business

**negocio** business (*establishment*); *pl.* business (*field*) (13); **hacer** (*irreg.*) **negocios** to do business; **hombre** (*m.*) / **mujer** (*f.*) **de negocios** businessman/businesswoman (13); **negocio particular** private business

**negro** *n.* black (2)

**negro/a** *adj.* **pimienta negra** black pepper (6)

**neoclásico/a** Neoclassical

**nervio** nerve; **nervios de acero** nerves of steel

**nervioso/a** nervous (2)

**nevar** (**ie**) to snow; **está nevando.** / **nieva.** it's snowing. (2)

**nevera** refrigerator

**ni** neither; nor; not even; **ni... ni...** neither . . . nor . . . (5); **ni modo** no way

**nicaragüense** Nicaraguan (P)

**niebla** fog (9)

**nieto/a** grandson/granddaughter (4); *pl.* grandchildren (4)

**nieve** *f.* snow (14)

**nilón** *m.* nylon

**niñez** *f.* childhood (9)

**ningún, ninguno/a** none, not any (5), no; **en ninguna parte** nowhere; **ningún lugar** nowhere

**niño/a** boy/girl; small child

**nivel** *m.* level

**no** no (P); not (P); **¿no?** right?; **no hay** there is/are not; **no hay de qué.** don't mention it. (P); **no muy bien.** not very well. (P); **no obstante** nevertheless; **no renovable** non-renewable (14); **no tener** (*irreg.*) **razón** to be wrong (3)

**Nóbel: Premio Nóbel** Nobel Prize

**noche** *f.* night; **buenas noches.** good evening. (*after evening meal*) (P); **de la noche** in the evening, at night (1); P.M.; **de noche** at night; **esta noche** tonight (1); **mesita de noche** nightstand (5); **por la noche** in the evening, at night (1)

**Nochebuena** Christmas Eve (11)

**Nochevieja** New Year's Eve (11)

**nocturno/a** *adj.* night, nocturnal

**nómada** *n. m., f.* nomad; *adj.* nomadic

**nombrar** to name

**nombre** *m.* name; **¿cuál es su nombre?** what's your (*form.*) name? (P); **¿cuál es tu nombre?** what's your (*fam.*) name? (P); **mi nombre es...** my name is . . . (P)

**noreste** *m.* northeast

**norma** rule, regulation

**noroeste** *m.* northwest

**norte** *m.* north; **al norte** (to the) north (8)

**Norteamérica** North America

**norteamericano/a** North American; *from Canada or the United States*; American, *from the United States*

**norteño/a** northern

**nos** *dir. obj. pron.* us (5); *indir. obj. pron.* to/for us (6); *refl. pron.* ourselves; **nos vemos.** see you later. (*lit.* we'll see each other.) (P)

**nosotros/as** *sub. pron.* we (P); *obj.* (*of prep.*) us

**nostálgico/a** nostalgic

**nota** note; grade; **sacar** (**qu**) **buenas/malas notas** to get good/bad grades (1)

**notar** to note, notice

**noticias** *pl.* news (15)

**noticiero** news report (15); newscast

**novecientos/as** nine hundred (4)

**novela** novel (11)

**novelista** *m., f.* novelist

**noveno/a** ninth (5)

**noventa** ninety (2); **ciento noventa y nueve** one hundred ninety-nine (4)

**noviazgo** courtship (12); engagement (12)

**noviembre** November (2)

**novio/a** boyfriend/girlfriend (1); fiancé/fiancée (12); bride/groom (12); **buscar** (**qu**) **novio/a por el Internet** to look for a boyfriend/girlfriend online, Internet dating (15); **pasar tiempo con el/la novio/a** to spend time with one's boyfriend/girlfriend (2)

**nube** *f.* cloud; **hay (muchas) nubes.** it's (very) cloudy. (2)

**nublado/a** cloudy; **está (muy) nublado.** it's (very) cloudy. (2)

**nuclear: energía nuclear** nuclear power (14)

**núcleo** nucleus; **núcleo urbano** city center

**nudo** knot

**nuera** daughter-in-law (4)

**nuestro/a(s)** *poss. adj.* our (1); *poss. pron.* ours (12)

**nueve** nine (P); **ciento noventa y nueve** one hundred ninety-nine (4)

**nuevo/a** new; **Año Nuevo** New Year's Day (11)

**número** number (P); **número ordinal** *gram.* ordinal number (5)

**numeroso/a** numerous, many

**nunca** never (5)

**nupcial** nuptial; **séquito nupcial** wedding party

**nutrición** *f.* nutrition

**nutrir** to nourish

**nutritivo/a** nutritional

# O

**o** *conj.* or; **o... o...** either . . . or . . . (5)

**obediente** obedient (4)

**obesidad** *f.* obesity

**objetivo** *n.* objective

**objeto** object; **objeto directo** *gram.* direct object; **objeto indirecto** *gram.* indirect object; **pronombre** (*m.*) **de objeto directo** *gram.* direct object pronoun (5);

**pronombre de objeto indirecto** *gram.* indirect object pronoun (6)

**obligación** *f.* obligation

**obligar (gu)** to force (*someone to do something*)

**obligatorio/a** compulsory, obligatory

**obra** work; **obra de arte** work of art (11); **obra de teatro** play (11); **obra maestra** masterpiece (11)

**observación** *f.* observation; **observación de pájaros** bird watching (9)

**observar** to observe

**obsesión** *f.* obsession

**obsesionado/a** obsessed

**obstante: no obstante** nevertheless

**obtener** (*like* **tener**) to obtain

**obvio/a** obvious; **es obvio que** it's obvious that (12)

**ocasión** *f.* occasion

**occidental** western

**océano** ocean (14); **Océano Atlántico/ Pacífico** Atlantic/Pacific Ocean

**ochenta** eighty (2)

**ocho** eight (P)

**ochocientos/as** eight hundred (4)

**ocio** leisure time

**octavo/a** eighth (5)

**octubre** October (2)

**ocupación** *f.* occupation

**ocupado/a** busy (2)

**ocupar** to occupy (9); to live in; to take up (*space*); **ocuparse de** to take care of

**ocurrir** to occur, to take place

**odio** hate (15)

**oeste** *m.* west; **al oeste** (to the) west (8)

**oferta** offer

**oficial** official

**oficina** (main) office (1); **edificio de oficinas** office building (8); **oficina de correos** post office (8)

**oficio** trade (13)

**ofrecer (zc)** to offer (6)

**ofrenda** *n.* offering

**oído** inner ear (12)

**oír** *irreg.* (*p.p.* **oído**) to hear (2)

**ojalá (que)** + *pres. subj.* hopefully (11)

**ojo** eye (12)

**ola** wave (14)

**olímpico/a** Olympic

**oliva: aceite** (*m.*) **de oliva** olive oil (6)

**olvidado/a** forgotten

**olvidar** to forget (*in accidental* **se** *construction*) (7); **olvidar(se) (de)** to forget (about)

**once** eleven (P)

**onda** wave; **qué buena onda** how cool; **ser** (*irreg.*) **buena onda** to be (a) cool (person); **ser mala onda** to be a jerk

**onomatopéyico/a** onomatopoeic

**opción** *f.* option

**ópera** opera (11)

**operar** to operate, run

**opinar** to express opinion

**opinión** *f.* opinion

**oportunidad** *f.* opportunity

**optar** to opt

**óptico/a** optic; **fibra óptica** fiber optics; optical fiber (15)

**optimista** *m., f.* optimist

**opuesto/a** *adj.* opposite

**oración** *f.* sentence

**orden** *m.* order

**ordenador** *m.* computer (*Sp.*)

**ordenar** to order (*in a restaurant*) (6)

**ordinal: número ordinal** *gram.* ordinal number (5)

**orégano** oregano

**oreja** ear (12)

**orgánico/a** organic (6)

**organismo** organism

**organización** *f.* organization (9)

**organizado/a** organized (13)

**organizar (c)** to organize

**órgano** organ

**orgullo** pride (15); arrogance (15)

**orgulloso/a** proud (4); **ser** (*irreg.*) **orgulloso/a** to be arrogant (15)

**orientación** *f.* orientation

**oriental** eastern

**orientarse** to get one's bearings

**origen** *m.* origin

**originar(se)** to originate

**originario/a** *adj.* originating; native

**orilla** shore (14)

**ornamentación** *f.* ornamentation

**oro** gold; **de oro** gold (7)

**orquesta** orchestra (11); **orquesta sinfónica** symphonic orchestra (11)

**ortiga** nettle

**ortográfico/a** *adj.* spelling

**os** *dir. obj. pron.* you (*pl. fam. Sp.*) (5); *indir. obj. pron.* to/for you (*pl. fam. Sp.*) (6); *refl. pron.* yourselves (*pl. fam. Sp.*)

**oscuro/a** dark (*color*) (7); dark; dim (5)

**oso** bear (14); **oso polar** polar bear (14)

**otavaleño/a** of or pertaining to Otavalo (Ecuador)

**otoño** fall (*season*) (2), autumn

**otro/a** other (P); another; **otra vez** again

**oveja** sheep (8)

**oxígeno** oxygen

**ozono** ozone; **capa de ozono** ozone layer (14)

## P

**paciencia** patience

**paciente** *n. m., f.* patient; *adj.* patient

**pacífico/a: (Océano) Pacífico** Pacific Ocean

**pacto** pact

**padecer (zc)** to suffer from; to undergo

**padrastro** stepfather (4)

**padre** *m.* father (4); *pl.* parents (4); **Día** (*m.*) **del Padre** Father's Day (11)

**padrino** godfather (4); *pl.* godparents (4)

**paella** Spanish dish with rice, shellfish, and often chicken and sausages, flavored with saffron

**pagado/a: vacaciones** (*f.*) **pagadas** paid vacation (13)

**pagano/a** pagan

**pagar (gu) (por)** to pay (for) (1); **pagar el agua** to pay the water (bill) (15); **pagar el alquiler** to pay the rent (15); **pagar el cable** to pay the cable TV (bill) (15); **pagar el celular** to pay the cell phone (bill) (15); **pagar el coche** to pay the car payment (15); **pagar el gas** to pay the (natural) gas (bill) (15); **pagar el Internet** to pay the Internet bill (15); **pagar el préstamo estudiantil** to pay the student loan (15); **pagar el satélite** to pay the satellite bill (15); **pagar el sistema de vigilancia** to pay the security system (bill) (15); **pagar el teléfono** to pay the telephone bill (15); **pagar la hipoteca** to pay the mortgage (15); **pagar la luz** to pay the electric bill (15); **pagar la matrícula** to pay tuition (15); **pagar las cuentas (médicas)** to pay the (medical) bills (15)

**página** page; **página Web** webpage (13)

**pago** payment; **pago anual/mensual/ semanal** annual/monthly/weekly payment (15)

**país** *m.* country (P); **País Vasco** Basque Country

**paisaje** *m.* landscape (14); scenery

**paja** straw; **de paja** straw (7)

**pájaro** bird; **observación** (*f.*) **de pájaros** bird watching (9)

**palabra** word (P); **palabra indefinida** *gram.* indefinite word (5); **palabra interrogativa** *gram.* question word (1); **palabra negativa** *gram.* negative word (5)

**palacio** palace (8); **Palacio Arzobispal** archbishop's residence

**paladar** *type of restaurant business, run out of the home*

**palmada** handclap

**palmera** palm tree (14)

**palo** stick; **palo de golf** golf club

**palomitas** *pl.* popcorn

**pampa** plain *(geography)*

**pan** *m.* bread (6); **pan integral** whole wheat bread (6); **pan tostado** toast (6)

**panadería** bakery

**Panamá** Panama; **sombrero Panamá** Panama hat

**panameño/a** Panamanian (P)

**panda** *m.* panda (14)

**pandereta** tambourine

**panel** (*m.*) **solar** solar panel (14)

**pantalla** (monitor) screen (15); **pantalla plana** flat screen; **televisión** (*f.*) **de pantalla ancha** wide-screen TV (15)

**pantalón** *m. s.* pants (7); **pantalón corto** shorts (7)

**pantano** wetlands (14); marsh (14); swamp

**papá** *m.* dad (1)

**papagayo** parrot (macaw) (14)

**papas** potatoes (*L.A.*) (6); **papas fritas** French fries (6); **puré** (*m.*) **de papas** mashed potatoes (6)

**papaya** papaya (6)

**papel** *m.* paper (1); role

**papelería** stationery store (7)

**paquete** *m.* package

**par** *m.* pair

**para** for (2); toward (4); **para + *inf.*** in order to (*do something*) (4); **para que + *subj.*** so that (14)

**parada** (bus/subway) stop (8); **hacer paradas** to make stops

**parador** *m. Sp.* parador (*state-owned hotel in historical buildings*)

**paraguas** *m. inv.* umbrella

**paraguayo/a** Paraguayan (P)

**parar** to stop (8)

**parcela** piece of land; plot

**parcial** partial; **empleo a tiempo parcial** part-time job (13)

**parecer** (zc) to seem; **parecerse** (a) to look like (each other) (9)

**parecido/a** similar

**pared** *f.* wall (1)

**pareja** partner (12); couple (12); **en parejas** in pairs; **pareja de hecho** common-law couple (12); domestic partner (12)

**paréntesis** *m.* parenthesis

**pariente** *m., f.* relative (4)

**parque** *m.* park (8); **parque nacional** national park (14); **parque zoológico** zoo (9)

**parrilla: a la parrilla** grilled

**parrillada** barbecue (*event*) (*Arg.*)

**parte** *f.* part; **en ninguna parte** nowhere; **por todas partes** everywhere (9)

**participación** *f.* participation

**participante** *m., f.* participant

**participar** to participate

**particular** particular; private; **negocio particular** private business

**partido** game (*single occurrence*) (2); match (*sports*)

**partir** to break; **a partir de** as of; from (*point in time*) on; beyond (4)

**pasa** raisin

**pasado** *n.* past

**pasado/a** *adj.* last; past; **el año pasado** last year (6); **el fin de semana pasado** last weekend; **el lunes (martes, miércoles,... ) pasado** last Monday (Tuesday, Wednesday, . . . ) (6); **el mes** (*m.*) **pasado** last month (6); **la semana pasada** last week (6); **pasado mañana** the day after tomorrow (1)

**pasajero/a** passenger (10)

**pasaporte** *m.* passport (10)

**pasar** to happen; to pass; to spend (*time*); **pasar la aspiradora** to vacuum (3); **pasar por el control de seguridad** to go through security (10); **pasar por la aduana** to go through customs (10); **pasar tiempo** to spend time (1); **pasar tiempo con el/la novio/a** to spend time with one's boyfriend/girlfriend (2); **pasar un rato** to spend some time (1); **pasarlo bien/mal** to have a good/ bad time (3); **pasarlo de maravilla** to have a great time; **pasarlo fenomenal** to have a great time

**pasarela** runway (*fashion*)

**pasatiempo** pastime (2)

**Pascua** Easter (11); **Pascua judía** Passover (11)

**pasear** to take a walk, stroll (2); **pasear con el perro** to take a walk/stroll with the dog (2); **pasear en barco** to go boating (9)

**paseo** walk, stroll; **dar** (*irreg.*) **un paseo** to take a stroll

**pasillo** hallway (5); **asiento de pasillo** aisle seat (10)

**pasión** *f.* passion (15)

**pasivo/a** passive

**pasmado/a** stunned

**paso** step

**pasta** pasta (6); **pasta de dientes** toothpaste

**pastel** *m.* cake (6); pie (6); *adj.* pastel (*colors*) (7); **pastel de cumpleaños** birthday cake

**pastilla** pill (12)

**pasto** pasture; fodder

**pastor** *m.* pastor; minister

**patata** potato

**paterno/a** paternal

**patinaje** *m.* skating

**patinar** to skate (2); **patinar en línea** to inline skate (2)

**patio** patio (5)

**patrimonio** patrimony; **Patrimonio Natural de la Humanidad** World Heritage Site (UNESCO)

**patriota** *m., f.* patriot

**patrón, patrona** patron; boss; **santo patrón, santa patrona** patron saint (11)

**pavimentado/a** paved

**pavo** turkey (6); **pavo real** peacock

**paz** *f.* peace (9)

**peatón, peatona** pedestrian

**pecho** chest (12)

**pedazo** piece

**pedido** *n.* order; **hacer** (*irreg.*) **un pedido** to place an order

**pedir** (i, i) to ask for (3); to order (3)

**pegar** (gu) to glue; to hit

**pelar** to peel

**pelear(se)** to fight (12)

**pelícano** pelican (14)

**película** movie; **ver** (*irreg.*) **una película** to watch a movie (3)

**peligro** danger; **especie** (*f.*) **en peligro de extinción** endangered species (14)

**peligroso/a** dangerous (14); **residuos peligrosos** hazardous waste (14)

**pelirrojo/a** redheaded (1)

**pelo** hair; **corte** (*m.*) **de pelo** haircut; **lavarse el pelo** to wash one's hair (5); **secarse** (qu) **el pelo** to dry off one's hair (5)

**pelota** ball

**peluquero/a** hairdresser (13)

**pena** pain; *pl.* sorrows; **darle** (*irreg.*) **pena** to make (*someone*) sad; **valer** (*irreg.*) **la pena** to be worth it

**pendiente** *adj.* pending

**península** peninsula (14); **Península Ibérica** Iberian Peninsula

**pensar** (ie) (en) to think (about) (3); **pensar** (ie) + *inf.* to plan to (*do something*) (3)

**peor** worse; worst

**pepino** cucumber

**pequeño/a** small (1)

**pera** pear (6)

**percusión** f. percussion

**perder (ie)** to lose (3); **perderse** to get lost; to miss (*a function, stop*)

**perdurar** to last, endure

**peregrinación** f. pilgrimage

**peregrino/a** pilgrim

**perejil** m. parsley

**perezoso/a** lazy (1)

**perfecto/a** perfect

**perfume** m. perfume (7)

**perfumería** perfume shop (7)

**periódico** newspaper (15); **periódico en línea** online newspaper (15)

**periodismo** journalism (1)

**periodista** m., f. journalist (13)

**periodístico/a** journalistic

**período** period (*of time*)

**perla** pearl; **de perlas** pearl (7)

**permanecer (zc)** to stay, remain

**permanente** permanent

**permiso** permission

**permitir** to permit, allow

**pero** conj. but (P)

**perro** dog; **pasear con el perro** to take a walk/stroll with the dog (2)

**persona** person (1)

**personaje** m. character; celebrity

**personal** n. personnel; adj. personal; **cuidado personal** personal care (12); **director(a) de personal** personnel director (13); **pronombre** (m.) **personal** gram. personal pronoun (P)

**personalidad** f. personality

**personalizar (c)** to personalize

**perspectiva** perspective

**pertenecer (zc) (a)** to belong (to) (9)

**peruano/a** Peruvian (P)

**pesa: levantar pesas** to lift weights (3)

**pesado/a** adj. heavy; boring

**pesar** to weigh

**pesca** fishing (9)

**pescado** fish (*prepared as food*) (6)

**pescar (qu)** to fish

**peseta** former currency of Spain

**pesimista** n. m., f. pessimist; adj. pessimistic

**peso** weight (*on a scale*); peso (*currency*)

**pesticidas** m. pesticides (14)

**pétalo** petal

**petite** petite (*size*)

**petróleo** petroleum (14); crude oil (14); **productos del petróleo** petroleum products (14)

**petrolero** oil tanker (14)

**petroquímico/a** petrochemical

**pez** m. (*pl.* **peces**) fish (*alive*) (8)

**picado/a** chopped; **carne** (f.) **picada** ground beef (6)

**picante** spicy (hot)

**picnic** m. picnic

**pico** peak

**pie** m. foot (12); **dedo del pie** toe (12)

**piedra** rock, stone; **aro de piedra** stone ring

**piel** f. skin; leather; **de piel** leather (7)

**pierna** leg (12)

**pieza** piece

**pijama** m., f. s. pajamas (7)

**pila** battery (14)

**pimentón dulce** paprika

**pimienta** pepper; **pimienta negra/roja** black/red pepper (6)

**pimiento** (bell) pepper

**piña** pineapple (6)

**pingüino** penguin (14)

**pintar** to paint (9)

**pinto: gallo pinto** black beans and rice dish of Costa Rica

**pintor(a)** painter (11)

**pintoresco/a** picturesque

**pintura** painting (11)

**pionero/a** pioneer

**piramidal** adj. pyramid

**pirata** m., f. pirate

**piscina** swimming pool (2); **nadar en la piscina** to swim in the swimming pool (2)

**piso** apartment (5); floor (*of a building*) (5); floor (*surface*); **barrer el piso** to sweep the floor (3); **bloque** (m.) **de pisos** block apartment building (5); **primer piso** second floor (5); **segundo piso** third floor (5); **trapear el piso** to mop the floor (3)

**pista** hint; rink; **pista de hielo** ice-skating rink

**pizarra** chalkboard

**pizarrón** m. whiteboard (1); **pizarrón blanco** whiteboard (1)

**plan** m. plan; **plan de jubilación** retirement plan (13)

**planchar** to iron; **planchar la ropa** to iron clothes (3)

**planear** to plan; **planear la jubilación** to plan one's retirement (15)

**planeta** m. planet

**plano** city map (8); blueprint

**plano/a** flat; **pantalla plana** flat screen

**planta** plant (14); floor (*of a building*); **planta baja** first (ground) floor (5); **planta salvaje** wild plant (14)

**plantación** f. plantation

**plantar** to plant

**plasma: televisor** (m.) **plasma** plasma television

**plástico** n. plastic; **bolsa de plástico** plastic bag (14); **envase** (m.) **de plástico** plastic container (14)

**plástico/a** adj. plastic; **artes** (f. but el **arte**) **plásticas** visual arts (11)

**plata** silver; **de plata** silver (7)

**plátano** banana; plantain

**platicar (qu)** to chat

**plato** plate (6); dish; **lavar los platos** to wash the dishes (3)

**playa** beach (14)

**plaza** plaza (2); town square; **plaza mayor** main square (*Sp.*)

**plegable** adj. folding

**plena** narrative musical form / dance from Puerto Rico

**pleno/a** full

**plomero/a** plumber (13)

**pluma** (fountain) pen

**población** f. population (8); **población densa** dense population (14)

**poblado** village

**pobre** poor

**pobreza** poverty

**poco** adv. little; **dentro de poco** in a little while; **poco a poco** little by little, gradually; **un poco (de)** a little bit (of)

**poco/a** little; few

**poder** n. power

**poder** irreg. to be able (3); can

**poderoso/a** powerful

**poema** m. poem

**poesía** poetry; **recitar poesía** to recite poetry (9)

**poeta** m., f. poet (11)

**polar: oso polar** polar bear (14)

**polea** pulley

**policía** m., f. police officer; f. police (*force*); **comisaría de policía** police station (8)

**política** n. politics

**político/a** n. politician; adj. political; **ciencias políticas** political science (1); **familia política** in-laws (4); **historia política** political history (9)

**pollo** chicken (6)

**polo** polo shirt (7)

**pomelo** grapefruit

**poner** irreg. (*p.p.* **puesto**) to put (2); to place (2); **poner a pruebas** to test; **poner la mesa** to set the table (3); **ponerle una inyección** to give (*someone*) a shot (12); **ponerse** to put on (*clothing*); **ponerse** + adj. to get, become + adj.; **ponerse al corriente** to catch up; **ponerse en contacto con** to get in touch with

**pontón: puente** (*m.*) **pontón** floating bridge

**pop: música pop** pop music (11)

**popularidad** *f.* popularity

**por** for (2); by (2); in (4); by means of (4); through (4); along (4); **hablar por teléfono** to speak on the phone (1); **llamar por teléfono** to call on the phone (1); **por año** yearly; per year; **por ciento** percent; **¡por Dios!** for heaven's sake! (9); **por ejemplo** for example (4); **por el contrario** on the contrary; **por eso** that's why (4); **por favor** please (4); **por fin** finally (4); **por la mañana** in the morning (1); **por la noche** in the evening, at night (1); **por la tarde** in the afternoon (1); **por lo general** generally (4); **por lo menos** at least (4); **por primera/última vez** for the first/last time (9); **¿por qué?** why? (3); **por si acaso** just in case (9); **por supuesto** of course (9); **por todas partes** everywhere (9)

**porcentaje** *m.* percentage

**porche** *m.* porch

**porfiria** Porphyria (*a group of rare genetic disorders*)

**porqué** *m.* reason why

**porque** *conj.* because (3)

**portafolios** *m. inv.* briefcase

**portátil: computadora portátil** laptop (1)

**porteño/a** *of/from Buenos Aires, Argentina*

**portero** goalkeeper

**portugués, portuguesa** Portuguese

**posada** inn (8)

**pose** *f.* pose

**poseer (y)** to own

**posesivo/a** possessive; **adjetivo posesivo** *gram.* possessive adjective (1); **posesivo tónico** *gram.* stressed possessive (12)

**posibilidad** *f.* possibility

**posible** possible; **es posible que** it's possible that (11)

**posición** *f.* position

**positivo/a** positive

**postal: tarjeta postal** postcard (10)

**posterior** later, subsequent

**postre** *m.* dessert (6)

**postular** to nominate; **postularse** to run for (*a political position*)

**potencia** power (*political*)

**practicar (qu)** to practice (1); **practicar el ala delta** to hang glide (9); **practicar la aromaterapia** to do aromatherapy (15); **practicar un deporte** to participate in a sport (1)

**práctico/a** practical

**pradera** meadow

**prado** meadow; field

**precaución** *f.* precaution

**preceder** to precede

**precio** price; **precio alto/bajo/fijo** high/low/fixed price (7)

**precioso/a** lovely; beautiful; precious

**precipicio** precipice

**preciso** necessary

**precocinado/a** precooked

**precolombino/a** pre-Columbian (9)

**predisposición** *f.* predisposition

**predominante** predominant

**predominar** to predominate

**preescolar** preschool

**preferencia** preference

**preferible** preferable

**preferido/a** favorite

**preferir (ie, i)** to prefer (3)

**pregunta** question; **hacer** (*irreg.*) **preguntas** to ask questions

**preguntar** to ask (*a question*) (6)

**prehispano/a** pre-Hispanic

**preinstalación** *f.* pre-installation

**prematuramente** prematurely

**premio** prize; award; **Premio Nóbel** Nobel Prize

**prenda** garment, article of clothing; **prenda de ropa** piece/article of clothing (7)

**prender** to turn on (*lights*)

**prensa** (the) press (15)

**preocupado/a** worried (2)

**preocupar** to worry (6); **preocuparse por** to worry about

**preparación** *f.* preparation

**preparar** to prepare (6); **prepararse** to get (*oneself*) ready

**preparativo** preparation

**preposición** *f. gram.* preposition (2); **preposición de lugar** *gram.* preposition of location (2)

**presa** dam (14)

**prescindir de** to do without (*something*)

**presencia** presence

**presenciado/a** witnessed

**presentación** *f.* introduction (P)

**presentar** to present

**presente** *n. m. gram.* present tense; *adj.* present

**preservación** *f.* preservation

**preservar** to preserve; to maintain

**presidente/a** president

**presión** *f.* pressure (15)

**préstamo** *n.* loan; **pagar (gu) el préstamo estudiantil** to pay the student loan (15)

**prestar** to loan (6); **prestar atención** to pay attention

**prestigio** prestige

**pretérito** *gram.* preterite (tense)

**prevenir** (*like* **venir**) to prevent

**previo/a** previous

**primario/a** primary; elementary; **escuela primaria** elementary school

**primavera** spring (2); **vacaciones** (*f.*) **de primavera** spring break (11)

**primer, primero/a** first (5); **a primera vista** at first sight; **por primera vez** for the first time (9); **primer piso** second floor (5); **primera clase** first class (10)

**primitivo/a** primitive

**primo/a** cousin (4); **primo/a segundo/a** second cousin (4)

**primordial** essential

**principal** *adj.* main; **dormitorio principal** master bedroom (5); **puerta principal** front door (5)

**principio** beginning; **a principios de** at the beginning of; **al principio** in the beginning, at first; **al principio de** at the beginning of

**prioridad** *f.* priority

**prisa** hurry; **tener** (*irreg.*) **prisa** to be in a hurry (3)

**prisión** *f.* prison

**privado/a** private

**privilegiado/a** privileged

**probable** probable; **es probable que** it's probable that (11)

**probar (ue)** to taste, try (6); to prove

**problema** *m.* problem; **problema ambiental** environmental problem (14)

**procedente** coming from

**proceder a** + *inf.* to proceed to (*do something*); **proceder de** to originate from

**procesado/a** processed

**procesador** *m.* processor

**procesión** *f.* procession (9)

**proceso** process

**producción** *f.* production

**producir** (*like* **conducir**) to produce

**productividad** *f.* productivity

**producto** product; **producto lácteo** dairy product (6); **productos del petróleo** petroleum products (14); **productos no reciclables** non-recyclable products (14); **productos químicos** chemical products (14)

**productor(a)** producer

**profesión** *f.* profession (13)

**profesional** professional

**profesor(a)** professor (1); teacher (1)

**profesorado** faculty (*academic*)

**profundo** *adv.* deeply; **respirar profundo** to breathe deeply (15)

**profundo/a** *adj.* profound

**programa** *m.* program

**programador(a)** programmer (13)

**progreso** progress

**prohibir (prohíbo)** to prohibit (11)

**prolongar (gu)** to prolong

**promedio** average

**promesa** promise

**prometer** to promise (6)

**promoción** *f.* promotion

**promover (ue)** to promote

**pronombre** *m. gram.* pronoun; **pronombre de objeto directo** *gram.* direct object pronoun (5); **pronombre de objeto indirecto** *gram.* indirect object pronoun (6); **pronombre personal** *gram.* personal pronoun (P)

**pronto** *adv.* soon; **hasta pronto.** see you soon. (P); **tan pronto como** *conj.* as soon as (13)

**propenso/a (a)** prone (to)

**propiedad** *f.* property (8)

**propietario/a** owner

**propina** tip (6), gratuity

**propio/a** *adj.* own

**proponer** (*like* **poner**) (*p.p.* **propuesto**) to propose, suggest

**proporcionar** to provide

**propósito** proposal; **conjunción** (*f.*) **de dependencia y propósito** *gram.* conjunction of contingency and purpose (14)

**protagonista** *m., f.* protagonist

**protección** *f.* protection

**proteger (j)** to protect (14)

**protegido/a** protected; **área** (*f. but* **el área**) **protegida** protected area

**proteína** protein

**prototipo** prototype

**provecho: buen provecho** bon appétit

**proveer (y)** (*p.p.* **proveído**) to provide

**provincia** province

**provisión** *f.* provision

**provocar (qu)** to provoke (14)

**próximo/a** next

**proyección** *f.* projection

**proyecto** project

**proyector** *m.* projector (13)

**prueba** test; quiz; proof; **poner** (*irreg.*) **a pruebas** to test; **tener** (*irreg.*) **pruebas** to have proof

**publicar (qu)** to publish

**público** *n.* public; people

**público/a** *adj.* public; **relaciones** (*f.*) **públicas** public relations (13)

**pueblo** town (8)

**puente** *m.* bridge (8); **puente pontón** floating bridge

**puerta** door (1); **puerta principal** front door (5)

**puerto** port

**puertorriqueño/a** Puerto Rican (P)

**pues** well

**puesto** job (13); position (13); stall (in a market) (7); **puesto callejero** street shop/stall

**puesto/a** (*p.p. of* **poner**) placed; (turned) on

**pulga** flea (*insect*)

**pulmones** *m.* lungs (12)

**puma** *m.* puma (14)

**punta** point; tip; punta (*dance of the Garífuna indigenous group*)

**punto** point; **en punto** sharp, exactly (*with time*) (1)

**puntual** punctual (13)

**pupusa** *pastry turnover from El Salvador*

**puré** (*m.*) **de papas** mashed potatoes (6)

**purificar (qu)** to purify; to clean

**puro/a** pure; clean; **aire** (*m.*) **puro** clean air (14)

## Q

**que** *rel. pron.* that, which, who; than; **así que** therefore, consequently; **hasta que** *conj.* until; **hay que** + *inf.* it's necessary to (*do something*); **lo que** what, that which; **más/menos... que** more/less . . . than; **ya que** *conj.* since

**¿qué?** what? (1); **¿a qué hora?** at what time? (1); **¿con qué frecuencia?** how often? (3); **no hay de qué.** don't mention it. (P); **¿por qué?** why? (3); **¿qué hora es?** what time is it? (1); **¿qué tal?** how's it going? (P); **¿qué tiempo hace?** what's the weather like? (2)

**¡qué... !** *interj.* what . . . !; **¡qué** + *adj.*! how + *adj.*!; **¡qué buena onda!** how cool!; **¡qué chévere!** cool!; **¡qué mala onda!** what a bummer!

**quechua** *m.* Quechua (*language indigenous to the region of the Andes*)

**quedar** to be located (*buildings*) (2); to leave (behind) (*in accidental* **se** *construction*) (7); to remain; **quedarse** to stay (*in a place*) (10); **quedarse en blanco** to go blank (*mind*)

**quehacer** *m.* chore (3); **quehacer doméstico** domestic chore (3)

**queja** complaint

**quejarse** to complain (12)

**quemar** to burn

**quena** Andean flute

**querer** *irreg.* to want (3); **quererse** to love each other (12); **quisiera** I would like (6)

**querido/a** dear

**queso** cheese (6)

**quetzal** *m.* quetzal bird (14)

**¿quién(es)?** who? (1), whom?; **¿con quién(es)?** with whom? (1)

**química** chemistry (1)

**químico/a** chemist (13); **productos químicos** chemical products (14)

**quince** fifteen (P); **menos quince** quarter to (1); **y quince** quarter past (1)

**quinceañera: fiesta de quinceañera** *young woman's fifteenth birthday party* (11)

**quinientos/as** five hundred (4)

**quinto/a** fifth (5)

**quipu** *m.* khipu (*lit. "talking knots", communication devices used by the Incas*)

**quisiera** I would like (6)

**quitar** to remove; **quitar la mesa** to clear the table (3); **quitarse** to take off (*clothing*); **quitarse el estrés** to remove stress (15)

**quizá(s)** perhaps

## R

**radio** *f.* radio (*medium*); **emisora de radio** radio station; **radio por satélite** satellite radio (15)

**raíz** (*pl* **raíces**) root

**rama** branch

**rana** frog (14)

**rap** *m.* rap (*music*)

**rapidez** *f.* quickness

**rápido** *adv.* fast; quickly

**rápido/a** *adj.* fast; quick

**raqueta** racket

**ráquetbol** *m.* racquetball

**raro/a** strange

**rascacielos** *m. inv.* skyscraper (8)

**rasgo** trait

**rato** time; **descansar un rato** to rest a bit (1); **pasar un rato** to spend some time (1); **ratos libres** free time (2)

**ratón** *m.* mouse (15)

**raya** stripe; **de rayas** striped (7)

**raza: Día** (*m.*) **de la Raza** Columbus Day (11)

**razón** *f.* reason; **no tener** (*irreg.*) **razón** to be wrong (3); **tener razón** to be right (3)

**razonable** reasonable

**real** royal; real; **pavo real** peacock

**realidad** *f.* reality

**realismo** realism

**realista** *m., f.* realist

**realizado/a** accomplished; performed; carried out

**realizar (c)** to carry out

**rebaja** price reduction (7)

**rebelde** *n. m., f.* rebel; *adj.* rebellious

**recepción** *f.* reception (*area in a hotel*) (10)

**recepcionista** *m., f.* receptionist (13)

**receptor** *m.* receiver

**receta** prescription (12); recipe

**recetar** to prescribe (12)

**rechazo** rejection

**recibir** to receive (1)

**reciclable** recyclable; **productos no reciclables** non-recyclable products (14)

**reciclado/a** recycled (14)

**reciclaje** *m.* recycling (14)

**reciclar** to recycle (14)

**recién** *adv.* recently; freshly; newly; **recién casado/a** newlywed

**reciente** recent

**recipiente** *m., f.* recipient

**recíproco/a** reciprocal; **verbo recíproco** *gram.* reciprocal verb (9)

**recitar** to recite; **recitar poesía** to recite poetry (9)

**reclamo de equipaje** baggage claim (10)

**reclutamiento** *n.* recruiting

**recoger (j)** to pick up; to collect; **recoger el equipaje** to pick up luggage (10)

**recomendable** advisable

**recomendación** *f.* recommendation

**recomendar (ie)** to recommend (6)

**reconocer (zc)** to recognize

**reconocido/a** (*p.p. of* **reconocer**) well-known

**reconocimiento** recognition

**reconstruir** (*like* **construir**) to rebuild; to reconstruct

**recopilar** to compile

**recordar (ue)** to remember

**recorrer** to travel around / go through (*a town/city*) (10)

**recorrido** tour (10); trip (10)

**recreación** *f.* recreation

**recuerdo** souvenir; memory

**recuperación** *f.* recovery

**recuperar** to recover

**recurso** resource; **recurso económico** financial resource; **recurso natural** natural resource (14); **recurso tecnológico** technological resource

**red** *f.* network; Internet; **red social** social network

**redondez** *f.* roundness

**redondo/a** round

**reducir** (*like* **conducir**) to reduce

**reemplazo** replacement

**referencia** reference

**referirse (ie, i) (a)** to refer (to)

**refinado/a** refined

**refinería** refinery

**reflejar** to reflect

**reflejo** reflection

**reflexionar (sobre)** to reflect (on)

**reflexivo/a** reflexive; **verbo reflexivo** *gram.* reflexive verb (5)

**reforestación** *f.* reforestation

**reforma** *n.* reform

**reformar** to reform

**reforzar (ue) (c)** to strengthen

**refresco** soft drink (6)

**refrigerador** *m.* refrigerator (5)

**refugio** refuge

**regalar** to give (*as a gift*) (6)

**regalo** gift (11)

**regatear** to haggle (7)

**regateo** *n.* haggling

**región** *f.* region

**regionalismo** regionalism (9)

**registrarse** to check in (10); to register

**regla** rule

**reglamentario/a** controlled (*substances*)

**regresar (a)** to return, go back (*to a place*) (1)

**regulación** *f.* regulation

**regular** *v.* to regulate; *adj.* regular; OK; **regular.** so-so. (P)

**reina** queen (9)

**reiniciarse** to restart

**reino** kingdom (9)

**reírse (i, i) (me río)** to laugh (12)

**relación** *f.* relationship (4); connection; **relación sentimental** emotional relationship (12); **relaciones públicas** public relations (13)

**relacionarse con** to be related to

**relajado/a** relaxed

**relajante** relaxing (6)

**relajarse** to relax (5)

**relámpago** lightning bolt (9)

**relatar** to relate, tell

**relativamente** relatively

**relevante** relevant

**relevo** relay

**religión** *f.* religion

**religioso/a** religious (11)

**reloj** *m.* clock (1); watch (1)

**remedio** remedy

**remontar (a)** to date back (to)

**remoto/a** remote

**renacentista** *adj.* Renaissance

**renacimiento** rebirth; revival

**rencoroso/a** resentful (15)

**rendimiento** performance (*of a person's body*)

**rendir (i, i)** to pay (*homage*)

**renovable** renewable (14); **no renovable** non-renewable (14)

**renovar (ue)** to renew

**renta** *n.* rent

**renunciar (a)** to resign (from) (*a job*) (13)

**reparación** *f.* repair; **taller** (*m.*) **de reparaciones** repair shop (8)

**reparar** to repair

**repartido/a** spread out

**repasar** to review

**repaso** *n.* review

**repente: de repente** suddenly

**repercusión** *f.* repercussion

**repetir (i, i)** to repeat

**repleto/a (de)** replete (with)

**réplica** aftershock (*earthquake*)

**reportero/a** reporter

**reposar** to rest

**representación** *f.* representation

**representante** *n., adj. m., f.* representative

**representar** to represent

**representativo/a** representative

**reproductor** *m.* player; **reproductor de DVD/empetrés** DVD/mp3 player

**reptil** *m.* reptile (14)

**república** republic (9)

**requerir (ie, i)** to require

**requisito** requirement

**res** *f.*: **carne** (*f.*) **de res** beef (6)

**resaca** hangover

**resaltar** to stand out

**rescatar** to rescue (9)

**rescate** *m.* rescue (9)

**reserva** reserve (14); **reserva biológica** biological reserve (10); **reserva ecológica** ecological reserve; **reserva marina** marine reserve; **reserva natural** refuge; natural reserve (14); **reserva zoológica** biological reserve

**reservación** *f.* reservation (6)

**resfriado** *n.* cold (12)

**resfriado/a** congested (12)

**resfriarse (me resfrío)** to catch a cold (12)

**residencia** dorm (1); residence; **residencia estudiantil** student dorm (1)

**residencial** residential

**residente** *m., f.* resident

**residir** to reside

**residuo** residue; **residuos peligrosos** hazardous waste (14)

**resistencia** resistance

**resolución** *f.* resolution

**resolver (ue)** (*p.p.* **resuelto**) to solve, resolve (14)

**respecto: (con) respecto a** with regard to, with respect to

**respetar** to respect

**respeto** respect (15)

**respetuoso/a** respectful (15)

**respirar** to breathe; **respirar profundo** to breathe deeply (15)

**respiratorio/a** respiratory

**responder** to respond

**responsabilidad** *f.* responsibility (13)

**responsable** responsible (4)

**respuesta** answer

**restaurado/a** restored

**restaurante** *m.* restaurant (6)

**restaurar** to restore

**resto** *n.* rest, remainder; *pl.* remains

**resucitar** to resuscitate

**resultado** result

**resultar** to result; to turn out

**resumen** *m.* summary

**resumir** to summarize

**retirar** to remove; **retirarse** to retire

**reto** challenge (15)

**retrato** portrait

**reunión** *f.* meeting; reunion

**reunirse (me reúno) (con)** to get together (with)

**reutilizar (c)** to reuse (14)

**revisar** to inspect (*luggage*) (10)

**revista** magazine (15); **revista en línea** online magazine (15)

**revolución** *f.* revolution

**revolucionario/a** revolutionary (9)

**revolver** (*like* **volver**) (*p.p.* **revuelto**) to stir

**revuelto/a** (*p.p. of* **revolver**): **huevos revueltos** scrambled eggs

**rey** *m.* king (9); **Día** (*m.*) **de los Reyes Magos** Feast of the Three Kings (Epiphany) (11)

**riachuelo** stream

**rico/a** rich; delicious

**rigidez** *f.* stiffness

**rígido/a** rigid

**rimel** *m.* mascara

**río** river (8)

**riqueza** wealth

**ritmo** rhythm; **ritmo de vida** pace of life (15)

**rito** rite, ritual

**ritual** *m.* ritual; *adj.* ritual

**robo** robbery

**roca** rock (14)

**rock** *m.* rock (music) (11)

**rockero/a** *n.* rock artist; *adj.* rock (*music*)

**rodeado/a (de)** surrounded (by)

**rodilla** knee (12)

**rojo** *n.* red (2)

**rojo/a** *adj.* red; **pimienta roja** red pepper (6)

**rol** *m.* role

**románico/a** Romanesque

**romano/a** *n., adj.* Roman

**romántico/a** romantic (6)

**romper** (*p.p.* **roto**) to break (7); **romper con** to break up with (12)

**ron** *m.* rum

**ropa** clothes (1); clothing (7); **doblar la ropa** to fold clothes (3); **lavar la ropa** to wash clothes (1); **planchar la ropa** to iron clothes (3); **prenda de ropa** piece/article of clothing (7); **ropa interior** lingerie, underwear (7); **secar (qu) la ropa** to dry clothes (3); **tender (ie) la ropa** to hang clothes (3)

**ropero** wardrobe (7)

**rosa** rose

**rosado** *n.* pink (2)

**rosado/a** *adj.* pink

**rostro** face

**roto/a** (*p.p. of* **romper**) broken

**router** *m.* router (15)

**rubio/a** blond(e) (1)

**rueda** wheel

**ruido** noise

**ruinas arqueológicas** archeological ruins (10)

**rural** rural (8); **turismo rural** rural tourism

**rústico/a: cabaña rústica** rustic cabin (10)

**ruta** route (10)

**rutina** routine

# S

**sábado** Saturday (1)

**sabana** savanna

**sabelotodo** know-it-all

**saber** *irreg.* to know (3); **saber** + *inf.* to know (*how to do something*); **saber de memoria** to know by heart

**sabroso/a** delicious

**sacar (qu)** to take out; **sacar buenas/malas notas** to get good/bad grades (1); **sacar fotos** to take photos (2); **sacar la basura** to take out the trash/garbage (3); **sacar un DVD** to check out a DVD (1)

**sacramento** sacrament

**sacrificado/a** sacrificed

**sacudir los muebles** to dust the furniture (3)

**sagrado/a** sacred

**sal** *f.* salt (6)

**sala** living room; **sala de espera** waiting room (10)

**salado/a** salty; **agua** (*f. but* **el agua**) **salada** salt water (14)

**salarial** *adj.* wage; salary

**salario** *n.* wage (13); salary, pay (13); **salario mínimo** minimum wage (13)

**salchicha** sausage (6)

**salida** departure (10); gate (10)

**salir** *irreg.* to go out (2); to leave (2); **¿en cuánto sale(n)?** how much is it (are they)? (7); **salir bien/mal** to turn out well/poorly; **salir con** to go out with (*someone*); **salir de** to leave from (*a place*); **salir para** to leave for (*a place*)

**salón** *m.* large room; living room (5); **salón de clase** classroom (1); **salón formal** living room

**salsa** sauce; salsa (*music*)

**saltar** to jump

**salto** *n.* jump; waterfall

**salud** *f.* health; **centro de salud** health center (8)

**saludable** healthy

**saludarse** to greet each other (9)

**saludo** greeting (P)

**salvadoreño/a** Salvadoran (P)

**salvaje** wild; **animal** (*m.*) **salvaje** wild animal (14); **planta salvaje** wild plant (14)

**san** Saint; **Día** (*m.*) **de San Valentín** St. Valentine's Day

**sancocho** *a type of soup*

**sandalias** sandals (7)

**sandía** watermelon

**sandinista** *n., adj.* Sandinista

**sándwich** *m.* sandwich (6)

**Sanfermines** *m. pl.* San Fermín Festival (Running of the Bulls) (11)

**sangre** *f.* blood (12)

**sanitario/a** sanitary

**sano/a** healthy (12)

**santo/a** saint; holy; **Día** (*m.*) **de Todos los Santos** All Saints' Day; **día del santo** one's saint day (11); **santo patrón, santa patrona** patron saint (11); **Semana Santa** Holy Week (11)

**saquear** to sack, plunder

**saqueo** *n.* plundering

**sartén** *f.* frying pan

**satélite** *m.* satellite (15); **pagar (gu) el satélite** to pay the satellite bill (15); **radio** (*f.*) **por satélite** satellite radio (15)

**sauna** sauna; **tomar una sauna** to spend time in a sauna (3)

**saxofón** *m.* sax(ophone)

**se** *refl. pron.* yourself (*form.*); himself/ herself; itself; yourselves (*form. Sp.; fam., form. elsewhere*); themselves

**secadora** dryer (3)

**secar (qu)** to dry; **secar la ropa** to dry clothes (3); **secarse** to dry off (5); **secarse el pelo** to dry off one's hair (5)

**sección** *f.* section

**secretario/a** secretary (13)

**secreto** secret

**sector** *m.* sector

**secular** secular

**secundario/a** secondary; **escuela secundaria** high school

**sed** *f.* thirst; **tener (*irreg.*) (mucha) sed** to be (very) thirsty (3)

**seda** silk; **de seda** silk (7)

**sede** *f.* seat (*government*)

**sedentario/a** sedentary

**seducir** (*like* **conducir**) to seduce

**segmento** segment

**seguida: en seguida** right away

**seguido/a (de)** *adj.* followed (by)

**seguir (i, i)** to continue (3); to follow (3); to go (8); to keep going (8); to pursue (*a career*); **seguir** + *gerund* to keep / still be (*doing something*) (3)

**según** according to (3)

**segundo/a** second (5); **primo/a segundo/a** second cousin (4); **segundo piso** third floor (5)

**seguridad** *f.* security; **control** (*m.*) **de seguridad** security; **pasar por el control de seguridad** to go through security (10)

**seguro** *n.* insurance; **seguro médico** health insurance (13)

**seguro/a** sure, certain; secure; **estar** (*irreg.*) **seguro/a (de)** to be sure (of) (11)

**seis** six (P)

**seiscientos/as** six hundred (4)

**selección** *f.* selection; team (*sports*)

**seleccionador(a)** coach; manager (*sports*)

**seleccionar** to choose, select

**selva** jungle (14)

**selvático/a** *adj.* jungle

**semáforo** traffic light (8)

**semana** week (1); **día** (*m.*) **de la semana** day of the week; **días de entre semana** weekdays (1); **entre semana** during the week (1); **fin** (*m.*) **de semana** weekend (1); **la semana pasada** last week (6); **la semana que viene** next week (1); **Semana Santa** Holy Week (11); **una vez a la semana** once a week (3)

**semanal** weekly; **pago semanal** weekly payment (15)

**semántico/a** semantic

**sembrador(a)** sower

**sembrar (ie)** to sow, plant

**semejante** similar

**semejanza** similarity

**semestre** *m.* semester

**semilla** seed

**seminario** seminary

**semisótano** semibasement

**señalar** to indicate

**sencillo/a** simple; **habitación** (*f.*) **sencilla** single room (10)

**senderismo** hiking (9)

**sendero** path (8)

**señor** *m.* man; Mr.; sir

**señora** woman; Mrs.; ma'am

**señorita** young woman; Miss; Ms.

**sentarse (ie)** to sit down

**sentimental** emotional (15); **relación** (*f.*) **sentimental** emotional relationship (12)

**sentimiento** feeling (15)

**sentir (ie, i)** to regret; to feel sorry; **sentir cariño por** to be fond of (12); **sentirse** to feel (5)

**separación** *f.* separation (12)

**separado/a** separated (4)

**separar** to separate; **separarse (de)** to separate (12); to get separated (from) (12)

**septiembre** September (2)

**séptimo/a** seventh (5)

**sequía** drought

**séquito** entourage; **séquito nupcial** wedding party

**ser** *n. m.* being; **ser humano** human being

**ser** *irreg.* to be (P); **¿cómo eres?** what are you (*s. fam.*) like? (P); **¿cómo es usted (Ud.)?** what are you (*s. form.*) like? (P); **¿cuál es su nombre?** what's your (*form.*) name? (P); **¿cuál es tu nombre?** what's your (*s. fam.*) name? (P); **¿de dónde eres?** where are you (*s. fam.*) from? (P); **¿de dónde es usted (Ud.)?** where are you (*s. form.*) from? (P); **es absurdo que** it's absurd that (11); **es cierto que** it's certain that (11); **es extraño que** it's strange that (11); **es importante que** it's important that (11); **es imposible que** it's impossible that (11); **es improbable que** it's improbable that (11); **es increíble que** it's incredible that (11); **es interesante que** it's interesting that (12); **es la una.** it's one o'clock. (1); **es mejor que** it's better that (12); **es necesario que** it's necessary that (11); **es obvio que** it's obvious that (12); **es posible que** it's possible that (11); **es probable que** it's probable that (11); **es una lástima que** it's a shame that (11); **es urgente que** it's urgent that (11); **es verdad que** it's true that (11); **mi nombre es...** my name is . . . (P); **¿qué hora es?** what time is it? (1); **sea cual sea** whatever; **ser arrogante** to be arrogant; **ser buena onda** to be (a) cool (person); **ser hora de** + *inf.* to be time to (*do something*); **ser mala onda** to be a jerk; **ser orgulloso/a** to be arrogant (15); **son las dos (tres, cuatro,... ).** it's two (three, four, . . . ) o'clock. (1); **soy...** I'm . . . (P); **soy de...** I'm from . . . (P)

**sereno/a** serene

**seriado** soap opera

**serie** *f. s.* series

**serio/a** serious

**serpiente** *f.* snake, serpent (14)

**serranía** mountainous region

**servicio** service; **servicio comunitario** community service; **servicio social** social service

**servilleta** napkin (6)

**servir (i, i)** to serve (3)

**sesenta** sixty (2)

**sesión** *f.* session

**setecientos/as** seven hundred (4)

**setenta** seventy (2); **los años setenta** the seventies

**severo/a** severe

**sexo** sex; gender

**sexto/a** sixth (5)

**si** if (1); **por si acaso** just in case (9)

**sí** yes (P)

**sicología** psychology (1)

**sicólogo/a** psychologist (13)

**sicu** *m.* siku, panpipe (*Andean musical instrument*)

**siempre** always (5)

**sien** *f.* temple (*anat.*)

**sierra** mountain range (14)

**siesta** nap (3); **dormir (ue, u) la siesta** to nap; **tomar una siesta** to take a nap (3)

**siete** seven (P)

**siglo** century (9)

**significado** *n.* meaning
**significar (qu)** to mean
**significativo/a** significant
**signo** sign
**siguiente** *adj.* following
**sílaba** syllable
**silencio** silence
**silla** chair (1)
**sillón** *m.* armchair (5)
**silvestre** wild; **flora y fauna silvestre** wild plant and animal life (14)
**simbolizar (c)** to symbolize
**símbolo** symbol
**simpático/a** nice (1)
**simplemente** simply
**simplificado/a** simplified
**sin** without; **sin amueblar** unfurnished (5); **sin embargo** however; nevertheless; **sin que** + *subj.* without (14)
**sinagoga** synagogue; **ir** (*irreg.*) **a la sinagoga** to go to the synagogue (3)
**sinceramente** sincerely
**sincretismo** syncretism
**sinfonía** symphony
**sinfónico/a** *adj.* symphony, symphonic; **música sinfónica** symphonic music (11); **orquesta sinfónica** symphonic orchestra (11)
**singular** single; singular, unique
**sino** but (rather); **sino que** but (rather)
**sinónimo** synonym
**sintetizar (c)** to synthesize
**síntoma** *m.* symptom (12)
**síquico/a** psychological
**sirvienta** maid
**sísmico/a** seismic
**sismo** earthquake
**sistema** *m.* system; **pagar (gu) el sistema de vigilancia** to pay the security system (bill) (15)
**sitio** site
**situación** *f.* situation
**situado/a** situated
**smog** *m.* smog (14)
**SMS** *m.* text message
**snowboarding** *m.* snowboarding; **hacer** (*irreg.*) **snowboarding** to snowboard
**sobre** *prep.* about; **sobre todo** especially; above all
**sobrecogimiento** awe
**sobredesarrollo** overdevelopment
**sobrellevar** to endure
**sobrepantalón** *m. s.* overpants
**sobrepasar** to exceed
**sobrepesca** *n.* overfishing

**sobrepoblación** *f.* overpopulation (14)
**sobrepoblado/a** overpopulated
**sobreviviente** *n. m., f.* survivor (9); *adj.* surviving
**sobrevivir** to survive (9)
**sobrino/a** nephew/niece (4); *m. pl.* nephews and nieces (4)
**sobrio/a** frugal
**social** social; **ciencia social** social science; **estatus** (*m.*) **social** social status; **red** (*f.*) **social** social network; **servicio social** social service
**socialista** socialist
**sociedad** *f.* society
**socio/a** associate
**sociología** sociology (1)
**sociólogo/a** sociologist
**sofá** *m.* sofa (5)
**software** *m.* software
**sois** you (*pl. fam. Sp.*) are (P)
**soja** soy
**sol** *m.* sun; sunshine; **hace (mucho) sol.** it's (very) sunny. (2); **tomar el sol** to sunbathe (2)
**solado** tiled (*floor*)
**solamente** only
**solar: energía solar** solar power (14); **panel** (*m.*) **solar** solar panel (14)
**solas: a solas** alone
**soldado** (male) soldier (13); **mujer** (*f.*) **soldado** (female) soldier (13)
**soledad** *f.* solitude
**solemne** solemn
**soler (ue)** + *inf.* to usually (*do something*) (3)
**solicitar** to apply for (13); **solicitar trabajo** to apply for a job (13)
**solicitud** *f.* application (13)
**sólido/a** solid; sound; steady
**sólo** *adv.* only (P)
**solo/a** *adj.* alone; single
**solsticio** solstice
**soltar (ue)** (*p.p.* **suelto**) to release, let (*something*) go
**soltero/a** single (4), unmarried
**solución** *f.* solution; **solución ambiental** environmental solution (14)
**solvencia** competence; **tener** (*irreg.*) **solvencia** to be solvent
**sombra** shadow
**sombrero** hat (7); **sombrero Panamá** Panama hat
**somos** we are (P)
**son** they are (P); you (*pl. form. Sp.; pl. fam., form. elsewhere*) are (P)
**sonar (ue)** to ring; to sound
**sonido** *n.* sound
**sonreír (i, i)** (**sonrío**) to smile (12)

**sonrisa** *n.* smile
**soñar (ue)** to dream
**sopa** soup (6)
**sopera** soup bowl, soup tureen (6)
**soroche** *m.* altitude sickness
**sorprender** to surprise (11)
**sorprendido/a** surprised (2)
**sorpresa** *n.* surprise; **fiesta de sorpresa** surprise party
**sostenible** sustainable
**soviético/a: Unión** (*f.*) **Soviética** Soviet Union
**soy** I am (P)
**su(s)** *poss. adj.* your (*s. form.*) (1); his (1); her (1); your (*pl. form. Sp.; pl. fam., form. elsewhere*) (1); their (1); **¿cuál es su nombre?** what's your (*form.*) name? (P)
**suave** mild; soft
**subcampeonato** runner-up championship game
**subir** to go up; to upload (13); **subir (a)** to climb; to get in/on (*a vehicle*) (10)
**subjetivo/a** subjective
**subjuntivo** *gram.* subjunctive
**substancia** substance
**subsuelo** subsoil
**subvencionado/a** *adj.* subsidized
**sucesión** *f.* succession (9)
**sucio/a** dirty (2)
**sucursal** branch (*of a business*)
**Sudamérica** South America
**sudamericano/a** South American
**suegro/a** father-in-law/mother-in-law (4)
**sueldo** salary (13); **aumento de sueldo** raise
**suelo** floor; soil; **contaminación** (*f.*) **del suelo** soil pollution (14)
**sueño** sleep; **tener** (*irreg.*) **sueño** to be sleepy (3)
**suerte** *f.* luck; **tener** (*irreg.*) **(mucha) suerte** to be (very) lucky (3)
**suéter** *m.* sweater (7)
**suficiente** enough
**sufrir** to suffer; to bear; **sufrir de estrés** to suffer from stress (15)
**sugerencia** suggestion
**sugerir (ie, i)** to suggest (6)
**sumar** to add (up)
**sumo/a** *adj.* utmost
**superar** to exceed; to overcome (9)
**supercremoso/a** extra creamy
**superficial** superficial
**superficie** *f.* surface
**superior** superior; greater; **educación** (*f.*) **superior** higher education
**supermercado** supermarket (6)

**supervisar** to supervise (13); to oversee (13)

**supervisor(a)** supervisor

**suponer** (like **poner**) (p.p. **supuesto**) to suppose, assume

**supuesto: por supuesto** of course (9)

**sur** m. south; **al sur** (to the) south (8)

**sureste** m. southeast

**surfear** to surf

**surfing: hacer** (irreg.) **surfing** to surf

**surgir (j)** to arise, emerge

**suroeste** m. southwest

**surrealismo** surrealism

**surrealista** surrealist

**suspender** to cancel; to suspend

**suspendido/a** suspended

**sustancia** substance

**sustantivo** gram. noun

**sustitución** f. substitution

**susto** fright

**suyo/a** poss. adj. your (s. form.; pl. form. Sp.; pl. fam., form. elsewhere) (12); his/her (12); its (12); their (12); poss. pron. yours (s. form.; pl. form. Sp.; pl. fam., form. elsewhere) (12); his/hers (12); its (12); theirs (12)

# T

**tabaco** tobacco

**tabla** chart, table

**tacita** little cup

**tacón** m. heel; **zapatos de tacón alto** high-heeled shoes (7); **zapatos de tacón bajo** flats (7)

**taíno/a** n., adj. Taino (pre-Columbian culture of the Caribbean)

**tal** such, such a; **con tal (de) que** + subj. provided that (14); **¿qué tal?** how's it going? (P); **tal vez** perhaps

**tala de árboles** tree felling (14)

**talento** talent

**talla** (clothing) size (7)

**tallado/a** carved; **tallado/a en madera** carved-wood (7)

**taller** m. workshop; **taller** (m.) **de reparaciones** repair shop (8)

**tamal** m. tamale

**tamaño** size

**tambalearse** to wobble

**también** also, too (1)

**tambor** m. drum

**tambora** drum (Afro-Caribbean percussion instrument)

**tampoco** neither (5); nor (5); not either

**tan** so; as; **tan... como** as . . . as (4); **tan pronto como** conj. as soon as (13);

**tango** dance and music of Argentina

**tanto** adv. so much; **tanto como** as much as (4)

**tanto/a** adj. as much, so much; such a; pl. so many, as many; **tanto/a/os/as... como** as much/many . . . as (4)

**tapa** appetizer

**tapar** to cover

**tardar** to take time

**tarde** f. afternoon; adv. late; **buenas tardes.** good afternoon. (until evening meal) (P); **de la tarde** in the afternoon (1); P.M.; **esta tarde** this afternoon (1); **más tarde** later; **por la tarde** in the afternoon (1)

**tarea** homework (1); chore; task

**tarima** dais, platform

**tarjeta** card; **tarjeta de crédito** credit card (6); **tarjeta de embarque** boarding pass (10); **tarjeta postal** postcard (10)

**tasa** rate

**taurino/a** adj. bullfighting

**taxi** m. taxi (8)

**taxista** m., f. taxi driver

**taza** (coffee) cup (6)

**tazón** m. bowl (6)

**te** dir. obj. pron. you (s. fam.) (5); indir. obj. pron. to/for you (s. fam.) (6); refl. pron. yourself (s. fam.)

**té** m. tea (6)

**teatro** theater (1); **obra de teatro** play (11)

**techo** roof

**teclado** keyboard (15)

**técnica** technique

**técnico/a** n. technician (13); adj. technical

**tecnología** technology (13)

**tecnológico/a** technological; **avance** (m.) **tecnológico** technological advance (15); **recurso tecnológico** technological resource

**tejano/a** Texan

**tejer** to weave (11)

**tejidos** woven goods (7)

**tela** fabric (7)

**tele** f. T.V.

**teleconferencia** teleconference (13)

**telefónico/a** adj. telephone, phone

**teléfono** telephone (1); **contestar el teléfono** to answer the phone (13); **hablar por teléfono** to speak on the phone (1); **llamar por teléfono** to call on the phone (1); **pagar (gu) el teléfono** to pay the telephone bill (15); **teléfono celular** cell (phone) (1); **teléfono fijo** landline; **teléfono móvil** cell phone

**telenovela** soap opera

**telerromance** m. soap opera

**teletrabajable** doable via telecommuting

**teletrabajo** n. telecommuting

**televisión** f. television; **mirar la televisión** to watch TV (1); **televisión de alta definición** HD TV (15); **televisión de pantalla ancha** wide-screen TV (15)

**televisor** m. television set; **televisor plasma** plasma television

**tema** m. subject, topic

**temblor** m. tremor

**tembloroso/a** trembling

**temer** to fear

**temperatura** temperature; **tomarle la temperatura** to take (someone's) temperature (12)

**templo** temple

**temporal** adj. time; part-time; **conjunción** (f.) **temporal** gram. temporal conjunction (13)

**temprano** adv. early

**tendencia** tendency

**tender (ie)** to hang; **tender la ropa** to hang clothes (3)

**tenedor** m. fork (6)

**tener** (irreg.) to have (3); **¿cuántos años tiene usted (Ud.)?** how old are you (s. form.)? (4); **¿cuántos años tienes?** how old are you (s. fam.)? (4); **no tener razón** to be wrong (3); **tener... años** to be . . . years old (3); **tener cuidado** to be careful (3); **tener don** (m.) **de gentes** to get along well with others (13); **tener éxito** to be successful (3); **tener frío** to be cold (3); **tener ganas de** + inf. to feel like (doing something) (3); **tener lugar** to take place (9); **tener miedo (de)** to be afraid (of) (3); **tener (mucha) sed** to be (very) thirsty (3); **tener (mucha) suerte** to be (very) lucky (3); **tener (mucho) calor/frío** to be (very) hot/cold (3); **tener náuseas** to be nauseous; **tener prisa** to be in a hurry (3); **tener pruebas** to have proof; **tener que** + inf. to have to (do something) (3); **tener razón** to be right (3); **tener solvencia** to be solvent; **tener sueño** to be sleepy (3); **tener una carrera** to have a career (15); **tenerle cariño a** to be fond of (12); **tenerle manía** to have it in (for someone) (15)

**tenis** m. tennis (2); **cancha de tenis** tennis court; **jugar (ue) (gu) al tenis** to play tennis; **zapatos de tenis** tennis shoes (7)

**tensión** f. tension

**tenso/a** tense

**terapia** therapy (15); **terapia de grupo** group therapy (15)

**tercer, tercero/a** third (5)

**termal** thermal; **aguas** (f. but **el agua**) **termales** hot springs; **baño termal** hot bath

**terminación** f. end

**terminar** to finish (1)

**término** term

**ternera** veal; **carne** (f.) **de ternera** veal

**terraza** terrace (5)

**terremoto** earthquake (9)

**terreno** land; territory

**terrestre** adj. land (14)

**territorio** territory (9)

**tertulia** n. social gathering (informal talk about politics, literature, and so on)

**tesis** f. thesis

**tesoro** treasure

**textil** textile

**texto** text; book; **libro de texto** textbook (1)

**ti** obj. (of prep.) you (s. fam.) (2)

**tiburón** m. shark (14)

**tico/a** n., adj. coll. Costa Rican

**tiempo** time; weather; **a tiempo** on time; **¿cuánto tiempo hace que… ?** how long has it been since . . . ?; **empleo a tiempo completo/parcial** full-/part-time job (13); **hace (muy) buen/mal tiempo.** it's (very) nice/bad out. (2); **manejar (bien/mal) el tiempo** to manage one's time (well/poorly) (15); **pasar tiempo** to spend time (1); **pasar tiempo con el/la novio/a** to spend time with one's boyfriend/girlfriend (2); **¿qué tiempo hace?** what's the weather like? (2); **tiempo libre** free time (2)

**tienda** store (6), shop; **tienda de comestibles** grocery store (6)

**tierra** land (8); soil (8); **Tierra** Earth (planet); **Madre Tierra** Mother Earth

**tigre** m. tiger (14)

**tila** lime (blossom) tea

**timbre** m. (door)bell, chime

**tímido/a** timid, shy

**tinto/a: vino tinto** red wine (6)

**tío/a** uncle/aunt (4); m. pl. aunts and uncles (4); **tío abuelo** great uncle

**típico/a** typical (1)

**tipo** type

**tira cómica** comic, comic strip

**tira y afloja** m. give and take

**tirolina** zipline (10)

**título** title; degree (professional)

**toalla** towel

**tocaor(a)** flamenco musician

**tocar (qu)** to play (a musical instrument) (1); to touch

**tocino** bacon (6)

**todavía** yet; still

**todo** adv. entirely; completely

**todo/a** n. whole; all; everything; m. pl. everybody; adj. all; every; each; **ante todo** above all; **Día** (m.) **de Todos los Santos** All Saints' Day; **por todas partes** everywhere (9); **sobre todo** especially; above all; **todo derecho** straight ahead (8); **todo el año** all year; **todo el día** all day; **todos los años** every year; **todos los días** every day (1)

**tolerante** tolerant

**tomar** to take (1); to drink (1); **tomar apuntes** to take notes (1); **tomar el sol** to sunbathe (2); **tomar helado** to eat ice cream (9); **tomar un café** to have a cup of coffee (3); **tomar una clase** to take a class (1); **tomar una copa** to have a drink (alcoholic) (3); **tomar una decisión** to make a decision; **tomar una sauna** to spend time in a sauna (3); **tomar una siesta** to take a nap (3); **tomarle la temperatura** to take (someone's) temperature (12)

**tomate** m. tomato (6)

**tónico/a: posesivo tónico** gram. stressed possessive (12)

**tono** tone

**tope** m. speed bump

**tópico** topic

**toque** m. touch; detail

**torear** to fight (bullfight)

**torero/a** bullfighter

**tormenta** storm (9)

**tornado** tornado (9)

**torneo** tournament

**toro** bull (8); **corrida de toros** bullfight (11)

**toronja** grapefruit (6)

**torpe** clumsy (4)

**torre** f. tower

**torrente** m. torrent

**torreón** m. tower

**torta** sandwich (Mex.)

**tortuga** turtle (14); **tortuga baula** leatherback sea turtle; **tortuga marina** sea turtle

**tos** f. cough (12)

**toser** to cough (12)

**tostado/a** toasted; **pan** (m.) **tostado** toast (6)

**tostón** m. fried plantain

**total** adj. total; complete; **en total** altogether

**totalidad** f. whole

**totora: balsa de totora** reed boat

**tour** m. tour, excursion

**trabajador(a)** hard-working (1)

**trabajar** to work (1); **trabajar en el jardín** to work in the garden/yard (3)

**trabajo** work (general) (1); **búsqueda de trabajo** job search (13); **Día** (m.) **del Trabajo** Labor Day; **horario de trabajo** work schedule (13); **lugar** (m.) **de trabajo** workplace (13); **solicitar trabajo** to apply for a job (13)

**tradición** f. tradition

**tradicional** traditional (6)

**traducir** (like **conducir**) to translate

**traductor(a)** translator (13)

**traer** irreg. (p.p. **traído**) to bring (2)

**tráfico** traffic (8)

**tragedia** tragedy

**traje** m. suit (7); **traje de baño** bathing suit (7)

**trajinera** flat-bottomed boat used in Xochimilco floating gardens, Mexico City

**trámite** m. step; procedure

**trance** m. trance

**tranquilizante** m. tranquilizer

**tranquilo/a** calm (4)

**transcurrir** to take place

**transferir (ie, i)** to transfer; to move

**transformar** to transform

**transgénico/a: alimentos transgénicos** genetically modified foods (15)

**tránsito** traffic

**transmitir** to transmit

**transportar** to transport

**transporte** m. transportation; **medio de transporte** mode of transportation (8)

**trapear** to mop; **trapear el piso** to mop the floor (3)

**tras** after

**trascendente** important, significant

**trascender (ie)** to transcend

**trasladar** to move

**trastero** junk room

**tratado** treaty (9)

**tratamiento** treatment; **tratamiento facial** facial treatment

**tratar de** to be about, deal with; **tratar de** + inf. to try to (do something)

**trato** treaty; pact; **trato hecho** it's a deal

**través: a través de** across; through; throughout

**travieso/a** mischievous (4)

**trece** thirteen (P)

**treinta** thirty (P); **y treinta** half past (1)

**treinta y cinco** thirty-five (2)

**treinta y cuatro** thirty-four (2)

**treinta y dos** thirty-two (2)

**treinta y nueve** thirty-nine (2)

**treinta y ocho** thirty-eight (2)

**treinta y seis** thirty-six (2)

**treinta y siete** thirty-seven (2)

**treinta y tres** thirty-three (2)

**treinta y uno** thirty-one (2)

**tremendo/a** tremendous

**tren** *m.* train (8); **tren ligero** light rail (14)

**tres** three (P); **ciento tres** one hundred three (4); **son las tres.** it's three o'clock. (1)

**trescientos/as** three hundred (4)

**tribu** *f.* tribe

**tribunal** court (*legal*)

**tributario** tributary

**trimestre** *m.* trimester

**tripulación** *f.* crew (*ship*)

**triste** sad (2)

**tristeza** sadness

**triunfar** to triumph

**trofeo** trophy

**trombón** *m.* trombone

**trompeta** trumpet

**tropical** tropical (6); **bosque** (*m.*) **tropical** tropical rainforest (14)

**trozo** piece

**tú** *sub. pron.* you (*s. fam.*) (P); **¿y tú?** and you (*s. fam.*)? (P)

**tu(s)** *poss. adj.* your (*s. fam.*) (1); **¿cuál es tu nombre?** what's your (*fam.*) name? (P)

**tuba** tuba

**tubo** tube

**tumba** tomb

**tundra** tundra

**túnel** *m.* tunnel

**turbina eólica** wind turbine (14)

**turismo** tourism (10); **turismo rural** rural tourism

**turista** *m., f.* tourist (10)

**turístico/a** *adj.* tourist

**turnarse** to take turns

**turno** turn

**tuyo/a** *poss. adj.* your (*s. fam.*) (12); *poss. pron.* yours (*s. fam.*) (12)

# U

**u** o (*used instead of* **o** *before words beginning with* **o-** *or* **ho-**)

**ubicación** *f.* position, location

**ubicado/a** located (8)

**últimamente** *adv.* recently, lately

**último/a** last; latest; **de última moda** fashionable (7); **la última vez que** the last (preceding) time that (6); **por última vez** for the last time (9)

**un(a)** *indef. art.* a, an (P); **un poco** a little (P)

**un, uno/a** one; **uno** one (*number*) (P); **ciento uno** one hundred one (4); **un millón (de)** one million (4); **una vez** once; **una vez a la semana / al mes** once a week/month (3)

**unos/as** *indef. art.* some (P)

**undimotriz: energía undimotriz** wave energy

**único/a** *adj.* only; unique; **hijo/a único/a** only child (4)

**unidad** *f.* unity

**unido/a** united; close (*relationship*) (4); **Estados Unidos** United States; **Naciones** (*f.*) **Unidas** United Nations

**unifamiliar** *adj.* single-family

**uniforme** *m.* uniform

**unión** *f.* association; alliance; union, joining (9); **Unión Soviética** Soviet Union

**unisex** unisex (7)

**universal** *adj.* universal; world

**universidad** *f.* university (1)

**universitario/a** *adj.* university

**universo** universe; world

**urbanización** *f.* urbanization

**urbano/a** urban (8); **desechos urbanos** urban waste (14); **núcleo urbano** city center

**urgente** urgent; **es urgente que** it's urgent that (11)

**uruguayo/a** Uruguayan (P)

**usar** to use

**uso** *n.* use; usage

**usted (Ud.)** *sub. pron.* you (*s. form.*) (P); *obj.* (*of prep.*) you (*s. form.*); **¿cómo es usted?** what are you like? (P); **¿cómo está usted?** how are you? (P); **¿cómo se llama usted?** what's your name? (P); **¿cuántos años tiene usted?** how old are you? (4); **¿de dónde es usted?** where are you from? (P); **¿y usted?** and you? (P)

**ustedes (Uds.)** *sub. pron.* you (*pl. form. Sp.; pl. fam., form. elsewhere*) (P); *obj.* (*of prep.*) you (*pl. form. Sp.; pl. fam., form. elsewhere*)

**usuario/a** user

**utensilio** utensil (6); *pl.* silverware (6)

**útil** *adj.* useful

**utilizar (c)** to utilize, use

**uvas** grapes (6)

# V

**va** (*pres. ind. of* **ir**) you (*s. form.*) go, are going; he/she/it goes, is going

**vaca** cow (8); **ve de vaca** *the letter v*

**vacaciones** *f.* vacation; **de vacaciones** on vacation (10); **estar** (*irreg.*) **de vacaciones** to be on vacation; **ir** (*irreg.*) **de vacaciones** to go on vacation (9); **vacaciones de primavera** spring break (11); **vacaciones pagadas** paid vacation (13)

**vaciar (vacío)** to empty

**vacuna** vaccine

**vainilla** vanilla (6)

**vais** (*pres. ind. of* **ir**) you (*pl. fam. Sp.*) go, are going

**Valentín: Día** (*m.*) **de San Valentín** St. Valentine's Day

**valer** *irreg.* to be worth; **¿cuánto vale(n)?** how much is it (are they) worth? (7); **valer la pena** to be worth it

**valeriana** valerian (*medicinal herb*)

**válido/a** valid

**valiente** brave (13)

**valle** *m.* valley (8)

**valor** *m.* value, worth

**valorar** to value

**vamos** (*pres. ind. of* **ir**) we go, are going

**van** (*pres. ind. of* **ir**) you (*pl. form. Sp.; pl. fam., form. elsewhere*) go, are going; they go, are going

**vapor** *m.* steam; **al vapor** steamed

**vaquero** cowboy

**vara** stick; rod

**variación** *f.* variation

**variado/a** varied (6); various

**variante** *f.* variant

**variar (varío)** to vary

**variedad** *f.* variety

**varios/as** several

**vas** (*pres. ind. of* **ir**) you (*s. fam.*) go, are going

**vasco** Basque (*language*)

**vasco/a** *n., adj.* Basque; **País** (*m.*) **Vasco** Basque Country

**vascuence** *m.* Basque (*language*)

**vaso** (water) glass (6)

**vasto/a** vast

**ve de vaca** *the letter v*

**vecindario** neighborhood (5)

**vecino/a** neighbor (5); *adj.* neighboring, next door

**vegetación** *f.* vegetation (14)

**vegetal** *adj.* vegetable

**vegetariano/a** vegetarian (6)

**vehículo** car

**veinte** twenty (P)

**veinticinco** twenty-five (P)

**veinticuatro** twenty-four (P)

**veintidós** twenty-two (P)

**veintinueve** twenty-nine (P)

**veintiocho** twenty-eight (P)

**veintiséis** twenty-six (P)

**veintisiete** twenty-seven (P)

**veintitrés** twenty-three (P)

**veintiún, veintiuno/a** *adj.* twenty-one; **veintiuno** twenty-one (*number*) (P)

**vejez** *f.* old age (9)

**vejiga** bladder; *a musical instrument made from a dried out animal bladder*

**vejigazo** *a musical blow to the* **vejiga** (*musical instrument*)

**vela** candle

**velocidad** *f.* speed; **gran velocidad** high speed

**vencer (z)** to overcome, conquer

**vendedor(a)** vendor (6); salesclerk

**vender** to sell (1)

**veneración** *f.* adoration

**venezolano/a** Venezuelan (P)

**venir** *irreg.* to come (3); **el lunes (martes, miércoles,… ) que viene** next Monday (Tuesday, Wednesday, . . . ) (1); **el mes que viene** next month; **la semana que viene** next week (1)

**venta** sale (7); *pl.* sales (*profession*)

**ventaja** advantage

**ventana** window (1)

**ventanilla: asiento de ventanilla** window seat (10)

**ventilación** *f.* ventilation

**ver** *irreg.* (*p.p.* **visto**) to see (2); to watch (2); **nos vemos.** see you later. (*lit.* we'll see each other.) (P); **ver un DVD** to watch a DVD (3); **ver una película** to watch a movie (3); **verse** to see each other (9)

**verano** summer (2)

**veras: ¿de veras?** really?

**verbo** *gram.* verb (P); **verbo de duda** *gram.* verb of doubt (11); **verbo de emoción** *gram.* verb of emotion (11); **verbo de voluntad** *gram.* verb of volition (desire) (11); **verbo recíproco** *gram.* reciprocal verb (9); **verbo reflexivo** *gram.* reflexive verb (5)

**verdad** *f.* truth; **es verdad que** it's true that (11); **¿verdad?** right?

**verdadero/a** true; real

**verde** green (2); **judía verde** green bean

**verdura** vegetable (6)

**vergüenza** shame; **darle** (*irreg.*) **vergüenza** to embarrass (*someone*)

**versión** *f.* version

**verter (ie)** to pour

**vestíbulo** lobby

**vestido** dress (7)

**vestimenta** clothes, clothing

**vestir (i, i)** to dress; **vestirse** to get dressed (5)

**veterinario/a** veterinarian (13)

**vez** *f.* (*pl.* **veces**) time, occurrence, occasion; **a la vez** at the same time; **a su vez** at the same time; **a veces** sometimes (P); **alguna vez** once; ever; **cada vez más** more and more; **cada vez menos** less and less; **de una vez** at once; **de vez en cuando** from time to time; **en vez de** instead of; **la última vez que** the last (preceding) time that (6); **otra vez** again; **por primera/última vez** for the first/last time (9); **tal vez** perhaps; **una vez a la semana / al mes** once a week/month (3); **una vez** once

**vía** route, way; means; roadway

**viajar** to travel (8)

**viaje** *m.* trip (10); **agencia de viajes** travel agency (10); **agente** (*m., f.*) **de viajes** travel agent; **de viaje** on a trip (10); **viaje de ida** one-way trip (10); **viaje de ida y vuelta** round trip (10)

**viajero/a** traveler; **cheque** (*m.*) **de viajero** traveler's check (10)

**vibrante** vibrant

**vicio** bad habit, vice (12)

**vida** life (9); **etapa de la vida** stage/period of life (9); **ritmo de vida** pace of life (15)

**vídeo** video

**videojuego** videogame (3); **jugar (ue) (gu) a los videojuegos** to play videogames (3)

**vidrio** glass (*material*); **envase** (*m.*) **de vidrio** glass container (14)

**viejo/a** old (4); **casco viejo** old quarter (*part of town*)

**viento** wind; **hace (mucho) viento.** it's (very) windy. (2)

**viernes** *m. inv.* Friday (1)

**vigilancia** vigilance; **pagar (gu) el sistema de vigilancia** to pay the security system (bill) (15)

**vigilar** to watch, keep an eye on

**vinagre** *m.* vinegar (6)

**vínculo** link, tie

**vino** wine (6); **vino blanco/tinto** white/red wine (6)

**violencia** violence

**violento/a** violent

**violeta** violet; **de color violeta** violet (9)

**violín** *m.* violin

**violoncelo** cello

**virgen** *n., adj. m., f.* virgin; **la Virgen** Virgin (Mary)

**virrey** *m.* viceroy (9)

**virtuosidad** *f.* virtuousness

**virtuoso/a** virtuous

**visado** visa (10)

**visigodo/a** Visigoth

**visión** *f.* vision

**visita** *n.* visit

**visitante** *m., f.* visitor

**visitar** to visit

**vista** view; **a primera vista** at first sight

**visto/a** (*p.p. of* **ver**) seen

**vital** vital (7); dynamic

**vitamina** vitamin

**vitrina** shop window

**viudo/a** widowed (4)

**vivienda** housing (5)

**vivir** to live (1)

**vivo/a** alive; brightly colored (7); **en vivo** live

**vocablo** word

**vocabulario** vocabulary

**volar (ue)** to fly (10)

**volcán** *m.* volcano (14)

**volcánico/a** volcanic

**vólibol** *m.* volleyball (1); **jugar (ue) (gu) al vólibol** to play volleyball (1)

**volumen** *m.* volume

**voluntad** *f.* wish, will; **verbo de voluntad** *gram.* verb of volition (desire) (11)

**voluntario/a** volunteer; **hacer** (*irreg.*) **de voluntario/a** to volunteer (15)

**volver (ue)** (*p.p.* **vuelto**) to return (*to a place*) (3); **volver + a + inf.** to (*do something*) again (3); **volverse + adj.** to become + *adj.* (12)

**vosotros/as** *sub. pron.* you (*pl. fam. Sp.*) (P); *obj.* (*of prep.*) you (*pl. fam. Sp.*)

**votar (por)** to vote (for)

**voy** (*pres. ind. of* **ir**) I go, am going

**voz** *f.* (*pl.* **voces**) voice; **en voz alta** aloud

**vuelo** flight (10); **asistente** (*m., f.*) **de vuelo** flight attendant

**vuelta** race (*cycling*); **a la vuelta** upon return(ing); **dar** (*irreg.*) **la vuelta** to turn around; **de vuelta** again; **viaje de ida y vuelta** round trip (10)

**vuestro/a(s)** *poss. adj.* your (*pl. fam. Sp.*) (1); *poss. pron.* yours (*pl. fam. Sp.*) (12)

**vulgar** vulgar; common

# W

**Web: página Web** webpage (13)

**WiFi: conexión** (*f.*) **WiFi** WiFi connection (15)

## Y

**y** *conj.* and (P); **y cuarto/quince** quarter past (1); **y media/treinta** half past (1); **¿y tú?** and you (*s. fam.*)? (P); **¿y usted (Ud.)?** and you (*s. form.*)? (P)

**ya** already; **ya no** no longer; **ya que** *conj.* since

**yerba** herb; **yerba medicinal** medicinal herb

**yerno** son-in-law (4)

**yo** *sub. pron.* I (P)

**yoga** *m.* yoga; **hacer** (*irreg.*) **yoga** to do yoga (3)

**yogur** *m.* yogurt (6)

**yuca** yucca

## Z

**zampoña** panpipe

**zanahoria** carrot (6)

**zapatería** shoe store (7)

**zapatos** shoes (7); **zapatos de tacón alto/bajo** high-heeled shoes / flats (7); **zapatos de tenis** tennis shoes (7)

**zócalo** main square; central plaza (*Mex.*)

**zona** area, zone; **zona ártica** Arctic region (14)

**zoológico/a: parque** (*m.*) **zoológico** zoo (9); **reserva zoológica** biological reserve

**zumo** juice (*Sp.*)

# A

a, an **un(a)** *indef. art.* (P); a little **un poco** (P)

ability **habilidad** *f.* (13)

able: to be able **poder** *irreg.* (3)

abroad **extranjero** (10)

absurd: it's absurd that **es absurdo que** (11)

accelerated **acelerado/a** (15)

accept **aceptar** (6)

accessory **complemento** (7); clothing accessory **complemento** (7)

according to **según** (3)

account: to manage one's accounts (online) **manejar las cuentas (por el Internet)** (15)

accountant **contador(a)** (13)

accounting **contabilidad** *f.* (1)

ache **dolor** *m.* (12)

achieve **alcanzar (c)** (9)

across from **enfrente de** *prep.* (5)

activity **actividad** *f.* (1)

actor **actor** *m.* (11)

actress **actriz** *f.* (11)

addict: drug addict **drogadicto/a** (12)

addiction **adicción** *f.* (12)

adjective **adjetivo** *gram.* (1); possessive adjective **adjetivo posesivo** *gram.* (1)

administer **administrar** (13)

administration: business administration **administración** *(f.)* **empresarial** (1)

adolescence **adolescencia** (9)

adopted son/daughter **hijo/a adoptivo/a** (4)

adorned **adornado/a** (11)

advance: technological advance **avance** *(m.)* **tecnológico** (15)

adverb **adverbio** *gram.* (8)

advise *v.* **aconsejar** (11)

advisor **consejero/a** (13)

aerobics: to do aerobics **hacer** *(irreg.)* **ejercicio aeróbico** (12)

affect *v.* **afectar** (14)

affection **cariño** (12)

affectionate **cariñoso/a** (4)

affirm **afirmar** (11)

afraid: to be afraid (of) **tener** *(irreg.)* **miedo (de)** (3)

after *conj.* **después de que** (13); *prep.* **después (de)** (1)

afternoon: good afternoon (*until evening meal*) **buenas tardes** (P);

in the afternoon **de la tarde** (1), **por la tarde** (1); this afternoon **esta tarde** (1)

again: to (*do something*) again **volver (ue)** (*p.p.* **vuelto**) + **a** + *inf.* (3)

age: old age **vejez** *f.* (9)

agency: travel agency **agencia de viajes** (10)

agricultural **agrícola** *m., f.* (8); agricultural tourism **agroturismo** (10)

agriculture **agricultura** (8)

ahead: straight ahead **derecho** (8); **todo derecho** (8)

air **aire** *m.* (14); air pollution **contaminación** *(f.)* **del aire** (14); clean air **aire puro** (14)

airplane **avión** *m.* (8)

airport **aeropuerto** (8)

aisle seat **asiento de pasillo** (10)

alcohol **alcohol** *m.* (12)

alcoholic **alcohólico/a** *n.* (12); alcoholic drink **bebida alcohólica** (6), **copa** (3)

along **por** (4)

alphabet **abecedario** (P)

also **también** (1)

always **siempre** (5)

amber **de ámbar** (7)

ambition **ambición** *f.* (15)

ambitious **ambicioso/a** (15)

anatomy **anatomía** (1)

and **y** (P); and you (*s. fam.*)? **¿y tú?** (P); and you (*s. form.*)? **¿y usted (Ud.)?** (P)

angry **enojado/a** (2)

animal: domesticated (farm) animal **animal** *(m.)* **doméstico** (8); plant and animal life **flora y fauna** (14); wild animal **animal salvaje** (14); wild plant and animal life **flora y fauna silvestre** (14)

annual payment **pago anual** (15)

answer *v.* **contestar** (1); to answer the phone **contestar el teléfono** (13)

anti-pollution **anticontaminante** (14)

apartment **apartamento** (5), **piso** (5); apartment building **edificio de apartamentos** (5); block apartment building **bloque** *(m.)* **de pisos** (5); studio apartment **estudio** (5)

apple **manzana** (6)

appliance **aparato doméstico** (3)

applicant **aspirante** *m., f.* (13)

application **solicitud** *f.* (13)

apply for (a job) **solicitar (trabajo)** (13)

April **abril** (2)

aquatic **acuático/a** (10)

Arabic (*language*) **árabe** *m.* (1)

archeological ruins **ruinas arqueológicas** (10)

archipelago **archipiélago** (14)

architect **arquitecto/a** (11)

architecture **arquitectura** (1)

Arctic region **zona ártica** (14)

are: how are you (*s. fam.*)? **¿cómo estás?** (P); how are you (*s. form.*)? **¿cómo está usted (Ud.)?** (P); they are **son** (P); you (*s. fam.*) are **eres** (P); you (*s. form.*) are **es** (P); you (*pl. fam. Sp.*) are **sois** (P); you (*pl. form. Sp.; pl. fam., form. elsewhere*) are **son** (P)

Argentine **argentino/a** (P)

argue **discutir** (12)

arm (*body*) **brazo** (12); (*weapon*) **arma** *f.* (*but* **el arma**) (9)

armchair **sillón** *m.* (5)

army **ejército** (9)

aromatherapy: to do aromatherapy **practicar (qu) la aromaterapia** (15)

arrival **llegada** (9)

arrive **llegar (gu)** (1)

arrogance **orgullo** (15)

arrogant: to be arrogant **ser** *(irreg.)* **orgulloso/a** (15)

art **arte** *f.* (*but* **el arte**) (1); art show **exposición** *f.* (11); arts and crafts **artesanías** (7); fine arts **bellas artes** (1); performing arts **artes escénicas** (11); School of Fine Arts **Facultad** *(f.)* **de Bellas Artes** (1); visual arts **artes plásticas** (11); work of art **obra de arte** (11)

article **artículo** (7); article of clothing **prenda de ropa** (7)

artist **artista** *m., f.* (11)

as: as . . . as **tan... como** (4); as much as **tanto como** (4); as much/many . . . as **tanto/a/os/as... como** (4); as soon as *conj.* **en cuanto** (13), **tan pronto como** (13)

ask **preguntar** (6); to ask a question **preguntar** (6); to ask for **pedir (i, i)** (3)

asleep: to fall asleep **dormirse (ue, u)** (5)

assassinate **asesinar** (9)

astronomy **astronomía** (1)

at **a** (1); at + *time* **a la(s)** + *time* (1); at least **por lo menos** (4); at night **de la noche** (1), **por la noche** (1); at what time? **¿a qué hora?** (1)

athlete **atleta** *m., f.* (13)

atmosphere **atmósfera** (14)

attach (*a document*) **adjuntar** (15)

attachment **adjunto** (15), **documento adjunto** (15)

attack **ataque** *m.* (9)

attend (*a class, event*) **asistir (a)** (1)

attendant: flight attendant **azafata** *m.,* *f.* (10)

August **agosto** (2)

aunt **tía** (4); aunts and uncles **tíos** (4)

authority **autoridad** *f.* (9)

available **disponible** (7)

avenue **avenida** (5)

avocado **aguacate** *m.* (6)

avoid **evitar** (14)

# β

back **espalda** (12)

backpack **mochila** (1)

backup (*information*) *v.* **almacenar** (15)

bacon **tocino** (6)

bad *adv.* **mal** (2); *adj.* **mal, malo/a** (1); bad habit **vicio** (12); it's (very) bad out. **hace (muy) mal tiempo.** (2); to get bad grades **sacar (qu) malas notas** (1); to have a bad time **pasarlo mal** (3)

bag: carry-on bag **maletín** *m.* (10); plastic bag **bolsa de plástico** (14)

baggage claim **reclamo de equipaje** (10)

balcony **balcón** *m.* (5)

ballet: ballet dancer **bailarín, bailarina** (11); classical ballet **ballet** (*m.*) **clásico** (11)

banana **banana** (6)

band **conjunto musical** (11)

bank **banco** (8)

banker **banquero/a** (13)

banking: Internet banking **manejar las cuentas por el Internet** (15)

baptism (*ceremony*) **bautizo** (4)

bar (*drinking establishment*) **bar** *m.* (8), **cantina** (8)

barber **barbero/a** (13)

baseball **béisbol** *m.* (1); to play baseball **jugar (ue) (gu) al béisbol** (1)

basket **canasta** (7)

basketball **basquetbol** *m.* (1); to play basketball **jugar (ue) (gu) al basquetbol** (1)

bathe (oneself) **bañar(se)** (5)

bathing suit **traje** (*m.*) **de baño** (7)

bathroom **baño** (5)

battery **pila** (14)

battle **batalla** (9)

bay **bahía** (14)

be **estar** *irreg.* (2); **ser** *irreg.* (P); to be (*doing something*) **estar** + *gerund*

(2); to be (very) hot **tener** (*irreg.*) **(mucho) calor** (3); to be (very) lucky **tener (mucha) suerte** (3); to be (very) thirsty **tener (mucha) sed** (3); to be . . . years old **tener... años** (3); to be able **poder** *irreg.* (3); to be afraid (of) **tener miedo (de)** (3); to be arrogant **ser orgulloso/a** (15); to be careful **tener cuidado** (3); to be cold **tener frío** (3); to be familiar with **conocer (zc)** (3); to be fond of **sentir (ie, i) cariño por** (12), **tenerle cariño a** (12); to be in a hurry **tener prisa** (3); to be located (*buildings*) **quedar** (2); to be right **tener razón** (3); to be sleepy **tener sueño** (3); to be successful **tener éxito** (3); to be sure (of) **estar seguro/a (de)** (11); to be up to date **estar al día** (15); to be wrong **no tener razón** (3)

beach **playa** (14)

beans **frijoles** *m.* (6); green beans **habichuelas** (6)

bear **oso** (14); polar bear **oso polar** (14)

because **porque** (3)

become + *adj.* **volverse (ue)** (*p.p.* **vuelto**) + *adj.* (12); to become independent **independizarse (c)** (9)

bed **cama** (3); to make the bed **hacer** (*irreg.*) **la cama** (3)

bedroom **dormitorio** (5); master bedroom **dormitorio principal** (5)

bee **abeja** (14)

beef **carne** (*f.*) **de res** (6); ground beef **carne picada** (6)

beer **cerveza** (6)

before *conj.* **antes de que** + *subj.* (14); *prep.* **antes (de)** (1)

begin **empezar (ie)** (3); to begin to (*do something*) **empezar** + **a** + *inf.* (3)

behind *prep.* **detrás de** (2); to leave behind (*in accidental* **se** *construction*) **quedar** (7)

beige **beige** (7)

believe **creer (y)** (*p.p.* **creído**) (2)

bellhop **botones** *m. inv.* (10)

belong (to) **pertenecer (zc) (a)** (9)

belt **cinturón** *m.* (7)

best friend **mejor amigo/a** (1)

better: it's better that **es mejor que** (12)

between **entre** *prep.* (3)

beyond **a partir de** (4)

bicycle: to ride a bicycle **andar** (*irreg.*) **en bicicleta** (1)

bilingual **bilingüe** (13)

bill **cuenta** (6); to pay the bills **pagar (gu) las cuentas** (15); to pay the cable TV bill **pagar el cable** (15); to pay the cell phone bill **pagar el celular** (15); to pay the electric

bill **pagar la luz** (15); to pay the Internet bill **pagar el Internet** (15); to pay the medical bills **pagar las cuentas médicas** (15); to pay the natural gas bill **pagar el gas** (15); to pay the satellite bill **pagar el satélite** (15); to pay the security system bill **pagar el sistema de vigilancia** (15); to pay the telephone bill **pagar el teléfono** (15); to pay the water bill **pagar el agua** (15)

billiards **billar** *m.* (3)

biodiversity **biodiversidad** *f.* (14)

biological reserve **reserva biológica** (10)

biologist **biólogo/a** (13)

biology **biología** (1)

bird: bird watching **observación** (*f.*) **de pájaros** (9); farm bird **ave** (*f. but* **el ave**) **de corral** (8); quetzal bird **quetzal** *m.* (14)

birthday **cumpleaños** *m. inv.* (4); young woman's fifteenth birthday party **fiesta de quinceañera** (11)

bit: to rest a bit **descansar un rato** (1)

black **negro** (2); black pepper **pimienta negra** (6)

blender **licuadora** (3)

block **cuadra** (8); block apartment building **bloque** (*m.*) **de pisos** (5)

blond(e) **rubio/a** (1)

blood **sangre** *f.* (12)

blouse **blusa** (7)

blue **azul** (2)

bluejeans **jeans** *m. pl.* (7)

Bluetooth earphone **auricular** (*m.*) **bluetooth** (15)

board *v.* **embarcar (qu) (en)** (10)

boarding pass **tarjeta de embarque** (10)

boat **barco** (8)

boating: to go boating **pasear en barco** (9)

body: human body **cuerpo humano** (12)

boil **hervir (ie, i)** (6)

Bolivian **boliviano/a** (P)

bolt: lightning bolt **relámpago** (9)

bookstore **librería** (1)

boots **botas** (7)

bore *v.* **aburrir** (6)

bored **aburrido/a** (2)

boring **aburrido/a** (1)

boss **jefe/a** (13)

bother **molestar** (6)

boulevard **bulevar** *m.* (5)

boutique *boutique* *f.* (7)

bowl **tazón** *m.* (6)

boyfriend **novio** (1); to look for a boyfriend online **buscar (qu) novio por el Internet** (15); to spend time with one's boyfriend **pasar tiempo con el novio** (2) bracelet **brazalete** m. (7)

brain **cerebro** (12)

brave **valiente** (13)

bread **pan** m. (6); whole wheat bread **pan integral** (6)

break **romper** (p.p. **roto**) (7); to break down (in accidental **se** construction) **descomponer** (like **poner**) (p.p. **descompuesto**) (7); to break up **desintegrar(se)** (9); to break up with **romper con** (12); spring break **vacaciones** (f. pl.) **de primavera** (11)

breakfast **desayuno** (6); to eat breakfast **desayunar** (1)

breathe deeply **respirar profundo** (15)

bricklayer **albañil** m. (13)

bride **novia** (12)

bridge **puente** m. (8)

bright **lleno/a de luz** (5)

brightly colored **vivo/a** (7)

bring **traer** irreg. (p.p. **traído**) (2)

brother **hermano** (4); half brother **medio hermano** (4)

brother-in-law **cuñado** (4)

brown **color** (m.) **café** (2)

brush one's teeth **lavarse los dientes** (5)

building **edificio** (1)

building: apartment building **edificio de apartamentos** (5); block apartment building **bloque** (m.) **de pisos** (5); office building **edificio de oficinas** (8)

bull **toro** (8); running of the bulls **encierro** (11); Running of the Bulls **Sanfermines** m. pl. (11)

bullfight **corrida de toros** (11)

bus **autobús** m. (8); bus station **estación** (f.) **de autobuses** (8); bus stop **parada (de autobuses)** (8)

bush **arbusto** (8)

business (field) **negocios** pl. (13)

business administration **administración** (f.) **empresarial** (1)

businessman **hombre** (m.) **de negocios** (13)

businesswoman **mujer** (f.) **de negocios** (13)

busy **ocupado/a** (2)

but **pero** conj. (P)

butter **mantequilla** (6)

butterfly **mariposa** (10)

buy **comprar** (1); to buy movie tickets online **comprar entradas de cine por el Internet** (15)

by **por** (2); by means of **por** (4)

## C

cabin: rustic cabin **cabaña rústica** (10)

cabinet: file cabinet **archivador** m. (13)

cable: to pay the cable TV **pagar (gu) el cable** (15)

cactus **cacto** (14)

cafeteria **cafetería** (1); cafeteria style restaurant **comedor** m. (8)

cake **pastel** m. (6)

calendar **calendario** (2)

call **llamar** (1); to call on the phone **llamar por teléfono** (1)

calm **tranquilo/a** (4)

camera: digital camera **cámara digital** (15)

camp v. **acampar** (9)

camping: to go camping **acampar** (9)

campus **campus** m. (1)

Canada Day **Día** (m.) **de Canadá** (11)

candies **dulces** m. (6)

canoe **canoa** (10)

cap **gorra** (7)

car **carro** (8), **coche** m. (5); electric car **carro/coche eléctrico** (14); hybrid car **carro/coche híbrido** (14); to pay the car payment **pagar (gu) el coche** (15)

caramel custard **flan** m. (6)

card: credit card **tarjeta de crédito** (6); playing cards **cartas** (3); to play cards **jugar (ue) (gu) a las cartas** (3)

cardboard **cartón** m. (14)

care: medical care **cuidado médico** (12); personal care **cuidado personal** (12); to take care of oneself **cuidarse** (12)

career **carrera** (15); to have a career **tener** (irreg.) **una carrera** (15)

careful: to be careful **tener** (irreg.) **cuidado** (3)

caribou **caribú** m. (14)

Carnival **Carnaval** m. (11); carnival mask **máscara de carnaval** (7)

carport **cochera** (5)

carrot **zanahoria** (6)

carry **llevar** (1)

carry-on (bag) **maletín** m. (10)

cartoons **dibujos animados** (9)

carved-wood **tallado/a en madera** (7)

case: in case **en caso de que** + subj. (14); just in case **por si acaso** (9)

cash **en efectivo** (6)

cat **gato** (4)

catch a cold **resfriarse (me resfrío)** (12)

cathedral **catedral** f. (8)

cattle **ganado** (8)

CD-ROM **CD-ROM** m. (15)

celebrate **celebrar** (11)

celebration **celebración** f. (11)

cell **celular** m. (1); cell phone **teléfono celular** (1); to pay the cell phone (bill) **pagar (gu) el celular** (15)

center: health center **centro de salud** (8)

central **céntrico/a** (5)

centrally located **céntrico/a** (5)

century **siglo** (9)

cereal **cereal** m. (6)

ceremony: civil ceremony **ceremonia civil** (4)

certain: it's certain that **es cierto que** (11)

chair **silla** (1)

challenge **reto** (15)

champagne **champaña** m. (6)

change: climate change **cambio climático** (14)

charismatic **carismático/a** (13)

charming **carismático/a** (13)

chat v. **charlar** (1)

cheap **barato/a** (7)

check **cuenta** (6); to check in **registrarse** (10); to check luggage **facturar el equipaje** (10); to check one's e-mail **leer (y) el e-mail** (1); to check out a DVD **sacar (qu) un DVD** (1); traveler's check **cheque** (m.) **de viajero** (10)

check-in counter **mostrador** m. (10)

check-up **chequeo** (12)

cheese **queso** (6)

chef **cocinero/a** (6)

chemical products **productos químicos** (14)

chemist **químico/a** (13)

chemistry **química** (1)

chest (anat.) **pecho** (12); chest of drawers **cómoda** (5)

chicken **pollo** (6)

child: only child **hijo/a único/a** (4)

childhood **niñez** f. (9)

children **hijos** (4)

Chilean **chileno/a** (P)

Chinese (language) **chino** (1)

chocolate **chocolate** m. (6)

choir **coro** (11)

chop (cut of meat) **chuleta** (6); pork chop **chuleta de cerdo** (6)

chore **quehacer** m. (3); domestic chore **quehacer doméstico** (3)

chorus (group) **coro** (11)

Christmas **Navidad** f. (11); Christmas Eve **Nochebuena** (11); Christmas tree **árbol** (m.) **de Navidad** (11)

chronicle **crónica** (9)

church **iglesia** (3); to go to church **ir** (irreg.) **a la iglesia** (3)

city map **plano** (8)

civil: civil ceremony **ceremonia civil** (4); civil war **guerra civil** (9)

civilization **civilización** f. (9)

claim: baggage claim **reclamo de equipaje** (10)

clam **almeja** (14)

class **clase** f. (1); (subject) **materia** (1); coach class **clase económica** (10); first class **primera clase** (10); to take a class **tomar una clase** (1)

classical: classical ballet **ballet** (m.) **clásico** (11); classical music **música clásica** (11)

classmate **compañero/a de clase** (1)

classroom **salón** (m.) **de clase** (1)

clay **de arcilla** (7)

clean adj. **limpio/a** (2); clean air **aire** (m.) **puro** (14); to clean the house **limpiar la casa** (3); to clean up the room **arreglar el cuarto** (3)

cleaner: vacuum cleaner **aspiradora** (3)

clear the table **quitar la mesa** (3)

clerk: file clerk **administrativo/a** (13)

client **cliente/a** (6)

climate change **cambio climático** (14)

climbing: mountain climbing **alpinismo** (9)

clinic **clínica** (1)

clock **reloj** m. (1)

cloning **clonación** f. (15)

close v. **cerrar (ie)** (3); adj. (relationship) **unido/a** (4); close friend **amigo/a íntimo/a** (15); close to prep. **cerca de** (2)

closet **armario** (5)

clothes **ropa** (1); to dry clothes **secar (qu) la ropa** (3); to fold clothes **doblar la ropa** (3); to hang clothes **tender (ie) la ropa** (3); to iron clothes **planchar la ropa** (3); to wash clothes **lavar la ropa** (1)

clothing **ropa** (7); article of clothing **prenda de ropa** (7); clothing accessory **complemento** (7); clothing size **talla** (7); piece of clothing **prenda de ropa** (7)

cloudy: it's (very) cloudy. **está (muy) nublado.** (2), **hay (muchas) nubes.** (2)

club: dance club **discoteca** (9)

clumsy **torpe** (4)

coach (person) **entrenador(a)** (13); coach (class) (travel) **clase** (f.) **económica** (10)

coast **costa** (14)

coat **abrigo** (7)

coconut **coco** (6)

coconut tree **cocotero** (14)

coffee **café** (3); coffee cup **taza** (6); coffee maker **cafetera** (5); coffee table **mesita** (5); to have a cup of coffee **tomar un café** (3)

cognate **cognado** (1)

cold **resfriado** (12); it's (very) cold. **hace (mucho) frío.** (2); to catch a cold **resfriarse (me resfrío)** (12)

colonial **colonial** (9); colonial era **época colonial** (9)

colonize **colonizar (c)** (9)

colony **colonia** (9)

color **color** m. (2)

colored: brightly colored **vivo/a** (7)

Colombian **colombiano/a** (P)

Columbus Day **Día** (m.) **de la Raza** (11)

combustion **combustión** f. (14)

come **venir** irreg. (3)

comfortable **cómodo/a** (7)

common-law couple **pareja de hecho** (12)

communicate (with each other) **comunicarse (qu)** (9)

community **comunidad** f. (8)

comparison **comparación** f. (4)

compassion **compasión** f. (13)

complain **quejarse** (12)

compose **componer** (like **poner**) (p.p. **compuesto**) (11)

composer **compositor(a)** (11)

computer **computadora** (1); computer laboratory **laboratorio de computadoras** (1); computer science **informática** (1)

concert **concierto** (11)

congested **resfriado/a** (12)

conjunction: conjunction of contingency and purpose **conjunción** (f.) **de dependencia y propósito** gram. (14); temporal conjunction **conjunción temporal** gram. (13)

connection: WiFi connection **conexión** (f.) **WiFi** (15)

conquer **conquistar** (9)

conqueror **conquistador(a)** (9)

conquest **conquista** (9)

conquistador **conquistador(a)** (9)

conservation **conservación** f. (14)

conservative **conservador(a)** (9)

conserve **conservar** (14)

contain **contener** (like **tener**) (6)

container: glass container **envase** (m.) **de vidrio** (14); plastic container **envase de plástico** (14)

content adj. **contento/a** (2)

contingency: conjunction of contingency and purpose **conjunción** (f.) **de dependencia y propósito** gram. (14)

continue **seguir (i, i)** (3)

convert **convertir (ie, i)** (9)

cook v. **cocinar** (3); n. **cocinero/a** (6)

cookie **galleta** (6)

cool: it's cool. **hace fresco.** (2)

copy: to make copies **hacer** (irreg.) **copias** (13)

coral reef **arrecife** (m.) **de coral** (14)

corn **maíz** m. (6)

corrupt **corrupto/a** (9)

cosmetics **cosméticos** pl. (7)

cost: how much does it (do they) cost? **¿cuánto cuesta(n)?** (7)

Costa Rican **costarricense** (P)

cotton **algodón** m. (7)

cough v. **toser** (12); n. **tos** f. (12); cough syrup **jarabe** m. (12)

counselor **consejero/a** (13)

count **contar (ue)** (6)

counter **mostrador** m. (10); check-in counter **mostrador** m. (10)

country **país** m. (P)

country(side) **campo** (5)

couple **pareja** (12); common-law couple **pareja de hecho** (12); married couple **matrimonio** (4)

course: of course **por supuesto** (9)

courtship **noviazgo** (12)

cousin **primo/a** (4); second cousin **primo/a segundo/a** (4)

cover **cubrir** (p.p. **cubierto**) (6)

cow **vaca** (8)

cozy **acogedor(a)** (6)

crab (animal) **cangrejo** (14)

cracker **galleta** (6)

crafts: arts and crafts **artesanías** (7)

crash (computer) **fallar** (15)

crazy **loco/a** (2)

cream: ice cream **helado** (6)

create **crear** (11)

credit card **tarjeta de crédito** (6)

crocodile **cocodrilo** (14)

cross **cruzar (c)** (8)

crude oil **petróleo** (14)

cruise (ship) **crucero** (10)

cry v. **llorar** (12)

Cuban **cubano/a** (P)

cube **cubículo** (13); office cube **cubículo** (13)

cup **taza** (6); coffee cup **taza** (6); to have a cup of coffee **tomar un café** (3)

current **actual** (7)

currently **actualmente** (8)

custard: caramel custard **flan** m. (6)

customs **aduana** (10); to go through customs **pasar por la aduana** (10)

cut the grass **cortar el césped** (3)

CV **currículum** m. (13)

cybernetic **cibernético/a** (15)

cycling **ciclismo** (9)

# D

dad **papá** (1)

daily **diario/a** (2)

dairy product **producto lácteo** (6)

dam **presa** (14)

dance v. **bailar** (1); n. **danza** (11); dance club **discoteca** (9); folkloric dance **baile** (m.) **folclórico** (11); traditional dance **baile** (m.) **folclórico** (11)

dancer **bailarín, bailarina** (11), **danzante** m., f. (11); ballet dancer **bailarín, bailarina** (11)

dangerous **peligroso/a** (14)

dark (lighting) **oscuro/a** (5); (color) **oscuro/a** (7)

dark-haired **moreno/a** (1)

dark-skinned **moreno/a** (1)

data: to enter data **anotar datos** (13)

date (calendar) **fecha** (2); (social) **cita** (12); to be up to date **estar** (irreg.) **al día** (15); to date from + time **datar de** + time (9)

dating: Internet dating **buscar (qu) novio/a por el Internet** (15)

daughter **hija** (4)

daughter: adopted daughter **hija adoptiva** (4)

daughter-in-law **nuera** (4)

day **día** m. (1); Canada Day **Día de Canadá** (11); Columbus Day **Día de la Raza** (11); day after tomorrow **pasado mañana** (1); day before yesterday **anteayer** (6); Day of the Dead **Día de los Muertos** (11); every day **todos los días** (1); Father's Day **Día del Padre** (11); Independence Day **Día de la Independencia** (11); Mother's Day **Día de la Madre** (11); New Year's Day **Año Nuevo** (11); one's saint day **día del santo** (11); Thanksgiving Day **Día de Acción de Gracias** (11)

daytrip **excursión** f. (10)

dead: Day of the Dead **Día** (m.) **de los Muertos** (11)

debt **deuda** (15)

decade **década** (9)

December **diciembre** m. (2)

declare **declarar** (9)

deeply: to breathe deeply **respirar profundo** (15)

deforestation **deforestación** f. (14)

delete **borrar** (15)

deliver **entregar (gu)** (6)

demanding adj. **exigente** (13)

demonstrative **demostrativo** gram. (4)

dense population **población** (f.) **densa** (14)

dentist **dentista** m., f. (12)

deny **negar (ie) (gu)** (11)

departure **salida** (10)

depression **depresión** f. (15)

describe **describir** (p.p. **descrito**) (1)

description **descripción** f. (P)

desert **desierto** (14)

design **diseño** (7)

designer **diseñador(a)** (13); fashion designer **diseñador(a) de modas** (13)

desire to (do something) **desear** + inf. (1); verb of desire **verbo de voluntad** gram. (11)

desk **escritorio** (1)

dessert **postre** m. (6)

destination **destino** (10)

destroy **destruir (y)** (9)

destruction **destrucción** f. (14)

develop **desarrollar** (14)

diamond adj. **de diamantes** (7)

dictatorship **dictadura** (9)

dictionary **diccionario** (1)

die **morir(se) (ue, u)** (p.p. **muerto**) (7)

difficult **difícil** (1)

digital camera **cámara digital** (15)

digitize **digitalizar (c)** (15)

dim **oscuro/a** (5)

dining room **comedor** m. (5)

dinner **cena** (6); to eat dinner **cenar** (1)

direct object pronoun **pronombre** (m.) **de objeto directo** gram. (5)

directions **direcciones** (8)

director **director(a)** (11); film director **cineasta** m., f. (11); personnel director **director(a) de personal** (13)

dirty **sucio/a** (2)

disaster: environmental disaster **desastre** (m.) **ambiental** (14); natural disaster **desastre natural** (9)

disco **discoteca** (9)

discount **descuento** (7)

discover **descubrir** (p.p. **descubierto**) (9)

discovered **descubierto/a** (p.p. of **descubrir**) (9)

disguise oneself **disfrazarse (c)** (11)

dish: to wash the dishes **lavar los platos** (3)

dishwasher **lavaplatos** m. inv. (3)

disintegrate **desintegrar(se)** (9)

disk: hard disk **disco duro** (13)

display emotion **emocionarse** (15)

dissolve **disolver (ue)** (p.p. **disuelto**) (9)

divorce **divorcio** (4)

divorced **divorciado/a** (4); to get divorced (from) **divorciarse (de)** (12)

dizzy **mareado/a** (12)

do **hacer** irreg. (p.p. **hecho**) (2); to do aerobics **hacer ejercicio aeróbico** (12); to do aromatherapy **practicar (qu) la aromaterapia** (15); to do yoga **hacer yoga** (3)

doctor **médico/a** (12)

dog: to take a walk with the dog **pasear con el perro** (2)

doll **muñeca** (9)

dolphin **delfín** m. (14)

domestic: domestic chore **quehacer** (m.) **doméstico** (3); domestic partner **pareja de hecho** (12)

domesticated animal **animal** (m.) **doméstico** (8)

Dominican **dominicano/a** (P)

dominos: to play dominos **jugar (ue) (gu) al dominó** (2)

donkey **burro** (8)

don't mention it. **no hay de qué.** (P)

door **puerta** (1); front door **puerta principal** (5)

dorm **residencia** (1); student dorm **residencia estudiantil** (1)

double room **habitación** (f.) **doble** (10)

doubt v. **dudar** (11); verb of doubt **verbo de duda** gram. (11)

down prep. **abajo** (5); to break down (in accidental **se** construction) **descomponer** (like **poner**) (7); to lie down **acostarse (ue)** (5)

download **bajar** (13)

downstairs **abajo** (5)

downtown **centro** (5)

draw v. **dibujar** (9)

drawers: chest of drawers **cómoda** (5)

drawing n. **dibujo** (11)

dress **vestido** (7)

dressed: to get dressed **vestirse (i, i)** (5)

dresser (furniture) **cómoda** (5)

drink v. **beber** (1), **tomar** (1); n. **bebida** (6), **copa** (3); alcoholic drink **bebida alcohólica** (6), **copa** (3); to have a drink (alcoholic) **tomar una copa** (3)

drive **conducir** irreg. (Sp.) (8), **manejar** (L.A.) (8); flash drive **lápiz** (m.) **de memoria** (15)

driver's license **carnet** (m.) **de conducir** (8)

drop (in accidental **se** construction) **caer** irreg. (7)

drug: drug addict **drogadicto/a** (12); to take drugs **drogarse (gu)** (12)

dry: to dry clothes **secar (qu) la ropa** (3); to dry off **secarse** (5); to dry off one's hair **secarse el pelo** (5)

dryer **secadora** (3)

during the week **entre semana** (1)

dust the furniture **sacudir los muebles** (3)

DVD: to check out a DVD **sacar (qu) un DVD** (1); to watch a DVD **ver** (irreg.) **un DVD** (3)

DVD-ROM **DVD-ROM** m. (15)

## E

eagle **águila** f. (but **el águila**) (14)
ear **oreja** (12); inner ear **oído** (12)
earphone: Bluetooth earphone **auricular** (m.) **bluetooth** (15)
earrings **aretes** m. (7)
earthquake **terremoto** (9)
east: (to the) east **al este** (8)
Easter **Pascua** (11)
easy **fácil** (1)
eat **comer** (1); to eat breakfast **desayunar** (1); to eat dinner **cenar** (1); to eat ice cream **tomar helado** (9); to eat lunch **almorzar (ue) (c)** (3)
ecological **ecológico/a** (14)
economics **economía** (1)
ecotourism **ecoturismo** (10)
educated: to get educated **formarse** (15)
education **educación** f. (1); **formación** (f.) **académica** (15); School of Education **Facultad** (f.) **de Educación** (1)
egg **huevo** (6)
eight **ocho** (P); eight hundred **ochocientos/as** (4)
eighteen **dieciocho** (P)
eighth **octavo/a** (5)
eighty **ochenta** (2)
either . . . or . . . **o... o...** (5)
electric: electric car **carro/coche** (m.) **eléctrico** (14); to pay the electric bill **pagar (gu) la luz** (15)
electrician **electricista** m., f. (13)
elephant **elefante** m. (14)
elevator **ascensor** m. (5)
eleven **once** (P)
e-mail **e-mail** m. (1); to read/check one's e-mail **leer (y) el e-mail** (1); to send an e-mail **mandar un e-mail** (6)
emotion: to display emotion **emocionarse** (15); verb of emotion **verbo de emoción** gram. (11)
emotional **emocional** (2), **sentimental** (15); emotional relationship **relación** (f.) **sentimental** (12)
empire **imperio** (9)
employee **empleado/a** (13)
employment **empleo** (15); to find stable employment **encontrar (ue) empleo estable** (15); to look for stable employment **buscar (qu) empleo estable** (15)
endangered species **especie** (f.) **en peligro de extinción** (14)
energy **energía** (14)
engagement **compromiso** (12); **noviazgo** (12)
engineer **ingeniero/a** (13)

engineering adj. **ingeniería** (1)
English (language) **inglés** m. (1)
enjoy **disfrutar (de)** (10)
enter data **anotar datos** (13)
enterprising adj. **emprendedor(a)** (13)
entertainment **distracción** f. (3)
environment **medio ambiente** (14)
environmental: environmental disaster **desastre** (m.) **ambiental** (14); environmental problem **problema** (m.) **ambiental** (14); environmental solution **solución** (f.) **ambiental** (14)
envy **envidia** (15)
Epiphany **Día** (m.) **de los Reyes Magos** (11)
Equatoguinean **ecuatoguineano/a** (P)
Equatorial Guinea: from Equatorial Guinea **ecuatoguineano/a** (P)
era: colonial era **época colonial** (9)
eraser (for pencil) **goma** (1); (for whiteboard) **borrador** m. (1)
establish **establecer (zc)** (9)
esteem: self-esteem **autoestima** (15)
Eve: Christmas Eve **Nochebuena** (11); New Year's Eve **Nochevieja** (11)
evening: good evening (after evening meal) **buenas noches** (P); in the evening **de la noche** (1), **por la noche** (1)
event **evento** (4)
every day **todos los días** (1)
everywhere **por todas partes** (9)
exactly **en punto** (1)
example: for example **por ejemplo** (4)
excited **emocionado/a** (2)
exercise v. **hacer** (irreg.) **ejercicio** (3)
exhibition **exposición** f. (11)
expense **gasto** (15)
expensive **caro/a** (7)
explain **explicar (qu)** (6)
explore **explorar** (9)
express oneself **expresarse** (15)
expression **expresión** f. (P); impersonal expression **expresión impersonal** gram. (11)
extend **extender (ie)** (9)
extra large (clothing size) **extra grande** (7)
eye **ojo** (12)

## F

fabric **tela** (7)
face: to wash one's face **lavarse la cara** (5)
factory **fábrica** (14)
fair **feria** (9)
fall (season) **otoño** (2); to fall asleep **dormirse (ue, u)** (5); to fall in love (with) **enamorarse (de)** (12)
family n. **familia** (4); adj. **familiar** (4)

fan **aficionado/a** (11)
far **lejos** (2); far from prep. **lejos de** (2)
farm **finca** (8); farm animal **animal** (m.) **doméstico** (8); farm bird **ave** (f. but **el ave**) **de corral** (8)
farmer **agricultor(a)** (8); farmer's field **huerta** (8)
fascinate **fascinar** (6)
fashion **moda** (7); fashion designer **diseñador(a) de modas** (13)
fashionable **de última moda** (7)
fat **gordo/a** (4)
father **padre** m. (4); Father's Day **Día** (m.) **del Padre** (11)
father-in-law **suegro** (4)
faucet **grifo** (14); to turn off the faucet **cerrar (ie) el grifo** (14)
feast **festividad** f. (11); Feast of the Three Kings **Día** (m.) **de los Reyes Magos** (11)
February **febrero** (2)
federal **federal** (9)
feel **sentirse (ie, i)** (5); to feel like (doing something) **tener** (irreg.) **ganas de + inf.** (3)
feeling **sentimiento** (15)
felling: tree felling **tala de árboles** (14)
female soldier **mujer** (f.) **soldado** (13)
fence n. **cerca** (8)
festival **feria** (9), **festival** m. (11); San Fermín Festival **Sanfermines** m. pl. (11)
festivity **festividad** f. (11)
fever **fiebre** f. (12)
fiancé(e) **novio/a** (12)
fiber: optical fiber **fibra óptica** (15)
field: farmer's field **huerta** (8)
fifteen **quince** (P)
fifteenth: young woman's fifteenth birthday party **fiesta de quinceañera** (11)
fifth **quinto/a** (5)
fifty **cincuenta** (2)
fight **pelear(se)** (12)
file v. **archivar** (13); n. **archivo** (15); file cabinet **archivador** m. (13); file clerk **administrativo/a** (13)
fill out (a form) **llenar** (13)
film director **cineasta** m., f. (11)
finally **por fin** (4)
find **encontrar (ue)** (3); to find out (about) **enterarse (de)** (15); to find stable employment **encontrar empleo estable** (15)
fine adv. **bien** (2); (response to greeting) **bien.** (P); fine arts **bellas artes** (1); School of Fine Arts **Facultad** (f.) **de Bellas Artes** (1)
finger **dedo** (12)

finish *v.* **terminar** (1)

fire *v.* **despedir** (*like* **pedir**) (13); *n.* **incendio** (9)

fireplace **chimenea** (5)

fireworks **fuegos artificiales** (11)

first **primer, primero/a** (5); first class **primera clase** (10); first floor **planta baja** (5); for the first time **por primera vez** (9)

fish (*prepared as food*) **pescado** (6); (*alive*) **pez** *m.* (*pl.* **peces**) (8)

fishing *n.* **pesca** (9)

five **cinco** (P); five hundred **quinientos/as** (4)

fixed **fijo/a** (7); fixed price **precio fijo** (7)

flag **bandera** (9)

flash drive **lápiz** (*m.*) **de memoria** (15)

flats (*shoes*) **zapatos de tacón bajo** (7)

flexible **flexible** (13)

flight **vuelo** (10); flight attendant **azafata** *m., f.* (10)

float: parade float **carroza** (11)

flood **inundación** *f.* (9)

floor (*of a building*) **piso** (5); first floor **planta baja** (5); ground floor **planta baja** (5); second floor **primer piso** (5); third floor **segundo piso** (5); to mop the floor **trapear el piso** (3); to sweep the floor **barrer el piso** (3)

flourish **florecer** (zc) (9)

flower shop **floristería** (7)

flu **gripe** *f.* (12)

fly *v.* **volar** (ue) (10)

fog **niebla** (9)

fold clothes **doblar la ropa** (3)

folklore **folclor** *m.* (11)

folkloric dance **baile** (*m.*) **folclórico** (11)

follow **seguir** (i, i) (3)

fond: to be fond of **sentir** (ie, i) **cariño por** (12), **tenerle** (*irreg.*) **cariño a** (12)

food **alimento** (6), **comida** (6); food item **comestible** *m.* (6); genetically modified foods **alimentos transgénicos** (15)

foot **pie** *m.* (12)

football **fútbol** (*m.*) **americano** (1); to play football **jugar** (ue) (gu) **al fútbol americano** (1)

for **para** (2); **por** (2); for example **por ejemplo** (4); for heaven's sake! **¡por Dios!** (9); for the first time **por primera vez** (9); for the last time **por última vez** (9)

force **fuerza** (9)

foreign languages **lenguas extranjeras** (1)

foreigner **extranjero/a** (10)

forest **bosque** *m.* (8)

forget (*in accidental* **se** *construction*) **olvidar** (7)

fork **tenedor** *m.* (6)

fortunately **afortunadamente** (8)

forty **cuarenta** (2)

fountain **fuente** *f.* (8)

four **cuatro** (P); four hundred **cuatrocientos/as** (4); it's four o'clock. **son las cuatro.** (1)

four-lane highway **autopista** (8)

fourteen **catorce** (P)

fourth **cuarto/a** (5)

free time **ratos libres** (2), **tiempo libre** (2)

freeway **autopista** (8)

French (*language*) **francés** *m.* (1); French fries **papas fritas** (6)

fresh water **agua** (*f. but* **el agua**) **dulce** (14)

Friday **viernes** *m. inv.* (1)

friend **amigo/a** (1); best friend **mejor amigo/a** (1); close friend **amigo/a íntimo/a** (15)

friendly **amable** (12)

friendship **amistad** *f.* (12)

fries: French fries **papas fritas** (6)

frog **rana** (14)

from **de** (P); from the **del** (*contraction of* **de** + **el**) (P)

front: front door **puerta principal** (5); in front of *prep.* **delante de** (5); in front of *prep.* **enfrente de** (2)

fruit **fruta** (6)

fuchsia **de fucsia** (7)

full-time job **empleo a tiempo completo** (13)

fun **divertido/a** (1); fun thing to do **diversión** *f.* (9)

furious **furioso/a** (2)

furnished **amueblado/a** (5)

furniture **muebles** *pl. m.* (3); to dust the furniture **sacudir los muebles** (3)

# G

gain: to gain independence **independizarse** (c) (9); to gain weight **engordar** (12)

game (*single occurrence*) **partido** (2)

garage **garaje** *m.* (5)

garbage **basura** (3); to take out the garbage **sacar** (qu) **la basura** (3)

garden **jardín** *m.* (3); to work in the garden **trabajar en el jardín** (3)

garlic **ajo** (6)

gas: gas station **gasolinera** (8); natural gas **gas** (*m.*) **natural** (14); to pay the (natural) gas (bill) **pagar** (gu) **el gas** (15)

gate (*airport*) **salida** (10)

generally **por lo general** (4)

genetically modified foods **alimentos transgénicos** (15)

geography **geografía** (1)

German (*language*) **alemán** *m.* (1)

get **conseguir** (*like* **seguir**) (3); to get along well with others **tener** (*irreg.*) **don** (*m.*) **de gentes** (13); to get along well/poorly (with each other) **llevarse bien/mal** (9); to get divorced (from) **divorciarse (de)** (12); to get dressed **vestirse** (i, i) (5); to get educated **formarse** (15); to get good/bad grades **sacar** (qu) **buenas/malas notas** (1); to get high **drogarse** (gu) (12); to get in/on (*a vehicle*) **subir (a)** (10); to get married (to) **casarse (con)** (12); to get off (of) (*a vehicle*) **bajarse (de)** (10); to get separated (from) **separarse (de)** (12); to get undressed **desvestirse** (*like* **vestir**) (5)

gift **regalo** (11)

girlfriend **novia** (1); to look for a girlfriend online **buscar** (qu) **novia por el Internet** (15); to spend time with one's girlfriend **pasar tiempo con la novia** (2)

give **dar** *irreg.* (6); to give (*as a gift*) **regalar** (6); to give (*someone*) a shot **ponerle** (*irreg.*) **una inyección** (12)

glacier **glaciar** *m.* (14)

glass **copa** (6); **vaso** (6); glass container **envase** (*m.*) **de vidrio** (14); water glass **vaso** (6); wine glass **copa** (6)

glide: to hang glide **practicar** (qu) **el ala delta** (9)

global warming **calentamiento global** (14)

gloves **guantes** *m.* (7)

go **ir** *irreg.* (2); **seguir** (i, i) (8); how's it going? **¿qué tal?** (P); to be going to (*do something*) **ir** + **a** + *inf.* (2); to go back (*to a place*) **regresar (a)** (1); to go boating **pasear en barco** (9); to go camping **acampar** (9); to go on a hike **dar** (*irreg.*) **una caminata** (9); to go on vacation **ir de vacaciones** (9); to go out **salir** *irreg.* (2); to go shopping **ir de compras** (7); to go through (*a town/city*) **recorrer** (10); to go through customs **pasar por la aduana** (10); to go through security **pasar por el control de seguridad** (10); to go to (*a class, event*) **asistir (a)** (1); to go to church **ir a la iglesia** (3); to go to the mosque **ir a la mezquita** (3); to go to the movies **ir al cine** (3); to go to the synagogue **ir a la sinagoga** (3)

goat **chivo** (8)

goddaughter **ahijada** (4)

godfather **padrino** (4)

godmother **madrina** (4)

godparents **padrinos** (4)

godson **ahijado** (4)

going: how's it going? **¿qué tal?** (P); to be going to (*do something*) **ir** (*irreg.*) + **a** + *inf.* (2)

gold *adj.* **de oro** (7)

golf **golf** *m.* (2)

good *adj.* **buen, bueno/a** (1); good *n.* (*merchandise*) **artículo** (7); good afternoon (*until evening meal*) **buenas tardes** (P); good evening (*after evening meal*) **buenas noches** (P); good morning (*until midday meal*) **buenos días** (P); to get good grades **sacar (qu) buenas notas** (1); to have a good time **pasarlo bien** (3); woven goods **tejidos** (7)

good-bye *n.* **despedida** (P); (*greeting*) **adiós** (P)

gorilla **gorila** *m.* (14)

government **gobierno** (9)

governor **gobernador(a)** (9)

grades: to get good/bad grades **sacar (qu) buenas/malas notas** (1)

grain **grano** (6)

grandchildren **nietos** (4)

granddaughter **nieta** (4)

grandfather **abuelo** (4)

grandmother **abuela** (4)

grandparents **abuelos** (4)

grandson **nieto** (4)

grapefruit **toronja** (6)

grapes **uvas** (6)

grass: to cut the grass **cortar el césped** (3)

gray **gris** (2)

green **verde** (2); green beans **habichuelas** (6)

greet each other **saludarse** (9)

greeting **saludo** (P)

groceries **comestibles** *m.* (6)

grocery store **tienda de comestibles** (6)

groom *n.* **novio** (12)

ground: ground beef **carne** (*f.*) **picada** (6); ground floor **planta baja** (5)

group: group therapy **terapia de grupo** (15); musical group **conjunto musical** (11)

Guatemalan **guatemalteco/a** (P)

guest: hotel guest **huésped(a)** (10)

gymnasium **gimnasio** (1)

# H

habit: bad habit **vicio** (12)

haggle **regatear** (7)

hair: to dry off one's hair **secarse (qu) el pelo** (5); to wash one's hair **lavarse el pelo** (5)

hairdresser **peluquero/a** (13)

half: half brother **medio hermano** (4); half past **y media/treinta** (1); half sister **media hermana** (4)

hallway **pasillo** (5)

ham **jamón** *m.* (6)

hamburger **hamburguesa** (6)

hammock **hamaca** (7)

hand: to hand in **entregar (gu)** (6); to shake hands with each other **darse** (*irreg.*) **la mano** (9); to wash one's hands **lavarse las manos** (5)

handbag **bolso** (7)

handsome **guapo/a** (1)

hang: to hang clothes **tender (ie) la ropa** (3); to hang glide **practicar (qu) el ala delta** (9)

happy **alegre** (2), **contento/a** (2); to be happy (about) **alegrarse (de)** (11)

hard disk **disco duro** (13)

hard-working **trabajador(a)** (1)

hat **sombrero** (7)

hate **odio** (15)

have **tener** *irreg.* (3); to have a career **tener una carrera** (15); to have a cup of coffee **tomar un café** (3); to have a drink (*alcoholic*) **tomar una copa** (3); to have a good/bad time **pasarlo bien/mal** (3); to have fun **divertirse (ie, i)** (7); to have it in (*for someone*) **tenerle manía** (15); to have just (*done something*) **acabar de** + *inf.* (10); to have to (*do something*) **tener que** + *inf.* (3)

hazardous waste **residuos peligrosos** (14)

HD TV **televisión** (*f.*) **de alta definición** (15)

he *sub. pron.* **él** (P); he is **es** (P)

head **cabeza** (12)

headache **dolor** (*m.*) **de cabeza** (12)

health: health center **centro de salud** (8); health insurance **seguro médico** (13)

healthy **sano/a** (12)

hear **oír** *irreg.* (*p.p.* **oído**) (2)

heart **corazón** *m.* (12)

heaven: for heaven's sake! **¡por Dios!** (9)

hello. **hola.** (P)

help **ayudar** (9)

hen **gallina** (8)

her *dir. obj. pron. f. s.* **la** (5); *poss. adj.* **su(s)** (1); **suyo/a(s)** (12); to/for her *indir. obj. pron.* **le** (6)

hers *poss. pron.* **suyo/a(s)** (12)

high: high plateau **altiplano** (14); high price **precio alto** (7); to get high **drogarse (gu)** (12)

high-heeled shoes **zapatos de tacón alto** (7)

highway **autopista** (8), **carretera** (8); four-lane highway **autopista** (8); two-lane highway **carretera** (8)

hike **caminata** (9); to go on a hike **dar** (*irreg.*) **una caminata** (9)

hiking *n.* **senderismo** (9)

hill **colina** (8)

him *dir. obj. pron. m. s.* **lo** (5); to/for him *indir. obj. pron.* **le** (6)

his *poss. adj.* **su(s)** (1); *poss. adj.* **suyo/a(s)** (12); *poss. pron.* **suyo/a(s)** (12)

history **historia** (1); political history **historia política** (9); world history **historia mundial** (9)

hobby **distracción** *f.* (3)

holiday **día** (*m.*) **festivo** (11)

Holy Week **Semana Santa** (11)

home: to maintain a home **mantener** (*like* **tener**) **una casa** (15)

homework **tarea** (1)

Honduran **hondureño/a** (P)

honest **honesto/a** (13), **íntegro/a** (13)

honeymoon **luna de miel** (12)

hopefully **ojalá** (**que**) + *pres. subj.* (11)

horse **caballo** (8)

horseback riding **equitación** *f.* (9)

hospital **hospital** *m.* (1)

hot: it's (very) hot. **hace (mucho) calor.** (2); to be (very) hot **tener** (*irreg.*) **(mucho) calor** (3)

hotel **hotel** *m.* (10); hotel guest **huésped(a)** (10)

house **casa** (3); to clean the house **limpiar la casa** (3)

housing **vivienda** (5)

how? **¿cómo?** (1); how are you (*s. fam.*)? **¿cómo estás?** (P); how are you (*s. form.*)? **¿cómo está usted (Ud.)?** (P); how many? **cuántos/as?** (P); how much? **¿cuánto?** (1); how much does it (do they) cost? **¿cuánto cuesta(n)?** (7); how much is it (are they)? **¿en cuánto sale(n)?** (7); how much is it (are they) worth? **¿cuánto vale(n)?** (7); how often? **¿con qué frecuencia?** (3); how old are you (*s. fam.*)? **¿cuántos años tienes?** (4); how old are you (*s. form.*)? **¿cuántos años tiene Ud.?** (4); how's it going? **¿qué tal?** (P)

hug each other **abrazarse (c)** (9)

human body **cuerpo humano** (12)

humanities **letras** (1)

humanity: School of Humanities **Facultad** (*f.*) **de Letras** (1)

hundred: one hundred **cien** (4); one hundred ninety-nine **ciento noventa y nueve** (4); one hundred three **ciento tres** (4); one hundred two **ciento dos** (4) hurricane **huracán** m. (9)

hurry: to be in a hurry **tener** (irreg.) **prisa** (3)

hurt **doler (ue)** (12)

husband **esposo** (1)

hybrid car **carro/coche** (m.) **híbrido** (14)

hydroelectric power **energía hidroeléctrica** (14)

## I

I sub. pron. **yo** (P); I am **soy** (P); I would like **me gustaría / quisiera** (6); I'm . . . **soy...** (P); I'm from . . . **soy de...** (P)

ice **hielo** (14); ice cream **helado** (6); to eat ice cream **tomar helado** (9)

iceberg **iceberg** m. (14)

if **si** (1)

illness **enfermedad** f. (12)

impersonal expression **expresión** (f.) **impersonal** gram. (11)

important: it's important that **es importante que** (11)

impossible: it's impossible that **es imposible que** (11)

improbable: it's improbable that **es improbable que** (11)

improve **mejorar** (14)

in **por** (4); in case **en caso de que** + subj. (14); in front of prep. **delante de** (5), **enfrente de** (2); in love (with) **enamorado/a (de)** (12); in order to (do something) **para** + inf. (4); in the afternoon **de la tarde** (1), **por la tarde** (1); in the evening **de la noche** (1), **por la noche** (1); in the morning **de la mañana** (1), **por la mañana** (1); just in case **por si acaso** (9)

incredible: it's incredible that **es increíble que** (11)

indefinite word **palabra indefinida** gram. (5)

independence **independencia** (9); Independence Day **Día** (m.) **de la Independencia** (11); to gain independence **independizarse (c)** (9)

independent: to become independent **independizarse (c)** (9)

indirect object pronoun **pronombre** (m.) **de objeto indirecto** gram. (6)

individual office **despacho** (1)

inexpensive **barato/a** (7)

infancy **infancia** (9)

inflexible **inflexible** (13)

inform **informar** (15)

ingredients **ingredientes** m. (6)

in-laws **familia política** s. (4)

inline skate **patinar en línea** (2)

inn **posada** (8)

inner ear **oído** (12)

insect **insecto** (14)

inside adv. **adentro** (5); prep. **dentro de** (5)

insist (on) **insistir (en)** (11)

inspect (luggage) **revisar** (10)

insurance: health insurance **seguro médico** (13)

interest v. **interesar** (6)

interesting **interesante** (1); it's interesting that **es interesante que** (12); to sound interesting (lit. to call out for one's attention) **llamar la atención** (6)

international **internacional** (6)

Internet: Internet banking **manejar las cuentas por el Internet** (15); Internet dating **buscar (qu) novio/a por el Internet** (15); Internet shopping **hacer** (irreg.) **las compras por el Internet** (15); to pay the Internet bill **pagar (gu) el Internet** (15); to surf the Internet **navegar (gu) en Internet** (1)

interpreter **intérprete** m., f. (13)

intervention **intervención** f. (9)

interview v. **entrevistar** (13); n. **entrevista** (13)

interviewer **entrevistador(a)** (13)

introduction **presentación** f. (P)

invade **invadir** (9)

invest in the stock market **invertir (ie, i) en la bolsa** (15)

iron clothes **planchar la ropa** (3)

irritated **irritado/a** (2)

island **isla** (14)

it dir. obj. pron. f. s. **la** (5); dir. obj. pron. m. s. **lo** (5); to/for it indir. obj. pron. **le** (6)

Italian (language) **italiano** (1)

item: food item **comestible** m. (6)

its poss. adj./pron. **suyo/a(s)** (12)

## J

jacket **chaqueta** (7)

jacuzzi **jacuzzi** m. (3)

jaguar **jaguar** m. (14)

January **enero** (2)

Japanese (language) **japonés** m. (1)

jazz **jazz** m. (11)

jealous **celoso/a** (12)

jeans **jeans** m. pl. (7)

jellyfish **medusa** (14)

jewelry **joyas** pl. (7)

jewelry store **joyería** (7)

job **empleo** (13), **puesto** (13); full-time job **empleo a tiempo completo** (13); job search **búsqueda de trabajo** (13); part-time job **empleo a tiempo parcial** (13); to apply for a job **solicitar trabajo** (13)

jog v. **correr** (1)

joining n. **unión** f. (9)

journalism **periodismo** (1)

journalist **periodista** m., f. (13)

judge n. **juez(a)** (13)

juice **jugo** (6)

July **julio** (2)

June **junio** (2)

jungle **selva** (14)

just in case **por si acaso** (9)

## K

keep (doing something) **seguir (i, i)** + gerund (3); to keep going **seguir** (8)

keyboard **teclado** (15)

king **rey** m. (9); Feast of the Three Kings **Día** (m.) **de los Reyes Magos** (11)

kingdom **reino** (9)

kiss each other **besarse** (9)

kitchen **cocina** (5)

kiwi **kiwi** m. (6)

knee **rodilla** (12)

knife **cuchillo** (6)

know **conocer (zc)** (3); **saber** irreg. (3)

knowledge **conocimiento** (13)

## L

laboratory **laboratorio** (1); computer laboratory **laboratorio de computadoras** (1)

ladle: soup ladle **cucharón** m. (6)

lagoon **laguna** (14)

lake **lago** (8)

lamp **lámpara** (5)

land n. **tierra** (8); adj. **terrestre** (14)

landfill **basurero** (14)

landscape **paisaje** m. (14)

languages **lenguas** (1); foreign languages **lenguas extranjeras** (1)

laptop **computadora portátil** (1)

large **gran, grande** (1); large (clothing size) **grande** (7); extra large (clothing size) **extra grande** (7)

laser **láser** m. (15)

last: for the last time **por última vez** (9); last Monday (Tuesday, Wednesday, . . . ) **el lunes (martes, miércoles,... ) pasado** (6); last month **el mes pasado** (6); last night **anoche** (6); the last time that **la última vez que** (6); last week **la semana pasada** (6); last year **el año pasado** (6) later: see you later **hasta luego** (P), **nos vemos** (*lit.* we'll see each other) (P)

laugh **reírse (i, i) (me río)** (12)

laundry room **lavadero** (5)

law **derecho** (1); **leyes** (1); School of Law **Facultad** (*f.*) **de Leyes** (1)

lawn: to mow the lawn **cortar el césped** (3)

lawyer **abogado/a** (13)

layer: ozone layer **capa de ozono** (14)

lazy **perezoso/a** (1)

learn **aprender** (1); to learn (about) **enterarse (de)** (15); to learn to (*do something*) **aprender a** + *inf.* (1)

least: at least **por lo menos** (4); the least . . . of/in **el/la/los/las menos... de** (4)

leather *adj.* **de cuero** (7), **de piel** (7)

leave **salir** *irreg.* (2); leave taking **despedida** (P); to leave (*in accidental* **se** *construction*) **quedar** (7); to leave behind (*in accidental* **se** *construction*) **quedar** (7)

left: the left (of) **a la izquierda (de)** (2)

leg **pierna** (12)

less: less . . . than **menos... que** (4); less than + *number* **menos de** + *number* (4)

lettuce **lechuga** (6)

liberal **liberal** (9)

librarian **bibliotecario/a** (1)

library **biblioteca** (1)

license: driver's license **carnet** (*m.*) **de conducir** (8)

lie down **acostarse (ue)** (5)

life **vida** (9); pace of life **ritmo de vida** (15); period of life **etapa de la vida** (9); (wild) plant and animal life **flora y fauna** (14); stage of life **etapa de la vida** (9)

lift weights **levantar pesas** (3)

light (*color*) **claro/a** (7); light rail **tren** (*m.*) **ligero** (14); traffic light **semáforo** (8)

lightning bolt **relámpago** (9)

like: "to like" (*lit.* to be pleasing) **gustar** (1); I would like **me gustaría / quisiera** (6); to feel like (*doing something*) **tener** (*irreg.*) **ganas de** + *inf.* (3); what are you (*s. fam.*) like? **¿cómo eres?** (P); what are you (*s. form.*) like? **¿cómo es usted (Ud.)?** (P); what's the weather like? **¿qué tiempo hace?** (2)

likewise **igualmente** (P)

line: to stand in line **hacer** (*irreg.*) **cola** (10)

lingerie **ropa interior** (7)

lion **león** *m.* (14)

listen to **escuchar** (1); to listen to music **escuchar música** (1)

literature **literatura** (1)

little: a little **un poco** (P)

live **vivir** (1)

living room **salón** *m.* (5)

loan **prestar** (6); to pay the student loan **pagar (gu) el préstamo estudiantil** (15)

lobster **langosta** (6)

local **local** *adj.* (6)

located **ubicado/a** (8); to be located (*buildings*) **quedar** (2)

location: preposition of location **preposición** (*f.*) **de lugar** *gram.* (2)

lodging **alojamiento** (10)

long: with long sleeves **de manga larga** (7)

look: to look for (something) **buscar (qu) (algo)** (1); to look for a boyfriend/girlfriend online **buscar novio/a por el Internet** (15); to look for stable employment **buscar empleo estable** (15); to look like (each other) **parecerse (zc) (a)** (9)

lose **perder (ie)** (3); to lose weight **adelgazar (c)** (12)

lot: parking lot **estacionamiento** (8)

love **amor** *m.* (12); in love (with) **enamorado/a (de)** (12); to fall in love (with) **enamorarse (de)** (12); to love (*lit.* to enchant) **encantar** (6); to love each other **amarse** (12), **quererse** *irreg.* (12)

low price **precio bajo** (7)

lucky: to be (very) lucky **tener** (*irreg.*) **(mucha) suerte** (3)

luggage **equipaje** *m.* (10); to check luggage **facturar el equipaje** (10); to pick up luggage **recoger (j) el equipaje** (10)

lunch **almuerzo** (6); to eat lunch **almorzar (ue) (c)** (3)

lungs **pulmones** *m.* (12)

luxury (*hotel*) **de lujo** *adj.* (10)

# M

macaw **papagayo** (14)

machine: washing machine **lavadora** (3)

magazine **revista** (15); online magazine **revista en línea** (15)

main office **oficina** (1)

maintain a home **mantener** (*like* **tener**) **una casa** (15)

major **carrera** (1)

make **hacer** *irreg.* (*p.p.* **hecho**) (2); to make copies **hacer copias** (13); to make the bed **hacer la cama** (3)

maker: coffee maker **cafetera** (5)

makeup **maquillaje** *m.* (7); to put on makeup **maquillarse** (5)

mall (*for shopping*) **centro comercial** (7)

man **hombre** *m.* (1)

manage **administrar** (13); to manage (*people*) **dirigir (j)** (13); to manage one's accounts (online) **manejar las cuentas (por el Internet)** (15); to manage one's time (well/poorly) **manejar (bien/mal) el tiempo** (15); to manage to (*do something*) **alcanzar (c) a** + *inf.* (9), **conseguir** (*like* **seguir**) + *inf.* (7)

manager **gerente** *m., f.* (10)

mango **mango** (6)

many: how many? **cuántos/as?** (P)

map: city map **plano** (8)

March **marzo** (2)

marital status **estado civil** (4)

marker **marcador** *m.* (1)

market **mercado** (6); stall in a market **puesto** (7); stock market **bolsa** (15); to invest in the stock market **invertir (ie, i) en la bolsa** (15)

marriage **matrimonio** (4)

married **casado/a** (4); married couple **matrimonio** (4)

marry **casarse (con)** (12)

marsh **pantano** (14)

mashed potatoes **puré** (*m.*) **de papas** (6)

mask **máscara** (7); carnival mask **máscara de carnaval** (7)

mass media **medios de comunicación** (15)

massage **masaje** *m.* (3)

master bedroom **dormitorio principal** (5)

masterpiece **obra maestra** (11)

material **material** *m.* (7)

math **matemáticas** *pl.* (1)

maturity **madurez** *f.* (9)

May **mayo** (2)

me *dir. obj. pron.* **me** (5); to/for me *indir. obj. pron.* **me** (6); with me **conmigo** (2)

meal **comida** (6)

mean *adj.* **antipático/a** (1)

means: by means of **por** (4)

meat **carne** *f.* (6)

media: mass media **medios de comunicación** (15)

medical care **cuidado médico** (12); to pay the medical bills **pagar (gu) las cuentas médicas** (15)

medicine **medicina** (1); School of Medicine **Facultad** (*f.*) **de Medicina** (1)

meditate **meditar** (15)

meditation **meditación** *f.* (3)

medium (*size*) **mediano/a** (7)

meet: it's a pleasure to meet you. **encantado/a.** (P), **mucho gusto.** (P)

melon **melón** *m.* (6)

mental well-being **bienestar** (*m.*) **mental** (15)

mention: don't mention it **no hay de qué** (P)

menu **menú** *m.* (6)

metal **metal** *m.* (14)

metallic **metálico/a** (7)

Mexican **mexicano/a** (P)

microwave **microondas** *m. inv.* (3); microwave oven **horno de microondas** (3)

midnight **medianoche** *f.* (1)

milk **leche** *f.* (6)

millennium **milenio** (9)

mine *poss. pron.* **mío/a(s)** (12)

mineral **mineral** *m.* (14)

minibus **camioneta** (8)

minimum wage **salario mínimo** (13)

mining **excavación** (*f.*) **minera** (14)

mint **menta** (6)

mischievous **travieso/a** (4)

mode of transportation **medio de transporte** (8)

model **modelo** *m., f.* (13)

modem **módem** *m.* (15)

modern **moderno/a** (7)

modified: genetically modified foods **alimentos transgénicos** (15)

mom **mamá** (1)

Monday **lunes** *m. inv.* (1); last Monday **el lunes pasado** (6); next Monday **el lunes que viene** (1); on Monday **el lunes** (1); on Mondays **los lunes** (1)

money: to save money **ahorrar dinero** (15)

monitor screen **pantalla** (15)

monkey **mono** (14)

month **mes** *m.* (2); last month **el mes pasado** (6); once a month **una vez al mes** (3)

monthly payment **pago mensual** (15)

mop the floor **trapear el piso** (3)

more . . . than **más... que** (4); more than + *number* **más de** + *number* (4)

morning: good morning (*until midday meal*) **buenos días** (P)

morning: in the morning **de la mañana** (1); in the morning **por la mañana** (1); this morning **esta mañana** (1)

mortgage **hipoteca** (15); to pay the mortgage **pagar (gu) la hipoteca** (15)

mosque: to go to the mosque **ir** (*irreg.*) **a la mezquita** (3)

most: the most . . . of/in **el/la/los/las más... de** (4)

mother **madre** *f.* (4); Mother's Day **Día** (*m.*) **de la Madre** (11)

mother-in-law **suegra** (4)

motorcycle **motocicleta** (8)

mountain **montaña** (8); mountain climbing **alpinismo** (9); mountain range **sierra** (14)

mouse **ratón** *m.* (15)

mouth **boca** (12)

movie theater **cine** *m.* (3); to buy movie tickets online **comprar entradas de cine por el Internet** (15); to watch a movie **ver** (*irreg.*) **una película** (3); to go to the movies **ir** (*irreg.*) **al cine** (3)

mow the lawn **cortar el césped** (3)

much: how much? **¿cuánto?** (1); how much does it (do they) cost? **¿cuánto cuesta(n)?** (7); how much is it (are they)? **¿en cuánto sale(n)?** (7); how much is it (are they) worth? **¿cuánto vale(n)?** (7); too much **demasiado** *adv.* (7)

mural **mural** *m.* (11)

murder *v.* **asesinar** (9)

mushrooms **champiñones** *m.* (6)

music **música** (1); classical music **música clásica** (11); pop music **música pop** (11); rock music **rock** *m.* (11); symphonic music **música sinfónica** (11); to listen to music **escuchar música** (1)

musical group **conjunto musical** (11)

musician **músico/a** (11)

my *poss. adj.* **mi(s)** (1); *poss. adj./pron.* **mío/a(s)** (12); my name is . . . **me llamo..., mi nombre es...** (P)

# N

name: my name is . . . **me llamo..., mi nombre es...** (P); what's your (*s. fam.*) name? **¿cómo te llamas?, ¿cuál es tu nombre?** (P); what's your (*s. form.*) name? **¿cómo se llama usted (Ud.)?, ¿cuál es su nombre?** (P)

name-brand **de marca** (7)

nap *n.* **siesta** (3); to take a nap **tomar una siesta** (3)

napkin **servilleta** (6)

national **nacional** (11); national park **parque** (*m.*) **nacional** (14)

nationalism **nacionalismo** (9)

nationality **nacionalidad** *f.* (P)

native (*person*) **indígena** (9)

natural **natural** (6); natural disaster **desastre** (*m.*) **natural** (9); natural gas **gas** (*m.*) **natural** (14); natural reserve **reserva natural** (14); natural resource **recurso natural** (14); to pay the natural gas (bill) **pagar (gu) el gas** (15)

nature **naturaleza** (10)

nauseated **mareado/a** (12)

necessary: it's necessary that **es necesario que** (11)

neck **cuello** (12)

necklace **collar** *m.* (7)

need to (*do something*) **necesitar** + *inf.* (1)

negative word **palabra negativa** *gram.* (5)

neighbor **vecino/a** (5)

neighborhood **barrio, vecindario** (5)

neither **tampoco** (5); neither . . . nor . . . **ni... ni...** (5)

nephew **sobrino** (4); nephews and nieces **sobrinos** (4)

nervous **nervioso/a** (2)

never **nunca, jamás** (5)

new: New Year's Day **Año Nuevo** (11); New Year's Eve **Nochevieja** (11)

news **noticias** (15); news report **noticiero** (15)

newspaper **periódico** (15); online newspaper **periódico en línea** (15)

next: next Monday (Tuesday, Wednesday, . . . ) **el lunes (martes, miércoles,... ) que viene** (1); next to **al lado de** (5); next week **la semana que viene** (1)

next-door **de al lado** (5)

Nicaraguan **nicaragüense** (P)

nice **simpático/a** (1); it's (very) nice out. **hace (muy) buen tiempo.** (2)

niece **sobrina** (4); nephews and nieces **sobrinos** (4)

night: at night **de la noche** (1), **por la noche** (1); last night **anoche** (6)

nightstand **mesita (de noche)** (5)

nine **nueve** (P); nine hundred **novecientos/as** (4)

nineteen **diecinueve** (P)

ninety **noventa** (2)

ninety-nine: one hundred ninety-nine **ciento noventa y nueve** (4)

ninth **noveno/a** (5)

no **no** (P); no one **nadie** (5)

none **ningún, ninguno/a** (5)

non-recyclable products **productos no reciclables** (14)

non-renewable **no renovable** (14)

noon **mediodía** *m.* (1)

nor **tampoco** (5); neither . . . nor . . . **ni... ni...** (5)

north: (to the) north **al norte** (8)

nose **nariz** *f.* (*pl.* **narices**) (12)

not **no** (P); not any **ningún, ninguno/a** (5); not very well **no muy bien** (P); not well **mal** *adv.* (2)

note: to take notes **tomar apuntes** (1)

notebook **cuaderno** (1)

nothing **nada** (5)

nourishment **alimento** (6)

novel **novela** (11)

November **noviembre** m. (2)

nuclear power **energía nuclear** (14)

number **número** (P); ordinal number **número ordinal** gram. (5)

nurse **enfermero/a** (12)

# O

o'clock: it's one o'clock. **es la una.** (1); it's two (three, four, . . .) o'clock. **son las dos (tres, cuatro,... ).** (1)

obedient **obediente** (4)

object: direct object pronoun **pronombre** (m.) **de objeto directo** gram. (5); indirect object pronoun **pronombre de objeto indirecto** gram. (6)

obtain **conseguir** (like **seguir**) (3)

obvious: it's obvious that **es obvio que** (12)

occupy **ocupar** (9)

ocean **océano** (14)

October **octubre** m. (2)

of **de** (1); of course **por supuesto** (9)

off: to dry off **secarse (qu)** (5); to dry off one's hair **secarse el pelo** (5)

offer v. **ofrecer (zc)** (6)

office **despacho** (1), **oficina** (1); individual office **despacho** (1); main office **oficina** (1); office building **edificio de oficinas** (8); office cube **cubículo** (13); post office **oficina de correos** (8)

often: how often? **¿con qué frecuencia?** (3)

oil **aceite** m. (6); oil tanker **petrolero** (14); olive oil **aceite de oliva** (6)

old **viejo/a** (4); old age **vejez** f. (9); how old are you (s. fam.)? **¿cuántos años tienes?** (4); how old are you (s. form.)? **¿cuántos años tiene Ud.?** (4); to be . . . years old **tener** (irreg.) **... años** (3)

older than **mayor que** (4)

olive oil **aceite** (m.) **de oliva** (6)

on: on a trip **de viaje** (10); on Monday (Tuesday, Wednesday, . . .) **el lunes (martes, miércoles...)** (1); on Mondays (Tuesdays, Wednesdays, . . .) **los lunes (martes, miércoles...)** (1); on top of **encima de** (2); on vacation **de vacaciones** (10)

once: once a month **una vez al mes** (3); once a week **una vez a la semana** (3)

one **uno** (P); it's one o'clock. **es la una.** (1); no one **nadie** (5); one hundred

**cien** (4); one hundred ninety-nine **ciento noventa y nueve** (4); one hundred three **ciento tres** (4); one hundred two **ciento dos** (4); one million **un millón (de)** (4); one thousand **mil** (4)

one-way trip **viaje** (m.) **de ida** (10)

onion **cebolla** (6)

online adj. **cibernético/a** (15); online magazine **revista en línea** (15); online newspaper **periódico en línea** (15); to buy movie tickets online **comprar entradas de cine por el Internet** (15); to look for a boyfriend/girlfriend online **buscar (qu) novio/a por el Internet** (15); to manage one's accounts online **manejar las cuentas por el Internet** (15); to shop online **hacer** (irreg.) **las compras por el Internet** (15)

only **sólo** adv. (P); only child **hijo/a único/a** (4)

open **abrir** (p.p. **abierto**) (1)

opera **ópera** (11)

optical fiber **fibra óptica** (15)

or: either . . . or . . . **o... o...** (5)

orange (color) **anaranjado** (2); (fruit) **naranja** (6)

orchard **huerta** (8)

orchestra **orquesta** (11); symphonic orchestra **orquesta sinfónica** (11)

order **pedir (i, i)** (3); (in a restaurant) **ordenar** (6); in order to (do something) **para** + inf. (4)

ordinal number **número ordinal** gram. (5)

organic **orgánico/a** (6)

organization **organización** f. (9)

organized **organizado/a** (13)

other **otro/a** (P); to get along well with others **tener** (irreg.) **don** (m.) **de gentes** (13)

ought to (do something) **deber** + inf. (3)

our poss. adj. **nuestro/a(s)** (1)

ours poss. pron. **nuestro/a(s)** (12)

outgoing **extrovertido/a** (4)

outside **afuera** (5)

outskirts **afueras** pl. (5)

oven **horno** (3); microwave oven **horno de microondas** (3)

overcome **superar** (9)

overpopulation **sobrepoblación** f. (14)

oversee **supervisar** (13)

owe **deber** (6)

ox **buey** m. (8)

ozone layer **capa de ozono** (14)

# P

pace of life **ritmo de vida** (15)

pack one's suitcases **hacer** (irreg.) **las maletas** (10)

paid vacation **vacaciones** (f.) **pagadas** (13)

pain **dolor** m. (12)

paint v. **pintar** (9)

painter **pintor(a)** (11)

painting **cuadro** (5), **pintura** (11)

pajamas **pijama** m., f. s. (7)

palace **palacio** (8)

palm tree **palmera** (14)

Panamanian **panameño/a** (P)

panda **panda** m. (14)

panel: solar panel **panel** (m.) **solar** (14)

pants **pantalón** m. (7)

papaya **papaya** (6)

paper **papel** m. (1)

parade **desfile** m. (9); parade float **carroza** (11)

Paraguayan **paraguayo/a** (P)

parents **padres** m. (4)

park **estacionar** (8)

park **parque** m. (8); national park **parque nacional** (14)

parking lot **estacionamiento** (8); parking place **estacionamiento** (8)

parrot **papagayo** (14)

participate in a sport **practicar (qu) un deporte** (1)

partner **pareja** (12); domestic partner **pareja de hecho** (12)

part-time job **empleo a tiempo parcial** (13)

party **fiesta** (2); to throw a party **hacer** (irreg.) **una fiesta** (2); young woman's fifteenth birthday party **fiesta de quinceañera** (11)

pass: boarding pass **tarjeta de embarque** (10)

passenger **pasajero/a** (10)

passion **pasión** f. (15)

passionate **apasionado/a** (15)

Passover **Pascua judía** (11)

passport **pasaporte** m. (10)

past: half past **y media/treinta** (1); quarter past **y cuarto/quince** (1)

pasta **pasta** (6)

pastel (colors) **pastel** adj. (7)

pastime **pasatiempo** (2)

path **sendero** (8)

patio **patio** (5)

patron saint **santo patrón, santa patrona** (11)

pay n. **salario** (13); to pay (for) **pagar (gu) (por)** (1); to pay the bills **pagar las cuentas** (15); to pay the cable TV (bill) **pagar el cable** (15); to pay the car payment **pagar el coche** (15); to pay the cell phone (bill) **pagar el celular** (15); to pay the electric bill **pagar la luz** (15); to pay the Internet bill **pagar el Internet** (15); to pay the medical bills **pagar las cuentas médicas** (15); to pay the mortgage **pagar la hipoteca** (15); to pay the (natural) gas (bill) **pagar el gas** (15); to pay the rent **pagar el alquiler** (15); to pay the satellite bill **pagar el satélite** (15); to pay the security system (bill) **pagar el sistema de vigilancia** (15); to pay the student loan **pagar el préstamo estudiantil** (15); to pay the telephone bill **pagar el teléfono** (15); to pay the water (bill) **pagar el agua** (15); to pay tuition **pagar la matrícula** (15)

payment: annual/monthly/weekly payment **pago anual/mensual/semanal** (15); to pay the car payment **pagar (gu) el coche** (15)

PDA **agenda electrónica** (15)

peas **guisantes** m. (6)

peace **paz** f. (9)

peach n. **durazno** (6)

pear **pera** (6)

pearl adj. **de perlas** (7)

pelican **pelícano** (14)

pen **bolígrafo** (1)

pencil **lápiz** m. (pl. **lápices**) (1)

penguin **pingüino** (14)

peninsula **península** (14)

people **gente** f. s. (4)

pepper: black pepper **pimienta negra** (6); red pepper **pimienta roja** (6)

performing arts **artes** (f.) **escénicas** (11)

perfume **perfume** m. (7); perfume shop **perfumería** (7)

period of life **etapa de la vida** (9)

person **persona** (1); young person **joven** m., f. (pl. **jóvenes**) (2)

personal: personal care **cuidado personal** (12); personal pronoun **pronombre** (m.) **personal** gram. (P)

personnel director **director(a) de personal** (13)

Peruvian **peruano/a** (P)

pesticides **pesticidas** m. (14)

pet **mascota** (4)

petroleum **petróleo** (14); petroleum products **productos del petróleo** (14)

pharmacist **farmacéutico/a** (13)

philosophy **filosofía** (1)

phone: cell phone **teléfono celular** (1); to answer the phone **contestar el teléfono** (13); to call on the phone **llamar por teléfono** (1); to pay the cell phone (bill) **pagar (gu) el celular** (15); to speak on the phone **hablar por teléfono** (1)

photographer **fotógrafo/a** (11)

photography **fotografía** (9)

photos: to take photos **sacar (qu) fotos** (2)

physical: physical state **estado físico** (2); physical well-being **bienestar físico** (15)

physically strong **fuerte físicamente** (13)

physicist **físico/a** (13)

physics **física** (1)

pick up luggage **recoger (j) el equipaje** (10)

pie **pastel** m. (6)

pig **cerdo** (8)

pill **pastilla** (12)

pineapple **piña** (6)

pink **rosado** (2)

pitcher **jarra** (6)

place v. **poner** irreg. (p.p. **puesto**) (2); n. **lugar** (1); parking place **estacionamiento** (8); to take place **tener** (irreg.) **lugar** (9)

plaid **de cuadros** (7)

plain n. (geographical) **llanura** (14); adj. **liso/a** (7)

plan: retirement plan **plan** (m.) **de jubilación** (13); to plan one's retirement **planear la jubilación** (15); to plan to (do something) **pensar (ie)** + inf. (3)

plant **planta** (14); (wild) plant and animal life **flora y fauna (silvestre)** (14); wild plant **planta salvaje** (14)

plastic: plastic bag **bolsa de plástico** (14); plastic container **envase** (m.) **de plástico** (14)

plate **plato** (6)

plateau: high plateau **altiplano** (14)

play v. (a game, sport) **jugar (ue) (gu) (a)** (1); v. (a musical instrument) **tocar (qu)** (1); n. (dramatic) **obra de teatro** (11); to play baseball **jugar al béisbol** (1); to play basketball **jugar al basquetbol** (1); to play cards **jugar a las cartas** (3); to play dominos **jugar al dominó** (2); to play football **jugar al fútbol americano** (1); to play pool **jugar al billar** (3); to play soccer **jugar al fútbol** (1); to play videogames **jugar a los videojuegos** (3); to play volleyball **jugar (ue) (gu) al vólibol** (1)

playing cards n. **cartas** (3)

playwright **dramaturgo/a** (11)

plaza **plaza** (2)

please **por favor** (4)

pleasure: it's a pleasure (to meet you). **encantado/a.** (P), **mucho gusto.** (P);

plumber **plomero/a** (13)

poet **poeta** m., f. (11)

poetry: to recite poetry **recitar poesía** (9)

polar bear **oso polar** (14)

police station **comisaría de policía** (8)

political: political history **historia política** (9); political science **ciencias políticas** (1)

polka-dotted **de lunares** (7)

pollute **contaminar** (14)

polluted **contaminado/a** (14)

pollution **contaminación** f. (14); air pollution **contaminación del aire** (14); soil pollution **contaminación del suelo** (14); water pollution **contaminación del agua** (14)

polo shirt **polo** (7)

pool **billar** m. (3); swimming pool **piscina** (2); to play pool **jugar (ue) (gu) al billar** (3); to swim in the swimming pool **nadar en la piscina** (2)

poorly: to get along poorly (with each other) **llevarse mal** (9); to manage one's time poorly **manejar mal el tiempo** (15)

pop music **música pop** (11)

population **población** f. (8); dense population **población densa** (14)

pork **carne** (f.) **de cerdo** (6); pork chop **chuleta de cerdo** (6)

position **puesto** (13)

possessive: possessive adjective **adjetivo posesivo** gram. (1); stressed possessive **posesivo tónico** gram. (12)

possible: it's possible that **es posible que** (11)

post office **oficina de correos** (8)

postcard **tarjeta postal** (10)

potatoes **papas** (L.A.) (6); mashed potatoes **puré** (m.) **de papas** (6)

pottery **cerámica** (7)

power **energía** (14); **fuerza** (9); hydroelectric power **energía hidroeléctrica** (14); nuclear power **energía nuclear** (14); solar power **energía solar** (14); wind power **energía eólica** (14)

practice **practicar (qu)** (1)

preceding: the preceding time that **la última vez que** (6)

pre-Columbian **precolombino/a** (9)

prefer **preferir (ie, i)** (3)

prepare **preparar** (6)

preposition **preposición** f., gram. (2); preposition of location **preposición de lugar** gram. (2)

prescribe **recetar** (12)

prescription **receta** (12)

press **prensa** (15)

pressure **presión** f. (15)

pretty **bonito/a** (1), **guapo/a** (1), **hermoso/a** (4)

price: fixed price **precio fijo** (7); high price **precio alto** (7); low price **precio bajo** (7); price reduction **rebaja** (7)

pride **orgullo** (15)

print v. **imprimir** (p.p. **impreso**) (15); n. **grabado** (11)

printer **impresora** (15)

probable: it's probable that **es probable que** (11)

problem: environmental problem **problema** (m.) **ambiental** (14)

procession **procesión** f. (9)

product: chemical products **productos químicos** (14); dairy product **producto lácteo** (6); non-recyclable products **productos no reciclables** (14); petroleum products **productos del petróleo** (14)

profession **profesión** f. (13)

professor **profesor(a)** (1)

programmer **programador(a)** (13)

prohibit **prohibir** (**prohíbo**) (11)

projector **proyector** m. (13)

promise v. **prometer** (6)

pronoun: direct object pronoun **pronombre** (m.) **de objeto directo** gram. (5); indirect object pronoun **pronombre de objeto indirecto** gram. (6); personal pronoun **pronombre personal** gram. (P)

property **propiedad** f. (8)

protect **proteger** (j) (14)

proud **orgulloso/a** (4)

provided that **con tal (de) que** + subj. (14)

provoke **provocar** (qu) (14)

psychologist **sicólogo/a** (13)

psychology **sicología** (1)

public relations **relaciones públicas** (13)

Puerto Rican **puertorriqueño/a** (P)

puma **puma** m. (14)

punctual **puntual** (13)

purple **morado** (2)

purpose: conjunction of contingency and purpose **conjunción** (f.) **de dependencia y propósito** gram. (14)

put **poner** irreg. (p.p. **puesto**) (2); to put on makeup **maquillarse** (5)

## Q

quality **calidad** f. (7)

quarter: quarter past **y cuarto/quince** (1); quarter to **menos cuarto/quince** (1)

queen **reina** (9)

question: question word **palabra interrogativa** gram. (1); to ask a question **preguntar** (6)

quetzal (bird) **quetzal** m. (14)

quit (doing something) **dejar de** + inf. (12)

## R

rabbit **conejo** (8)

radio: satellite radio **radio** (f.) **por satélite** (15)

rail: light rail **tren ligero** (14)

railway **ferrocarril** m. (8)

rainforest: tropical rainforest **bosque** (m.) **tropical** (14)

raining: it's raining. **está lloviendo.** / **llueve.** (2)

raise **aumento** (13)

range: mountain range **sierra** (14)

reach **alcanzar (c)** (9)

read **leer (y)** (p.p. **leído**) (1); to read one's e-mail **leer el e-mail** (1)

receive **recibir** (1)

reception (area in a hotel) **recepción** f. (10)

receptionist **recepcionista** m., f. (13)

reciprocal verb **verbo recíproco** gram. (9)

recite poetry **recitar poesía** (9)

recommend **recomendar (ie)** (6)

recycle **reciclar** (14)

recycled **reciclado/a** (14)

recycling **reciclaje** m. (14)

red **rojo** (2); red pepper **pimienta roja** (6); red wine **vino tinto** (6)

redheaded **pelirrojo/a** (1)

reduction: price reduction **rebaja** (7)

reef **arrecife** m. (14); coral reef **arrecife de coral** (14)

reflexive verb **verbo reflexivo** gram. (5)

refrigerator **refrigerador** m. (5)

refuge **reserva natural** (14)

region: Arctic region **zona ártica** (14)

regionalism **regionalismo** (9)

relations: public relations **relaciones** (f.) **públicas** (13)

relationship **relación** f. (4); emotional relationship **relación sentimental** (12)

relative **pariente** m., f. (4)

relax **relajarse** (5)

relaxing adj. **relajante** (6)

religious **religioso/a** (11)

remove stress **quitarse el estrés** (15)

renewable **renovable** (14)

rent: to pay the rent **pagar (gu) el alquiler** (15)

repair shop **taller** (m.) **de reparaciones** (8)

report n. **crónica** (9); **informe** m. (13); news report **noticiero** (15); to write reports **escribir informes** (13)

reptile **reptil** m. (14)

republic **república** (9)

rescue v. **rescatar** (9); n. **rescate** m. (9)

resentful **rencoroso/a** (15)

reservation **reservación** f. (6)

reserve **reserva** (14); biological reserve **reserva biológica** (10)

resign (from) (a job) **renunciar (a)** (13)

resolve **resolver (ue)** (p.p. **resuelto**) (14)

resource: natural resource **recurso natural** (14)

respect **respeto** (15)

respectful **respetuoso/a** (15)

responsibility **responsabilidad** f. (13)

responsible **responsable** (4)

rest v. **descansar** (1); to rest a bit **descansar un rato** (1)

restaurant **restaurante** m. (6); cafeteria style restaurant **comedor** m. (8); roadside restaurant **comedor** (8)

résumé **currículum** (m.) (13)

retire **jubilarse** (13)

retired **jubilado/a** (4)

retirement plan **plan** (m.) **de jubilación** (13); to plan one's retirement **planear la jubilación** (15)

return (to a place) **regresar (a)** (1), **volver (ue)** (p.p. **vuelto**) (3)

reuse **reutilizar (c)** (14)

revolutionary **revolucionario/a** (9)

rice **arroz** m. (6)

ride v. **montar en** (8); ride a bicycle **andar** (irreg.) **en bicicleta** (1)

riding: horseback riding **equitación** f. (9)

right: to be right **tener** (irreg.) **razón** (3); to the right (of) **a la derecha (de)** (2)

ring **anillo** (7)

river **río** (8)

road **camino** (8)

roadside restaurant **comedor** m. (8)

roasted **asado/a** (6)

rock **roca** (14); rock music **rock** m. (11)

romantic **romántico/a** (6)

room **cuarto** (3); double room **habitación** (f.) **doble** (10); laundry room **lavadero** (5); living room **salón** m. (5); single room **habitación sencilla** (10); to tidy/clean up the room **arreglar el cuarto** (3); waiting room **sala de espera** (10)

roommate **compañero/a de cuarto** (1)

rooster **gallo** (8)

round trip **viaje** (m.) **de ida y vuelta** (10)

route **ruta** (10)

router **router** *m.* (15)

rug **alfombra** (5)

ruin: archeological ruins **ruinas arqueológicas** (10)

run **correr** (1)

run out of (*in accidental* **se** *construction*) **acabar** (7)

running of the bulls **encierro** (11); Running of the Bulls **Sanfermines** (11)

rural **rural** (8)

rustic cabin **cabaña rústica** (10)

# S

sad **triste** (2)

saint: one's saint day **día** (*m.*) **del santo** (11); patron saint **santo patrón, santa patrona** (11)

sake: for heaven's sake! **¡por Dios!** (9)

salad **ensalada** (6)

salary **salario** (13), **sueldo** (13)

sale **venta** (7)

salt **sal** *f.* (6); salt water **agua** (*f. but* **el agua**) **salada** (14)

Salvadoran **salvadoreño/a** (P)

San Fermín Festival **Sanfermines** *m. pl.* (11)

sand **arena** (14)

sandals **sandalias** (7)

sandwich **sándwich** *m.* (6)

satellite **satélite** *m.* (15); satellite radio **radio** (*f.*) **por satélite** (15); to pay the satellite bill **pagar (gu) el satélite** (15)

Saturday **sábado** (1)

sauna: to spend time in a sauna **tomar una sauna** (3)

sausage **salchicha** (6)

save (*a file*) **guardar** (13); to save (as) **guardar (como)** (15); to save money **ahorrar dinero** (15)

say **decir** *irreg.* (*p.p.* **dicho**) (6); to say good-bye to each other **despedirse** (*like* **pedir**) (9)

scan *v.* **escanear** (15)

scanner **escáner** *m.* (15)

scared **asustado/a** (2)

schedule **horario** (13); work schedule **horario de trabajo** (13)

school **escuela** (8); School of Education **Facultad** (*f.*) **de Educación** (1); School of Fine Arts **Facultad de Bellas Artes** (1); School of Humanities **Facultad de Letras** (1); School of Law **Facultad de Leyes** (1); School of Medicine **Facultad de Medicina** (1); School of Science **Facultad de Ciencias** (1)

science **ciencia** (1); computer science **informática** (1); political science **ciencias políticas** (1); School of Science **Facultad** (*f.*) **de Ciencias** (1)

scientist **científico/a** (13)

screen **pantalla** (15); monitor screen **pantalla** (15)

script **guión** *m.* (11)

sculpt **esculpir** (11)

sculptor **escultor(a)** (11)

sculpture **escultura** (7)

sea **mar** *m.* (14)

seagull **gaviota** (14)

seahorse **caballo marino** (14)

seal **foca** (14)

search: job search **búsqueda de trabajo** (13)

seashell **concha** (14)

season **estación** *f.* (2)

seat **asiento** (10); aisle seat **asiento de pasillo** (10); window seat **asiento de ventanilla** (10)

second **segundo/a** (5); second cousin **primo/a segundo/a** (4); second floor **primer piso** (5)

secretary **secretario/a** (13)

security: to go through security **pasar por el control de seguridad** (10); to pay the security system (bill) **pagar (gu) el sistema de vigilancia** (15)

see **ver** *irreg.* (*p.p.* **visto**) (2); see you later. **hasta luego.** (P), **nos vemos.** (*lit.* we'll see each other.) (P); see you soon. **hasta pronto.** (P); see you tomorrow. **hasta mañana.** (P); to see each other **verse** (9)

self-esteem **autoestima** (15)

selfish **egoísta** (15)

selfishness **egoísmo** (15)

sell **vender** (1)

send **mandar** (6); to send an e-mail **mandar un e-mail** (6)

separate (from) *v.* **separarse (de)** (12)

separated **separado/a** (4); to get separated (from) **separarse (de)** (12)

separation **separación** *f.* (12)

September **septiembre** *m.* (2)

serpent **serpiente** *f.* (14)

serve **servir (i, i)** (3)

serving bowl **cuenco** (6)

set the table **poner** (*irreg.*) **la mesa** (3)

settle **establecerse (zc)** (9)

seven **siete** (P); seven hundred **setecientos/as** (4)

seventeen **diecisiete** (P)

seventh **séptimo/a** (5)

seventy **setenta** (2)

shake hands with each other **darse** (*irreg.*) **la mano** (9)

shame: it's a shame that **es una lástima que** (11)

shark **tiburón** *m.* (14)

sharp **en punto** (1)

shave **afeitarse** (5)

she *sub. pron.* **ella** (P); she is **es** (P)

sheep **oveja** (8)

shell **concha** (14)

shellfish **mariscos** *pl.* (6)

shelves **estantería** (5)

ship: cruise ship **crucero** (10)

shirt **camisa** (7); polo shirt **polo** (7)

shoe: shoe store **zapatería** (7); high-heeled shoes **zapatos de tacón alto** (7); shoes **zapatos** (7); tennis shoes **zapatos de tenis** (7)

shop: flower shop **floristería** (7); repair shop **taller** (*m.*) **de reparaciones** (8); to shop online **hacer** (*irreg.*) **las compras por el Internet** (15)

shopping: Internet shopping **hacer** (*irreg.*) **las compras por el Internet** (15); to go shopping **ir** (*irreg.*) **de compras** (7)

shore **orilla** (14)

short (*height*) **bajo/a** (1); with short sleeves **de manga corta** (7)

shortage **escasez** *f.* (14)

shorts **pantalón** (*m.*) **corto** (7)

shot: to give (*someone*) a shot **ponerle** (*irreg.*) **una inyección** (12)

should (*do something*) **deber** + *inf.* (3)

shoulder **hombro** (12)

show *v.* **mostrar (ue)** (3); *n.* **espectáculo** (11)

shower *n.* **ducha** (5); to take a shower **ducharse** (5)

shrimp **camarones** *m. pl.* (6)

siblings **hermanos** (4)

sick **enfermo/a** (2); **mal** *adv.* (2)

sidewalk **acera** (8)

sign *v.* **firmar** (13)

silk *adj.* **de seda** (7)

silver *adj.* **de plata** (7)

silverware **utensilios** (6)

sing **cantar** (1)

singer **cantante** *m., f.* (11)

single **soltero/a** (4); single room **habitación** (*f.*) **sencilla** (10)

sink **lavabo** (5)

sister **hermana** (4); half sister **media hermana** (4)

sister-in-law **cuñada** (4)

six **seis** (P); six hundred **seiscientos/as** (4)

sixteen **dieciséis** (P)

sixth **sexto/a** (5)

sixty **sesenta** (2)

size **talla** (7); clothing size **talla** (7)

skate *v.* **patinar** (2); to inline skate **patinar en línea** (2)

skill **destreza** (13)

skirt **falda** (7)

sky **cielo** (9)

skycap **maletero/a** (10)

skyscraper **rascacielos** *m. inv.* (8)

slave **esclavo/a** (9)

sleep **dormir (ue, u)** (3)

sleepy: to be sleepy **tener** (*irreg.*) **sueño** (3)

sleeve: with long sleeves **de manga larga** (7); with short sleeves **de manga corta** (7)

small **chico/a** (7); **pequeño/a** (1)

smart **listo/a** (4)

smile **sonreír (i, i) (sonrío)** (12)

smog **smog** *m.* (14)

smoke *v.* **fumar** (12); *n.* **humo** (14)

snack *v.* **merendar (ie)** (6)

snake **serpiente** *f.* (14)

snow *n.* **nieve** *f.* (14)

snowing: it's snowing. **está nevando. / nieva.** (2)

so that **para que** + *subj.* (14)

soccer **fútbol** *m.* (1); to play soccer **jugar (ue) (gu) al fútbol** (1)

sociology **sociología** (1)

socks **calcetines** *m.* (7)

sofa **sofá** *m.* (5)

soft drink **refresco** (6)

soil **tierra** (8); soil pollution **contaminación** (*f.*) **del suelo** (14)

solar: solar panel **panel** (*m.*) **solar** (14); solar power **energía solar** (14)

soldier **soldado** (13); female soldier **mujer** (*f.*) **soldado** (13)

solution: environmental solution **solución** (*f.*) **ambiental** (14)

solve **resolver (ue)** (*p.p.* **resuelto**) (14)

some **algún, alguno/a(s)** (5); **unos/as** *indef. art.* (P)

someone **alguien** (5)

something **algo** (5)

sometimes **a veces** (P)

son **hijo** (4); adopted son **hijo adoptivo** (4)

song **canción** *f.* (11)

son-in-law **yerno** (4)

soon: as soon as *conj.* **en cuanto** (13), **tan pronto como** (13); see you soon **hasta pronto** (P)

so-so **regular** (P)

sound interesting (*lit.* to call out for one's attention) **llamar la atención** (6)

soup **sopa** (6); soup ladle **cucharón** *m.* (6); soup tureen **sopera** (6)

south: (to the) south **al sur** (8)

Spanish **español(a)** (P); Spanish (*language*) **español** *m.* (1)

speak **hablar** (1); to speak on the phone **hablar por teléfono** (1)

speakers **altavoces** *m.* (15)

specialty store **boutique** *f.* (7)

species: endangered species **especie** (*f.*) **en peligro de extinción** (14)

spectator **espectador(a)** (11)

spend: to spend some time **pasar un rato** (1); to spend time **pasar tiempo** (1); to spend time in a sauna **tomar una sauna** (3); to spend time with one's boyfriend/girlfriend **pasar tiempo con el/la novio/a** (2)

spew **arrojar** (14)

spider **araña** (14)

spinach **espinacas** *pl.* (6)

spoon **cuchara** (6)

sport: to participate in a sport **practicar (qu) un deporte** (1)

spring **primavera** (2); spring break **vacaciones** (*f.*) **de primavera** (11)

stability **estabilidad** *f.* (9)

stable: to look for / to find stable employment **buscar (qu) / encontrar (ue) empleo estable** (15)

stadium **estadio** (1)

stage **escenario** (11); stage of life **etapa de la vida** (9)

stall **puesto** (7); stall in a market **puesto** (7)

stand in line **hacer** (*irreg.*) **cola** (10)

state: physical state **estado físico** (2)

station: bus station **estación** (*f.*) **de autobuses** (8); gas station **gasolinera** (8); police station **comisaría de policía** (8)

stationary store **papelería** (7)

statistics **estadística** (1)

statue **estatua** (8)

status: marital status **estado civil** (4)

stay **estadía** (10); stay (*in a hotel*) **alojarse** (10), stay (*in a hotel*) **hospedarse** (10); stay (*in a place*) **quedarse** (10)

steak **bistec** *m.* (6)

stepbrother **hermanastro** (4)

stepdaughter **hijastra** (4)

stepfather **padrastro** (4)

stepmother **madrastra** (4)

stepsister **hermanastra** (4)

stepson **hijastro** (4)

still be (*doing something*) **seguir (i, i)** + *gerund* (3)

stock: stock market **bolsa** (15); to invest in the stock market **invertir (ie, i) en la bolsa** (15)

stockings **medias** *pl.* (7)

stomach **estómago** (12)

stomachache **dolor** (*m.*) **de estómago** (12)

stop *v.* **parar** (8); *n.* **parada** (8); (*layover*) **escala** (10); bus stop **parada (de autobuses)** (8); subway stop **parada (de metro)** (8); to stop (*doing something*) **dejar de +** *inf.* (12)

store **tienda** (6); grocery store **tienda de comestibles** (6); jewelry store **joyería** (7); shoe store **zapatería** (7); specialty store **boutique** *f.* (7); stationary store **papelería** (7); toy store **juguetería** (7)

storm **tormenta** (9)

story **cuento** (9)

stove **estufa** (3)

straight (*direction*) **derecho** (8); straight ahead **(todo) derecho** (8)

strange: it's strange that **es extraño que** (11)

straw *adj.* **de paja** (7)

strawberry **fresa** (6)

street **calle** *f.* (2)

stress **estrés** *m.* (12); to remove stress **quitarse el estrés** (15); to suffer from stress **sufrir de estrés** (15)

stressed possessive **posesivo tónico** *gram.* (12)

stretch **estirarse** (15)

striped **de rayas** (7)

stroll: to take a stroll (with the dog) **pasear (con el perro)** (2)

strong: physically strong **fuerte físicamente** (13)

student **estudiante** *m., f.* (1); student dorm **residencia estudiantil** (1); student union **centro estudiantil** (1); to pay the student loan **pagar (gu) el préstamo estudiantil** (15)

studio apartment **estudio** (5)

study *v.* **estudiar** (1); *n.* **despacho** (5)

style **estilo** (7); cafeteria style restaurant **comedor** *m.* (8)

subject **materia** (1)

suburbs **afueras** *pl.* (5)

subway **metro** (8); subway stop **parada (de metro)** (8)

successful: to be successful **tener** (*irreg.*) **éxito** (3)

succession **sucesión** *f.* (9)

suffer from stress **sufrir de estrés** (15)

sugar **azúcar** *m.* (6)

suggest **sugerir (ie, i)** (6)

suit **traje** *m.* (7); bathing suit **traje de baño** (7)

suitcase **maleta** (10); to pack one's suitcases **hacer** (*irreg.*) **las maletas** (10)

summer **verano** (2)

sunbathe **tomar el sol** (2)

Sunday **domingo** (1)

sunny: it's (very) sunny. **hace (mucho) sol.** (2)

supermarket **supermercado** (6)

supervise **supervisar** (13)

sure: to be sure (of) **estar** (*irreg.*) **seguro/a (de)** (11)

surf the Internet **navegar (gu) en Internet** (1)

surprise **sorprender** (11)

surprised **sorprendido/a** (2)

survive **sobrevivir** (9)

survivor **sobreviviente** (9)

sweater **suéter** *m.* (7)

sweep the floor **barrer el piso** (3)

swim **bañarse** (5), **nadar** (2)

swimming **natación** *f.* (2); swimming pool **piscina** (2); to swim in the swimming pool **nadar en la piscina** (2)

symphonic: symphonic music **música sinfónica** (11); symphonic orchestra **orquesta sinfónica** (11)

symptom **síntoma** *m.* (12)

synagogue: to go to the synagogue **ir** (*irreg.*) **a la sinagoga** (3)

syrup: cough syrup **jarabe** *m.* (12)

system: to pay the security system (bill) **pagar (gu) el sistema de vigilancia** (15)

## T

table **mesa** (1); coffee table **mesita** (5); to clear the table **quitar la mesa** (3); to set the table **poner** (*irreg.*) **la mesa** (3)

tablecloth **mantel** *m.* (6)

take **tomar** (1); to take a class **tomar una clase** (1); to take a nap **tomar una siesta** (3); to take a shower **ducharse** (5); to take a stroll/walk (with the dog) **pasear (con el perro)** (2); to take care of oneself **cuidarse** (12); to take drugs **drogarse (gu)** (12); to take notes **tomar apuntes** (1); to take out the garbage/trash **sacar (qu) la basura** (3); to take photos **sacar fotos** (2); to take place **tener** (*irreg.*) **lugar** (9); to take (someone's) temperature **tomarle la temperatura** (12)

tall **alto/a** (1)

tanker: oil tanker **petrolero** (14)

taste *v.* **probar (ue)** (6)

taxi **taxi** *m.* (8)

tea **té** *m.* (6)

teacher **maestro/a** (13), **profesor(a)** (1)

technician **técnico/a** (13)

technological advance **avance** (*m.*) **tecnológico** (15)

technology **tecnología** (13)

teeth: brush one's teeth **lavarse los dientes** (5)

teleconference **teleconferencia** (13)

telephone **teléfono** (1); to pay the telephone bill **pagar (gu) el teléfono** (15)

tell **contar (ue)** (6); **decir** *irreg.* (*p.p.* **dicho**) (6)

temperature: to take (someone's) temperature **tomarle la temperatura** (12)

temporal conjunction **conjunción** (f.) **temporal** *gram.* (13)

ten **diez** (P)

tennis **tenis** *m.* (2); tennis shoes **zapatos de tenis** (7)

tenth **décimo/a** (5)

terrace **terraza** (5)

territory **territorio** (9)

textbook **libro de texto** (1)

than: less . . . than **menos... que** (4); less than + *number* **menos de** + *number* (4); more . . . than **más... que** (4); more than + *number* **más de** + *number* (4); older than **mayor que** (4); younger than **menor que** (4)

thank you. **gracias.** (P)

Thanksgiving Day **Día** (*m.*) **de Acción de Gracias** (11)

that *adj.* **ese/a** (4); *pron.* (*concept, unknown thing*) **eso** (4); that (over there) *adj.* **aquel, aquella** (4); that (over there) *pron.* (*concept, unknown thing*) **aquello** (4); that one *pron.* **ese/a** (4); that one (over there) *pron.* **aquel, aquella** (4); that which *rel. pron.* **lo que** (6); that's why **por eso** (4)

the el *def. art. m. s.;* la *def. art. f. s.;* los *def. art. m. pl.;* las *def. art. f. pl.* (P)

theater **drama** (11); **teatro** (1); movie theater **cine** *m.* (3)

their *poss. adj.* **su(s)** (1); *poss. adj./pron.* **suyo/a(s)** (12)

them *dir. obj. pron. m. pl.* **los**; *dir. obj. pron. f. pl.* **las** (5); to/for them *indir. obj. pron.* **les** (6)

therapy **terapia** (15); group therapy **terapia de grupo** (15)

there: there is/are **hay** (P); there was/were **hubo** (7);

these *adj.* **estos/as** (4); these ones *pron.* **estos/as** (4)

they **ellos/as** (P)

thin **delgado/a** (4)

thing **cosa** (3); fun thing to do **diversión** *f.* (9)

think (about) **pensar (ie) (en)** (3)

third **tercer, tercero/a** (5); third floor **segundo piso** (5)

thirsty: to be (very) thirsty **tener** (*irreg.*) **(mucha) sed** (3)

thirteen **trece** (P)

thirty **treinta** (P)

this *adj.* **este/a** (4); this *pron.* (*concept, unknown thing*) **esto** (4); this afternoon **esta tarde** (1); this morning **esta mañana** (1); this one *pron.* **este/a** (4)

those *adj.* **esos/as** (4); those (ones) *pron.* **esos/as** (4); those (ones) (over there) *pron.* **aquellos/as** (4); those (over there) *adj.* **aquellos/as** (4)

thousand **mil** (4)

three **tres** (P); Feast of the Three Kings (Epiphany) **Día** (*m.*) **de los Reyes Magos** (11); it's three o'clock. **son las tres.** (1); one hundred three **ciento tres** (4); three hundred **trescientos/as** (4)

thrive **florecer (zc)** (9)

throat **garganta** (12)

through **por** (4)

throw: to throw a party **hacer** (*irreg.*) **una fiesta** (2); to throw out **arrojar** (14)

Thursday **jueves** *m. inv.* (1)

ticket **billete** *m.* (*Sp.*) (10), **boleto** (*L.A.*) (10); to buy movie tickets online **comprar entradas de cine por el Internet** (15)

tidy up the room **arreglar el cuarto** (3)

tie **corbata** (7)

tiger **tigre** *m.* (14)

time: at what time? **¿a qué hora?** (1); for the first time **por primera vez** (9); for the last time **por última vez** (9); free time **ratos libres** (2), **tiempo libre** (2); the last/preceding time that **la última vez que** (6); time period **época** (9); to have a good/bad time **pasarlo bien/mal** (3); to manage one's time (well/poorly) **manejar (bien/mal) el tiempo** (15); to spend some time **pasar un rato** (1); to spend time **pasar tiempo** (1); to spend time in a sauna **tomar una sauna** (3); to spend time with one's boyfriend/girlfriend **pasar tiempo con el/la novio/a** (2); what time is it? **¿qué hora es?** (1)

tip **propina** (6)

tired **cansado/a** (2)

toast *n.* **pan** (*m.*) **tostado** (6); to toast (to) **brindar (por)** (11)

today **hoy** (1)

toe **dedo del pie** (12)

toilet **inodoro** (5)

tomato **tomate** *m.* (6)

tomorrow **mañana** (1); see you tomorrow **hasta mañana** (P); the day after tomorrow **pasado mañana** (1)

tonight **esta noche** (1)

too **también** (1); too much **demasiado** *adv.* (7)

tooth **diente** *m.* (12)

toothache **dolor** (*m.*) **de muela** (12)

top: on top of **encima de** (2)

tornado **tornado** (9)

tour **excursión** *f.* (10), **recorrido** (10)

tourism **turismo** (10); agricultural tourism **agroturismo** (10)

tourist **turista** *m., f.* (10)

toward **para** (4)

town **pueblo** (8)

townhouse **casa adosada** (5)

toy **juguete** *m.* (9); toy store **juguetería** (7)

trade **oficio** (13)

traditional **tradicional** (6); traditional dance **baile** (*m.*) **folclórico** (11)

traffic **circulación** *f.* (8), **tráfico** (8); traffic light **semáforo** (8)

train **tren** *m.* (8)

trainer **entrenador(a)** (13)

translator **traductor(a)** (13)

transportation: mode of transportation **medio de transporte** (8)

trash **basura** (3); to take out the trash **sacar (qu) la basura** (3)

travel **viajar** (8); to travel around (*a town/city*) **recorrer** (10); travel agency **agencia de viajes** (10)

traveler's check **cheque** (*m.*) **de viajero** (10)

treaty **tratado** (9)

tree **árbol** *m.* (8); Christmas tree **árbol de Navidad** (11); coconut tree **cocotero** (14); palm tree **palmera** (14); tree felling **tala de árboles** (14)

trip **recorrido** (10), **viaje** *m.* (10); on a trip **de viaje** (10); one-way trip **viaje de ida** (10); round trip **viaje de ida y vuelta** (10)

tropical **tropical** (6); tropical rainforest **bosque** (*m.*) **tropical** (14)

truck **camión** *m.* (8)

true: it's true that **es verdad que** (11)

try **probar (ue)** (6)

T-shirt **camiseta** (7)

tsunami **maremoto** (9)

Tuesday **martes** *m. inv.* (1); last Tuesday **el martes pasado** (6); next Tuesday **el martes que viene** (1); on Tuesday **el martes** (1); on Tuesdays **los martes** (1)

tuition: to pay tuition **pagar (gu) la matrícula** (15)

tuna **atún** *m.* (6)

turbine: wind turbine **turbina eólica** (14)

tureen: soup tureen **sopera** (6)

turkey **pavo** (6)

turn **doblar** (8); to turn off the faucet **cerrar (ie) el grifo** (14)

turtle **tortuga** (14)

TV: HD TV **televisión** (*f.*) **de alta definición** (15); to pay the cable TV (bill) **pagar (gu) el cable** (15); to watch TV **mirar la televisión** (1); wide-screen TV **televisión de pantalla ancha** (15)

twelve **doce** (P)

twenty **veinte** (P)

twenty-eight **veintiocho** (P)

twenty-five **veinticinco** (P)

twenty-four **veinticuatro** (P)

twenty-nine **veintinueve** (P)

twenty-one **veintiuno** (P)

twenty-seven **veintisiete** (P)

twenty-six **veintiséis** (P)

twenty-three **veintitrés** (P)

twenty-two **veintidós** (P)

twin **gemelo/a** (4)

two **dos** (P); it's two o'clock. **son las dos.** (1); one hundred two **ciento dos** (4); two hundred **doscientos/ as** (4); two million **dos millones (de)** (4); two thousand **dos mil** (4)

two-lane highway **carretera** (8)

typical **típico/a** (1)

## U

ugly **feo/a** (1)

uncle **tío** (4); aunts and uncles **tíos** (4)

under **debajo de** (2)

understand **comprender** (1), **entender (ie)** (3)

understanding *adj.* **comprensivo/a** (13)

underwear **ropa interior** (7)

undressed: to get undressed **desvestirse (i, i)** (5)

unfortunately **desafortunadamente** (8), **desgraciadamente** (8)

unfurnished **sin amueblar** (5)

union **unión** *f.* (9); student union **centro estudiantil** (1)

unisex **unisex** (7)

university **universidad** *f.* (1)

unless *conj.* **a menos que** + *subj.* (14)

unselfish **altruista** *m., f.* (15)

unselfishness **altruismo** (15)

until **hasta que** *conj.* (13)

up **arriba** (5); to be up to date **estar** (*irreg.*) **al día** (15); to break up with **romper con** (12)

upload **subir** (13)

upright (*righteous*) **íntegro/a** (13)

upstairs **arriba** (5)

urban **urbano/a** (8); urban waste **desechos urbanos** (14)

urgent: it's urgent that **es urgente que** (11)

Uruguayan **uruguayo/a** (P)

us *dir. obj. pron.* **nos** (5); to/for us *indir. obj. pron.* **nos** (6)

usually: to usually (*do something*) **soler** + *inf.* (3)

utensil **utensilio** (6)

## V

vacation: on vacation **de vacaciones** (10); paid vacation **vacaciones** (*f.*) **pagadas** (13); to go on vacation **ir** (*irreg.*) **de vacaciones** (9)

vacuum *v.* **pasar la aspiradora** (3); vacuum cleaner **aspiradora** (3)

valley **valle** *m.* (8)

vanilla **vainilla** (6)

varied **variado/a** (6)

vegetable **verdura** (6)

vegetarian **vegetariano/a** (6)

vegetation **vegetación** *f.* (14)

vendor **vendedor(a)** (6)

Venezuelan **venezolano/a** (P)

verb **verbo** *gram.* (P); reciprocal verb **verbo recíproco** *gram.* (9); reflexive verb **verbo reflexivo** *gram.* (5); verb of desire **verbo de voluntad** *gram.* (11); verb of doubt **verbo de duda** *gram.* (11); verb of emotion **verbo de emoción** *gram.* (11); verb of volition **verbo de voluntad** *gram.* (11)

very: not very well **no muy bien** (P); very well **muy bien** (P)

veterinarian **veterinario/a** (13)

vice **vicio** (12)

viceroy **virrey** *m.* (9)

videogame **videojuego** (3); to play videogames **jugar (ue) (gu) a los videojuegos** (3)

village **aldea** (8)

vinegar **vinagre** *m.* (6)

visa **visado** (10)

visual arts **artes** (*f.*) **plásticas** (11)

vital **vital** (7)

volcano **volcán** *m.* (14)

volition: verb of volition **verbo de voluntad** *gram.* (11)

volleyball **vólibol** *m.* (1); to play volleyball **jugar (ue) (gu) al vólibol** (1)

volunteer *v.* **hacer** (*irreg.*) **de voluntario/a** (15)

## W

wage **salario** (13); minimum wage **salario mínimo** (13)

wait *v.* **esperar** (11)

waiter **mesero** (6)

waiting room **sala de espera** (10)

waitress **mesera** (6)

wake up **despertarse (ie)** (5)

walk *v.* **caminar** (1); to take a walk (with the dog) **pasear (con el perro)** (2)

wall **pared** *f.* (1)

wallet **cartera** (7)

want **querer** *irreg.* (3); to want to (*do something*) **desear** + *inf.* (1)

war **guerra** (9); civil war **guerra civil** (9)

wardrobe **ropero** (7)

warming: global warming **calentamiento global** (14)

warrior **guerrero/a** (9)

wash: to wash clothes **lavar la ropa** (1); to wash one's face/hands/hair **lavarse la cara / las manos / el pelo** (5); wash the dishes **lavar los platos** (3)

washer **lavadora** (3)

washing machine **lavadora** (3)

waste **desperdiciar** (14); hazardous waste **residuos peligrosos** (14); urban waste **desechos urbanos** (14)

watch *v.* **ver** *irreg.* (*p.p.* **visto**) (2); *n.* **reloj** *m.* (1); to watch a DVD **ver un DVD** (3); to watch a movie **ver una película** (3); to watch TV **mirar la televisión** (1)

watching: bird watching **observación** (*f.*) **de pájaros** (9)

water **agua** *f.* (*but* **el agua**) (6); *adj.* **acuático/a** (10); fresh water **agua dulce** (14); salt water **agua salada** (14); to pay the water (bill) **pagar (gu) el agua** (15); water glass **vaso** (6); water pollution **contaminación** (*f.*) **del agua** (14)

wave **ola** (14)

we *sub. pron.* **nosotros/as** (P); we are **somos** (P)

weapon **arma** *f.* (*but* **el arma**) (9)

weather: what's the weather like? **¿qué tiempo hace?** (2)

weave **tejer** (11)

webpage **página Web** (13)

wedding **boda** (4)

Wednesday **miércoles** *m. inv.* (1); last Wednesday **el miércoles pasado** (6); next Wednesday **el miércoles que viene** (1); on Wednesday **el miércoles** (1); on Wednesdays **los miércoles** (1)

week **semana** (1); during the week **entre semana** (1); Holy Week **Semana Santa** (11); last week **la semana pasada** (6); next week **la semana que viene** (1); once a week **una vez a la semana** (3)

weekdays **días** (*m.*) **de entre semana** (1)

weekend **fin** (*m.*) **de semana** (1)

weekly payment **pago semanal** (15)

weight: to gain weight **engordar** (12); to lift weights **levantar pesas** (3); to lose weight **adelgazar (c)** (12)

welcome: you're welcome **de nada** (P)

welcoming *adj.* **acogedor(a)** (6)

well **bien** *adv.* (2); not very well **no muy bien** (P); to get along well (with each other) **llevarse bien** (9); to get along well with others **tener** (*irreg.*) **don** (*m.*) **de gentes** (13); to manage one's time well **manejar bien el tiempo** (15); very well **muy bien** (P)

well-being: physical/mental well-being **bienestar físico/mental** (15)

well-lit **lleno/a de luz** (5)

west: (to the) west **al oeste** (8)

wetlands **pantano** (14)

whale **ballena** (14)

what? **¿cuál(es)?** (1); **¿qué?** (1) ; *rel. pron.* **lo que** (6); at what time? **¿a qué hora?** (1); what are you (*s. fam.*) like? **¿cómo eres?** (P); what are you (*s. form.*) like? **¿cómo es usted (Ud.)?** (P); what time is it? **¿qué hora es?** (1); what's the weather like? **¿qué tiempo hace?** (2); what's your (*s. fam.*) name? **¿cómo te llamas?, ¿cuál es tu nombre?** (P); what's your (*s. form.*) name? **¿cómo se llama usted (Ud.)?, ¿cuál es su nombre?** (P)

wheat: whole wheat bread **pan** (*m.*) **integral** (6)

when **cuando** (2)

when? **¿cuándo?** (1)

where? **¿dónde?** (1); where (to)? **¿adónde?** (2); where are you (*s. fam.*) from? **¿de dónde eres?** (P); where are you (*s. form.*) from? **¿de dónde es usted (Ud.)?** (P)

which? **¿cuál(es)?** (1)

white **blanco** (2); white wine **vino blanco** (6)

whiteboard **pizarrón** (*m.*) **(blanco)** (1)

who? **¿quién(es)?** (1)

whole wheat bread **pan integral** (6)

whom?: with whom? **¿con quién(es)?** (1)

why: that's why **por eso** (4)

why? **¿por qué?** (3);

wide-screen TV **televisión** (*f.*) **de pantalla ancha** (15)

widowed **viudo/a** (4)

wife **esposa** (1)

WiFi connection **conexión** (*f.*) **WiFi** (15)

wild animal **animal** (*m.*) **salvaje** (14); wild plant **planta salvaje** (14); wild plant and animal life **flora y fauna silvestre** (14)

wind: wind power **energía eólica** (14); wind turbine **turbina eólica** (14)

window **ventana** (1); window seat **asiento de ventanilla** (10)

windy: it's (very) windy. **hace (mucho) viento.** (2)

wine **vino** (6); red wine **vino tinto** (6); white wine **vino blanco** (6); wine glass **copa** (6)

winter **invierno** (2)

wireless **inalámbrico/a** (15)

with **con** (1); with short/long sleeves **de manga corta/larga** (7); with whom? **¿con quién(es)?** (1)

without **sin que** + *subj.* (14)

woman **mujer** *f.* (1); young woman's fifteenth birthday party **fiesta de quinceañera** (11)

wooden **de madera** (7)

wool *adj.* **de lana** (7)

word **palabra** (P); indefinite word **palabra indefinida** *gram.* (5); negative word **palabra negativa** *gram.* (5); question word **palabra interrogativa** *gram.* (1)

work *v.* **trabajar** (1); *n.* (*general*) **trabajo** (1); to work in the garden **trabajar en el jardín** (3); to work in the yard **trabajar en el jardín** (3); work of art **obra de arte** (11); work schedule **horario de trabajo** (13)

workplace **lugar** (*m.*) **de trabajo** (13)

world **mundial** *adj.* (9); world history **historia mundial** (9)

worried **preocupado/a** (2)

worry *v.* **preocupar** (6)

worth: how much is it (are they) worth? **¿cuánto vale(n)?** (7)

write **escribir** (*p.p.* **escrito**) (1); to write reports **escribir informes** (13)

writer **escritor(a)** (11)

wrong: to be wrong **no tener** (*irreg.*) **razón** (3)

## Y

yard **jardín** *m.* (3); to work in the yard **trabajar en el jardín** (3)

year **año** (3); last year **el año pasado** (6); New Year's Day **Año Nuevo** (11); New Year's Eve **Nochevieja** (11); to be . . . years old **tener** (*irreg.*)**... años** (3)

yell *v.* **gritar** (12)

yellow **amarillo** (2)

yes **sí** (P)

yesterday **ayer** (6); the day before yesterday **anteayer** (6) yoga: to do yoga **hacer** (*irreg.*) **yoga** (3)

yogurt **yogur** *m.* (6)

you *subj. pron.* **tú** *s. fam.*, **usted (Ud.)** *s. form.*, **vosotros/as** *pl. fam. Sp.*, **ustedes (Uds.)** *pl. form. Sp.; pl. fam., form. elsewhere* (P); *dir. obj. pron.* **te** *s. fam.*, **lo/la** *s. form.*, **os** *pl. fam. Sp.*, **los/las** *pl. form. Sp.; pl. fam., form. elsewhere* (5); *obj. (of prep.)* **ti** *s. fam.*, **usted (Ud.)** *s. form.*, **vosotros/as** *pl. fam. Sp.*, **ustedes (Uds.)** *pl. form. Sp.; pl. fam., form. elsewhere* (2); and you (*s. fam.*)? **¿y tú?** (P); and you (*s. form.*)? **¿y usted (Ud.)?** (P); how are you (*s. fam.*)? **¿cómo estás?** (P); how are you (*s. form.*)? **¿cómo está usted (Ud.)?** (P); thank you **gracias** (P); to/for you *indir. obj. pron.* **te** *s. fam.*, **le** *s. form.*, **os** *pl. fam. Sp.*, **les** *pl. form. Sp.; pl. fam., form. elsewhere* (6); you (*s. fam.*) are **eres** (P); you (*s. form.*) are **es** (P); you (*pl. fam. Sp.*) are **sois** (P); you (*pl. form. Sp.; pl. fam., form. elsewhere*) are **son** (P); you (*s. fam.*); with you **contigo** (2)

you're welcome **de nada** (P)

young: young person **joven** *m., f.* (*pl.* **jóvenes**) (2); young woman's fifteenth birthday party **fiesta de quinceañera** (11)

younger than **menor que** (4)

your *poss. adj.* **tu(s)** *s. fam.*, **su(s)** *s. form., pl. form. Sp.; pl. fam., form. elsewhere*, **vuestro/a(s)** *pl. fam. Sp.* (1); *poss. adj.* **tuyo/a(s)** *s. fam.*, **suyo/a(s)** *s. form., pl. form. Sp.; pl. fam., form. elsewhere*, **vuestro/a(s)** *pl. fam. Sp.* (12)

yours *poss. pron.* **tuyo/a** *s. fam.* **suyo/a(s)** *s. form., pl. form. Sp.; pl. fam., form. elsewhere*, **vuestro/a(s)** *pl. fam. Sp.* (12)

youth **juventud** *f.* (9)

# Z

zero **cero** (P)

zipline **tirolina** (10)

zoo **parque** (*m.*) **zoológico** (9)

# Credits

## Text Credits

# Index

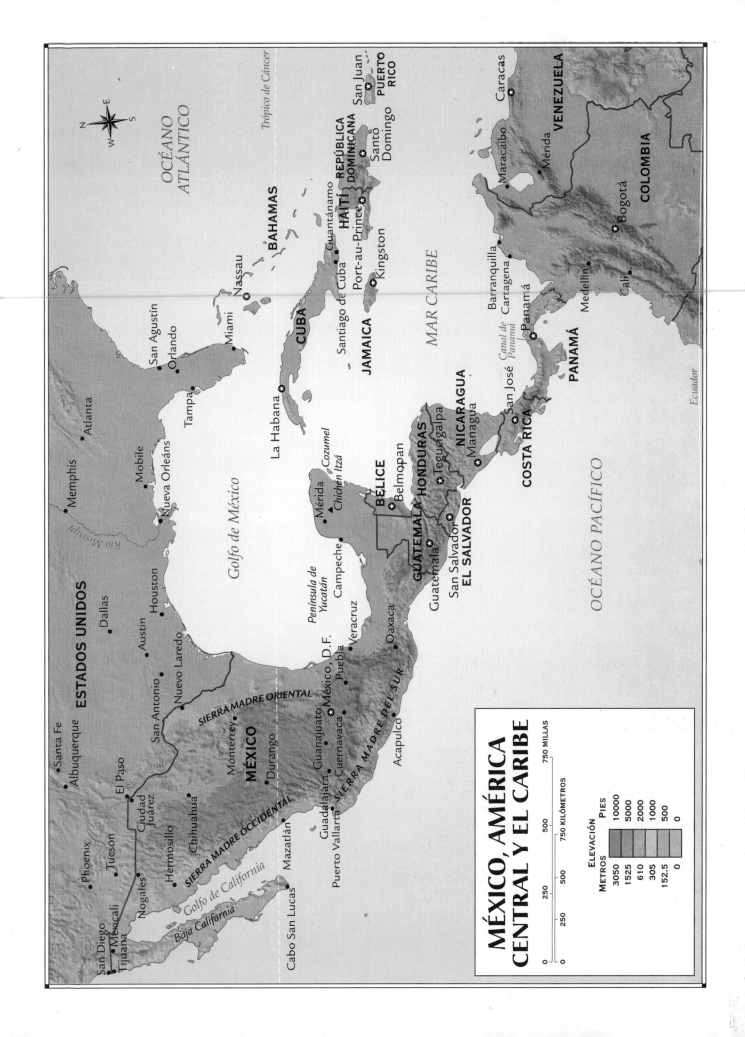

# MÉXICO, AMÉRICA CENTRAL Y EL CARIBE

**ELEVACIÓN**

| METROS | PIES |
|--------|------|
| 3050 | 10000 |
| 1525 | 5000 |
| 610 | 2000 |
| 305 | 1000 |
| 152.5 | 500 |
| 0 | 0 |

OCÉANO ATLÁNTICO

Trópico de Cáncer

**ESTADOS UNIDOS**

Santa Fe
Albuquerque
Phoenix
Tucson
San Diego
Tijuana
Mexicali
Nogales
El Paso
Ciudad Juárez
Hermosillo
Chihuahua
Nuevo Laredo
San Antonio
Austin
Dallas
Houston
Monterrey
Durango
Memphis
Atlanta
Mobile
Nueva Orleáns
Tampa
San Agustín
Orlando
Miami

*Río Misisipi*

*Río Grande*

**MÉXICO**

Mazatlán
Cabo San Lucas
*Baja California*
*Golfo de California*
Puerto Vallarta
Guadalajara
Guanajuato
México, D.F.
Cuernavaca
Puebla
Veracruz
Acapulco
Oaxaca

**SIERRA MADRE OCCIDENTAL**
**SIERRA MADRE ORIENTAL**
**SIERRA MADRE DEL SUR**

*Golfo de México*

*Península de Yucatán*
Mérida
Cozumel
▲ Chichén Itzá
Campeche

Nassau
**BAHAMAS**

La Habana
**CUBA**
Santiago de Cuba
Guantánamo

**JAMAICA**
Kingston

Port-au-Prince
**HAITÍ**
**REPÚBLICA DOMINICANA**
Santo Domingo
San Juan
**PUERTO RICO**

*MAR CARIBE*

**BELICE**
Belmopan
**GUATEMALA**
Guatemala
**HONDURAS**
Tegucigalpa
San Salvador
**EL SALVADOR**
**NICARAGUA**
Managua
**COSTA RICA**
San José
Canal de Panamá
**PANAMÁ**
Panamá

Barranquilla
Cartagena
Maracaibo
Medellín
Cali
Bogotá
**COLOMBIA**

Mérida
Caracas
**VENEZUELA**

*Ecuador*

*OCÉANO PACÍFICO*

0  250  500  750 MILLAS
0  250  500  750 KILÓMETROS

NICARAGUA

MAR CARIBE

COSTA
RICA

PANAMÁ

Barranquilla

Maracaibo

Caracas

*Río Orinoco*

VENEZUELA

GUYANA

Georgetown

Paramaribo

OCÉANO
ATLÁNTICO

Medellín

Bogotá

Cayenne

Cali

COLOMBIA

GUAYANA FRANCESA

SURINAM

Quito

ECUADOR

Ecuador

Guayaquil

Manaus

Belém

*Río Amazonas*

OCÉANO
PACÍFICO

PERÚ

C
O
R
D
I
L
L
E
R
A

Lima

Machu Picchu

BRASIL

Recife

Cuzco

*Lago Titicaca*

OCÉANO PACÍFICO

Isla Pinta

Isla Marchena

BOLIVIA

Arequipa

La Paz

Brasília

Isla San Salvador

Isla Santa Cruz

Sucre

Isla
Isabela

Isla San
Cristóbal

D
E

Puerto
Baquerizo
Moreno

ISLAS
GALÁPAGOS
(ECUADOR)

L
O
S

PARAGUAY

São Paulo

Antofagasta

0       100 MILLAS

Asunción

Puerto Iguazú

Rio de Janeiro

*Trópico de
Capricornio*

0       100 KILÓMETROS

CHILE

A
N
D
E
S

*Río Paraná*

0       8 MILLAS

0       8 KILÓMETROS

Córdoba

OCÉANO
ATLÁNTICO

Cabo
Cummings

Valparaíso

Rosario

Hanga Roa

Santiago

URUGUAY

Montevideo

Mataveri

OCÉANO
PACÍFICO

ARGENTINA

Buenos
Aires

*Río de la Plata*

Cabo Sur

ISLA DE PASCUA
(CHILE)

Concepción

Bahía Blanca

OCÉANO
PACÍFICO

San Carlos de
Bariloche

AMÉRICA DEL SUR

Islas
Malvinas

Punta Arenas

Estrecho de
Magallanes

0       250       500       750 MILLAS

Tierra del Fuego

0    250    500    750 KILÓMETROS

Cabo de Hornos

ELEVACIÓN

METROS       PIES

3050          10000

1525          5000

610           2000

305           1000

152.5         500

0             0